COST-BENEFIT ANALYSIS: CONCEPTS AND PRACTICE

COST-BENEFIT ANALYSIS: CONCEPTS AND PRACTICE

Anthony E. Boardman
University of British Columbia

David H. Greenberg
University of Maryland, Baltimore County

Aidan R. Vining
Simon Fraser University

David L. Weimer
University of Rochester

Prentice Hall
Upper Saddle River, NJ 07458

Library of Congress Cataloging-in-Publication Data

Cost benefit analysis: concepts and practice / Anthony Boardman...
[et al.].
    p. cm.
    Includes bibliographical references and index.
    ISBN 0-13-519968-9 (case)
        1. Cost effectiveness.   I. Boardman, Anthony E.
HD47.4.C669   1996
658.15'54—dc20   95-37859
                                                           CIP

Executive Editor: Leah Jewell
Assistant Editor: Teresa Cohan
Editor-in-Chief: Jim Boyd
Director of Production and Manufacturing: Joanne Jay
Associate Managing Editor: Carol Burgett
Production Editor: Louise Rothman
Production Services Manager: Lorraine Patsco
Interior Design/Page Layout: Annie Bartell and John Nestor
Illustrations: Warren Fischbach
Cover Designer: Bruce Kenselaar
Copy Editor: Donna E. Mulder
Buyer: Paul Smolenski
Marketing Manager: Susan McLaughlin

 © 1996 by Prentice-Hall, Inc.
A Simon & Schuster Company
Upper Saddle River, New Jersey 07458

Printed in the United States of America

10   9   8   7   6   5   4   3

ISBN 0-13-519968-9

PRENTICE-HALL INTERNATIONAL (UK) LIMITED, *London*
PRENTICE-HALL OF AUSTRALIA PTY. LIMITED, *Sydney*
PRENTICE-HALL CANADA INC., *Toronto*
PRENTICE-HALL HISPANOAMERICANA, S.A., *Mexico*
PRENTICE-HALL OF INDIA PRIVATE LIMITED, *New Delhi*
PRENTICE-HALL OF JAPAN, INC., *Tokyo*
SIMON & SCHUSTER ASIA PTE, LTD., *Singapore*
EDITORA PRENTICE-HALL DO BRASIL, LTDA., *Rio de Janeiro*

To

Barbara, Linda, Melanie, and Ulrike

CONTENTS

10 ■ ESTIMATING AND VALUING IMPACTS FROM OBSERVED BEHAVIOR   292

11 ■ CONTINGENT VALUATION: USING SURVEYS TO ELICIT INFORMATION ABOUT COSTS AND BENEFITS   345

12 ■ SHADOW PRICES FROM SECONDARY SOURCES   377

13 ■ COST-EFFECTIVENESS ANALYSIS AND COST-UTILITY ANALYSIS   395

14 ■ DISTRIBUTIONALLY WEIGHTED COST-BENEFIT ANALYSIS   411

15 ■ HOW ACCURATE IS CBA?   428

A SELECTED COST-BENEFIT ANALYSIS BIBLIOGRAPHY   445

AUTHOR INDEX   473

SUBJECT INDEX   479

PREFACE

Collaborative academic projects often take longer than originally anticipated, not just because of the normal delays of coordinating the efforts of busy people, but also because initially modest goals can become more ambitious as participants delve into their subject. We confess to both these sins. Our original plans made in 1990 were very modest. We intended to use an expanded version of the chapter on benefit-cost analysis in the text *Policy Analysis: Concepts and Practice* by David Weimer and Aidan Vining as the conceptual foundation for a collection of cases. Our goal was to produce a book that would be conceptually sound, practically oriented, and easily accessible to both students and practitioners. Though our final product is far different in form and content than we initially planned, we believe that we have produced such a book.

Our plans evolved for a number of reasons. Perhaps most importantly, through our teaching of undergraduate and graduate students as well as our experiences training government employees, we realized that many topics demanded extended treatment if the essential basics were to be effectively conveyed and solid foundations laid for further learning of advanced topics. We also decided that fully integrating illustrations and examples with concepts and methods is pedagogically superior to presenting independent cases. The result is a series of chapters that develop conceptual foundations, methods of application, and extensions of cost-benefit analysis through numerous practical examples and illustrations.

We wrote this book with three main audiences in mind. First, we intend it for use in courses on public-sector decision making offered in graduate programs in public policy analysis, urban planning, public administration, business, economics, public health, and environmental studies. Second, we envision it being used at the undergraduate level either as a primary text for a course on cost-benefit analysis or as a supplementary text for economics courses in public finance, public-sector economics, and policy analysis. Third, we intend it to be useful to policy analysts and public managers as both a general introduction and as a starting point for exploring advanced topics. In order to be appropriate for these diverse audiences, we have emphasized clear discussion over formal mathematics, and application over abstract theory. Nevertheless, we think that we have covered important, if difficult, conceptual issues in adequate detail both as a framework for thoughtful application and as a basis for further study. The latter has led us to include ample endnotes pointing to more advanced sources.

Though our decision to develop the book as a comprehensive and fully integrated treatment of cost-benefit analysis has engaged us in a much longer project than we originally anticipated, the process has been a rewarding one for us. We were forced to think more deeply about some topics that we thought we had already mastered and to develop others with which none of us was very familiar. We did this enjoyably together through numerous exchanges of drafts and during several intensive work sessions at the University of British Columbia. Among us, old friendships were strengthened and new ones were developed.

Our project was also made more productive and enjoyable by our many colleagues who gave us advice, comments, encouragement, or information. We thank here just a few people who were particularly helpful: Marcus Berliant, Edward Bird, James Brander, Eric Hanushek, Robert Havemen, Stanley Engerman, Doug Landin, Ted Miller, Bernhard Schwab, Walter Oi, W.G. Waters II, and Michael Wolkoff. We also thank Roy T. Gobin, Loyola University, Chicago; George T. Fuller, Wagner Graduate School, New York University; Ruth Shen, San Francisco State University; and Larry Karp, University of California at Berkeley, who wrote thoughtful reviews at the request of the publisher. Of course, they are not responsible for any errors that remain.

1

INTRODUCTION
TO COST-BENEFIT ANALYSIS

In the Affair of so much Importance to you, wherein you ask my Advice, I cannot for want of sufficient Premises, advise you *what* to determine, but if you please I will tell you *how*. When those difficult Cases occur, they are difficult, chiefly because while we have them under Consideration, all the Reasons *pro* and *con* are not present to the Mind at the same time; but sometimes one Set present themselves, and at other times another, the first being out of Sight. Hence the various Purposes or Inclinations that alternately prevail, and the Uncertainty that perplexes us.

To get over this, my Way is, to divide half a Sheet of Paper by a Line into two Columns; writing over the one *Pro*, and over the other *Con*. Then during three or four Days Consideration, I put down under the different Heads short Hints of the different Motives, that at different Times occur to me, *for* or *against* the Measure. When I have thus got them all together in one View, I endeavour to estimate their respective Weights; and where I find two, one on each side, that seem equal, I strike them both out. If I find a Reason *pro* equal to some two Reasons *con*, I strike out the three. If I judge some two Reasons *con*, equal to some three Reasons *pro*, I strike out the five; and thus proceeding I find at length where the Ballance lies; and if after a Day or two of farther consideration, nothing new that is of Importance occurs on either side, I come to a Determination accordingly. And, tho' the Weight of Reasons cannot be taken with the Precision of Algebraic Quantities, yet, when each is thus considered, separately and comparatively, and the whole lies before me, I think I can judge better, and am less liable to make a rash Step; and in fact I have found great Advantage from this kind of Equation, in what may be called *Moral* or *Prudential Algebra*.

—B. Franklin, London, September 19, 1772[1]

INDIVIDUAL VERSUS SOCIAL COSTS AND BENEFITS

Benjamin Franklin's advice about how to make a personal decision illustrates many of the features of cost-benefit analysis (CBA). These include a systematic categorization of impacts as benefits (pros) and costs (cons), valuing in dollars (assigning weights), and then determining the *net benefits* of the proposal relative to the status quo (net benefits equal benefits minus costs).

When we as individuals talk of costs and benefits, we naturally tend to consider only our *own* costs and benefits. To oversimplify, we choose between alternative courses of action according to which has the largest individual net benefits. Similarly, in evaluating various investment alternatives, firms tend to consider only those costs (expenditures) and benefits (revenues) that flow to them. In cost-benefit analysis we try to consider *all of the costs and benefits to society as a whole*. For this reason, some people refer to CBA as *social* cost-benefit analysis.

Stated at this level of abstraction, it is unlikely that many people would disagree with CBA. In practice, however, there are disagreements, which are of two types. First, social critics including philosophers, libertarians, some political economists, and socialists have disputed the fundamental utilitarian assumptions of CBA that the sum of individual utilities should be maximized and that it is possible to trade off utility gains for some against utility losses for others. These critics are not prepared to make trade-offs between one person's benefits and another person's costs. Second, participants in the public policy-making process (analysts, bureaucrats, and politicians) may disagree about such practical issues as whether certain given impacts are costs or benefits, what those impacts will be over time, how to monetize (attach a dollar value to them), and how to make trade-offs between the present and the future.

Our purpose in this chapter is to provide a nontechnical but reasonably comprehensive overview of CBA. Though we introduce a number of key concepts, we do so informally, returning to discuss them more thoroughly in subsequent chapters. Therefore, this chapter is best read without great concern about definitions and technical details.

THE PURPOSE AND USES OF CBA[2]

The broad purpose of CBA is to help social decision making. More specifically, the objective is to facilitate the more efficient allocation of society's resources. As we will see, where markets work well, individual self-interest will lead to an efficient allocation of resources. Consequently, government analysts and politicians bear the burden of providing a rationale for any governmental interference with private choice. Economists lump these rationales under the general heading of *market failures*. Where markets fail there is a prima facie rationale for government intervention. But it is no more than that. One must be able to demonstrate the superior efficiency of a particular intervention relative to the alternatives, including the status quo. For this purpose, we use CBA.

There are two major types of cost-benefit analysis that aid government resource allocation decisions in distinct ways. *Ex ante* CBA, which is just standard CBA as the term is commonly used, assists in the decision about whether scarce social resources should be allocated by government to a specific policy, whether program, project, or regulation. Thus, its contribution to public policy decision making is direct, immediate, and bureau specific. *Ex post* analysis is conducted at the end of a project.[3] At the end, all of the costs are "sunk" in the sense that they measure how much has already been given up to do the project; also, there is less uncertainty about what the actual benefits and costs were (apart from measurement errors). The value of such analyses is broader and less immediate as they provide information not only about the particular intervention but also about the "class" of such interventions. In other words, such analyses contribute to "learning" by government managers, politicians, and academics about whether particular classes or types of projects are worthwhile. Eventually the weight of evidence may lead to a policy change. For example, a whole range of CBAs in the 1960s and 1970s of industry-specific economic regulation showed that the costs of regulation often exceeded the benefits, paving the way for deregulation initiatives in the 1980s.[4]

In practice, many CBA studies are performed during the course of the life of a project, that is, *in medias res*. Some elements of such studies are similar to an *ex ante* analysis, while others are similar to an *ex post* analysis.

There is also a fourth class of CBA—one that compares *ex ante* predictions with *ex post* measurements or, more likely, with *in medias res* estimates *for the same project*. This comparative class of CBA is most useful to policymakers for learning about the efficacy of CBA as a decision-making and evaluative tool. Unfortunately, CBA comparisons appear to be almost nonexistent in the academic literature. In fact, we are unable to find any disinterested published *ex post* or *in medias res* analysis that is compared to an objective *ex ante* analysis of the same or very similar project.[5] (In Chapter 15 we will provide an example of such a comparison.) The lack of comparison CBAs is not as surprising as it may appear because the constituencies for *ex ante* CBA are frequently different from those for *ex post* or *in medias res* CBA.

It is useful to elaborate on the values of the four different classes of CBA discussed previously: *ex ante*, *ex post*, *in medias res*, and *ex ante/ex post* or *ex ante/in medias res* comparisons. Table 1.1 summarizes the important ways in which different classes of analysis serve different purposes.

Project-Specific Decision Making

Ex ante analysis is most useful for deciding whether resources should be allocated to a particular project. For ongoing projects where it is feasible to shift resources to alternative uses, an *in medias res* analysis can also be used for decision-making purposes. It is rare that such analysis will lead to termination of a project nearing completion because costs tend to come before benefits in investment projects, and the subsequent benefits will usually exceed the subsequent costs. However, it can happen. Recently a Canadian Environmental Assessment Panel recommended the decommissioning of a

TABLE 1.1   VALUE OF DIFFERENT CLASSES OF CBA

Value	Class of Analysis			
	Ex Ante	*In Medias Res*	*Ex Post*	*Ex Ante/Ex Post* or *Ex Ante/In Medias Res* Comparison
Resource allocation decision for this project	Yes—helps to select best project or make "go" versus "no-go" decisions, if accurate	If low sunk costs, can still shift resources. If high sunk costs, usually recommends continuation	Too late—the project is over	Same as *in medias res* or *ex post* analysis
Learning about actual value of specific project	Poor estimate— high uncertainty about future benefits and costs	Better—reduced uncertainty	Excellent— although some errors may remain. May have to wait long for study	Same as *in medias res* or *ex post* analysis
Contributing to learning about actual value of similar projects	Unlikely to add much	Good— contribution increases as performed later. Need to adjust for uniqueness	Very useful— although may be some errors and need to adjust for uniqueness. May have to wait long for project completion.	Same as *in medias res* or *ex post* analysis
Learning about omission, fore-casting, measure-ment and eval-uation errors in CBA	No	No	No	Yes, provides information about these errors and about the accuracy of CBA for similar projects

Source: Anthony E. Boardman, Wendy L. Mallery, and Aidan R. Vining, "Learning from *Ex Ante/Ex Post* Cost-Benefit Comparisons: The Coquihalla Highway Example," *Socio-Economic Planning Sciences*, 28, no. 2 (June 1994), 69–84, Table 1, p. 71. Reprinted with kind permission from Elsevier Science Ltd, The Boulevard, Langford Lane, Kidlington OX5 1GB, UK.

just completed dam on the basis of an *in medias res* analysis which showed that, with continuation, future environmental costs exceeded future benefits.[6] Because *ex post* analysis is conducted at the end of the project, it is obviously too late to reverse resource allocation decisions with respect to that particular project.

Learning About the Value of the Specific Project

In the early stages of a project there is considerable uncertainty about the actual consequences and, consequently, about the true net benefits. As time goes by uncertainty decreases and more is known about the true value of the project. At the end, all impacts have occurred. In general, *ex post* studies are more accurate than *in medias res* studies, which are more accurate than *ex ante* studies.

Learning About the Potential Benefits of Similar Projects

Ex post analyses not only provide information about a particular policy intervention but, more importantly, about similar interventions as well. Thus, they provide information for analysts conducting *ex ante* analyses of similar policies. Furthermore, *ex post* analyses potentially contribute to learning by political and bureaucratic decision makers, as well as policy researchers, about whether particular kinds of projects are worthwhile. The U.S. federal government has explicitly induced learning by sponsoring and requiring evaluation of a variety of "pilot tests," "demonstration projects," and "social experiments" including, for example, various welfare reform demonstrations that were conducted by different states during the 1980s.[7] Eventually the weight of evidence may lead to a policy change.[8] *In medias res* analyses provide similar learning: Analyses of ongoing regulatory policies contributed to deregulation in the trucking, airline, and telecommunications industries.[9]

The degree of societal learning from *in medias res* and *ex post* analyses depends on the *representiveness* of a particular project. This is crucial for realistic assessment of the usefulness of CBA.[10] For example, CBAs of experiments involving new surgical procedures or pharmaceutical products are usually representative. Lessons from many projects, however, are not as generalizeable as they appear.[11] For example, there may be scale-related effects for either benefits or costs (the proposed intervention is usually at least several orders of magnitude bigger than the experiment).[12] Also the proposed program usually has a more extended time frame than the experiment, which may increase the incentives for behavioral changes that increase costs or reduce benefits.

Learning About the Efficacy of CBA

Comparisons of *ex ante* with either *in medias res* or *ex post* analyses are most useful for learning about the value of CBA itself. First, they help estimate the level of confidence one can place in subsequent CBAs. That is, they provide a measure of *ex ante* precision. This information is useful for decision-making purposes. Second, comparison studies help explain the divergence between expected and realized benefits and costs. In Chapter 15, we describe four important dimensions of accuracy: omission errors, forecasting errors, measurement errors, and valuation errors.

THE DEMAND FOR CBA

The demand for CBA is illustrated by Executive Order 12291, issued by President Reagan in early 1981. This requires that a regulatory impact analysis (RIA) accompany every major regulatory initiative (over $100 million in cost) from government agencies. (An RIA is essentially a cost-benefit analysis that also identifies distributional and fairness considerations.) In the spring of 1995 the U.S. House of Representatives passed legislation that requires considerably more elaborate CBAs to be performed prior to regulations being promulgated. Moreover, before the regulations are issued, the CBAs could be challenged in the courts or by petition to the regulatory agency. This legislation was being debated by the Senate at the time this book was completed.

Nearly all other Western industrialized countries have similar protocols covering broad ranges of programs or specific program areas. For example, Canada's Federal-Provincial Fraser River Flood Control Agreement recognizes that before any dike construction can take place, projects have to be determined to be engineeringly sound and economically viable. Economic viability is determined by CBA.

The demand for *ex post* analysis tends not to be so explicit—there are no mandatory requirements that it be done. Nonetheless, resource allocation decisions often draw heavily on such analyses. For example, President Clinton's State of the Union Address on February 17, 1993, emphasized the relationship between *ex post* CBAs of specific Head Start programs (i.e., educational programs for low-income preschool children) and his intention to increase funding and expand the scope of such programs.

As public officials face citizen resistance to raising taxes, they are forced increasingly to ensure that government works more efficiently and effectively. In practice, this may provide an impetus toward the increased use of CBA and related methods to make more efficient resource allocation decisions. Such trends are contemporaneous with more concern for the environment, which calls for the valuation of all social costs and benefits, rather than just government expenditures. But, as we will see, there are enormous pressures working against the correct use of CBA including ignorance of correct methods, and bureaucratic and political incentives to distort it.

CLIENTS FOR THIS BOOK

We write this book first of all for people who want to know how to do CBA—current and future analysts. Second, it is for people who want to know how to interpret CBA—in other words, clients of CBAs. We think clients can be helped in two ways. In the narrow sense clients should be well enough informed to evaluate specific CBAs. They should be able to judge whether or not a CBA has been conducted well: Does it meet professional standards? In the broad sense, clients' primary need may be to understand the collection of CBAs in a given policy area. Here the purpose is to evaluate CBA studies well enough to have a sense of the conclusions of the literature in specific areas such as employment training or environmental regulation. In order to do this well, one has to understand the basic principles of CBA.

THE BASIC STEPS OF CBA ILLUSTRATED USING A HIGHWAY EXAMPLE

The best way to get a feel for what CBA involves is to walk through a relatively straightforward example. First, we go through the basic steps of CBA using an example to illustrate how they should be performed. Second, we retrace our steps pointing out the realities and practical difficulties associated with actually doing each step. The conceptual and practical issues that we touch on drive most of the rest of this book. Do not worry if concepts are unfamiliar to you; this is a dry run. Subsequent chapters explain the concepts clearly.

CBA may look intimidating and complex. You may not know where to start. To help make CBA more manageable, we break it down into nine basic steps, as summarized in Table 1.2.

Imagine a cost-benefit analyst working for the State of Texas in 1986 has been asked to perform a CBA of a new highway between Amarillo and Austin (this is hypothetical!), called the AA Highway. This four-lane divided freeway would extend for 195 kilometers, significantly reducing travel time between the two cities. The analyst's results are presented in Table 1.3. How did she get them? We will go through the nine steps, one at a time.

1. Decide whose benefits and costs count (standing).   Following the steps in Table 1.2, the analyst must first decide who has standing, that is, whose benefits and costs should be counted. In this case, she was not in a position to decide this; her superiors were. They wanted the analysis done from the Texan perspective, but also asked her to take a global perspective. The global perspective counts all of the benefits and costs to everyone, irrespective of where they reside. Thus, it includes benefits (and costs) to Californians, Mexicans, and even tourists from the United Kingdom. The state perspective counts only the benefits and costs that accrue to Texas residents. These include costs and benefits that are borne by the Texas government. The two perspectives are shown in the table.

2. Select the portfolio of alternative projects.   Step 2 requires the analyst to specify the set of alternative projects. In this simple example the highway department was interested in only two alternatives to the status quo: one with tolls and one without. The toll was set by the highway department; it ranged from $40 for large trucks to $8 for cars. Combining the with-toll and without-toll alternatives with the two different perspectives on standing gives us the four columns in Table 1.3, labeled A through D.

TABLE 1.2   CONCEPTUALLY CBA IS SIMPLE

1.   Decide whose benefits and costs count (standing).
2.   Select the portfolio of alternative projects.
3.   Catalogue potential (physical) impacts and select measurement indicators.
4.   Predict quantitative impacts over the life of the project.
5.   Monetize (attach dollar values to) all impacts.
6.   Discount for time to find present values.
7.   Sum: Add up the benefits and costs.
8.   Perform sensitivity analysis.
9.   Recommend the alternative with the largest net social benefits.

TABLE 1.3   AMARILLO-AUSTIN HIGHWAY CBA (1986 $ MILLION)

	No Tolls		With Tolls	
	A Global Perspective	B State Perspective	C Global Perspective	D State Perspective
Project Benefits:				
Time and Operating Cost Savings	389.8	292.3	290.4	217.8
Terminal Value of Highway	53.3	53.3	53.3	53.3
Safety Benefits (Lives)	36.0	27.0	25.2	18.9
Alternative Routes Benefits	14.6	10.9	9.4	7.1
Toll Revenues	—	—	—	37.4
New Users	0.8	0.6	0.3	0.2
Total Benefits	494.5	384.1	378.6	334.7
Project Costs:				
Construction	338.1	338.1	338.1	338.1
Maintenance	7.6	7.6	7.6	7.6
Toll Collection	—	—	8.4	8.4
Toll Booth Construction	—	—	0.3	0.3
Total Costs	345.7	345.7	354.4	354.4
Net Social Benefits	148.8	38.4	24.2	-19.7

Source: Adapted from Anthony Boardman, Aidan Vining, and W.G. Waters, II, "Costs and Benefits through Bureaucratic Lenses: Example of a Highway Project," *Journal of Policy Analysis and Management*, 12, no. 3 (Summer 1993), 532–555, Table 1, p. 537.

3. Catalogue potential (physical) impacts and select measurement indicators.

Step 3 requires the analyst to catalogue the physical impacts of the alternatives and to specify the impacts' units. We use the term *impacts* broadly to include both required resources and outputs of the projects. The anticipated beneficial impacts were time saved and reduced vehicle operating costs for travelers on the new highway ("Time and Operating Cost Savings" in Table 1.3); the residual value after the discounting period of 20 years ("Terminal Value of Highway"); accidents avoided (including lives saved) due to drivers switching to the shorter, safer new highway ("Safety Benefits"); reduced congestion on the existing alternative routes ("Alternative Routes Benefits"); revenues collected from tolls ("Toll Revenues"); and benefits accruing to newly generated traffic ("New Users"). The anticipated cost impacts were construction costs ("Construction"); additional maintenance and snow removal ("Maintenance"); toll collection ("Toll Collection"); and toll booth construction and maintenance ("Toll Booth Construction").

Specification of impact category indicators occurs simultaneously with specification of the impact categories. There are no particular difficulties in this study in specifying measurement indicators of each impact category that is used. For example, number of lives saved per year, person-hours of travel time saved, and dollar value of gasoline saved are reasonably straightforward.

Observe that to facilitate presentation, some impacts have been identified as being costs, while others have been labeled as benefits. For example, time saved is a benefit, while construction expenditure is a cost. Again, note that impacts refer to both inputs (which are typically costs) and outputs (which are typically benefits).

4. Predict quantitative impacts over the life of project. This project, like almost all projects, has impacts over extended periods of time. The fourth task is to predict for each alternative project the level of all impacts over the life of that project, and sometimes beyond it. We need to estimate how many people will use each highway under the with-tolls and no-tolls alternatives, and what proportion of these users are Texans. In this example, one must predict or calculate for different categories of drivers (trucks, passenger cars on business, passenger cars on vacation) and for all alternatives over time:

- The number of vehicle-trips on the new highway.
- The number of vehicle-trips on the old roads.
- The total amount of time users save.
- The total amount of vehicle operating costs and wear-and-tear that users save.

One must also predict:

- How many accidents are avoided and lives saved.
- The frequency and severity of rainstorms, tornadoes, and other factors that affect maintenance costs.

Each impact must be predicted over the life of the project. Here we present an example of how the analyst predicted how many lives the new highway would save each year:

Shorter distance:

130 vkm × 0.027 lives lost per vkm	= 3.5 lives/year
Safer (4-lane versus 2-lane):	
313 vkm × 0.027 lives lost per vkm × 0.33	= 3.0 lives/year
Total lives saved[13]	= 6.5 lives/year

There are two components. First, the new highway is shorter than existing alternative routes. Hence, it is expected that drivers will avoid 130 million vehicle-kilometers (vkm) of driving and evidence provided by the state suggests that, on average, there are 0.027 deaths per million vehicle-kilometers. The shorter distance is expected, therefore, to save 3.5 lives per year. The new highway is also predicted to be safer per kilometer driven. It is expected that 313 million vehicle-kilometers will be driven each year on the new highway. Based on previous traffic engineering evidence, the analyst estimated that the new highway would lower the fatal accident rate by one-third. Consequently, the new highway is expected to save 3.0 lives per year due to being safer. Combining the two components, 6.5 lives are saved per year.

5. Monetize (attach dollar values to) all impacts. The analyst now has to monetize each of the impact units described previously. *Monetization* means value in dollars. Specifically, we need to monetize time saved, a *statistical* life saved, and accidents avoided. One would like to find such values in a "catalogue" that, for example, provides one with the monetary value of an hour of leisure saved, the value of an hour saved by a person on business, and the value of an hour saved by a truck driver. Ideally, each estimate should be location specific and time specific. Thus, in our example, it should pertain to Texas in 1986. Some examples of the dollar values per unit used in this CBA are:

- Leisure time saved per vehicle = 25 percent of gross wage × average number of passengers = $6.68 per vehicle-hour.
- Business time saved per vehicle = $12 per vehicle-hour.
- Truck drivers' time saved per vehicle = $14 per vehicle-hour.
- Value of a life saved = $500,000 per life.

These estimates were based on previously published estimates of the value of time and the value of life, topics that are discussed in depth in Chapter 12.

6. Discount for time to find present values. For any project that has either costs or benefits arising over extended periods (years), we need a method to aggregate the benefits and costs that occur at different times. Future benefits and costs are discounted relative to present benefits and costs in order to obtain their *present values*. The need to discount arises due to most people's preference to consume now rather than later. Discounting has nothing to do with inflation per se, although inflation must be taken into account. A cost or benefit accruing in year t is converted to its present value by dividing it by $(1+d)^t$, where d is the social discount rate. As discussed in Chapter 5, the choice of the appropriate social discount rate is a contentious issue. In the highway example the analyst used a real (inflation-adjusted) social discount rate of 7.5 percent to calculate present values.

7. Sum: add up benefits and costs. The basic decision rule for a single alternative (relative to the status quo) is simple: Add up the present value of benefits (B), add up the present value of costs (C), and see which is larger. If benefits exceed costs, then proceed with the project. If not, stay with the status quo. In short, the analyst would recommend proceeding with the project if:

$$\text{NPV} = B - C > 0.$$

In other words, *when there is only one potential project, proceed with that project if the net present value of social benefits (NPV) is positive.*

When there is more than one alternative to the status quo, the rule is slightly more complicated: *Select the project with the highest NPV.*

The bottom line in our highway example is that projects A, B, and C have positive NPVs. The with-toll alternative from the Texas perspective (D) is the only one that does not. We should emphasize that these estimates are "expected" NPVs, based on our best predictions and valuations.

8. Perform sensitivity analysis. As discussed in Chapter 6, sensitivity analysis is an attempt to deal with uncertainty. One can perform sensitivity analysis with respect to both prediction of impacts and their valuation per unit of impact. For example, the analyst may be uncertain about the predicted number of lives saved and about the appropriate dollar value to place on a statistical life saved. One can also perform sensitivity analysis with respect to standing and the social discount rate. In this example, the analyst performed sensitivity analysis on the standing issue by comparing global against state NPVs.

9. Recommend the alternative with the largest net social benefits. In this case, three of the alternative projects have positive NPVs and one has a negative NPV. The latter indicates that from a Texan perspective it would be more efficient to "do nothing" (not build the proposed AA highway) at this time than to build it and charge tolls. Sometimes the status quo is the best alternative. Here, however, from a global perspective both the with-tolls and without-tolls alternatives are preferable to the status quo. Based on the preceding analysis, the analyst will recommend the selection of A above C or B above D, that is, the project with the largest NPV. In short, the no-toll alternatives are superior.

This result gives a flavor of the possibly counterintuitive recommendations that CBA can support. In this case, tolls lower the NPV because they deter people from using the highway, and so fewer people enjoy the benefits.[14]

Keep in mind that A is not directly comparable to B (and C is not directly comparable to D) because A and C represent different levels of standing from B and D. In this example, the global NPVs (A and C) are larger than the state NPVs (B and D) primarily because the benefits are higher while costs are the same. But this is beside the point. The issues of standing must be determined independently of which level of analysis obtains the highest NPV.

THE REALITY OF CBA

The highway example illustrates how to perform the basic steps of CBA. Yet, at each step, there are potential difficulties. We want to give you a taste for the practical difficulties of performing CBA. One factor that helps us to do this is the fact that the highway on which this example is based was actually built, with tolls, in 1987. But look for it in British Columbia, not in Texas![15]

In this section, we focus on those difficulties inherent in doing CBA well; we recognize a whole host of other difficulties is created by political and behavioral biases and other factors. We deal with these later in this chapter.

We should stress right up front that it takes many resources (time, skill, and money) to do CBA well, especially where the alternative projects are large and complex, and have unique features. The costs involved may be very large. For example,

TABLE 1.4   THE REALITIES OF DOING CBA

---

1. Decide whose benefits and costs count.

    Contentious whether global, national, state, or local perspective is appropriate.

2. Select the portfolio of alternative projects.

    Potentially infinite, the analyst must select a reasonable subset.

3. Catalogue potential (physical) impacts and select measurement indicators.

    Difficult to identify specific impacts where unresearched scientific or biological processes are involved.
    True impacts may be unobservable.

4. Predict quantitative impacts over the life of the project.

    Prediction is difficult, especially over long periods for complex systems.

5. Monetize (attach dollar values to) all impacts.

    Where there are no appropriate market values, one needs "catalogues" that rarely exist. Often the most
    important benefits are the most difficult to measure.

6. Discount for time to find present values.

    Different theories suggest different social discount rates.

7. Sum: Add up the benefits and costs.

    Some argument about the appropriate decision criterion.

8. Perform sensitivity analysis.

    Potentially infinite—analyst has to choose a reasonable subset.

9. Recommend the alternative with the largest net social benefits.

    This is usually easy! It normally does not present any practical analytical difficulties, just political ones.
    The one exception is where sensitivity analysis shows that NPV estimates are very uncertain.

Thomas Hopkins reports that a recent analysis of the costs and benefits of reducing lead in gasoline cost the Environmental Protection Agency (EPA) roughly $1 million.[16] On average, the EPA spends approximately $700,000 for a major CBA, that is, for the analysis of projects with compliance cost in excess of $100 million annually.[17] Large-scale evaluations of training programs, of which CBA is one component, often run into millions of dollars.

To illustrate the realities of performing CBA well, we return to our nine steps, this time focusing on the difficulties. These are summarized in Table 1.4.

1. Decide whose benefits and costs count. It is sometimes contentious whether an analysis should be performed from the global, national, state, or local perspective. While the federal government usually performs analyses taking only national costs and benefits into account, critics argue that many issues should be analyzed from a global perspective. Recent environmental issues that fall into this category include ozone depletion, greenhouse gases, and acid rain. At the other extreme, local governments typically want to ignore costs and benefits that occur in the adjacent municipality or are borne by higher levels of government. Our highway example deals with this issue by analyzing costs and benefits from both a global perspective and a Texas perspective.

2. Select the portfolio of alternative projects. In our highway example, there were only two alternatives—with tolls and without tolls—relative to the status quo.

But the range of alternatives is potentially infinite, varying on a large number of dimensions. Some dimensions on which new alternatives could have differed include:

- Timing: The highway could have been delayed until a later date.
- Surface: The highway could have been surfaced in bitumen rather than concrete.
- Routing: The highway could have taken quite different routes.
- Size: The highway could have been two lanes or six lanes, rather than four lanes.
- Tolls: The toll could have been higher or lower.
- Wild Animal Friendliness: The highway could have been built with or without "Armadillo Crossings."

Changing the highway on just one of these dimensions would generate a new alternative. Changing two or three simultaneously greatly increases the number of alternatives. In general, if there were n dimensions, each with k possible values, there would be k^n alternatives. For example, if there were three dimensions, each with three possible values, there would be 27 mutually exclusive alternatives. With four dimensions, each with three possible values, there would be 81 alternatives! Neither decision makers nor analysts can cognitively handle comparisons among such a large number of alternatives.[18]

In practice, CBA analysts evaluate *only one project at a time*. In the preceding discussion all of the alternatives pertain to a specific highway between Austin and Amarillo. There is usually no attempt to compare the net social benefits of this project to alternative highway projects or, even more broadly, to health care, antipoverty, or national defense projects. As a practical matter, full optimization is impossible. In theory, CBA compares the net benefits of investing resources in a particular project with the net benefits of *hypothetical* projects that would be displaced if the project under evaluation were to proceed. *If, however, a particular project would displace a specific alternative rather than hypothetical ones, it should be evaluated relative to the specific alternative.* Thus, if government decided resources could be used only for the highway project or for a health-care project, then the highway project should be compared with the health-care project, not the status quo.

The limited nature of the comparisons sometimes frustrates politicians and decision makers who imagine that CBA is a *deus ex machina* that will rank *all* policy alternatives. On the other hand, as we discuss in subsequent chapters, the weight of CBA evidence can and does help in making broad social choices across policy areas.

Even if the analyst focuses on only one project (with few or many alternatives), there can be no guarantee that the analyst will select the optimal alternative. Even local optimization may not be possible. As we stated earlier, the analyst will recommend the project with the largest NPV among those evaluated. This point is illustrated in Figure 1.1.

Consider a project for which the alternatives vary along an output scale (Q). The benefits and costs associated with alternative scales are represented by the functions $B(Q)$ and $C(Q)$, respectively. The benefits increase as the scale increases, but at a decreasing rate. On the other hand, costs increase at an increasing rate. A small-scale

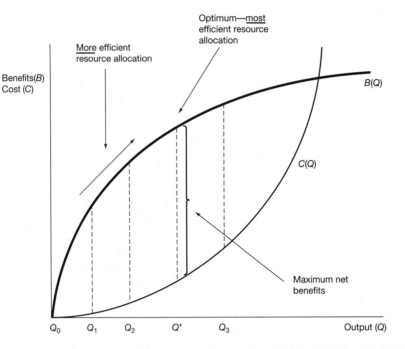

Moving from Q_0 toward Q^* increases efficiency; that is: NPV(Q^*) > NPV(Q_2) > NPV(Q_1) > NPV(Q_0)

Moving beyond Q^* reduces efficiency, but Q_3 is more efficient than Q_0: NPV(Q^*) > NPV(Q_3) > NPV(Q_0)

Figure 1.1   CBA Seeks More Efficient Resource Allocation

project (for example, Q_1) has positive net benefits. As the scale increases, the net benefits increase up to the optimal scale, Q^*. As the scale is increased beyond Q^*, the net benefits are positive but are decreasing. The net benefits are zero where the cost curve and benefit curve intersect and are negative for larger-scale projects.

Suppose there is no program now (current output level is Q_0). The analyst may compare the status quo with only two alternative output levels Q_1 and Q_2. (These are the alternatives of the project.) Given the benefit and cost functions, output level Q_2 is preferred to output level Q_1, which, in turn, is preferred to the status quo, Q_0. The analyst will therefore recommend adoption of Q_2. As the figure shows, however, net social benefits are maximized at output level Q^*; this is the optimum scale. Adoption of the optimum was not recommended because it was not among the set of evaluated alternatives. Thus, the analyst has chosen a more efficient alternative to the status quo, but not the most efficient alternative.

The analyst cannot be certain that she has included the optimum output level in the set of alternatives for two reasons. First, she cannot know what the optimum is until after she has performed the analysis. Second, even after beginning to estimate costs and benefits, cognitive capacity limitations, often summarized as *bounded rationality* problems, may hinder the analyst from even considering the optimal alternative.[19] These cognitive factors become an increasingly important issue when (1) project benefits and costs vary simultaneously on many dimensions, (2) the benefit and cost functions are discontinuous or complex (for example, with interaction terms), and (3) when there is uncertainty about the interactions or the functional forms. In practice, these cognitive limitations are always a factor to some extent. In the example depicted in Figure 1.1, this problem is unlikely to be of major importance because the NPVs depend only on scale, and the functional relationships $B(Q)$ and $C(Q)$ are assumed known and are relatively simple and smooth.

Another practical reason for not considering the optimum stems from budgetary or political constraints, which limit the choice set. In the example illustrated by Figure 1.1, projects in excess of size Q_2, including Q^*, may have been excluded because of budgetary or political considerations. We stress, however, that this should not be considered a weakness of CBA itself, but rather of the political process that selects projects.

In practice, it is useful initially to consider an expanded choice set. A brainstorming session can be very valuable at an early stage to expand the range of consideration.

3. Catalogue potential (physical) impacts and select measurement indicators. In the highway example, identifying impacts was relatively straightforward, although a critic might argue that some impacts were omitted. Some impact categories that the analyst did not include were: health impacts from automobile emissions, impacts on the population of armadillos and other animals, and changes in scenic beauty.

From a CBA perspective, we are only interested in the relationship between an impact and individual utility. In CBA, so-called impacts that do not have any value to human beings are not counted. (The big caveat is that this only applies where human beings have the relevant knowledge and information to make rational valuations.) In order to treat something as an impact, we have to know that there is a cause-and-effect relationship between some physical outcome of the project and human beings with standing. For some impacts, this relationship is so obvious that we do not think about it explicitly. For example, we do not question the existence of a causal relationship between motor vehicle usage and accidents that result in morbidity and mortality. Of course, this still requires us to estimate the exact functional form of the relationship, specifying the level (quantity) of morbidity and mortality under each alternative.

For other impacts, the causal relationships may not be so obvious. What about the impact of exhaust fumes from vehicle usage of the highway on drivers' blood pressure? Demonstrating such cause-and-effect relationships often involves extensive scientific research concerning the impact of airborne lead on blood pressure, whether exposure to secondary smoke raises lung cancer rates, or whether organochlorines harm game fish.

In many CBAs, what we suspect to be the most important impacts may depend upon unresearched, preliminary, or contradictory scientific or biological knowledge. A recent example that illustrates this problem is the controversy surrounding the effect of chlorinated organic compounds in bleached pulp mill effluent on wildlife. While an earlier Swedish study found such a link, a recent Canadian study found none.[20]

One current, highly publicized controversy that demonstrates how widely opinions can vary is provided by the northern spotted owl. While some experts feel the costs of logging are relatively minor, Jonathan Rubin and his colleagues have argued the costs may be very large:

> Biologically, the owl is an indicator for old-growth temperate ecosystems: the trees, associated plant communities, and wildlife species that find their optimal habitat in these forests. If the spotted owl cannot survive, its extinction could represent a lack of viability for old-growth habitat itself. Elimination of an ecosystem, itself a unique resource, clearly has greater costs for society than mere extinction of the owl.[21]

In some circumstances, the true impact is unobservable. For example, one may never know exactly how many crimes (or crimes avoided) can be attributed to an intervention. However, we usually have access to alternative indicators, such as changes in arrest rates or changes in conviction rates. In practice, the analyst will probably have to choose one of these surrogates (although one could instead take a weighted average of several). Choice of a specific indicator will usually depend on data availability: what is easy to measure and to monetize. Bear in mind that all indicators involve some slippage of information. Furthermore, remember that the valuation should be consistent with the chosen indicator. For example, the valuation of an arrest should be lower than the valuation of a conviction of the guilty party so that one would obtain similar estimates of crime impacts from using either indicator.

Watch out for impact categories where two different groups of people view what is apparently the same impact in opposite ways. Actually, this is mainly a question of valuation—some may view the impact as a benefit while others may view it as a cost. Consider, for example, "flooded land" as a potential impact category. Residents of the flood plain will generally view floods as a cost, while duck hunters will regard them as a benefit. In such circumstances, it is more useful to have two impact categories— one for damaged homes, another for recreation—even though in reality these are simply opposite valuations of the same impact. Sometimes such differences in valuations flag issues relevant to standing or the issue of weighting costs or benefits that accrue to particular individuals or groups. (Chapter 14 is devoted to distributional weighting.)

4. Predict quantitative impacts over the life of the project.   One odd feature of the cost-benefit literature is that hardly anybody discusses the fact that prediction is both essential and very difficult! Most textbooks focus on theoretical issues, assuming that demand and supply curves are known. But they often are not. How good are analysts at predicting the impacts? Surprisingly, as we discussed earlier, there are almost no published examples in which a CBA has first been performed before a project was undertaken (*ex ante*) and then verified in terms of predictive accuracy at the end of the project (*ex post*). Consequently, the predictive capability of CBA and, therefore, its value as a practical tool are somewhat unproven.

This issue is so important that Chapter 15 is devoted largely to it and related issues. As discussed there, current evidence suggests that in the actual highway project on which our example is broadly based, usage levels and therefore benefits are considerably higher than predicted, but so were costs! Even this understates the problem. There were errors within benefit categories, which did not show up in the aggregate dollar benefit as they offset each other. In general, prediction is especially difficult where projects have long time horizons or relationships among variables are complex.

Many of the realities associated with actually doing steps 3 and 4 are brilliantly summarized by Kenneth Boulding's poem on dam building in the Third World, presented in Exhibit 1.1. Many of his points deal with omission of impact categories due to misunderstanding or ignorance of cause-and-effect relationships and to prediction errors. He also makes points about the distribution of costs and benefits, which we discuss later.

■   **EXHIBIT 1.1   A BALLAD OF ECOLOGICAL AWARENESS**

> The cost of building dams is always underestimated,
> There's erosion of the delta that the river has created,
> There's fertile soil below the dam that's likely to be looted,
> And the tangled mat of forest that has got to be uprooted.
>
> There's the breaking up of cultures with old haunts' and habits' loss,
> There's the education programme that just doesn't come across,
> And the wasted fruits of progress that are seldom much enjoyed
> By expelled subsistence farmers who are urban unemployed.
>
> There's disappointing yield of fish, beyond the first explosion;
> There's silting up, and drawing down, and watershed erosion.
> Above the dam the water's lost by sheer evaporation;
> Below, the river scours, and suffers dangerous alteration.
>
> For engineers, however good, are likely to be guilty
> Of quietly forgetting that a river can be silty,
> While the irrigation people too are frequently forgetting
> That water poured upon the land is likely to be wetting.
>
> Then the water in the lake, and what the lake releases,
> Is crawling with infected snails and water-borne diseases,
> There's a hideous locust breeding ground when water level's low,
> And a million ecologic facts we really do not know.
>
> There are benefits, of course, which may be countable, but which
> Have a tendency to fall into the pockets of the rich,
> While the costs are apt to fall upon the shoulders of the poor.
> So cost-benefit analysis is nearly always sure
> To justify the building of a solid concrete fact,
> While the Ecologic Truth is left behind in the Abstract.

—Kenneth E. Boulding

Reprinted with the kind permission of Mrs. Boulding.

5. Monetize (attach dollar values to) all impacts.   Many of the most intuitively important impacts are intangible or are very difficult to value in monetary terms. The value of life is an obvious example. Environmental issues are also contentious. In CBA, value is measured in terms of "willingness-to-pay." As we discuss in Chapter 3, where markets exist and work well (don't "fail") willingness-to-pay can be determined from the appropriate demand curve. Naturally, problems arise where markets do not exist. In such cases, obtaining a value for just a few impact categories can be a life's work. Scholars have spent many person-years trying to determine the appropriate value of a saved life. In practice, most CBA analysts do not reinvent these wheels but instead draw upon previous research. Ideally, analysts would like to have "catalogues" of appropriate values to attach to impacts where no market values exist. Unfortunately, such catalogues rarely exist, although, as we show in Chapter 12, considerable progress is being made in this regard.

In the highway example, a saved life was valued at $500,000 in 1986 dollars. Recently a consensus has begun to emerge that the appropriate value of life is considerably higher, closer to $2 million in 1986 dollars.[22]

Some government agencies and critics of CBA are unwilling to attach a monetary value to life, which forces them to use an alternative method of analysis. Cost-effectiveness analysis and multigoal analysis, which we discuss in Chapters 2 and 13, are two possibilities.

6. Discount for time to find present values. The *social discount rate* is the rate at which analysts should discount the benefits and costs accruing at different times. Different theories suggest different values for the social discount rate. Many learned tomes have been written on this subject. We summarize this literature in Chapter 5. Unfortunately, for the practically oriented analyst, there is a lot of theoretical disagreement. The value of the social discount rate is thus a good candidate for sensitivity analysis. Sometimes the discount rate for use in a CBA is mandated by a government authority (e.g., the Office of Management and Budget, the General Accounting Office, Ministry of Finance or Treasury Board). Often, for example, the specified real (inflation-adjusted) discount rate is 10 percent. But many economists regard this rate as much too high and advocate a lower rate.

7. Sum: Add up the benefits and costs. There is some disagreement about the appropriateness of using the maximization of NPV of social benefits as a decision rule. Potential alternatives include the internal rate of return and the benefit-cost ratio. This is one area with more heat than light. The appropriate criterion to use is the NPV of social benefits, which requires only summation of the discounted benefits and costs. There is no disagreement on the merits of this method; it always gives the correct answer.

Arguments about whether it is appropriate to aggregate *all* of the impacts often turn out to reflect deeper disagreements concerning the choice of appropriate analysis methods. For example, if the analyst is not prepared to monetize the value of life, then she cannot sum all of the project's impacts and will be forced to adopt an alternative method to CBA, such as cost-effectiveness analysis.

8. Perform sensitivity analysis. Potentially, every assumption in a CBA can be varied infinitely. In practice, one has to use judgment and focus on those assumptions that are potentially most important for the results. But this can mean that CBA is vulnerable to the judgment biases of the analyst. Nevertheless, carefully thought-out scenarios are usually more informative than a mindless varying of assumptions.

9. Recommend the alternative with the largest net social benefits. This one is easy! It does not present any practical difficulties. Note, however, that the analyst makes a recommendation, not a decision. CBA concerns how resources *should* be allocated; it is normative. It does not claim to be a positive (i.e., descriptive) theory of how resource allocation decisions are actually made. Such decisions are made in political and bureaucratic arenas. CBA is only one input to this political decision-making process—one that attempts to push it toward more efficient resource allocation.

BUREAUCRATIC AND POLITICAL "LENSES"[23]

Thus far we have introduced CBA and discussed the prediction difficulties associated with performing CBA. But we have assumed implicitly that CBA is unconstrained by bureaucratic and political processes. This approach is reasonable given that CBA is based on normative principles: It proposes how resource allocation decisions should be made. Theoretically, its value cannot be countered by pointing out that real-world decisions are not always consistent with CBA; indeed, such arguments make the case for more explicit efforts to use CBA. In practice, however, if CBA never had an influence on real-world decisions, it obviously would lack a bit of oomph. CBA does have influence—as we discussed earlier, demand for it is growing. But CBA frequently gets distorted when bureaucrats and politicians get their hands on it. Certainly a *positive theory* of government, that is, analysis of how decisions are actually made, must take this reality very seriously. But some commentators have raised this to a *normative theory*, that is, analysis of how decisions "should" get made. We are not going to get into this debate here (except to the extent that our normative biases are clear). Rather, our purpose is to illustrate some of the perspectives of bureaucrats and politicians and how they distort CBA.

In a world that was perfect apart from market failures, governments would seek to produce perfect CBAs. But government analysts are also individuals who have a tendency to see "costs" and "benefits" from self-interested or agency-interested perspectives.

The major point of this section is that the bureaucratic role has a strong influence on what many government employees think CBA is, and should be, about. Bureaucratic perceptions of what constitutes "benefits" and "costs" appear to be based primarily on their bureaucratic role; specifically, whether they are "analysts," "spenders," or "guardians."[24] These labels are indicative of the perspective they bring to project evaluation in government. The analysts' perspective can be represented by standard CBA, which we have already presented in Table 1.3. Guardians and spenders have quite different lenses.

Most government employees have not taken, and will not take, formal courses in CBA analysis and, therefore, they will go on believing that what they think is CBA is, in fact, CBA. Even employees schooled in standard CBA may modify their orientation toward those of guardians or spenders as a consequence of the immediacy of their daily bureaucratic roles. The perceptions of guardians and spenders have important impacts on policy outcomes.

Guardians

Guardians tend to be found in central budgetary agencies, such as the U.S. Office of Management and Budget, and in controllership or accounting functions within line agencies. They tend to have a bottom-line budgetary orientation. Their natural tendency is to equate benefits with revenue inflows to their agency or other governmental coffers and costs with revenue outflows from their spending agency or other governmental coffers. Thus, they engage in revenue-expenditure analysis. Guardians have a natural tendency to regard CBA as naive, impractical, and, worst of all in their eyes, a tool whereby spenders can justify whatever it is they want to spend.

For guardians within line agencies, the picture is more complex because they have dual allegiances. Many are prone to cognitive dissonance: They are most likely to describe themselves as being unsure of whether they are guardians, spenders, or both.

The conceptual lens of "pure" guardians can be illustrated by the way they tend to look at the costs and benefits of the AA Highway. Table 1.5 summarizes how a state-based guardian would evaluate the no-toll highway alternative (from column B of Table 1.3) and the corresponding with-toll alternative (from column D of Table 1.3). To guardians, all toll revenues are benefits, whether paid by state residents or by nonresidents. Construction costs are a cost, because they are an outlay by state government. Because guardians seek to minimize net budgetary expenditures, their preference, not surprisingly, is for the with-toll alternative. Indeed, their gut reaction is to consider raising tolls, irrespective of its effect on levels of use or its impact on social benefits.

How does the guardians' perspective differ from CBA? Most importantly, guardians ignore nonfinancial social benefits, in this case $384.1 million for the no-toll alternative and $297.3 million for the toll alternative. In general, they ignore important impacts valued by consumers and producers such as time saved and lives saved. When guardians control the post office, it is easy to understand why one has to wait so long to buy a stamp and post a letter. Neither your time nor my time figures into their calculations.

In this particular example, all social costs happen to represent governmental budgetary costs and so there is no difference between the CBA cost figures and those used by guardians. In other situations, however, there might be considerable differences between social costs and guardians' costs. This can be illustrated by their treatment of the cost of labor in job-creation programs. Guardians consider financial remuneration to labor as the cost, while CBA analysts would consider the loss of leisure time as the cost if the workers would otherwise be unemployed.

Another manifestation of this point concerns the treatment of resources, such as land or buildings, that are currently owned or leased very cheaply by the government. Ignoring their value in other uses, guardians tend to treat them as free to government itself because they do not require additional budgetary outlays.

Guardians ignore costs not borne by their level of government (e.g., costs borne by users or by local authorities), whether financial or nonfinancial. Thus, guardians ignore the loss suffered by Texans from paying tolls. In aggregate, guardians treat these toll revenues as a benefit, while in CBA they would be a transfer involving off-

TABLE 1.5   AA HIGHWAY FROM A STATE GUARDIAN'S PERSPECTIVE (1986 $ MILLION)

	No Tolls	With Tolls
Revenues ("Benefits"):		
Toll revenues from Texas residents	0	112.1
Toll revenues from non-Texas residents	0	37.4
	0	149.5
Expenditures ("Costs"):		
Construction	338.1	338.1
Maintenance	7.6	7.6
Toll collection	—	8.4
Toll booth construction	—	0.3
	345.7	354.4
Net Revenue-Expenditure "Benefits"	-345.7	-204.9

Source: Adapted from Anthony Boardman, Aidan Vining, and W.G. Waters, II, "Costs and Benefits through Bureaucratic Lenses: Example of a Highway Project," *Journal of Policy Analysis and Management*, 12, no. 3 (Summer 1993), 532–555, Table 2, p. 539.

setting costs and benefits; that is, they would be treated as having no effect on net benefits. Furthermore, guardians would tend to ignore nonfinancial social costs, if there were any, in the same way that they ignore nonbudgetary social benefits. To them, congestion and pollution are not relevant costs.

Guardians treat subsidies from other governments (e.g., the federal government) as a benefit because these funds reduce what the state must expend. This ignores the fact that, in practice, the federal government may have earmarked a fixed transfer budget of funds for Texas: Funds used for one purpose may reduce the amount available for other purposes. If so, none of these federal funds should be treated as a benefit from the state perspective.

Finally, guardians generally want to use a high discount rate. One reason is that because of their financial background or the agency's culture, they want to use a financial market discount rate, which is generally higher than the appropriate social discount rate. A second reason stems from their distrust of spenders who, in their view, overestimate benefits, underestimate costs, and generally use money less efficiently than the private sector. Guardians know that using a high discount rate will make it more difficult to justify projects advocated by spenders, because in most of these projects costs occur early and benefits occur late.

Spenders

Spenders tend to come from service or line departments. Some service departments, such as transportation, may be involved with large physical projects, while social service departments, such as health, welfare, or recreation, make large human capital investments. Some service departments, such as housing, make both types of expenditures. The views of spenders are somewhat more variegated than those of guardians because the constituencies of particular agencies are highly varied. Nevertheless, there are major commonalities. Most importantly, spenders have a natural tendency to regard expenditures on constituents as benefits rather than as costs. Thus, for example, they typically see expenditures on labor as benefits rather than costs. Spenders regard themselves as builders or professional deliverers of government-mandated services. As spenders focus on providing projects or services to particular groups in society, we characterize their behavior as constituency-support. Table 1.6 summarizes how spenders in the state highway department view the no-tolls versus the with-tolls alternatives.

Spenders view pecuniary and nonpecuniary benefits *received by* their constituents (residents of Texas in this example) as benefits. Most importantly, they treat money spent on construction workers who built the highway as a benefit. Thus, they think of both project benefits *and* project costs as benefits. With this method of accounting, both the with-tolls and no-tolls highway alternatives generate huge net constituency benefits. In general, spenders tend to support *any* alternative rather than the (no project) status quo. Thus, the mistrust of spenders by guardians is perfectly understandable. Guardians and spenders almost always oppose one another.

Spenders view monetary outlays *paid by* Texan highway users (also their constituents) as costs; for example, they treat tolls paid by Texan highway users as costs. Table 1.6 shows that spenders tend to favor the nontoll road primarily because a toll is a cost for some of their constituents. Indeed, spenders normally do not favor "user pay" fees, unless the agency keeps the toll revenue within its own budget or the payers are nonconstituents.

If spenders could keep the tolls, then they would face a dilemma: Tolls would reduce constituency benefits, but they would increase the agency's budget. Generally, spenders behave as if they are budget-maximizing bureaucrats.[25] When part of an agency's budget flows from clients (i.e., user fees), it faces a trade-off between budget maximization and constituency-support maximization.

TABLE 1.6   AA HIGHWAY FROM A STATE SPENDER'S PERSPECTIVE (1986 $ MILLION)

	No Tolls	With Tolls
Constituency "Benefits":		
Project Costs (from CBA)	345.7	354.4
Project Benefits (from CBA)	384.1	334.7
	729.8	689.1
Constituency "Costs":		
Toll Revenues from Texas Residents	—	112.1
Net Constituency "Benefits"	729.8	577.0

Source: Adapted from Anthony Boardman, Aidan Vining, and W.G. Waters, II, "Costs and Benefits through Bureaucratic Lenses: Example of a Highway Project," *Journal of Policy Analysis and Management*, 12, no. 3 (Summer 1993), 532–555, Table 3, p. 542.

In general, as Robert Haveman and others have pointed out, politicians prefer projects that concentrate benefits on particular interest groups and camouflage costs or diffuse them widely over the population.[26] In practice, politicians and spenders weight each impact category by the strength of the connection that constituents are expected to make between an impact and the particular spending department. If the spending agency perceives that it will receive no credit for expenditure on particular benefits, it will tend to ignore them. Because people almost always notice expenditures on themselves, such "benefits" are invariably treated as important and are heavily weighted.[27] Thus, for example, construction jobs are heavily weighted. The net result is that for many projects expenditure benefits are weighted more strongly than social benefits.

Spenders treat some inputs as neither benefits nor costs. In particular, assets that are currently owned by the state government are simply ignored. In support of the Tellico Dam, for example, the Tennessee Valley Authority (TVA) argued that "since the farm land behind the dam had already been purchased, the value of this land should be considered a sunk cost, even though the land has yet to be flooded and could be resold as farm land if the project was not completed."[28] In the AA highway example, spenders would tend not to include any cost for the land on which the highway was built if it were already owned by the state government.

Spenders treat (relatively recent) past expenditures on an *ongoing* project as investments that provided (and may continue to provide) constituency benefits. For the same reason, spenders believe completion of the project is worthwhile, even in the presence of negative information about real economic costs.

Another set of reasons for completion is indirect, stemming from the "pull-through" effect from the political sponsors. There may be strong political support for continuation of a venture even though it may not be justifiable on efficiency grounds. Politicians do not treat sunk costs as sunk because the political net benefits of completion are generally positive. For example, even though the Tellico Dam in Tennessee was 90 percent complete, the incremental costs still exceeded the benefits.[29] Nonetheless, Congress decided to complete the project. Why? Politicians may believe that the project is beneficial to them in the sense that it is an investment that continues to buy ongoing support. Furthermore, as an added impetus for completion, Jerry Ross and Barry Staw note that "[n]ot only may those directly involved with a project work to maintain it, but other units interdependent or politically aligned with a threatened project can be expected to provide support."[30]

Spenders also tend to favor projects that involve large, irreversible, capital-intensive investments. For example, spenders tend to favor urban rail systems over buses. Once in place these assets cannot be easily redeployed to other uses or markets so the system will almost certainly remain in operation and constituents are guaranteed to receive some benefits. At the same time, the lower operating costs normally associated with such projects allow for lower prices. In turn, this may foster relatively high usage levels, which spenders think may contribute to political support.

The perspective of spenders concerning market efficiency has a bearing on the way they view many aspects in CBA. To spenders, markets are almost always inefficient. They act as if they believe unemployment is high and most project expenditures on labor will go to the unemployed. If one could demonstrate to spenders that a person who will be employed by the project is currently employed elsewhere, then they would tend to argue that this worker's vacated job will be filled by an unemployed worker. Thus, even if the money did not go directly to an unemployed worker, there would eventually be a job "created" for an unemployed worker. Spenders implicitly do not accept that project resources are diverted from other potentially productive uses that also involve jobs.

Spenders regard project expenditures as inherently beneficial to the community: Creating jobs stimulates the economy directly and indirectly through multiplier (secondary) effects.[31] In the extreme it gives rise to a "Midas touch" of project evaluation: First declare the expenditures (costs) to be a "benefit," and then multiply these expenditures by a multiplier, and any government project can be self-evidently justified as producing "benefits" greater than "costs."

Spenders generally favor using a low social discount rate. They prefer a low discount rate because, typically, most benefits occur later while most costs are up-front. While a lower discount rate does not tremendously affect near-term benefits, it raises the present value of benefits that are further off in time and, therefore, raises the total NPV.

With guardians looking over spenders' shoulders, how can spenders generate political support for the projects they favor? One way is to overestimate usage levels and therefore benefits.[32] In addition to straight overestimation, spenders tend to use aforementioned multipliers to boost benefits. The other obvious way spenders generate political support is to underestimate expenditures (costs). All of these efforts are attempts to reduce guardian opposition and increase political feasibility.

CONCLUSION

In this initial chapter, we have provided a broad overview of many of the most important issues in CBA. We deal with these issues in more detail in subsequent chapters. At this point, do not worry if you can only see CBA "through the glass, darkly." Do not worry if you cannot entirely follow the AA highway analysis. Our desire was to give you a taste for the practical reality. We think that it is important to provide the reader with a sense of the reality of CBA before dealing with the technical issues.

CBA is often taught in a way that is completely divorced from political reality. We wish to avoid this mistake. CBA is a normative tool, not a description of how political and bureaucratic decision makers actually make decisions. Yet, because CBA disregards the demands of politicians, spenders, guardians, and interest groups, it is not surprising that there are tremendous pressures to ignore it or, alternatively, to adapt it to the desires of various constituencies or interest groups. Thus, correct CBA is no more than a "voice" for rational decision making.

EXERCISES FOR CHAPTER 1

1. Imagine that you live in a city that currently does not require bicycle riders to wear helmets. Furthermore, imagine that you enjoy riding your bicycle without wearing a helmet.
   a. From your perspective, what are the major costs and benefits of a proposed city ordinance that would require all bicycle riders to wear helmets?
   b. What are the categories of costs and benefits from society's perspective?
2. The effects of a tariff on imported kumquats can be divided into the following categories: tariff revenues received by the treasury ($8 million); increased use of resources to produce more kumquats domestically ($6 million); the value of reduced consumption by domestic consumers ($4 million); and increased profits received by domestic kumquat growers ($5 million). A CBA from the national perspective would find costs of the tariff equal to $10 million—the sum of the costs of increased domestic production and forgone domestic consumption ($6 million + $4 million = $10 million). The increased profits received by domestic kumquat growers and the tariff revenues received by the treasury simply reflect higher prices paid by domestic consumers on the kumquats that they continue to consume and, hence, count as neither benefits nor costs. Thus, the net benefits of the tariff are negative (-$10 million). Consequently, the CBA would recommend against adoption of the tariff.
   a. Assuming the agriculture department views kumquat growers as its primary constituency, how would it calculate net benefits if it behaves as if it is a spender?
   b. Assuming the treasury department behaves as if it is a guardian, how would it calculate net benefits if it believes that domestic growers pay profit taxes at an average rate of 20 percent?

NOTES

[1]"Letter to Joseph Priestley," in *Benjamin Franklin: Representative Selections, with Introduction, Bibliography and Notes*, Frank Luther Mott and Chester E. Jorgenson (New York: American Book Company, 1936), pp. 348–349. We would like to thank our colleague, Ken MacCrimmon, for bringing this quote to our attention; see Kenneth R. MacCrimmon, "An Overview of Multiple Objective Decision Making," in *Multiple Criteria Decision Making*, James L. Cochrane and Milan Zeleny eds. (Columbia: University of South Carolina Press, 1973), pp. 18–44 at p. 27.

[2]This section draws upon Anthony E. Boardman, Wendy L. Mallery, and Aidan R. Vining, "Learning from *Ex Ante/Ex Post* Cost-Benefit Comparisons: The Coquihalla Highway Example," *Socio-Economic Planning Sciences*, 28, no. 2 (June 1994), 69–84.

[3]We often use the term *project* generically. Our discussion applies more generally to policies, programs, regulations, demonstrations, and other government interventions.

[4]See Robert Hahn and John A. Hird, "The Costs and Benefits of Regulation: Review and Synthesis," *Yale Journal of Regulation*, 8, no. 1 (Winter 1991), 233–278.

[5]Thus, we do not include CBAs by the World Bank of its own projects. In fact, evidence suggests that the World Bank does not actually use CBA much; see Nathaniel H. Leff, "The Use of Policy-Science Tools in Public-Sector Decision Making: Social Benefit-Cost Analysis in the World Bank," *Kyklos*, 38, no. 1 (1985), 60–76.

[6]Federal Environmental Assessment Review Office, *Oldman River Dam: Report of the Environmental Assessment Panel*, Ottawa, Ontario, May 1992.

[7]For summaries of the *workfare* evaluations, see Judith M. Gueron and Edward Pauly, *From Work to Welfare* (New York: Russell Sage Foundation, 1991), and David Greenberg, "Conceptual Issues in Cost-Benefit Analysis of Welfare-to-Work Programs," *Contemporary Policy Issues*, 10, no. 4 (October 1992), 51–63.

[8]See Martha Derthick and Paul J. Quirk, *The Politics of Deregulation* (Washington, DC: The Brookings Institution, 1985), and Carol H. Weiss, "Evaluation for Decisions: Is Anybody There? Does Anybody Care?" *Evaluation Practice*, 9, no. 1 (1988), 5–20.

[9]See, for example, Hahn and Hird, "The Costs and Benefits of Regulation: Review and Synthesis."

[10]Of course, other criteria may determine whether evaluative research actually gets used; see the preceding paragraph. For a review of evaluative research utilization in policy analysis, see David H. Greenberg and Marvin B. Mandell, "Research Utilization in Policymaking: A Tale of Two Series of Social Experiments," *Journal of Policy Analysis and Management*, 10, no. 4 (Fall 1991), 633–656.

[11]Robinson G. Hollister, Peter Kemper, and Rebecca A. Maynard, eds., *The National Supported Work Demonstration* (Madison, WI: University of Wisconsin, 1984).

[12]See Thomas K. Glennan, Jr., "Evaluating Federal Manpower Programs: Notes and Observations," in *Evaluating Social Programs: Theory, Practice and Politics*, Peter H. Rossi and Walter Williams (New York: Seminar Press, 1972).

[13]Of course, some additional deaths will occur as a result of more people traveling by road between the two cities. This additional cost is netted out against the generated traffic benefits.

[14]As we will discuss in Chapter 3, on congested highways positive tolls may in fact increase the net social benefits.

[15]The example itself is roughly based on W.G. Waters II and Shane Meyers, "Benefit-Cost Analysis of a Toll Highway: British Columbia's Coquihalla," *Journal of the Transportation Research Forum*, 28, no. 1 (1987), 434–443.

[16]Thomas D. Hopkins, "Economic Analysis Requirements as a Tool of Regulatory Reform: Experience in the United States," Statement presented to the Sub-Committee on Regulations and Competitiveness Standing Committee on Finance, House of Commons, Ottawa, September 15, 1992, p. 10.

[17]U.S. Environmental Protection Agency, *EPA's Use of Benefit-Cost Analysis: 1981–1986*, EPA-230-05-87-028, Office of Policy, Planning and Evaluation, August 1987, pp. 1–3.

[18]G.A. Miller, "The Magical Number Seven, Plus or Minus Two: Some Limits on Our Capacity for Processing Information," *Psychological Review*, 65, no. 1 (1956), 81–97.

[19]For the seminal writing on this topic, see Herbert A. Simon, *Models of Man* (New York: Wiley, 1957).

[20]These studies are discussed by Robert Williamson, "Pulp Cleanup May Be Waste of Money," *Toronto Globe and Mail*, December 23, 1992, pp. A1, A6.

[21]Jonathan Rubin, Gloria Helfand, and John Loomis, "A Benefit-Cost Analysis of the Northern Spotted Owl," *Journal of Forestry*, 89, no. 12 (December 1991), 25–30, at p. 26.

[22]Ted R. Miller, "The Plausible Range for the Value of Life—Red Herrings Among the Mackerel," *Journal of Forensic Economics*, 3, no. 3, (1990), 17–39.

[23]This section draws heavily upon Anthony Boardman, Aidan Vining, and W.G. Waters, II, "Costs and Benefits through Bureaucratic Lenses: Example of a Highway Project," *Journal of Policy Analysis and Management*, 12, no. 3 (Summer 1993), 532–555.

[24]This terminology was introduced by Sanford Borins and David A. Good, "Spenders, Guardians and Policy Analysts: A Game of Budgeting Under the Policy and Expenditure Management System," Toronto, Case Program in Canadian Administration, Institute of Public Administration of Canada, 1987 (revised 1989).

[25]See, for example, William A. Niskanen, "Bureaucrats and Politicians," *Journal of Law and Economics*, 18, no. 3 (December 1975), 617–643, and André Blais and Stéphane Dion, eds., *The Budget-Maximizing Bureaucrat: Appraisals and Evidence* (Pittsburgh, PA: University of Pittsburgh Press, 1991). For various reasons, senior spenders may be more interested in the discretionary budget or "budget-shaping" than in budget maximizing; see Patrick Dunleavy, *Democracy, Bureaucracy and Public Choice*

(Englewood Cliffs, NJ: Prentice Hall, 1992). They may, therefore, be willing to support projects that involve considerable "contracting out" and other activities that may not be budget maximizing per se.

[26]Robert H. Haveman, "Policy Analysis and the Congress: An Economist's View," *Policy Analysis*, 2, no. 2 (Spring 1976), 235–250.

[27]Barry R. Weingast, et al. refer to this phenomenon as the "Robert Moses effect" after the "famous New Yorker who appreciated it and exploited it so effectively." See Barry R. Weingast, Kenneth A. Shepsle, and Christopher Johnsen, "The Political Economy of Benefits and Costs: A Neoclassical Approach to Distributive Politics," *Journal of Political Economy*, 89, no. 4 (August 1981), 642–664, at p. 648.

[28]Robert D. Behn, "Policy Analysis and Policy Politics," *Policy Analysis*, 7, no. 2 (Spring 1981), 199–226, at p. 213, n. 27.

[29]R.K. Davis, "Lessons in Politics and Economics from the Snail Darter," in *Environmental Resources and Applied Welfare Economics: Essays in Honor of John V. Krutilla*, ed. Vernon K. Smith (Washington, DC: Resources for the Future, 1988), pp. 211–236.

[30]Jerry Ross and Barry M. Staw, "Expo 86: An Escalation Prototype," *Administrative Science Quarterly*, 31, no. 2 (June 1986), 274–297, at p. 278.

[31]One reason why some spenders attach so much importance to multipliers is because they have a basic grounding in input-output analysis, but they do not clearly understand the fundamental distinction between economic and social impact analyses, and evaluation studies; see W.G. Waters, II, "Impact Studies and the Evaluation of Public Projects," *Annals of Regional Science*, 10, no. 1 (March 1976), 98–103.

[32]See, for example, John F. Kain, "The Use of Straw Men in the Economic Evaluation of Rail Transport Projects," *American Economic Review, AEA Papers and Proceedings*, 82, no. 2 (May 1992), 487–493, and Linda R. Cohen and Roger G. Noll, eds., *The Technology Pork Barrel* (Washington, DC: The Brookings Institution, 1991).

2

CONCEPTUAL FOUNDATIONS
OF COST-BENEFIT ANALYSIS

It seems only natural to think about the alternative courses of action we face as individuals in terms of their costs and benefits. Is it appropriate to evaluate public policy alternatives in the same way? The CBA of the highway sketched in the first chapter suggests some of the practical difficulties analysts typically encounter in measuring costs and benefits. Yet, even if analysts can measure costs and benefits satisfactorily, evaluating alternatives solely in terms of their net benefits may not always be appropriate. An understanding of the conceptual foundations of CBA provides a basis for determining when CBA can be appropriately used as a decision rule, when it can usefully be part of a broader analysis, and when it should be avoided.

At the heart of CBA is the concept of allocative efficiency. In this chapter we provide a nontechnical introduction to Pareto efficiency and we explain its central importance to CBA. Doing so enables us to distinguish CBA from other analytical frameworks. It also provides a basis for understanding the various philosophical objections commonly made against the use of CBA for decision making.

CBA AS A MEASURE OF ALLOCATIVE EFFICIENCY

CBA can be thought of as providing a protocol for measuring *allocative efficiency*.[1] Though we develop a more formal definition of allocative efficiency in the following section, it can be thought of as a situation in which resources, such as land, labor, and capital, are deployed in their highest valued uses in terms of the goods and services they create. In situations in which analysts care only about the efficiency of alternative policies, CBA allows them to make direct comparisons. Even when other values are important, CBA serves as a yardstick that can be used to provide information about the relative efficiency of alternative policies. Indeed, analysts rarely encounter situations in which efficiency is not one of the relevant values. Critical evaluation of these assertions requires a precise definition of efficiency.

Pareto Efficiency

A simple and intuitively appealing definition of efficiency underlies modern welfare economics and CBA: *Pareto efficiency. An allocation of goods is Pareto efficient if no alternative allocation can make at least one person better off without making anyone else worse off.* An allocation of goods is inefficient, therefore, if an alternative allocation can be found that does make at least one person better off without making anyone else worse off. One would have to be malevolent not to want to achieve Pareto efficiency.

Figure 2.1 illustrates the concept of Pareto efficiency in a simple situation involving the allocation of a fixed amount of money between two persons. Imagine that the two persons will receive any total amount of money of up to $100 if they agree on how to split it between themselves. Assume that if they do not agree, then each person receives just $25. The vertical axis measures the amount of money received by person 1 and the horizontal axis measures the amount of money received by person 2. The point labeled $100 on the vertical axis represents the outcome in which person 1 gets the entire $100. Similarly, the point labeled $100 on the horizontal axis represents the outcome in which person 2 gets the entire $100. The line connecting these two extreme points, which we call the *potential Pareto frontier*, represents all the feasible splits between the two persons that allocates the entire $100. Splits involving less than $100 lie within the triangle formed by the potential Pareto frontier and the axes. Such a point is the one labeled ($25, $25). This point represents the status quo in the sense that it gives the amounts the two persons receive if they do not reach an agreement about splitting the $100. The segment of the potential Pareto frontier that gives each person at least as much as the status quo is called the *Pareto frontier*.

The lightly shaded triangle formed by the lines through the status quo point and the Pareto frontier represents all the alternative allocations that would make at least one of the persons better off than the status quo without making the other worse off. The feasibility of these points means that the status quo is not Pareto efficient. Movement to any one of these points is called a *Pareto improvement*. Any Pareto improvement that does not lie on the potential Pareto frontier would leave open the possibility of further Pareto improvements and thus not provide a Pareto efficient allocation. Only on the potential Pareto frontier is it impossible to make a feasible reallocation that makes one person better off without making the other person worse off.

Returning to the initial situation, it should be clear that the segment of the potential Pareto frontier that guarantees at least $25 dollars to each person represents all the Pareto efficient allocations in this situation. Each of these points makes a Pareto improvement over the status quo and leaves no opportunity for further improvements. The segment of the potential Pareto frontier that represents actual Pareto improvements depends upon the status quo. We return later to the significance of the difference between the potential and actual Pareto frontier in our discussion of criticisms of CBA.

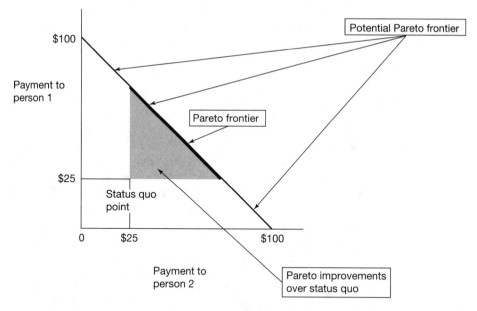

Figure 2.1 Pareto Efficiency

Net Benefits and Pareto Efficiency

The link between net benefits and Pareto efficiency is straightforward: *If a policy has positive net benefits, then it is possible to find a set of transfers, or "side payments," that makes at least one person better off without making anyone else worse off.* A full understanding of this link requires some reflection on how one measures benefits and costs in CBA. In particular, it requires one to consider *willingness-to-pay* as the method for valuing the impacts of a policy and opportunity cost as the method for valuing the resources required to implement the policy. Though we develop these important concepts more fully in the next chapter in the context of market exchange, the simple introductions that follow provide the basis for understanding the link between net benefits and Pareto efficiency.

  Willingness-to-pay.   Consider a proposed policy that would produce impacts of relevance to three people. Assume that these people make honest revelations of their assessments of the values of the impacts. Through a series of questions, we elicit the payments that each person would have to make or to receive under the policy so that he or she were indifferent between the status quo on one hand and the policy with the payments on the other. So, for example, imagine that person 1 honestly reveals that she would be indifferent between the status quo and paying $100 to have the policy implemented. Similarly, person 2 might say that he is indifferent between the status quo and paying $200 to have the policy implemented. These values are the willingness-to-pay of persons 1 and 2 for the policy. Unlike persons 1 and 2, assume that person 3 does not like the impacts of the proposed policy and would have to receive a payment of $250 if the policy were implemented to feel just as well off as he did under the status quo; it is the amount that would have to be given to the person in conjunction with the proposed policy so that he is indifferent between it and the status quo. The negative of this amount (-$250) would be the willingness-to-pay of person 3 for the policy.

The algebraic sum of these willingness-to-pay values is the appropriate measure of the net benefits of the impacts of the policy. In this example, the willingness-to-pay amounts can be divided into $300 of benefits ($100 + $200) accruing to persons 1 and 2 and $250 of costs (-$250) accruing to person 3. The net benefits are thus positive and equal to $50. If these were the only three persons affected by the policy, and if the policy required no resources to implement, then the $50 would be the appropriate measure of net benefits from the perspective of CBA. Simple implementation of the policy would not be Pareto efficient because person 3 would be made worse off with respect to the status quo. But we can easily imagine altering the policy so that it would be Pareto efficient. For example, imagine that person 3 receives $75 from person 1 and $175 from person 2 as part of the policy. Now person 1 is better off than the status quo ($100 of benefits minus $75 given to person 3), person 2 is better off ($200 of benefits minus $175 given to person 3), and person 3 is no worse off ($250 of costs from the policy minus $250 of benefits in the form of compensation from persons 1 and 2).

The key point is that if and only if the aggregate net benefits of the policy as measured by the willingness-to-pay of affected individuals are positive, then there exist sets of contributions and payments that make the policy a Pareto improvement over the status quo.

Opportunity cost. The implementation of policies usually requires the use of some valuable inputs that could be used to produce other things. For example, implementing a policy to build a bridge across a river would require the use of labor, steel, concrete, construction machinery, and land that could be used to produce other things of value to people. The concept of *opportunity cost* is used in CBA to place a dollar value on the inputs required to implement policies. *The opportunity cost of using an input to implement a policy is its value in its best alternative use.* Opportunity cost measures the value of what society must forgo to use the input to implement the policy.

Return to the example of the three persons whose aggregate willingness-to-pay for the policy was $50. Imagine that the policy requires inputs that have an opportunity cost of $75. That is, if the policy were implemented, then some other members of society would have to give up goods valued at $75. In this case, the policy does not generate enough net benefits to the three persons to allow them to compensate those who must forgo the $75 of goods—the net benefits to society as a whole are negative $25 ($50 of net benefits to the three persons minus $75 in opportunity costs to the rest of society). Thus, the policy could not be made Pareto efficient because it does not produce enough benefits to permit all those who bear costs to be compensated fully. If the opportunity cost were only $20 instead of $75, then net benefits to society would be $30 and it would be possible to compensate all those who bear costs so that no one is made worse off, and some people are made better off, by the policy. In general, if the net benefits of a policy are positive, then it is potentially Pareto improving.

USING CBA FOR DECISION MAKING

The connection between net benefits and Pareto efficiency should now be clear. *As long as analysts value all impacts in terms of willingness-to-pay and all required inputs in terms of opportunity costs, then the sign of the net benefits indicates whether or not it would be possible to compensate those who bear costs sufficiently so that no one is made worse off.* Positive net benefits indicate the potential for compensation to make the policy Pareto efficient; negative net benefits indicate the absence of this potential.

One could imagine the following decision rule for CBA: Adopt only policies that are actually Pareto efficient. In other words, only policies that yielded some positive benefits after actually providing full compensation to all those who bear costs would be adopted so that there would be no losers, only winners. Though very appealing conceptually, such a rule would be extremely difficult to apply in practice for a number of reasons. First, it would place great informational burdens on analysts not just to measure aggregate costs and benefits, which can often be inferred from observing prices and quantities in markets, but also to measure costs and benefits for each person—a task that would generally render CBA too costly to use. Second, once the distribution of costs and benefits at the individual level were known, the administrative costs of actually making specific transfers for each government policy would almost certainly be high. Third, it is very difficult to operate a practical system of compensation payments that does not distort the investment and work behavior of households. Fourth, the requirement that everyone be fully compensated would create a strong incentive for people to find ways to overstate the costs and understate the benefits that they expect to receive from policies, complicating the already difficult task of inferring people's true willingness-to-pay values. The "actual Pareto efficiency" principle in practice would thus result in society forgoing many policies that offer positive net benefits and the diversion of much effort toward the seeking of unjustified compensation.

Potential Pareto Efficiency

CBA utilizes an alternative decision rule with somewhat less conceptual appeal, but much greater feasibility, than the actual Pareto efficiency rule. It is based on what is known as the Kaldor-Hicks criterion: A policy should be adopted if and only if those who will gain *could* fully compensate those who will lose and still be better off.[2] The Kaldor-Hicks criterion provides the basis for the *potential Pareto efficiency* rule: *Adopt only policies that have positive net benefits.* As long as net benefits are positive, it is at least possible that losers could be compensated so that the policy *potentially* could be Pareto improving. In terms of Figure 2.1, any point on the potential Pareto frontier would pass the potential Pareto efficiency rule while only those points on the potential Pareto frontier that guarantee at least $25 to each person (the heavily shaded segment of the potential Pareto frontier) pass the actual Pareto efficiency rule.

Several justifications, aside from feasibility, are commonly offered in defense of the potential Pareto efficiency rule. First, by always choosing policies with positive net benefits, society maximizes aggregate wealth. This indirectly helps those who are worse off in society because richer societies have greater capability for helping their poorest members and, if redistribution is a normal good (that is, other things equal, people want more of it as their wealth increases), members of society have a greater willingness to help.[3] Second, it is likely that different policies will have different sets of winners and losers. Thus, if the rule is consistently applied to government activity, then costs and benefits will tend to average out across people so that each person is likely to realize positive net benefits from the full collection of policies. Third, as we discuss later in this chapter, the rule stands in contrast to the incentives in representative political systems to give too much weight to costs and benefits that accrue to organized groups (so-called *stakeholders*) and too little weight to costs and benefits that accrue to unorganized interests. Its use in public discourse may thereby reduce the chances that Pareto inefficient policies will be adopted. Fourth, if a more equal distribution of wealth or income is an important goal, then it is possible to address it directly through transfers after a large number of efficiency-enhancing policies have been adopted. In other words, redistribution can at least in theory be done "wholesale" with a single redistribution program rather than "retail" with each of many policies.

Application of the Decision Rule in Practice

In situations in which policies have independent effects and there are no constraints on inputs, the CBA decision rule is simple: *Adopt all policies that have positive net benefits.* A more general version of the rule applies in situations involving multiple policies that may enhance or interfere with each other: *Choose the combination of policies that maximizes net benefits.* Physical, budgetary, and other constraints may limit the combinations of policies that are feasible.

Policies are sometimes *mutually exclusive*. For example, we cannot drain a swamp to create agricultural land and simultaneously preserve it as a wildlife refuge. When all the available policies are mutually exclusive, efficiency is maximized by choosing the one with the largest net positive benefits. Consider the list of projects in Table 2.1, for example. Interpret the costs and benefits as being expressed in terms of present values, so that they can be directly compared with dollars of current consumption. Suppose we could choose any combination of projects, then we should simply choose all those with positive net benefits—namely, projects A, B, C, and D. Assume, however, that all projects are mutually exclusive, except C and D which can be built together to obtain synergistic gains. By taking the combination of C and D to be a separate project, we can consider all the projects on the list to be mutually exclusive. Looking down the column labeled "Net Benefits," we see that project B offers the largest net benefits and therefore should be the one selected.

Analysts often compare programs in terms of *benefit-cost ratios*. Note that project B, which offers the largest net benefits, does *not* have the largest ratio of benefits to costs. Project A has a benefit-cost ratio of 10, while project B has a benefit-cost ratio of only 3. Nevertheless, project B should be selected because it offers larger net ben-

TABLE 2.1   CHOOSING AMONG PROJECTS: NET BENEFITS VERSUS BENEFIT-COST RATIOS

	Costs	Benefits	Net Benefits	Benefits/Costs
No project	0	0	0	—
Project A	1	10	9	10
Project B	10	30	20	3
Project C	4	8	4	2
Project D	3	5	2	1.7
Projects C and D	7	21	14	3
Project E	10	8	−2	0.8

(1) No constraints: Choose A, B, and combination C and D (net benefits equal 43).

(2) All projects mutually exclusive: Choose B (net benefits equal 20).

(3) Costs cannot exceed 10: Choose A and combination C and D (net benefits equal 23).

Source: Adapted from David L. Weimer and Aidan R. Vining, *Policy Analysis: Concepts and Practice* (Englewood Cliffs, NJ: Prentice Hall, 1992), Figure 9.9.

efits than project A. This comparison shows how the benefit-cost ratio can sometimes confuse the choice process when the projects under consideration are of different scale. Furthermore, the benefit-cost ratio is sensitive to whether negative willingness-to-pay amounts are subtracted from benefits or added to costs. For example, imagine that the cost of 10 for project B was opportunity costs and the benefits of 30 consist-ed of 40 for one group and -10 for another. Treating the negative willingness-to-pay as a cost rather than as a negative benefit would leave the net benefits unchanged but would lower the benefit-cost ratio from 3 to 2. Thus, benefit-cost ratios are subject to manipulation. For these reasons, we recommend that analysts avoid using benefit-cost ratios and rely instead on net benefits to rank policies.

Note that projects C and D are shown as synergistic. That is, the net benefits from adopting both together exceed the sum of the net benefits from adopting each one independently. Such might be the case if project C were a dam that created a reser-voir that could be used for recreation as well as hydroelectric power and D were a road that increased access to the reservoir. Of course, projects can also interfere with each other—for instance, the dam might reduce the benefits of a downstream recreation project. The important point is that care must be taken to determine interactions among projects so that the combinations of projects providing the greatest net bene-fits in aggregate can be readily identified.

Return to Table 2.1 and interpret the listed costs as public expenditures exactly equal to opportunity costs and the listed benefits as the willingness-to-pay values for all project effects. Now assume that, while none of the projects are mutually exclusive in a physical sense, total public expenditures (costs) cannot exceed 10 because of a budget constraint that is binding for political reasons. If project B is selected, then the budget constraint is met and net benefits of 20 result. If project A and the combination of projects C and D are selected instead, then the budget constraint is also met, but net benefits of 23 result. No other feasible combination offers larger net benefits. Thus, under the budget constraint, net benefits are maximized by choosing projects A and the combination of C and D.

LIMITATIONS OF CBA: OTHER ANALYTICAL APPROACHES

It is important for analysts to realize the limitations of CBA. Two types of circumstance make CBA inappropriate for decision making. First, technical limitations may make it impossible to quantify and then monetize all relevant impacts as costs and benefits. Second, goals other than efficiency may be of relevance to the policy. For example, some policies are intended to affect the equality of outcomes or opportunity. Nevertheless, CBA is often a useful yardstick for measuring efficiency even when it is not an appropriate decision rule.

Technical Limitations to CBA

CBA in its pure form requires that all impacts relevant to efficiency be quantified and made commensurate through monetization. Only when all the costs and benefits are expressed in dollars can the Kaldor-Hicks criterion be applied by the calculation of net benefits. Limitations in theory, data, or analytical resources, however, may make it impossible for the analyst to measure and value all impacts of a policy as commensurate costs and benefits. It may still be desirable to do a qualitative cost-benefit analysis, or, if all but one important effect can be monetized, to switch from CBA to cost-effectiveness analysis. A brief description of each of these alternative approaches follows.

Qualitative CBA. The advice given by Benjamin Franklin at the beginning of Chapter 1 can be thought of as a prescription for qualitative CBA. In conducting qualitative CBA, the analyst monetizes as many of the impacts as possible. The analyst then makes qualitative estimates of the relative importance of the remaining costs and benefits. Consider, for instance, a program to plant trees along an urban highway. The cost of the program, which consists only of the expenditures that must be made to hire a contractor to plant and to maintain the trees, can be directly monetized. The benefits, however, include a number of effects that are likely to be very difficult to monetize: the visual pleasure the trees give to motorists, the reduction of noise in adjoining neighborhoods, and the filtering of pollutants from the air. With sufficient resources, the analyst would be able to estimate these benefits through a variety of techniques such as surveys of motorists and comparisons with the effects of other noise reduction programs on property values. But because the program involves relatively small costs, it is unlikely that such efforts would be justified. Instead, a reasonable approach would be to list these benefits with rough estimates of their order of magnitude.

Analysts who lack the time, data, or other resources needed to value all relevant impacts directly may be able to make use of estimates found in other CBAs or economic research. For example, most analysts doing CBA do not directly estimate people's willingness-to-pay for reductions in mortality risk. Instead, as discussed in Chapters 10 and 12, they rely on econometric studies investigating how people trade such things as money, wages, and time for changes in levels of risk.

When possible, analysts should quantify the impacts, that is, estimate the numeric values of the nonmonetized impacts of the policy. For example, consider the CBA of a proposed regulation to restrict commercial fishing practices so that fewer dolphins will be killed per ton of tuna harvested. The regulation produces a benefit because some people have a positive willingness-to-pay for dolphin deaths avoided. Actually monetizing, that is, measuring the willingness-to-pay, is a difficult task that very well might not be feasible for the analyst responsible for conducting the CBA. The analyst may be able, however, to predict the number of dolphins saved by the regulation. Doing so increases the usefulness of the qualitative CBA for others by conveying the magnitude of the impact of the regulation. Additionally, the client or other users of the analysis may be able to provide estimates of the willingness of people to pay for each dolphin saved so that a fully monetized CBA becomes feasible.

Cost-effectiveness analysis. Analysts can often quantify impacts, but not monetize them all. If the analyst is unable or unwilling to monetize the major benefit, then cost-effectiveness analysis may be appropriate. Because not all of the impacts can be monetized, it is not possible to estimate net benefits. The analyst can, however, construct a ratio involving the quantitative, but nonmonetized, benefit and the total dollar costs. A comparison of this ratio across alternative policies is the basis of cost-effectiveness analysis. The comparison allows the analyst to rank policies in terms of the cost-effectiveness criterion. However, unlike the net benefits criterion of CBA, it does not directly allow the analyst to conclude that the highest-ranked policy contributes to greater efficiency.

Return to the qualitative CBA of the fishing regulation discussed earlier. Imagine that, exclusive of the benefit of avoided dolphin deaths, all the impacts could be monetized to a net cost of c dollars. If the number of avoided dolphin deaths were n_d, then the analyst could construct a cost-effectiveness ratio for the regulation, n_d/c, which can be interpreted as the average number of dolphins saved per dollar of opportunity cost borne. (Alternatively, the analyst could construct the cost-effectiveness ratio as c/n_d, which would be interpreted as the average dollar cost per dolphin saved.) Now imagine a number of alternative regulations, each of which involves some quantity of net costs to save some number of dolphins. A cost-effectiveness ratio can be calculated for each of these programs to facilitate comparison across alternative regulations.

Making use of the cost-effectiveness ratios requires that some additional information be brought to bear. If the objective is to save as many dolphins as possible at a net cost of no more than c^*, then the analyst should select the most effective regulation from among those with net costs of less than c^*. Alternatively, if the objective is to save at least n_d^* dolphins, then the analyst should select the regulation with the lowest cost from among those regulations saving at least n_d^*. This is not necessarily the alternative with the best cost-effectiveness ratio.

Analysts often encounter situations in which they themselves or their clients are unable or unwilling to monetize impacts such as human lives saved, injuries avoided, and the acres of old-growth forest preserved. Because cost-effectiveness analysis may be useful in these situations, we consider it in greater depth in Chapter 13.

The Relevance of CBA When Goals Other Than Efficiency Matter

One value, Pareto efficiency, underlies CBA. The general public, politicians, and even economists, however, very often consider other values to be relevant to social problems and the public policies proposed to solve them. Though efficiency almost always is one of the relevant values in policy analysis, other values such as equality of opportunity, equality of outcome, expenditure constraints, political feasibility, and national security, for instance, may be as, or even more, important values. Indeed, the spenders and guardians we met in Chapter 1 behave as if they are responding to goals other than efficiency. When values in addition to efficiency are relevant, as well as when efficiency is the only value, but relevant impacts cannot be monetized, *multigoal analysis* provides the appropriate framework. In the special case in which efficiency and equality of outcome are the only relevant values, *distributionally weighted CBA* may be an appropriate technique.

Multigoal analysis.   The most general analytical framework is multigoal analysis. At the heart of multigoal analysis lies the notion that all policy alternatives should be compared in terms of all the relevant values. Though multigoal analysis can be prescribed as a number of distinct steps,[4] three of its aspects are especially important. First, the analyst must move from relevant values to general goals to specific objectives that can be used as yardsticks for evaluating alternative policies. For example, the value of human dignity may imply a goal of improving equality of opportunity, which might be expressed as quantifiable objectives such as increasing participation in higher education and expanding work force participation. Second, the analyst must evaluate each alternative policy, including the status quo, with respect to each of the objectives. Third, as no policy alternative is likely to dominate the others in terms of all the objectives, the analyst usually can only make a recommendation to adopt one of the alternatives by carefully considering and making a subjective judgment concerning the trade-offs in the achievement of objectives it offers relative to the other alternatives.

As a simple example, consider a multigoal analysis of alternative income transfer policies intended to help poor families. The analyst might construct the worksheet shown in Table 2.2 as a checklist for keeping track of the relevant goals. Efficiency and the quality of life of poor families are appropriate values that can be immediately "translated" into the substantive goals of increasing economic efficiency and improving the quality of life of the poorest families. The goal of achieving political feasibility might be added to take account of the fact that a consensus on the relative importance of the substantive goals among politicians is unlikely—in this example, it can be thought of as an instrumental goal that is valuable not for its own sake but because it helps achieve the substantive goals. The major efficiency impacts are likely to be work disincentives for the recipients of aid and the real resource costs of administering the aid policy. If both of these impacts could be monetized, then the objective for measuring efficiency would simply be the sum of the net benefits of these two impacts

TABLE 2.2   EVALUATION MATRIX WORKSHEET FOR ALTERNATIVE FAMILY AID POLICIES

		Policy Alternatives		
Goals	Objectives	Policy A (status quo)	Policy B	Policy C
Increase efficiency	Increase work incentives			
	Reduce administrative costs			
Improve quality of life of poorest families	Reduce number of families below poverty line			
	Reduce number of one-parent families			
	Increase educational achievement of family members			
Achieve political feasibility	Maximize probability of adoption of required legislation			

as measured in CBA. If either one of them could not be monetized, however, then efficiency would be stated in terms of two objectives corresponding to the two impacts. The goal of improving the quality of life of poor families would probably be expressed in terms of such objectives as reducing the number of families below the poverty line, reducing the number of one-parent families, and increasing the educational achievement of family members. The objective associated with the additional goal of political feasibility might be maximizing the probability of passage of legislation required to implement the policy.

Before selecting among the alternative policies, the analyst should fill in *all* the cells of a matrix like the one shown in Table 2.2. Each cell would contain a prediction of the effect of a particular policy in terms of a particular criterion. By filling in all the cells, the analyst seeks to gain a comprehensive comparison of the alternatives across all the criteria.

Note that one can think of CBA, qualitative CBA, and cost-effectiveness analysis as special cases of multigoal analysis. In the case of CBA, there is one goal (increase efficiency) with one objective (maximize net benefits) so that the evaluation matrix has only one row and the choice among alternatives is trivial (simply select the policy with the largest net benefits). In the case of qualitative CBA, there is also one goal but, because all relevant impacts cannot be monetized, it corresponds to several objectives, one for each impact. In the case of cost-effectiveness analysis, the goal of efficiency is often combined with some other goal such as satisfying a constraint on monetary costs or achieving some target level of reduction in the quantified but nonmonetized impact.

■ **EXHIBIT 2.1**

In its evaluation of alternative strategies for improving ports and airports, the Hong Kong government developed the following goals and associated objectives:

GOAL	SUBSUMED OBJECTIVES
Economic Performance	• Maximize net benefits • Maximize confidence in Hong Kong's future • Minimize detrimental impact on Hong Kong's economy • Ensure strategies fall within limits of government's resource availability
Environmental and Social Impact	• Minimize disturbance to existing communities (including noise) • Minimize disturbance to local economies • Minimize detrimental impact on recreational opportunities • Minimize detrimental impact on landscape and ecology • Minimize detrimental impact on water quality • Minimize detrimental impact on air quality • Maximize opportunities for replanning of and improvement to existing urban areas
Programming	• Provide facilities in line with forecast demand • Minimize uncertainty of program
Flexibility and Robustness	• Minimize detrimental impact of the following eventualities: 　　Port demand not reaching forecast levels 　　Airport demand growth not reaching forecast levels 　　Port demand growth exceeding forecast rates 　　Delays in provision of facilities or other transport infrastructure 　　Siltation of North Lantau Channel more serious than forecast 　　Closure of a major transportation link • Optimize capacity to accommodate expansion in port, airport and associated uses: 　　As forecast for the period 2006 to 2011 　　Beyond 2011
Financial Performance	• Maximize net present value of public sector investment • Maximize the opportunity for major project packages to be financially viable

The government evaluated three combinations of airport and port facilities in terms of these goals and objectives. The measurement of net economic benefits, the first objective under the goal of "Economic Performance," was a CBA that included the opportunity costs of land and capital, revenues from non-Hong Kong users, and the benefits of accommodating greater air passenger demand as its major components. The objectives under

"Financial Performance" were addressed by comparing government expenditures and revenues under each of the alternatives.

Source: Government Secretariat, Land and Works Branch, *Ports & Airport Development Strategy* (Hong Kong: Government Printer, December 1989).

Distributionally weighted CBA. If both efficiency and equality of income are relevant goals, and their relative importance can be quantified, then distributionally weighted CBA provides an alternative decision rule to the maximization of net benefits. Instead of considering aggregate net benefits as in standard CBA, net benefits are calculated for each of several relevant groups distinguished by income, wealth, or some similar characteristic of relevance to a distributional concern. The net benefits of each group are multiplied by a weighting factor, selected by the analyst to reflect some distributional goal, and then summed to arrive at a number that can be used to rank alternative policies.

Table 2.3 compares standard and distributionally weighted CBA for two projects affecting two groups of people. In the upper panel, which shows standard CBA, the net benefits accruing to groups A and B receive equal weight, resulting in the selection of project I. In the lower panel, the net benefits accruing to group A are weighted three times as heavily as the benefits accruing to group B, resulting in the selection of project II.

The major problem analysts encounter in doing distributionally weighted CBA is arriving at an appropriate and acceptable set of weights. One general approach,

TABLE 2.3   STANDARD VERSUS DISTRIBUTIONALLY WEIGHTED CBA

1. Standard CBA

	Net Benefits		
Projects	Group A	Group B	Aggregate Net Social Benefits
I	10	50	60
II	20	30	50
Weights	1	1	Selection: Project I

2. Distributionally Weighted CBA

	Net Benefits		
Projects	Group A	Group B	Aggregate Net Social Benefits
I	10	50	80
II	20	30	90
Weights	3	1	Selection: Project II

which takes as a desirable social goal increasing equality of wealth, involves making the weights inversely proportional to wealth (or income) to favor policies that tend to equalize wealth (or income) in the population.[5] Another general approach, which takes as a desirable social goal the raising of the position of the least advantaged in society, involves placing a higher weight on the net benefits of those with incomes or wealth below some threshold levels than on those with incomes or wealth above the threshold. As reasonable arguments can be made in support of each of these approaches, the absence of a consensus about appropriate weights is not surprising.[6]

Obviously, developing weights that allow a single quantitative criterion for ranking alternative policies makes the choice among policy alternatives very easy. Yet this ease is achieved only by making an assumption that forces efficiency and equality of outcome to be fully commensurate. Dissatisfaction with the strong assumptions required to do this has led a number of analysts to suggest that distributionally weighted CBA should always be done in conjunction with standard CBA to make clearer the efficiency implications of the selected weights.[7] In doing so, the study becomes in effect a multigoal analysis, raising the question of whether an explicit treatment of efficiency and equality as separate goals might not be a more appropriate framework when both efficiency and distributional concerns are important. Cost-effectiveness analysis might also provide a more reasonable approach than distributionally weighted CBA by posing the question in terms of achieving the most desirable redistribution possible for some fixed level of net cost.[8]

FUNDAMENTAL ISSUES RELATED TO WILLINGNESS-TO-PAY

Fundamental issues arise with respect to the interpretation of willingness-to-pay as a measure of benefits. One of these issues concerns the *dependence of willingness-to-pay on the distribution of wealth* in society. The other issue, known as *standing*, concerns whose willingness-to-pay counts in the aggregation of benefits.

Dependence of Willingness-to-Pay on the Distribution of Wealth

The willingness of a person to pay to obtain a policy impact certainly depends on the wealth that she or he has available. Consequently, the sum of the willingness of persons to pay, the benefit measure in CBA, depends on their levels of wealth. If the distribution of wealth in society were to be changed, then it would be likely that the sum of people's willingness-to-pay would change as well, perhaps altering the ranking of alternative policies in terms of their net benefits.

The dependence of net benefits on the distribution of wealth would not pose a conceptual problem if losers from adopted policies were *actually* compensated so that it would be certain a Pareto improvement resulted. From a utilitarian perspective, Pareto improvement guarantees that the sum of utilities of individuals in society increases. In application of the Kaldor-Hicks criterion, however, it is possible that an adopted policy could actually lower the sum of utilities if people with different levels of wealth had different *marginal utilities of money*.[9] As an illustration, consider a policy that gives $10 of benefits to a person with high wealth and inflicts $9 of costs on a person with low wealth. If the low-wealth person's marginal utility of money is higher than that of the high-wealth person, then it is possible that the utility loss of the low-wealth person could outweigh the utility gain of the high-wealth person. Thus, while the Pareto principle allows us to avoid interpersonal utility comparisons by guaranteeing increases in aggregate utility for policies with positive net benefits, the Kaldor-Hicks criterion does not do so.

The implication of the dependence of willingness-to-pay on wealth is that the justification for the Kaldor-Hicks criterion weakens for policies that concentrate costs and benefits on different wealth groups. Policies with positive net benefits that concentrate costs on low-wealth groups may not increase aggregate utility; moreover, policies with negative net benefits that concentrate benefits on low-wealth groups may not decrease aggregate utility. However, if the Kaldor-Hicks criterion is consistently applied, and adopted policies do not produce consistent losers or winners, then the overall effects of the policies taken together will tend to make everyone better off. Hence, concerns about reductions in aggregate utility would be unfounded.

Critics of CBA sometimes question the validity of the concept of Pareto efficiency itself because it depends on the status quo distribution of wealth. Returning to Figure 2.1, note that the location of the Pareto frontier would change if the location of the status quo point were changed. Some have advocated the formulation of a *social welfare function* that maps the utility, wealth, or consumption of all individuals in society into an index that ranks alternative distributions of goods.[10] In this broader framework incorporating distributional values, an efficient policy is one that maximizes the value of the social welfare function. But how does society determine the social welfare function? Unfortunately, conceptual and practical difficulties preclude the formulation of a social welfare function through any fair collective choice procedure.[11] In practice, it must therefore be provided subjectively by the analyst as in distributionally weighted CBA. We believe that it is usually better to keep the subjective distributional values of analysts explicit by doing multigoal analysis rather than to use a subjective index of social welfare. As an alternative, analysts can report net benefits by wealth or income group as well as for society as a whole.

Dependence of Net Benefits on Assumptions About Standing

The question of whose willingness-to-pay should count in the aggregation of net benefits has come to be known as the issue of standing.[12] It has immediate practical importance in at least three contexts: the jurisdictional definition of society, the exclusion of socially unacceptable preferences, and the inclusion of the preferences of future generations. A recognition of social constraints, rights, and duties often helps answer the question of standing.

Jurisdictional definition of society. The most inclusive definition of society encompasses all people, no matter where they live or to which government they owe allegiance. Analysts working for the United Nations or some other international organization might very well adopt such a universalistic, or global, perspective. Yet for purposes of CBA, most analysts define society at the national level. The basis for this restriction in jurisdiction is the notion that the citizens of a country share a common constitution, formal or informal, that sets out fundamental values and rules for making collective choices. In a sense, they consent to being a society. Furthermore, they accept that the citizens of other countries have their own constitutions that make them distinct societies.

The distinction between universal and national jurisdiction becomes relevant in the evaluation of policies whose impacts spill over national borders. For example, if U.S. analysts adopt the national-level jurisdiction as defining society, then they would not attempt to measure the willingness of Canadian residents to pay to avoid pollution originating in the United States that exacerbates acid rain in Canada. In principle, the willingness of U.S. citizens to pay to reduce acid rain in Canada should be included in the CBA, though in practice, it would be very difficult to measure.

As in the highway example discussed in Chapter 1, a similar issue arises with respect to subnational units of government. As a simpler illustration, consider a city that is deciding whether or not to build a convention center. Assume that a CBA from the national perspective (giving standing to everyone in the country) predicts that the project will generate $1 million in benefits (which all accrue to city residents), $2 million in costs (which are also borne by city residents) and, therefore, negative $1 million in net benefits (or $1 million in net costs). Also assume, however, that through an intergovernmental grants program, the national government will repay the city's $2 million of costs resulting from this particular project. The grant appears to the city residents as a $2 million benefit offsetting $2 million in local costs. Thus, from the perspective of the city, the convention center generates $1 million in net benefits rather than $1 million in net costs.

One can make an argument that the city should treat its residents as the relevant society and, hence, should not give standing to nonresidents. The city government has a charter to promote the welfare of its residents. The city by itself can do relatively little to affect national policy—even if it does not take advantage of all the opportunities offered by the national government, other cities probably will. Furthermore, analysts who do not adopt the city's perspective risk losing influence, a possibility of special concern to analysts who earn their living by selling advice to the city.

Adopting the subnational perspective, however, makes CBA a less valuable decision rule for public policy. We believe that analysts should generally conduct CBA from at least the national perspective. They may, of course, also conduct a parallel CBA from the subnational perspective as a response to the interests of their clients. If major impacts spill over national borders, then the CBA should be done from the international as well as the national perspective.

Jurisdictional membership. Deciding the level of jurisdiction defining society leaves open a number of questions about who should be counted as members of the jurisdiction. For example, almost all analysts agree that citizens of their country living abroad should have standing. With respect to noncitizens in their country, most analysts would probably give standing to those who were in the country legally. Less consensus exists with respect to the standing of other categories of people: Should illegal aliens have standing? What about the children of illegal aliens?

One source of guidance for answering these sorts of questions is the system of legally defined rights.[13] For example, a ruling by the courts that the children of illegal aliens are entitled to access publicly funded education might encourage the analyst to give these children standing in CBA. Reliance on legally defined rights to determine standing, however, is not always morally acceptable. It would not have been right to deny standing in CBA to slaves in the antebellum United States, nonwhites in apartheid South Africa, or Jews in Nazi Germany simply because they lacked legal rights. Therefore, legal rights alone cannot fully resolve the issue of standing in CBA.

One other issue of membership deserves brief mention. CBA is anthropocentric. Only the willingness-to-pay of people counts. Neither flora nor fauna have standing. That is not to say that their "interests" have no representation. Many people are willing to pay to preserve species, and some are even willing to pay to preserve individual animals or plants. As discussed in Chapter 8, it is conceptually correct within the CBA framework to take account of these willingness-to-pay amounts, though effectively doing so is very often beyond our analytical reach.

Exclusion of socially unacceptable preferences.   People sometimes hold preferences that society seeks to suppress through widely supported legal sanctions. For instance, though some people would be willing to pay for the opportunity to have sexual relations with children, most countries attempt to thwart the expression of such preferences through strict criminal penalties. Should such socially unacceptable preferences be given standing in CBA?

One approach to answering this question adds duties and prohibitions to legal rights as sources of guidance about social values. Together they can be thought of as social constraints that should be taken into account in CBA just as the analyst takes account of physical and budgetary constraints.[14] Clear and widely accepted legal sanctions may help identify preferences that should not have standing.

An important application arises in estimating the net benefits of policies that are intended to reduce the amount of criminal behavior in society. Some analysts count reductions in the monetary returns to crime as a cost borne by criminals, offsetting the benefits of reduced criminal activity enjoyed by their previous victims.[15] As the returns from crime are illegal and widely viewed as wrong, however, the social constraint perspective argues against treating them in this manner.

The issue of the standing of preferences can be especially difficult for analysts to resolve when they are dealing with foreign cultures. Consider, for instance, the CBA of a program to bring water to poor communities in Haiti.[16] Analysts found that husbands had a negative willingness-to-pay for the time that their wives saved from easier access to water. By contemporary standards in most urban settings, people would generally regard these preferences as unworthy. Yet in the cultural context of rural Haiti at the time, they were quite consistent with prevailing norms. Should these preferences of husbands have standing? In practice, lack of data to estimate willingness-to-pay amounts for this sort of impact usually spares analysts from having to answer this difficult question.

Inclusion of the preferences of future generations. Some policies adopted today, such as the disposal of nuclear wastes or the restoration of wilderness areas, may have impacts on people not yet born. Though we believe that these people should have standing in CBA, there is no way to measure their willingness-to-pay directly because they are not yet here to express it.[17] How serious a problem does this pose for CBA?

The absence of direct measures of the willingness of future generations to pay for policy impacts is unlikely to be serious in most circumstances for two reasons. First, because few policies involve impacts that appear only in the far future, the willingness-to-pay of people alive today can be used to predict how future generations will value them. Second, as most people alive today care about the well-being of their children, grandchildren, and great-grandchildren, whether or not they have yet been born, they are likely to include the interests of these generations to some extent in their own valuations of impacts. Indeed, because people cannot predict with certainty the place that their future offspring will hold in society, they are likely to take a very broad view of future impacts.

In Chapters 5 and 8, we return to the question of the standing of future generations when we discuss social discounting and existence value.

CONCERNS ABOUT THE ROLE OF CBA IN THE POLITICAL PROCESS

The most vocal critics of CBA fear that it subverts democratic values. Some see the monetizing of impacts as a profane attempt to place a price on everything. Others see CBA as undermining democracy. Though these fears are largely unfounded, they deserve explicit consideration by advocates of CBA.

Does CBA Debase the Terms of Public Discourse?

A number of objections have been raised to the effort made in CBA to value all policy impacts in terms of dollars: Pricing goods not normally traded in markets—for example, life itself—decreases their perceived value by implying that they can be compared to goods that are traded in markets; pricing such goods reduces their perceived value by weakening the claim that they should not be for sale in any circumstance; and pricing all goods undercuts the claim that some goods are "priceless."[18] The language and conceptual frameworks that people use almost certainly affect the nature of debate to some extent. It is not clear, however, how influential the technical concepts of economics are in actually shaping public discourse. In any event, the correct interpretation of how nonmarket goods are monetized largely undercuts the charge that CBA debases public discourse.

Consider the issue of the monetization of the value of life. On the surface it may appear that economists are implying that a price can be put on someone's life. A closer look, which we provide in Chapters 10 and 12, indicates that the value of life estimated by economists really is a measure of how much people are willing to pay to reduce their risk of death; in other words, it is the value of a *statistical life,* the willingness-to-pay to avoid risks that will result on average in one less death in a population. It is appropriate to use the value of a statistical life in assessing proposed policies that change the risk of death that people face; it may not be appropriate to place a dollar value on the life of any particular person.

Every day people voluntarily make trade-offs between changes in the risk of death and other values: driving faster to save time increases the risk of being involved in a fatal traffic accident; eating fatty foods is pleasurable, but increases the risk of fatal heart disease; skiing is exhilarating, but risks fatal injury. Is it profane to take account of these preferences in valuing the impacts of public policies? Most economists would answer no. Indeed, valuing statistical lives seems less profane than attempting to place a dollar value on a specific person by estimating the person's forgone future earnings, a procedure employed by courts in cases of wrongful death.

Does CBA Undermine Democracy?

Some critics of CBA charge that it undermines democracy by imposing the single value of efficiency on public policy. Their charge would be justified if the appropriate comparison were between a world in which public policy is determined solely through democratic processes that gave equal weight to all interests and a world in which public policy is determined strictly through the application of CBA. But this is an inappropriate comparison for two reasons. First, actual governmental processes fall far short of "ideal democracy." Second, at most, CBA has modest influence in public policy making.[19]

The interests of vocal constituencies, often those who can organize themselves in anticipation of obtaining concentrated benefits or avoiding concentrated costs, typically receive great attention from those in representative governments who wish to be reelected or advance to higher office. Less vocal constituencies usually have their interests represented less well. The interests of many of these less vocal constituencies are often better reflected in CBA. For example, CBA takes account of the individually small, but in aggregate large, costs borne by consumers because of government price-support programs that raise prices to the benefit of a small number of well-organized agricultural producers. But CBA rarely serves as the decision rule for public policy. Indeed, it is difficult to identify important public policies selected solely on the basis of CBA.

A realistic assessment of representative democracy and the current influence of CBA should allay concerns that the latter is subverting the former. To the extent it is influential, CBA probably contributes to more democratic public policy by paying attention to diffuse interests typically underrepresented in representative governments. It would have to become very much more influential before it could possibly be viewed as undermining democratic processes. Despite our hopes that the readers of this book will help make the use of CBA more prevalent, we have no concerns about it being too influential in the near future.

CONCLUSION

CBA is a method for determining if proposed policies could potentially be Pareto improving: Positive net benefits make it at least possible to compensate those who bear costs so that some people are made better off without making anyone else worse off. Willingness-to-pay and opportunity cost are the guiding principles for measuring costs and benefits. In the next chapter, we explain how willingness-to-pay and opportunity cost can be inferred from market behavior.

EXERCISES FOR CHAPTER 2

1. Many experts claim that, although VHS is now dominant, Betamax is a superior video recorder technology. Assume that these experts are correct, so that, all other things equal, a world in which all video recorders were Betamax technology would be Pareto superior to a world in which all video recorders were VHS technology. Yet it seems implausible that a policy that forced a switch in technologies would be even potentially Pareto improving. Explain.

2. Let's explore the concept of willingness-to-pay with a thought experiment. Imagine a specific sporting, entertainment, or cultural event that you would very much like to attend—perhaps a World Cup match, the seventh game of the World Series, a Garth Brooks concert, or Kathleen Battle performance.

   a. What is the most you would be willing to pay for a ticket to the event?
   b. Imagine that you won a ticket to the event in a lottery. What is the minimum amount of money that you would be willing to accept to give up the ticket?
   c. Imagine that your income were 50 percent higher than it is now, but that you didn't win a ticket to the event. What is the most you would be willing to pay for a ticket?
   d. Do you know anyone who would sufficiently dislike the event that they would not use a free ticket unless they were paid to do so?
   e. Do your answers suggest any possible generalizations about willingness-to-pay?

3. How closely do government expenditures measure opportunity cost for each of the following program inputs?

   a. Time of jurors in a criminal justice program that requires more trials.
   b. Land to be used for a nuclear waste storage facility, which is owned by the government and located on a military base.
   c. Labor for a reforestation program in a small rural community with high unemployment.
   d. Labor of current government employees who are required to administer a new program.
   e. Concrete that was previously poured as part of a bridge foundation.

4. Three mutually exclusive projects are being considered for a remote river valley: Project R, a recreational facility, has estimated benefits of $10 million and costs of $8 million; project F, a forest preserve with some recreational facilities, has estimated benefits of $13 million and costs of $10 million; project W, a wilderness area with restricted public access, has estimated benefits of $5 million and costs of $1 million. In addition, a road could be built for a cost of $4 million that would increase the benefits of project R by $8 million, increase the benefits of project F by $5 million, and reduce the benefits of project W by $1

million. Even in the absence of any of the other projects, the road has estimated benefits of $2 million.

    a. Calculate the benefit-cost ratio and net benefits for each possible alternative to the status quo. Note that there are seven possible alternatives to the status quo: R, F, and W, both with and without the road, and the road alone.

    b. If only one of the seven alternatives can be selected, which should be selected according to the CBA decision rule?

5. An analyst for the navy was asked to evaluate alternatives for forward-basing a destroyer flotilla. He decided to do the evaluation as a CBA. The major categories of costs were related to obtaining and maintaining the facilities. The major category of benefit was reduced sailing time to patrol routes. The analyst recommended the forward base with the largest net benefits. The admiral, his client, rejected the recommendation because the CBA did not include the risks to the forward bases from surprise attack and the risks of being unexpectedly ejected from the bases because of changes in political regimes of the host countries. Was the analyst's work wasted?

6. Because of a recent wave of jewelry store robberies, a city increases police surveillance of jewelry stores. The increased surveillance costs the city an extra $500,000 per year, but as a result, the amount of jewelry that is stolen falls. Specifically, without the increase in surveillance, jewelry with a retail value of $1 million would have been stolen. This stolen jewelry would have been fenced by the jewelry thieves for $600,000.

What is the net *social* benefit resulting from the police surveillance program?

NOTES

[1]Unless otherwise stated, we intend efficiency to mean *allocative efficiency,* as defined in this section. A broader interpretation of efficiency, which we discuss in a later section, is the maximization of a specific social welfare function that explicitly ranks alternative allocations.

[2]Nicholas Kaldor, "Welfare Propositions of Economics and Interpersonal Comparisons of Utility," *Economic Journal*, 49, no. 195 (September 1939), 549–552; John R. Hicks, "The Valuation of the Social Income," *Economica*, 7, no. 26 (May 1940), 105–124. The principle can also be stated as suggested by Hicks: Adopt a policy if and only if it would not be in the self-interest of those who will lose to bribe those who will gain not to adopt it.

[3]Those who are worse off in society may or may not have been the ones who have borne the net costs of public policies. This argument thus shifts the focus from fairness with respect to particular policies to the relative position of those in society who are worse off for whatever reason.

[4]For a detailed presentation of multigoal analysis, see David L. Weimer and Aidan R. Vining, *Policy Analysis: Concepts and Practice* (Englewood Cliffs, NJ: Prentice Hall, 1992), Chapter 8.

[5]For a demonstration of the application of various measures of vertical and horizontal equality, see Marcus C. Berliant and Robert P. Strauss, "The Horizontal and Vertical Equity Characteristics of the Federal Individual Income Tax," in *Horizontal Equity, Uncertainty, and Economic Well-Being*, eds. Martin David and Timothy Smeeding (Chicago: University of Chicago Press, 1985), 179–211.

[6]The fact that people routinely donate to charities suggests that, other things equal, most people would be willing to pay something to obtain a distribution of wealth that is more favorable to the currently poor. Ironically, CBA provides a conceptual way to place a dollar value on alternative distributions of wealth: the sum of the willingness of the individual members of society to pay for moving from the status

quo distribution of wealth to an alternative one. Unfortunately, it is usually impractical to elicit willingness-to-pay amounts of this sort.

[7]For example, Harberger proposes that a dual test be applied: The policy should have positive weighted and unweighted net benefits. Arnold C. Harberger, "On the Use of Distributional Weights in Social Cost-Benefit Analysis," *Journal of Political Economy*, 86, no. 2 part 2 (April 1978), S87–S120.

[8]For an excellent development of this approach, see Edward M. Gramlich and Michael Wolkoff, "A Procedure for Evaluating Income Distribution Policies," *Journal of Human Resources*, 14, no. 3 (Summer 1979), 319–350.

[9]The marginal utility of money is how much a person's utility changes for a small increase in the person's wealth. Economists generally assume declining marginal utility of money. That is, as a person's wealth increases, each additional dollar produces smaller increases in utility.

[10]Abram Bergson [as Burk], "A Reformulation of Certain Aspects of Welfare Economics," *Quarterly Journal of Economics*, 52, no. 2 (February 1938), 310–334.

[11]Tibor Scitovsky, "The State of Welfare Economics," *American Economic Review*, 51, no. 3 (June 1951), 301–315; Kenneth Arrow, *Social Choice and Individual Values*, 2nd ed. (New Haven, CT: Yale University Press, 1963). Of course, even basic CBA implies an underlying social welfare function that is subject to the limitations of any social choice rule. See, for example, Charles Blackorby and David Donaldson, "A Review Article: The Case Against the Use of the Sum of Compensating Variations in Cost-Benefit Analysis," *Canadian Journal of Economics*, 23, no. 3 (1990), 471–494.

[12]The seminal work is Dale Whittington and Duncan MacRae, Jr., "The Issue of Standing in Cost-Benefit Analysis," *Journal of Policy Analysis and Management*, 5, no. 4 (Summer 1986), 665–682.

[13]Richard O. Zerbe, Jr., "Comment: Does Benefit-Cost Analysis Stand Alone? Rights and Standing," *Journal of Policy Analysis and Management*, 10, no. 1 (Winter 1991), 96–105.

[14]For a development of the notion of social constraints in CBA, see William N. Trumbull, "Who Has Standing in Cost-Benefit Analysis?" *Journal of Policy Analysis and Management*, 9, no. 2 (Spring 1990), 201–218. For a more general treatment of institutional constraints and social welfare, see Daniel W. Bromley, *Economic Interests and Institutions: The Conceptual Foundations of Public Policy* (New York: Basil Blackwell, 1989).

[15]David A. Long, Charles D. Mallar, and Craig V.D. Thornton, "Evaluating the Benefits and Costs of the Job Corps," *Journal of Policy Analysis and Management*, 1, no. 1 (Fall 1981), 55–76.

[16]For a discussion of this case from the perspective of a number of issues of standing of preferences, see Duncan MacRae, Jr. and Dale Whittington, "Assessing Preferences in Cost-Benefit Analysis: Reflections on Rural Water Supply Evaluation in Haiti," *Journal of Policy Analysis and Management*, 7, no. 2 (Winter 1988), 246–263.

[17]See Daniel W. Bromley, "Entitlements, Missing Markets, and Environmental Uncertainty," *Journal of Environmental Economics and Management*, 17, no. 2 (September 1989), 181–194.

[18]Steven Kelman, "Cost-Benefit Analysis: An Ethical Critique," *Regulation* (January/February 1981), 33–40.

[19]Alan Williams, "Cost-Benefit Analysis: Bastard Science? And/Or Insidious Poison in the Body Politick?" *Journal of Public Economics*, 1, no. 2 (1972), 199–226; Aidan R. Vining and David L. Weimer, "Welfare Economics as the Foundation for Public Policy Analysis: Incomplete and Flawed but Nevertheless Desirable," *Journal of Socio-Economics*, 21, no. 1 (Spring 1992), 25–37.

3

VALUING BENEFITS
AND COSTS WHEN DEMAND
AND SUPPLY CURVES
ARE KNOWN

The objective of a cost-benefit analysis of a government policy is to sum all the benefits resulting from the policy and subtract all the associated costs. Doing this requires that the values of all these benefits and costs first be measured in monetary terms. Although in practice, as suggested in Chapter 1, this is often difficult to accomplish, in principle, it would be a relatively straightforward exercise if all the pertinent demand and supply curves were known. The reason for this is that the areas under demand and supply curves provide measures of consumer and producer surpluses.[1] Under most circumstances, it is the changes in consumer and producer surpluses that result from a government policy that provide conceptually correct measures of the monetary value of the policy's benefits and costs.

In this chapter, we first discuss very briefly why conceptually correct measures of benefits and costs—that is, the measures described in the rest of the chapter—are often not used in actual studies and what the implications of this are. We then review some of the major concepts from microeconomic theory that are especially pertinent to CBA, with particular emphasis on producer and consumer surplus. We next describe the valuation of resources—that is, the inputs—used in government policies. In doing this, we stress the concept of opportunity costs and, hence, the use of supply curves and producer surplus. Finally, we examine how the output from or outcomes of government policies can be valued, emphasizing the use of the concept of willingness-to-pay and, thus, demand curves and consumer surplus.

The chapter also includes two appendices. Appendix 3A briefly examines when consumer surplus, as it is conventionally estimated empirically, provides an adequate approximation of the conceptually correct measure of consumer willingness-to-pay. Appendix 3B provides brief explanations of common types of market failures includ-

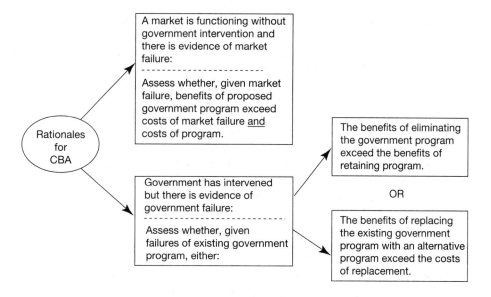

Figure 3.1 The Rationales for CBA

ing monopoly, externalities, and public goods. This appendix does not aspire to be a comprehensive discussion of market failures, rather it is an overview. For a comprehensive discussion of market failures, we recommend the companion volume to this book by David Weimer and Aidan Vining.[2]

The reason for discussing market failures in this book is that their presence provides the prima facie rationale for most, although not all, CBAs. If markets worked perfectly, Pareto efficiency would be obtained without government intervention; that is, a set of prices would arise that distributes resources to firms and goods to individuals in such a way that it would not be possible to find a reallocation that would make at least one person better off without also making at least one other person worse off. It is only when markets fail that there are grounds for such interventions and, hence, a need for CBA. CBA may also be conducted on existing government policies. In this case, the analyst is essentially assessing whether the current policy is inefficient—that is, whether the current policy exhibits "government failure."[3] These two rationales for CBA, market failure and government failure, are summarized in Figure 3.1.

ACTUAL VERSUS CONCEPTUALLY CORRECT
MEASURES OF BENEFITS AND COSTS

In most CBAs, the measures of benefits and costs actually used differ from the conceptually correct measures to some extent. Hence, one purpose of examining the conceptually correct measures of the benefits and costs of a government policy is so that they can serve as a benchmark against which the measures used in real studies can be compared. So that we can focus on this objective in this chapter, we typically ignore the problems inherent in actually deriving demand and supply curves needed to measure benefits and costs, an issue we take up in detail in Chapters 9 to 11. Instead we focus on how the conceptually correct measures of benefits and costs would be obtained if the necessary curves were known.

Before turning to the conceptually correct measures, it is helpful to examine briefly why they often differ from the measures used in actual studies. A fundamental reason is that it is often convenient to use observed prices in valuing benefits and costs. However, as illustrated later in this chapter and examined in detail in Appendix 3B, whenever a government policy involves the production of a public good, or an externality or monopoly power is present, market-set prices may not provide good indicators of the social value of benefits and costs. There are other situations in which a market-set price does not even exist. To mention just one example: Persons entering parks in the U.S. National Park system pay a fee, but this fee is set by the Park Service, not by the market. Consequently, it is unlikely that it bears a very strong relation to the value of the benefits visitors actually receive from visiting the parks. Thus, a continuum exists. At one end of this continuum are values that can be measured in terms of prices that are set in well-functioning, competitive markets. At the other end is the complete absence of market exchanges that can be used to value benefits and costs resulting from a government policy.

In cases in which observed prices fail to reflect the social value of a good accurately or observed prices do not exist, an approach called *shadow pricing* is often used in measuring benefits and costs. That is, analysts adjust observed prices or assign values when observed prices do not exist. They attempt to come as close as possible to measuring the value that those receiving benefits from a government project place on them or the lost value to those who incur its costs. For example, prices charged by paper factories may understate the true social cost of paper if the production process generates pollution. Given such circumstances, an analyst conducting a CBA may adjust the market price upward to account for the negative externality resulting from the pollution. Another important example of shadow pricing is the considerable effort that economists have put into attempting to place an appropriate value (that is, price) on human life. Similarly, economists have also put much effort into trying to determine the social value of recreational areas such as public parks.

We indicate numerous additional situations in this chapter when shadow pricing is required and at several junctures suggest approaches that can be taken toward obtaining shadow prices. In Chapters 9-11, we describe additional techniques that are used to obtain shadow prices for purposes of CBA.

Although numerous shadow pricing techniques exist, it is still frequently the case that the measures of benefits and costs used in actual studies differ from their conceptually correct counterparts. There are several reasons for this:

1. As discussed in Chapter 15, errors are sometimes made in CBA. In some instances, for example, the distinction between the measure being used and the conceptually correct measure is sufficiently subtle that it is inadvertently overlooked. In such instances, those conducting the study may be unaware that their

results are incorrect and do not even attempt to utilize appropriate shadow pricing techniques.

2. It is often difficult to derive an appropriate shadow price. In some studies, consequently, the difference between the actual and the correct measure may be potentially serious, but it is technically infeasible or beyond the time and resources available to those conducting the study to do much about it. In the most extreme instances, even determining the conceptually correct measures of value is so complex and daunting as to put it beyond the grasp of analysts. But even when shadow prices are used, the resulting measures of benefits and costs may still vary from their conceptually correct counterparts. When this is the case, it is at least incumbent upon those conducting the study to point out why and how the study results may be biased.

3. There may be reason to think that differences between the actual and the correct measures are sufficiently minor that the study results are not very much affected. In such instances, shadow pricing may not be necessary.

A PRIMER ON WELFARE ECONOMIC CONCEPTS

The purpose of this section is to review some of the major concepts in microeconomic theory that apply to CBA, especially to the measurement of individual benefits and costs. Most of these concepts should be somewhat familiar from previous exposure to economics—indeed, some such exposure is assumed. In the course of the review, we attempt to indicate the relevance of each concept to CBA. For purposes of simplicity, the presence of perfect competition is assumed throughout this section. Specifically, it is assumed that there are so many buyers and sellers in each market that none can individually affect prices, that buyers and sellers can easily enter and exit from each market, that the goods sold in each market are homogeneous (i.e., identical), that there is an absence of transaction costs in buying and selling in each market, that information is perfect, and that private costs and benefits are identical to social costs and benefits (i.e., that there are no externalities). Measuring benefits and costs when some of these assumptions do not hold and, consequently, various forms of market failure are present is considered later in this chapter and in Appendix 3B.

Demand Curves

A standard assumption in economics is that demand curves slope downward. The reasoning behind, and the importance of, this assumption to CBA will become clear as we proceed. A downward sloped demand curve is illustrated as line *D* in Figure 3.2.

The rationale for the downward slope is based upon the principle of *diminishing marginal utility*; each additional unit of the good is valued slightly less highly by a consumer than the preceding unit. And for that reason, a consumer is willing to pay less for another unit than for the preceding unit. Indeed, at some point, a consumer would be unwilling to pay anything for an additional unit; his or her demand would be sated.

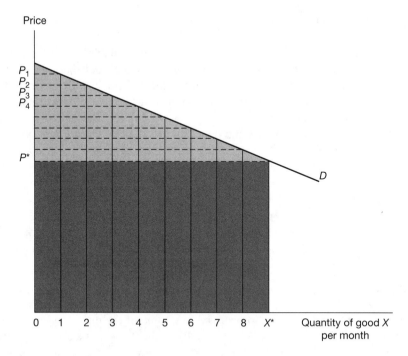

Figure 3.2   Consumer Gross Benefits and Consumer Surplus

This notion that demand curves indicate how much people are willing to pay for various quantities of a good is absolutely critical to understanding both demand curves and the principle behind putting values on benefits in CBA. For that reason, it is useful briefly to reexamine willingness-to-pay (WTP), a concept that was originally introduced in Chapter 2. To do this, we switch from looking at how individual consumers value a good to how all the potential consumers of the good in an economic society value it in aggregate. Figure 3.2 illustrates the demand curve for these consumers.

Figure 3.2 indicates that there is at least one member of society who is willing to pay a price of P_1 for one unit of good X. Similarly, there is at least one who would pay a price of P_2 for the second unit of X, and there is someone who would pay P_3 for the third unit of X, and so forth.[4] The message from this exercise should be obvious: The area under the demand curve—in other words, the sum of all the small rectangles—closely approximates the willingness-to-pay for X by all the members of society. Thus, the lightly shaded area plus the darkly shaded area in Figure 3.2 approximates society's willingness-to-pay for a given amount of X—say, X^*. To put it just a little differently, the lightly and darkly shaded areas approximate the total *gross benefits* society would receive from consuming X^* units of good X.

Now, of course, under most circumstances, people actually have to pay something to consume good X. Let us assume that the competitive market sets the price of X at P^*. Thus, consumers pay P^*X^*, the darkly shaded area, to the producers. In this case, the *net benefits* from consuming good X—that is, gross benefits less payments required to purchase X^* units of good X—equal the area below the demand curve but above the price line. This lightly shaded area is called *consumer surplus*.

When demand curves are known, consumer surplus is one of the basic concepts used in CBA to value impacts. The reason why consumer surplus is so important to CBA is that, under most circumstances, changes in consumer surplus can appropriately be used as reasonable approximations of the willingness-to-pay for policy changes. That is, as stated in Chapter 2, the algebraic sum of willingness-to-pay values is the appropriate measure of the benefits of a policy. In Appendix 3A, we examine the circumstances under which changes in consumer surplus do provide close approximations to willingness-to-pay values and the circumstances under which they do not. The major conclusion from Appendix 3A is that in most instances such approximations are sufficiently accurate for CBA purposes.

Changes in consumer surplus.   To see how the concept of consumer surplus can be used in CBA, consider a policy that results in a price change. For example, as shown in Figure 3.3(a), a policy that reduces the price of good X from P^* to P_1 would result in a "benefit" to consumers (that is, an increase in consumer surplus) equal to the area of the shaded trapezoid P^*ABP_1. Similarly, as shown in Figure 3.3(b), a policy that increases the price of good X from P^* to P_2 would impose a "cost" on consumers (a loss in consumer surplus) equal to the area of the shaded trapezoid P_2ABP^*.

If the values of the change in the price and the change in the quantity of good X that is consumed are both known, and the demand curve is linear, then the change in consumer surplus can be readily computed on the basis of the following formula:

$$\Delta CS = \Delta P(X^*) + 1/2\Delta X(\Delta P) \tag{3.1}$$

where ΔCS is the *absolute* value of the change in consumer surplus resulting from a price change, ΔP is the absolute magnitude of the price change (i.e., $P^* - P_1$ or $P_2 - P^*$), and ΔX is the absolute value of the change in the quantity of X demanded as a result of the price change (i.e., $X_1 - X^*$ or $X^* - X_2$).

Sometimes the value of ΔX is not directly known, but an estimate of the *price elasticity of demand* is available. The price elasticity of demand, e_d, is defined as the percentage change in quantity divided by the percentage change in price and can be computed as follows:[5]

$$e_d = (\Delta X/\Delta P)(P^*/X^*) \tag{3.2}$$

When the value of the change in the quantity is not known, but the price elasticity of demand is, the change in consumer surplus can be computed by using a slight modification of equation (3.1):[6]

$$\Delta CS = \Delta P(X^*) + 1/2[(\Delta X/\Delta P)(P^*/X^*)](\Delta P)(X^*)(\Delta P/P^*)$$

$$= \Delta P(X^*)[1 + 1/2(\Delta P/P^*)e_d] \tag{3.3}$$

Now let us assume that the price increase from P^* to P_2 shown in Figure 3.3(b) results from a government-imposed excise tax, where each unit of X has been taxed by an amount equal to the difference between the old and the new price $(P_2 - P^*)$. In

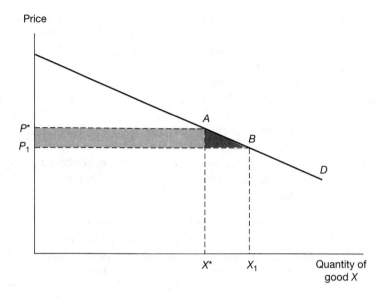

Figure 3.3(a)   Change in Consumer Surplus Due to a Price Decrease

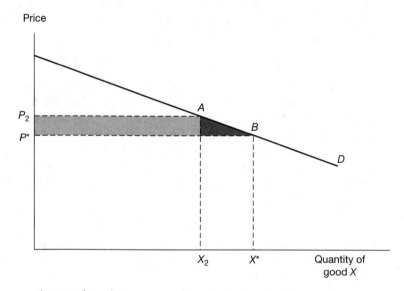

Figure 3.3(b)   Changes in Consumer Surplus Due to a Price Increase

this case, the rectangular part of the trapezoid in Figure 3.3(b)—which is the tax revenue collected—can be viewed as a *transfer*: money that is transferred from consumers of X to the government. It is called a transfer because from the perspective of society as a whole its net impact is zero. The tax imposes a cost on consumers of X, but this cost is offset by an identical benefit received by the government.[7]

The triangular part of the trapezoid, however, is a *pure cost* of the tax. That is, consumers lose consumer surplus, but there is no offsetting benefit to some other part of society. This pure loss in consumer surplus is an example of *deadweight loss*.[8] It results from the distortion in economic behavior from the competitive equilibrium. The tax causes some consumers to purchase less output than they would in the absence of the tax because, inclusive of the tax, the price of the good now exceeds these consumers' willingness-to-pay. Thus, those consumers who in the absence of the tax would collectively have purchased $X^* - X_2$ of the good, and received the consumer surplus represented by the triangular area, lose this consumer surplus. In general, there will always be a deadweight loss if a government imposes a tax on a competitive market. In principle, *if a government project is funded through a new tax, the resulting deadweight loss—but not the tax revenue—should be counted as part of the cost of the project.* We consider this subject further later in the chapter.

Individual versus market demand curves. Just one more point concerning demand curves remains to be mentioned: the relationship between the demand curves of individual consumers in a market and the demand curve for the entire market. The market demand curve for a private good is simply the horizontal sum of the individual demand curves. Individual demand curves indicate the amount of the good each consumer would want to purchase at each price. By adding together all these quantities at each price, which graphically corresponds to summing the demand curves for individuals horizontally, the market demand curve is obtained. This is important for cost-benefit purposes because it implies that a market demand curve can appropriately be used to measure the effect of a price change on the total consumer surplus of all buyers in the market. In other words, total consumer surplus is just the sum of the surpluses of each of the individual consumers in the market and, consequently, changes in total consumer surplus approximate the sum of all the willingness-to-pay values associated with a given price change.

Supply Curves

Figure 3.4 presents a standard U-shaped *marginal cost curve* for an individual firm. The curve pertains to costs in the short run, when at least one factor of production—say, capital—is fixed. Thus, as output expands and increasing amounts of the variable factors of production, such as labor, are used with the fixed factor, diminishing returns must eventually occur. This implies, as is shown in the diagram, that at least part of the marginal cost curve must slope upward.[9]

For purposes of CBA, it is important to recognize that this upward sloping segment of the firm's marginal cost curve corresponds to the firm's *supply curve*.[10] The reason for this is that at any given price, the upward sloping curve segment determines how much output the firm will produce per period. For example, at a price of P^*, the firm would maximize profit by producing at X^*. If it produced more output than X^*, it would take in less in additional revenue than the additional cost it would incur. And if it produced less output than X^*, it would lose more in revenue than it would save in costs. (If the firm wishes to maximize its profits, it would not produce where the

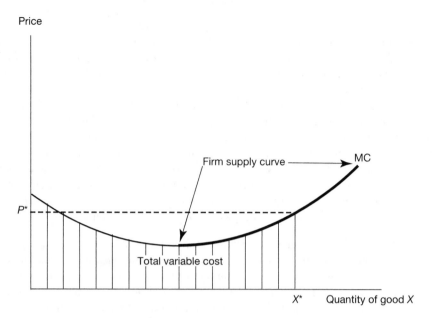

Figure 3.4 Individual Firm Supply Curve

downward sloping segment of the marginal cost curve intersects the price line because by continuing to expand output past this point, until output reaches X^*, it can increase revenues by more than it increases costs.)

Just as the demand curve indicates the willingness-to-pay for each additional unit of a good consumed, the marginal cost curve indicates the additional cost incurred to produce each additional unit of a good. This means that the area under the marginal cost curve represents the total variable cost of producing a given amount of good X—say, X^*.

It is important to emphasize that the variable costs we are considering are opportunity costs, the value of what is given up by a decision, not accounting costs. For example, if the owner of the firm represented in the diagram could earn $80,000 working for someone else, but actually withdraws only $50,000 from the firm each year for personal use, it is the $80,000 figure that should be counted as costs incurred by the firm. This amount is the appropriate measure of opportunity costs—what at least one member of society gives up to work at the firm.

As indicated in Chapter 2, the notion of opportunity costs is critical to CBA. The cost of a project includes the opportunity costs incurred by various members of society so that the project can command the resources it requires. Thus, for CBA purposes, we are interested in the value of the goods and services the resources used by the firm could have produced in their next best use. Consequently, the cost curve in Figure 3.4 should be viewed as drawn under the assumption that the owners of all the production factors the firm uses are paid prices equal to their opportunity costs. Moreover, for such factors as capital and entrepreneurship, these opportunity costs are defined to include a *normal return*[11] because these factors would receive such a return in their best alternative use.[12]

Similar to the case of demand curves, a market supply curve can be derived by summing horizontally the individual supply curves for all the individual firms in a market. These individual supply curves indicate how much output each firm in a market is willing to sell at each price. Thus, the individual supply curves provide the information required to determine the total supply available to the market at each price.

A market supply curve is illustrated in Figure 3.5. As in the case of the supply curves for individual firms, the area under this curve indicates the total variable costs—that is, the opportunity costs—incurred in producing a given amount of output—say, X^*. In other words, this area, $0abX^*$, is the minimum revenue that firms in the market must receive before they would be willing to produce the output amount X^*. However, at a price of P^*, these firms actually receive total revenues that exceed this minimum requirement, an amount that is equal to the area represented by the rectangular area, $0P^*bX^*$. The difference between this rectangular area and the area under the supply curve, that is, the area aP^*b, is called *producer surplus*. Or viewed slightly differently, the sum of total producer surplus and opportunity costs—that is, areas $aP^*b + 0abX^*$—corresponds to total revenues.

Producer surplus is the supply-side equivalent to consumer surplus. Just as changes in prices resulting from government policies have impacts on consumers that can be valued in terms of changes in consumer surplus, price changes also result in impacts on producers that can be valued in terms of changes in producer surplus. For example, a decrease in price from P^* to P_1 decreases producer surplus by P^*bcP_1 to P_1ca and an increase in price to P_2 increases producer surplus by P^*bdP_2 to P_2da.

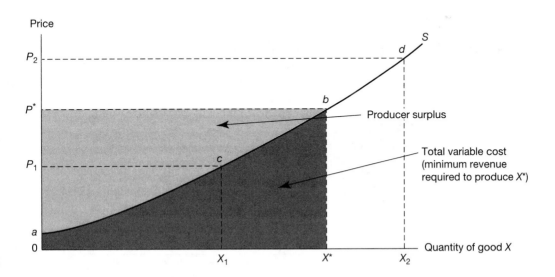

Figure 3.5   Market Supply Curve

It is important to recognize that producer surplus is not identical to firm profits. Producer surplus is the difference between total revenues and *variable* (or opportunity) costs, while firm profit is the difference between total revenues and *total* costs—where total costs include fixed, as well as variable, costs.[13]

Social Surplus and Allocative Efficiency

The sum of consumer surplus and producer surplus is called *social surplus*. Social surplus is illustrated in Figure 3.6, which depicts both a market demand and supply curve in the same graph. In this graph, which once again is drawn under an assumption of perfect competition, equilibrium occurs at a price of P^* and a quantity of X^*. Social surplus, given this equilibrium, is the large triangular area, *abc*, between the demand and supply curves. Viewed slightly differently, social surplus can be defined as the difference between the area under the demand curve (i.e., the gross benefits received by consumers of output X^*) and the area under the supply curve (the opportunity cost of the resources required to produce X^*). If the equilibrium output, X^*, is produced, social surplus—that is, benefits less costs—is maximized.

To reiterate a point made earlier, under well-functioning perfectly competitive markets and in the absence of market failures, the market equilibrium maximizes social surplus. Hence, Pareto efficiency will be obtained: It will not be possible to make someone better off without making someone else worse off. Indeed, an equilibrium point, such as X^*, is said to be *allocatively efficient* because anything that interferes with the competitive process and causes too few or too many resources to be allocated to the production of a good will reduce social surplus. For example, anything that causes output to be different from this equilibrium level—for instance, to be at

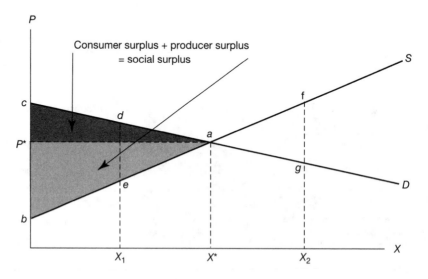

Figure 3.6   Social Surplus

either X_1 or X_2—is an *economic distortion* that shrinks the area of social surplus. Therefore, at least some people will be worse off.

The losses in social surplus (which at X_1 would equal the triangular area *ade* and at X_2 would equal the triangular area *afg*) are deadweight losses, reductions in allocative efficiency. A deadweight loss represents a net cost to society attributable to a distortion. Thus, any government policy that tends to move the market away from the perfectly competitive equilibrium (e.g., imposition of a tax) imposes a social cost by increasing deadweight loss. And a government policy that moves a distorted market toward the perfectly competitive equilibrium produces a social benefit by reducing deadweight loss.

This simple model of economic welfare can also be used to examine how the social benefits or costs that result from government policies are distributed among different economic groups in society. For example, suppose that the perfectly competitive market shown in Figure 3.7 is initially in equilibrium at a price of P^* and a quantity of X^*. At the point of equilibrium, *b*, the price paid by consumers equals the marginal cost of producing the good represented in Figure 3.7 because the supply curve in the figure corresponds to the marginal cost curve. *Allocative efficiency can be obtained only when the price paid by consumers equals the marginal cost to society.*[14]

Now assume that a law is passed guaranteeing sellers a price of P_T. Such a policy actually exists in otherwise competitive agricultural markets in the United States, such as those for corn and cotton, and is known as *target pricing*. At a target price of P_T, sellers desire to sell a quantity of X_T. However, buyers are willing to pay a price

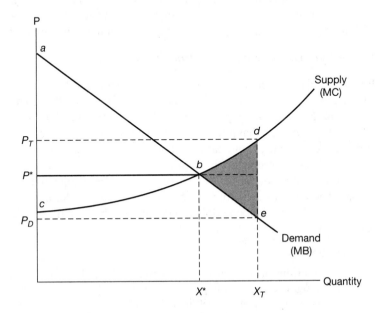

Figure 3.7   The Efficiency of Perfect Markets

of only P_D for this quantity so this becomes the effective market price. Under target pricing, this gap between P_T and P_D is filled by subsidies paid to sellers by the government. Since the marginal cost of producing X_T exceeds the willingness of consumers to pay for this quantity of X, a deadweight loss, corresponding to area bde, results from the policy.

The policy, however, affects buyers, sellers, and taxpayers differently. Since buyers pay a price of only P_D under the policy, but sellers are paid a price of P_T, total consumer surplus increases from area abP^* to area aeP_D, while total producer surplus increases from area P^*bc to area $P_T dc$. Thus, buyers gain area P^*beP_D, while sellers gain area $P_T dbP^*$. Taxpayers, through government-provided subsidies, pay for these benefits to buyers and sellers from the policy. The value of these subsidies, which is the cost of the policy to taxpayers, is represented by area $P_T deP_D$. Note that these subsidies exceed the combined gains of the buyers and sellers by the area bde, the total deadweight loss resulting from the policy. While area bde represents the net social loss resulting from the policy, the remainder of the subsidies—areas P^*beP_D and $P_T dbP^*$—represent transfers from taxpayers to buyers and to sellers respectively. While these transfers are a cost to taxpayers, they are benefits to both buyers and sellers in this market. Because the benefits and costs associated with transfers are fully offsetting, they are typically treated in CBA as having no net impact on society.

The proportion of each dollar given up by one group in society (e.g., taxpayers) that as a result of deadweight loss (or administrative costs) does not accrue as transfers to any other group (e.g., consumers or producers) is sometimes called *leakage*. In the target pricing example illustrated in Figure 3.7, leakage would be measured as $bde/P_T deP_D$. Notice that in this particular example, leakage occurs in the expenditure of tax revenues on a government program. In the following subsection, we discuss additional leakage that occurs in raising tax revenues for government programs.

Deadweight Loss of Financing Through Taxes

Earlier in this chapter, we indicated that a tax on a good, such as an excise tax, typically results in deadweight loss; that is, social surplus is lost in transferring the tax revenue from consumers and producers to the government. This loss (or leakage) occurs whenever there is a behavioral response to a tax—for example, an excise tax on a consumption good causes purchases of the good to fall somewhat or a tax on earnings causes workers to reduce their work hours somewhat. The marginal value of the forgone consumption or forgone hours of work is the deadweight loss of the tax. As a consequence of this loss, the social cost of raising a dollar of revenue through an excise tax is larger than one dollar, sometimes substantially larger.[15] A numeric illustration of this is provided in Exhibit 3.1.

■ **EXHIBIT 3.1**

The following table, which was adopted with modifications from a study by Edgar Browning, is based on a hypothetical society with only five households. The idea is to tax everyone to obtain $1,350 in additional revenue, and then distribute this equally to everyone. The net effect, as shown in column 6, is a total transfer of $270 from the two richest households to the two poorest households. The real incomes of the two poorest households increase by $240 in aggregate, while the real incomes of the three richest households decrease by $390. Thus, it costs $1.63 for every dollar transferred, ignoring administrative costs.

For purposes of the illustration, it is assumed that all households initially work 2,000 hours a year and face a marginal tax rate of 40 percent. Thus, as indicated in column 1, the gross before-tax hourly wage rate of household A is $5 ($10,000/2,000), but its after-tax net wage rate is only $3 ($5 × 0.6). The gross and net hourly wage rates for the remaining four households may be similarly computed. It is further assumed that the compensated labor supply elasticity for all households is 0.15, a value that is consistent with empirical estimates presented in Chapter 9. In other words, it is assumed that a 1 percent change in net wages will cause households to change their hours worked by 0.15 percent. Suppose now that the government introduces a separate income tax of 1 percent that increases each household's marginal tax rate from 40 percent to 41 percent. This reduces each household's net after-tax wage rate by 1.67 percent (i.e., 0.01/0.60 = 0.0167). As a consequence, hours worked fall by 0.25 percent (0.15 × 0.0167 = 0.0025), or 5 hours per year. Hence, as shown in column 3, earnings also fall by 0.25 percent.

Net additional tax revenue is given in column 4. For example, household A initially paid taxes of $4,000 ($10,000 × 0.4), while after the new income tax, it paid taxes of about $4,090 ($9,975 × 0.41), an increase of approximately $90. The total of $1,350 in additional tax revenue is divided equally and $270 is distributed to each household. The net transfer (column 5– column 4) is given in column 6.

Column 7 presents the total change in disposable income, which is obtained by adding columns 3 and 6. The net incomes of the three richest households have been reduced by $570 in aggregate, while the net incomes of the two poorest families have been increased by a total of only $195. But all the families are now working less and enjoying more leisure. Assuming that the value of additional leisure equals the after-tax net wage rate, household A receives a leisure gain valued at $15 ($3 × 5 hours), household B receives a leisure gain valued at $30 ($6 × 5 hours), and so forth. The total change in real income (including the value of the gain in leisure) is given in column 8. The real incomes of households A and B increase by $240 in aggregate, while the incomes of households C, D, and E decrease by $390.

THE MARGINAL COST OF REDISTRIBUTION

Household (1)	Initial (Gross) Earnings (2)	Change in Earnings (3)	Net Add-itional Tax Revenue[*] (4)	Transfer (5)	Net Transfer (6)	Change in Disposable Income (7)	Change in Real Income (8)
A	10,000	−25	90	270	180	155	170
B	20,000	−50	180	270	90	40	70
C	30,000	−75	270	270	0	−75	−30
D	40,000	−100	360	270	−90	−190	−130
E	50,000	−125	450	270	−180	−305	−230
Total	150,000	−375	1,350	1,350	0	−375	−150

*These figures are rounded to the nearest $10.

Source: Edgar K. Browning, "The Marginal Cost of Redistribution," *Public Finance Quarterly,* 21 no. 1 (January 1993), 3–32, Table 1 at p. 5. Reprinted by permission of Sage Publications, Inc.

Economists refer to the social surplus lost from raising an additional dollar of tax revenue as the *marginal excess burden of taxation* (MEB). Several studies provide estimates of MEB for specific taxes and countries.[16] Charles Ballard, John Shoven, and John Whalley provide the most comprehensive study of MEB in terms of the types of taxes covered.[17] They estimate an overall MEB for the U.S. tax system of between 17 and 56 cents, depending upon assumptions about the elasticities of labor supply and savings. For a less extreme range of assumptions, they find that the MEB for income taxes ranges from 16 to 31 cents,[18] the MEB for capital taxation at the industry level ranges from 18 to 46 cents, and the MEB for taxes on commodities without externalities ranges from 4 to 12 cents.

Which MEB is relevant to CBA? With respect to federal projects, it is probably reasonable to view income taxes as the marginal tax source, suggesting that the appropriate MEB would be around 25 cents. With respect to local projects, the marginal tax source is more reasonably viewed as the property tax. Though comparable estimates of the MEB of the property tax are not available, they are probably less distorting than income taxes. Therefore, a lower MEB for locally funded projects would probably be reasonable.

Assume that you have an acceptable estimate of the MEB for a government for which you are evaluating a proposed project. How would you take the MEB into account? You would apply the *shadow price of tax dollars*, (1 + MEB), *to those costs and benefits that represent decrements or increments to the government's financial position, in other words, to the government's expenditures or revenues.* At least conceptually, these expenditures or revenues increase or decrease the amount of tax revenue that, other things equal, would be required to achieve the same aggregate financial position.

Five categories of costs and benefits can be distinguished. First, *costs that represent expenditures by the government should be multiplied by the shadow price of tax dollars.* Second, *benefits that accrue as revenue to the government should also be multiplied by the shadow price of tax dollars.* Third, *costs that accrue as losses in social surplus exclusive of government expenditures should **not** be multiplied by the shadow price of tax dollars.* Fourth, *benefits that accrue as gains in social surplus exclusive of government revenue should **not** be multiplied by the shadow price of tax dollars.* Fifth, *transfers, which otherwise either would not be recorded as costs and benefits or would be recorded as exactly offsetting costs and benefits, should be recorded and multiplied by the shadow price of tax dollars if they represent increments or decrements to government cash flow.* In other words, project-specific taxes or subsidies must be multiplied by the shadow price of tax dollars; they do not "cancel out." Thus, care should be taken to enumerate all costs and benefits, including transfers.

VALUING INPUTS: OPPORTUNITY COSTS

Public policies usually require resources (i.e., inputs) that could be used to produce other goods or services instead. Public works projects such as dams, bridges, highways, and subway systems, for example, require labor, materials, land, and equipment.

Similarly, social service programs typically require professional employees, computers, telephones, and office space; and wilderness preserves, recreation areas, and parks require at least land. The resources used for these purposes obviously cannot be used to produce other goods and services. Almost all public policies incur opportunity costs. Conceptually, these costs equal the value of the goods and services that would have been produced had the resources used to implement them been used instead in the best alternative way. These opportunity costs, as seen in the preceding section, are represented by areas under supply curves. These areas are the theoretically appropriate measures of the costs of the inputs.

As a practical matter, the most obvious and natural way to measure the value of the resources used by a public project is simply as the direct budgetary outlay needed to purchase the resources. Often the dollar figures needed for this purpose are conveniently available from accounting records. Under certain circumstances, the direct budgetary outlay is also identical to the conceptually appropriate opportunity cost measure, but under other circumstances, it is not. To determine when it is and when it is not permissible to use budgetary outlays, we compare the conceptually appropriate measure of costs with the direct budgetary outlay measure of costs in three alternative market situations: (1) when the market for a resource is efficient (i.e., there are no market failures) and purchases of the resource for the project will have a negligible effect on the price of the resource; (2) when the market for the resource is efficient, but purchases for the project will have a noticeable effect on prices; and (3) when the market for the resource is inefficient (i.e., there is a market failure). As will be seen, in the first of these situations, budgetary expenditures accurately measure project opportunity costs; in the second situation, budgetary outlays generally slightly overstate project opportunity costs; and in the third situation, expenditures may substantially overstate or understate project opportunity costs.

Before beginning, it may be helpful to make a general point concerning opportunity costs: The relevant determination is what must be given up today and in the future, *not* what has already been given up. The latter costs are *sunk* and, unlike variable costs, are not represented by the area under supply curves. For instance, suppose that you are asked to evaluate a decision to complete a bridge after construction has already begun. What is the opportunity cost of the steel and concrete that is already in place? It is not the original expenditure made to purchase them. Rather, it is the value of these materials in their current best alternative use. This value is most likely measured by the maximum amount for which the steel and concrete could be sold as scrap. Conceivably, the cost of scrapping the materials may exceed their value in any alternative use so that salvaging them would not be justified. Indeed, if salvage is necessary, say for environmental or other reasons, then the opportunity cost of the materials will be negative (and thus counted as a benefit, an avoided cost) when calculating the net gains of *continuing* construction. In situations where resources that have already been purchased have exactly zero scrap value (the case of labor already expended, for instance), the costs are entirely sunk and are not relevant to decisions concerning future actions.

Measuring Opportunity Cost in Efficient Markets with Negligible Price Effects

Perfectly elastic supply curves. An example of this is when a government agency running a training program for unemployed workers purchases pencils for trainees. Assuming an absence of failures in the market for pencils, and that the agency buys only a small proportion of the total pencils sold in the market, the agency is realistically viewed as facing a horizontal supply curve for pencils. Thus, the agency's purchases will have a negligible effect on the price of pencils; it can purchase additional pencils at the price they would have cost in the absence of the training program.

This situation is depicted in Figure 3.8. If a project purchases q' units of the input factor represented in the diagram (e.g., pencils), the demand curve, D, would shift horizontally to the right by q'.[19] As implied by the horizontal supply curve, marginal costs remain unchanged and, hence, the price remains at P_0. The area under the supply curve represents the opportunity cost of the factor and P_0 is the opportunity cost of one additional unit of the factor. Consequently, the opportunity cost to society of the q' additional units of the factor needed by the project is simply the original price of the factor times the number of units purchased (i.e., P_0 times q'). In Figure 3.8, this is represented by the shaded rectangle abq_1q_0. Thus, the amount that the agency must pay to purchase additional pencils equals the opportunity cost of the resources used to produce

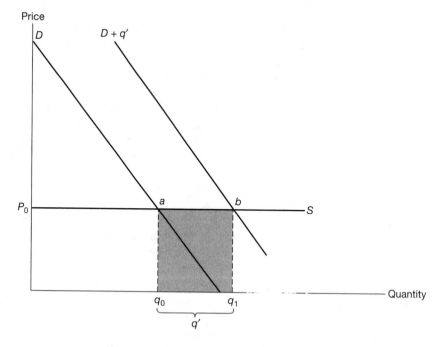

Figure 3.8 Opportunity Costs With No Price Effects

them. In other words, if the q' units of the factor were not used for purposes of the project, then P_0 times q' worth of goods could be produced elsewhere in the economy.

What is important about the situation just described is that the social cost of the units of the factor needed by the project, the shaded rectangular area in Figure 3.8, is identical to the budgetary outlay required to purchase the units; both are equal to P_0 times q'. *Because most factors have neither steeply rising nor declining marginal cost curves, it is often reasonable to interpret expenditures on project inputs as equal to their social cost.* This at least is the case when the quantity of the resource purchased makes only a small addition to the total demand for the resource, and where, in addition, there is no reason to suspect the existence of significant market failures.

Perfectly inelastic supply curves.   Now let us examine a government purchase of a parcel of land—say, for a park—rather than pencils. We assume that, unlike the pencils, the quantity of land is fixed at A acres. Thus, the government faces a vertical rather than horizontal supply curve. In addition, in this example, we assume that if the government does not purchase the land, it will be sold in one-acre parcels to private buyers who will build houses on it.

This situation is represented in Figure 3.9, where S is the supply curve and D the private-sector demand curve. Thus, if the owners of the land sell it in the private market, they receive the amount represented by the rectangle $PbAO$. Now let us assume that the government secures all A units of the land at the market price through its eminent domain powers, paying owners the market price of P. Thus, the government's budgetary cost is represented in Figure 3.9 by area $PbAO$.

Here, however, the government's budgetary outlay understates the opportunity cost of removing the land from the private sector. The reason is that the potential private buyers of the land lose consumer surplus (triangle aPb in Figure 3.9) as a result of the

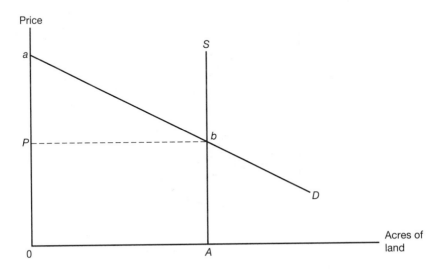

Figure 3.9   Opportunity Costs With Inelastic Supply

government taking away their opportunity to purchase land, a real loss that is not included in the government's purchase price. The full cost of the land if it is purchased by the government is represented in Figure 3.9 by *all* of the area under the demand curve to the left of the vertical supply curve, not only the rectangular area below the price line.[20]

Measuring Opportunity Costs in Efficient Markets with Noticeable Price Effects

It is possible that even when a resource required by a project is purchased in an essentially efficient market, such a large quantity of the resource is required that its price is bid up. This can occur, for example, if the construction of a very large dam requires massive amounts of concrete. In such a situation, the project should be viewed as facing an upward sloping supply curve for the resource input. Such a supply curve is illustrated in Figure 3.10. In this example, project purchases of q' units of the resource would shift the demand curve, D, to the right. Because the supply curve, S, is upward sloping, the equilibrium price rises from P_0 to P_1, indicating that the large purchase causes the marginal cost of the resource to rise. The price increase causes the original buyers in the market to decrease their purchases from q_0 to q_2. However, total purchases, including those made by the project, expand from q_0 to q_1. Thus, the q' units of the resource purchased by the project come from two distinct sources: (1) units bid away from their previous buyers; and (2) additional units sold in the market.

Total project expenditures on the resource are equal to P_1 times q'. In Figure 3.10, these expenditures are represented by areas $B + C + G + E + F$, which together form a rectangle. Unlike the case where the price of the resource does not change,

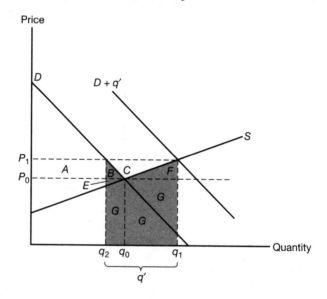

Figure 3.10   Opportunity Costs With Price Effects

however, this expenditure does not correspond to the opportunity cost of using q' units of the resource. The price change must be taken into account in computing the opportunity cost. In doing this, *the general rule is that opportunity cost equals expenditure less (plus) any increase (decrease) in social surplus occurring in the factor market.* In other words, budgetary outlays on a resource do not equal opportunity costs when the outlays cause a change in social surplus in the market for the resource.

To understand why, first look at the areas labeled A and B in Figure 3.10. These two areas represent a decrease in the consumer surplus of the original buyers because of the price increase. However, sellers gain more in producer surplus as a result of the price increase than the original buyers lose—a gain represented by areas $A + B + C$. Part of the gain in producer surplus, namely the area represented by $A + B$, merely offsets the loss in consumer surplus and, hence, is a transfer from buyers to sellers. However, area C represents a net gain in social surplus.[21] To measure the social cost of the project's purchase of the resource, this net gain in social surplus must be subtracted from the project's total budgetary outlay on the resource, areas $B + C + G + E + F$. Thus, the net social cost of the project's purchase of q' units of the resource is represented by areas $B + G + E + F$.

It is interesting to examine the distributional implications of the project's purchase of resources in a bit more detail. The preceding analysis shows that three separate groups in the economy would be affected: the sellers of the resource, the original buyers, and the agency responsible for the project itself. This agency presumably represents the interest of taxpayers. The differential effects of the purchase are displayed in the following accounting ledger:

	BENEFITS	COSTS
Original Buyers		$A + B$
Sellers	$A + B + C$	
Agency		$B + C + G + E + F$
Net Social Cost		$B + G + E + F$

The basic point here is that when prices change, budgetary outlays do not equal social costs. In the example shown in Figure 3.10, they differ by area C. As an examination of the figure suggests, however, unless the rise in prices is quite substantial, this area will be small relative to total budgetary costs. This suggests that in many instances budgetary outlays will provide a pretty good approximation of true social cost.

If prices do go up substantially, however, budgetary costs must be adjusted for CBA purposes. If the demand and supply curves are linear (or can be reasonably assumed to be approximately linear), the amount of this adjustment—that is, the area represented by C—can be readily calculated. It equals the amount of the factor purchased for the project, q', multiplied by $1/2(P_1 - P_0)$, half the difference between the new and the old prices.[22] Alternatively, the opportunity cost of purchasing the resource for the project can be computed directly as the amount purchased multiplied by the average of the new and old prices—that is, $1/2(P_1 + P_0) \times q'$.[23] The average of the new and old prices is the shadow price that reflects the social opportunity cost of purchasing the resource more accurately than either the old price or the new price alone.

It is useful to recognize that the social cost of using a resource for a project or program does not necessarily depend upon the mechanism that a government uses to obtain it. Suppose, for example, that instead of paying the market price for q' units of the resource represented in Figure 3.10, the government instead first orders supplying firms to increase their prices to the original buyers in the market from P_0 to P_1, thereby causing sales to these buyers to fall from q_0 to q_2. Next suppose that the government orders these firms to supply q' units to the government at the additional cost required to produce them. The social surplus loss resulting from the price increase to the original buyers is area $B + E$, which is the deadweight loss attributable to the increase. The social opportunity cost of producing the additional q' units of the resource for the government, which in this case corresponds to the government's budgetary expenditure, is the trapezoidal area $G + F$. Thus, the total social cost that results from the government's directive is $B + G + E + F$. This social cost is exactly the same as the social cost that results when the government purchases the resource in the same manner as any other buyer in the market. Notice, however, that this time the government's budgetary outlay, $G + F$, is smaller, rather than larger, than the social opportunity cost of using the resource.

Measuring Costs in Inefficient Markets

As indicated earlier in this chapter, in an efficient market price equals marginal social cost. Whenever price does not equal marginal social cost, allocative inefficiency results. As discussed in Appendix 3B, a variety of circumstances can lead to inefficiency: absence of a working market; market failures (e.g., public goods, externalities, natural monopolies, markets with few sellers, and information asymmetries); and distortions due to government interventions (such as taxes, subsidies, regulations, price ceilings, and price floors). Any of these distortions can arise in factor markets, complicating the estimation of opportunity cost.

Because of space limitations, it is possible to examine only three of these distortions here. First, we consider the situation in which the government purchases an input at a price below the factor's opportunity cost. Second, we examine the case in which the government hires from a market in which there is unemployed labor. Third, we explore the situation in which the government purchases inputs for a project from a monopolist. In each of these situations, shadow pricing is needed to measure accurately the opportunity cost of the input the government uses.

Purchases at below opportunity costs.   Consider a proposal to establish more courts so that more criminal trials can be held. Budgetary costs include the salaries of judges and court attendants, rent for courtrooms and offices, and perhaps expenditures for additional correctional facilities (because the greater availability of trial capacity leads to more imprisonment). For these factors, budgetary costs may correspond well to social opportunity costs. However, the budget may also include payments to jurors, payments that typically just cover commuting expenses. If any compensation is paid to jurors for their time, it is usually set at a nominal *per diem* not related to the value of their time, as, say, reflected by their wage rates. Thus, budgetary outlay to jurors almost certainly understates the opportunity cost of jurors' time. Consequently, some form of shadow pricing is necessary. A better estimate of jurors' opportunity cost is, for example, their commuting expenses plus the number of juror-hours times either the average or the median hourly wage rate for the locality. The commuting expenses estimate should include the actual resource costs of transporting jurors to the court, not just out-of-pocket expenses; the hourly wage rate times the hours spent on jury duty provides a measure of the value of goods forgone because of lost labor.

Hiring unemployed labor. We have stressed that assessing opportunity costs in the presence of market failures or government interventions requires a careful accounting of social surplus changes. Analysis of the opportunity cost of workers hired for a government project who would otherwise be unemployed illustrates the kind of effort that is required.

Let us examine the opportunity costs of labor in a market in which minimum wage laws, union bargaining power, or some other factor creates a wage floor that keeps the wage rate above the market clearing level and, consequently, there is unemployed labor.[24] Notice that we are focusing here on a very specific form of unemployment: that which occurs when the number of workers who desire jobs at the wage paid in particular labor markets exceeds the number of workers employers are willing to hire at that wage. Workers who are unemployed for this reason are sometimes said to be *in surplus*. We focus on surplus workers so that we can examine their opportunity costs when they are hired for a government project. This issue is of particular importance because there are some government projects that are specifically designed to put surplus workers to work and numerous other projects that are likely to hire such workers. Of course, there are other forms of unemployment than the type emphasized here. For example, some persons are briefly unemployed while they move from one job to another.

Before discussing how the opportunity cost of surplus labor might be measured, it may be useful to consider more explicitly the extent to which the labor hired to work on a government project reduces the number of unemployed workers.[25] Say, for example, a project hires 100 workers. How many fewer workers will be unemployed as a result? In considering this question, it is important to recognize that the project does not have to hire directly from the ranks of the unemployed. Even if the project hires 100 employed persons, this will result in 100 job vacancies, some of which may be filled by the unemployed. If the unemployment rate for the type of workers hired for the project (as determined by their occupation and geographic location) is very high (say, over 10 or 15 percent), the number of unemployed workers may fall by nearly 100. But if the unemployment rate for the workers is low (below 5 or 6 percent), most of the measured unemployed are probably between jobs rather than in surplus. As a consequence, the project is likely to cause little reduction in the number of persons who are unemployed. Instead the project will draw its work force from those employed elsewhere or out of the labor force. At moderate rates of unemployment

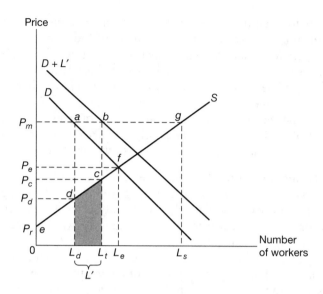

Figure 3.11   Opportunity Cost With a Price Floor

(between 5 and 10 percent), the reduction in the number of unemployed persons will probably be well under 100, but substantially above zero.

Figure 3.11 depicts a situation in which a government project reduces unemployment. In this figure, the preproject demand schedule for labor, D, and the supply schedule for labor, S, intersect at P_e, the equilibrium price in the absence of the wage floor, P_m. At the wage floor, L_s workers desire employment, but only L_d workers are demanded so that $L_s - L_d$ workers are unemployed. Now, imagine that L' workers are hired for a government project at a wage of P_m. This shifts the demand schedule to the right by L'. As long as L' is less than the number of unemployed laborers, price remains at the floor.

We now consider five alternative measures of the social cost of hiring the L' unemployed workers. All five of these measures are subject to criticism. Indeed, it is not obvious that, as a practical matter, it is possible to obtain an accurate value of the social cost of hiring the unemployed. However, some of the alternative methods described here provide better approximations of the true social cost than others.

1. Alternative A.   It is sometimes suggested that because the unemployed are not working, there are zero opportunity costs in putting them to work. This treats the unemployed, however, as if their time is valueless. This is clearly inappropriate on two grounds. First, many unemployed persons are in fact engaged in productive enterprises such as job search, child care, and home improvements. Second, even if they were completely at leisure, leisure itself has value to those who are enjoying it. Consequently, few, if any, unemployed persons are willing to work at a zero wage. Indeed, the supply curve in Figure 3.11 represents the value that various individuals— both those who are employed and those who are unemployed—place on their time when they are not employed. For example, an individual located at point f would only be willing to accept employment at a price of P_e or greater. Thus, P_e provides a measure of the value that this person places on his or her time—in other words, his or her opportunity cost of giving up leisure time to work. Similarly, individuals located on the supply curve at points c and d value their time at P_c and P_d, respectively. As Figure 3.11 indicates that no individual is willing to work at a price below P_r, and P_r has a positive value, the figure implies that the opportunity cost of hiring the unemployed must be above zero. However, as suggested by the fact that the probabilities of illness, divorce, and suicide all increase with unemployment, while job skills deteriorate, this opportunity cost could, in practice, be very low for many unemployed persons.

2. Alternative B.   Figure 3.11 indicates that total budgetary expenditure on labor for this project is P_m times L', which equals the area of rectangle abL_tL_d. This budgetary outlay for labor, however, is likely to overstate substantially the true social cost of hiring workers for the project. As implied by the supply curve in Figure 3.11, although employed workers are paid a price of P_m, most would be willing to work for less. This difference between the value they place on their time, as indicated by the supply curve, and P_m, the price they are actually paid while employed, is producer (i.e., worker) surplus. To obtain a measure of the social cost of hiring workers for the project, this producer surplus must be subtracted from the budgetary expenditure on labor. Alternative B fails to do this.

3. Alternative C.   As the project expands employment in the market represented by Figure 3.11 from L_d to L_t, one might assume that the trapezoid $abcd$ represents producer surplus enjoyed by the newly hired. Given this assumption, one would subtract area $abcd$ from area abL_tL_d to obtain a measure of the social cost of hiring workers for the project. Thus, the social cost would be measured as the shaded trapezoid cdL_dL_t, the area under the supply curve between L_d and L_t. This shaded area would equal the opportunity cost of the newly hired workers—that is, the value of the time they give up when they go to work.

4. Alternative D.   One shortcoming of alternative C is that it is implicitly based on an assumption that all the unemployed persons hired for the project value their time at less than P_c and at greater than P_d. In other words, this approach assumes that these workers are all located between points c and d on the supply curve. However, there is no basis for such an assumption. Indeed, it is quite likely that some of the hired unemployed persons value their time at well above P_c and that others value their time at well under P_d. In fact, the figure implies that unemployed persons who value their time as low as P_r and as high as P_m would be willing to work on the project because the project would pay them a price of P_m! Thus, perhaps, a better assumption is that the unemployed persons who would actually get hired for the project are distributed more or less equally along the supply curve between points e and g, rather than being confined between points d and c. This assumption implies that the unemployed persons who are hired for the project value their time by no more than P_m, by no less than

P_r, and, on average, by $1/2(P_m + P_r)$. Thus, the social cost of hiring L′ workers for the project would be computed as equal to $1/2(P_m + P_r) \times L'$.

5. Alternative E.   One practical problem with using alternative D in an actual CBA is that the value of P_r—the lowest price at which any worker represented in Figure 3.11 would be willing to accept employment—is unlikely to be known. Given this, some assumption about the value of P_r must be made. One possible, although not very plausible, assumption is that the supply curve passes through the origin and, hence, the value of P_r equals zero. If we once again assume that the unemployed persons who are hired for the project are distributed more or less equally along the supply curve between the point at which it intersects the vertical axis and point g, this implies that the unemployed persons who are hired for the project value their time by no more than P_m, by no less than zero, and, on average, by $1/2(P_m + 0) = 1/2P_m$. Hence, the social cost of hiring workers for the project would be computed as $1/2P_m \times L'$. Note that the estimate provided by this computation is equal to one-half the government's budgetary outlay. While this cost estimate would be smaller and almost certainly less accurate than that computed using alternative D, it is usually much more readily obtained for use in actual studies. Given our preceding argument that nonwork time has a positive value, it is probably best viewed as providing a practical lower-bound estimate of the true project social costs for labor, while the full value of project budgetary cost for labor (alternative B) provides an easily obtained upper-bound estimate.

Purchases from a monopoly.   We now turn to a final example of measuring the social cost of project or program purchases in an inefficient market: the purchase of an input supplied by a monopoly. In this circumstance, a government agency's budgetary outlay overstates the true social costs resulting from the purchase. This overstatement occurs because the price of the input exceeds the social cost of producing it. As a consequence, a substantial share of the revenues a monopolist receives are transfers or *monopoly rents*. Thus, in principle, a CBA should not use the budgetary outlay as a measure of social cost.

Figure 3.12 illustrates a government agency's purchase of an input from a monopoly. Prior to the purchase, the input is produced at level Q_1, where the monopolist's marginal cost and marginal revenue curves intersect. The price at Q_1, as determined by the demand curve, is P_1. Now, as a result of the agency's purchase of Q' units, the monopolist's demand curve and the marginal revenue curve shift to the right. The price of the input increases to P_2 and the quantity sold increases to Q_2. At the new price, the agency purchases a quantity equal to the distance between Q_3 and Q_2, while the original buyers in the market reduce the quantity they purchase by an amount equal to the distance between Q_1 and Q_3.

As in our previous examples, the direct budgetary cost of the agency's purchase equals the price times the quantity purchased: $P_2(Q_2 - Q_3)$. In Figure 3.12, this is represented by the rectangle between Q_3 and Q_2 and bounded by P_2 (i.e., areas $A + C + G + E$). However, these budgetary costs overstate the true social cost. To find the true social cost of the agency's purchase, one must examine the effects of the purchase on the monopolist and the original buyers of the input, as well as on the agency's revenues.

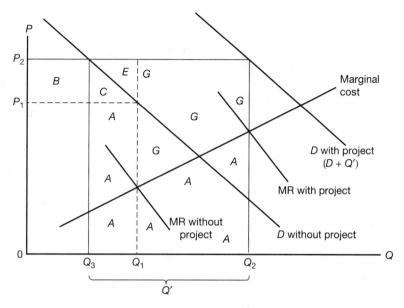

Figure 3.12   Opportunity Costs When Buying from a Monopoly

Because the monopolist sells more of the input at higher prices, its producer surplus increases. This increase has two parts: (1) that resulting from the higher price the monopolist now receives for the units that it previously sold (which is represented in Figure 3.12 by areas $B + C + E$); and (2) that resulting from the additional units that the monopolist now sells (area G). Thus, as can be seen from Figure 3.12, part of the cost to the agency—areas $C + G + E$—is a transfer to the monopolist.

Original buyers in the market are clearly worse off as a result of the agency's purchase, because they now have to pay a higher price for the input. In measuring their loss of consumer surplus, it is the original demand curve that is pertinent because this is the curve that reflects the original buyers' willingness-to-pay for the input. Thus, the total loss in consumer surplus by the original buyers, all of which is a transfer to the monopolist, is equal to areas $B + C$.

The following distributional accounting ledger summarizes the effects of the purchase:

	BENEFITS	COSTS
Original Buyers		$B + C$
Monopolistic Seller	$B + C + G + E$	
Agency		$A + C + G + E$
Net Social Cost		$A + C$

The major conclusion of this analysis is that in the case of input purchases from a monopolist, budgetary expenditures are larger than the social costs. The reason is that the price the monopoly charges exceeds the marginal cost of producing the input. Consequently, in conducting a CBA, the government's budgetary cost should, in principle, be adjusted downward through shadow pricing. In practice, however, the error that would result from using the unadjusted budgetary expenditures would often not be very large. As an examination of Figure 3.12 suggests, the size of the bias—that is, areas $G + E$—depends on the extent to which the price the monopoly charges exceeds its marginal costs—in other words, on how much monopoly power it actually has. And this, in turn, depends on how steeply sloped the demand curve is. Thus, before an analyst develops shadow prices, a sometimes difficult undertaking, he or she should ask whether it is really necessary to do so.

The general rule.   Other market distortions also affect opportunity costs in predictable ways. It is useful to summarize the direction of the bias created by some of these distortions. In factor markets in which supply is taxed, direct expenditure outlays overestimate opportunity cost; in factor markets in which supply is subsidized, expenditures underestimate opportunity cost. In factor markets exhibiting positive externalities of supply, expenditures overestimate opportunity cost; in factor markets exhibiting negative externalities of supply, expenditures underestimate opportunity costs. To determine opportunity costs in such cases, apply the general rule: *Opportunity cost equals direct expenditures on the factor minus (plus) gains (losses) in social surplus occurring in the factor market.*

VALUING OUTCOMES: WILLINGNESS-TO-PAY

The valuation of policy outcomes should be based on the concept of willingness-to-pay: *Benefits are the sums of the maximum amounts that people would be willing to pay to gain outcomes that they view as desirable; costs are the sums of the maximum amounts that people would be willing to pay to avoid outcomes that they view as undesirable.*[26] Estimating changes in social surpluses that occur in relevant markets enables us to take account of these costs and benefits.

To estimate these changes in social surplus, it is critical to distinguish between two types of markets: *primary markets* and *secondary markets*. Primary markets refer to markets that are directly affected by a policy—for example, the effect of a training program for carpenters on the labor market for carpenters. Secondary markets are markets that are indirectly affected—for example, the effect of the training program for carpenters on the market for hammers.

One reason this distinction is important is because in conducting CBAs of government policies, there is a natural tendency to list as many effects of the policies as one's imagination permits. For example, an improvement in public transportation in a particular city may reduce downtown pollution and congestion. It may also reduce the demand for automobile repairs, parking places, and gasoline. Finally, automobiles previously used for purposes of commuting may become available for use by other family members. Such effects are often referred to as *secondary, second-round, spill-over, side effects,* or *indirect effects*.

To assess secondary effects, one must first determine which impacts occur in primary markets and which occur in secondary markets. For instance, the reductions in pollution and congestion mentioned earlier suggest the existence of a distorted primary market due to externalities. If they are important, then such effects should be accounted for in a CBA. On the other hand, effects on the demand for auto repairs, parking places, and gasoline occur in secondary markets and, as will be seen, can often be ignored in conducting CBA. The effect of public transportation on the availability of automobiles to other family members may also be viewed as occurring in a secondary market, a market in which supply consists of family-owned vehicles and the demand side of the market consists of the remaining members of the family. For reasons discussed later, it may be possible to ignore this effect.

In the remainder of this section, we not only distinguish between primary and secondary markets but also between efficient and distorted markets. Thus, we examine the valuation of policy outcomes in four different types of markets: (1) efficient primary markets; (2) distorted primary markets; (3) efficient secondary markets; and (4) distorted secondary markets.

Valuing Benefits in Efficient Primary Markets

Valuation of gross benefits is relatively straightforward when a policy affects the supply schedules of goods in efficient markets.[27] Under these circumstances, the rule is: *The gross social benefits of a policy equal net revenue generated by the policy plus the change in social surplus resulting from the policy.* We examine two common situations where this rule is applicable. First, we consider policies that directly affect the quantity of a good available to consumers. For example, a publicly operated day-care center shifts the supply schedule to the right—more day care is offered to consumers at each price. This results in direct reductions in costs to consumers. Second, we consider policies that shift the supply schedule down by altering the price or availability of some input used to produce the good. For example, deepening a harbor so that it accommodates large, efficient ships and thereby reducing the cost of transporting bulk commodities to and from the port for shipping companies. Here there are direct reductions in costs to producers.

Direct reductions in costs to consumers.   Figure 3.13 shows the gross benefits that result when a project directly increases the available supply of a good in a market, but the increase is so small that the price of the good is unaffected. Under these circumstances, the government may be treated like other competitors in an efficient market. Hence, as shown in the figure, it faces a horizontal demand schedule, D, for the good at the market price, P_0. If the project directly adds a quantity, q', to the market, then the supply schedule as seen by consumers shifts from S to $S + q'$.[28] Because the demand curve is horizontal, the price of the good and, hence, social surplus are unaffected by the shift in the supply curve. However, if consumers must purchase the additional units of the good from the project, the project receives revenue equal to P_0 times q', the area of rectangle q_0abq_1.[29] These revenues are the only gross benefits that accrue from the project selling q' units in the market.

Figure 3.14 differs from Figure 3.13 because it is based on the assumption that the government adds a sufficiently large quantity of a good to a market to reduce the

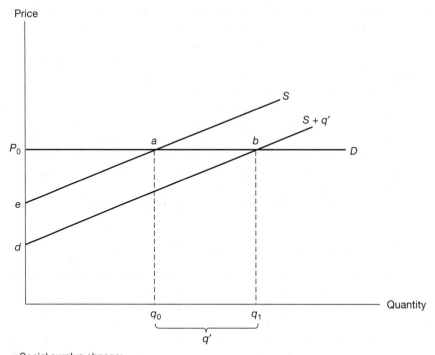

Social surplus change:

(a) Direct supply of q' by project: gain of project revenue equal to area of rectangle q_0abq_1

(b) Supply schedule shift through cost reduction: gain of trapezoid *abde*

Figure 3.13   Measuring Benefits in an Efficient Market with No Price Effects

price of the good. Thus, the demand schedule, D, in Figure 3.14 is shown as downward sloping. The intersection of the demand schedule and the supply schedule, S, indicates the equilibrium price, P_0, prior to the project. The equilibrium price of the good falls to P_1 after the government enters the market by providing the q' units of the good. This time, because of the reduction in costs to consumers, there is a change in social surplus. If consumers must purchase the additional units of the good from the project, then the gain in consumer surplus corresponds to the area of trapezoid P_0abP_1. Because private-sector suppliers continue to operate on the original supply schedule, S, they suffer a loss of producer surplus equal to the area of trapezoid P_0acP_1. Thus, the net gain in social surplus equals the area of triangle abc, which is lightly shaded. In addition, the project receives revenue equal to the area of rectangle q_2cbq_1. The sum of project revenues and the gain in social surplus in the market equals area q_2cabq_1, which is the total gross benefits from the project selling q' units in the market.

What benefits would accrue if q' units of the good were instead distributed free to selected consumers? If the price of the good does not change, as in the situation depicted in Figure 3.13, the answer is straightforward: As a result of receiving q' units of the good free, consumers gain surplus equal to the area of rectangle q_0abq_1, an area

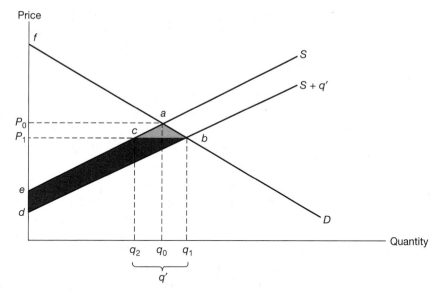

Social surplus change:

(a) Direct supply of q' by project: gain of triangle *abc*
    plus project revenue equal to area of rectangle q_2cbq_1
(b) Supply schedule shift through cost reduction: gain
    of trapezoid *abde*

Figure 3.14 Measuring Benefits in an Efficient Market

that exactly corresponds to the revenues that would have accrued had the project's output been sold.

The answer is more complex if the increase in the supply of the good causes its price to fall, the situation shown in Figure 3.14. Under these circumstances, if the q' units are given only to those consumers who would have valued these units at P_1 or higher, then the project gross benefit measure is again exactly the same as it would have been had the output been sold. As before, the reduction in price from P_0 to P_1 results in an increase in social surplus equal to area *abc*. With free distribution, however, no revenue accrues to the project. Instead, as a result of receiving q' units of the good free, consumers enjoy an additional surplus equal to the area of rectangle q_2cbq_1. Thus, total gross benefits from the project once again equal the area of trapezoid q_2cabq_1.

It is more likely, however, that if q' units of the good are distributed for free, some would go to consumers who are located below point *b* on the market demand curve shown in Figure 3.14. In other words, some would be distributed to consumers in greater quantities than they would have purchased at price P_1. If the recipients of these excess units keep some of them, area q_2cabq_1 overestimates the project's benefit because these persons value their marginal consumption of these excess units at less than P_1.[30] Area q_2cabq_1 approximates project benefits, however, if recipients of the excess units sell them to others who would have been willing to buy them at a price of P_1 (provided the transaction costs associated with the sale of the excess units are minimal).

Suppose, for example, that a project provides previously stockpiled gasoline to low-income consumers during an oil supply disruption (an in-kind subsidy). Some low-income households will find themselves with more gasoline than they would have purchased on their own at price P_1; therefore, they will try to sell the excess. Doing so will be relatively easy if access to the stockpiled gasoline is provided through legally transferable coupons; it would obviously be much more difficult if the gasoline had to be physically taken away by the low-income households. If the gasoline could be costlessly traded among consumers using coupons, then we would expect the outcome to be identical to one in which the gasoline is sold in the market and the revenue given directly to low-income consumers.

Reductions in costs to producers. We now turn to a different type of public-sector project: those, such as harbor deepening, that lower the private sector's cost of supplying a market. Figure 3.14 can again be used to analyze this situation. In this case, however, the supply schedule shifts to $S + q'$, not because the project directly supplies q' to the market, but rather because reductions in their marginal costs allow private-sector firms to offer q' additional units profitably at each price.[31] As in the case of direct supply of q', the new equilibrium price is P_1. Thus, the gain in consumer surplus corresponds to the area of trapezoid P_0abP_1. The change in producer surplus corresponds to the difference in the areas of triangle P_0ae (the producer surplus with supply schedule S) and triangle P_1bd (the producer surplus with supply schedule $S + q'$). Area P_1ce is common to the two triangles and therefore cancels. Hence, producers enjoy a net gain in surplus equal to area $ecbd$ minus area P_0acP_1. Adding this gain to the gain in consumer surplus, area P_0abP_1, means that the gain in social surplus resulting from the project equals the area of trapezoid $abde$. (That is, area $ecbd$ + area P_0abP_1 – area P_0acP_1 = area $ecbd$ + area abc = area $abde$.[32]) Because no project revenue is generated, area $abde$ alone is the gross benefit of the project.[33]

The straightforward measurement of gross benefits, which is illustrated in Figure 3.14, depends on two important assumptions: that the market is efficient and that effects in other markets can be ignored. We next turn to situations in which these conditions do not hold.

Valuing Benefits in Distorted Primary Markets

If market failures or government interventions distort the relevant product market, then project benefits should continue to be measured as changes in social surplus resulting from the project plus net revenues generated by the project. However, complications arise in determining the correct social surplus changes. For example, consider a program that subsidizes the purchase of rodent extermination services in a poor neighborhood. One mechanism for doing this is to provide to residents of the neighborhood vouchers that are worth a certain number of dollars for each unit of extermination services they purchase. After subtracting the face value of these vouchers from what they charge neighborhood residents for their services, exterminators would be reimbursed the voucher face value by the government.

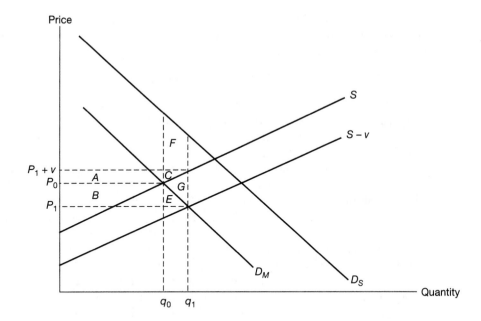

Gain to consumers in target neighborhood: $B + E$
Gain to consumers in nearby neighborhood: $C + G + F$
Gain to producers: $A + C$
Program costs: $A + B + C + G + E$
Net benefits: $C + F$

Figure 3.15   Social Benefits for Direct Supply of a Good with a Positive Externality

By increasing the use of extermination services, such a program may well result in a positive externality:[34] The fewer rodents in the neighborhood, the easier it is for residents in adjoining neighborhoods to control their own rodent populations. This situation is illustrated in Figure 3.15, where the market demand schedule, D_M, is shown as understating the social demand schedule, D_S. Thus, the market equilibrium price, P_0, and quantity, q_0, are both too low from the social perspective.

What are the social benefits of a program that makes vouchers worth v dollars per unit of extermination service available to residents of a poor neighborhood? As implied by Figure 3.15, when the vouchers become available, residents of the poor neighborhood face a supply schedule that is below the original market supply schedule, S, by v dollars. As a consequence of a voucher-induced shift in the supply schedule, neighborhood residents increase their purchases of extermination services from q_0 to q_1, paying an effective price of P_1. Consumers in the targeted neighborhood enjoy a surplus gain equal to the area of trapezoid $B + E$; producers, who now receive a higher supply price of $P_1 + v$, enjoy a surplus gain equal to the area of trapezoid $A + C$; and people in the surrounding neighborhoods, who enjoy the positive externality, gain surplus equal to the area of parallelogram $C + G + F$—the area between the market and social demand schedules over the increase in consumption. The program must pay out v times q_1 in subsidies, which equals the area of rectangle $A + B + C + G + E$. Subtracting this program cost from the gains in social surplus in the market yields gross program benefits: the area of trapezoid $C + F$.[35]

Valuing Benefits in Efficient Secondary Markets

Complements and substitutes.   Secondary market effects most often result because government policies affect the prices of goods in primary markets, and this, in turn, noticeably affects the demand for other goods. These latter goods are referred to as *complements* and *substitutes*.

Consider the following example. Stocking a lake near a city with game fish lowers the effective price of access to fishing grounds for the city's residents. They will not only fish more but also demand more bait and other fishing equipment. We say that access to fishing grounds and fishing equipment are complements because a decrease (increase) in the price of one will result in an increase (decrease) in the demand for the other. In contrast, fishing might very well be a substitute for golfing so that as the price of fishing goes down (up), the demand for golfing goes down (up).

If government policies in primary markets affect the demand for goods in secondary markets, prices in these secondary markets may or may not change as a result. We first discuss the simpler situation in which prices do not change. We then analyze the more complex situation in which prices do change in secondary markets.

Efficient secondary market effects without price changes.   Because most goods have substantial numbers of complements and substitutes, many government projects cause effects in large numbers of secondary markets. Accounting for all these effects would obviously impose an enormous burden on analysts. Fortunately, however, such effects can often be ignored in CBA without substantially biasing the estimates of net benefits. When can we ignore secondary market effects on complements and substitutes? *We can and indeed should ignore impacts in undistorted secondary markets as long as prices in these markets do not change.* The reason for this is that in the absence of price adjustments in secondary markets in response to price changes in primary markets, impacts are typically fully measured in primary markets. Measuring the same effects in both markets is therefore usually unnecessary; in fact, doing so will result in *double counting*. Thus, for example, if we have no reason to believe that prices in the fishing equipment market change, then the increased consumption of fishing equipment is not relevant to the CBA of a project that increases access to fishing grounds.

A closer look at the fishing example should make the rule for the treatment of secondary markets clearer. Panel (a) in Figure 3.16 shows the market for "fishing days." Prior to the stocking of the nearby lake, the effective price of a day of fishing (largely the time costs of travel) was P_{F0}, the travel cost to a lake much further away. Once fishing is available at the nearby lake, the effective price falls to P_{F1} and, as a consequence, the number of days spent fishing by local residents rises from q_{F0} to q_{F1}.[36] The resulting increase in social surplus equals the area of trapezoid $P_{F0}abP_{F1}$, the gain in consumer surplus. We measure this gain in consumer surplus using the demand schedule for fishing, D_F. As is customary in textbooks, this demand schedule should be viewed as the relation between price and quantity that would exist in the primary market *if* the prices of all secondary goods were held constant. Later we discuss the importance of this assumption.

Now consider the market for new fishing equipment. The decline in the effective price of fishing days shifts the demand schedule for new fishing equipment from D_{E0} to D_{E1} as shown in panel (b) of Figure 3.16. If the supply schedule is perfectly

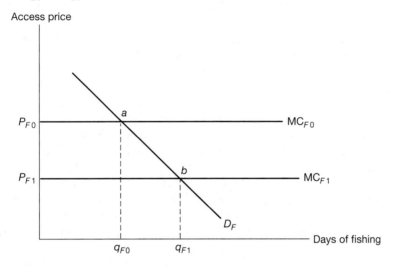

Figure 3.16(a)   Primary Market: Market for Fishing Days

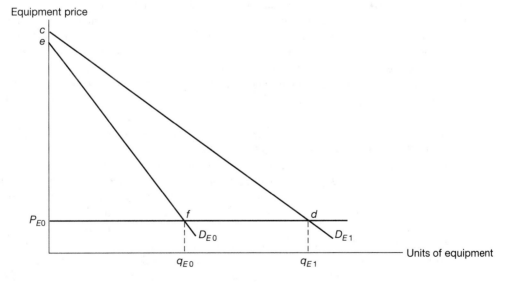

Figure 3.16(b)   Secondary Market: Market for Fishing Equipment (No Price Effect)

elastic, the likely case when the local market accounts for only a small fraction of regional or national demand, then the shift in demand will not increase the price of fishing equipment.

Does this shift in demand for fishing equipment represent a change in consumer welfare that should be counted in a CBA of the fish stocking project? In other words, should the gap between the old and new demand curves that is above the price line be counted as an additional increase in consumer surplus? It is tempting to treat the increase in consumer surplus from efP_{EO} to cdP_{EO} in panel (b) as an additional increase in social benefits that should be added to $P_{F0}abP_{F1}$ in panel (a), but this should not be done. As we show later, doing so would result in double counting. As long as price does not change in the equipment market as a result of stocking the lake, the social surplus change in the fishing market measures the entire benefit from the stocking project.[37]

To see this, first consider fishers who already own all the fishing equipment they need at the time the lake is stocked and, hence, are not presently in the market for fishing equipment. The value that these persons place on their existing fishing equipment will tend to increase as a result of stocking the nearby lake. However, because they are not in the market for new fishing equipment, the gap between the old and new demand curves for new fishing equipment does not reflect this increase. Of course, the willingness of these persons to pay for fishing days will presumably be higher than it otherwise would have been as a result of the fact that they will not have to incur new expenditures for fishing equipment. But any additional increase in consumer surplus that these fishers enjoy as a result of already owning fishing equipment at the time the nearby lake is stocked will already be reflected by the primary market demand curve for fishing days, which will be further to the right than it otherwise would be. It cannot show up in the secondary market for fishing equipment.

Now consider individuals who do not own fishing equipment at the time the lake is stocked but are now induced to make such purchases. The gap between the two demand curves in panel (b) of Figure 3.16 does accurately reveal the increased value that these persons place on fishing equipment. That is, these people are now willing to pay more for fishing equipment, and indeed they will buy more fishing equipment. It is the only way they can fully realize surplus gains from the stocking project. But this expenditure is obviously not an additional benefit from the stocking project. Just like the fishers who already own fishing equipment, the increase in consumer surplus that these persons receive from the stocking project is fully reflected by the primary market demand curve for fishing days. This includes any consumer surplus that they receive from their purchases of fishing equipment. Thus, counting the gap between the two demand curves in panel (b), as well as the increase in consumer surplus shown in panel (a), as benefits would result in counting the same benefits twice.

Persons who do not own fishing equipment at the time the lake is stocked would be even better off if, like the current owners of fishing equipment, they did not have to buy new equipment in order to take advantage of the newly stocked lake. Thus, everything else being equal, willingness-to-pay for fishing days is presumably greater among those who already own fishing equipment than among those who must purchase it. The increase in consumer surplus that results from the stocking project for both groups, even if different from one another, will be fully reflected in the primary market demand curve for fishing days.

Efficient secondary market effects with price changes.[38]   The situation is more complex when the supply schedule in the secondary market is upward sloping. To see this, we examine the effect of stocking the lake on the demand for golfing. In Figure 3.17, panel (a) once again shows the demand for fishing days, while panel (b) now shows the demand for golfing days. As before, the reduction in the price of fishing days from P_{F0} to P_{F1} as a result of stocking the lake causes an increase in social surplus equal to the area $P_{F0}abP_{F1}$ (for the moment ignore demand curves D_{F1} and D^*).

As fishing and golf are presumed to be substitutes, a reduction in the price for fishing days from P_{F0} to P_{F1} would cause the demand for golfing to fall. Thus, the demand curve for golfing in panel (b) would shift to the left from D_{G0} to D_{G1}. As previously emphasized, by itself this shift does not represent a change in consumer surplus that is not already fully accounted for in measuring the change in consumer surplus in the primary market. Golfers are obviously not made worse off by stocking the lake, although some may now place a lower valuation on golf. Instead, by itself, the shift in demand merely indicates that in the absence of golf, the consumer surplus gains from stocking the lake would have been even larger. The existence of golf is reflected by the location of the demand curve for fishing days, which is further to the left than it would have been if golf were not available as a substitute for fishing.

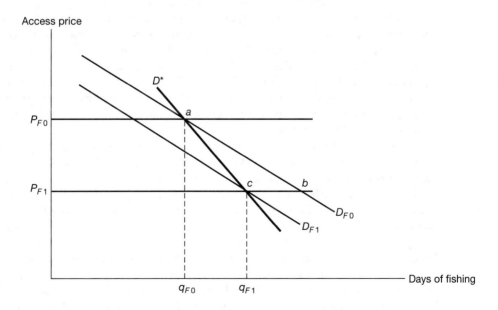

Figure 3.17(a)   Primary Market: Market for Fishing Days

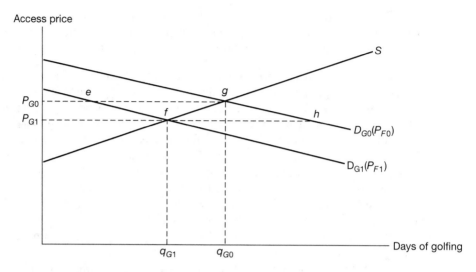

Figure 3.17(b) Secondary Market: Market for Golfing Days (Price Effects)

The shift of demand from D_{G0} to D_{G1}, however, causes the fees for golf course use to fall from P_{G0} to P_{G1}. This, in turn, results in an increase in consumer surplus, one represented by the area $P_{G0}efP_{G1}$, that has not previously been taken into account. In addition, the fall in golfing fees also causes a reduction in producer surplus equal to area $P_{G0}gfP_{G1}$. As the reduction in producer surplus exceeds the increase in consumer surplus, a net loss in social surplus equal to the area of triangle efg results.[39]

Should this loss in social surplus in the golfing market be subtracted from the social surplus gain in the fishing market in measuring net gains from the project? It is frequently unnecessary to do so. The reason is that the increase in consumer surplus gain in the fishing market is often likely, in practice, to be measured as the area $P_{F0}acP_{F1}$ rather than as the area $P_{F0}abP_{F1}$. If measured in this way, the increase in consumer surplus in the fishing market would be understated by the triangular area abc, but this triangle tends to approximate closely triangle efg, the net loss in social surplus in the golfing market.

To see why the consumer surplus gain in the fishing market may, in practice, be measured as the area $P_{F0}acP_{F1}$ rather than as the area $P_{F0}abP_{F1}$, one must recognize that our fishing story does not end with the shift in the demand curve in the secondary market. If golf and fishing are substitutes, the reduction in golf course fees will cause people to switch from fishing to golf and the demand for fishing days will fall. This is shown in panel (a) as a leftward shift in the demand curve for fishing days from D_{F0} to D_{F1}. By itself, this shift does not cause any further changes in social surplus; because we have assumed that the supply of fishing days is perfectly elastic, prices in the market for fishing days are unaffected. Note, however, that by drawing a line between the original and the final equilibrium points in panel (a) of Figure 3.17—that is, between points a and c—one can derive a special type of demand curve, D^*.

This demand curve, which is sometimes called an *observed* or an *equilibrium* demand curve,[40] indicates what the demand for fishing days will be once prices in other markets, including the market for golfing days, have fully adjusted to the change in prices in the market for fishing days. Thus, D^* differs from the demand curves D_{F0} and D_{F1}, which as mentioned earlier, indicate the number of fishing days demanded at each price for fishing days, *holding the prices of all other goods constant*. As it is typically very difficult statistically to hold the prices of secondary goods constant while measuring the relation between price and quantity demanded in a primary market, empirically estimated demand curves—the ones actually observed and available for use in a CBA—often resemble equilibrium demand curves such as D^* instead of "textbook-style" demand curves such as D_{F0} and D_{F1}.[41]

Thus, as suggested earlier, the equilibrium demand curve, D^*, is the one that is likely to be used, in practice, to obtain a measure of the increase in social surplus resulting from the reduction in the price of fishing days. However, the resulting measure, $P_{F0}acP_{F1}$, understates the true measure of the gain in social surplus in the primary market, $P_{F0}abP_{F1}$, by the triangular area *abc*. But, as previously suggested, area *abc* provides a good approximation of area *efg* in panel (b),[42] the area that should be subtracted from area $P_{F0}abP_{F1}$ to obtain an accurate measure of the overall net gains from stocking the lake. In other words, area *abc* represents part of the benefits from the fish stocking project and area *efg* an approximately offsetting cost of the project. Hence, by using the equilibrium demand curve to measure the change in social surplus, we incorporate social surplus changes that occur in the market for golfing days, as well as those that occur in the market for fishing days. We do not have to obtain separate measures of the surplus changes that occur in secondary markets.[43]

This is important because it illustrates a more general point: By using an equilibrium demand curve for the primary market—the type of demand curve that is often empirically estimated, and hence, available—one can often capture the effects in *both* the primary market and all secondary markets of policy interventions initiated in the primary market. Thus, we can restate our earlier rule concerning project impacts in secondary markets: *We can and indeed should ignore effects in undistorted secondary markets, regardless of whether or not there are price changes, if we are measuring benefits in the primary market using empirically measured demand schedules that do not hold prices in secondary markets constant.*

This conclusion carries an important policy lesson. It is frequently tempting for advocates of a policy to claim benefits exist in secondary markets. When society is broadly defined, however, such claims cannot be justified unless the secondary market is distorted. Only when standing is restricted to some group smaller than society as a whole do undistorted secondary markets appear as sources of positive benefits.[44] For example, in evaluating the stocking project from the narrow perspective of the local county, one might count as a benefit increases in revenues received by local businesses resulting from nonresidents buying fishing equipment in the county. Keep in mind, however, that from the broader social—or national—perspective, these revenues simply represent a transfer from nonresidents to residents. This point is illustrated in a very different context in Exhibit 3.2, where an equilibrium demand curve is used in assessing the effects of a policy that restrained automobile imports.

■ EXHIBIT 3.2

In 1981, under strong pressure from the Reagan administration and the U.S. Congress, the Japanese government agreed to limit the number of automobiles shipped to the United States. This so-called voluntary restraint agreement (VRA) was motivated by the notion that because Japanese imports were substitutes for U.S.-produced automobiles, a reduction in the number of imports would increase the sales of domestically produced cars.

A CBA of the VRA for automobiles, as well as other similar import restraint agreements, can be conducted with the aid of the model illustrated in the diagrams that appear in this exhibit. In this model, the market for cars imported to the United States from Japan is viewed as the primary market, as it is the market where the policy action was directed, while the market for U.S.-produced automobiles is viewed as the secondary market. In the diagrams, D_J and S_J represent the demand and supply schedules for Japanese imports in the absence of the VRA, while D_{US} and S_{US} represent their counterparts in the market for domestically produced automobiles. Thus, in the absence of the VRA, Q_J cars would have been imported from Japan to the United States and sold at price of P_J, while Q_{US} domestically produced autos would have been purchased at a price of P_{US}. The diagrams reflect the fact that in 1981 Japanese imports were considerably less expensive, on average, than their American counterparts. The flat supply curve for Japanese automobiles is based on the assumption that the Japanese were willing to supply as many cars as American consumers were willing to purchase at a price of P_J.

The VRA set a ceiling on the number of cars the Japanese could export to the United States at Q', thereby substantially reducing the number of Japanese automobiles available to American consumers. As a result, the price of Japanese imports increased to P'_J. Because imported and domestic automobiles are substitutes, the higher price of Japanese automobiles caused an upward shift in the demand for domestic automobiles to D'_{US}, increasing their price to P'_{US} and their quantity to Q'_{US}. The increased price of domestic autos, in turn, caused the demand schedule for Japanese imports to shift to D'_J, prompting an additional increase in their price to P''_J.

Based on the equilibrium demand curve in the primary market, D^*_J, it can be seen that the VRA resulted in deadweight loss equal to the triangular area abc. In addition, because of the higher prices paid for Japanese automobiles, Japanese automobile producers received a transfer from U.S. consumers corresponding to the rectangular area $P''_J acP_J$. Based on information about the prices and sales of imported and domestic automobiles under the VRA and empirical estimates of the slopes of the relevant supply and demand schedules, David G. Tarr and Morris E. Morkre calculated that in 1981 the deadweight loss equaled $155 million and the transfer equaled $753 million. If Japanese automobile producers are not given standing, and the very nature of the VRA suggests that they should not be, the sum of these two figures, $908 million, was the total social cost of the VRA in 1981. Similar costs also occurred in each of the following years until 1985, when the policy was dropped.

As pointed out in the text, by using the equilibrium demand curve, we need only focus on the primary market to determine the effects of a policy on *social* surplus. By doing this, however, we ignore the beneficiaries of the VRA, U.S. auto producers and workers. Indeed, producer surplus in the market for U.S. automobiles, the secondary market in our

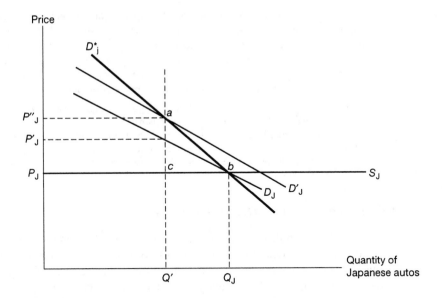

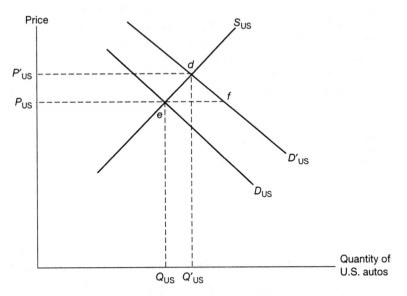

Figure 3.2(a) for Exhibit   Japansese Automobiles (Primary Market)
Figure 3.2(b) for Exhibit   U.S. Automobiles (Secondary Market)

analysis, increased by area $P'_{US}deP_{US}$. This increase, however, was more than offset by the decrease in consumer surplus that occurred in the secondary market, area $P'_{US}dfP_{US}$. (As suggested in the text, the difference between the increase in producer surplus and the decrease in consumer surplus in the secondary market—area *def*—is taken into account by using the equilibrium demand curve to measure the VRA's impacts in the primary market.) Thus, unless U.S. consumers, like Japanese auto producers, are given no stand-ing in the analysis, a VRA policy *must* decrease social surplus. In fact, as pointed out by Jose A. Gomez-Ibanez, Robert A. Leone, and Stephen A. O'Connell, over the long run a VRA can even hurt domestic auto producers and workers—for example, by encouraging Japanese producers to circumvent limits on the *number* of imports by selling high-price rather than low-price autos and by setting up production plants in the United States.

Source: David G. Tarr and Morris E. Morkre, *Aggregate Costs to the United States of Tariffs and Quotas on Imports: General Tariff Cuts and Removal of Quotas on Automobiles, Steel, Sugar, and Textiles* (Washington, DC: Bureau of Economics Staff Report to the Federal Trade Commission, 1984), 54–74, and Jose A. Gomez-Ibanez, Robert A. Leone, and Stephen A. O'Connell, "Restraining Auto Imports: Does Anyone Win?" *Journal of Policy Analysis and Management*, 2, no. 2 (1983), 196–219.

Valuing Benefits in Distorted Secondary Markets

Unfortunately, when distortions exist in secondary markets and, consequently, market prices do not equal social marginal costs, use of equilibrium demand curves in prima-ry markets does not allow one to value fully effects that occur in these markets. To see why, examine Figure 3.18, a slightly altered version of panel (b) of Figure 3.16. This new figure is based on the assumption that the market price of fishing equipment, P_{E0}, underestimates the marginal social cost by x cents. (Think of the equipment as lead sinkers, some of which eventually end up in the lake, where they poison ducks and other wildlife. The x cents would then represent the value of the expected loss of wildlife from the sale of another sinker.) In this case, the expansion of consumption involves a social surplus loss equal to x times $(q_{E1} - q_{E0})$ and represented in Figure 3.18 by the shaded rectangle. This loss, which is not reflected at all by market demand or

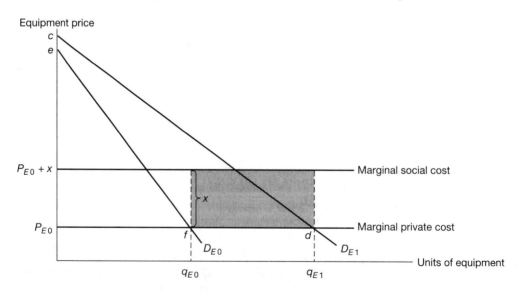

Figure 3.18   Distorted Secondary Market: Market for Fishing Equipment (No Price Effect)

supply curves in the fishing market, should be subtracted from the benefits occurring in that market in order to obtain an accurate measure of net gains from the program.

Another type of distortion in secondary markets is imposed by the presence of taxes. For example, Figure 3.19 illustrates local produce markets for beef and chicken, which are substitutes for one another. For simplicity, the supply curves in both markets are assumed to be perfectly elastic. In the absence of any taxes on these products, the price of beef (the primary good) would be P_B and the price of chicken (the secondary good) would be P_C.

For purposes of our illustration, let us assume that chicken is currently subject to a tax of t_C cents per pound, but beef is not presently taxed. Given this situation, the existing demand schedules for beef and chicken are represented by D_{B0} and D_{C0}, respectively. As panel (b) of Figure 3.19 indicates, the tax on chicken provides the government with revenue equal to the rectangular area *fgji*, but reduces consumer surplus by the area of trapezoid *fgki*. Thus, the tax on chicken results in deadweight loss equal to the triangular area *gkj*.

Now assume that the government is considering imposing a tax of t_B cents per pound on beef. As indicated in panel (a), if the new tax is adopted, the government will collect revenue represented by the rectangular area *abde*, but consumers of beef will lose surplus equal to the area of trapezoid *abce*. Consequently, imposition of the new tax will result in deadweight loss in the beef market equal to the triangular area *bcd*.

However, the increase in the market price of beef shifts the demand curve for chicken, a substitute, from D_{C0} to D_{C1}. For reasons discussed previously, this shift does not represent a change in consumer surplus. But the shift does cause an increase

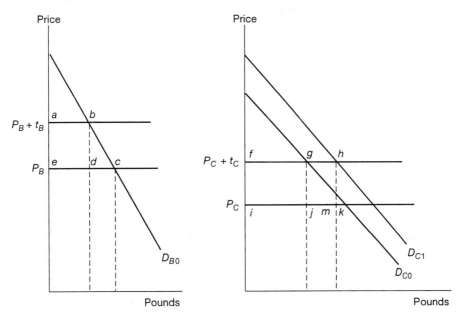

Figure 3.19(a)   Market for Beef   **Figure 3.19(b)**   Market for Chicken

in the sale of chickens, resulting in an increase in tax revenues collected by the government. This increase, which is represented in panel (b) by area *ghmj*, is a benefit from the tax imposed on beef that could conceivably more than offset the deadweight loss occurring in the beef market.

The important lesson from this illustration is that, unlike situations in which there are no distortions in secondary markets, benefits and costs of a policy intervention cannot be fully measured by observing only those effects that occur in primary markets. Effects that occur in distorted secondary markets should, in principle, be valued separately. Yet, in practice, it may be very difficult to do so. Estimation problems usually preclude accurate measurement of welfare changes that occur in secondary markets. Estimating own-price effects (how quantity demanded changes as the price of the good changes) is often difficult; estimating cross-price effects (how the quantity demanded of good *Y* changes as the price of good *Z* changes) is more difficult yet. Consequently, we are rarely very confident of predictions of demand shifts in secondary markets. Moreover, when secondary markets are distorted, it is also very difficult to measure the size of the distortions. (Recall the *x*-cent loss of wildlife from the sale of another sinker. How is the value of *x* to be estimated?) But such measures are usually needed if program effects in distorted secondary markets are to be taken into account.

Fortunately, price changes in most secondary markets are likely to be small. Most goods are neither strong complements nor strong substitutes. Hence, large price changes in the primary markets are usually necessary to produce noticeable demand shifts in the secondary markets. Thus, even when secondary markets are distorted, ignoring these markets may result in little bias to CBA.

CONCLUSION

Many of the key concepts from this chapter are summarized in Table 3.1. As the table indicates, changes in social surplus serve as the basis for measuring the costs and benefits of policies. The concept of opportunity cost helps us value the inputs that policies divert from private use; the concept of willingness-to-pay helps us value policy outputs. The key to valuing outputs is to identify the primary markets in which they occur. When the outputs are not traded in organized markets, ingenuity is often needed to infer supply and demand schedules (remember the market for "fishing days"). For this purpose, various shadow pricing techniques, such as those discussed in Chapters 9, 10, and 11, are often needed. Costs and benefits that occur in undistorted secondary markets are typically very difficult to value, but generally need not, indeed, should not, be added to costs and benefits that are measured in primary markets. Doing so will usually result in double counting.

TABLE 3.1   RULES FOR MEASURING SOCIAL BENEFITS AND COSTS OF GOVERNMENT INTERVENTIONS IN MARKETS

TYPE OF INTERVENTION	EFFICIENT MARKETS	INEFFICIENT MARKETS
Purchases from factor markets	If supply curve is flat, value cost as direct budgetary expenditure [example: purchase materials from a competitive national market]	Value costs as direct budgetary expenditure less (plus) any increase (decrease) in social surplus in market
[concept: value costs as the opportunity cost of the purchased resources]	If supply curve is not flat, value cost as direct budgetary expenditure less (plus) any increase (decrease) in social surplus in market [example: purchases of materials from a competitive local market]	[examples: hiring unemployed labor; purchases of materials from a monopoly]
Changes in costs to consumers or producers in primary markets	Value change as net change in social (i.e., consumer and producer) surplus plus (less) any increase (decrease) in government revenues	Value change as net change in social (i.e., consumer, producer, and third-party) surplus plus (less) increase (decrease) in government revenues
[concept: value benefits as willingness-to-pay for the change and costs as willingness-to-pay to avoid the change]	[example: government provision of goods and services to consumers or producers]	[example: tax or subsidy in market with externality]
Changes in quantities exchanged in secondary markets as a result of government intervention in primary or factor markets	If prices do not change in secondary market, ignore secondary market impacts	Costs or benefits resulting directly from increases in the size of the distortion should, in principle, be measured Other impacts in secondary market should be ignored if prices do not change.
	If prices do change, but benefits in primary market are measured using a demand curve with other market prices held constant, then social surplus changes in the secondary market will always represent reductions in social surplus that should be subtracted from changes in the primary market. But if benefits in the primary market are measured using a demand curve that does not hold other prices constant, ignore secondary market impacts.	
[concepts: commodities exchanged in secondary markets are typically complements of or substitutes for commodities exchanged in primary markets; most impacts in secondary markets can be valued in primary markets]	[example: price changes in primary market cause demand curve shifts in competitive secondary market]	[example: price changes in primary market causes demand curve shift in secondary market with externality]

These rules pertain only to measuring impacts of government interventions on society as a whole. Issues associated with standing are ignored in the rules.

APPENDIX 3A

CONSUMER SURPLUS AND WILLINGNESS-TO-PAY

In Chapter 3, we assert that under most circumstances, estimates of changes in consumer surplus, as measured by demand curves, can be used in CBA as reasonable approximations of individuals' willingness-to-pay for or willingness-to-pay to avoid the effects of policy changes. In this appendix, we examine the circumstances under which measured changes in consumer surplus do in fact provide a close approximation to willingness-to-pay and the circumstances under which they do not. For purposes of illustration, we specifically focus on the link between the amount a consumer would be willing to pay to avoid a given price increase and estimates based on the demand curve of the loss in the consumer's surplus resulting from the price increase.

COMPENSATING VARIATION

The maximum amount of money that a consumer would be willing to pay to avoid a price increase is the amount required to return him to the same level of utility he enjoyed prior to the change in price, an amount called *compensating variation*.[1] If the consumer had to spend any more than the value of his compensating variation, then he would be worse off paying to avoid the increase than allowing it to occur. If he could spend any less, then he would be better off paying to avoid the increase, rather than allowing it to occur. Hence, for a loss in consumer surplus resulting from a price increase to equal the consumer's willingness-to-pay to avoid the price increase, it has to correspond exactly to the compensating variation value associated with the price increase.

These assertions are most readily demonstrated by an indifference curve analysis. Such an analysis is presented in panel (a) of Figure 3.A1. This diagram represents a consumer who faces a world with only two goods, X and Y. The straight lines in the diagram are budget constraints. The particular budget constraint that the consumer faces depends upon the consumer's income level and on the relative prices of goods X and Y. The greater the consumer's income, the more of X and Y he can afford and, consequently, the greater the distance the budget constraint will be from the origin, O. Thus, for example, the budget constraint JK represents a higher income level than the budget constraint GI. The slope of the consumer's budget constraint indicates how many additional units of Y can be obtained if one less unit of X is purchased. Thus, holding everything else constant, the slope of the budget constraint is negative and depends upon the price of X relative to the price of Y. Consequently, if the price of X rises relative to that of Y, the consumer's budget constraint will become more steeply sloped, changing, for example, from budget constraint GH to budget constraint GI. As can be seen, such a change indicates that a larger number of units of Y can be purchased in exchange for each unit of X that the consumer gives up.

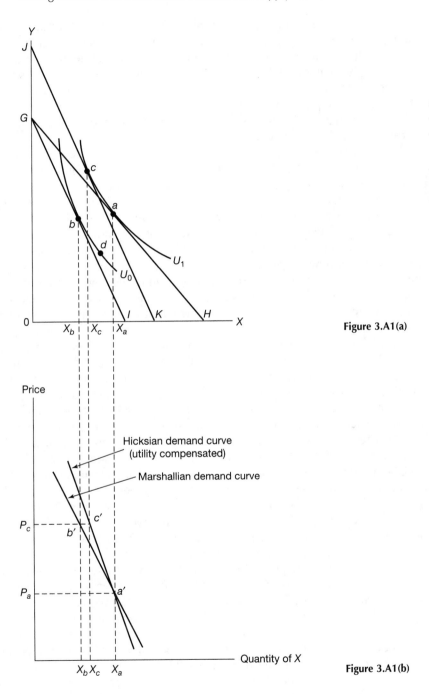

Figure 3.A1(a)

Figure 3.A1(b)

The curved lines in Figure 3.A1(a) are *indifference curves*. All points along a single indifference curve represent combinations of goods X and Y that provide the consumer with equal levels of utility. Thus, the consumer is indifferent between points b and d on U_0 or points a and c on U_1. The further an indifference curve is from the origin, the greater the level of utility. Thus, the consumer would prefer any point on indifference curve U_1 (e.g., point a) to any point on indifference curve U_0 (e.g., point b). This is not surprising in this case because more of both good X and good Y would be consumed at point a than at point b.

The indifference curves in Figure 3.A1(a) are negatively sloped because any movement along an indifference curve definitionally represents a situation whereby an increase in the consumption of one good is offset by a sufficient reduction in the consumption of the other good such that the consumer's level of utility is left unchanged.[2] Were the individual to consume either more of both goods or less of both goods, his level of utility would obviously change. The fact that the indifference curves are convex in shape (i.e., they bend inward toward the origin) reflects *diminishing marginal utility*—as the consumer consumes more of one good, he becomes increasingly less willing to give up consumption of an additional unit of the other good. For example, the convex shape of indifference curve U_0 implies that at point b the consumer would be willing to give up more units of Y in order to consume one additional unit of X than he would at point d.

Now let us assume that good X in Figure 3.A1(a) is a product on which the consumer spends only a small fraction of his total income—for example, movie tickets—and good Y is a composite good on which the consumer spends all the rest of his income. Under these circumstances, good Y is a reasonable approximation of the consumer's total money income. Consequently, the slope of a budget constraint in the figure would indicate the price of good X—that is, the amount of money income (i.e., good Y) the consumer would have to give up to obtain one more unit of X.

Assume that the consumer initially faces budget constraint GH. He will then choose point a on indifference curve U_1. Point a represents an equilibrium because the consumer cannot increase his utility by moving to any alternative point and, hence, has no incentive to do so.[3] Now assume that as a result of a government policy, the price of good X is doubled.[4] This changes the consumer's equilibrium to point b on a more steeply sloped budget constraint, GI, and a lower indifference curve, U_0. Thus, the consumer's consumption of good X falls from X_a to X_b.[5]

If the consumer were paid a lump sum of money sufficient to compensate him entirely for the price increase in X, this would shift the budget constraint in a parallel movement from GI to JK, allowing him to move back to the original indifference curve, U_1. However, the consumer would now choose point c (rather than a) and would consume X_c of the good (rather than X_a). As the vertical distance between the two parallel budget constraints (i.e., the difference between points G and J on the vertical axis) represents the amount of good Y—that is, money income—that the consumer would have to be paid in order to lose no utility as a result of the price increase, this distance measures the compensating variation associated with the price increase.

As asserted previously, this compensating variation value is the maximum amount that the consumer would be willing to pay to avoid the price increase. To see this, suppose that the price increase occurs and that the consumer is fully compensated for it. Now imagine that if he is willing to pay all the compensation he received—that is, the full value of his compensating variation—the price increase will be revoked. Will he accept or reject this offer? He will, in fact, be indifferent to it. If he accepts the offer, then he will return to his initial equilibrium at point a on indifference curve U_1; and if he rejects it, then he will remain at point c, which is also on U_1. Thus, the compensation value represents the maximum amount the consumer would be willing to pay to avoid the price increase. If he could pay a bit less to revoke the price increase, then he would definitely do so. If he had to pay a bit more, then he would prefer to accept the increase.

INCOME AND SUBSTITUTION EFFECTS

Given the information contained in Figure 3.A1(a), the total effect of the increase in the price of X on the consumer's demand for good X—that is, the change from X_a to X_b—can be decomposed into two separate effects: a *compensated substitution effect* and an *income effect*.[6] The compensated substitution effect is represented in Figure 3.A1(a) as the change in demand from X_a to X_c. It allows us to examine the effect of a change in the price of X on the demand for X *if* the individual were exactly compensated for any losses of utility he suffers as a result of the price increase and, as a consequence, remained on indifference curve U_1. The compensated substitution effect always causes the demand for a good to change in the opposite direction from a change in the price of the good. For example, holding the consumer's level of utility constant, an increase in the price of good X causes him to substitute some of the now relatively less expensive good Y for good X. Hence, as shown in the figure, X_c is smaller than X_a.

The income effect is represented in Figure 3.A1(a) as the change in demand from X_c to X_b and results because the increase in the price of good X reduces the consumer's disposable income. If, as the diagram implies, X is a *normal good*—that is, if purchases of the good and disposable income are positively related—the consumer will purchase less of it. Hence, X_b is smaller than X_c. Thus, like the substitution effect, the income effect associated with the price increase will also cause the consumer to reduce his demand for the good.

DEMAND CURVES

Because the slopes of the budget constraints in Figure 3.A1(a) indicate both the old and the new prices of good X and the points tangent to these budget constraints with indifference curves indicate the amount of the good that the consumer wants at each price, the figure provides information about two points along the consumer's demand curve for X. Indeed, as we know the quantity of output the consumer would demand after the price increase, both if his utility were held constant and if it were not, we can actually determine the location of pairs of points along two different demand curves. These two pairs of points appear in Figure 3.A1(b) as points a' and c' and as points a' and b', respectively. If we assume that the demand curves are linear, we can simply draw a straight line between the two points in each pair to derive the entire demand curves.

The line in Figure 3.A1(b) that connects points a' and b' is a conventional demand curve of the sort usually emphasized in textbooks. This demand curve, which is known as a *Marshallian demand curve*, incorporates both the substitution and income effects associated with changes in the price of good X. Statistical efforts by economists to estimate relations between the price of a good and quantities purchased, holding income, other prices, and other factors constant, are attempts to estimate Marshallian demand curves empirically.

The demand curve in Figure 3.A1(b) that connects points a' and c' keeps utility constant as the price of good X changes and, thus, incorporates only the compensated substitution effect associated with price changes. This demand curve is sometimes called the *utility-compensated* or the *Hicksian demand curve*. Because Hicksian demand curves are unaffected by income effects, they are usually, as is the case in Figure 3.A1(b), more steeply sloped than Marshallian demand curves. Because of the difficulty of holding utility constant, unlike Marshallian demand curves, Hicksian demand curves cannot usually be directly estimated using statistical techniques.[7]

EQUIVALENCE OF CONSUMER SURPLUS
AND COMPENSATING VARIATION

Movements up the Hicksian demand curve—say from P_a to P_c—are equivalent to allowing the price to increase while compensating the consumer with a lump-sum payment of just sufficient size to permit him to remain on his original indifference curve. This lump-sum payment can be measured graphically as either the vertical distance between the two parallel budget constraints in Figure 3.A1(a) (i.e., as the difference between money income at points G and J) or as the change in consumer surplus indicated by the Hicksian demand curve in Figure 3.A1(b) (the area $P_a a' c' P_c$). Thus, the change in consumer surplus resulting from a price change measured with a Hicksian demand curve exactly equals the consumer's compensating variation—that is, the maximum amount the consumer would be willing to pay to avoid the price increase.

Hence, it is Hicksian demand curves that permit measurement of the compensating variation associated with price changes. However, as pointed out earlier, it is Marshallian curves that are more often available for use in actually conducting CBA. To the extent these two demand curves differ, using a Marshallian demand curve to measure consumer surplus will result in a biased estimate of compensating variation and, therefore, of willingness-to-pay. As can be seen from Figure 3.A1(b), the two alternative demand curves do produce different measures of consumer surplus, one that differs by the triangular area $a'b'c'$. For a price increase, the change in consumer surplus is smaller if measured with the Marshallian demand curve than with a Hicksian demand curve; for a price reduction, it is larger.

As previously suggested, the difference between the two types of demand curves is that the Marshallian curve incorporates the income effects associated with price changes, as well as the substitution effects, while the Hicksian curve incorporates only the latter. Thus, the biased estimate of willingness-to-pay that results from using Marshallian rather than Hicksian demand curves to measure consumer surplus depends upon the size of the income effect associated with a price change. *Usually this income effect and, hence, the bias are small and can be safely ignored.*[8] This, at least, is the case if the price change is moderate and the good in question accounts for a fairly small part of total consumption. Thus, CBAs of government policies that affect corn, cotton, tobacco, and gasoline prices will generally be little affected by use of Marshallian rather than Hicksian demand curves. However, *the bias could be of some importance for a CBA of a government policy that would result in large price changes in such consumption goods as housing or automobiles or in big changes in wage rates.* Consequently, except for a few instances when it clearly seems inappropriate to do so, throughout the rest of this book, we shall assume that the income effects associated with various policy changes are sufficiently small that consumer surpluses that are measured by using Marshallian demand curves provide reasonable approximations of willingness-to-pay.

APPENDIX 3B

MARKET FAILURES

Correction of market failures provides much of the justification for the sorts of policy interventions that are often the subject of CBA. Therefore, this appendix provides a brief overview of market failures. The four major types of market failures we examine are: monopoly, information asymmetry, externalities, and public goods.

MONOPOLY

It is useful to examine monopoly first because it is an excellent example of a topic discussed in Chapter 3: deviations from competitive equilibriums that result in deadweight loss.[1] One key to understanding monopoly is to recognize that because, by definition, a monopolist is the only firm in its market, it views the market demand curve as the demand schedule for its output. Because market demand curves are downward sloping, if the monopolist sells all its output at the same price, then it can sell an additional unit of output only by reducing its price on every unit it sells. Consequently, the monopolist's marginal revenue—that is, the additional revenue it receives for each additional unit of output it sells—is less than the selling price of that output. For example, if a monopolist could sell four units of output at a price of $10 but must reduce its price to $9 in order to sell five units, its revenue would increase from $40 to $45 as a result of selling the fifth unit. Therefore, the $5 in marginal revenue it receives from the fifth unit is less than the $9 selling price of the unit.

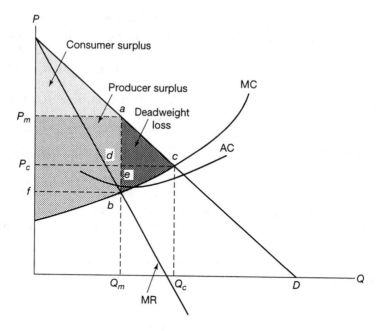

Figure 3.B1 Monopoly

Thus, as shown in Figure 3.B1, the monopolist's marginal revenue curve is located below its demand curve. Given this situation, the monopolist would maximize profit by producing at Q_m, where its marginal cost equals its marginal revenue. At this output level, the price it can charge, P_m, is determined by the demand curve it faces.[2]

As in the competitive case, the social surplus generated by the output produced and sold by the monopolist is represented graphically by the area between the demand curve and the marginal cost curve that is to the left of the equilibrium point. The social surplus above the price line (i.e., the consumer surplus) is captured by buyers. And that below the price line (the producer surplus) is captured by the monopolist.[3] Although the term *monopolist* is sometimes used pejoratively, in a CBA, any increase in producer surplus received by a monopolist that results from a government policy is counted as a benefit of the policy. The rationale is that owners of monopolies, like consumers and the owners of competitive firms, are part of society; therefore, benefits accruing to them "count."

The Social Cost of Monopoly

Notice that, unlike perfect competition, social surplus is not maximized if the monopolist is left to its own devices. This is because the monopolist does not produce at the competitive level, Q_c, where the marginal cost curve intersects the demand curve, and does not charge the competitive price, P_c. This lost social surplus, which is represented in Figure 3.B1 by the triangular area *abc*, is deadweight loss that results from monopolistic behavior. Were it possible for the government to break the monopoly into a large number of competing firms so that a competitive outcome resulted,[4] two things would happen: First, the deadweight loss would disappear and social surplus would increase by the area *abc*. In CBA, this is counted as a benefit. Second, because the competitive price, P_c, is less than the monopolistic price, P_m, consumers would capture that part of the monopolist's producer surplus that is represented by the rectangular area $P_m a d P_c$. In CBA, this is viewed as a transfer.

Natural Monopoly

So far, we have been focusing on a general form of monopoly. We now turn to a specific type of monopoly: *natural monopoly*. The essential characteristic of natural monopolies is that their fixed costs are very large relative to their variable costs; public utilities, roads, and bridges all provide good examples. As shown in Figure 3.B2, these large fixed costs cause average costs to be very large at small amounts of output and, as the fixed component of costs becomes spread over increasing amounts of output, to continue to fall over a large range of output. This, in turn, means that over a wide range of output, average costs will exceed marginal costs. Indeed, in Figure 3.B2, average costs exceed marginal costs over what we shall term the *relevant range of output*—that is, the range between the first unit of output and the amount consumers would demand at a zero price, Q_0.

In principle, marginal costs could be either rising or falling over the relevant output range, but for the sake of simplicity, we have drawn the marginal cost curve as horizontal. The important point is that it is below total average cost over the relevant range, so that it pulls average cost down. Hence, average costs continue to fall over the relevant range of output. As a result, unit costs would be lower under a natural monopoly

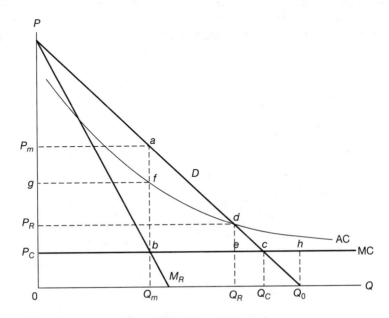

Figure 3.B2 Natural Monopoly

than under competition. However, allocative efficiency would not result if the monopoly maximized profits by setting prices at P_m.

INFORMATION ASYMMETRY

The term *information asymmetry* implies that information about a product or a job may not be equal on both sides of a market. For example, sellers may have more information concerning how well made or safe a product is than buyers, doctors may know more about needed care than patients, or employers may know more about working conditions than their workers.

The implications of information asymmetry are easy to show in a diagram. To do this, we focus on the case in which sellers of a product have more information than buyers. Such a situation is represented by the two demand curves that appear in Figure 3.B3. One of these curves, D_i, represents how much of the product buyers would desire if they had full information concerning it, while the other demand curve, D_u, indicates how much they actually desire, given their lack of full information. In other words, the two demand curves represent, respectively, willingness-to-pay with and without full information concerning the product. They indicate that if buyers had full information, their willingness-to-pay would diminish.[5]

In principle, it is possible that D_u could be to the left of D_i, rather than to the right of it as shown in Figure 3.B3. This would occur if instead of desiring more of the product in the absence of information concerning it than they would with the information, consumers desire less of it. In practice, however, such situations are unlikely to continue for long because strong incentives would exist for sellers to eliminate such information asymmetry by providing buyers with the needed information, thereby increasing their demand for the product. But when the actual demand curve is to the right of

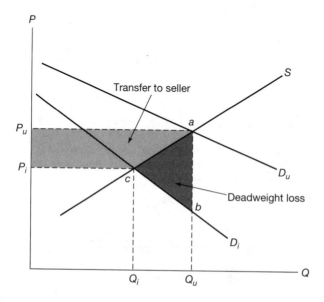

Figure 3.B3
Information Assymmetry

the fully informed demand curve, the incentive, in contrast, is for sellers to withhold the information.

The diagram shows that there are two effects of information asymmetry. First, by raising the price and the amount of the good purchased, information asymmetry increases producer surplus and reduces consumer surplus, resulting in a transfer from consumers to sellers. This transfer is shown in Figure 3.B3 by the trapezoidal area $P_u a c P_i$. Second, by increasing the amount of the good sold relative to the full information case, information asymmetry results in deadweight loss, which is shown in the figure as the triangular area *abc*.

It is useful to discuss when information asymmetry is likely to be important—that is, when the benefits of government intervention may exceed the costs. This largely depends upon two factors: First, the ease with which consumers can obtain the information for themselves; and second, whether third parties that could provide the missing information are likely to arise through market forces. To discuss these factors, it is helpful to distinguish among three types of products: (1) search goods, (2) experience goods, and (3) postexperience goods.[6]

Search goods. Search goods are products with characteristics that consumers can learn about by examining them prior to purchasing them. For example, a student who needs a notebook for a class can go to the bookstore and easily learn pretty much everything he or she wants to know about the characteristics of alternative notebooks. Under such circumstances, information asymmetry is unlikely to be a serious problem.

Experience goods. Experience goods are products about which consumers can obtain full knowledge, but only after purchasing and experiencing them. Good examples are tickets to a movie, a meal at a new restaurant, a new television set, and a house. At least to a degree, information asymmetry concerning many such products takes care of itself. For example, once consumers have been to a restaurant, they acquire some information concerning the expected quality of the meal should they eat there again. Warranties, which are typically provided for televisions and many other major consumer durables, serve a similar purpose. In addition, market demand for information about experience goods often prompts third parties to provide information for a price. This reduces information asymmetry. For example, newspaper reviews provide information about movies and restaurants; in the United States, *Consumer Reports* provides information about television sets and many other goods; and inspection services examine houses prior to purchase.

Postexperience goods. It is in the case of postexperience goods that government intervention to reduce information asymmetry is most likely to be efficiency-enhancing. The reason for this is that even well after consumers purchase and consume such goods, they may not learn about their important characteristics—for example, adverse health effects associated with a prescription drug or a new automobile with a defective part. Employee exposure to an unhealthy chemical by an employer is similar. In these cases, information asymmetry may persist for long periods of time, even until the health of some people is ruined. Moreover, since the needed information is often expensive to gather and private-sector parties willing to pay for it may not exist, markets are unlikely to produce third parties that provide the necessary information.

EXTERNALITIES

An externality is an effect that production or consumption has on third parties—in other words, on people not involved in the production or consumption of the good. It is a by-product of production or consumption for which there is no market. Standard examples include pollution caused by a factory and the pleasure derived from a neighbor's beautiful garden. Table 3.B1 provides examples of each of four distinct types of externalities: positive and negative externalities that occur in the production process; and positive and negative externalities that occur in the consumption process.[7] We first examine a negative externality (i.e., one that imposes social costs) and then a positive externality (one that produces benefits).

TABLE 3.B1   EXAMPLES OF FOUR TYPES OF EXTERNALITIES

Source	Positive	Negative
Production Process	Private timber forests provide scenic view or "birding" to nature lovers	Air pollution from factories harm lungs of people living nearby
Consumption Process	Immunization by persons against contagious disease helps protect others	Cigarette smoke from smoker harms lungs of nonsmoker

Source: Adapted from David L. Weimer and Aidan R. Vining, *Policy Analysis: Concepts and Practice* (Englewood Cliffs, NJ: Prentice Hall, 1992), Figure 3.11.

Negative Externalities

Figure 3.B4 illustrates a market in which the production process results in a negative externality—for example, air or water pollution emitted by factories. The supply curve, S^*, reflects only the private marginal costs incurred by the suppliers of the good, while the second supply curve, $S^\#$, incorporates the costs that the negative externality imposes on third parties, as well as the private marginal costs incurred by suppliers. The gap between these two curves can be viewed as the amount those subjected to the negative externality—for example, pollution—would be willing to pay to avoid it. In other words, it represents the costs imposed by the externality on third parties.

The size of this gap depends in part upon whether the market somehow compensates third parties for the negative externality. For example, the gap would be smaller if homeowners were able to purchase their houses at lower prices because of pollution in their area than if they were not.

Figure 3.B4 indicates that, if left to its own devices, the market sets too low a price for the good (P^* versus $P^\#$) because it fails to take account of the cost to third parties of producing the good. As a result, too much output is produced (Q^* instead of $Q^\#$). This causes deadweight loss, which in the diagram is represented by the triangu-

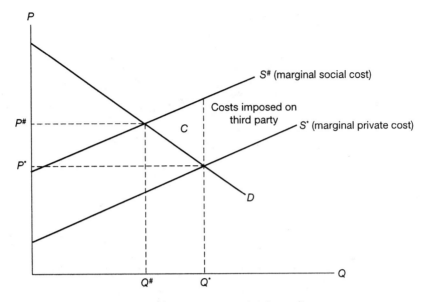

Figure 3.B4　Negative Externality

lar area labeled *C*. This deadweight loss reflects the fact that for each unit of additional output produced in excess of $Q^{\#}$, marginal social costs (shown by the supply curve $S^{\#}$) increasingly exceed marginal social benefits (shown by the demand curve *D*).

Positive Externalities

Now let us look at a positive externality—for example, a lumber company that plants trees that are enjoyed by nature lovers prior to their being harvested. This situation is represented in Figure 3.B5. In this diagram, the demand curve, D^{*}, represents the willingness-to-pay for the lumber produced by the trees. To take account of the benefits received by the nature lovers, we must add a second demand curve to the diagram, $D^{\#}$. The gap between these two demand curves represents the willingness-to-pay of nature lovers for the pleasant view.

As timber companies do not capture the third-party benefits represented by the gap between the two demand curves, they base their decisions on curve D^{*}. Thus, the market-set price, P^{*}, is lower than the price that would be optimal for society, $P^{\#}$. As a result, too little output is produced (Q^{*} versus $Q^{\#}$), generating the deadweight loss shown in Figure 3.B5 as the triangular area *C*.

PUBLIC GOODS

Once produced, public goods—for example, flood control projects or national defense—are there for everyone. No one can or, indeed, should be excluded from enjoying their benefits. In that sense, public goods may be regarded as a special type of positive externality. Like other positive externalities, private markets, if left to their own devices, tend

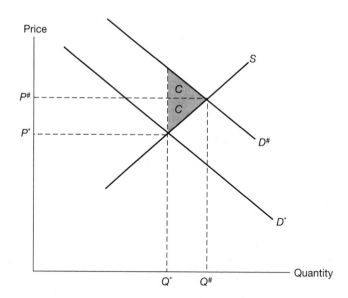

Figure 3.B5   Positive Externality

to produce less public goods than is socially optimal. In their purest form, public goods have two key attributes: They are *nonexcludable* and they are *nonrivalrous*.

Nonexcludability

A good is nonexcludable if it is impossible, or at least highly impractical, for one person to maintain control over its use.[8] Supplied to one consumer, it is available for all consumers, a phenomena sometimes called *jointness in supply*. For example, unless overcome by physical force, a purchaser of a hamburger can exclude others from taking a bite; but it would be very difficult for a user of the light emitted from a particular streetlight to keep others from using that light. Hence, the hamburger is excludable and streetlight is nonexcludable.

The reason nonexcludability causes market failure is easy to see. Once a nonexcludable good such as streetlight or national defense exists, it is there for everyone to use. Because there is no way to charge for its use, a *free-rider problem* results. As a consequence, there is no incentive for the private sector to provide it. Usually it must be publicly provided, if it is going to be provided at all.

Nonrivalry in Consumption

Nonrivalry implies that one person's consumption of a good does not keep someone else from also consuming it; more than one person can obtain benefits from a given level of supply at the same time. For example, one person's use of streetlight to help her see at night does not diminish the ability of another person to use the same light. But if one person eats a hamburger, another cannot consume the same hamburger. The hamburger is rivalrous; streetlight is nonrivalrous. Thus, unlike the hamburger, even if it were feasible to exclude a second person from using streetlight, it would be inefficient to do so because the marginal cost of supplying light to the second person is zero.

Although the reason nonrivalry causes market failure is more complex than why nonexcludability causes market failure, it can be examined by contrasting how a *total marginal benefit curve*—that is, a curve that reflects the incremental benefits to consumers from each additional unit of a good that is available for their consumption— is derived for a rivalrous good with how such a curve is derived for a nonrivalrous good. To do this graphically as easily as possible, we assume that there are only two potential consumers of each of the two goods. Thus, Figure 3.B6 displays two graphs: one for the rivalrous good (hamburgers) and one for the nonrivalrous good (streetlight). Each graph contains three curves: a demand curve representing consumer A's willingness-to-pay (d_A); a demand curve representing consumer B's willingness-to-pay (d_B); and a total marginal benefit (MB) curve, which is derived from the demand curves for the two consumers.

The total marginal benefit curve for the rivalrous good is equivalent to a market demand curve. To derive this curve, the two demand curves for individual consumers are summed horizontally. For example, at a price of P^*, consumer A would want to consume q_1 and consumer B would want q_2 of the good. Total market demand for the good at a price of P^* is equal to $q_1 + q_2$, a total of Q^*. Thus, willingness-to-pay for (or equivalently, marginal benefits from) the last unit of the total of Q^* units consumed is P^*. Notice that until the price falls below $P^{\#}$, the marginal benefit curve would correspond to B's demand curve because A would not demand any of the good.

The total marginal benefit curve for the nonrivalrous good, in contrast to that for the rivalrous good, is derived by adding the demand curves for individual consumers vertically rather than horizontally. At an output level of Q^*, for example, total willingness-to-pay (i.e., the total marginal benefits from the last unit of good that is made available) is equal to $p_a + p_b$ or P^*. Notice that at output levels above $Q^{\#}$, consumer A's willingness-to-pay falls to zero and, consequently, the marginal benefit curve corresponds to consumer B's demand curve.

The reason the demand curves for individual consumers must be summed horizontally in the presence of rivalry and vertically in its absence can be clarified through use of a numerical example. If at a price of $2 consumer B wanted to buy two hamburgers and consumer A one, total demand would equal three hamburgers. But if at a price of $1,000 B wanted two streetlights on the block on which he and A both lived, but A wanted only one, two streetlights would completely satisfy the demands of both. Thus, the total demand for a nonrivalrous good cannot be determined by summing the quantity of the good each consumer desires at a given price. It must be determined instead by summing each consumer's willingness-to-pay for a given quantity of the good. Hence, although A and B would have a different willingness-to-pay for the two streetlights—A's might be less than $1,000 and B's more than $1,000—their total demand for the two streetlights can be determined by adding A's willingness-to-pay for two lights to B's.

The distinction between how the total demand for rivalrous and nonrivalrous goods are determined has an important implication. In the case of the rivalrous good,

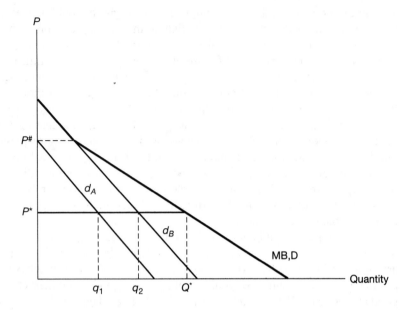

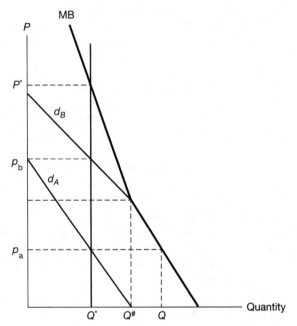

Figure 3.B6(a)   Rivalrous Good (e.g., hamburgers)
Figure 3.B6(b)   Nonrivalrous Good (e.g., streetlight)

consumers will reveal to the market how much they want. For example, if the price of hamburgers is set at P^*, consumer A will actually purchase q_1 of the good and consumer B will purchase q_2. But in the case of a nonrivalrous good, there is no market mechanism that causes consumers to reveal how much output they would purchase at different prices. For example, if the price of streetlight is at p_b, consumer B would be willing to purchase Q^* of the good. But if B did that, A would not purchase any, because, as a result of B's purchase, he could consume all he wanted. In other words, A would free ride on B. Because of this free-rider problem, B might refuse to make any purchases until A agreed to make some sort of contribution.[9]

When only a small group of people is involved, they may be able to work out the free-rider problems caused by the nonexcludability and nonrivalry of public goods through negotiations. For example, a neighborhood association might make arrangements for installing and paying for streetlights. But notice that this is not really a market solution. And even when negotiations do take place, too much or too little of the good may be produced. For example, if consumers A and B are to be charged for streetlight on the basis of their willingness-to-pay, they both will probably try to convince each other that they place a low value on streetlights, regardless of how each actually values it. It is therefore difficult to determine where the total marginal benefit curve for a public good is located, even if only a small group of people is involved. When a large group of people all share a good that is nonexcludable and nonrivalrous—for example, national defense—negotiations become impractical. Consequently, if the good is going to be produced at all, the government must almost certainly intervene by either producing the good itself or subsidizing its production.

Pure Public Goods versus Other Public Goods

Because streetlight is almost both nonrivalrous in consumption and nonexcludable, it is close to being a pure public good. A hamburger, in contrast, is a *pure private good*. There are other goods, however, that are either nonrivalrous or nonexcludable, but not both. For example, an uncrowded road is essentially nonrivalrous in nature. One person's use of it does not keep another from using it. But it is excludable. Both individuals could be required to pay a toll to use it. Hence, it is sometimes called a *toll good*. Fish in international waters provide an example of a good that is rivalrous but nonexcludable. Fish move around so it is difficult to preclude fishers from access to some particular type of fish, say, tuna. But if a fisher catches a particular tuna, then it is no longer available to other fishers. This type of good is called an *open access resource*. Goods that are either nonrivalrous or nonexcludable, but not both, do not exhibit all of the characteristics of public goods, but do exhibit some of these characteristics.[10] However, for the sake of brevity, we have focused on pure public goods—that is, those that are both nonrivalrous and nonexcludable. Examples of goods that are close to being pure public goods are streetlight, police protection, flood control, and national defense.

As suggested by the preceding analysis, because of both nonrivalry and nonexcludability, actual markets for pure public goods are unlikely to exist. However, marginal benefit and marginal cost curves, which are analogous to market demand and supply curves, do exist. We have already shown how a marginal benefit curve for a public

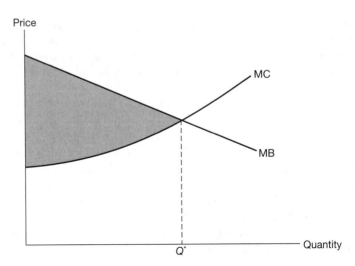

Figure 3.B7 Marginal Benefit and Marginal Cost Curves for a Public Good

good is derived. And, as in the case of a private good, the marginal cost curve for a public good simply reflects the costs of producing each incremental unit of the good.

The marginal benefit and cost curves for a pure public good are illustrated in Figure 3.B7. Social welfare is maximized when marginal benefits equal marginal costs, while deadweight loss results at either smaller or larger output amounts. Thus, the diagram implies that society would be best off if $Q*$ of the good were produced and consumed. However, because of the absence of a true market, little or none of the public good represented in the diagram would be produced without government intervention, or at least some sort of negotiation process. Thus, in the absence of government intervention or negotiations, society would forgo most or all the social surplus represented by the shaded triangular area. Even if the government does intervene or negotiations take place, however, there is no guarantee that output of the good will be at $Q*$. Instead, because the marginal benefit curve for a pure public good is inherently unknowable, too much or too little of it may be produced.[11]

EXERCISES FOR CHAPTER 3

1. A person's demand for gizmos is given by the following equation:

$$q = 6 - 0.5p + 0.0001I$$

where q is the quantity demanded at price p when the person's income is I.
Assume initially that the person's income is $40,000.

    a. At what price will demand fall to zero? (This is sometimes called the *choke price* because it is the price that chokes off demand.)

    b. If the market price for gizmos is $10, how many will be demanded?

    c. At a price of $10, what is the price elasticity of demand for gizmos?

  d. At a price of $10, what is the consumer surplus?

  e. If price rises to $12, how much consumer surplus is lost?

  f. If income were $60,000, what would be the consumer surplus loss from a price rise from $10 to $12?

2. At the current market equilibrium, the price of a good equals $30 and the quantity equals 10 units. At this equilibrium, the price elasticity of supply is 1.5. Assume that the supply schedule is linear.

  a. Use the price elasticity and market equilibrium to find the supply schedule. (Hint: the supply schedule has the following form: $q = a + (\Delta q/\Delta p)p$. First, find the value of $\Delta q/\Delta p$, and then, find the value of a.)

  b. Calculate the producer surplus in the market.

  c. Imagine that a policy results in price falling from $30 to $20. By how much does producer surplus fall?

  d. What fraction of the lost producer surplus is due to the reduction in the quantity supplied and what fraction is due to the fall in price received per unit sold?

3. Consider a low-wage labor market. Workers in this market are not presently covered by the minimum wage, but the government is considering implementing such legislation. If implemented, this law would require employers in this market to pay workers a $5 hourly wage. Suppose all workers in this market are equally productive, the current market clearing wage rate is $4 per hour, and that at this market clearing wage there are 600 employed workers. Further suppose that under the minimum wage legislation, only 500 workers would be employed and 300 workers would be unemployed. Finally, assume that the market demand and supply schedules are linear and that the market reservation wage, the lowest wage at which any worker in the market would be willing to work, is $1.

  Compute the dollar value of the impact of the policy on employers, workers, and society as a whole.

4. Suppose the government is considering an increase in the toll on a certain stretch of highway from $.40 to $.50. At present, 50,000 cars per week use that highway stretch; after the toll is imposed, it is projected that only 40,000 cars per week will use the highway stretch.

  a. Assuming that the marginal cost of highway use is constant (i.e., the supply curve is horizontal) and equal to $.40 per car, what is the net cost to society attributable to the increase in the toll? (Hint: The toll increase will cause the supply curve, not the demand curve, to shift.)

  b. Because of the reduced use of the highway, the government would reduce its purchases of concrete from 20,000 tons per year to 19,000 tons per year. Thus, if the price of concrete were $25 per ton, the government's cost savings would be $25,000. However, the government's reduced demand for concrete causes its market price to fall from $25 per ton to $24.50 per ton. Moreover, because of this reduction in price, the purchases of concrete by nongovernment buyers increase by 300 tons per year. Assuming that the factor market for concrete is competitive, can the government's savings of $25,000 be appropriately used as the measure of the *social* value of the cost savings that result from the government purchasing less concrete? Or would shadow pricing be necessary?

  c. Because of the reduced use of the highway, demand in the secondary market for subway rides increases. Assuming that the price of subway rides is set equal to the marginal cost of operating the subway and marginal costs are constant (i.e., the supply curve is horizontal), and no externalities result from the reduced use of the highway and the increased use of the subway, are there additional costs or benefits due to the increased demand for subway rides? Why or why not?

    d. Because of the reduced use of the highway, demand in the secondary market for gasoline falls—indeed, by 30,000 gallons per year. As we realize, there is a stiff tax on gasoline, one that existed prior to the new toll. Assuming that the marginal cost of producing gasoline is $1 per gallon, that these marginal costs are constant (i.e., the supply curve is constant), that no externalities result from the consumption of gasoline, and that the gasoline tax adds 30 percent to the supply price, are there any additional costs or benefits due to this shift? If so, how large are they?

5. A country imports 3 billion barrels of crude oil per year and domestically produces another 3 billion barrels of crude oil per year. The world price of crude oil is $18 per barrel. Assuming linear schedules, economists estimate the price elasticity of domestic supply to be 0.25 and the price elasticity of domestic demand to be –0.1 at the current equilibrium.

    a. Consider the changes in social surplus that would result from imposition of a $6 per barrel import fee on crude oil that would involve annual administrative costs of $50 million. Assume that the world price will not change as a result of the country imposing the import fee, but that the domestic price will increase by $6 per barrel. Also assume that only producers, consumers, and taxpayers within the country have standing. Determine the quantity consumed, the quantity produced domestically, and the quantity imported after the imposition of the import fee. Then estimate the annual social net benefits of the import fee.

    b. Imagine that the government realizes 20 percent of the increase in the producer surplus of domestic oil firms as revenue collected through its corporate income tax. Assume that this revenue plus the revenue collected from the import fee less its administration costs is used to reduce domestic taxes. Reestimate the social net benefits of the import-fee assuming that the marginal excess burden of the tax system in the country is .25 overall, but the marginal excess burden of the corporate tax revenue induced by the import fee is zero.

    c. The reduction in the country's demand for imports may affect the world price of crude oil. Assuming that the import fee reduces the world price from $18 to $16 per barrel, and thus, the after-tax domestic price is $16 + $6 = $22 per barrel, a net increase in domestic price of $4 per barrel, repeat the analysis done in parts a and b.

6. Prior to the imposition of the import fee analyzed in question 5, the country annually consumed 900 million short tons of coal, all domestically mined, at a price of $22 per short ton. How would the CBA done in question 5 change if, after imposition of the import fee, the following circumstances are assumed to result from energy consumers switching from crude oil to coal?

    a. Annual consumption of coal rises by 40 million short tons, but the price of coal remains unchanged.

    b. Annual consumption of coal rises by 40 million short tons and the price of coal rises to $23 per short ton. In answering this question, assume that the prices of other goods, including coal, were *not* held constant in estimating the demand schedule for crude oil.

    c. Annual consumption of coal rises by 40 million short tons and the price of coal rises to $23 per short ton. In answering this question, assume that the prices of other goods, including coal, were held constant in estimating the demand schedule for crude oil. Also assume that the demand curve for coal is completely inelastic.

    d. The market price of coal underestimates its marginal social cost by $5 per short ton because the coal mined in the country has a high sulphur content that produces smog when burned. In answering this question, assume that, as in question 6.a, the annual consumption of coal rises by 40 million short tons, but the price of coal remains unchanged.

7. Imagine that all the crude oil imports to the country are made by ships owned by its nationals. The Association of Petroleum Shippers argues that the reduction in imports resulting from the import fee discussed in question 5 will drive down the price of shipping services and thereby inflict a loss on them. The Committee for Energy Independence, which favors the import fee, argues that the reduction in shipping prices will benefit consumers of shipping services. Which argument is correct? In preparing an answer, make the following assumptions: The import fee will reduce the quantity of imported crude oil from 3 billion to 2.5 billion barrels per year; the reduction in barrels shipped will drive per barrel shipping costs down from $1 per barrel to $.75 per barrel; and the elasticity of demand in the shipping market at the new equilibrium ($.075, 2.5 billion barrels) is –0.3. Also assume that the shipping market is undistorted and that the prices of other goods, including shipping services, were held constant in estimating the demand schedule for crude oil.

NOTES

[1]Producer surplus and consumer surplus are defined a bit later in this chapter.

[2]David L. Weimer and Aidan R. Vining, Policy Analysis: Concepts and Practice, 2nd ed. (Englewood Cliffs, NJ: Prentice Hall, 1992). For a theoretical treatment of externalities, public goods, and club goods see Richard Corres and Todd Sandler, *The Theory of Externalities, Public Goods and Club Goods*, (New York: Cambridge University Press, 1986).

[3]For a detailed examination of government failures, see Weimer and Vining (2nd edition), Chapter 6.

[4]Note that viewed in this fashion, the relation depicted in Figure 3.2 is called an *inverse demand curve*; that is, price is viewed as a function of quantity, rather than the other way around, as is more ordinarily the case. One can envision deriving an inverse demand curve through an auction in which bids are taken on the first unit of a good offered for sale, then on the second unit, then the third unit, and so forth, with successively lower bids obtained for each additional unit of the good that is offered. This kind of auction is called a Dutch auction. Apparently, in years past, it was common in Holland to have a mechanical "clock" with hands that started at the bid made on the previous unit and swept through successively lower bids until stopped by an individual who wished to make a bid.

[5]If the value of e_d is greater than one and, hence, the percentage change in quantity demanded is greater than the percentage change in price, then demand is said to be *relatively elastic*. On the other hand, if the value of e_d is less than one and, hence, the percentage change in quantity demanded is smaller than the percentage change in price, then demand is said to be *relatively inelastic*. If the value approaches infinity (i.e., the demand curve is horizontal), then demand is said to be *perfectly elastic*, while if the value is zero (the demand curve is vertical), then demand is said to be *completely inelastic*.

[6]The use of elasticity estimates in conducting CBAs is further described in Chapter 10.

[7]The government is not, of course, the ultimate beneficiary of the tax revenues. This depends on the projects and programs that are funded by the tax revenues.

[8]Deadweight loss (DWL) may be defined more formally in terms of Figures 3.3(a) and (b) as follows:

$$DWL = \int_{x^*}^{x_1} (MSB - MSC)dx, \qquad \text{if } X^* < X_1$$

$$DWL = \int_{x_2}^{x^*} (MSB - MSC)dX, \qquad \text{if } X_2 < X^*$$

where MSB is marginal social benefits and MSC is marginal social costs.

When the elasticity of demand (e_d) is known, the change in deadweight loss resulting from a price change—for example, one imposed by a tax—can be computed by using the formula:

$$\Delta DWL = 1/2P^*x^*(\Delta P/P^*)^2 e_d$$

Notice that this formula is similar to Equation (3.3).

[9]Over longer periods of time, fewer factors of production are fixed so that supply schedules tend to be flatter.

[10]More precisely, the firm's supply curve is the upward sloping segment of its marginal cost curve that is above its average variable cost curve. If the firm were producing below its average variable cost curve, it could not cover its variable costs and, as a consequence, would shut down. It should also be noted that in the absence of perfect competition (for example, in the case of monopoly), the upward sloping segment of a firm's marginal cost curve is not its supply curve. This point is further discussed in Appendix 3B.

[11]By normal return, we simply mean the market price or rate of return that each unit of a resource commands under perfect competition.

[12]Thus, because we are presently assuming the existence of perfect competition and well-functioning markets, social opportunity costs, as we have defined them, correspond to private economic costs. In the absence of perfect competition (or, as discussed in Appendix 3B, if externalities exist), private economic costs may differ from the costs that using resources imposes on society. These latter costs, *social opportunity costs,* are the relevant cost measure for purposes of CBA. The use of shadow pricing to obtain appropriate measures of social opportunity costs when markets are distorted is discussed later in this chapter.

[13]In the long run all the factors of production are free to vary. Consequently, in the long run, producer surplus does correspond to firm profits. Moreover, long-run market supply curves tend to be flatter (i.e., more elastic) than short-run market supply curves, both because all the factors of production are free to vary and because firms can enter and exit from the market. Consequently, the long-run impacts of price increases on producer surplus will be larger than the short-run impacts, while the opposite will be true of price decreases.

[14]In this discussion, we are assuming perfect competition and, hence, that marginal private costs equal marginal social costs. Later in this chapter, as well as in Appendix 3B, we consider situations where marginal private costs do not equal marginal social costs—for example, when externalities exist.

[15]In this section, we continue to assume perfect competition. If prior to being taxed, however, a good was overconsumed from the social perspective—for example, as a result of a negative externality— then the introduction of a tax could increase efficiency by reducing the overconsumption. In this case, the marginal welfare cost of raising a dollar of taxes would be less than one dollar. More generally, as discussed later in the chapter, the efficiency implications of interventions depend on the distortions already in the market. For example, Charles Ballard demonstrates that when labor markets for low-income groups are distorted by high effective marginal tax rates, redistributing through wage subsidies can actually result in efficiency gains. Charles L. Ballard, "The Marginal Efficiency Cost of Redistribution," *American Economic Review,* 78, no.5 (December 1988), 1019–1033.

[16]For example, see Edgar K. Browning, "The Marginal Cost of Public Funds," *Journal of Political Economy*, 84, no. 2 (April 1976), 283–298 and "On the Marginal Welfare Cost of Taxation," *American Economic Review*, 77, no. 1 (March 1987), 11–23; Harry Campbell, "Deadweight Loss and Commodity Taxation in Canada," *Canadian Journal of Economics*, 8, no. 3 (August 1975), 441–446; Charles E. Stuart, "Swedish Tax Rates, Labor Supply, and Tax Revenues," *Journal of Political Economy*, 89, no. 5 (October 1981), 1020–1038.

[17]Charles L. Ballard, John B. Shoven, and John Whalley, "General Equilibrium Computations of the Marginal Welfare Costs of Taxes in the United States," *American Economic Review*, 75, no.1 (March 1985), 128–138.

[18]In a recent article, Charles L. Ballard and Don Fullerton ["Distortionary Taxes and the Provision of Public Goods," *Journal of Economic Perspectives*, 6, no. 3 (1992), 117–131] suggest that, under certain assumptions, the MEB of taxes on earned income could actually be negative. The two most important of

these assumptions are that labor supply curves are backward bending and that the public goods purchased with the tax revenues have no effect on labor supply.

[19]Notice that in all the examples previously discussed in this chapter only the price of a good changed. Consequently, the demand curve for the good did not shift. Instead, there was a movement along the curve, causing a change in the *quantity demanded*. If instead, something other than prices changes—for example, a new project results in a need for additional pencils—the demand curve shifts and there is a change in *demand*.

[20]If the government were to purchase only a small part of the fixed supply of land on the open market, its budgetary outlay would very closely approximate the opportunity cost of removing the land from the private sector. In this case, the government's entry into the market would bid up the price of the land slightly, crowding potential private-sector land buyers who are just to the left of point *b* on the demand curve out of the market. These buyers would lose a negligible amount of surplus. In addition, those private-sector buyers who remain in the market would pay a slightly higher price. Hence, surplus would be transferred between these buyers and the sellers of the land.

[21]There is a natural tendency of those who are promoting a particular government project (e.g., a dam or a recreational area) to emphasize the potential benefits to those who must supply resources to the project. Our analysis suggests that in well-functioning markets these benefits only occur if the price of these resources increases, and even then, part of the benefits to the suppliers of the resources is offset by increases in costs to the original buyers of the resources. Note, however, that the analysis is based on the assumption that the resources used in the project would be fully employed even in the absence of the project. As will be seen later in this chapter, if this assumption does not hold, additional project benefits can then accrue to suppliers of resources.

[22]This formula is based on a bit of geometry. The triangular area *C* equals one-half the rectangular area from which it is formed, $B + C + F$. Thus, area *C* is equivalent to $1/2(P_1 - P_0) \times q'$.

[23]This amount is derived as follows:

$$P_1 q' - 1/2(P_1 - P_0)q' = 1/2(P_0 + P_1)q'.$$

[24]For a discussion of various forms of wage rigidity that result in unemployment, see Ronald G. Ehrenberg and Robert S. Smith, *Modern Labor Economics: Theory and Public Policy*, 5th ed. (New York: Harper Collins College Publishers, 1994), Chapter 16.

[25]For more detailed discussions of these issues, see Robert H. Haveman, "Evaluating Public Expenditure Under Conditions of Unemployment," in *Public Expenditure and Policy Analysis*, 3rd ed., Robert H. Haveman and Julius Margolis eds. (Boston: Houghton Mifflin Company, 1983), pp. 167–182, and E.J. Mishan, *Cost-Benefit Analysis*, 4th ed. (London: Unwin Hyman, 1988), pp. 325–329.

[26]As mentioned in Chapter 1, sometimes in a CBA a policy outcome that people would be willing to pay to avoid is referred to as a *negative benefit*, rather than as a *cost*. These two terms can be viewed as equivalent.

[27]The term *gross benefits* is used because we are ignoring the inputs needed to increase the supply of goods. Measurement of the social cost of these resources was discussed in the previous section. *Net benefits* would be obtained by subtracting these values from gross benefits.

[28]As in the case of the demand curve, a change in price only causes a movement along the supply curve, a change in *quantity supplied*. But a project that provides more of a good increases the supply of the good, resulting in a shift of the supply curve.

[29]The rectangle $q_0 a b q_1$ also, of course, represents a cost to those consumers who purchase the good from the government. This "cost," however, is exactly offset by benefits that these persons enjoy in consuming the good and, consequently, can be ignored in our analysis.

[30]Note that this issue is similar to one we encountered in measuring the cost of hiring unemployed workers to work on a government project. Just as workers may be appropriately viewed as distributed along a labor market supply curve so may consumers of a good be appropriately viewed as located along a product market demand curve.

[31]This assumes, of course, that the market is sufficiently competitive and the firms in it are sufficiently efficient that all of the cost savings are passed on to consumers in the form of a price decrease.

[32]An alternative method of measuring the gain in social surplus is simply to compare total social surplus with and without the project. In the absence of the project, total social surplus would be represented by the triangular area *fae*, while in the presence of the project, total social surplus would be represented by the triangular area *fbd*. Subtracting the smaller triangle from the larger triangle, we again find that the net gain in social surplus equals the trapezoidal area *abde*.

[33]Notice that in this instance we are once again ignoring expenditures the government incurs in purchasing inputs needed to undertake the project. Hence, we are again measuring gross benefits rather than net benefits.

[34]For greater detail concerning externalities, see Appendix 3B.

[35]In this example, gross program benefits only differ from net program costs by the administrative costs required to operate the program. Also notice that in the context of the example the rule that gross project benefits equals changes in social surplus plus net revenues generated by the project continues to hold once it is recognized that in this instance *net* revenues are actually negative.

[36]Notice that, in this example, we are assuming that the price of fishing equals the marginal social cost of fishing and that marginal social costs are constant. This, in turn, implies that there are no producer surplus or externalities in the primary market (e.g., highway congestion does not result because of increased travel to the newly stocked lake).

[37]As discussed in greater detail in Chapter 10, in situations in which we cannot measure social surplus changes in primary markets, we may try to infer them from the demand shifts in secondary markets. For example, imagine that we have no information to help us determine the demand schedule for fishing days, but that we do have information to help us predict how the demand schedule for fishing equipment will change. For lack of a direct measure of benefits, we might take the difference between the social surplus in the fishing equipment market after the project (based on demand schedule D_{E1}) and the social surplus in the equipment market prior to the project (based on demand schedule D_{E0}). We would then apply some scaling factor to correct for underestimation that results from the fact that not all the consumer surplus from fishing will be reflected in the equipment market. (Some fishers will fish with old equipment and self-collected bait—their surplus will not appear in the equipment market. Moreover, equipment and bait comprise only some of the inputs to fishing.)

[38]For a useful analysis that uses a somewhat different approach than the one presented in this subsection but reaches very similar conclusions, see Herbert Mohring, "Maximizing, Measuring, and Not Double Counting Transportation-Improvement Benefits: A Primer on Closed- and Open-Economy Cost-Benefit Analysis," *Transportation Research*, 27, no. 6 (1993), 413–424.

[39]As advocates of a policy often claim benefits in secondary markets, it is somewhat ironic that demand shifts in undistorted secondary markets that cause price changes *always* involve losses in social surplus. This can be seen by using panel (b) in Figure 3.17 to illustrate the case of an outward shift in demand in a secondary market, as well as the case of an inward shift in demand. Simply take D_{G1} as the original demand schedule and D_{G0} as the postproject demand schedule. Using the postproject demand schedule for measuring social surplus changes, we see that the price increase from P_{G1} to P_{G0} results in a producer surplus increase equal to the area of trapezoid $P_{G1}fgP_{G0}$ and a consumer surplus loss equal to the area of $P_{G1}hgP_{G0}$ so that social surplus falls by the area of triangle *fgh*.

[40]See Richard E. Just, Darrell L. Hueth, and Andrew Schmitz, *Applied Welfare Economics and Public Policy* (Englewood Cliffs, NJ: Prentice Hall, 1982), Chapter 9.

[41]For greater detail concerning this point, see Just, Hueth, and Schmitz, pp. 200–213.

[42]Indeed, under certain assumptions, areas *abc* and *efg* will almost exactly equal one another. The most important of these assumptions is that the price changes in the two markets represented in Figure 3.17 are small and that no income effects result from these price changes. If there are no income effects, there will be symmetry in substitution between the two goods. In other words, their cross-substitution effects will be equal. That is, $\partial q_F/\partial P_G = \partial q_G/\partial P_F$. Given this approximate equality, $\Delta P_F \cdot \Delta q_F \approx \Delta P_G \cdot \Delta q_G$. Hence,

area *abc* approximately equals area *efg*. Typically, income effects do occur as a result of price changes, but as discussed in Appendix 3A, these effects tend to be very small for most goods. Consequently, one would anticipate that area *abc* would generally closely approximate area *efg*.

[43]Separate measures would have to be obtained, however, to examine how benefits and costs were distributed among various groups. For example, area *abc* is a gain to consumers, while area *efg* is a loss to producers. To the extent these two areas are equal, they represent a transfer of surplus from producers to consumers. In addition, surplus corresponding to area $P_{G0}efP_{G1}$ is also transferred from producers to consumers.

[44]Promoters of localized recreational facilities—for example, the advocates of building new sports stadiums, museums, and parks—sometimes refer to such benefits as *multiplier effects*. They argue that persons from outside the community who take advantage of these facilities will make purchases from nearby businesses and that these businesses will, in turn, also spend their newly gained revenues nearby, and this, in turn, will generate still more revenues that will be spent locally, and so forth. In a full employment national economy, these multiplier effects are only relevant when standing is restricted to residents of a specific geographic area because they only occur as a result of consumers shifting their spending from one area to another. Moreover, even localized multiplier effects generally tend to be relatively small. First, local businesses are often owned by nonresidents. Second, many of the purchases by local businesses are made outside the local area. Thus, expenditures made within a local area readily dissipate elsewhere.

APPENDIX A NOTES

[1]An alternative to compensating variation as the money metric for measuring welfare changes is equivalent variation, the amount of money that if paid by the consumer would cause him to lose just as much utility as the price increase. The major points made in this appendix are valid for either measure. We focus on compensating variation because it has a somewhat more natural interpretation than equivalent variation. George W. McKenzie argues, however, that only equivalent variation satisfies all the desirable properties of a money metric for social welfare. See George W. McKenzie, *Measuring Economic Welfare: New Methods* (New York: Cambridge University Press, 1983).

Although compensating variation and equivalent variation are appropriate measures of the welfare changes resulting from price increases or decreases, it has been argued that either *compensating surplus* or *equivalent surplus* is more appropriately used when the quantity of a good, rather than its price, increases or decreases. In this appendix, we focus on price rather than quantity changes. For a discussion of when each of the four welfare change measures are most appropriately used, as well as a useful graphical presentation of each, see V. Kerry Smith and William H. Desvousges, *Measuring Water Quality Benefits* (Boston: Kluwer-Nijhoff Publishing, 1986), Chapter 2.

[2]The slope of an indifference curve is called the *marginal rate of substitution*, where the

$$\text{marginal rate of substitution} = \left. \frac{\partial Y}{\partial X} \right|_{\overline{U}} < 0$$

and $\overline{U}$ indicates that utility is being held constant.

[3]At equilibrium, the marginal rate of substitution will equal the ratio of the price of good X to the price of good Y.

[4]Thus, in Figure 3.A1(a), $OI = 1/2OH$ or $I = 1/2H$.

[5]Depending on the slopes of the indifference curves, the consumption of good Y could either increase or decrease. As shown in Figure 3.A1(a), it slightly decreases in this particular example.

[6]In calculus notation, this decomposition can be represented as follows:

$$\frac{dX}{dP} = \left. \frac{dX}{dP} \right|_{\overline{U}} - X \left. \frac{dX}{dY} \right|_{\overline{P}}$$

This equation is known as the *Slutsky equation*. The first term to the right of the equal sign is the substitution effect, where utility is held constant. The second term is the income effect, where prices are held constant, and X is the amount of the good consumed prior to the price change.

[7]It is sometimes possible, however, to approximate Hicksian demand curves indirectly by first obtaining estimates of the relation between quantity purchased and prices *and* the relation between quantity purchased and income and then (as implied by the preceding footnote) use the Slutsky equation to derive the income-compensated (rather than the utility-compensated) relation between prices and quantity purchased [e.g., see Robin W. Boadway and Neil Bruce, *Welfare Economics* (Oxford, United Kingdom: Basil Blackwell Ltd, 1984), pp. 219–220]. In practice, however, this is not always feasible. Thus, it is estimates of Marshallian demand curves that are most often available and used for purposes of CBA.

[8]For analyses of the size of the bias, see Boadway and Bruce, *Welfare Economics*, pp. 216–219; Julian M. Alston and Douglas M. Larson, "Hicksian vs. Marshallian Welfare Measures: Why Do We Do What We Do?" *American Journal of Agricultural Economics*, 75 (August 1993), 764-769; and Robert D. Willig, "Consumer's Surplus Without Apology," *American Economic Review*, 66, no. 4 (September 1976), 589-597.

APPENDIX B NOTES

[1]There are, of course, other types of markets in which individual firms have market power—for example, those characterized by oligopoly or monopolistic competition. We focus on markets characterized by monopoly, and especially natural monopoly, because government intervention is most likely to occur in these markets.

[2]Notice that while quantity is determined along the monopolist's marginal cost curve, price is not. Thus, unlike a perfectly competitive firm's marginal cost curve, a monopolist's marginal cost curve cannot be interpreted as its supply curve.

[3]As was true of competitive firms, producer surplus is not identical to profits. To calculate profits, fixed costs must be subtracted from producer surplus. Profits can be determined in Figure 3.B1 by use of the average cost curve, AC, a curve that reflects both variable and fixed costs. Specifically, profits are represented by the rectangular area $P_m aef$.

[4]There are, of course, alternative policies that the government might adopt in response to the monopoly. For example, it might tax the monopolist's profits, regulate the prices the monopolist charges, or operate the monopoly as a state-owned enterprise.

[5]The two demand curves are drawn closer together at high prices than at low prices to imply that at higher prices buyers would go to more trouble to obtain additional information about the product than at lower prices. Whether or not this is actually the case, however, is not essential to the analysis.

[6]For a more extensive discussion of these three types of products, see Vining and Weimer, "Information Asymmetry Favoring Sellers: A Policy Framework," *Policy Sciences*, Vol. 21, No. 4, (1988), 281–303.

[7]Externalities may occur for a wide variety of reasons. For example, some result because a particular type of manufacturing technology is used (e.g., air pollution caused by smokestack industry). Others arise because of interdependencies (or synergies) between producers and consumers or different groups of producers (e.g., beekeepers who provide pollination services for nearby fruit growers). Still other externalities occur because of networking (e.g., the larger the number of persons who purchase a particular type of automobile, the greater the number of qualified service garages available to each buyer).

[8]When it is feasible to do so, private firms attempt to make nonexcludable goods excludable. One example of this is scramblers used by certain television cable networks.

[9]The free-rider problem is also closely linked to difficulties in remedying problems resulting from externalities. For example, because clean air is both nonrivalrous and nonexcludable, in the absence of government intervention, there is limited incentive for the private sector to produce clean air by reducing air pollution.

[10]*Common property resources* are similar to open access goods except that the set of potential users is clearly defined. For an extensive discussion of such goods, see David L. Weimer and Aidan R. Vining, *Policy Analysis: Concepts and Practice* (Englewood Cliffs, NJ: Prentice Hall, 1992), 45–57. Two additional publications that focus on common property resource goods are Elinor Ostrom, *Governing the Commons* (New York: Cambridge University Press, 1990), and Glenn Stevenson, *Common Property Economics* (New York: Cambridge University Press, 1991).

4

BENEFITS AND COSTS IN
DIFFERENT TIME PERIODS:
THE MECHANICS
OF DISCOUNTING

Both private and public decisions can have important consequences that extend over time. When consumers buy houses, automobiles, or education, they generally expect to accrue benefits and incur costs over a number of years. When the government builds a dam, subsidizes job training, regulates carbon dioxide emissions, or leases the outer continental shelf for oil exploration, it sets in motion consequences for society that extend over many years. Often analysts have to compare projects with different flows of benefits and costs arising over different time periods. Formally, they have to make intertemporal (across time) comparisons. To do this, analysts *discount* future costs and benefits so that all costs and benefits are in a common metric—the present value. Thus, they can measure and compare the net social benefits of each policy alternative using the net present value criterion.

Most analysts realize that future costs and benefits should be discounted in some way. But, surprisingly, there is evidence that some governmental clients are not as familiar with the concept as one might expect. For example, a recent survey of 90 U.S. municipalities with populations over 100,000 found that only 43 percent use discounting in evaluating projects. Those that do discount employ a variety of rationales, but generally use a real discount rate of around 3 percent.[1]

This chapter deals with practical issues one must know in order to compute net present values. It assumes implicitly that the *social discount rate*, the rate at which analysts should discount the benefits and costs of a societal (government) project, is known. As we discuss in Chapter 5, this is a reasonable assumption as analysts often operate in circumstances in which the discount rate has been set equal to a particular value.

Specifically, the sections of this chapter cover the following topics: the basics of discounting; the difference between nominal and real discount rates; the timing of benefits and costs; terminal values; comparing projects with different time frames; relative price changes; and sensitivity analysis in discounting. Appendix 4A presents some shortcut methods for calculating present values, future values, and net present values, focusing on annuities and perpetuities. Appendix 4B demonstrates how to calculate present values when interest is compounded more frequently than once per period. These topics are essentially uncontroversial. Readers who are familiar with capital budgeting techniques may want to skip over these issues and move to Chapter 5.[2]

BASICS OF DISCOUNTING

Compounding and Discounting over Two Periods Only

Consider the following project. You have the opportunity to buy several cases of vintage wine for $10,000. You know that the wine will sell for $11,000 one year from now. Should you invest in this project? (We assume that you will not drink the wine: The purpose is investment not consumption!) As a preliminary, it is often useful to lay out the annual benefits and costs of investing in the project as in Table 4.1. You want to compare the $10,000 cost now with the $11,000 benefit you would receive a year from now. There are three ways to do this, each of which give the same answer.

Using future values.   This method compares what you would receive if you invested in the project with what you would get if you invested your money elsewhere. It illustrates the basic idea of *simple compounding*. We present this method first because the idea of simple compounding is intuitively appealing for anyone who has ever had a savings account.

Suppose you use your $10,000 to buy a bond or T-bill (treasury bill)[3] at interest rate i. Then, next year, you will have $10,000(1 + i)$. This amount is called the *future value* (FV) because it is an amount that you will receive in the future. Formally,

$$FV = \$10,000(1 + i) \qquad (4.1)$$

You can compare this future value with the $11,000 you would receive if you had invested in the project, and pick whichever project gives you more one year from now. If, for example, the interest rate on the T-bill is 8 percent, then $i = 0.08$ and $FV = \$10,000(1 + 0.08) = \$10,800$, which is less than $11,000. Consequently, you would be well advised to buy the wine.

TABLE 4.1   BENEFITS AND COSTS OF BUYING WINE

YEAR	ANNUAL BENEFIT	ANNUAL COST	ANNUAL NET BENEFIT
0	0	10,000	−10,000
1	11,000	0	11,000

Using present values.   We now switch from compounding to discounting. This captures the same idea but makes the comparison now, today, rather than in the future. Specifically, this method compares the current value of what you would receive if you invested in the project with what you actually have now. To return to the wine example, this method determines the amount of money today that would yield $11,000 next year assuming that you could invest the money at interest rate i; that is, it discounts the future benefits of the project to obtain its *present value* (PV):

$$PV = \frac{\$11,000}{(1+i)} \qquad (4.2)$$

You can then compare this with the $10,000 you have now, and choose whichever project gives the most today. As equation (4.2) demonstrates, discounting is the opposite of compounding.

Returning to our example, in order to have $11,000 in one year when you could invest money at 8 percent, you would need today

$$PV = \frac{\$11,000}{(1+0.08)} = \$10,185.19$$

In other words, the present value of $11,000 received one year from now when the interest rate is 8 percent is $10,185.19. This is the present value of investing in the wine. Since this amount is more than $10,000, you should invest in the wine.

Using net present values.   Third, calculate the overall value of the project—the net benefit—and see whether or not it is positive. Specifically, the *net present value* (NPV) of the project equals the present value of all of its cash flows, both positive (benefits) and negative (costs):

$$NPV = -\$10,000 + \frac{\$11,000}{(1+i)}$$

You can then compare the NPV of the project with $0. As we discussed in Chapter 2, if the NPV is positive, then you should proceed with the project; if it is negative, then you should not. This is usually slightly simpler, although equivalent to, comparing the present value of the benefits with the present value of the costs.

For example, if the interest rate is 8 percent, then the NPV of buying the wine is

$$NPV = -\$10,000 + \frac{\$11,000}{(1 + 0.08)} = -\$10,000 + \$10,185.19 = \$185.19$$

Because the NPV is positive you should buy the wine.

Implicitly, the positive NPV decision rule assumes there is no other alternative with a higher NPV. *If there are multiple alternatives, then one should select the alternative with the highest NPV.* In such situations calculating the NPV of each project is considerably easier than trying to keep track of the separate benefits and costs of each alternative.

The foregoing example also assumed that you had $10,000 available which you could either use to buy the wine or you could invest at interest rate i. Sometimes analysts calculate NPVs of projects for which the government may not have all the cash immediately available and it may have to borrow some funds. *Implicitly, analysts assume that the government can borrow or lend at the same interest rate i. Under this assumption it does not matter whether the government currently has the money or not: the NPV rule still holds.*

Compounding and Discounting over Multiple Years

We now generalize these results across many years.[4] Suppose that you are thinking about leaving your $10,000 in the bank for five years in order to buy a car which you will need at that time. Suppose that the interest rate is 15 percent and interest is compounded annually. The amounts at the beginning of each year and end of each year are shown in Table 4.2. When there is more than one year and interest earned in one year is reinvested to earn additional interest (*interest on the interest*) in subsequent years, the interest received is called *compound interest* and the process is called *compounding interest*. Throughout the main body of this chapter we assume interest is compounded once annually. In Appendix 4B, we discuss more frequent compounding.

Future values over multiple years.   In general, if an amount X is invested for n years and interest is compounded annually at i percent per annum, then the future value is:[5]

$$FV = \$X(1 + i)^n \tag{4.3}$$

For example, suppose $50 is invested for four years with interest compounded annually at 8 percent. Then the future value is:

$$FV = \$50(1 + 0.08)^4 = \$68.02$$

TABLE 4.2   INVESTMENT OF $10,000 COMPOUNDED AT 15 PERCENT PER ANNUM

Year	Beginning of Year $	End of Year $
1	10,000.00	11,500.00
2	11,500.00	13,225.00
3	13,255.00	15,208.80
4	15,208.80	17,490.10
5	17,490.10	20,113.60

The term $(1 + i)^n$, which gives the future value of \$1 in n years at annual interest rate i, is called the *compound interest factor*. Most finance textbooks include an appendix of compound interest factors. Many pocket calculators have this function, as do most computer spreadsheet programs.

There is a handy rule for computing approximate future values called the rule of 72. Money roughly doubles when $100i \times n = 72$. For example, if the interest rate is 8 percent, then your money doubles in $72/8 = 9$ years. Similarly, the rule tells us that if you want your money to double in ten years, then you need an interest rate of at least $72/10 = 7.2$ percent.

Present value over multiple years.   Now consider present values, which require discounting rather than compounding. Suppose that a rich uncle leaves you a coupon-clipped bond[6] with a face value of \$100,000 that matures in four years. As usual, you would prefer the cash now. If the interest rate is 7 percent, what is the current market value of the bond (ignoring transaction costs and taxes)? From equation (4.3) we can see that, in general, the present value of \$X received n years from now with interest computed annually at i percent is:

$$PV = \frac{\$X}{(1 + i)^n} \tag{4.4}$$

The term $1/(1 + i)^n$, which equals the present value of \$1 received in n years when the interest rate is i, is called the *present value factor* or the *discount factor*. Again, these factors are available in most finance textbooks and in computer spreadsheet programs. Using this formula, the present value of the coupon-clipped bond is:

$$PV = \frac{\$100,000}{(1 + 0.07)^4} = \$76,289.52$$

This is somewhat less than the amount you had in mind!

For another illustration, consider the following two projects: project I yields \$1,050 one year from now; project II yields \$550 one year from now and \$540 two years from now. Which project do you prefer? Assume an interest rate of 5 percent. The present values of the projects are:

$$PV(I) = \frac{\$1,050}{(1 + 0.05)^1} = \$1,000$$

$$PV(II) = \frac{\$550}{(1 + 0.05)^1} + \frac{\$540}{(1 + 0.05)^2} = \$523.81 + \$489.80 = \$1,013.61$$

Applying discounting rules, the PV of project II is larger than the PV of project I. Assuming that you could borrow or invest money at 5 percent, you would be better off if you chose project II.

Net present value of a CBA project. We have now introduced all of the material on basic compounding needed for CBA. *Analysts evaluate projects using the net present value criterion.* By definition, the net present value (NPV) of a project equals the present value of the benefits minus the present value of the costs:

$$\text{NPV} = \text{PV}(B) - \text{PV}(C) \tag{4.5}$$

Equivalently, the NPV of a project equals the present value of the net benefits. To understand the equivalence, consider a project with an expected life of n years. Let,

$$B_t = \text{total benefits arising in year } t \ (t = 0, 1, 2, \ldots, n)$$
$$C_t = \text{total costs arising in year } t \ (t = 0, 1, 2, \ldots, n)$$

The annual net benefits equal the difference between annual total benefits and annual total costs, that is, $B_t - C_t \ (t = 0, 1, 2, \ldots, n)$. The present value of the net benefits of a project is given by:

$$\text{NPV} = B_0 - C_0 + \frac{B_1 - C_1}{(1 + i)^1} + \cdots + \frac{B_{n-1} - C_{n-1}}{(1 + i)^{n-1}} + \frac{B_n - C_n}{(1 + i)^n}$$

More generally, for a project that may last indefinitely (represented by the symbol ∞ for infinity),

$$\text{NPV} = \sum_{t=0}^{\infty} \frac{B_t - C_t}{(1 + i)^t} \tag{4.6}$$

Alternatively, separating costs and benefits:

$$\text{NPV} = \sum_{t=0}^{\infty} \frac{B_t}{(1+i)^t} - \sum_{t=0}^{\infty} \frac{C_t}{(1+i)^t} \tag{4.7}$$

which is in the form of equation (4.5).

The preceding discounting formulas assume that all benefits and costs arise only at the end of a year. Impacts are assumed to arise immediately ($t = 0$), or at the end of the first year ($t = 1$), or at the end of the second year ($t = 2$), and so on. Of course, there is essentially no practical distinction between an impact that occurs on the last day of one year and a similar-sized impact that occurs on the first day of the next year.

If all of the costs of a project occur immediately ($t = 0$) and all of the benefits occur over the ensuing n years ($t = 1, 2, \ldots, n$), then equation (4.6) simplifies to:

$$\text{NPV} = -C_0 + \frac{B_1}{(1 + i)^1} + \cdots + \frac{B_{n-1}}{(1 + i)^{n-1}} + \frac{B_n}{(1 + i)^n}$$

$$\text{NPV} = -C_0 + \sum_{t=1}^{n} \frac{B_t}{(1 + i)^t} \tag{4.8}$$

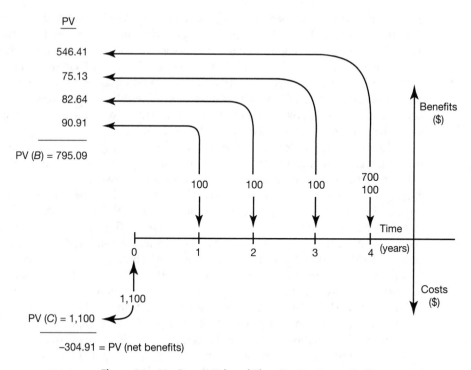

Figure 4.1 Net Present Value of Choosing Car X over Car Y

The following simple example illustrates the mechanics of discounting. Suppose that you are a graduate student planning to buy an automobile to use during four years of graduate school. You have narrowed your choice to two alternatives that, financial considerations aside, you like equally well. Although car X initially costs $1,100 more than car Y, it offers better gasoline mileage (30 miles per gallon compared to 20 miles per gallon) and it has a $700 higher expected resale value when it is four years old. You expect to drive 6,000 miles in each of the next four years. Additionally, you expect the price of gasoline to remain constant at $1 per gallon. Therefore, car X would save $100 per year in gasoline costs relative to car Y.[7] The benefits and costs of car X relative to car Y are represented on a time graph in Figure 4.1.

If interest rates are 10 percent, then the present value of the benefits of choosing car X over car Y are $795.09, but the present value of the costs are $1,100 so that the net present value of buying car X over car Y is –$304.91. In other words, you would obtain a higher net benefit by choosing car Y.

REAL VERSUS NOMINAL DOLLARS

Conventional private-sector financial analysis measures revenues, expenditures, net income, assets, liabilities, and cash flows in terms of historical monetary units. Such units are referred to as nominal dollars (sometimes called *current dollars*). If you have ever listened to an older person reminisce, then you probably know that a dollar purchased more in 1970 than it does now—"a dollar's not worth a dollar anymore!" For example, nominal per capita disposable personal income in the United States was $3,521 in 1970 and $16,236 in 1990, but you could not buy four and one-half times as much on an average income in 1990 as you could on an average income in 1970. The purchasing power of a dollar declines with price inflation. In order to control for declining purchasing power of a dollar due to inflation, we sometimes convert nominal dollars to *real dollars* (sometimes called *constant dollars*).

To obtain real, or constant, dollar measures, analysts adjust for changes in inflation. In effect, analysts *deflate* dollars to account for higher prices. The Consumer Price Index (CPI) is the most commonly used *deflator*.[8] It is expressed as the ratio of the cost of purchasing a standard market basket of goods in a particular year to the cost of purchasing the same basket of goods in some base year, multiplied by 100. For instance, from Table 4.3 one can see the cost of a basket of goods in 1990 was 1.307 times the average cost of purchasing a similar basket in 1982–84 in the United States. Similarly, the cost of a basket of goods in 1970 was 0.388 times the average cost of purchasing a similar basket in 1982–84. Consequently, the cost of a basket of goods in 1990 was 1.307/0.388 = 3.37 times the cost in 1970. Returning to our example, one can see that while nominal incomes increased by 361 percent between 1970 and 1990, the CPI increased by 237 percent, so that real incomes increased by only 37 percent during this period in the United States.[9]

In practice, analysts may face the complication that they observe interest rates expressed in terms of nominal dollars but they project benefits and costs as real dollars. Care must be taken to ensure that the units of measure of impacts are consistent with the units of measure of the discount rate. The rule is: *If benefits and costs are measured in nominal dollars, then the analyst should use a nominal discount rate; if benefits and costs are measured in real dollars, then the analyst should use a real discount rate.* Both methods result in the same answer.

When analysts use a real discount rate, they must first convert amounts measured in nominal dollars to equivalent amounts in real dollars in some base year. Suppose, for example, an analyst wants to convert nominal incomes to real incomes using 1987 as the base year. Using the CPI deflator from Table 4.3, real per capita disposable personal income in 1970 expressed in 1987 dollars was:

$$\$(3,521/0.388) \times 1.136 = \$10,309$$

and real per capita disposable personal income in 1990 expressed in 1987 dollars was:

$$\$(16,236/1.307) \times 1.136 = \$14,112$$

The CPI for Canada is presented in Table 4.4.

A Practical Example: Garbage Trucks

A practical example illustrates the basic issues in moving from market interest rates, which are nominal rates, to the appropriate real discount rate. Consider a city that uses a rural landfill to dispose of solid refuse. By adding larger trucks to the refuse fleet,

TABLE 4.3   THE U.S. CONSUMER PRICE INDEX (CPI)

YEAR	CPI*,**	% CHANGE IN CPI
1960	29.6	1.7
1961	29.9	1.0
1962	30.2	1.0
1963	30.6	1.3
1964	31.0	1.3
1965	31.5	1.6
1966	32.4	2.9
1967	33.4	3.1
1968	34.8	4.2
1969	36.7	5.5
1970	38.8	5.7
1971	40.5	4.4
1972	41.8	3.2
1973	44.4	6.2
1974	49.3	11.0
1975	53.8	9.1
1976	56.9	5.8
1977	60.6	6.5
1978	65.2	7.6
1979	72.6	11.3
1980	82.4	13.5
1981	90.9	10.3
1982	96.5	6.2
1983	99.6	3.2
1984	103.9	4.3
1985	107.6	3.6
1986	109.6	1.9
1987	113.6	3.6
1988	118.3	4.1
1989	124.0	4.8
1990	130.7	5.4
1991	136.2	4.2
1992	140.3	3.0
1993	144.5	3.0
1994	148.2	2.4

* A composite index for all items.

** The base period, when the CPI = 100, was 1982–1984.

Source: U.S. Bureau of the Census, *Statistical Abstract of the United States 1994* (Washington, DC: U.S. Government Printing Office), Table Nos. 747 and 748; U.S. Bureau of Labor Statistics, *CPI Detailed Report* (Washington, DC: U.S. Department of Labor, May 1995), Table 24.

TABLE 4.4   THE CANADIAN CONSUMER PRICE INDEX (CPI)

YEAR	CPI*,**	% CHANGE IN CPI
1962	24.2	1.3
1963	24.6	1.7
1964	25.1	2.0
1965	25.7	2.4
1966	26.6	3.5
1967	27.6	3.8
1968	28.7	4.0
1969	30.0	4.5
1970	31.0	3.3
1971	31.9	2.9
1972	33.4	4.7
1973	36.0	7.8
1974	39.9	10.8
1975	44.2	10.8
1976	47.5	7.5
1977	51.3	8.0
1978	55.9	9.0
1979	61.0	9.1
1980	67.2	10.2
1981	75.5	12.4
1982	83.7	10.9
1983	88.5	5.7
1984	92.4	4.4
1985	96.0	3.9
1986	100.0	4.2
1987	104.4	4.4
1988	108.6	4.0
1989	114.0	5.0
1990	119.5	4.8
1991	126.2	5.6
1992	128.1	1.5
1993	130.4	1.8
1994	130.7	0.2

* A composite index for all items.

** The base period, when the CPI = 100, was 1986.

Adapted from: Statistics Canada, *The Consumer Price Index*, Catalogue No. 62-001, 74 no. 3 (March 1995), Table 4, p. 18 (for 1976–1994); Statistics Canada, *Consumer Prices and Price Indexes* (Ottawa: Ministry of Supply and Services), Table 8, p. 22 (for 1969–1975) and Statistics Canada, *The Consumer Price Index*, Catalogue 62-001, 54, no. 3 (March 1976), Table 4, p. 7 (for 1961–1968). Reproduced by authority of the Minister of Industry, Statistics Canada. Readers wishing additional information on data provided through the cooperation of Statistics Canada may obtain copies of related publications by mail from: Publication Sales, Statistics Canada, Ottawa, Ontario, KlA 0T6, by calling (613) 951-7277 or toll-free 800-267-6677. Readers may also facsimile their order by dialing (613) 951-1584.

the city would be able to save $100,000 in disposal costs during the first year after purchase and *equivalent* amounts in each successive year of use. The trucks would be purchased today for $500,000 and would be sold after four years. (The city expects to open a resource recovery plant in four years that will obviate the need for landfill disposal.) The city can currently borrow money at a market interest rate of 10 percent. People generally expect that inflation will be 4 percent. Should the city buy the trucks? As usual, the answer should be "yes" if the NPV is positive (assuming there are no other alternatives that might have a higher NPV). Is it? In the following sections we work through this example in some detail.

The Advantage of Working in Real Dollars

As we mentioned earlier, analysts must decide whether to work in real dollars or nominal dollars. In the private sector it is more natural to work in nominal dollars. Interest rates and other market data are in nominal dollars, pro forma income and cash flow projections make more sense in nominal dollars, and the tax system is based on nominal amounts. However, *for CBA it is usually easier and more intuitively appealing to estimate benefits and costs in real dollars.* For the garbage truck example, the yearly benefits and costs in real dollars are given in column 2 of Table 4.5. Here it is assumed that annual savings are the same in real terms each year. This would apply, for example, if the purchased trucks transported exactly the same amount of garbage each year. If the trucks transported different amounts of garbage each year, then the differences may be hidden, or at least not immediately obvious, when using nominal dollars. The differences would, however, be quite clear when using real dollars.

Implicitly, this example assumes that the *relative valuations* (prices) of wages, gasoline, and other components that figure into the benefit calculations do not change over time—this issue is discussed later in this chapter. If the amount transported is not expected to change, but relative prices are expected to change over time, then the

TABLE 4.5   THE NET PRESENT VALUE OF INVESTMENT IN NEW GARBAGE TRUCKS

EVENT	ANNUAL BENEFITS AND COSTS (In Real Dollars)	ANNUAL BENEFITS AND COSTS (In Nominal Dollars)
0. Purchase	−500,000	−500,000
0. Annual Savings	100,000	100,000
1. Annual Savings	100,000	104,000
2. Annual Savings	100,000	108,160
3. Annual Savings	100,000	112,486
4. Liquidation	200,000	233,972
NPV	28,252*	28,252**

* Using a real discount rate of 5.769231 percent.

** Using a nominal discount rate of 10 percent.

Source: Adapted from David L. Weimer and Aidan R. Vining, *Policy Analysis: Concepts and Practice*, 2nd ed. (Englewood Cliffs, NJ: Prentice Hall, 1992), p. 280.

effects of these relative price changes can be seen immediately when using real dollars. They may not be so clear when using nominal dollars. Thus, in general, it is more informative to use real dollars than to use nominal dollars.

In this example, it is also assumed that all benefits (and costs) occur at the beginning of each year. Thus, all of the first year's benefits occur now ($t = 0$), all of the second year's benefits occur in one year's time ($t = 1$), and so on. This assumption may not be realistic. We will show later in this chapter how to estimate the NPV of the project when we assume the benefits or costs arise at different times.

Finally, note that it is assumed the city sells the trucks in four years' time ($t = 4$) for $200,000 in real terms. In other words, the city would receive a check in the amount of $200,000 in four years if there were no inflation in the interim. This is called the *real liquidation value*. To estimate such a number, one could use the current market price of four-year-old trucks in the same condition as one expected the city's trucks to be in after four years' time. This is intuitively easier than predicting the value of the truck in four years' time in nominal dollars.

Calculating the real discount rate.   In order to calculate the NPV of the proposed investment, analysts apply a real discount rate to future costs and benefits that are expressed in real dollars. Projecting costs and benefits in real dollars (that is, ignoring inflation) is natural, as shown previously. The difficulty arises in determining the appropriate real discount rate. The market interest rate is a nominal rate, incorporating the expected rate of inflation—lenders do not want to be repaid in less valuable dollars.[10] If analysts decide that the market interest rate facing the decision maker is the appropriate discount rate, then, because it is nominal, they must adjust for the expected inflation rate to arrive at the appropriate real discount rate. The real discount rate (r) *approximately* equals the nominal discount rate (i) minus the expected rate of inflation (m): $r \simeq i - m$. For example, if the nominal discount rate is 10 percent and inflationary expectations are 4 percent, then the real discount rate is approximately 6 percent. More precisely, as we will show later, the real discount rate should be computed thus:[11]

$$r = (i - m)/(1 + m) \qquad (4.9)$$

For our city, which faces a nominal discount rate of 10 percent and expects a 4 percent inflation rate, the real discount rate is 5.77 percent.[12] Applying this real discount rate to the annual real costs and benefits in the middle column of Table 4.5 yields an NPV equal to $28,252. Thus, as long as no alternative equipment configuration offers a greater NPV, the city should purchase the larger trucks. A time line for the NPV calculation is presented in Figure 4.2.

What is the expected rate of inflation?   Obviously, CBA analysts cannot know precisely how price inflation will change the purchasing power of future dollars, but they must obtain an estimate. A common approach is to assume that the rate of inflation will continue at its current level, but this may be quite unreasonable. A more appropriate way to estimate the expected inflation rate is to assume that real long-term bond yields will remain stable and to subtract this yield from the current long-term bond yield. For exam-

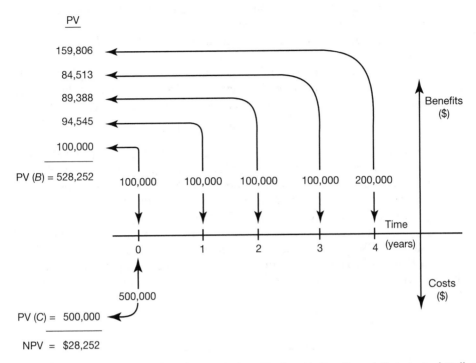

Figure 4.2   Net Present Value of Purchasing Garbage Trucks with Benefits and Costs in Real Dollars Using a Real Discount Rate of 5.77 Percent

ple, if the yield on long-term bonds is currently 10 percent and the real long-term bond yield has been about 2 percent and is expected to remain at that rate, this suggests that the market expects inflation will average 8 percent over the long term. If the project will last only 3 years, then a reasonable estimate of inflation during this period can be obtained by subtracting the historical real yield on 3 year bonds from the current yield on bonds that will mature in 3 years.

There are a variety of potential secondary sources for the expected inflation rate including the OECD (Organization for Economic and Cultural Development) or central governments' departments of finance or statistics (or their equivalent). Each week *The Economist* presents recent changes in consumer prices and the results of a poll of consumer price forecasts for the current year and the following year for major industrialized countries. Other sources include publications from the American Statistical Association and from reputable investment firms.

Using Nominal Dollars

If analysts take the nominal market interest rate facing the city as the appropriate discount rate, then they must predict future costs and benefits in inflated dollars. The right-hand column of Table 4.5 shows the anticipated benefits and costs of this project in nominal dollars, assuming a 4 percent annual inflation rate. As mentioned earlier, this example assumes implicitly that wage rates, gasoline prices, and other prices that figure into the benefit calculations increase at the same rate as the general price level.

To convert from real dollars to nominal dollars, simply inflate the real dollars by the expected rate of inflation. Explicitly, if $X denotes the real value in year 0 dollars of an amount received in year n, then the nominal value in year n dollars is:

$$\text{Nominal value} = \$X(1 + m)^n \qquad (4.10)$$

where m is the expected rate of inflation. For instance, the $100,000 of savings realized by the third year in real year 0 dollars is equivalent to $112,486 of savings in nominal year 3 dollars, if inflation is constant over the period at 4 percent. Notice that the city expects to receive $233,972 when it sells the trucks at the end of the fourth year. This is called the *nominal liquidation value* of the trucks.

Using the 10 percent market interest rate seen by the city as the nominal discount rate, the NPV of the benefits and costs in nominal (current) dollars is $28,252, as shown in Figure 4.3. Thus, discounting real costs and benefits with the real discount rate is equivalent to discounting nominal costs and benefits with the nominal discount rate.[13]

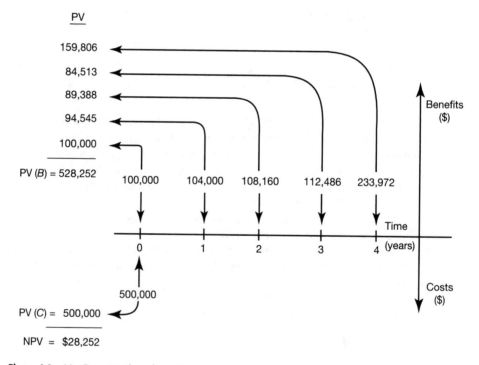

Figure 4.3 Net Present Value of Purchasing Garbage Trucks with Benefits and Costs in Nominal Dollars Using a Nominal Discount Rate of 10 Percent

TIMING OF BENEFITS AND COSTS

The foregoing example assumes that the annual benefits and costs occur at the beginning of each period. Often it is more appropriate to assume that the benefits or costs occur at the end of each period. Under the assumption that the annual benefits occur at the end of each year, as shown in Figure 4.4, the NPV of the garbage truck project falls considerably from $28,253 to $8,155. In percentage terms this is a substantial drop relative to the previous NPV. It indicates that the assumptions analysts make about the timing of benefits and costs can greatly affect the NPV.

To obtain more accurate results, benefits or costs that actually arise immediately or within the first six months of a project could be treated as if they corresponded to $t = 0$, those that arise more than six months but less than eighteen months later could correspond to $t = 1$, and so on. Alternatively, benefits or costs that arise during the first year could be treated as if they occurred at $t = 0.5$ (six months), those that arise during the second year could be treated as if they occurred at $t = 1.5$ (eighteen months), and so on. For more information about how to calculate the present value of benefits or costs that arise at different times during the discounting period, as well as for multiple compounding in each year, see Appendix 4B.

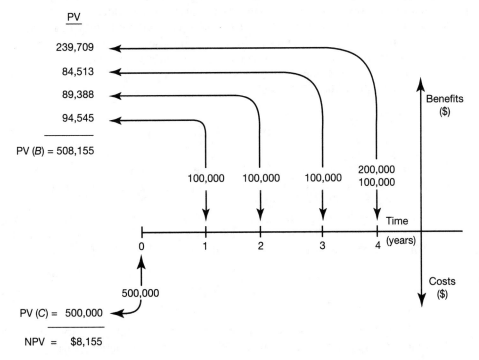

Figure 4.4 Net Present Value of Purchasing Garbage Trucks with Benefits Arising at the End of Each Year (Benefits and Costs in Real Dollars Using a Real Discount Rate of 5.77 Percent)

TERMINAL VALUES

The formula for calculating the NPV—equation (4.6)—makes clear that in theory *all the benefits or costs of a project should be measured, even when they extend indefinitely.* In practice, however, analysts usually discount benefits and costs over finite time horizons. Typically, analysts select a discount period that extends over the presumed life of the project. But, even though the project is complete from an engineering or administrative perspective, social benefits or costs may continue to flow from the project for many more years. For example, the benefits of infrastructure investments tend to accrue well after the end of the original project for which they were constructed. The impacts of a highway may continue to exist for centuries. In England, for example, cars travel on roads that were laid out by the Romans—more than 15 centuries ago. The Great Wall of China continues to generate tourism benefits even though it is truly ancient. The same issue also arises in human capital investment programs, especially training and health programs. For example, preschool training programs may benefit participants throughout their entire lives, years after they participated in the program; some benefits may even accrue to their children. All of these impacts (if material!) should be included in a CBA. But, in practice, how should analysts handle them?

One way is to forecast all of the benefits and costs indefinitely, that is, to estimate equation (4.6) directly. But, as the previous examples illustrate, the practical forecasting difficulties of estimating equation (4.6) directly may be horrendous.

In practice, analysts try to work around these forecasting problems by calculating a *terminal value* or, synonymously, a *residual value*, which reflects the present value of the social impacts that arise after the end of the discounting period.[14] Using terminal values, the NPV is calculated:

$$\text{NPV} = \sum_{t=0}^{n} \frac{b_t - c_t}{(1 + r)^t} + T(n) \tag{4.11}$$

where the first term on the right hand side of equation (4.11) is the present value of the benefits and costs during the discounting period of n years and $T(n)$ is the present value of the terminal value after n years.

In theory, using a finite discounting period and an appropriate terminal value should give results identical to equation (4.6). Indeed, these methods are identical if $T(n)$ is the present value of the net social benefits that arise after n years:

$$T(n) = \sum_{t=n+1}^{\infty} \frac{b_t - c_t}{(1 + r)^t} \tag{4.12}$$

In theory, the choice of the end of the discounting period is arbitrary. For example, the following equations give identical NPVs, all equal to equation (4.6):

$$\text{NPV} = \sum_{t=0}^{10} \frac{b_t - c_t}{(1 + r)^t} + T(10) \tag{4.13}$$

$$\text{NPV} = \sum_{t=0}^{20} \frac{b_t - c_t}{(1 + r)^t} + T(20) \tag{4.14}$$

$$\text{NPV} = \sum_{t=0}^{30} \frac{b_t - c_t}{(1 + r)^t} + T(30) \tag{4.15}$$

if $T(n)$ is estimated by equation (4.12). The only difference between these formulas is that the discounting period is different; specifically, it ends after 10 years in equation (4.13), after 20 years in equation (4.14), and after 30 years in equation (4.15). As the discounting period lengthens and the NPV of the project during the discounting period changes, the terminal value changes by an equal amount in the opposite direction so the NPV of the project is unchanged.

Alternative Methods for Handling Terminal Values

In practice, however, $T(n)$ is not usually computed by equation (4.12). There are five practical methods of calculating terminal values. Obviously, the estimated NPV will vary according to the method used.

Using terminal values based on salvage value or liquidation value.   For public-sector projects that have private-sector characteristics, the liquidation value or salvage value may be used as a terminal value. In the garbage trucks example we discussed earlier, the municipality will liquidate the trucks after four years for $200,000 in real dollars. In effect, we used this liquidation value as the terminal value.

This approach is easy when one can readily obtain estimates of the liquidation value of items, as one can for equipment and buildings. However, many public-sector projects have no meaningful salvage value because there is no market for the kinds of assets they involve.

Even if a liquidation value is readily available, it may not accurately reflect the social cost. The market liquidation value or salvage value is the appropriate terminal value only when the salvage value obtained in the market equals the social value of the asset at the time the community decides to sell it *and* there are no subsequent social benefits and costs that should be attributed to the project. Again, these conditions do not pertain to many public-sector projects.

Using terminal values based on depreciated value.   The second method recognizes that the stream of benefits and costs from a capital-oriented project is directly related to its depreciated value. Indeed, by definition, the value of an asset equals the present value of the net benefits that it generates. Rather than focus on estimating the stream of benefits and costs, this method focuses on estimating the depreciated value.[15]

It is important to emphasize that here we are referring to real (i.e., economic) depreciation, not accounting depreciation. There may be a huge difference. Economic depreciation concerns the decline in the economic value of an asset over time. In contrast, accounting depreciation is largely determined for tax or reporting purposes. Tax authorities may allow companies to take 100 percent depreciation in one year, in which case a company can write off 100 percent of the cost of an investment, even though the investment itself may yield benefits that extend over decades. Thus, the depreciated accounting value may bear no relationship to the reduced usefulness or the amount of wear and tear of an asset. *Accounting depreciation should never be included as a cost (expense) in CBA.*

Using economic depreciation value is applicable where there is no market for some capital item so that it remains in the public sector. However, this method suffers from three problems:

1. Estimating economic depreciation rates can be very difficult. Different assets depreciate at different rates. For example, aircraft are maintained at near 100 percent efficiency until they fall apart; in contrast, the efficiency of railroads initially declines very quickly and then decreases at a decreasing rate.

2. The amount of economic depreciation is often endogenous: Depreciation is affected by how the asset is used (and maintained) in the project. If maintenance is at a high level, then an asset may continue to perform at 100 percent efficiency for many years. If maintenance is at a low level, then it may start to fall apart quickly. Thus, a capital asset's useful life depends on the project itself.

3. The rate at which a piece of equipment or a project actually declines may bear no relationship to the stream of social benefits and costs that it generates. For example, an aircraft may be maintained at 100 percent efficiency but, if it is in "mothballs" and nobody flies in it, the social benefits may be zero.

Using terminal values based on initial construction cost.   This method estimates the terminal value based on initial construction costs. In the highway example we presented in Chapter 1, we assumed a useful life of the highway of 20 years. The value at the predicted end of the highway's useful life of all subsequent benefits and costs were assumed to equal 75 percent of initial construction costs ($0.75 \times \$338.1$ million = \$253.58 million.) That is, the future value of the highway in 20 years was assumed to equal \$253.58 million, which has a present value of \$59.6 million. Consequently, according to the method basing terminal values on initial construction cost, the terminal value is \$59.6 million. In effect, this method is a special case of using depreciated values.

When using this method, the analyst must select some proportion of the initial construction costs to use as a terminal value. There is no direct evidence to suggest that the net social benefits that can be attributed to a highway after 20 years is related to initial construction costs at all. The 75 percent figure is quite arbitrary. This method then is not intuitively appealing.

Using terminal values based on simple projections.   Yet another method estimates the terminal value based on simple extrapolations of benefits and costs. Consider, for example, a proposed dike that may last indefinitely. Assume annual net benefits have been calculated for the first 35 years so that it is necessary to estimate a terminal value for the thirty-fifth year. Suppose the net benefits of the dike are $895,000 in the thirty-fifth year (in real dollars). If it is assumed that these net bene-fits will remain constant indefinitely and that the real discount rate is 7 percent, then using equation (4A.3) in Appendix 4A, the formula for the PV of a perpetuity, the aggregate value in the thirty-fifth year of these net benefits equals $12.785 million. The terminal value based on this method equals the PV of these net benefits, which is $1.2 million.

Terminal values obtained by this method are usually very sensitive to the dis-count rate. Illustratively, if the real discount rate were 5 percent, then the aggregate value in the thirty-fifth year of the subsequent net benefits would be $17.9 million, which has a PV of $3.4 million. This terminal value is almost three times higher than the one obtained assuming a 7 percent discount rate.

What if net benefits grew at 1 percent per annum? Using equation (4A.5) in Appendix 4A, the formula for the PV benefits that grow at a constant rate, the termi-nal value would be $1.5 million, assuming a 7 percent discount rate, and would be $4.2 million assuming a 5 percent discount rate.

For many government projects, especially training programs, it is reasonable to assume that the annual net benefits decay at a constant rate after some date. In this case equation (4A.5) can be used with a negative growth rate. If, to continue using the preceding example, net benefits declined at 1 percent per annum, then the terminal value would be $737,000, assuming a 7 percent discount rate.

Setting the terminal value equal to zero.   A final method chooses a fairly long discounting period and ignores subsequent social benefits and costs. In effect, this method assumes the net benefits of the project beyond a finite time horizon are zero. In practice, this assumption may apply reasonably well to private-sector decisions which involve only private benefits and costs. But, in the public sector, where exter-nalities and nonpecuniary benefits and costs matter, and projects often continue to have impacts over many years, this method may omit important benefits or costs if the time horizon is too short.

Summary and Conclusion Concerning Terminal Values

The analyst must decide simultaneously on the discounting period (time horizon) and the method for calculating the terminal value. In theory, the terminal value is designed to capture all subsequent benefits and costs beyond the discounting period. In practice, computation of a terminal value may be quite ad hoc. The estimated terminal value may bear little relation to the theoretically correct amount.

The length of the discounting period and the method for calculating the terminal value may be interdependent. If, for example, the analyst is going to assume the ter-minal values are zero, then he or she should use a relatively long discounting period. If the analyst is using one of the other methods, then it makes sense to break at the end of the project's useful life or project horizon, that is, when almost all of the initial cap-ital has depreciated and major additional capital investments are required in order to provide any significant subsequent social value. In practice, for physical projects this information is usually provided by engineers. For a highway, it may be 20 years; for a dike, it may be 35 years. But, it is often hard to determine *ex ante* the expected useful economic life of a road, a dike, or an aircraft. In practice, the predicted period of useful life may be quite arbitrary.

Where projects have private-sector characteristics and assets can be liquidated easily, it may be relatively straightforward to obtain an appropriate terminal value. It is more difficult to calculate an accurate terminal value for projects with indefinite lives. Assuming terminal values are proportional to construction costs is easy, but this approach lacks a strong conceptual foundation. Calculating the terminal value based on relatively simple projections of subsequent social benefits and costs is more theoretically appealing. Furthermore, there is strong evidence that, for medium-to long-term (over many years) periods, simple forecasting models predict better than more complicated models. Thus, this method may do at least as well as rather complicated direct estimations of equation (4.6). The final method ignores all of the social costs and benefits beyond some arbitrary date. For many public-sector projects, this assumption is unacceptable.

COMPARING PROJECTS WITH DIFFERENT TIME FRAMES

Lack of Comparability Between Projects with Different Time Frames

Consider the following example.[16] An electric utility company is considering two alternative proposals for new sources of energy. One is a major hydroelectric dam (HE) lasting 70 years; the other is a thermal power plant (TP) lasting 35 years. These proposals are summarized in Table 4.6.[17] Suppose the appropriate real social discount rate is 5 percent.

TABLE 4.6   CHARACTERISTICS OF TWO ALTERNATIVE ENERGY PROPOSALS

Characteristics	Hydro	Thermal
Generating Capacity (Mwh)	100	100
Annual Generation (Gwh/yr)	500	500
Capital Costs (10^6\$)	100	50
Annual Benefits (10^6\$/yr)	10.0	10.0
Annual Operating and Maintenance Costs (10^6\$/yr)	3.5	2.8
Annual Fuel Costs (10^6\$/yr)	0	3
Useful Life of Plant (years)	70	35

Note: Kwh = kilowatt hours (10^3 watt hours)

  Mwh = megawatt hours (10^6 watt hours)

  Gwh = gigawatt hours (10^9 watt hours)

Source: Deirdre Fahy and Bernhard Schwab, "Electro," Faculty of Commerce and Business Administration, University of British Columbia.

Using equation (4.8), the NPVs of the two alternatives (in millions of dollars) are:[18]

$$NPV \text{ (HE)} = -100 + \sum_{t=1}^{70} \frac{6.50}{(1.05)^t} = \$25.73 \tag{4.16}$$

$$NPV \text{ (TP)} = -50 + \sum_{t=1}^{35} \frac{4.20}{(1.05)^t} = \$18.77 \tag{4.17}$$

On the basis of these calculations, the hydroelectric project appears better. But these projects are not commensurable because the life of the hydroelectric dam is twice that of the thermal power plant. There are two methods for evaluating projects with different time frames: rolling over the shorter project and the equivalent annual net benefit method. They always lead to the same conclusion, as we illustrate.

Rolling Over the Shorter Project

What happens in 35 years if the utility chooses the thermal power plant? One option is to build another thermal power plant. The NPV of back-to-back thermal power plants is:

$$NPV \text{ (2TP)} = 18.77 + \frac{18.77}{(1.05)^{35}} = \$22.17 \tag{4.18}$$

The PV of two back-to-back thermal power plants equals the PV of the first power plant of $18.77 million plus the PV of the second power plant, which equals the PV of $18.77 million received in 35 years. The difference between the NPV of back-to-back thermal power plants and the NPV of only one thermal power plant is $3.40 million. In effect, we would have arrived at the same figure if we had evaluated building only one thermal plant, but assigned a terminal value of $3.40 million to this project.

The NPV of the alternative of back-to-back thermal power plants is still less than the NPV of the larger and longer hydroelectric project. Thus, under the preceding assumptions, the hydroelectric project is best.

Notice here that one project is twice as long as the other so that when one project is done twice (i.e., "rolled over") it now has the same length as the initially longer project. Thus, they are comparable. If project A were two-thirds the length of project B, then the analyst should compare three project As back to back with two project Bs back to back.

Equivalent Annual Net Benefit Method

An equivalent method of comparing projects of unequal length is the *equivalent annual net benefit method* (EANB). The EANB equals the NPV of each initial alternative divided by the *annuity factor* that has the same life as the project. The result is an amount that, if received each year for the life of the project, would have the same NPV as the project. This conversion makes it possible to compare two or more projects with different lengths when they might be continually repeated. For example, dividing the NPVs given by equations (4.16) and (4.17) by the appropriate annuity factors gives:[19]

$$EANB(HE) = \$25.73/19.343 = \$1.330$$
$$EANB(TP) = \$18.77/16.374 = \$1.146$$

The equivalent annual net benefit is $1.33 million for the hydroelectric alternative and $1.15 million for the thermal power alternative. As before, the utility is better off with the hydroelectric alternative, assuming continuous replacement.

It is easy to confirm the equivalence of the EANB method and the roll-over method just described: The ratio of the NPVs of one hydro plant to back-to-back thermal plants equals the ratio of the EANBs for the hydro plant to the thermal plant (1.16).

Uncertainty and Quasi-Option Value

But in 35 years it may not be necessary or appropriate to build a second thermal power plant with exactly the same characteristics as the first. In fact, in 35 years' time, available technology will probably enable the utility to produce electricity at a fraction of the cost of the thermal plant, both in terms of capital cost and annual operating and maintenance costs. The PV of these savings is difficult to know with precision. Suppose, for illustrative purposes, construction costs *and* annual operating and maintenance costs of a new type of thermal plant in 35 years will be half the present costs in real terms. In this case, the NPV of an (old) thermal plant (TP) followed by a new thermal plant (NTP) would be:[20]

$$NPV\,(NTP\,|\,TP) \;=\; 18.77 + \frac{66.70}{(1.05)^{35}} \;=\; \$30.86 \qquad (4.19)$$

Under these assumptions, the old thermal plant followed by a new thermal plant alternative would be better than the hydroelectric alternative.

One could go further and argue that in 35 years a completely different technology may be available or the needs of the utility may be completely different. This can be thought of as a relative price change, which we discuss in the following section. The main point, however, is that while the hydroelectric alternative locks the utility in for 70 years, the thermal power plant has more flexibility. Chapter 7 discusses this topic in depth. For the time being, we shall treat the increased flexibility as an additional benefit, called *quasi-option* value, that can either be incorporated into the terminal value or, preferably, treated as a separate term. Comparison of equations (4.16) and (4.17) shows that if the PV of the quasi-option value associated with the thermal power plant exceeds $6.96 million, then the thermal power plant is the superior alternative. Equation (4.18) and the illustrative calculation in equation (4.19) indicates that this option value is at least $3.4 million and could be much higher.

RELATIVE PRICE CHANGES

Earlier in this section, we discussed how to handle expected price changes due to inflation (general price increases), but we assumed relative valuations and prices remained constant. In this section we discuss how to handle anticipated relative price changes.

The importance of this issue can be seen by observing how the net benefits of the thermal project discussed previously depend critically on the relative price of coal. Suppose you were faced in 1980 with the data in Table 4.7. How would the past relative price changes affect your recommendation concerning the thermal or hydroelectric power plants? On average, from 1974 to 1979, thermal coal prices increased significantly faster than the CPI. Based on these data, it might have been reasonable to assume that the relative price of coal would continue to increase. If the NPV of the thermal alternative is computed under this assumption, then it would look even less attractive than before and the hydroelectric project would look even more attractive than before.[21]

The importance of relative price changes is well illustrated by a CBA of a coal development project in British Columbia to supply Japanese customers.[22] Consider Table 4.8. The second, third, and fourth columns contain the benefits, costs, and net benefits, respectively, according to the CBA prepared by the provincial government of British Columbia (roughly equivalent to a state government in the United States).[23] Overall, the net benefits were estimated to be $330 million. The main beneficiaries of this project were expected to be the Canadian National Railway, which is the state-owned railway company, and the Canadian federal government, which would receive corporate taxes. Here corporate taxes and royalties are treated as a benefit to government, but a cost to industry; thus, they "net out." The British Columbia provincial government was also expected to benefit from royalties and higher corporate taxes, but it would pay for the Tumbler Ridge Branchline, which involved extending the provincially owned railway system to

TABLE 4.7   ANNUAL CHANGES IN THE PRICE OF THERMAL COAL AND THE CPI

Year	Change in the Purchase Price Index of Thermal Coal (%)	Change in the Consumer Price Index (%)
1974	51.92	10.90
1975	41.77	10.80
1976	8.88	7.51
1977	7.34	8.00
1978	17.74	8.95
1979	8.90	9.13
Arithmetic Average	22.80	9.20
Geometric Average*	16.78	9.13

* When calculating the mean change in an index that is given as percentage points it is more meaningful to calculate the geometric mean rather than the arithmetic mean. The geometric mean (GM) of n numbers is obtained using the formula: $GM = (X_1 X_2, \ldots, X_n)^{1/n}$.

TABLE 4.8   NORTH EAST COAL DEVELOPMENT PROJECT

	Benefits ($ million)	Costs ($ million)	Net Benefits		
			Base Case ($ million)	90% Base Price ($ million)	90% Base Price and Quantity ($ million)
Mining Sector	3,316	3,260*	56	−146	−240
Transport Sector					
Trucking	33	33	0	0	0
Canadian National Railway	504	358	146	146	121
B.C. Railway	216	202	15	15	6
Port Terminal	135	150	−15	−15	−23
Analysis and Survey	11	11	0	0	0
British Columbia**					
Royalties	77	0	77	69	62
Corporate Taxes	154	0	154	125	107
Producer Surplus (Labor)	25	0	25	25	25
Environment	10	5	5	5	5
Highways***	0	88	−88	−88	−88
Tumbler Ridge Branchline	91	267	−176	−176	−185
Canada					
Corporate Taxes	132	0	132	107	92
Highways, Port Navigation	0	26	−26	−26	−26
Producer Surplus (Labor)	25	0	25	25	25
Totals	4,729	4,400	330	66	−119

* Includes taxes and royalties.
** Excluding impacts included elsewhere.
*** Highways, electric power, townsite.
Source: Based on W.W. Waters, II, "A Reanalysis of the North East Coal Development," (undated), Tables 2 & 3. All figures in millions of 1980 dollars, assuming a 10 percent real discount rate with the discounting period ending in 2003 and no terminal value.

the North East Coal Development Project. The mining sector would benefit in terms of increased producer surplus. Also, this project was expected to create jobs for unemployed workers in British Columbia and the rest of Canada. The present value of the producer surplus to labor was estimated to be $25 million at both the provincial and federal levels. Notice that the analysis does not include any consumer surplus, as all of the coal would be exported.

The fifth column contains the expected net benefits to each sector if the price of coal were to fall to 90 percent of the base price. Under this assumption, the aggregate net benefits would fall by $264 million from $330 million to $66 million, a substantial change. If the price of coal were to fall to 90 percent of the base price and Japanese customers were to cut back their purchases of coal to 90 percent of their expected orders, then the overall net benefits would fall by $449 million from $330 million to –$119 million, as shown in column 6.[24] Thus, relatively small changes in relative prices and in quantities purchased have a huge impact on the NPV of this project.

In this example the benefits and costs are broken down by sector to illustrate distributional impacts. The main anticipated "winners" were the Canadian National Railway (CNR) and the federal government of Canada. If the price of coal fell by 10 percent, then the mining sector would lose money. Also, the rest of the residents of British Columbia would switch from being marginal "winners" to marginal "losers," largely because royalties and corporate taxes would decrease while the costs of highways and the Tumbler Ridge Branchline are fixed. If the price and quantity levels were to fall to 90 percent of the anticipated levels, then the mining sector would lose badly.

SENSITIVITY ANALYSIS IN DISCOUNTING

Sensitivity analysis can be performed with respect to many parameters—individually or jointly. In Chapters 6 and 7 we consider the conceptual foundations of dealing with uncertainty in detail. Here we focus on the sensitivity of the decision to changes in the discount rate and the terminal value. These two parameters often drive a CBA.

There are two ways of getting a handle on the problem. The best way is to systematically vary each parameter and recalculate the NPV as the parameters vary. The second way is to find the breakeven discount rate and the breakeven terminal value.

Varying the Discount Rate and the Terminal Value

The most informative way to do sensitivity analysis on a parameter is to vary it around the best estimate of its value and observe the impact on NPV. To illustrate, return to the garbage trucks example given in Table 4.5. The city employed a real discount rate of 5.77 percent. If it had used 4 percent instead, then the NPV would have been about $48,500 rather than $28,252. If instead the city had used 8 percent, then the NPV would have been about only $4,720. At a discount rate of 8.5 percent, the NPV would be negative. As long as the city believes that the correct discount rate is between 4 and 8 percent, the project has a positive NPV.

Figure 4.5 plots the NPV against real discount rates that range from zero to 12 percent. It is constructed by simply repeating the calculation of the NPV using different discount rates—a process that is very easy to do with a spreadsheet program on a personal computer. Note that the curve slopes downward indicating that the NPV declines as the interest rate increases. This is a common feature of projects that have the costs early and the benefits later. Using a higher discount rate results in a lower NPV as the future benefits are discounted more than are the more immediate costs.

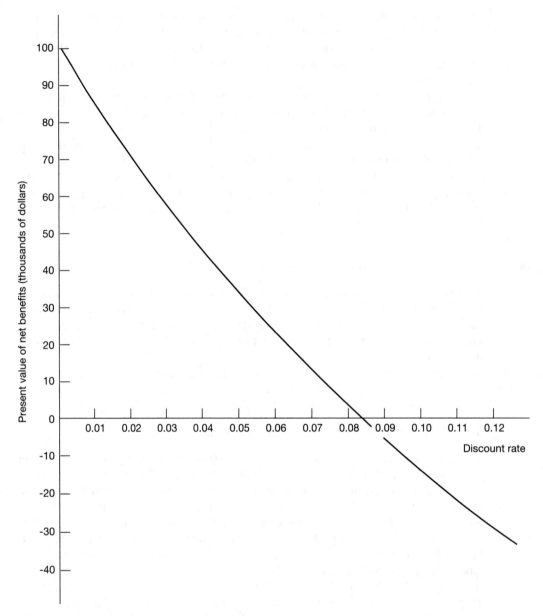

Figure 4.5   NPV of Purchasing New Garbage Trucks as a Function of the Real Discount Rate

Source: David L. Weimer and Aidan R. Vining, *Policy Analysis: Concepts and Practice,* 2nd ed. (Englewood Cliffs, NJ: Prentice Hall, 1992), p. 282.

Now consider changes in the estimated terminal value of the garbage trucks. The city assumed it would receive $200,000 when it sold the trucks in four years. If it realized only $150,000 from the sale of the trucks, then the NPV for the project would decline from $28,252 to –$11,700. If the city realized $225,000 from the sale of the trucks, the NPV would increase to $48,228. Using a computer spreadsheet it is easy to construct a graph similar to Figure 4.5 with the NPV on the vertical axis and the terminal value on the horizontal axis. This graph slopes upward reflecting the fact that the NPV increases as the terminal value increases.

With personal computers it is easy to examine simultaneous changes in the discount rate and the terminal value. Figure 4.5 shows how the NPV changes as the discount rate changes, assuming the terminal value equals $200,000. We can quite easily assume a different terminal value and recompute the curve showing the new relationship between the NPV and the discount rate. If we assume a higher terminal value, then the curve in Figure 4.5 will shift to the right, maintaining a similar curvature. If we assume a terminal value lower than $200,000, then this curve will shift to the left. Thus, we can examine simultaneously the impact on the NPV of changes in the discount rate and the terminal value.

Finding the Breakeven Discount Rate and the Breakeven Terminal Value

For many projects there will be some discount rate at which the NPV just equals zero. This rate, which is called the *internal rate of return* (IRR), can be read off Figure 4.5 at the point at which the curve representing the present value of net benefits crosses the horizontal axis. In this example, it is about 8.4 percent.[25]

The IRR can be presented to decision makers with the following advice: *Choose the project if you believe that the social discount rate is less than the internal rate of return; reject the project if you believe that the social discount rate is greater than the internal rate of return.* There are, however, a number of potential problems with using the IRR for decision making. First, it may not be unique; that is, there may be more than one discount rate at which the NPV is zero. This problem only arises when annual net benefits change more than once from positive to negative (or vice versa) during the discount period. Second, IRRs are percentages, not dollar values. Therefore, in general, they cannot be added across alternative projects. This is a scale problem which always arises with the use of ratios, including IRRs and benefit-cost ratios. Nonetheless, the IRR conveys useful information to other analysts who want to know how sensitive the results are to any particular discount rate.

Similarly, it is easy to compute the terminal value at which the NPV equals zero. In this example, the *breakeven terminal value* is $164,642, which implies the city would just breakeven on the project if it sold the trucks at the end of year 4 for $164,642. Obviously, the project has a positive NPV if the terminal value is greater than $164,642 and has a negative NPV if the terminal value is less than $164,642.

CONCLUSION

This chapter presents the main issues concerning the mechanics of discounting in CBA. It assumes that the appropriate discount rate is known. In fact, determination of the appropriate discount rate to use in CBA is a highly contentious issue, which we discuss in Chapter 5.

APPENDIX 4A

SHORTCUT FORMULAS FOR CALCULATING FVs, PVs, AND NPVs

In many circumstances it is possible to estimate FVs, PVs, or NPVs using shortcut formulas. This section considers four common situations: annuities, perpetuities, benefits (or costs) that grow or decline at a constant rate over a finite number of years, and benefits (or costs) that grow or decline at a constant rate in perpetuity.

Future value of an annuity.   An *annuity*, usually denoted by *A*, pays an equal, fixed amount each year for a number of years. Usually, the payments occur at the end of each year. Suppose, for example, that you receive payments of $50 per annum for the next five years, interest is 8 percent, and all interest is reinvested at 8 percent. Assuming all payments are received at the end of each year, how much will you have accumulated at the end of five years? It is often useful to visualize this type of problem through a *time graph*, as shown in Figure 4.A1. As the figure shows, the future value of this annuity equals $293.33.

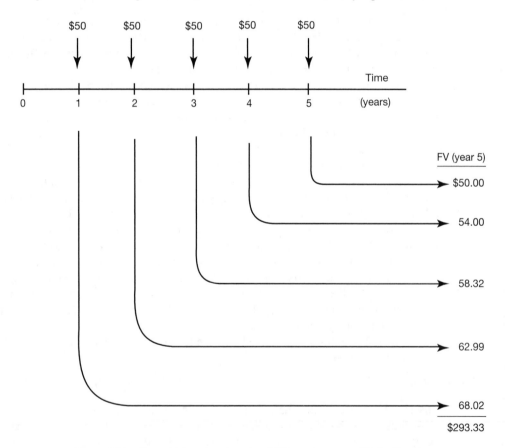

Figure 4.A1   Future Value of an Annuity of $50 per Annum at 8% for Five Years

In general, the future value of an annuity of $A per annum for n years with interest at i percent is given by:

$$FV = \$A(1 + i)^{n-1} + A(1 + i)^{n-2} + \ldots + A(1 + i)^2 + A(1 + i) + A$$
$$= \$A[(1 + i)^{n-1} + (1 + i)^{n-2} + \ldots + (1 + i)^2 + (1 + i) + 1]$$

It can be shown that:

$$FV = \$A \frac{(1 + i)^n - 1}{i} \tag{4A.1}$$

To illustrate use of the formula, observe that the future value of an annuity of $400 per year for 20 years with the interest rate at 6 percent is:

$$FV = \$400 \frac{(1 + 0.06)^{20} - 1}{0.06} = \$14,714.24$$

As a second illustration of the formula, suppose a person plans to retire in ten years and through annual savings wants to have accumulated $800,000 by that time. Also suppose that she has already accumulated $200,000. She wants to know how much she needs to set aside each year to achieve her objective if funds can be invested at 12 percent per annum. First, note that whatever additional amounts she saves, the original $200,000 will have grown to $621,170, using equation (4A.1). Consequently, she needs to accumulate $178,830 through additional savings. Substituting this amount and other known values into equation (4A.1) gives:

$$FV = \$X \frac{(1 + 0.12)^{10} - 1}{0.12} = \$178,830$$

Solving this equation for X tells us that she needs to save $10,190 per year for the next ten years.

The term $((1 + i)^n - 1)/i$ from equation (4A.1) gives the future value of an annuity of $1 per year for n years with interest at i percent. Tables of these formulas are available in finance textbooks and they are contained in many pocket calculators and computer spreadsheet programs. Returning to the preceding example, these tables tell us that the future value of an annuity of $1 for ten years at 12 percent is 17.55. Dividing $178,830 by 17.55 gives $10,190, the same amount we obtained earlier.

Present Value of an Annuity

Quite frequently in CBA the annual (gross) benefits or the annual net benefits are the same amounts each year; thus, they can be treated like an annuity. A simple formula gives the present value of an annuity. Suppose, for illustrative purposes, a friend has won a lottery which pays $10,000 per year for the next four years (with payments being at the end of each year). If the interest rate is 6 percent, what is the present value of this lottery prize? Again, for this type of problem, it is useful to draw a time graph, as shown in Figure 4.A2. The figure shows, in this case, the present value equals $34,651.06.

But there is an easier method. In general, the present value of an annuity of $A per annum (with payments received at the end of each year) for n years with interest at i percent is given by:

$$PV = \frac{\$A}{(1 + i)^1} + \frac{\$A}{(1 + i)^2} + \cdots + \frac{\$A}{(1 + i)^{n - 1}} + \frac{\$A}{(1 + i)^n}$$

It can be shown that:

$$PV = \$A \, \frac{1 - (1 + i)^{-n}}{i} \tag{4A.2}$$

The term $((1 - (1 + i)^{-n})/i)$, which equals the present value of an annuity of $1 per year for n years when the interest rate is i, is called an *annuity factor*. Most finance texts include tables of annuity factors, and they are contained in most computer spreadsheet programs. *It is important to note, however, that many computer spread-*

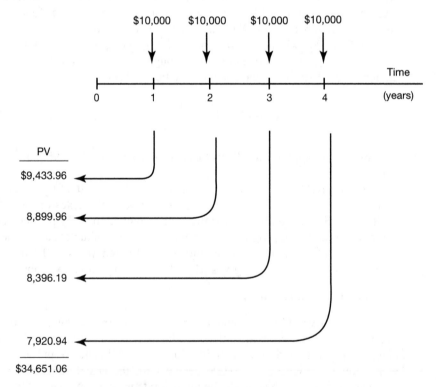

Figure 4.A2   Present Value of an Annuity of $10,000 per Year for Four Years at 6%

sheet programs assume that annuity payments occur at the beginning of each period (year) rather than at the end of each period (year). This is contrary to equation (4A.2) and to standard practice.

Returning to our example, we can now use equation (4A.2) to determine the PV of the lottery:

$$PV = \$10,000 \; \frac{1 - (1 + 0.06)^{-4}}{0.06}$$

$$PV = \$10,000 \times 3.4651056$$

$$PV = \$34,651.06$$

which is the same answer calculated previously.

As another example of calculating the present value of an annuity, suppose you own a bond that has a face value of $100,000 and matures in exactly five years' time. The interest rate paid on the bond is 9 percent so that $9,000 is paid to you on the same date each year. Suppose you have just received this year's interest payment and wish to calculate the PV of the bond, including future interest payments, but not including the $9,000 you have just received. The market interest rate is 5 percent. One way to solve this problem is to use equation (4A.2) to determine the present value of the annual interest payments and then use equation (4.4) to determine the present value of the $100,000:

PV of $9,000/year for 5 years at 5%   = 9,000 × 4.3295   = $38,965.29

PV of $100,000 in 5 years at 5%
with annual compounding   = 100,000 × 0.7835   = $78,352.62

PV = $117,317.91

Alternatively, you could use equation (4.6):

$$PV = \frac{9,000}{1.05} + \frac{9,000}{(1.05)^2} + \frac{9,000}{(1.05)^3} + \frac{9,000}{(1.05)^4} + \frac{109,000}{(1.05)^5}$$

$$= 8,571.43 + 8,163.27 + 7,774.54 + 7,404.32 + 85,404.35$$

$$= \$117,317.91$$

Note that the last term in the latter method includes the final interest payment *and* the principal repayment. It should be clear that both methods give the right answer, but the first method is usually easier for this type of problem.

It is informative to note how the present value of an annuity varies with time and the interest rate. *The present value of an annuity decreases as interest rates increase, and vice versa.* This is a partial explanation for why bond prices rise as interest rates fall, as they did in the United States between 1988 and 1993. It also partially explains why bond prices fall as interest rates rise, as they did in Canada between 1993 and 1995. Another important observation is that *annuity payments received after the twen-*

tieth year add little to the present value when interest rates are 10 percent or higher. Thus, benefits received more than 20 years in the future will not have a large impact on the present value of the benefits of projects with relatively constant benefits streams. Arguments along these lines have a tendency to reduce the value of investments in long-term projects like reforestation.

Present Value of a Perpetuity

When an annuity continues indefinitely, it is called a *perpetuity*. The present value of $A received (at the end of) each year in perpetuity is given by:[1]

$$PV = \frac{\$A}{i} \tag{4A.3}$$

For example, the present value of a perpetuity of $2,000 per year when interest rates are 8 percent is:

$$PV = \frac{\$2,000}{0.08} = \$25,000$$

When interest rates are 10 percent, the present value of a perpetuity is very easy to calculate: It equals the perpetual annuity multiplied by ten. For example, the present value of a perpetuity of $80,000 per year is $800,000 if the interest rate is 10 percent.

The Present Value of Benefits (or Costs) that Grow or Decline at a Constant Rate

Sometimes the gross benefits or net benefits of a project grow annually at a constant rate. If Bt denotes the gross benefits in year t, then assuming they grow at a constant annual growth rate, g, gross benefits in year t will be:

$$Bt = B_1(1 + g)^{t-1} \qquad t = 1,2,\ldots \tag{4A.4}$$

Under these circumstances the present value of the total benefits over n years can be shown to be:

$$PV(B) = \frac{B_1}{1 + g} \times \frac{1 - (1 + i_0)^{-n}}{i_0} \qquad (\text{if } i > g) \tag{4A.5}$$

where

$$i_0 = \frac{i - g}{1 + g} \qquad \text{and } i > g \tag{4A.6}$$

In other words, the PV of a benefit stream that starts at B_1 and grows at a constant rate g for n years when interest rates are i is equivalent to the PV of an annuity of $B_1/(1+g)$ for n years when interest rates are i_0, where i_0 is given by equation (4A.6).

To illustrate how to calculate the present value of a stream of annual benefits that grow at a constant rate, consider a town that is considering the construction of a dike whose benefits will last 20 years. The expected benefits of the proposed project in the first year are $50,000. Due to anticipated in-migration these benefits are expected to grow at 2 percent per annum. If the interest rate is 6 percent, then the expected present value of the benefits is:

$$PV(B) = \frac{50,000}{1.02} \times \frac{1 - (1 + 0.0392)^{-20}}{0.0392} = \$671,112$$

If there is no growth in benefits, then using equation (4A.2), $PV(B) = \$573,496$. This example illustrates that even quite small growth rates can have large impacts on NPVs.

Equation (4A.5) only holds if the interest rate exceeds the growth rate: $i > g$. If $i \leq g$, then it cannot be used. Importantly, though, it can be used if g is negative, that is, if benefits decline at a constant rate. Of course, equation (4A.5) pertains also to costs that change at a constant rate as well as to benefits that change at a constant rate.

Present Value of Benefits (or Costs) that Grow or Decline at a Constant Rate in Perpetuity

If initial benefits of B_1 grow at a constant rate g indefinitely and the interest rate equals i, then the PV is given by:[2]

$$PV(B) = \frac{B_1}{i - g} \qquad (\text{if } i > g) \qquad\qquad (4A.7)$$

As before, this formula only holds if $i > g$.

APPENDIX 4B

DISCOUNTING WITH MULTIPLE COMPOUNDING IN EACH PERIOD

Future Value with Multiple Compounding in a Year

Thus far we have assumed that interest is calculated only once each period, with a period being a year. In practice, mortgages, savings accounts, and other investments compound interest more frequently than once a year.

Suppose we can invest $1,000, the annual interest rate is 15 percent, but interest is compounded semiannually, that is, every six months. How much will we have at the end of the year? With an annual interest rate of 15 percent but with semiannual compounding, we earn 7.5 percent interest every six months. Therefore, at the end of the first six-month period, we would have:

$$\$1,000 \,(1 + 0.075) = 1,000 \,(1.075) = \$1,075$$

If we left the money in the bank for another six months, then we would end the year with:

$$\$1,075 \ (1.075) = \$1,155.63$$

This example illustrates that investing for one year at 15 percent annual interest with semiannual compounding is equivalent to investing for two years at 7.5 percent per annum compounded once a year:

$$1,000\left(1 + \frac{0.15}{2}\right)^2 = 1,000(1.075)^2 = \$1,155.63$$

Basically, when interest is compounded semiannually, there are twice as many *periods* as before. However, *during each period* the interest rate is only half the annual rate.

A comparison of the amount realized with semiannual compounding to the amount obtained with annual compounding shows that as interest is compounded more frequently, the future value increases more quickly. This occurs because as interest is compounded more frequently, interest is earned sooner on the interest. Thus, the effective annual interest rate with multiple compounding is higher than the effective annual rate with single compounding. In this example, the *effective annual interest rate*, which is the interest rate that would have to obtain if interest were compounded annually in order to yield the same amount as multiple compounding, is 15.563 percent.

In general, the future value of $\$X$ *in one year* at interest rate i compounded k times a year is

$$FV = \$X \left(1 + \frac{i}{k}\right)^k$$

It follows that the future value of $\$X$ *in n years* with interest rate i compounded k times per year is

$$FV = \$X \left[\left(1 + \frac{i}{k}\right)^k\right]^n$$

$$= \$X \left(1 + \frac{i}{k}\right)^{nk}$$

(4B.1)

To illustrate the application of equation (4B.1) suppose, for example, your local bank offers two savings accounts: One provides interest of 10 percent calculated daily (DIS), the other provides interest of 11.5 percent calculated monthly (MS). If you deposit $\$1,000$ to each account, how much would accumulate in each account in two years?

$$FV(DIS) = \$1,000\left(1 + \frac{0.10}{365}\right)^{(2 \times 365)} = \$1,221.37$$

$$FV(MS) = \$1,000\left(1 + \frac{0.115}{12}\right)^{(2 \times 12)} = \$1,257.22$$

Future Value with Continuous Compounding

If interest is compounded continuously, then the future value of $X in n years with interest rate i is given by:

$$FV = \$Xe^{in} \qquad (4B.2)$$

where e is the base of the natural logarithm, which equals 2.71828 to five decimal places.[1]

For example, suppose you put $1,000 into a savings account for two years. If interest is compounded continuously and the interest rate is 10 percent, then the future value will be:

$$FV = \$1,000 \ e^{(0.10 \times 2)} = \$1,221.40$$

If the interest rate is 11.5 percent, then the future value will be:

$$FV = \$1,000 \ e^{(0.115 \times 2)} = \$1,258.60$$

As one would expect, continuous compounding yields slightly larger amounts than daily or monthly interest compounding, which we computed earlier. However, over a two-year period, the difference is not very much.

Present Value with Multiple Compounding in a Year

Suppose your parents want you to visit them in a year and at that time the trip will cost $1,000. How much do you need to set aside now in order to buy the ticket in a year if the current interest rate is 15 percent, and interest is compounded twice a year? If you had $X now, then with semiannual compounding you would have $X\left(1 + \dfrac{0.15}{2}\right)^{2}$ in a year, so you should set this amount equal to $1,000 and solve for $X:

$$\$X\left(1 + \frac{0.15}{2}\right)^{2} = \$1,000$$

$$\$X = \frac{1,000}{\left(1 + \dfrac{0.15}{2}\right)^{2}} = \$865.33$$

Thus, the present value of $1,000 in a year with interest at 15 percent compounded semiannually is $865.33. This is how much you would need to have now.

In general, the present value of $Y *in one year* with interest rate i compounded k times a year is

$$PV = \frac{Y}{\left(1 + \dfrac{i}{k}\right)^k}$$

The present value of $Y in n years at interest rate i compounded k times a year is

$$PV = \frac{Y}{\left(1 + \dfrac{i}{k}\right)^{nk}} \tag{4B.3}$$

To illustrate use of this formula, imagine that a coupon-clipped bond with $10,000 face value will mature in two years from today. The market interest rate is 10 percent and interest is compounded twice a year. Using equation (4B.3), the present value of the bond is:

$$PV = \frac{10,000}{\left(1 + \dfrac{0.10}{2}\right)^{2 \times 2}} = \frac{10,000}{(1.05)^4} = \$8,227.02$$

For another illustration, consider a corporation that sells $10,000 par value of its 8 percent, two-year bonds. Interest is paid semiannually. If the market interest rate is 10 percent, the present value of the interest payments is:

$$\text{PV of \$400 received in 6 months} = \frac{400}{1 + 0.05} = 380.95$$

$$\text{PV of \$400 received in 12 months} = \frac{400}{(1 + 0.05)^2} = 362.81$$

$$\text{PV of \$400 received in 18 months} = \frac{400}{(1 + 0.05)^3} = 345.54$$

$$\text{PV of \$400 received in 24 months} = \frac{400}{(1 + 0.05)^4} = 329.08$$

$$\text{PV of bond interest} = 1,418.38$$

The present value of the bond equals the present value of the principal ($10,000 received in two years) plus the present value of the interest payments. Therefore, the PV of the bond = $8,227.02 + $1,418.38 = $9,645.40. This is the market value of the bond: It would sell at a discount of $354.60.

Present Value with Continuous Compounding

If interest is compounded continuously, then the present value of $Y received in n years' time with interest rate i is given by:

$$PV = \frac{Y}{e^{in}} \tag{4B.4}$$

For example, the present value of $10,000 received in 12 years' time with interest at 8 percent, compounded continuously, is:

$$PV = \frac{10,000}{e^{0.08 \times 12}} = \frac{10,000}{2.612} = \$3,829$$

EXERCISES FOR CHAPTER 4

1. A highway department is considering building a temporary bridge to cut travel time during the three years it will take to build a permanent bridge. The temporary bridge can be put up in a few weeks at a cost of $740,000. At the end of three years, it would be removed and sold for scrap at a net *cost* of $81,000, estimated as the net cost of a similar operation done today. Based on estimated time savings and wage rates, fuel savings, and reductions in risks of accidents, department analysts predict that the benefits in real dollars would be $275,000 during the first year, $295,000 during the second year, and $315,000 during the third year. Departmental regulations require use of a real discount rate of 6 percent.
   a. Calculate the present value of net benefits assuming that the benefits are realized at the end of each of the three years.
   b. Calculate the present value of net benefits assuming that the benefits are realized at the beginning of each of the three years.
   c. Calculate the present value of net benefits assuming that the benefits are realized in the middle of each of the three years.
   d. Calculate the present value of net benefits assuming that half of each year's benefits are realized at the beginning of the year and the other half at the end of the year.
   e. Does the temporary bridge pass the net benefits test?
2. A government data processing center has been plagued in recent years by complaints from employees of back pain. Consultants have estimated that upgrading office furniture at a net cost of $425,000 would reduce the incidence and severity of back injuries each year, allowing the center to avoid medical care that currently costs $68,000. They estimate that the new furniture would also provide yearly benefits of avoided losses in work time and employee comfort worth $18,000. The furniture would have a useful life of five years, after which it

would have a positive salvage value equal to 10 percent of its initial net cost. The consultants made their estimates of avoided costs assuming that they would be treated as occurring at the beginning of each year.

In its investment decisions, the center uses a nominal discount rate of 9.5 percent and an assumed general inflation rate of 4 percent. It expects the inflation rate for medical care to run between 4 percent and 6 percent but is uncertain as to the exact rate. In other words, it is uncertain as to whether the cost of medical care will inflate at the same rate as other prices or rise 2 percent faster. Should the center purchase the new furniture?

3. A town's recreation department is trying to decide how to use a piece of land. One option is to put up basketball courts with an expected life of eight years. Another is to install a swimming pool with an expected life of 24 years. The basketball courts would cost $180,000 to construct and yield net benefits of $40,000 at the end of each of the eight years. The swimming pool would cost $2.25 million to construct and yield net benefits of $170,000 at the end of each of the 24 years. Each project is assumed to have zero salvage value at the end of its life. Using a real discount rate of 5 percent, which project offers larger net benefits?

4. The environmental protection agency of a county would like to preserve a piece of land as a wilderness area. The current owner has offered to lease the land to the county for 20 years in return for a lump-sum payment of $1.1 million, which would be paid at the beginning of the 20-year period. The agency has estimated that the land would generate $110,000 per year in benefits to hunters, bird watchers, and hikers. Assume that the lease price represents the social opportunity cost of the land and that the appropriate real discount rate is 6 percent.

   a. Assuming that the yearly benefits, which are measured in real dollars, accrue at the end of each of the 20 years, calculate the net benefits of leasing the land.

   b. Some analysts in the agency argue that the annual real benefits are likely to grow at a rate of 2 percent per year due to increasing population and county income. Recalculate the net benefits assuming that they are correct.

5. Imagine that the current owner of the land in the previous exercise was willing to sell the land for $2 million. Assuming this amount equaled the social opportunity cost of the land, calculate the net benefits if the county were to purchase the land as a permanent wildlife refuge. In making these calculations, first assume a zero annual growth rate in the $110,000 of annual real benefits; then assume that these benefits grow at a rate of 2 percent per year.

NOTES

[1]Richard O. Zerbe, Jr. and Dwight Dively, "How Municipal Governments Set Their Discount Rate: Do They Get It Right?" manuscript, University of Washington, October 1990.

[2]For an excellent book that covers most of the issues discussed in this chapter, see Stephen A. Ross and Randolph W. Westerfield, *Corporate Finance* (St. Louis, MO: Times Mirror/Mosby College Printing, 1988). Of course, this finance textbook does not have a CBA focus.

[3]A T-bill is a short-term bond issued by the Treasury Department of the U.S. government. Usually, the minimum size is $100,000. It yields an interest rate that is slightly higher than the rate offered by banks on personal savings accounts. Some banks offer a "T-bill Account," which enables customers with less than $100,000 (but more than some specified minimum) to earn almost the same rate as that given on T-bills.

[4]Technically speaking, we are discounting over multiple *periods* rather than multiple years. But, because in almost all applications the period of discounting is a year and it is easier to think of years rather than periods, we use the term *years*. For multiple discounting during each period, see Appendix 4B.

[5]For example, consider the future value in two years. At the end of the first year one would have $FV_1 = \$X(1 + i)$. At the end of the second year, one would have $FV_2 = \$[X(1 + i)](1 + i) = \$X(1 + i)^2$.

[6]Some bonds pay interest in the form of coupons that are initially attached to the bond. Whenever interest payments are due, typically every six months, a coupon is removed from the bond and exchanged for interest. This process may continue until the bond matures. Alternatively, at any time prior to maturity, the coupons may be removed from the bond and sold separately. The remaining part of the bond is called a coupon-clipped bond. It yields no interest because all of the interest coupons have literally been clipped off and sold.

[7]$\{[\$1/g]\times[6,000 \text{ m}]/[20\text{m}/g]\} - \{[\$1/g]\times[6,000 \text{ m}]/[30\text{m}/g]\} = \$100$.

[8]A broader measure is the implicit deflator for gross national product (GNP), which is the ratio of GNP measured at current prices to GNP measured at prices in some base year. Whereas CPI is based on a standard market basket of consumer goods, the implicit deflator for GNP is a comprehensive price index.

[9]16,236/1.307 versus 3,521/0.388.

[10]The market interest rate also includes a factor for the uncertainty associated with future inflation, which is called the inflation risk premium. As there is no simple analytic solution for the size of this premium, we ignore this factor.

[11]In financial economics, this relationship is known as the Fisher effect.

[12]From equation (4.9), $(0.10 - 0.04)/(1 + 0.04) \approx 5.77$. More accurately, the real discount rate is 5.769231 percent, which is the rate used in the NPV calculations in this example in order to ensure that the results for the real and nominal methods are identical.

[13]It is easy to show that analysts will arrive at the same NPV as long as they consistently use either real dollars and a real discount rate or nominal dollars and a nominal discount rate. Recall that the NPV for a project is given by equation (4.6), and suppose that these benefits (B_t) and costs (C_t) are nominal dollars and i is the nominal discount rate. Now define b_t as real benefits, c_t as real costs, r as the real discount rate, and let m denote the expected inflation rate. Substituting equation (4.10) into equation (4.6) gives:

$$\text{NPV} = \sum_{t=0}^{\infty} \frac{B_t - C_t}{(1 + i)^t} = \sum_{t=0}^{\infty} \frac{(b_t - c_t) \times (1 + m)^t}{(1 + i)^t}$$

Setting $\dfrac{1}{(1 + r)} = \dfrac{(1 + m)}{(1 + i)}$ gives the NPV formula expressed in real dollars:

$$\text{NPV} = \sum_{t=0}^{\infty} \frac{b_t - c_t}{(1 + r)^t}$$

This formula is equivalent to equation (4.6) with the benefits and costs expressed in nominal dollars. Finally, note that rearranging the equation that introduces the real discount rate in this footnote gives equation (4.9) the formula for converting a nominal discount rate to a real discount rate.

[14]Terminal values are well understood in the context of the private-sector capital budgeting literature. See, for example, Peter Lusztig and Bernhard Schwab, *Managerial Finance in a Canadian Setting* (Toronto: Butterworths, 1988), Chapter 8: Capital Budgeting, especially pp. 310–311. See also pp. 976–979.

[15]For a discussion about how to measure depreciated capital, see Charles R. Hulten, "The Measurement of Capital," Chapter 4 in *Fifty Years of Economic Measurement: The Jubilee of the Conference on Research in Income and Wealth*, eds. Ernst R. Berndt and Jack E. Triplett (Chicago: The University of Chicago Press, 1990), pp. 119–152.

[16]This example is based on the "Electro" case by Deirdre Fahy and Bernhard Schwab, Faculty of Commerce and Business Administration, University of British Columbia.

[17]Implicitly, we assume that the terminal value of each plant is zero.

[18]Both of these projects yield benefits that are the same each year. In effect, they are *annuities*. Shortcut formulas for calculating the present values of annuities are given in Appendix 4A.

[19]The annuity factor for the hydroelectric project is the present value of an annuity of $1 per year for 70 years using an interest rate of 5 percent which, by equation (4A.2), equals 19.343. Similarly, the annuity factor for the thermal project is the present value of $1 per annum for 35 years at an interest rate of 5 percent, which is 16.374.

[20]The NPV of the new thermal plant at the time it is started is given by

$$NPV(NTP) = -25 + \sum_{t=1}^{35} \frac{5.60}{(1.05)^t} = \$66.70$$

[21]Parenthetically, the price of thermal coal took a dive! In retrospect, the thermal power plant would have been superior for this reason alone. This example illustrates the problem of estimating future prices based on simple extrapolations rather than performing a thorough analysis of the coal industry.

[22]An initial study was prepared by the government of British Columbia, "A Benefit-Cost Analysis of the North East Coal Development," Ministry of Industry and Small Business, 1982. The sensitivity analyses were prepared by W.W. Waters, II, "A Reanalysis of the North East Coal Development," Working paper, University of British Columbia (undated).

[23]The initial study made shadow price adjustments for foreign exchange earnings. These are excluded from Table 4.8 because, according to Waters, they are probably inappropriate.

[24]This scenario of declining prices and declining quantities sold is quite plausible for this project. The major Japanese customers were simultaneously encouraging development of Australian and other sources. If these sources come on line at the same time there would be a worldwide excess supply, internationally determined coal prices would fall, and demand for B.C. coal would also fall.

[25]Again, a computer spreadsheet program is very useful in searching for the IRR through trial and error. Start with a low rate that gives a positive NPV. Also pick a high rate that gives a negative NPV. Pick a rate midway between these two. If the NPV is negative, then choose a rate between the midpoint value and the lower one. If the NPV is positive, then choose a new value between the midpoint value and the higher one. Repeat this process until you find the rate that gives a zero NPV after rounding. This rate is the internal rate of return.

APPENDIX A NOTES

[1]This follows immediately by taking the limit of equation (4A.2) as *n* goes to infinity.

[2]Some students of finance will recognize this model as the Gordon growth model for valuing stocks whose dividends exhibit this property; see M. Gordon, *The Investment, Financing and Valuation of the Corporation* (Homewood, IL: Richard D. Irwin, 1962), pp. 46–47. It is also known as the dividend growth model.

APPENDIX B NOTES

[1]Formally, $e = \text{Lim} (1 + \frac{1}{n})^n$, as $n \rightarrow \infty$.

5

THE SOCIAL
DISCOUNT RATE

This chapter deals with the theoretical issues pertaining to selection of an appropriate social discount rate. It is possible to do CBA and, more particularly, discounting without knowing this theory in any detail. Indeed, as we discuss later in this chapter, many government departments and agencies require their analysts to use a prescribed real discount rate. But, of course, without the conceptual foundation we present in this chapter, you would not be able to give advice or answer questions about the selection or level of the discount rate.

Choice of the social discount rate method is one of the most controversial and important topics within CBA. As Robert Lind points out, the social discount rate "has critical implications for the federal budget, for regional development, for technological choices, for the environment, and for the size of government."[1]

We divide this chapter into the following sections: the theory behind the social discount rate assuming perfect markets; alternative social discount rate methods in the absence of perfect markets; and the social discount rate in actual practice.[2] Appendix 5A discusses adjusting the social discount rates for risk.

THE THEORY BEHIND THE APPROPRIATE SOCIAL
DISCOUNT RATE METHOD IN PERFECT MARKETS

To understand the theoretical foundation of discounting, we must recognize that it is rooted in the preferences of individuals. As individuals, we tend to prefer to consume more immediate benefits to ones occurring in the more distant future. We also face an opportunity cost of forgone interest when we spend dollars today rather than invest them for future use. These two considerations of importance to individual decisions, the *marginal rate of time preference* and the *marginal rate of return on private invest-ment*, provide a basis for deciding how costs and benefits realized by society in the future should be discounted so that they are comparable to costs and benefits realized by society today.

A third element concerns the issue of intergenerational trade-offs and discount-ing of impacts that occur in the distant future. At one extreme some philosophers have argued that there should be no discounting at all; that is, the social discount rate should be zero. We will discuss this position and related issues in the next section. For this section, however, we will ignore them.

The objective of discounting for time is to put all costs and benefits in a common metric so that the net benefits of policies can be measured. The standard approach involves expressing costs and benefits occurring in the future in terms of how much they could contribute to losses and gains of current consumption. In other words, as described in Chapter 4, it discounts future consumption to arrive at their present values.

There is wide consensus among economists that the costs and benefits of public programs should be discounted for time at a positive rate. However, there is less agree-ment about what this positive rate should be because there is no consensus about the appropriate method for discounting in the imperfect markets that we face in the real world. Unfortunately, policy analysts do not have the luxury of waiting for these issues to be resolved. Therefore, we present in this and subsequent sections the vari-ous conceptual issues that arise in discussions of social discount rates and rules of thumb for resolving them in practice.

In this section, we discuss the core building blocks; specifically, the marginal rate of time preference and the marginal return on private investment. It is useful to first show that in perfect markets these rates equal market interest rates so that, in theory, there is no problem.

An Individual Consumer's Marginal Rate of Time Preference

Most of us would be unwilling to lend someone $100 today in return for a promise of payment of $100 in a year's time. We generally value $100 today more than the promise of $100 next year—even if we are certain that the promise will be carried out and that there will be no inflation. Perhaps $90 is the most that we would be willing to lend today in return for a promise of payment of $100 in a year's time. If so, then we say that the present value of receiving $100 next year is $90. We can think of the $90 as equivalent to the future payment discounted back to the present. Economists refer to our preference to consume sooner rather than later as *time preference*. The rate at which current individuals make marginal trade-offs is called the *marginal rate of time preference* (MRTP).

The concept of time preference can be easily understood in the context of bor-rowing and lending. Imagine that you are a graduate student who will receive a stipend of $5,000 this year and $9,000 next year. Your rich uncle offers to give you some money and asks you if you would rather have $1,000 this year or $1,200 next year. If you are indifferent between the gifts, then you have a MRTP of 20 percent—you are just willing to sacrifice $200 additional consumption next year in order to consume the extra $1,000 this year rather than next year.[3]

Absent a rich uncle, you might be able to consume more today through borrowing. Although most banks may not be interested in lending you money because they fear you may not pay them back, let us assume that your local credit union will lend to you at an annual interest rate of 10 percent. That is, you can borrow $1,000 if you promise to pay it plus $100 in interest next year. If you were willing to give up $200 to get an additional $1,000 immediately from your uncle, you surely would take advantage of the loan that requires you to give up only $100 in consumption next year in order to consume $1,000 more this year rather than next year. Once you take the loan, you have $6,000 to spend this year and $7,900 to spend next year. Now that you have reduced the gap between what you have to spend this year relative to next year, you probably have an MRTP of less than 20 percent. After taking the loan, and if given the choice, you would now probably take a gift of $1,200 next year over a gift of $1,000 this year. If so, this indicates your MRTP is less than 20 percent. This example illustrates that your MRTP changes as you shift consumption from one year to another year.

Equality of Discount Rates in Perfect Markets

As long as you can borrow as much as you like, you can shift consumption from the future to the present until your MRTP falls to the rate of interest you must pay. If banks offer a rate of interest in excess of your MRTP, then you will happily defer some consumption to the future. For example, if you are indifferent between an additional $1,000 today and $1,050 next year, but can deposit $1,000 for one year to obtain an additional $1,060 next year, then you would want to make the deposit. Only when the rate of interest you earn just equals your MRTP will you be indifferent between spending and depositing an additional dollar.

MRTP equals the market interest rate.   It is easy to show that in a competitive, undistorted capital market the MRTP equals the market interest rate. Suppose that a consumer's utility is a function of consumption in two periods (usually years): C_1 denotes consumption in the first period and C_2 denotes consumption in the second period. The consumer maximizes his or her utility subject to a budget constraint in which I denotes income and i the market interest rate:

$$\text{Max } U(C_1, C_2) \tag{5.1}$$

$$\text{s.t. } C_1 + \frac{C_2}{1+i} = I \tag{5.2}$$

This problem is represented diagrammatically in Figure 5.1. The curves labeled U^1 and U^2 are *indifference curves*; that is, the consumer is indifferent among the consumption levels in the two periods corresponding to all of the points on one of these curves.[4] U^2 is higher than U^1; that is, the preference directions are north and east. The (absolute value of the) slope of the indifference curves equals the consumer's *mar-*

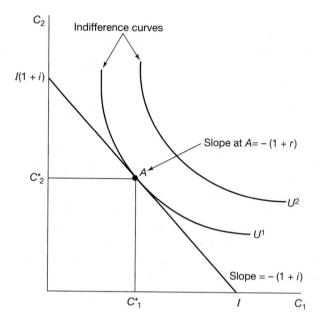

Figure 5.1 Equality of MRTP and the Interest Rate

ginal rate of substitution (MRS) between C_1 and C_2.[5] Furthermore, by definition, the marginal rate of substitution equals $1 + r$, where r is the marginal rate of time preference. As we discussed at the beginning of this section, in the relevant range, $r > 0$, and thus the (absolute value of the) slope of the indifference curve is greater than one, reflecting the fact that consumers require more in the next period in order to give up consumption in this period. Indeed, r measures how much more the individual requires in the next period in order to give up a dollar of consumption in this period. Note that r, the consumer's marginal rate of time preference, changes as he or she moves along an indifference curve and consumption shifts from one period to another.

This utility maximization problem supposes that the consumer receives all of his or her income in the first period and can invest all or part of it at interest rate i.[6] Thus, the consumer could spend all of his or her income in year 1 which means $C_1 = I$ and $C_2 = 0$; the consumer could spend all of it in year 2 in which case $C_1 = 0$ and $C_2 = (1 + i)I$; or the consumer could consume at any other points on the budget constraint represented by the straight line with slope $-(1 + i)$. In other words, each additional unit of consumption in period 1 costs $(1+i)$ units of consumption in period 2; each additional unit of consumption in period 2 costs $1/(1+i)$ units of consumption in period 1.

To determine the optimal consumption levels, we find the point at which the budget constraint is tangential to an indifference curve. Rewriting the budget constraint, equation (5.2), thus:

$$C_2 = I(1 + i) - (1 + i)C_1 \qquad (5.3)$$

shows that the slope of the budget constraint equals $-(1 + i)$. The (absolute value of the) slope of the budget constraint exceeds 1, indicating that the consumer earns positive interest at rate i on the part of his or her income that he or she saves this year. In Figure 5.1, the optimal consumption levels are at point A where the slope of the indifference curve, $-(1 + r)$, equals the slope of the budget constraint, $-(1 + i)$, that is, where $r = i$. Thus, at the optimum, the market interest rate, i, equals the consumer's MRTP, r.[7] (As shown in Figure 5.1, the consumer's optimal consumption levels of C_1 and C_2 are C_1^* and C_2^*.)

This result holds generally for people without extreme preferences over consumption in the two periods.[8] Thus, every individual has an MRTP equal to the market interest rate that he or she faces. Because all consumers face the same market interest rate in an economy with a perfect capital market, all consumers have the same MRTP. As everyone is willing to trade current and future consumption at the same rate when markets are perfect, it is natural to interpret the market interest rate as the social discount rate, that is, as the appropriate social rate for discounting changes in social surplus occurring in different periods. Later we discuss the appropriateness of interpreting market interest rates as social discount rates when markets are not perfect.

Rate of return on private investment equals the market interest rate. We now present a more general two-period model that incorporates production as well as consumption. In this model, the decision maker is able to shift production as well as consumption between periods.

Suppose that you are the economics minister of a small country. Further suppose initially that there is no borrowing or lending, which implies that you consume what you produce in each period. The curve connecting points X_1 and X_2 in Figure 5.2 indicates the various combinations of current (period 1) and future (period 2) production that your country's economy could achieve. By using available domestic resources to their fullest potential, your country could obtain any combination of production on the curve connecting X_1 and X_2. (The locus of these combinations is called the *production possibility frontier* for your economy.) If all effort is put into current production, then X_1 can be produced in period 1, but production will fall to zero in period 2. Similarly, if all effort is put into preparing production in period 2, then X_2 will be available in period 2 but there is no production in period 1.

Neither of these extremes is attractive. Indeed, suppose U^1 and U^2 are what you believe to be indifference curves for your country. You consider any point to the northeast of one of these indifference curves better than any point on it. For analogous reasons to those discussed in the previous section, you will choose point m on the production possibility frontier. This combination of production and consumption in the two periods makes your country best off, given that there is no borrowing or lending. At this point the slope of the production possibility curve, which is called the *marginal rate of transformation*, equals the slope of the indifference curve, which equals the marginal rate of substitution.

Now suppose that foreign banks are willing to lend or borrow at an interest rate i. That is, the banks are willing to either loan or borrow one dollar's worth of produc-

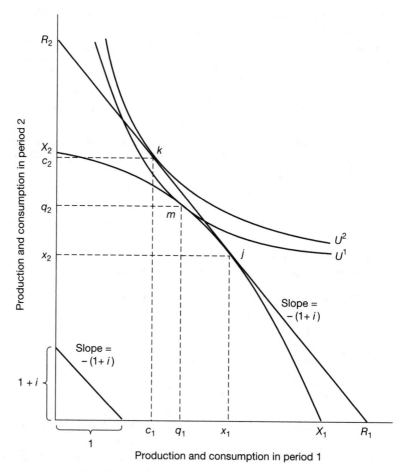

Figure 5.2   Optimal Levels of Production and Consumption in a Two-Period Model
with Borrowing and Lending
Source: Adapted from Weimer and Vining, p. 226

tion in period 1 in return for the promise of repayment of $(1+i)$ dollars worth of production in period 2. You realize that, with access to this capital market, you can
expand your country's consumption possibilities. For instance, if you produced at
point j on the production possibility frontier in Figure 5.2, then you could achieve a
consumption combination anywhere along the line with slope $-(1+i)$ going through
point j by either borrowing or lending. This line is shown as connecting points R_1 and
R_2, where R_2 equals $(1+i)R_1$. For example, in period 1 your country could produce x_1
and consume c_1. It could then lend the difference $(x_1 - c_1)$ so that in period 2 it could
consume c_2, consisting of x_2 in domestic production and c_2-x_2 (equal to $[1+i][x_1-c_1]$)
in repaid loans. Thus, as a result of borrowing and lending, your country's *consumption possibility frontier* expands from the original production possibility frontier connecting X_1 and X_2 to the discount line connecting R_1 and R_2.

The most favorable production possibility results from choosing the production combination such that the discount line is just tangent to the production possibility frontier. Point j happens to be the point of tangency. At this point the marginal rate of transformation equals the slope of the discount line. The most desirable consumption opportunity is shown as point k, which is on indifference curve U^2, the one with the highest utility that can be reached along the consumption possibility frontier. Specifically, utility is maximized at the point at which the marginal rate of substitution equals the slope of the discount line. Thus, in equilibrium, the marginal rate of transformation equals the marginal rate of substitution, which equals the slope of the discount line.

The key to understanding discounting in CBA is to recognize that at point j in Figure 5.2 (and point A in Figure 5.1) you are indifferent between having one additional unit of consumption in period 1 and $(1+i)$ additional units in period 2. Thus, in evaluating policies that make small changes to your consumption in the two periods, you should treat one dollar of change in consumption in period 1 as equivalent to $1/(1+i)$ dollars of change in consumption in period 2. This is equivalent to taking the present value of the changes.

ALTERNATIVE SOCIAL DISCOUNT RATE METHODS IN THE ABSENCE OF PERFECT MARKETS

In a world with perfect capital markets, such as the one illustrated in Figure 5.2, every *consumer* is willing to trade between marginal current and marginal future consumption at the market rate of interest. At the same time, the rate at which *firms* (the private economy) transform marginal current production into marginal future production (the marginal rate of return on private investment) also equals the market rate of interest. Thus, there appears to be one market rate of interest that is the appropriate social discount rate. In perfect markets, individuals' marginal rate of time preference, the rate of return on private investment, and the (bank's) market interest rate are all equal.

The situation becomes immensely more complicated when we relax our assumption of a perfect capital market and, therefore, of a single market interest rate. Taxes and other distortions, such as risk and transaction costs, lead to divergence between the rate of return on investment and the rate at which consumers are willing to trade current and future consumption. Suppose that consumers are willing to trade marginal current and marginal future consumption at a rate of 6 percent.[9] If they face an income tax of 25 percent and firms face a profits tax of 50 percent, then they will only invest in projects that earn a return of at least 16 percent. (The firm returns 8 percent to the investor after the profit tax is paid; the investor retains 6 percent after paying the income tax.) Which if any of these rates is the correct social discount rate? There are four possible methods to use to determine the social discount rate: the marginal social rate of time preference, the marginal social opportunity cost of capital, weighted average method, and the shadow price of capital.

Marginal Social Rate of Time Preference Method (SRTP)

In the simple capital market model developed in Figure 5.2, consumers maximize the present value of their consumption opportunities by equating their marginal rate of time preference to the rate of return on savings. In a world with taxation, consumers maximize the present value of consumption by equating their marginal rate of time preference to their *real, after-tax rate of return on savings.* Economists commonly take the interest rate on treasury bills as the nominal pretax rate of return on savings. This rate is converted to an after-tax rate by multiplying it by one minus the marginal income tax rate and then adjusting for inflation to give the real after-tax rate of return on savings.[10]

As an illustration, take the yield in 1989 on treasury bills of three-year constant maturity, 8.55 percent, as a starting point. The U.S. marginal tax rate on income for middle-income taxpayers was 28 percent, so that the after-tax yield was $[(1 - 0.28) \times (0.0855)] = 6.2$ percent. Taking 4.6 percent as the expected rate of inflation gives a real after-tax yield of $[(0.062 - 0.046)/(1 + 0.046)] = 1.5$ percent. *Calculations of this sort generally lead to estimates of the individual marginal rate of time preference in the range of just above 0 to 4 percent.*

When estimating the marginal rate of time preference, care must be taken not to be misled by short-run fluctuations in market interest rates. Averaging real market interest rates over several periods is more likely to give a reasonable starting point for making inferences about the MRTP. From a practical perspective, Robert Hartman explains that when analysts at the Congressional Budget Office considered how to estimate the marginal rate of time preference, they decided that they did not want a procedure that gave unstable estimates: "We did not want to have to explain why the MX missile was a good idea last month, but not now."[11]

The *social rate of time preference* (SRTP) is the rate at which *society* is willing to exchange consumption now for more consumption in the future. There are two fundamental problems. One problem is that different individuals may have different MRTPs. A second problem is that the marginal *social* rate of time preference may differ from the marginal *individual* rate of time preference, the rate we computed earlier. There are some reasons to believe that the social rate may be lower, although it could be higher. One reason for a lower rate, as Kenneth Arrow and Robert Lind argue, is that collective risk aggregates and nullifies risks to individuals.[12] This argument is developed more fully in Chapter 7.

Factors affecting an individual's MRTP   Individual time preference depends on many factors. Most people have positive time preference. Other things being equal, they will only give up present consumption in exchange for greater amounts of future consumption. Why? Obviously risk concerning our future circumstances is a factor. The present is certain, while the future is not—a bird in the hand is worth two in the bush. There is, for example, the risk of death. If you think you have only a short time to live, then you will value the present very highly because, quite literally, there may be no tomorrow for you. Thus, it is reasonable to expect that older people have a higher MRTP rate than younger people.[13] Of course, even if you knew you were going to die, you might want to leave something to your children or to others; that is, people may want to leave *bequests*. Thus, MRTPs are usually not extremely high.

Individuals' MRTPs may also be affected by their expectation of future income levels. We would rather consume now if we expect to have more income in the future, because our marginal utility of consumption will be lower in the future.[14] Thus, for example, students probably have a high MRTP. On the other hand, persons near retirement may have a negative MRTP: They may keep saving even if the market interest rate is zero because they think they will need the money.

Individuals may have different marginal rates of time preference over different goods. For example, Jan Olsen suggests that it is possible that individual MRTPs for health differs from that for "ordinary consumption goods."[15] Others have suggested that we might have a high MRTP for mainframe computers but a low MRTP for clean air, clean water, or biological diversity.[16] Part of the reason for the different MRTPs may be due to the longevity of different goods: Computers have relatively short useful lives while environmental goods have long time horizons. We discuss this issue further in the following section.

Intergenerational issues and declining social discount rates. One reason why the social discount rate may be lower than the individual MRTP is that individuals have finite lives, but society does not.[17] Consequently, current individuals may not sufficiently take into account the consumption possibilities or desires of future generations. Those yet unborn do not have a direct voice in current markets, yet we may believe that they should have standing in our (current) CBA.[18] The willingness of people to pass inheritances to their children and to pay to preserve unique resources gives indirect standing to future generations. However, future generations may be underrepresented in current markets. To the extent that the interests of future generations remain underrepresented, an argument can be made for using a social discount rate lower than the individual MRTP (and the private economy's marginal return on investment).

One argument that has been put forward for why future generations should not be given any more weight than they already have is that they will inherit a growing stock of capital and knowledge that will compensate them for the current consumption of natural resources. In the past, successive generations have tended to enjoy higher standards of living than their parents. If this trend continues, it is legitimate to ask why this current generation should subsidize a richer subsequent generation.[19] However, there is increasing evidence that current "Generation Xers" may not be as well off as immediately preceding generations. Thus, it is not so easy to argue that the current generation can consume existing natural resources and future generations will be compensated for them.

The intergenerational issue is particularly relevant when evaluating projects, such as the storage of nuclear wastes or reforestation, that have consequences far into the future. Consider, for example, the following two streams of benefits ($ millions):

	1996	1997	1998	$\cdots$	2031	2032	2033	$\cdots$	∞	NPV
A)	100	100	100		100	100	100		100	1,000
B)	151	100	100		100	0	0		0	1,014

Intuitively, one might think that stream A yields higher benefits than stream B: It yields $100 million per year indefinitely, thereby being identical to stream B from 1997 to 2031 and superior from year 2032 onward. It has lower benefits than stream B only in the first year. Nonetheless, at a discount rate of 10 percent, stream A has a lower NPV than stream B.

Thus far, we have used *constant discounting*; that is, a constant social discount rate *i* has been applied to all impacts, whenever they occur. With constant discounting, impacts that arise in year *n* are weighted by the present value factor $a(n) = (1 + i)^{-n}$, which declines geometrically. Thus, impacts that occur far in the future have a low weight.

At the other extreme, some philosophers have argued that the social discount rate should be zero, which, in effect, implies nondiscounting. According to this view, one that we do not share, society is indifferent between, for example, $100 today and $100 in a century. Future events have exactly the same weight as current events.

Charles Harvey and others have suggested that a potentially reasonable alternative is to use declining discount rates, that is, to decrease the discount rate for impacts that occur further in the future, with the discount rate tending to zero as the timing of the impacts tends to infinity.[20] For example, *proportional discounting* assumes the present value factor is given by:

$$a(n) \ = \ \frac{b}{b + n} \quad n \geq 0 \tag{5.4}$$

for some parameter *b*>0.

Motivation for declining discount rates is based on declining individual MRTPs over longer time periods or, in other words, decreasing timing aversion. The idea is that we attach less importance to the difference between the same impact separated by a fixed number of periods as both periods are shifted further into the future. Exhibit 5.1 presents evidence that individual MRTPs for saving lives now versus saving lives in the future decline as the time horizon extends further into the future. After reviewing the recent literature on counterexamples to constant discounting, George Loewenstein and Drazen Prelec conclude that "unlike the EU [expected utility] violations, which in many cases can only be demonstrated with a clever arrangement of multiple choice problems (e.g., the Allais paradox), the counterexamples to DU [constant discounting] are simple, robust, and bear directly on central aspects of economic behavior."[21]

Analysts are not in agreement about how to resolve this issue. The case for the use of declining social discount rates has been made recently, but it has not yet been widely accepted. In our view, *for projects with long time horizons, the social discount rate should be lower than the MRTP of currently living people.* However, despite the evidence of declining MRTPs over time, we do not advocate the use of nonconstant discount rates.

■ **EXHIBIT 5.1**

Maureen Cropper and colleagues have conducted surveys to measure how participants are willing to tradeoff lives saved today with lives saved in the future. In round numbers, this research suggests that people are indifferent between one life saved today and two lives saved in five years' time, three lives saved in ten years' time, six lives saved in 25 years' time, 11 lives saved in 50 years' time, and 44 lives saved in 100 years' time. More precisely, and expressing the results in terms of MRTP, the research found an implicit marginal rate of time preference of 16.8 percent over a five-year horizon, 11.2 percent over a ten-year horizon, 7.4 percent over a 25-year horizon, 4.8 percent over a 50-year horizon, and 3.8 percent over a 100-year horizon. These results suggest that individual MRTPs are significantly greater than zero, but they decline as the time horizon extends further into the future.

Source: Maureen L. Cropper, Sema K. Aydede, and Paul R. Portney, "Rates of Time Preference for Saving Lives," *American Economic Review: Papers and Proceedings*, 82, no. 2 (May 1992), 469–472.

Irreversibility and merit goods. Some have argued that society is myopic in the sense that it makes choices now that it later regrets. This line of argument is used to try to justify public provision of so-called *merit goods*, such as educational television, theater, and the arts. In general, we are not convinced by this argument. While it is relevant when society makes an *irreversible* decision that it may later regret, we show in our discussion of quasi-option value in Chapter 7 that such myopia can be corrected by more explicit modeling of the decision problem. Thus, myopia should not be handled by adjusting the social discount rate.

Marginal Social Opportunity Cost of Capital (SOC)

The government and the private sector compete for the same pool of funds. Efficient allocation of resources requires that, at the margin, investments in the government sector should yield the same return as investments in the private sector. If not, then total welfare could be increased by allocating resources to the sector yielding the higher returns. Evaluation of government projects should, therefore, use the marginal social opportunity cost of funds in the private sector or, for short, the social opportunity cost of capital (SOC). As a first approximation, economists measure the SOC by *the marginal before-tax rate of return on private investment*. For example, as discussed in detail later, the average real, before-tax return on investments during the 1970s and 1980s was more than 10 percent. As pointed out previously, due to tax distortions and risk, this method usually leads to a higher social discount rate than the SRTP method.

There are a number of factors that should be taken into consideration when using the rate of return on private investment for the SOC. All of them suggest that *in certain situations, the average real pretax rate of return should be adjusted downward*. First, we should use the *marginal* pretax rate of return rather than the *average* pretax rate of return. The marginal rate of return will be lower than the average because rational businesspeople will make their best deals first. Second, private-sector rates of return are determined in markets that may be distorted by externalities and monopolistic pricing. If, in the aggregate, the private sector generates negative externalities, then we should use a lower rate of return. Similarly, if market power enables firms to restrict output and to increase prices above socially optimal levels, then we should adjust downward private-sector returns on investment. Third, since the private sector must compensate investors for risk, the average return on investment incorporates a risk premium. On average, public-sector projects may have less risk than the private-sector projects—a topic that we take up in the following section. Consequently, the average return on investment should be adjusted down to obtain an applicable rate for public-sector projects. Finally, as we have mentioned before, we must consider the uses to which resources would actually be put if the project were not implemented. Would the money be available for the private sector, or would the government invest it elsewhere? If the resources would otherwise be used where they would earn a return lower than the marginal pretax rate of return, then the analyst should use a lower discount rate.

Weighted Average Method (WAM)

Notwithstanding the problems identified earlier, one way economists have proposed the social discount rate be calculated is in terms of the source of the resources that are used in a particular project.[22] If the resources for the public project come entirely at the expense of current private consumption, then the marginal social rate of time preference (SRTP) is appropriate. If the source of the resources used in the public project is entirely at the expense of current private investment, then the marginal rate of return on private investment (SOC) is appropriate. More generally, according to this method, *the social discount rate equals an average of the SOC and SRTP weighted in proportion to the source of the resources in terms of lost private investment and lost consumption.* In short, the social discount rate using the weighted average method (WA) is given by:

$$WA = (\alpha)SOC + (1 - \alpha)SRTP \qquad (5.5)$$

where α equals the proportion of resources (costs) displacing private investment, and $(1 - \alpha)$ equals the proportion of resources (costs) displacing current consumption.

In addition to the problems that pertain to the SRTP and SOC methods that we have already discussed, there are problems determining α. For each project individually and for all government projects in aggregate, economists disagree about whether public investment detracts primarily from current private consumption (savings), private investment (real capital formation), or from some other source (loans from foreigners). Arnold Harberger, for instance, argues that because marginal public expenditures are typically financed by borrowing, public investment fully displaces private investment.[23] Accepting this "crowding out" hypothesis, we might use some market measure, such as the rate of return on corporate Aaa bonds, as the first approximation for the nominal social discount rate.[24] However, the apparent absence of a link between borrowing by the U.S. federal government and interest rates has led some economists to argue that public expenditures are being financed by foreign capital rather than by forgone domestic private investment.[25] Thus, "crowding out" may be much less than dollar for dollar.

For Canada, Glenn Jenkins proposed weights of 75 percent for displaced private domestic investment, 20 percent for incremental foreign funding, and only 5 percent for displaced domestic consumption.[26] In a critique, David Burgess suggests that the proportion of foreign funding may have been higher than 50 percent.[27] However, given the current enormous size of Canada's debt, few would argue that it will be this high in the future!

Even if we know α for the initial investment period, the project may generate future returns that can either be invested or consumed. We should therefore adjust α to reflect how future returns are actually used.

In theory, each project should be evaluated by its own discount rate, which depends on the source of the resources from which it draws. In practice, governments generally wish to set a single social discount rate so that decision makers do not have to evaluate the appropriateness of the rate selected for each individual project.

Finally, we should point out that care must be taken over nomenclature. Some authors refer to the *weighted average method* as the *social opportunity cost of capital*. Conceptually, this different terminology actually makes more sense because the social opportunity cost represents the loss to society from using the resources for a government project instead of consuming them, investing them, or borrowing them. Many people think the funds for a government project come exclusively at the expense of private-sector investment so that the marginal social opportunity cost of capital always equals the marginal rate of return on private investment.

Shadow Price of Capital Method (SPC)

Rather than use the preceding methods, a conceptually attractive alternative is to convert all costs and benefits to their corresponding changes in consumption, and then use the marginal rate of time preference as the discount rate.[28] Analysts usually estimate benefits directly in terms of additions to consumption. Costs, on the other hand, may accrue as reductions in either consumption or private investment. Those costs that accrue as reductions in private investment must be valued in terms of the stream of consumption that would have resulted had the investment not been displaced.

The procedure for converting forgone investment to its equivalent in streams of forgone consumption involves finding the *shadow price of capital*. The "shadow" in the phrase emphasizes that the price of capital in terms of consumption cannot be directly observed in a market but instead must be inferred. Four parameters are relevant in determining the SPC: (1) the pretax gross (before depreciation) rate of return on private capital, w, which indicates the yield on a unit of capital each year; (2) the depreciation rate, δ, which indicates the natural rate of decline in the value of a unit of capital per year; (3) the gross savings rate, s, which measures the fraction of gross return on investment that is reinvested; and (4) the marginal rate of time preference, d. Assuming a geometrically depreciating capital stock, Randolph M. Lyon derives the following expression for θ, the shadow price of capital:[29]

$$\theta = \frac{w - sw}{d + \delta - sw} \tag{5.6}$$

Despite the simplicity of this expression, calculating the SPC is far from clear-cut because we do not know with certainty the appropriate values of the four parameters. Nevertheless, we can demonstrate how one could make a rough calculation from readily available sources for 1989.

We begin with the depreciation rate, δ, which is needed for our inference of the pretax gross rate of return on private capital. Unlike our estimates of the other parameters, we are forced to go beyond readily available macroeconomic data to come up with even a rough figure. Researchers have analyzed the relative prices of new and used equipment and structures to estimate economic depreciation rates.[30] Their analysis suggests that the depreciation rate for equipment used in manufacturing is 13.3 percent and the depreciation rate for structures used in manufacturing is 3.4 percent.[31] Weighting these rates by the relative proportions of equipment (67 percent) and structures (33 percent) in the capital stock gives an average depreciation rate of $[(0.67) \times (0.133) + (0.33) \times (0.034)] = 10$ percent.[32]

Consider next the pretax gross rate of return on private capital, w. We might take the average rate of return on Aaa corporate bonds as the after-tax net rate of return on capital. In 1989, this rate was 9.26 percent.[33] But the marginal U.S. federal corporate tax rate is 34 percent and the median marginal state corporate tax rate is 6 percent.[34] Combining these rates while taking account of the deductibility of state taxes as business expenses yields a total marginal tax rate of 38 percent.[35] Thus, investment funded by corporate bonds cannot have a pretax net rate of return of less than $[0.0926/(1 - 0.38)] = 14.9$ percent. As this is a nominal rate of return, we must adjust it for expected price inflation in 1989. Assuming that the market in 1989 correctly estimated the actual rate of price inflation, we could use 4.8 percent, the percentage change in the consumer price index (see Table 4.3), as the expected rate of inflation in 1989. Adjusting for expected inflation yields $[(0.149 - 0.048)/(1 + 0.048)] = 9.6$ percent as the before-tax net real rate of return on private investment. To obtain the gross rate of return we must add to this net rate of return, our estimate of the rate of depreciation, which is 10 percent.[36] The result is a pretax gross real rate of return on capital of 19.6 percent.

Next consider the gross savings rate, s. As a rough measure, we take the ratio of net private domestic investment ($771.2 billion in 1989) to the gross domestic product ($5,163.2 billion in 1989) to obtain a gross savings rate of 15 percent.

Table 5.1 displays the shadow prices of capital for various values of the marginal rate of time preference, and for three different values of the pretax gross rate of return on private capital, assuming the gross savings rate is 15 percent and the depreciation rate is 10 percent. Column 3 gives the shadow price of capital under the assumption the pretax rate of return on private capital is 19.6 percent, which is our estimated return. Column 2 gives the shadow prices under the assumption that marginal state and local taxes are zero so that w equals 18.8 percent; column 4 instead assumes that marginal state and local taxes are 10 percent so that w equals 20.3 percent.[37]

TABLE 5.1 THE SHADOW PRICE OF CAPITAL (θ) AS A FUNCTION OF THE REAL MARGINAL
RATE OF TIME PREFERENCE (d) AND THE PRETAX GROSS RATE OF RETURN (w)

Marginal rate of	Pretax gross rate of return (w)		
time preference (d)	0.188	0.196	0.203
0.00	2.23	2.36	2.48
0.01	1.95	2.07	2.17
0.02	1.74	1.84	1.92
0.03	1.57	1.66	1.73
0.04	1.43	1.51	1.58
0.05	1.31	1.38	1.44
0.06	1.21	1.28	1.33
0.07	1.13	1.18	1.24
0.08	1.05	1.11	1.15
0.09	0.99	1.04	1.08
0.10	0.93	0.98	1.02

Gross savings rate (s) = 0.15; Depreciation rate (δ) = 0.10.

Illustration of the Four Social Discounting Methods

A simple example illustrates the four social discounting methods discussed earlier.
Imagine that a temporary bypass to ease traffic congestion during the reconstruction
of a major highway would cost $5 million in capital costs and $2 million in time lost
by neighborhood residents during its first year of operation. During the first year and
each of four subsequent years, the bypass would generate $2 million (real) in time sav-
ings to roadway users.[38] Assume that the scrap value of the bypass just equals the cost
of removing it at the end of the fifth year. Is the bypass economically efficient?

To answer this question, we assume the marginal rate of time preference for all
residents and for society equals 4 percent and calculate the NPV in four ways.

Marginal social rate of time preference method (SRTP). First, we use the
SRTP of 4 percent as the social discount rate and assume a shadow price of capital of
one. Given these assumptions, the NPV equals $2.26 million.

Social opportunity cost of capital (SOC). Second, if we use the real net rate
of return on private investment of 9.6 percent we estimated previously as the social
discount rate and assume a shadow price of capital of one, then the NPV of the project is $1.40 million, smaller than when we discounted with the marginal rate of time
preference but still positive.

Weighted average method (WAM). Third, let us assume that the full $5 million
in capital costs is at the expense of private investment, while the $2 million in time costs
to neighborhood residents represents a loss of consumption. These sources of costs
might be taken as weights in finding a composite discount rate based on the SOC and
the SRTP: [(5/7)×(0.096) + (2/7)×(0.04)] = 0.080. Again, assuming that the shadow

price of capital equals one, this composite social discount rate yields a present value of net benefits for the project of $1.62 million. As noted previously, this sort of weighting procedure has been suggested in the literature. Nevertheless, the selection of weights seems arbitrary. Imagine, for instance, that capital and consumption costs occurred in different proportions in later years. What then would be the appropriate weights?

Shadow price of capital method (SPC).   Fourth, let us consider the shadow price of capital approach. The first step involves applying the appropriate shadow price to all costs that come at the expense of private investment—if benefits added to the value of private capital, then they would also be converted to their equivalent consumption value by applying the shadow price. In the example at hand, the only effect on private investment is the loss of $5 million in the first year. The SPC consistent with an SRTP of 4 percent in Table 5.1 is 1.51, assuming the pretax gross rate of return equals 19.6 percent. Therefore, the first period costs would be [(1.51)×($5 million) + $2 million] = $9.55 million. This can be interpreted as the value of the stream of consumption forgone because of the project. Now discounting the annual benefits using the SRTP of 4 percent as the social discount rate yields a present value for the benefits of $9.26 million. Therefore, the proposed project has a negative present value of net benefits (–$0.29 million). In other words, the shadow price of capital approach in this case indicates that the project would be inefficient because it involves net costs.

Note that although the other three discounting approaches indicate that building the bypass would be efficient (assuming no alternative exists offering a larger present value of net benefits), the shadow price of capital approach indicates that building the bypass would not be efficient. The discrepancy results in this case because such a large fraction of the costs of the project was assumed to be at the expense of private investment. Shifting $1 million in costs from forgone investment to forgone consumption would be sufficient to yield positive net benefits under the shadow price of capital approach. Similarly, positive net benefits would result if benefits were assumed to represent increments to investment rather than consumption. For example, instead of all the benefits coming from the time savings of commuters, some benefits might result if a nearby delivery service could avoid buying additional trucks because of the time savings offered by the bypass.

Conclusion on Social Discounting Methods in the Absence of Perfect Markets

Several practical implications follow from accepting, as we do, the conceptual validity of the shadow price of capital approach to discounting. First, *if **all** costs and benefits are measured as increments to consumption, then these costs and benefits should be discounted at the marginal rate of time preference*. Second, *if **all** costs and benefits are measured as increments to private investment, then these costs and benefits should be discounted at the marginal rate of time preference with the resulting present value of net benefits multiplied by the shadow price of capital to obtain the present value of net social benefits*. Note that in this case the magnitude of the shadow price is irrelevant to the question of whether the present value of net social benefits is positive. It would be relevant, however, in comparing the project to an alternative that does not measure *all* costs and benefits as increments to private investment. Third, *when some costs and benefits are measured as increments to consumption and others are measured as increments to private investment, applying the shadow price of capital is essential for determining whether or not the present value of net social benefits is positive.* Unfortunately, costs and benefits often cannot be definitively classified as increments to either consumption or private investment. Therefore, *the sensitivity of the present value of net social benefits to changes in classification should be investigated when employing the shadow price of capital approach.*

Our presentation of the issues involved in this section should make clear that analysts are unlikely ever to have complete confidence in whatever discounting procedure they use. In the case of the more simple discounting methods, choice of the appropriate social discount rate requires judgment. Taking account of the shadow price of capital demands that even more parameters, which cannot be known with certainty, be specified. It is almost always desirable, therefore, for analysts to test the sensitivity of their results to changes in the parameters used in discounting, as described earlier in this chapter.

THE SOCIAL DISCOUNT RATE IN ACTUAL PRACTICE

The actual practice of discounting often diverges substantially from theory. Most practitioners realize that future costs and benefits should be discounted in some way. Standard practice ignores the distinction between increments to consumption and increments to capital. In other words, the shadow price of a dollar of capital is assumed to be one dollar of consumption. Practitioners then focus on the question of what social discount rate to use.

As we discussed in Chapter 1, spenders, guardians, and analysts will tend to favor different discount rates. In general, guardians tend to view government expenditures as crowding out private investment; consequently, they tend to argue for a social discount rate approximating the rate of return on private investment. Spenders view government expenditures as reducing current consumption or act as if they hold this view and, therefore, tend to argue for a social discount rate approximating the marginal rate of time preference.

When costs precede benefits, as is the case for most projects, those who favor such projects may argue for a low rate while those who oppose them may argue for a high rate. In many practical situations, however, debate is ruled out because the discount rate is prescribed by government review and monitoring agencies. As these rates are set by guardians, they tend to be higher than social discount rates based on the theory presented previously in this chapter.

Table 5.2 shows the discounting rules used by three of the primary oversight agencies of the U.S. federal government. The Office of Management and Budget (OMB) generally requires most agencies to use a *real* discount rate of 10 percent—a rate that might, as we discussed earlier, best be interpreted as close to the real, before-tax rate of return on private investment.[39] For projects with long-term benefits or ben-

**TABLE 5.2   DISCOUNTING OF REAL COSTS AND BENEFITS BY THREE FEDERAL
                      OVERSIGHT AGENCIES**

Application	Agency		
	Office of Management and Budget (OMB)	Congressional Budget Office (CBO)	General Accounting Office (GAO)
General Public Investment	10% real; agencies must justify use of alternative rate	theory: real yield of Treasury debt; guideline: 2% plus or minus 2%;	average yield on Treasury debt maturing between one year and the life of the project less the forecast inflation rate
Investment in Water Projects	nominal Treasury long-term borrowing rate applied to *real* net benefits	lower (higher) for projects with returns negatively (positively) correlated with gross national product	
Lease-Purchase Decisions	real Treasury borrowing rate plus one-eigth percent	real Treasury borrowing rate	
Asset Divestitures	real market interest rates for comparable private ventures	real market interest rates for comparable private ventures	

Source: Based on discussion in Randolph M. Lyon, "Federal Discount Rate Policy, the Shadow Price of Capital, and Challenges for Reforms," *Journal of Environmental Economics and Management*, 18, no. 2, part 2 (March 1990), S29–S50.

efits that accrue after a lag in project costs, the OMB procedure may substantially underestimate the NPV relative to the shadow price of capital approach or any other of the methods discussed previously.[40]

For water-related projects—long a focus of pork barrel politics—the actual standards are much lower. Specifically, OMB requires agencies to apply the estimated average cost of federal borrowing as determined by the Secretary of the Treasury—a nominal rate—to the *real* costs and benefits of water projects![41] Ironically, because *nominal* borrowing rates have been below 10 percent in recent years, this conceptually incorrect procedure might, in practice, be more appropriate than the use of 10 percent as the real discount rate.

The OMB rules for investment projects differ markedly from those used by the Congressional Budget Office (CBO). CBO views the marginal rate of time preference as the appropriate discount rate and recommends that 2 percent, plus or minus 2 percent, be used. Obviously, many projects that would have positive present values of net benefits using the CBO procedure would have negative present values of net benefits under OMB's 10 percent rule.

The General Accounting Office (GAO) adopts a more flexible approach, basing its discount rate on the real rate of interest on federal borrowing. Perhaps it is best thought of as the cost to the government of borrowing rather than as either the rate of return on private investment or the marginal rate of time preference.

At a particular moment in time, GAO uses the same rate for all applications. CBO and OMB, on the other hand, use different rules for evaluating lease-purchase decisions and asset divestitures. Each treats lease-purchase decisions as purely revenue-expenditure questions. Rather than attempting to take account of the social or financial effects on society as a whole, the focus is on the financial position of the government. Real revenues and expenditures to the government are discounted at the real Treasury borrowing rate, or at this rate plus one-eighth of a percentage point. Because neither the shadow price of capital nor the marginal excess tax burden need to be considered explicitly when all costs and benefits are measured as changes to government revenue, this approach is reasonable from a social perspective in the sense that it involves discounting the cash flows of projects at the risk-free rate of return.

In the case of the divestiture of government-owned assets that produce revenue streams, CBO and OMB turn to market interest rates for comparable private ventures as the discount factor to avoid a curious result: If both the market and the government shared a common estimate of the revenue stream, then the government, using a discount rate lower than the market rate of interest, would always obtain a higher PV of the asset than would the potential private purchasers. Consequently, the government would never divest! Of course, the government might divest if private owners thought they could realize a more favorable revenue stream through better management than the government so that their bids would be higher than the PV to the government, even when the government discounted at a lower rate.

Since 1976, the Canadian (Federal) Treasury Board Secretariat, like the OMB, has recommended use of a 10 percent real social discount rate, with sensitivity analysis at plus or minus five percentage points.[42] Provincial government guidelines in Canada have tended to follow suit.[43] As in the United States, this is a "financial" discount rate. The rationale for the 10 percent real discount rate draws extensively on research by Glenn Jenkins who used a social opportunity cost of capital approach with 75 percent weight on displaced private investment that would have earned a real social rate of return of 11.45 percent, 20 percent weight on incremental foreign funding at a social cost of 6.11 percent, and 5 percent weight on incremental displaced domestic consumption at a social time preference rate of 4.14 percent.[44] David Burgess and others have argued that this 10 percent real rate is too high.[45] Although some Canadian government agencies have indicated a willingness in recent years to use slightly lower rates (usually 8 percent), monitoring agencies continue to require high real social discount rates.

CONCLUSION

Discounting for time is fundamental to the proper practice of CBA. By now, most policy analysts realize the importance of discounting. Common practice, however, often does not reflect theory. Few analysts employ the shadow price of capital approach. In view of the difficulties one faces in applying these concepts, we must not be too critical. Indeed, we should be humble about whatever procedure we use, presenting the sensitivity of our results to changes in parameter values.

APPENDIX 5A

SHOULD THE SOCIAL DISCOUNT RATE BE ADJUSTED FOR RISK?

In Chapter 6 we consider how to take account of uncertainty about the magnitude of costs and benefits that will be realized in future years. The basic notion is that costs and benefits can be estimated for each of a number of mutually exclusive contingencies. Assigning probabilities to each of these contingencies allows the analyst to calculate expected values (averages) for each period. If we assume risk neutrality (indifference between lotteries and certain payments equal to the expected values of the lotteries), then discounting these expected values for time in the standard way allows us to interpret the present value of expected net social benefits as the appropriate objective function for determining if policies are efficient.

As we discuss in Chapter 7, however, a complication arises because we generally assume that individuals are risk averse (i.e., they prefer guaranteed payments to uncertain amounts with the same expected value). Risk aversion among individuals raises the question of how we should treat risky projects. Though we will answer this question more thoroughly in Chapter 7, this appendix focuses on whether and how the social discount rate should be adjusted for risk.

Economists have expressed divergent views on whether the social discount rate should reflect project risk.[1] The controversy can be resolved to some extent by reference to the capital asset pricing model (CAPM). The basic idea of this model is that *investors* have to be compensated for risk. Individual investments are subject to two types of risk. One type of risk is *unique risk* (or *specific risk, residual risk,* or *unsystematic risk*), which pertains exclusively to a particular investment. This risk can be avoided by portfolio diversification, that is, by holding shares in a fairly large number of different investments. The second type of risk is called *market risk* or *systematic risk*. This risk cannot be avoided by portfolio diversification. It arises because of economywide changes that affect all investments, including the market portfolio, to some extent. Stock prices, for example, tend to move in the same direction.

Formally, the CAPM states that, in equilibrium, the expected rate of return on an asset equals the risk-free rate plus an amount that compensates for systematic risk:

$$E(r_i) = r_f + [E(r_m) - r_f]\beta_i \tag{5A.1}$$

where $E(r_i)$ is the expected rate of return on individual asset i, $E(r_m)$ is the expected rate of return to the market portfolio, r_f is the risk-free rate of return or the rate of return on a risk-free asset, such as high-grade corporate bonds or T-bills, $E(r_m) - r_f$

equals the market risk premium, and β_i is a measure of systematic risk for individual asset i. Often the systematic risk for a security is called its beta.

This model is represented graphically in Figure 5.A1. In equilibrium, all investments lie on the security market line with the expected return of an investment varying in direct proportion to its systematic risk, β_i. It can be shown that

$$\beta_i = \frac{\text{Cov } (r_i, r_m)}{\sigma_m^2} - \rho_{im} \frac{\sigma_i}{\sigma_m} \tag{5A.2}$$

Thus, a security's systematic risk—its beta—equals the covariance of the security's own rate of return with the market portfolio divided by the variance in the market rate of return. Setting $r_i = r_m$ and substituting equation (5A.2) into equation (5A.1) indicates that the market portfolio has a beta of one. An investment that is uncorrelated with the market portfolio has a beta of zero and, as shown by equation (5A.1), has an expected return equal to r_f, the risk-free rate of return.

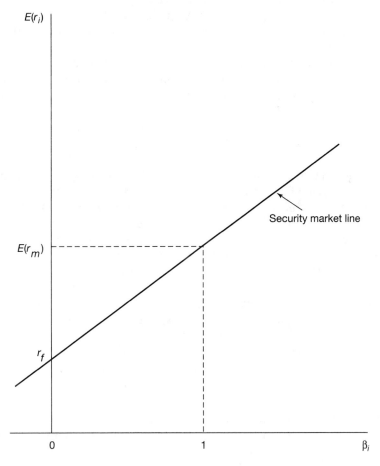

Figure 5.A1 The Capital Asset Pricing Model

Private-sector Capital Budgeting Implications of the CAPM

The private-sector capital budgeting implications of the CAPM are straightforward, at least in theory.[2] The first step is to ascertain a proposed investment's beta. This varies according to the correlation between the project's net benefits and the market portfolio, as shown in equation (5A.2). Indeed, this could be calculated using equation (5A.2) if the appropriate data were available. More likely, the analyst would use simple rules of thumb. Projects that tend to perform better than the market portfolio in good times and worse than the market portfolio in bad times (for instance, cyclical stocks) have betas greater than one. Investments that are highly correlated with the market portfolio have betas close to one. Investments that are weakly, positively correlated with the market portfolio have betas between zero and one. Investments that are uncorrelated with the market portfolio, so-called risk-free investments, have a beta equal to zero. Investments that are negatively correlated with the market portfolio, such as countercyclical stocks, have negative betas.

The second step is to estimate the right-hand side of equation (5A.1), which can be interpreted as the expected rate of return for an investment with the same systematic risk as the one under consideration or, more briefly, as the appropriate risk-adjusted rate of return. This requires knowing the risk-free rate (r_f), for which one can use interest rates on treasury bills or a similar security. It also requires an estimate of the market risk premium, $E(r_m) - r_f$.[3] If, for example, an investment's beta equals 0.5, the risk-free rate equals 3 percent, and the market risk premium equals 8 percent, then the expected rate of return for an investment in this risk class is

$$E(r_i) = 3 + 8(0.5) = 7 \text{ percent}$$

If the expected internal rate of return (IRR) of the proposed investment exceeds the expected rate of return for an investment in this risk class, then one should proceed with the investment. If the IRR is less than the appropriate risk-adjusted rate of return, then one should not proceed with the investment. In this particular example, we would proceed with the investment if its expected IRR is greater than 7 percent and would not proceed if its expected IRR is less than 7 percent.

An alternative capital budgeting approach discounts the expected cash flows of the investment at the appropriate risk-adjusted rate of return, in this example 7 percent. If the resultant NPV is positive, then the investment should proceed; otherwise, it should not. Formally, suppose the expected net benefits (cash flows) of a proposed investment all arise in one year's time and are denoted $E(NB)$. Then the present value of the investment is:

$$E(NPV) = \frac{E(NB)}{1 + r_f + [E(r_m) - r_f]\beta_i} \tag{5A.3}$$

Equation (5A.3) is referred to as the risk-adjusted present value formula. It is similar to equation (4.6) where $i = r_f + [E(r_m) - r_f]\beta_i$, the appropriate risk-adjusted discount rate.

Use of the CAPM in CBA

Now consider a potential government project as a possible new investment. Society may be risk adverse and want to reduce the total risk associated with national social income. Consequently, it is appropriate to evaluate an investment using a discount rate that depends on the covariance of that investment with national social income or, more simply, national income. All of the rules developed previously can now be applied straightforwardly. *Government projects with expected net benefits that are negatively (or positively) correlated with national income should be discounted at a rate lower (higher) than the risk-free rate.* Here, of course, we are taking correlation as a rough measure of the project's beta which, in practice, will be difficult to estimate accurately.

In general, the benefits and the costs of infrastructure projects, such as developing ports and building highways, are likely to be positively correlated with national income. Consequently, these projects should be discounted using a higher rate than normal. The benefits and costs of job-creation projects are likely to be negatively correlated with national income. These projects should be discounted using a lower rate than normal.

As a practical rule of thumb, some authors suggest that you adjust the riskless discount rate downward only when the expected net benefits of a project are likely to be highly negatively correlated with national income and the project has a long time horizon. If the correlation is not highly negative, then substantial adjustment is likely to be unwarranted; if the project has a short time horizon, then the lower discount rate is unlikely to affect the magnitude of the present value of net social benefits dramatically. Worrying about adjusting discount rates for risk is probably only worthwhile in practice for clearly negative correlations and long time horizons. So, for example, if we expect national income to be highly negatively correlated with the world price of oil, and we expect the net benefits of an oil stockpiling program to be positively correlated with the world price of oil, then the expected net benefits of the stockpiling program will probably be negatively correlated with national income. Therefore, if the time horizon of the stockpiling program is long, then downward adjustment of the riskless discount rate would be justified. Unfortunately, the state of the art does not allow us to determine the exact magnitude of the adjustment.

Summary and Limitations of the CAPM for CBA

According to the CAPM, the variance of a project (project risk) is not relevant to the choice of a discount rate. Systematic project risk matters, not unsystematic project risk, which can be diversified away. The contribution of a particular project to the total risk associated with national income is essentially given by the beta of that investment, which depends on the covariance of that project with national income, not its variance.

There are some limitations of the CAPM. First, the CAPM is basically a two-period model, which casts doubt on its applicability to CBA. Second, in practice it is hard to obtain precise estimates of project betas.

EXERCISES FOR CHAPTER 5

1. The following table gives cost and benefit estimates in real dollars for dredging a navigable channel from an inland port to the open sea.

Year	Dredging and Patrol Costs ($)	Savings to Shippers ($)	Value of Pleasure Boating ($)
0	2,548,000	0	0
1	60,000	400,000	60,000
2	60,000	440,000	175,000
3	70,000	440,000	175,000
4	70,000	440,000	175,000
5	80,000	440,000	175,000
6	80,000	440,000	175,000
7	90,000	440,000	175,000

The channel would be navigable for seven years, after which silting would render it unnavigable. Local economists estimate that 75 percent of the savings to shippers would be directly invested by the firms, or their shareholders, and the remaining 25 percent would be used by shareholders for consumption. The social marginal rate of time preference is assumed to be 2 percent, the marginal rate of return on private investment is assumed to be 10 percent, and the shadow price of capital is assumed to be 1.90.

Assuming that the costs and benefits accrue at the end of the year they straddle, calculate the present value of net benefits of the project using each of the following methods:

a. Discount at the marginal rate of return on private investment, as suggested by the U.S. Office of Management and Budget.

b. Discount at the marginal social rate of time preference, as suggested by the U.S. Congressional Budget Office.

c. Discount using the shadow price of capital method and assuming that all government expenditures come at the expense of private investment.

d. Discount using the shadow price of capital method and assuming that 90 percent of government expenditures come at the expense of private investment and 10 percent at the expense of private consumption.

2. An analyst for a municipal public housing agency explained the choice of a discount rate as follows: "Our agency funds its capital investments through nationally issued bonds. The effective interest rate that we pay on the bonds is the cost that the agency faces in shifting revenue from the future to the present. It is therefore the appropriate discount rate for the agency to use in evaluating alternative investments." Comment on the appropriateness of this discount rate.

3. Assume the following: Society faces a marginal excess burden of raising public revenue equal to MEB; the shadow price of capital equals P_c; public borrowing displaces private investment dollar for dollar; and public revenues raised though taxes displace investment at the savings rate, s, and consumption at the rate, $1-s$. Consider a public project involving a large initial capital expenditure, C, followed by a stream of benefits that are entirely consumed, B.

    a. Discuss how you would apply the shadow price of capital method to the project if it is financed fully out of current taxes.

    b. Discuss how you would apply the shadow price of capital method to the project if it is financed fully by public borrowing, which is later repaid by taxes.

    c. Discuss how you would apply the shadow price of capital method to the project if it is fully self-financed through fees charged to beneficiaries.

NOTES

[1]Robert C. Lind, "A Primer on the Major Issues Relating to the Discount Rate for Evaluating National Energy Projects," in *Discounting for Time and Risk in Energy Policy*, Robert C. Lind, et al., (Washington, DC: Resources for the Future, 1982), pp. 21–94 at p. 8.

[2]Throughout this chapter we assume that inflation is zero so that the real social discount rate equals the nominal social discount rate.

[3]Assume here, in order to reveal your true preferences, that there is no arbitrage opportunity; that is, you could not borrow or lend money. Arbitrage means that you can simultaneously buy something in one market and sell it in another market and thereby make a guaranteed profit. If interest rates were less than 20 percent and arbitrage were allowed, you could say that you would rather have the $1,200 next year and then immediately borrow between $1,000 and $1,200 from the bank. Thus, you would say you would prefer to have the $1,200 next year even though you would actually prefer to have $1,000 now.

[4]Along an indifference curve,

$$dU = \frac{\partial U}{\partial C_1} dC_1 + \frac{\partial U}{\partial C_2} dC_2 = 0$$

[5]Formally, MRS $\equiv -\dfrac{dC_2}{dC_1}\bigg|_{U=constant} = \dfrac{\partial U / \partial C_1}{\partial U / \partial C_2}$

[6]It would make no conceptual difference if the consumer received income in both periods.

[7]Formally, we set up the following Lagrangian:

$$L = U(C_1, C_2) + \lambda[I - C_1 - \frac{C_2}{1 + i}]$$

and then take derivatives with respect to C_1 and C_2:

$$L_{c_1} = \frac{\partial U}{\partial C_1} - \lambda = 0$$

$$L_{c_2} = \frac{\partial U}{\partial C_2} - \frac{\lambda}{1 + i} = 0$$

Consequently,

$$\frac{\partial U / \partial C_1}{\partial U / \partial C_2} = 1 + i$$

Now, by definition,

$$\text{MRS} \equiv \frac{\partial U / \partial C_1}{\partial U / \partial C_2} = 1 + r$$

where r = marginal rate of time preference. Therefore, $r = i$ at equilibrium.

[8]Formally, the result holds as long as the problem has an interior solution. A very impatient person has an MRTP > i; diagrammatically, this problem has a corner solution on the C_1-axis. For simplicity, we shall ignore this possibility.

[9]We take this example from Robert C. Lind, "A Primer on the Major Issues Relating to the Discount Rate for Evaluating National Energy Projects," in *Discounting for Time and Risk in Energy Policy*, Robert C. Lind, et al., (Washington, DC: Resources for the Future, 1982), pp. 21–94.

[10]Let d = the nominal, before-tax rate of return on savings and t = tax rate. Then the after-tax return on savings = $d(1 - t)$. Further, let i = rate of inflation and r = the real, after-tax return on savings. Now,

$$\frac{1 + i}{1 + d(1 - t)} = \frac{1}{(1 + r)} \text{ . Therefore, } r = \frac{d(1 - t) - i}{(1 + i)} \text{ .}$$

[11]Robert W. Hartman, "One Thousand Points of Light Seeking a Number: A Case Study of CBO's Search for a Discount Rate Policy," *Journal of Environmental Economics and Management*, 18, no. 2, part 2 (March 1990), S3–S7, at S5.

[12]Kenneth J. Arrow and Robert C. Lind, "Uncertainty and the Evaluation of Public Investment Decisions," *American Economic Review*, 60, no. 3 (June 1970), 364–378.

[13]See Maureen L. Cropper, Sema K. Aydede, and Paul R. Portney, "Rates of Time Preference for Saving Lives," *American Economic Review*, 82, no. 2 (May 1992), 469–472, who found a positive relationship between age and the marginal rate of time preference but could find no significant relationship between respondents' MRTP and their sex, education, marital status, or income.

[14]A related reason why some would rather consume now stems from a belief that technological progress will make things better in the future.

[15]Jan Abel Olsen, "On What Basis Should Health be Discounted?" *Journal of Health Economics*, 12, no. 1 (1993), 39–53.

[16]See, for example, Paul C. Stern, "Blind Spots in Policy Analysis: What Economics Doesn't Say about Energy Use," *Journal of Policy Analysis and Management*, 5, no. 2 (Winter 1986), 200–227, especially pp. 207–209, for a discussion of differences in the implicit discount rates for different household appliances.

[17]Social attitudes regarding the present versus the future might differ collectively from individual perception. That is, collectively we place a greater weight on the future than we do in personal consumption decisions.

[18]For a discussion of this issue, see Daniel W. Bromley, "Entitlements, Missing Markets, and Environmental Uncertainty," *Journal of Environmental Economics and Management*, 17, no. 2 (September 1989), 181–194.

[19]As Groucho Marx asked: "What has posterity done for us?"

[20]The reasonableness of this is developed in Charles M. Harvey, "The Reasonableness of Non-Constant Discounting," *Journal of Public Economics*, 53, no. 1 (1994), 31–51. Harvey refers to declining discount rates as *slow discounting*.

[21]George Loewenstein and Drazen Prelec, "Anomalies in Intertemporal Choice: Evidence and an Interpretation," *Quarterly Journal of Economics*, 107, no. 2 (May 1992), 573–597 at p. 574.

[22]Agnar Sandmo and Jacques H. Drèze, "Discount Rates for Public Investment in Closed and Open Economies," *Economica*, 38, no. 152 (November 1971), 395–412.

[23]Arnold C. Harberger, "The Discount Rate in Public Investment Evaluation," *Conference Proceedings of the Committee on the Economics of Water Resource Development* (Denver, Co: Western Agricultural Economics Research Council, Report No. 17, 1969).

[24]For a demonstration of how to move from market rates to the social discount rate under the Harberger hypothesis, see Steve H. Hanke and James Bradford Anwyll, "On the Discount Rate Controversy," *Public Policy*, 28, no. 2 (Spring 1980), 171–183.

[25]Robert C. Lind, "Reassessing the Government's Discount Rate Policy in Light of New Theory and Data in a World Economy with a High Degree of Capital Mobility," *Journal of Environmental Economics and Management*, 18, no. 2, part 2 (March 1990), S8–S28.

[26]See Glenn Jenkins, "The Measurement of Rates of Return and Taxation for Private Capital in Canada," in *Benefit Cost and Policy Analysis*, eds. William A. Niskanen et al. (Chicago: Aldine, 1973), 211–245 and Glenn P. Jenkins, *Capital in Canada: Its Social and Private Performance 1965–1974*, Discussion Paper No. 98, Economic Council of Canada (Ministry of Supply and Services Canada, 1977).

[27]David F. Burgess, "The Social Discount Rate for Canada: Theory and Evidence," *Canadian Public Policy*, 7, no. 3 (Summer 1981), 383–394.

[28]David F. Bradford, "Constraints on Government Investment Opportunities and the Choice of Discount Rate," *American Economic Review*, 65, no. 5 (December 1975), 887–899. See also the *Journal of Environmental Economics and Management*, vol. 18S (1990).

[29]Randolph M. Lyon, "Federal Discount Policy, the Shadow Price of Capital, and Challenges for Reforms," *Journal of Environmental Economics and Management*, 18, no. 2, part 2 (March 1990), S29–S50, Appendix I.

[30]Charles R. Hulten and Frank C. Wykoff, "The Measurement of Economic Depreciation," in *Depreciation, Inflation, and the Taxation of Income from Capital*, Charles R. Hulten ed. (Washington, DC: Urban Institute Press, 1981), pp. 81–125.

[31]Mervyn A. King and Don Fullerton, eds., *The Taxation of Income from Capital: A Comparative Study of the United States, the United Kingdom, Sweden, and West Germany* (Chicago: University of Chicago Press, 1984), pp. 214–215.

[32]Bureau of the Census, *Statistical Abstract of the United States, 1990* (Washington, DC: U.S. Government Printing Office, 1990), p. 743.

[33]*Economic Report of the President, 1991* (Washington, DC: U.S. Government Printing Office, 1991), pp. 368–369.

[34]Median marginal state corporate tax rate was calculated from Table 22 of the Advisory Commission on Intergovernmental Relations, *Significant Features of Fiscal Federalism*, 1 (January 1990), 60–62. In addition to the marginal state corporate tax rate, corporations pay, on average, about 2 percent in real property taxes.

[35]Let x be the marginal state rate and y be the marginal federal rate. On each dollar of return, the firm pays x to the state and $(1 - x)y$ to the federal government so that the total marginal rate is $x + (1 - x)y = x + y - xy$. Thus, for our example, the marginal tax rate equals $0.34 + 0.06 - (0.34 \times 0.06) = 0.38$.

[36]As we discuss in Chapter 4, CBA does not treat depreciation (or capital cost allowance for taxation purposes) as an expense. However, the private sector does treat depreciation (capital cost allowance) as a cost (an expense) and deducts it from cash flows in order to arrive at net taxable income. Because depreciation does not entail cash outlays, we should "add it back" to net taxable income in order to obtain comparable cash flows (or, as in our example, add the depreciation rate to the pretax net return on net income in order to obtain comparable pretax gross rates of return). Adding the depreciation rate after adjusting for the marginal tax rate is consistent with the assumption that depreciation is fully deductible from cash flows in order to derive at net taxable income. If it were not, then it would be appropriate to add depreciation to the bond rate before adjusting for taxes. In our example, we assume implicitly that the average capital cost allowance rate equals the average physical rate at which assets depreciate. As we discuss in Chapter 4, the accounting depreciation of the capital assets involved with any particular project may differ significantly from the physical (economic) depreciation of these assets. But it is probably reasonable to assume these rates are similar on average.

[37]Assuming marginal state and local taxes are zero, investment funded by corporate bonds cannot have a pretax net rate of return of less than $0.0926/(1 - 0.34) = 14.03$ percent. Adjusting for expected infla-

tion yields $(0.1403 - 0.048)/1.048 = 8.8$ percent. Adding the estimated rate of depreciation of 10 percent gives an estimate of w of 18.8 percent. Assuming marginal state and local taxes are 10 percent, investment funded by corporate bonds cannot have a pretax net rate of return of less than $0.0926/(1 - 0.406) = 15.59$ percent. Adjusting for expected inflation yields $(0.1559 - 0.048)/1.048 = 10.3$ percent. Adding the estimated rate of depreciation of 10 percent gives an estimate of w of 20.3 percent.

[38]This illustration assumes that all costs and benefits occur on the first day of each period. Therefore, a net benefit of –$5 million occurs immediately, and annual net benefits of $2 million occur one, two, three, and four years from today. If it is more reasonable to assume the costs or benefits occur at the end of each period, then an adjustment must be made as we discuss in Chapter 4.

[39]See Office of Management and Budget, Circular A-94, March 1972. This rate was reaffirmed in 1978 and 1988.

[40]Jeffrey A. Kolb and Joel D. Scheraga, "Discounting the Benefits and Costs of Environmental Regulations," *Journal of Policy Analysis and Management*, 9, no. 3 (Summer 1990), 381–390. The authors argue for applying the shadow price of capital approach through two steps: first, annualizing project costs over the expected lifetime of the project and, second, discounting by the marginal rate of time preference (p. 384).

[41]See Office of Management and Budget, "Principles, Standards, and Procedures for Water and Related Land Resource Planning" and S.80-A of the U.S. Water Resources Development Act of 1974.

[42]See Treasury Board Secretariat, *Benefit-Cost Analysis Guide* (March 1976).

[43]See, for example, Verne W. Loose, ed., *Guidelines for Benefit-Cost Analysis*, Environment and Land Use Committee Secretariat (Victoria, British Columbia: The Queen's Printer, June 1977).

[44]See Glenn Jenkins, "The Measurement of Rates of Return and Taxation for Private Capital in Canada," in *Benefit Cost and Policy Analysis*, eds. William A. Niskanen et al. (Chicago: Aldine, 1973), pp. 211–245 and Glenn P. Jenkins, *Capital in Canada: Its Social and Private Performance 1965–1974*, Discussion Paper No. 98, Economic Council of Canada (Ministry of Supply and Services Canada, 1977).

[45]David F. Burgess, "The Social Discount Rate for Canada: Theory and Evidence," *Canadian Public Policy*, 7, no. 3 (Summer 1981), 383–394.

APPENDIX NOTES

[1]See, for example, Kenneth J. Arrow and Robert C. Lind, "Uncertainty and the Evaluation of Public Investment Decisions," *American Economic Review*, 60, no. 3 (June 1970), 364–378, who argue for using a riskless rate, and Martin J. Bailey and Michael C. Jensen, "Risk and the Discount Rate for Private Investment," in *Studies in the Theory of Capital Markets*, ed. Michael C. Jensen (New York: Praeger, 1972), pp. 269–293, who argue in favor of using a rate that varies with risk.

[2]For the implications of the CAPM to private-sector capital budgeting, see Mark E. Rubinstein, "A Mean-Variance Synthesis of Corporate Financial Theory," *Journal of Finance*, 28, no. 1 (March 1973), 167–181.

[3]A well-respected finance text suggests that $E(r_m) - r_f = 8.3$ percent; see Richard Brealey and Stewart Myers, *Principles of Corporate Finance*, 2nd ed. (New York: McGraw-Hill, 1984), p. 131. However, this may be too high.

6

DEALING
WITH UNCERTAINTY:
EXPECTED VALUE
AND SENSITIVITY ANALYSIS

Cost-benefit analysis requires us to predict the future. Whether or not it is desirable to begin a project depends on what we expect will happen after we have begun. But, as mere mortals, we rarely are able to make precise predictions about the future. Indeed, in many situations analysts can be certain that circumstances largely beyond their clients' control, such as epidemics, floods, bumper crops, or fluctuations in international oil prices, will greatly affect the benefits and costs that would be realized from proposed policies. How can analysts reasonably take account of these uncertainties in CBA?

In this chapter, we sketch two ways of dealing with uncertainty: *expected value analysis* and *sensitivity analysis*. Expected value analysis is a way of taking account of the dependence of benefits and costs on the occurrence of specific contingencies, or "states of the world." Sensitivity analysis is a way of acknowledging uncertainty about the values of important parameters in our predictions. Sensitivity analysis should be a component of almost *any* CBA; expected value analysis should be used when it is reasonable to conceptualize the future in terms of a number of distinct contingencies of relevance to predictions of costs and benefits.

EXPECTED VALUE ANALYSIS

One can imagine several types of uncertainty about the future. At the most profound level, one might not be able to specify the full range of relevant circumstances that may occur. Indeed, the human and natural worlds are so complex that one cannot hope to anticipate every possible future circumstance. Yet, in many situations of relevance to one's daily life and public policy, it is reasonable to characterize the future in terms of a number of distinct contingencies. For example, in deciding whether or not to take an umbrella to work, one might reasonably divide the future into two contingencies: Either it will or will not rain sufficiently to make the umbrella useful. Of course, other relevant contingencies can be imagined—it will be a dry day, but one may or may not be the victim of an attempted mugging in which the umbrella would prove valuable in self-defense. Yet if these additional contingencies are extremely unlikely, it is often reasonable to leave them out of one's model of the future. Modeling the future as a set of relevant contingencies involves yet another narrowing of uncertainty: How likely are each of the contingencies? If one is willing to assign probabilities of occurrence to each of the contingencies, then uncertainty about the future becomes a problem of *risk*. Problems of risk can be incorporated into CBA through expected value analysis.

Contingencies and Their Probabilities

Modeling uncertainty as risk begins with the specification of a set of *contingencies* that are *exhaustive* and *mutually exclusive*. Contingencies can be thought of as possible events, outcomes, or states of the world such that one and only one of the relevant set of possibilities will actually occur. What makes a set of contingencies the basis of an appropriate model for conducting a CBA of a policy?

One important consideration is that the contingencies capture the full range of likely variation in net benefits of the policy. So, for example, in evaluating an oil stockpile for use in the event of an oil price shock sometime in the future, one would want to consider at least two contingencies: There never will be an oil price shock (a situation in which the policy is likely to result in net losses) and there will be a major price shock (a situation in which the policy is likely to result in net gains).

Another consideration is how well the contingencies represent the possible outcomes between the extremes. In some circumstances, the possible contingencies can be listed exhaustively so that they are fully representative. More often, however, they sample an infinite number of possibilities. In these circumstances, each contingency can be thought of as a *scenario*—a description of a possible future. Do the specified contingencies provide a sufficient variety of scenarios to convey the possible futures adequately? If so, then the contingencies are representative.

Figure 6.1 illustrates the representation of a continuous scale with discrete contingencies. The horizontal axis gives the number of inches of summer rainfall in an agricultural region. The vertical axis gives the net benefits of a water storage system, which increase as the amount of rainfall decreases. Imagine that an analyst were to represent uncertainty about rainfall with only two contingencies: "excessive" and "deficient." The excessive contingency assumes 22 inches of rainfall, which would yield zero net benefits from the storage system. The deficient contingency assumes zero inches of rainfall, which would yield $4.4 million in net benefits. If the relationship between rainfall and net benefits follows the straight line labeled A, and all the rainfall amounts between zero and 22 are equally likely, then the average of net benefits over the full continuous range would be $2.2 million. If the analyst assumed that each of the contingencies were equally likely, then the average over the two contingencies would also be $2.2 million so that using two scenarios would be adequately representative.[1]

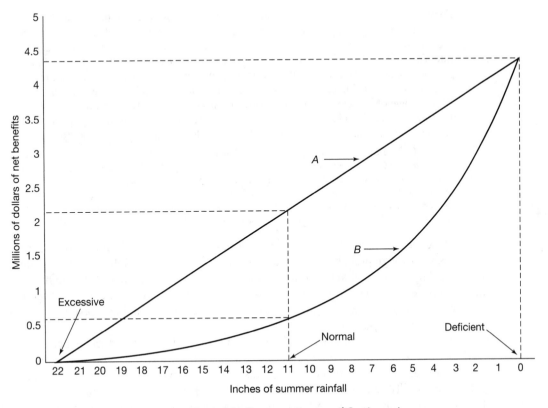

Figure 6.1   Representativeness of Contingencies

Now imagine that the net benefits follow the curved line labeled B. Again assuming that all rainfall amounts between zero and 22 inches are equally likely, the average of net benefits over the full continuous range would only be about $1.1 million, so that using only two contingencies would grossly overestimate the average net benefits from the storage system. Adding "normal" as a contingency that assumes 11 inches of rainfall and averaging net benefits over all three contingencies yields net benefits of $1.6 million, more representative than the average calculated with two contingencies, but still a considerable overestimate. Even more contingencies are desirable. For example, moving to five equally spaced contingencies gives an average of $1.3 million, much closer yet to the average over the continuous range.[2]

■ **EXHIBIT 6.1**

In their evaluation of alternative government oil stockpiling programs in the early 1980s, Glen Sweetnam and colleagues at the U.S. Department of Energy modeled the uncertainty surrounding oil market conditions with five contingencies: *slack market*—oil purchases for the U.S. stockpile of up to 1.5 million barrels per day (mmb/d) could be made without affecting the world oil price; *tight market*—oil purchases increase world price at the rate of $3.60 per mmb/d; *minor disruption*—loss of 1.5 mmb/d from the world market; *moderate disruption*—loss of 6.0 mmb/d; *major disruption*—loss of 12.0 mmb/d.

For each of the 24 years of their planning horizon, they assumed that the probabilities of each of the contingencies occurring depended only on the contingency that occurred in the previous year. For each year, they calculated the social surplus in the U.S. oil market conditional on each of the five market contingencies and change in the size of the stockpile.

The model they constructed allowed them to answer the following questions: For any current market condition and stockpile size, what change in stockpile size maximizes the present value of expected net benefits? How much storage capacity should be constructed? How fast should it be added? The model and the answers it provided were influential in policy debates concerning expansion of the U.S. stockpile, the Strategic Petroleum Reserve.

SOURCES: Glen Sweetnam, "Stockpile Policies for Coping with Oil-Supply Disruptions," in *Policies for Coping with Oil-Supply Disruptions*, eds. George Horwich and Edward J. Mitchell (Washington, DC: American Enterprise Institute for Public Policy Research, 1982), pp. 82–96. On the role of the model in the policy-making process, see Hank C. Jenkins-Smith and David L. Weimer, "Analysis as Retrograde Action: The Case of Strategic Petroleum Reserves," *Public Administration Review*, 45, no. 4 (July/August 1985), 485–494.

Once we have specified a tractable but representative set of contingencies, the next task is to assign probabilities of occurrence to each of them. To be consistent with the logical requirement that the contingencies taken together are exhaustive and mutually exclusive, the probabilities that we assign must sum to exactly one. Thus, if there are three contingencies, C_1, C_2, and C_3, we must assign corresponding probabilities p_1, p_2, and p_3 such that $p_1+p_2+p_3 = 1$.

The probabilities may be based solely on historically observed frequencies, on subjective assessments by clients, analysts, or other experts based on a variety of information and theory, or on both.[3] For example, return to the contingencies in Figure 6.1: agriculturally "excessive," "normal," and "deficient" precipitation in a river valley for which a water storage system has been proposed. The national weather service may be able to provide data on average annual rainfall over the last century that allows an analyst to estimate the probabilities of the three levels of precipitation from their historical frequencies. If such data were not available, then the analyst would have to base the probabilities on expert opinion, comparison with similar valleys in the region for which data are available, or some other subjective assessment. As such subjective assessments are rarely made with great confidence, it is especially important to investigate the sensitivity of the results to the particular probabilities chosen.

Calculating the Expected Value of Net Benefits

The specification of contingencies and their respective probabilities allows us to calculate the *expected net benefits* of a policy. We do so by first predicting the net benefits of the policy under each contingency and then taking the weighted average of these net benefits over all the contingencies, where the weights are the respective probabilities that the contingencies occur. Specifically, for n contingencies, let B_i be the benefits under contingency i, C_i be the costs under contingency i, and p_i be the probability of contingency i occurring, then the expected net benefits, $E[NB]$, are given by the formula:

$$E[NB] = p_1(B_1-C_1) + ... + pn(Bn-C_n) \qquad (6.1)$$

which is just the expected value of net benefits over the n possible outcomes.[4]

Figure 6.2 draws attention to the important assumption that underlies the use of expected costs and benefits in CBA: Expected values are equivalent to certain amounts of the same size called *certainty equivalents*. The upper branch represents an alternative course of action with different net benefits under each of three contingencies: NB_1 occurring with probability P_1, NB_2 occurring with probability P_2, and NB_3 occurring with probability P_3. For concreteness, imagine that the upper branch represents the decision to replace an obsolete fossil fuel power plant with a nuclear one. If it is completed early (contingency 1 with P_1=.1), then it will yield large net benefits (NB_1=$10 billion). If it is completed on time (contingency 2 with P_2=.4), then it will yield moderate net benefits (NB_2=$5 billion). If it is completed late (contingency 3 with P_3=.5), then it will yield negative net benefits (NB_3=–$2 billion). Thus, the expected net benefit from the decision to build the nuclear plant is $E(NB_U)$=$2 billion [(.1)($10 billion)+(.4)($5 billion)+(.5)(–$2 billion)].

The lower branch represents the decision to replace the obsolete facility with a new fossil fuel plant. Assume that it guarantees a net benefit, NB_L, of $2 billion.

In CBA, it is common practice to treat expected values like $E(NB_U)$ and certain amounts like NB_L as fully commensurate. Thus, because they each equal the same amount, $2 billion, CBA would rank them as equally efficient. Chapter 7 considers the appropriateness of treating expected values and certainty equivalents as commensurate. It explains that doing so is not conceptually correct in measuring willingness-to-pay in circumstances in which individuals face uncertainty. Nevertheless, it argues that in practice, *treating expected values and certain amounts as commensurate is generally reasonable when either the pooling of risk over the collection of policies, or the pool-*

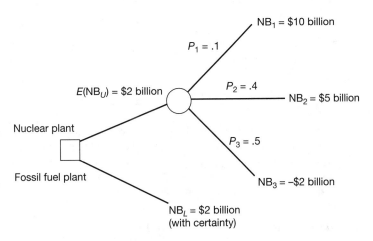

Basic assumption of applied CBA:

Expected values are commensurate with certain amounts of the same size. (CBA is indifferent between the upper and lower branches.)

Figure 6.2   Expected Value and Its Certainty Equivalent

ing of risk over the collection of persons affected by a policy, will make the actually realized values of costs and benefits close to their expected values. For example, a policy that affects the probability of highway accidents involves reasonable pooling of risk across many drivers so that realized values will be close to expected values. In contrast, a policy that affects the risk of nuclear accident does not involve pooling so that the realized value of accident costs may be very far from their expected value. As discussed in Chapter 7, such unpooled risk may require an adjustment to expected benefits called option value.

■ **EXHIBIT 6.2**

Hepatitis B poses a serious risk to health-care workers. A CBA of a proposed regulation that would require employers to offer free vaccination to workers exposed 12 or more times per year to the hepatitis B virus involved the estimation of a large number of probabilities, including rates of exposure, vaccination effectiveness, postexposure treatment effectiveness, natural immunity, worker turnover, and voluntary participation. The estimated expected cost to an individual who develops hepatitis B ($21,000) was based on the probabilities of various acute and chronic conditions involving different medical costs, lost employment, and reduced life expectancy:

Acute Disease	Probability	Cost/Case ($)
Subclinical	.330	0
Mild, not hospitalized	.420	380
Moderate, not hospitalized	.200	3,900
Severe, hospitalized	.050	30,000
Chronic Disease		
No chronic symptoms	.956	0
Chronic persistent hepatitis	.020	2,000
Chronic active hepatitis	.020	865,000
Primary hepatic cancer	.004	300,000

Measuring benefits as avoided costs of medical care, prophylaxis, and lost productivity yield annual net benefits for the regulation of $63.6 million.

Source: Josephine A. Mauskopf, Cathy J. Bradley, and Michael T. French, "Benefit-Cost Analysis of Hepatitis B Vaccine Programs for Occupationally Exposed Workers," *Journal of Occupational Medicine*, 33, no. 6 (June 1991), 691–698.

Decision Trees and Expected Net Benefits

The basic procedure for expected value analysis, taking weighted averages over contingencies, can be directly extended to situations in which costs and benefits accrue over multiple years, as long as the risks in each year are independent of the realizations of risks in previous years. Consider, for example, a CBA of a dam with a 20-year life. Assume that the costs and benefits of the dam depend only on the contingencies of below-average rainfall and above-average rainfall in the current year. Additionally, if the analyst is willing to make the plausible assumption that the amount of rainfall in any year does not depend on the rainfall in previous years, then the analyst can simply calculate the present value of expected net benefits for each year and calculate the present value of this stream of net benefits in the usual way.

The basic expected value procedure cannot be so directly applied when either the net benefits accruing under contingencies or the probabilities of the contingencies depend on the contingencies that have previously occurred. For example, above-average rainfall in one year may make the irrigation benefits of a dam less in the next year because of accumulated ground water. In the case of a policy to reduce the costs of earthquakes, the probability of a major earthquake may change each year depending on the mix of earthquakes that occurred in the previous year.

Such situations require a more flexible framework for handling risk than basic expected value analysis. *Decision analysis* provides the needed framework.[5] Though it takes us too far afield to present decision analysis in any depth here, we sketch its general approach and present a simple illustration that demonstrates its usefulness in CBA. A number of book-length treatments of decision analysis are available for those who wish to pursue this topic in more depth.[6]

Decision analysis proceeds in two basic stages. First, one specifies the logical structure of the decision problem in terms of sequences of decisions and realizations of contingencies using a diagram, called a *decision tree*, that links an initial decision (the trunk) to final outcomes (branches). Second, one works backward from final outcomes to the initial decision, calculating expected values of net benefits across contingencies and pruning dominated branches (i.e., eliminating branches with lower expected values of net benefits).

Consider a vaccination program against a particular type of influenza that involves various costs.[7] The objective of minimizing costs is equivalent to maximizing net benefits. The costs of the program result from immunization expenditures and possible adverse side effects; the benefits consist of the adverse health effects that are avoided if an epidemic occurs. This flu may infect a population over the next two years before sufficient immunity develops worldwide to stop its spread. Figure 6.3 presents a simple decision tree for a CBA of this vaccination program. The tree should be read from left to right to follow the sequence of decisions, denoted by □, and random selections of contingencies, denoted by O. The tree begins with a decision node, the square labeled 0 at the extreme left. The upper bough represents the decision to implement the vaccination program this year; the lower bough represents the decision not to implement the program this year.

Upper bough: the vaccination program. Follow the upper bough first. If the program is implemented, then it will involve direct administrative costs, C_a, and the costs of adverse side effects, such as contracting the influenza from the vaccine itself, suffered by those who are vaccinated, C_s. Note that C_s, like most of the other costs in this example, is itself an expected cost based on the probability of the side effect, the cost to persons suffering the side effect, and the number of persons vaccinated. The

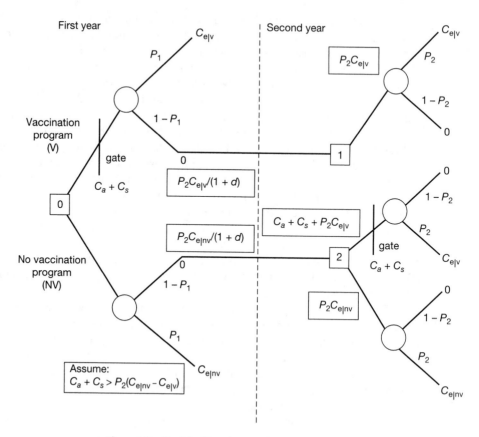

Figure 6.3 Decision Tree for Vaccination Program Analysis

solid vertical line on the bough can be thought of as a toll gate at which point the program costs, $C_a + C_s$, are incurred. A chance node, represented by a circle, appears next. Either the influenza infects the population (the upper branch, which occurs with probability P_1 and results in costs $C_{e|v}$, where the subscript should be read as "epidemic occurs given the vaccination program has been implemented") or the influenza does not infect the population (the lower branch, which occurs with probability $1 - P_1$ and results in zero costs at that time). If the influenza does occur, then the population will be immune in the next year. Thus, the upper branch does not continue. If the influenza does not occur, then there is still a possibility that it might occur in the next year. Therefore, the lower branch continues to the second year, where the square labeled 1 notes the beginning of the second year. It leads directly to another chance node that specifies the two contingencies in the second year: The influenza infects the population (the upper subbranch, which occurs with probability P_2 and results in costs $C_{e|v}$) or the influenza does not infect the population (the lower subbranch, which occurs with probability $1 - P_2$ and results in zero costs).[8]

Lower bough: no vaccination program. We now return to the initial decision node and follow the lower bough representing no vaccination program in the first year. Initially there is no cost associated with this decision. A chance node follows with two branches: Either the influenza infects the population (the lower branch, which occurs with probability P_1 and results in costs C_{elnv}) or the influenza does not infect the population (the upper branch, which occurs with probability $1-P_1$ and results in zero costs).[9] If the influenza does occur, then there is no need to consider the next year. If it does not occur, then the tree continues to decision node 2: Either implement the vaccination program in the second year (the upper subbranch crossing the gate where program costs C_a+C_s are incurred) or do not implement it (the lower subbranch).

If the program is implemented, then a chance node occurs: The influenza infects the population (the lower twig, which occurs with probability P_2 and results in costs C_{elv}) or the influenza does not infect the population (the upper twig, which occurs with probability $1-P_2$ and results in zero costs). We complete the tree by considering the parallel chance node following the decision not to implement the program: The influenza infects the population (the lower twig, which occurs with probability P_2 and results in costs C_{elnv}) or the influenza does not infect the population (the upper twig, which occurs with probability $1-P_2$ and results in zero costs).

Solving the decision tree. To solve the decision problem, we work from right to left, replacing chance nodes with their expected costs and pruning off parallel nodes that are dominated. Consider the chance node following decision node 1. Its expected cost, calculated by the expression $P_2C_{elv}+(1-P_2)0$, equals P_2C_{elv}.

Now consider the chance nodes following decision node 2. The lower chance node, following a decision not to implement the vaccination program, has an expected cost of P_2C_{elnv}. The upper chance node has an expected cost of P_2C_{elv}, to which must be added the certain payment of program costs so that the full expected cost of implementing the vaccination program in the second year is $C_a+C_s+P_2C_{elv}$. We can now compare the expected cost of the two possible decisions at node 2: P_2C_{elnv} versus $C_a+C_s+P_2C_{elv}$. Assume that program costs are greater than the expected cost reduction from the vaccine, that is, $C_a+C_s>P_2(C_{elnv}-C_{elv})$, then P_2C_{elnv} is smaller than $C_a+C_s+P_2C_{elv}$ so that not implementing the program dominates implementing it.[10] We can now prune off the upper sub-branch. If we reach decision node 2, then we know that we can obtain expected second-year costs of P_2C_{elnv}.

At decision node 0 the expected costs of implementing the vaccination program (i.e., following the upper bough) consist of direct costs plus the expected costs of the following chance node, which now has the payoffs C_{elv} if there is an epidemic and the discounted expected value of node 1, $P_2C_{elv}/(1+d)$, if there is not an epidemic. Note that because this latter cost occurs in the second year, it is discounted using rate d. Thus, the present value of expected costs from implementing the vaccination program is given by

$$EC_v = C_a + C_s + P_1C_{elv} + (1-P_1)P_2C_{elv}/(1+d) \tag{6.2}$$

where the last term incorporates the expected costs from the second year.

The expected costs of not implementing the vaccination program are calculated in the same way: The payoff if there is not an epidemic becomes the discounted expected costs from decision node 2, $P_2 C_{\text{elnv}}/(1+d)$; the payoff if there is an epidemic is still C_{elnv}. Therefore, the expression

$$EC_{\text{nv}} = P_1 C_{\text{elnv}} + (1-P_1)P_2 C_{\text{elnv}}/(1+d)$$

gives the present value of expected costs of not implementing the program.

The final step is to compare the present values of expected costs for the two possible decisions at node 0. We prune the bough with the larger present value of expected costs. The remaining bough is the optimal decision.

As an illustration, suppose that we have gathered data suggesting the following values for parameters in the decision tree: $P_1=.4$, $P_2=.2$, $d=.05$, $C_{\text{elv}}=.5C_{\text{elnv}}$ (the vaccination program cuts the costs of influenza by half), $C_a=.1C_{\text{elnv}}$ (the vaccination costs 10 percent of the costs of the influenza), and $C_s=.01C_{\text{elnv}}$ (the side-effect costs are 1 percent of the costs of the influenza). For these values, $EC_{\text{v}}=.367C_{\text{elnv}}$ and $EC_{\text{nv}}= .514C_{\text{elnv}}$. Therefore, the vaccination program should be implemented in the first year because $EC_{\text{v}} < EC_{\text{nv}}$.

Calculating expected net benefits of the vaccination program. Returning explicitly to CBA, we can recognize the benefits of the vaccination program as the costs it avoids. Thus, the present value of expected net benefits of the vaccination program is simply $EC_{\text{nv}} - EC_{\text{v}}$, which in the numerical illustration presented previously equals $0.147C_{\text{elnv}}$. In Chapter 7, we return to the question of the appropriateness of expected net benefits as a generalization of net benefits in CBA.

Extending Decision Analysis

Decision analysis can be used to structure much more complicated analyses than the CBA of the vaccination program. Straightforward extensions include: more than two alternatives at decision nodes, more than two contingencies at chance nodes, more than two periods of time, and different probabilities of events in different periods. For example, analyses of the U.S. oil stockpiling program typically involve trees so large that they can only be fully represented and solved by computers.[11] Even in less complex situations, however, decision analysis can be very helpful in showing how risk should be incorporated into the calculation of expected net benefits.

SENSITIVITY ANALYSIS

Whether or not we structure a CBA explicitly in terms of contingencies and their probabilities, we always face some uncertainty about the magnitude of the impacts we predict and the values we assign to them. Our basic analysis usually submerges this uncertainty by using our most plausible estimates of these unknown quantities. These estimates comprise what is called the *base case*. The purpose of sensitivity analysis is to acknowledge the underlying uncertainty. In particular, it should convey how sensitive predicted net benefits are to changes in assumptions. If the sign of net benefits does not change when we consider the range of reasonable assumptions, then our analysis is *robust* and we can have greater confidence in its results.

Large numbers of unknown quantities, the usual situation in CBA, make the brute force approach of looking at all combinations of assumptions unfeasible. For example, the vaccination program analysis, which we further develop in the next section, involves 17 different uncertain numerical assumptions. If we looked at just three different values for each assumption, there would still be over 129 million different combinations of assumptions to consider.[12] Even if we could compute net benefits for all these combinations, we would still face the daunting task of sorting through the results and communicating them in an effective way.

We illustrate here three more manageable approaches to doing sensitivity analysis. First, we demonstrate *partial sensitivity analysis*: How do net benefits change as we vary a single assumption while holding all others constant? Partial sensitivity is most appropriately applied to what the analyst believes to be the most important and uncertain assumptions. It can be used to find the values of numerical assumptions at which net benefits equal zero, or just break even. Second, we consider *worst- and best-case analysis*: Does any combination of reasonable assumptions reverse the sign of net benefits? Analysts are generally most concerned about situations in which their most plausible estimates yield positive net benefits, but they want to know what would happen in a worst case involving the least favorable, or most conservative, assumptions. Third, we present *Monte Carlo sensitivity analysis*: What distribution of net benefits results from treating the numerical values of key assumptions as draws from probability distributions? The mean and variance, or spread, of the distribution of net benefits convey information about the riskiness of the project.

A Closer Look at the Vaccination Program Analysis

We illustrate these techniques by considering a more detailed specification of the costs relevant to the decision analysis of the vaccination program presented in Figure 6.3. We analyze a hypothetical program to vaccinate some residents of a county against a possible influenza epidemic.[13]

Consider the following general description of the program. Through an advertising and outreach effort by its Department of Health, the county expects to be able to recruit a large fraction of persons, mainly older residents in poor health who are at high mortality risk from influenza, and a much smaller fraction of the general population for vaccination. As the vaccine is based on a live virus, some fraction of those vaccinated will suffer an adverse reaction that, in effect, converts them to high-risk status and gives them influenza, a cost included in C_s. As the vaccine does not always confer immunity, often because it is not given sufficiently in advance of the exposure to the influenza virus, its effectiveness rate is less than 100 percent. Everyone who contracts the influenza must be confined to bed rest for a number of days. Analysts can value this loss as the average number of hours of work lost times the average wage rate for the county, though this procedure might overestimate the opportunity costs of time for older persons and underestimate the cost of the unpleasantness of the influenza symptoms for both groups. They can place a dollar value on the deaths caused by the influenza by multiplying the number of expected deaths times

TABLE 6.1   BASE-CASE VALUES FOR VACCINATION PROGRAM CBA

Parameter	Value [Range]	Comments
County Population (N)	380,000	Total population in the county
Fraction High Risk (r)	.06 [.04,.08]	One-half population over age 64
Low-Risk Vaccination Rate (v_l)	.05 [.03,.07]	Fraction of low-risk persons vaccinated
High-Risk Vaccination Rate (v_h)	.60 [.40,.80]	Fraction of high-risk persons vaccinated
Adverse Reaction Rate (α)	.03 [.01,.05]	Fraction vaccinated who become high risk
Low-Risk Mortality Rate (m_l)	.00005 [.000025,.000075]	Mortality rate for low-risk infected
High-Risk Mortality Rate (m_h)	.001 [.0005,.002]	Mortality rate for high-risk infected
Herd Immunity Effect (θ)	1.0 [.5,1.0]	Fraction of effectively vaccinated who contribute to herd immunity effect
Vaccine Effectiveness Rate (e)	.75 [.65,.85]	Fraction of vaccinated who develop immunity
Hours Lost (t)	24 [18,30]	Average number of work hours lost to illness
Infection Rate (i)	.25 [.20,.30]	Infection rate without vaccine
First-Year Epidemic Probability (p_1)	.40	Chance of epidemic in current year
Second-Year Epidemic Probability (p_2)	.20	Chance of epidemic next year
Vaccine Dose Price (q)	$9/dose	Price per dose of vaccine
Overhead Cost (o)	$120,000	Costs not dependent on number vaccinated
Opportunity Cost of Time (w)	$12/hour	Average wage rate in the county
Value of Life (L)	$3,000,000	Assumed value of life
Discount Rate (d)	.05	Real discount rate
Number High-Risk Vaccinations (V_h)	13,680	High-risk persons vaccinated: $v_h r N$
Number Low-Risk Vaccinations (V_l)	17,860	Low-risk persons vaccinated: $v_l(1-r)N$
Fraction Vaccinated (v)	.083	Fraction of total population vaccinated: $rv_h + v_l(1-r)$

the dollar value of life. The various numerical assumptions for the analysis appear in Table 6.1. Notice, for example, that the base case value used for each saved life is $3 million.

The benefits of vaccination arise through two impacts. First, those effectively vaccinated are immune to the influenza. Thus, the program targets persons with high mortality risk because they benefit most from immunity. Second, through what is known as the *herd immunity* effect, a positive externality, vaccinated persons reduce the risks of infection to those not vaccinated—thus, some low-risk persons are recruited for vaccination to increase the total fraction of the population that is vaccinated.[14] These two effects cause the expected costs of the epidemic with vaccination, C_{elv}, to be less than the expected costs of the epidemic without the vaccination program, C_{elnv}.

Table 6.2 relates the specific numerical assumptions in Table 6.1 to the parameters in Figure 6.3. From Table 6.2, we can see that the direct program costs, C_a, depend on the overhead (i.e., fixed) costs, o, and cost per vaccination, q, times the number of vaccinations given $(V_h + V_l)$. The costs of side effects, C_s, depend on the adverse reaction rate, α, the number vaccinated, and the cost per high-risk infection, $wt + m_h L$, where wt is the opportunity cost of lost labor and $m_h L$ is the cost of loss of life. The costs of the epidemic without the vaccination program, C_{elnv}, depend on the infection rate, i, the number of high-risk susceptibles, rN, and low-risk susceptibles, $(1-r)N$, and the costs per high- and low-risk infections. Finally, the cost of the epidemic with the vaccination program, C_{elv}, depends on the postvaccination infection rate, $i - \theta ve$, the number of high-risk individuals remaining susceptible, $rN - eV_h$, the number of low-risk individuals remaining susceptible, $(1-r)N - eV_l$, and the costs per low- and high-risk infections. Working through these formulas yields expected net benefits equal to $7.718 million (see Table 6.2) for the base-case assumptions presented in Table 6.1.

Partial sensitivity analysis. An important assumption in the analysis is the probability that the epidemic occurs. In the base case, we assumed that the probability of the epidemic in the next year, given no epidemic in the current year, p_2, is one-half the probability of the epidemic in the current year, p_1. To investigate the relationship between net benefits and the probability of epidemic, we vary p_1 (and, hence, by the preceding assumption, p_2) holding all other base-case values constant. Specifically, we vary p_1 from zero to 0.5 by increments of 0.05. We thereby isolate the marginal partial effect of changes in probability on net benefits.

The results of this procedure are displayed as the line labeled $L = \$3$ million in Figure 6.4. This label reminds us of another base-case assumption, the value of life equals $3 million, which we vary next. Because the equations underlying the calculation of net benefits were embedded in a spreadsheet on a personal computer, it was easy to generate the points needed to draw this line by simply changing the values of p_1 and recording the corresponding net benefits.

TABLE 6.2   FORMULAS FOR CALCULATING THE NET BENEFITS OF VACCINATION PROGRAM

Variable	Value (millions of dollars)	Formula
C_a	0.404	$o + (V_h + V_l)q$
C_s	3.111	$\alpha(V_h + V_l)(wt + m_h L)$
C_{elnv}	57.855	$i[rN(wt + m_h L) + (1-r)N(wt + m_l L)]$
C_{elv}	36.014	$(i - \theta ve)\{(rN - eV_h)(wt + m_h L) + [(1-r)N - eV_l](wt + m_l L)\}$
EC_v	22.036	$C_a + C_s + p_1 C_{elv} + (1-p_1)p_2 C_{elv}/(1+d)$
EC_{nv}	29.754	$p_1 C_{elnv} + (1-p_1)p_2 C_{elnv}/(1+d)$
$E[NB]$	7.718	$EC_{nv} - EC_v$

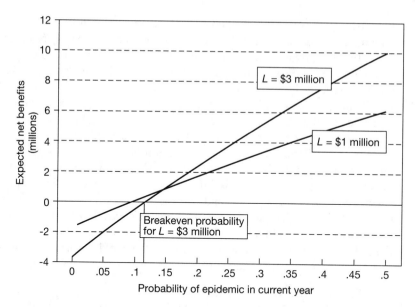

Figure 6.4   Expected Net Benefits of Vaccination

As expected, this line is upward sloping: The higher the probability of the epidemic, the larger the net benefits of the vaccination program. Note that for values of p_1 less than about .11, net benefits become negative (i.e., it lies below the solid horizontal line). In other words, if we think that the probability of the epidemic in the current year is less than .11, and we are willing to accept the other base-case assumptions, then we should not implement the program. The probability at which net benefits switch sign is called the *breakeven value*. Finding and reporting breakeven values for various parameters is often a useful way to convey their importance.

The line labeled L=$1 million repeats the procedure changing the base-case assumption of the value of life from $3 million per life to $1 million per life.[15] The graph thus conveys information about the impact of changes in two assumptions: Each line individually gives the marginal impact of epidemic probability; looking across lines conveys information about the impact of changes in the assumed value of life. As this illustration suggests, we can easily consider the sensitivity of net benefits to changing two assumptions at the same time by constructing families of curves in a two-dimensional graph. Though computers make it feasible to produce graphs that appear three dimensional, the added information that these graphs convey may confuse the viewer.

Figure 6.5 considers one more example of partial sensitivity analysis. It repeats the investigation of the marginal impact of epidemic probability on net benefits for two different assumptions about the size of the herd immunity effect, θ. The upper curve is for the base case that assumes a full herd immunity effect (θ=1). The lower curve assumes that only one-half of the effect occurs (θ=.5), perhaps because the pop-

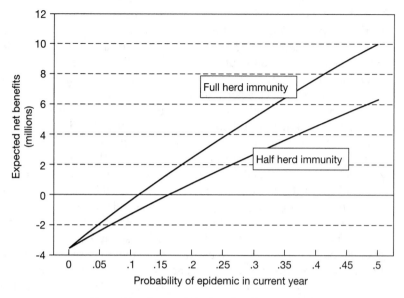

Figure 6.5   Expected Net Benefits of Vaccination

ulation does not mix sufficiently uniformly for the simple model of herd immunity assumed in the base case to apply. (Both cases return to the base-case assumption of $3 million per life saved.) Note that the breakeven probability rises to over 0.15 for the weaker herd immunity effect. Of course, we could give primary focus to the herd immunity effect by graphing net benefits against the size of the herd immunity effect, holding epidemic probability constant.

A thorough investigation of sensitivity ideally considers the partial marginal impacts of changes in each of the important assumptions. Unfortunately, there is a "chicken and egg" problem: Identifying the important assumptions often cannot be done before actually doing the sensitivity analysis because importance depends on the marginal response of net benefits to changes in assumptions, as well as the plausible range of the assumptions. In the analysis of the vaccination program, for example, partial sensitivity analysis might well be warranted for most of the assumptions presented in Table 6.1.

Worst- and best-case analysis.   The base-case assumptions, which generally assign the most plausible numerical values to unknown parameters, produce an estimate of net benefits that we think is most representative. In the vaccination program example, these assumptions yield fairly large positive net benefits. We can put a plausible lower bound on net benefits by considering the least favorable of the plausible range of values for each of the assumptions. In this way, we can calculate a pessimistic prediction of net benefits. Also, we can calculate an optimistic prediction of net benefits by using the most favorable assumptions. It should be kept in mind, however, that if the ranges really are plausible, then the probability of actually realizing net benefits as extreme as either the worst or the best case gets very small as the number of parameters gets large.

Worst-case analysis acknowledges that society, or specific decision makers, may be risk averse. That is, they often care not just about expected net benefits, the appropriate consideration in most cases, but also about the possible "downside." Furthermore, as we point out in Chapters 1 and 15, there are often cognitive limitations and bureaucratic incentives to generate optimistic forecasts. Worst-case analysis provides a useful check against these biases.

As a demonstration of worst-case analysis, we take the lower end of each of the ranges presented in Table 6.1 for r, v_l, v_h, m_l, m_h, θ, e, t, and i, and the higher end of the range for α. For example, we assume that r, the fraction of the population at high mortality risk, equals .04 rather than the base-case value of .06. (For the time being, we keep p_1, p_2, q, o, w, L, and d at their base-case values.) With worst-case assumptions, net benefits fall to $0.101 million. Though still positive, this more conservative estimate is almost two orders of magnitude (10^2) less than under the base-case assumptions.

Return to the question of the sensitivity of net benefits to the probability of epidemic. The breakeven probability rises from about 11 percent under the base-case assumptions to almost 37 percent under the more conservative worst-case assumptions. In other words, expected net benefits would no longer be positive if we assessed the probability of an epidemic to be only slightly less likely than 0.4, the assumed value under the base case.

Care must be taken in determining which are the most conservative assumptions. Under the base-case assumptions, for example, net benefits increase as our assumed value of life increases. Under the conservative assumptions, however, net benefits decrease as the value of life increases. This reversal in the direction of the marginal impact of the value of life occurs because the higher rate of adverse reactions, α, under the conservative case is sufficiently large so that the expected number of deaths is greater with the vaccination program (1.8 deaths) than without it (1.7 deaths).

More generally, caution is warranted when net benefits are a nonlinear function of a parameter. In such cases, the value of the parameter that either minimizes or maximizes net benefits may not be at the extreme of its plausible range. Close inspection of partial sensitivity graphs generally give a good indication of the general nature of the relationship, though they can sometimes be misleading because they depend on the particular assumed values of all other parameters. A more systematic approach is to inspect the functional form of the model used to calculate net benefits. When a nonlinear relationship is present, extreme values of assumptions may not necessarily result in extreme values of net benefits. Indeed, inspection of Table 6.2 indicates that net benefits are a quadratic function of vaccination rates v_l and v_h because they depend on C_{elv} which involves the product of direct effects and the herd effect. Under the base-case assumptions, for instance, net benefits would be maximized if all high-risk persons were vaccinated and 46 percent of low-risk persons were vaccinated. As these rates are well above those that could realistically be obtained by the program, we can reasonably treat the upper and lower bounds of vaccination rates as corresponding to extreme values of net benefits.

If the base-case assumptions generate negative net benefits, then it would have been reasonable to see if more optimistic, or best-case, assumptions produce positive net benefits. If the best-case prediction of net benefits is still negative, then we can be very certain that policy should not be adopted. If it is positive, then we may want to see if combinations of somewhat less optimistic assumptions can also sustain positive net benefits.

Monte Carlo sensitivity analysis.   Partial and extreme case sensitivity analyses have two major limitations. First, they may not take account of all the available information about assumed values of parameters. In particular, if we believe that values near the base-case assumptions are more likely to occur than values near the extremes of their plausible ranges, then the worst and best cases are highly unlikely to occur because they require the joint occurrence of a large number of independent low-probability events. Second, these techniques do not directly provide information about the variance, or spread, of the statistical distribution of realized net benefits. If we cannot distinguish between two policies in terms of expected values of net benefits, we may be more confident in recommending the one with the smaller variance because it has a higher probability of producing realized net benefits near the expected value.

Monte Carlo analysis provides a way of overcoming these problems. The name suggests the casinos of that famous gambling resort. It is apt because the essence of the approach is playing games of chance many times to elicit a distribution of outcomes. For many years Monte Carlo analysis has played an important role in the investigation of statistical estimators whose properties cannot be adequately determined through mathematical techniques alone. The falling opportunity cost of computing, especially the greater availability of flexible spreadsheet software for microcomputers, makes Monte Carlo analysis feasible for an ever increasing number of practicing policy analysts.

The basic steps for doing Monte Carlo analysis are as follows. First, specify probability distributions for all the important uncertain quantitative assumptions. For the Monte Carlo analysis of the vaccine program, we focus on the ten parameters with expressed ranges in Table 6.1. If we do not have theory or empirical evidence that suggests a particular distribution, then it is sometimes reasonable to specify a uniform distribution over the range. That is, we assume that any value between the upper and lower bound of plausible values is equally likely. For example, we assume that the distribution of the fraction of the population at risk, r, is uniformly distributed between .04 and .08. Often, though, we believe that values near the most plausible estimate should be given more weight. For example, assume that analysts believe that hours lost due to influenza follows a normal distribution. They could center it at the best estimate of 24 hours and set the standard deviation at 3.06 so that there is only a 5 percent chance of values falling outside the plausible range of 18 to 30 hours. (See Appendix 6.A for a brief discussion of working with probability distributions on spreadsheets.)

As discussed in Chapter 10, analysts can sometimes estimate unknown parameters statistically. They might then wish to use their 95 percent confidence intervals as their ranges. Commonly used regression models allow analysts to approximate the distribution of an unknown parameter as normal with mean and standard deviation given by their empirical estimates.

Second, we execute a trial by taking a random draw from the distribution for each parameter to arrive at a set of specific values for computing realized net benefits. For example, in the case of the vaccination program analysis, analysts have to determine which contingencies occur in the two periods. To determine if an epidemic occurs in the current year, they take a draw from a Bernoulli distribution with probability p_1. To implement this on a typical computer spreadsheet, they can draw from a distribution uniformly distributed between zero and one and compare it to the probability of an epidemic in the current year. If the random draw is smaller (larger) than the probability, then they assume that an epidemic does (not) occur in the current year. If an epidemic does not occur in the current year, then they follow a similar procedure to determine if an epidemic occurs in the second year. Three mutually exclusive realizations of net benefits are possible:

Epidemic in neither year: NB $= -(C_a + C_s)$

Epidemic in current year: NB $= -(C_a + C_s) + (C_{elnv} - C_{elv})$

Epidemic in next year: NB $= -(C_a + C_s) + (C_{elnv} - C_{elv})/(1 + d)$

where the values of the costs on the left-hand side depend on the particular values of the parameters drawn for this trial.

Note that these estimates of NB no longer involve expectations with respect to the contingencies of epidemics, though the cost estimates themselves are expected values. For each random draw, only one combination of contingencies can actually occur. (As discussed in Chapter 7, the epidemic poses a collective risk to the population, while the costs result from the realizations of independent risks to individuals in the population.)

Third, we repeat the trial described in the second step many times to produce a large number of realizations of net benefits. The average of the trials provides an estimate of the expected value of net benefits. An approximation of the probability distribution of net benefits can be obtained by breaking the range of realized net benefits into a number of equal increments and counting the frequency with which trials fall into each one. The resulting histogram of these counts provides a picture of the distribution. The more trials that go into the histogram, the more likely it is that the resulting picture gives a good representation of the true distribution of realized net benefits. Underlying this faith is the *law of large numbers*, which tells us that, as the number of trials approaches infinity, the frequencies will converge to the true underlying probabilities.

Figure 6.6 presents a histogram of 1,000 replications of random draws from the bracketed assumptions in Table 6.1. As noted earlier, the assumed distributions are all uniform except that for hours lost, w, which follows a normal distribution, and whether or not the epidemic occurs, which follows a Bernoulli distribution. The height of each bar is proportional to the number of trials that had net benefits falling in the corresponding increment.

The average of net benefits over the 1,000 trials is $5.48 million. This differs from our base-case calculation of $7.72 million because the base-case value of the herd immunity factor, θ, was set at one rather than at the middle of the plausible range. Repeating the Monte Carlo procedure with the herd immunity factor set to one yields

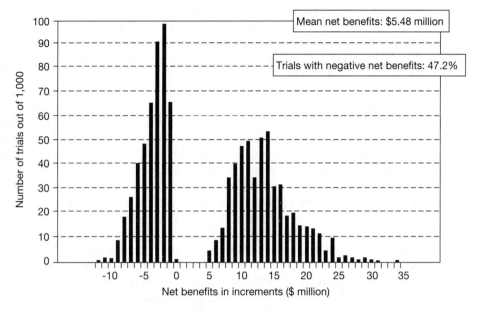

Figure 6.6   Histogram of Realized Net Benefits

an average of realized net benefits of $7.47 million, which is very close to the base-case calculation of expected net benefits.

In general, *if the calculation of net benefits involves sums of random variables, using their expected values yields the expected value of net benefits. If the calculation involves sums and products of random variables, then using their expected values yields the expected value of net benefits only if the random variables are uncorrelated.* In the Monte Carlo approach, correlations among variables can be taken into account by drawing parameter values from either multivariate or conditional distributions rather than from independent univariate distributions as in this example. Finally, *if the calculation involves ratios of random variables, then even independence (i.e., an absence of correlations) does not guarantee that using their expected values will yield the correct expected value of net benefits.* In this latter situation, the Monte Carlo approach is especially valuable because it provides a way of estimating the correct expected net benefits.

The histogram provides a visual display of the entire distribution of net benefits so that its spread and symmetry can be easily discerned. The trials themselves can be used to calculate directly the sample variance, standard error, and other summary statistics describing net benefits.

An interesting application of Monte Carlo analysis is the investigation of how reductions in the variances of assumptions affect the variance in the realized net benefits. For example, suppose an agency is deciding whether or not it is worthwhile to invest analytical resources in conducting a study that would reduce the estimate of the variance of hours lost. One could replicate the analysis with a smaller assumed variance of hours lost and compare the variance of the resulting distribution of realized net benefits with the distribution in Figure 6.6. A necessary condition for the investment of analytical resources to be worthwhile is a meaningful change in the distribution of realized net benefits.

The most striking feature of the histogram is that it portrays a bimodal distribution. If an epidemic occurs in either year, then the vaccination program in the first year has positive net benefits and it is as if we are drawing only from the right-most hump of the distribution. If an epidemic occurs in neither year, then the vaccination program has negative net benefits and it is as if we are drawing from the left-most hump of the distribution. The assumed probabilities of epidemic in the two years leads us to expect positive net benefits 52 percent of the time $[p_1+(1-p_1)p_2]$, which is close to the 52.8 percent of trials with positive net benefits in the Monte Carlo analysis.

The Monte Carlo results presented in Figure 6.6 treated several parameters as if they were certain. Most importantly, it treated the values of time and life as certain. As suggested in Chapter 10, we are in fact uncertain about these values. One approach would be to repeat the Monte Carlo analysis treating these parameters as random variables as well. In effect, we would be mixing uncertainty about predicted effects with uncertainty over how we value those effects. In some situations, this may be appropriate, but here it would probably be clearer to distinguish between these two types of uncertainty. To take account of our uncertainty about how we should value effects, we can simply repeat the original Monte Carlo analysis for a number of combinations of fixed values of time and life. Our results would be a collection of histograms like Figure 6.6 that would provide the basis for assessing how sensitive our assessment of net benefits is to changes in these critical values.

CONCLUSION

Uncertainty inheres to some degree in every CBA. Through expected value analysis, we attempt to average over the possible contingencies to arrive at expected net benefits as a plausible prediction of net benefits. In situations not explicitly involving risk, we often assume parameter values that are more appropriately thought of as draws from probability distributions rather than as certain parameters. The purpose of sensitivity analysis is to determine how net benefits change if these parameters deviate from their assumed values. Partial sensitivity analysis, the most commonly used approach, focuses attention on the consequences of alternative assumptions about key parameters. Extreme-case analysis examines whether combinations of plausible assumptions exist that reverse the sign of net benefits. Monte Carlo analysis attempts to estimate the distribution of net benefits by explicitly treating assumed parameter values as random variables. It is especially useful when the risk of the policy is of particular concern and the parameters have nonuniform distributions or the formula for the calculation of net benefits involves the parameters in other than simple sums. While the nature of the policy under consideration and the resources available to the analysts attempting to estimate its benefits and costs determine the appropriate form of sensitivity analysis, every CBA should be subjected to tests of its sensitivity to the assumptions it employs.

APPENDIX 6A

DOING MONTE CARLO SENSITIVITY ANALYSIS WITH A SIMPLE SPREADSHEET

Spreadsheets greatly reduce the labor needed to conduct sensitivity analysis. Usually the calculation of net benefits can be organized so that partial sensitivity analysis can be done by simply changing the value of a single spreadsheet cell. Though specialized software is available for doing Monte Carlo analysis, with a bit of effort it can be done with any simple spreadsheet that provides a random number generator.

Generating Random Variables

Most spreadsheets provide a function for generating random variables that are distributed uniformly from zero to one. To generate uniform random variables with other ranges, one simply multiplies the draw from the random variable uniformly distributed from zero to one by the desired range and then adds the minimum value. So, for example, to get the appropriate random variable for the fraction of high-risk persons in the population, r in Table 6.1, use the following formula: $.04+(.08-.04)z$ where z is the uniform random variable with range zero to one.

Some other distributions can be generated directly from the uniform distribution. For example, to obtain draws from an exponential distribution, one would simply take the natural logarithm of the uniformly distributed random variable and multiply it by the negative of the desired expected value of the exponential distribution. Yet the most useful distribution, the normal, cannot be directly generated by a simple formula in most spreadsheets.

The Central Limit Theorem motivates a procedure for generating normally distributed random variables. Very loosely speaking, sums of almost any sort of random variables tend to look normal. One can obtain fairly good approximations of draws from a standardized normal random variable through the Teichroew procedure.[1] First, sum 12 uniform random variables. Second, subtract six from the resulting sum to center it at zero. Third, divide the resulting difference by four to get a random variable we will call y. Fourth, the following polynomial yields a standardized normal random variable:

$$3.949846138y + 0.252408784y^3 + 0.076542912y^5$$
$$+ 0.008355968y^7 + 0.029899776y^9$$

These steps can be implemented as a formula in a single cell and copied to other cells as needed. For spreadsheets with macro capability, a macro can be written to implement this procedure. Indeed, macros that generate columns of normally distributed and other random variables make Monte Carlo analysis much faster.

The standardized normal distribution can be given any expected value and variance through simple transformations: Add a constant equal to the desired expected value and multiply by the square root of the desired variance. A range of 3.92 standard deviations includes 95 percent of the area of the normal distribution. To get the random variable we used in the Monte Carlo analysis for hours lost, t in Table 6.1, we added 24 to the standardized normal and multiplied it by $(30-18)/3.92$ so that there was only a 5 percent chance that a value of t would be generated outside the range 18 to 30.

Most books on mathematical statistics indicate how random variables distributed as chi-square, Student's t, F, and multivariate normal can be generated using combinations of normally distributed random variables. Similarly, the gamma distribution and the discrete Poisson distribution can be generated from exponential distributions. Discussion of these methods here would take us too far afield.

Steps in Monte Carlo Sensitivity Analysis

Once procedures have been developed for generating appropriately distributed random variables, the conduct of Monte Carlo analysis is straightforward, though, depending on the capabilities of the spreadsheet and the hardware upon which it operates, perhaps tedious. A simple approach follows.

First, construct a row of appropriate random variables and the formulas that use them to compute net benefits. The last cell in the row should contain net benefits.

Second, copy the entire row a number of times so that the last column of the resulting block contains different realizations of net benefits. Most spreadsheet and hardware arrangements should be able to handle blocks of about 100 rows without memory or time problems.

Third, save the realizations in a separate location.

Fourth, repeat steps 2 and 3 until an adequate number of realizations have been accumulated. In some spreadsheets, step 2 can be accomplished by simply entering a "recalculate" command. The adequate number depends on the variances of the random variables and the degree of confidence desired in the distribution of realized net benefits.

Fifth, analyze the accumulated realizations along the lines of Figure 6.6.

EXERCISES FOR CHAPTER 6

1. The initial cost of constructing a permanent dam (i.e., a dam that is expected to last forever) is $425 million. The annual net benefits will depend on the amount of rainfall: $18 million in a "dry" year, $29 million in a "wet" year, and $52 million in a "flood" year.

   Meteorological records indicate that over the last 100 years there have been 86 "dry" years, 12 "wet" years, and 2 "flood" years. Assume the annual benefits, measured in real dollars, begin to accrue at the end of the first year. Using the meteorological records as a basis for prediction, what are the net benefits of the dam if the real discount rate is 5 percent?

2. Use several alternative discount rate values to investigate the sensitivity of the present value of net benefits of the dam in exercise (1) to the assumed value of the real discount rate.

3. The prevalence of a disease among a certain population is .40. That is, there is a 40 percent chance that a person randomly selected from the population will have the disease. An imperfect test that costs $250 is available to help identify those who have the disease before actual symptoms appear. Those who have the disease have a 90 percent chance of a positive test result; those who do not have the disease have a 5 percent chance of a positive test. Treatment of the disease before the appearance of symptoms costs $2,000 and inflicts additional costs of $200 on those who do not actually have the disease. Treatment of the disease after symptoms have appeared costs $10,000.

   The government is considering the following possible strategies with respect to the disease:

S1. Do not test and do not treat early.

S2. Do not test and treat early.

S3. Test and treat early if positive and do not treat early if negative.

Find the treatment/testing strategy that has the lowest expected costs for a member of the population.

In doing this exercise, the following notation may be helpful: Let D indicate presence of the disease, ND absence of the disease, T a positive test result, and NT a negative test result.

Thus, we have the following information:

$$P(D) = .40, \text{ which implies } P(ND) = .60$$
$$P(T|D) = .90, \text{ which implies } P(NT|D) = .10$$
$$P(T|ND) = .05, \text{ which implies } P(NT|ND) = .95$$

This information allows calculation of some other useful probabilities:

$$P(T) = P(T|D)P(D)+P(T|ND)P(ND) = .39 \text{ and } P(NT) = .61$$
$$P(D|T) = P(T|D)P(D)/P(T) = .92 \text{ and } P(ND|T) = .08$$
$$P(D|NT) = P(NT|D)P(D)/P(NT) = .07 \text{ and } P(ND|NT) = .93$$

4. In exercise (3) the optimal strategy involved testing. Does testing remain optimal if the prevalence of the disease in the population is only .05? Does your answer suggest any general principle?

5. (Use of a spreadsheet program to do this exercise is strongly recommended.)

A town with a population of 164,250 persons who live in 39,050 households is considering introducing a recycling program that would require residents to separate paper from their household waste so that it can be sold rather than buried in a landfill like the rest of the town's waste. Two major benefits are anticipated: revenue from the sale of waste paper and avoided tipping fees (the fee that the town pays the owners of landfills to bury its waste). Aside from the capital costs of specialized collection equipment, household containers, and a sorting facility, the program would involve higher collection costs, inconvenience costs for households, and disposal costs for paper that is collected but not sold. The planning period for the project has been set at eight years, the expected life of the specialized equipment.

The following information has been collected by the town's sanitation department:

Waste Quantities: Residents currently generate 3.6 pounds of waste per person per day. This daily per capita amount has grown over the last 20 years at an average of 0.02 pounds per year. Small or no increases in the last few years, however, raise the possibility that levels realized in the future will fall short of the trend.

Capital Costs: The program would require an initial capital investment of $1,688,000. Based on current resale values, the scrap value of the capital at the end of eight years is expected to be 20 percent of its initial cost.

Annual Costs: The department estimates that the separate collection of paper will add an average of $6/ton to the cost of collecting household waste. Each ton of paper collected and not sold would cost $4 to return to the landfill.

Savings and Revenues: Under a long-term contract, tipping fees are currently $45 per ton with annual increases equal to the rate of inflation. The current local market price for recycled paper is $22/ton but has fluctuated in recent years between a low of $12 per ton and a high of $32 per ton.

Paper Recovery: The fraction of household waste made up of paper has remained fairly steady in recent years at 32 percent. Based on the experience of similar programs in other towns, it is estimated that between 60 and 80 percent of paper included in the program will be separated from other waste and 80 percent of the paper that is separated will be suitable for sale, with the remaining 20 percent of the collected paper returned to the waste stream for landfilling.

Household Separation Costs: The sanitation department recognized the possibility that the necessity of separating paper from the waste stream and storing it might impose costs on households. An average of 10 minutes per week per household of additional disposal time would probably be needed. A recent survey by the local newspaper, however, found that 80 percent of respondents considered the inconvenience of the program negligible. Therefore, the department decided to assume that household separation costs would be zero.

Discount Rate: The sanitation department has been instructed by the budget office to discount at the town's real borrowing rate of 6 percent. It has also been instructed to assume that annual net benefits accrue at the end of each of the eight years of the program.

a. Calculate an estimate of the present value of net benefits for the program.
b. How large would annual household separation costs have to be per household to make the present value of net benefits fall to zero?
c. Assuming that household separation costs are zero, conduct a worst-case analysis with respect to the growth in the quantity of waste, the price of scrap paper, and the percentage of paper diverted from the waste stream.
d. Under the worst-case assumptions of part (c), how large would the average yearly household separation costs have to be to make the present value of net benefits fall to zero?
e. Investigate the sensitivity of the present value of net benefits to the price of scrap paper.
f. Discuss how you would structure a Monte Carlo analysis of the present value of net benefits of the program.

NOTES

[1]A more realistic assumption (e.g., rainfall amounts closer to the center of the range are more likely) would not change this equality as long as the probability density function of rainfall is symmetric around 11 inches.

[2]The representativeness is very sensitive to the particular shape of the probability density function of rainfall. The use of two contingencies would be even less representative if amounts of rainfall near 11 inches were more likely than more extreme amounts.

[3]Bayes' theorem provides a rule for updating subjective probability estimates on the basis of new information. Let A and B be events. A basic axiom of probability theory is that

$$P(A \text{ and } B) = P(A|B)P(B) = P(B|A)P(A)$$

where $P(A \text{ and } B)$ is the probability of both A and B occurring, $P(A)$ is the probability of A occurring, $P(B)$ is the probability of B occurring, $P(A|B)$ is the conditional probability that A occurs given that B has occurred, and $P(B|A)$ is the conditional probability of B occurring given that A has occurred. It follows directly from the axioms that

$$P(A|B) = P(B|A)P(A)/P(B)$$

which is the simplest statement of Bayes' rule.

Its application is quite common in diagnostic tests. For example, we may know the frequency of a disease in the population, $P(A)$, the probability that a test will yield a positive result if randomly given to a member of the population, $P(B)$, and the conditional probability that, given the disease, the test will be positive, $P(B|A)$. We would thus be able to calculate, $P(A|B)$, the conditional probability that someone with a positive test has the disease.

Discussions of Bayes' rule can be found in almost any introductory text on probability and statistics. For a more advanced treatment, see S. James Press, *Bayesian Statistics: Principles, Models, and Applications* (New York: John Wiley and Sons, 1989).

[4]In the case of a continuous underlying dimension, such as price, the expected value of net benefits is calculated using integration, the continuous analog of addition. Let $NB(x)$ be the net benefits given some particular value of x, the underlying dimension. Let $f(x)$ be the probability density function over x. Then

$$E[NB] = \int NB(x)f(x)dx$$

where the integration is over the range of x.

[5]The term *decision analysis* was originally used to include both choice under risk (statistical decision analysis) and games against strategic opponents (game theory). Now it is commonly used to refer only to the former.

[6]We recommend Howard Raiffa, *Decision Analysis: Introductory Lectures on Choices under Uncertainty* (Reading, MA: Addison-Wesley, 1969), Morris H. DeGroot, *Optimal Statistical Decisions* (New York: McGraw-Hill, 1970), Robert L. Winkler, *Introduction to Bayesian Inference and Decision* (New York: Holt, Rinehart and Winston, 1972), and Robert D. Behn and James W. Vaupel, *Quick Analysis for Busy Decision Makers* (New York: Basic Books, 1982) as general introductions. For more direct application to CBA, see Miley W. Merkhofer, *Decision Science and Social Risk Management: A Comparative Evaluation of Cost-Benefit Analysis, Decision Analysis, and Other Formal Decision-Aiding Approaches* (Boston: D. Reidel Publishing Company, 1987).

[7]This example is hypothetical, though concern about influenza epidemics has been the subject of public policy debate in recent years. See, for example, Richard E. Neustadt and Harvey V. Fineberg, *The Swine Flu Affair: Decision-Making on a Slippery Disease* (Washington, DC: U.S. Government Printing Office, 1978), and David S. Fedson, "The Influenza Vaccination Demonstration Project: An Expanded Policy Goal," *Infection Control and Hospital Epidemiology*, 11, no. 7 (July 1990), 357–361.

[8]Note that in this example the probability of an epidemic in the second year is conditional on whether or not an epidemic occurred in the first year. If an epidemic has occurred in the first year, then the population gains immunity and there is zero probability of an epidemic in the second year. If an epidemic has not occurred, then there is some positive probability, p_2, that one will occur in the second year.

[9]Note the assumption that the probability of the influenza reaching the population, p_1, is independent of whether or not this particular population is vaccinated. This would not be a reasonable assumption if the vaccination were to be part of a national program that reduced the chances that the influenza would reach this population from some other vaccinated population.

[10]In this particular problem, it will never make sense to wait until the second year to implement the program if it is going to be implemented at all. If, however, the risk of side effects were expected to fall in the second year, say, because a better vaccine would be available, then delay could be optimal. In terms of the decision tree, we could easily model this alternative scenario by using different values of Cs in the current and next years.

[11]For a discussion of the application of decision analysis to the stockpiling problem, see David L. Weimer and Aidan R. Vining, *Policy Analysis: Concepts and Practice* (Englewood Cliffs, NJ: Prentice Hall, 1992), Chapter 12.

[12]Calculating the number of combinations: $3^{17} = 129,140,163$.

[13]For examples of CBA applied to hepatitis vaccine programs, see Josephine A. Mauskopf, Cathy J. Bradley, and Michael T. French, "Benefit-Cost Analysis of Hepatitis B Vaccine Programs for Occupationally Exposed Workers," *Journal of Occupational Medicine*, 33, no. 6 (June 1991), 691–698; Gary M. Ginsberg and Daniel Shouval, "Cost-Benefit Analysis of a Nationwide Neonatal Inoculation Programme against Hepatitis B in an Area of Intermediate Endemicity," *Journal of Epidemiology and Community Health*, 46, no. 6 (December 1992), 587–594; and Murray Krahn and Allan S. Detsky, "Should Canada and the United States Universally Vaccinate Infants against Hepatitis B?" *Medical Decision Making*, 13, no. 1 (January–March 1993), 4–20.

[14]Call the basic reproductive rate of the infection R_0. That is, each primary infection exposes R_0 individuals to infection. If i is the fraction of the population no longer susceptible to infection because of previous infection, then the actual reproductive rate is $R=R_0(1-i-v)$, where v is the fraction of the population effectively vaccinated. If R falls below one, then the infection dies out because, on average, each infection generates less than one new infection. Assuming that the population is homogeneous with respect to susceptibility to infection and that infected and noninfected individuals uniformly mix in the population, a rough estimate of the ultimate i for the population is given by the formula $i=1-1/R_0-v$ where $1-1/R_0$ is the estimate of the infection rate in the absence of the vaccine. For an overview, see Roy M. Anderson and Robert M. May, "Modern Vaccines: Immunisation and Herd Immunity," *The Lancet*, no. 8690 (March 1990), 641–645; and Joseph W.G. Smith, "Vaccination Strategy," in *Influenza, Virus, Vaccines, and Strategy*, Philip Selby ed. (New York: Academic Press, 1976), pp. 271–294.

[15]The $L=$ \$3 million and $L=$\$1 million lines cross because lives are at risk both from the vaccination side effects and from the epidemic. At low probabilities of epidemic, the expected number of lives saved from vaccination is negative so that net benefits are higher for lower values of life. At higher probabilities of epidemic, the expected number of lives saved is positive so that net benefits are higher for higher values of life.

APPENDIX NOTE

[1]For an explanation of the Teichroew procedure and methods for generating many other distributions from uniform random variables, see Thomas H. Naylor, Joseph L. Balintfy, Donald S. Burdick, and Kong Chu, *Computer Simulations Techniques* (New York: John Wiley & Sons, 1966).

7

OPTION PRICE, OPTION VALUE, AND QUASI-OPTION VALUE

In the actual practice of CBA, analysts almost always apply the Kaldor-Hicks criterion to expected net benefits in circumstances involving significant risks. They typically estimate changes in social surplus conditional on particular contingencies occurring, and then they compute an expected value over the contingencies. Economists, however, now generally consider *option price*, the amount that individuals are willing to pay for policies prior to the realization of contingencies, to be the theoretically correct measure of willingness-to-pay in circumstances of uncertainty. Whereas consumer surplus can be thought of as an *ex post* measure of welfare change in the sense that individuals value policies as if contingencies have actually occurred, option price is an *ex ante* welfare measure in the sense that consumers value policies without knowing which contingency will occur. These measures generally differ from one another. In this chapter, we consider the implications of the common use of expected social surplus, rather than option price, as the method for measuring benefits.

The central concern of this chapter is the conceptually correct measure of willingness-to-pay in circumstances in which individuals face uncertainty. Individuals may face uncertainties about their demand for a good, the supply of a good, or both. With respect to demand, one may be uncertain about one's future income, utility function (tastes), and the prices of other goods. For example, one's utility from skiing may depend on the sturdiness of one's knees, a physical condition that cannot be predicted with certainty. With respect to supply, one may be uncertain about the future quantity, quality, or price of a good. For example, the increase in the quality of fishing that will result from restocking a lake with game fish depends on such variable factors as weather and spills of toxic chemicals, and hence, is uncertain to some degree.

In contrast to Chapter 6, we limit our attention to uncertainties of direct relevance to individuals. We ignore uncertainties that are not of direct individual relevance, but instead arise because analysts must make predictions about the future to estimate measures of willingness-to-pay. In the context of the CBA of the vaccination program discussed in Chapter 6, for example, the probability of epidemic, the probability an unvaccinated individual will be infected, the probability a vaccinated individual will be infected, and the probability a vaccinated individual will suffer a side effect are exactly the sort of uncertainties considered in this chapter. The analyst's uncertainties about the magnitude of these probabilities, the appropriate shadow price of time, or the number of people who will choose to be vaccinated were adequately addressed in the discussion of sensitivity analysis presented in Chapter 6. Though these analytical uncertainties are usually of greatest practical concern in CBA, we seek here to provide the conceptual foundation required for understanding the appropriate measure of costs and benefits when individuals face significant uncertainties.

This chapter has four major sections. The first section introduces option price and clarifies its relationship to expected surplus. The second section introduces the concept of *option value*, the difference between option price and expected surplus, and reviews the theoretical literature that attempts to determine its sign. Although sometimes thought of as a conceptually distinct category of benefits, option value is actually an adjustment to account for the fact that benefits are usually measured in terms of expected surplus rather than in terms of option price. The third section provides a general assessment of the appropriateness of the use of expected surplus as a proxy for option price. The final section considers *quasi-option value*, a purported benefit category that captures the value of preserving options by delaying decisions until a future time when more information is available. Quasi-option value is best thought of as an adjustment to net benefits to account for misspecification of the decision problem facing the analyst rather than as a conceptually distinct category of benefits.

EX ANTE *WILLINGNESS-TO-PAY: OPTION PRICE*[1]

Viewing benefits (or costs) in terms of the willingness of individuals to pay to obtain desirable (or avoid undesirable) policy impacts provides a clear perspective on the appropriateness of treating expected net benefits as if they were certain amounts. By identifying the conceptually correct method for valuing uncertain costs and benefits, we can better understand the circumstances under which the use of expected net benefits is more or less appropriate.

There is now a near consensus among economists that the conceptually correct way to value the benefits of a policy in circumstances involving risk is to sum the *ex ante* amounts that individuals would be willing to pay to obtain the policy. In other words, we would rely on individuals to assess for themselves how they would trade payments that are certain for combinations of contingent payments.[2]

Imagine that each person, knowing the probabilities of each of the contingencies, would give a truthful answer to the following question: Prior to knowing which contingency will actually occur, what is the maximum amount that you would be willing to pay to obtain the policy? The answer to this question is what economists call the person's *option price* for the policy. If we think of the policy as a lottery having probabilities of various payoffs to the person, then the option price is the person's *certainty equivalent* of the lottery. By summing the option prices of all persons, we obtain the aggregate benefits of the policy, which can then be compared to its opportunity cost in the usual way. If the opportunity cost is not dependent on which contingency actually occurs, then we have fully taken account of risk by comparing the aggregate willingness-to-pay, which is independent of the contingency that actually occurs, with the certain opportunity cost.

Remember that in actual CBA, analysts typically measure benefits by first estimating the social surplus under each contingency and then taking the expected value of these amounts using the probabilities of the contingencies. How does this expected surplus measure compare to the option price? Assuming that individuals are risk averse, expected surplus can either underestimate or overestimate option price depending on the sources of risk. For an individual who is risk averse and whose utility function depends only on income, *expected surplus will underestimate option price for policies that reduce income risk and overestimate option price for policies that increase income risk.* The excess of option price over expected surplus for risk-reducing projects in the first of these circumstances can be thought of as the "insurance benefit" of the policy.

Table 7.1 shows the contingent payoffs for a policy, building a temporary dam that provides water for irrigation and thereby reduces the income risk faced by a farmer. Without the dam, the farmer will have income of $100 if it is wet and $50 if it is dry during the growing season; with the dam, the farmer's income will be $110 if it is wet and $100 if it is dry. Assuming that the dry and wet contingencies are equally likely, the variance of the farmer's income without the dam is $625 and the variance with the dam is only $25.[3] Contingent upon it being wet, the farmer would be willing to pay up to $10 to have the dam. Contingent upon it being dry, the farmer would be willing to pay up to $50 to have the dam. These amounts, $10 and $50, are the farmer's contingent surpluses for the dam. The farmer's expected surplus is thus $30, the expected value of these amounts.[4]

To find the farmer's option price, we first calculate the expected utility, EU, without the dam. We then find the certain payment with the dam that gives the farmer the expected utility without the dam. If we assume for illustrative purposes that the farmer's utility is given by the natural log of his or her income as in Table 7.1, then the expected utility without the dam equals 4.26 and the option price for the dam is $34.20, which exceeds the expected surplus of $30. Thus, if the opportunity cost of the project were $32 and the farmer were the only beneficiary, the common practice of using expected surplus would lead us to reject building the dam when, in fact, the option price indicates that building the dam would increase the farmer's utility.

The relationship between expected surplus and option price for the farmer is illustrated in Figure 7.1. The vertical axis indicates willingness-to-pay amounts if it is dry; the horizontal axis represents willingness-to-pay amounts if it is wet. The *willingness-to-pay locus* (the curved line) shows all of the combinations of contingent

TABLE 7.1   EXAMPLE OF A RISK-REDUCING PROJECT

	Policy		Probability of Contingency
Contingency	Dam	No Dam	
Wet	110	100	.5
Dry	100	50	.5
Mean	105	75	
Variance	25	625	

Surplus point:	$U(110 - S_w) = U(100)$ implies $S_w = 10$
	$U(100 - S_d) = U(50)$ implies $S_d = 50$
Expected surplus:	$E(S) = .5\ S_w + .5\ S_d = 30$
Expected utility of no dam:	$EU = .5\ U(100) + .5\ U(50)$
Willingness-to-pay locus:	(δ_w, δ_d) such that
	$.5\ U(110 - \delta_w) + .5\ U(100 - \delta_d) = EU$
Option price:	$.5\ U(110 - OP) + .5\ U(100 - OP) = EU$
	$EU = 4.26$ and $OP = 34.2$
	for $U(c) = \ln(c)$, where c is net income.
Comparison:	$OP > E(S)$

payments for the dam, based on knowledge of the probabilities of the contingencies but prior to knowing which one will actually occur, which give the farmer the same expected utility with the dam as without it.[5]

It may be helpful to think of the willingness-to-pay locus in the following way: Imagine that the government offers to build the dam if you sign a contract that states that you will pay the government X_d if it is dry and X_w if it is wet—this is a contingent contract because its terms depend on events that will not be known until sometime in the future. If you are just indifferent between signing and not signing this contract, then the amounts X_d and X_w give a point on your willingness-to-pay locus. The rest of the points on the locus represent other combinations of contingent payments that would also leave you indifferent between signing and not signing the contract.

The dotted line, which represents equal willingness-to-pay amounts under the contingencies, is called the *certainty line*. Again thinking in terms of a contract specifying future payments, a point on the certainty line can be thought of as specifying the same payment no matter whether it is wet or dry. The option price occurs where the willingness-to-pay locus intersects the certainty line. That is, the option price is the maximum certain payment that would be made to obtain the policy.

The surplus point always lies on the willingness-to-pay locus. The line passing through it with slope equal to the negative of the ratio of the probabilities of the contingencies is called a *fair bet line*.[6] All the points on the fair bet line have the same expected value. The point at which the fair bet line running through the surplus point intersects the certainty line gives the expected surplus.[7]

As long as the cost of the project does not depend on the contingency that occurs, it would be represented as a point on the certainty line. Only if the option price

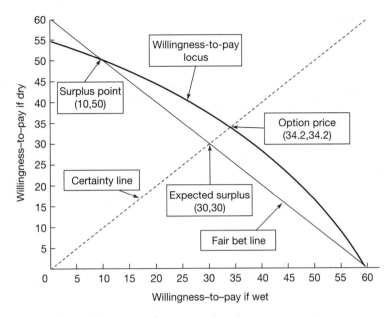

Figure 7.1   Risk-Reducing Project: Expected Surplus and Option Price

lies further to the northeast along the certainty line than does the cost would the project increase the farmer's welfare.

Figure 7.2 provides an alternative graphical representation of option price. The curved line gives the farmer's utility as a function of income. In the absence of a dam, the farmer realizes income of $50 dollars if it is dry and $100 if it is wet. Because the probabilities of wet and dry are each one-half, the expected utility of no dam can be found as the point midway between the utilities of these no-dam incomes. The point on the vertical axis labeled EU = 4.26 is exactly A away from each of the contingent utilities. As it is midway between them, it equals the expected utility. If the dam is built, then the farmer realizes income of $100 if it is dry and $110 if it is wet. The option price for the dam is how much income the farmer could give up for certain with the dam to obtain the same expected utility as without it. The arrows marked OP=34.2 shift the contingent incomes with the dam by subtracting $34.2 from each so that the net contingent incomes are $65.8 and $75.8. The utilities of these net incomes are each B away from 4.26 so that their expected utility equals the expected utility of no dam. Thus, either no dam or a dam with a certain payment of $34.2 gives the farmer the same expected utility.

Table 7.2 describes a policy involving construction of a bridge in an earthquake-prone area, which involves an increase in income risk. As shown in the table and illustrated in Figure 7.3, the expected surplus of $84 exceeds the option price of $71.1. Thus, if the opportunity cost of the bridge were a certain $75 and the person were the only beneficiary, the option price indicates that building it would reduce the person's expected utility if he or she actually had to pay the opportunity cost of its construction. Hence, the bridge should not be built even though the expected surplus from building it is positive.

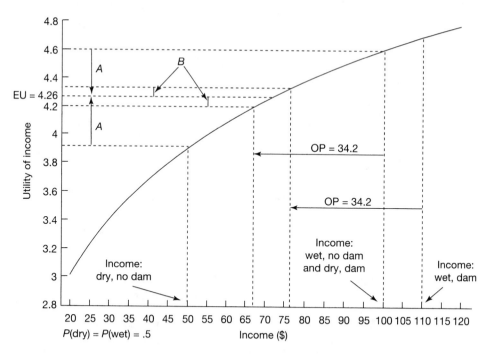

Figure 7.2 Utility Function and Option Price for Risk-Decreasing Project

These comparisons show option price rather than expected surplus to be the appropriate benefit measure in circumstances of uncertainty. Is this generally true? The answer to this question requires a clearer specification of the institutional environment of policy choice.

The key consideration concerns the availability of insurance against the risks in question. *If complete and actuarially fair insurance is unavailable against the relevant risks, then option price is the conceptually correct measure of benefits.* Insurance is complete if individuals can purchase sufficient coverage to eliminate their risks entirely. It is actuarially fair if its price depends only on the true probabilities of the relevant contingencies. In the case of two contingencies, with the probability of contingency 1 equal to p and the probability of contingency 2 equal to $1 - p$, actuarially fair insurance would allow the individual to trade contingent income in contingency 1 for contingent income in contingency 2 at a price of $p / (1 - p)$. For example, if p equals .2, then the price of insurance equals .25 (.2/.8) so that to increase income in contingency 2 by \$25, the individual would have to give up \$100 in contingency 1. Graphically, the availability of actuarially fair insurance means that individuals could move along the fair bet lines shown in Figures 7.1 and 7.3 through purchases of insurance.

Complete and actuarially fair insurance is rarely available in the real world.[8] The problem of *moral hazard*, the changes in risk-related behavior of insurees induced by insurance coverage, encourages profit-maximizing insurers to limit coverage through copayments.[9] Insurers may be unwilling to provide full insurance against losses to

TABLE 7.2   EXAMPLE OF A RISK-INCREASING PROJECT

	Policy		Probability of Contingency
Contingency	Bridge	No Bridge	
No earthquake	200	100	.8
Earthquake	100	80	.2
Mean	180	96	
Variance	1600	64	

Surplus point:	$U(200 - S_n) = U(100)$ so $S_n = 100$
	$U(100 - S_e) = U(80)$ so $S_e = 20$
Expected surplus:	$E(S) = .8\ S_n + .2\ S_e = 84$
Expected utility of no bridge:	$EU = .8\ U(100) + .2\ U(80)$
Willingness-to-pay locus:	(δ_n, δ_e) such that
	$.8\ U(200 - \delta_n) + .2\ U(100 - \delta_e) = EU$
Option price:	$.8\ U(200 - OP) + .2\ U(100 - OP) = EU$
	$EU = 4.56$ and $OP = 71.1$
	for $U(c) = \ln(c)$ where c is net income.
Comparison:	$OP < E(S)$

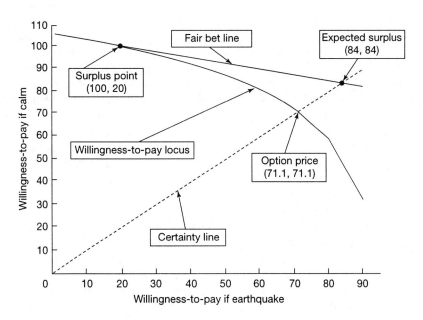

Figure 7.3   Risk-Increasing Project: Expected Surplus and Option Price

unique assets that cannot be easily valued in markets.[10] When insurees have better information about their true risks than insurers, the problem of *adverse selection* may result in either the combining of low- and high-risk persons in the same price pool or the limiting of the extent of coverage to induce high risks to reveal themselves.[11] Routine administrative costs, as well as efforts to control moral hazard and adverse selection, inflate prices above the actuarially fair levels. Limited pools of insurees or uncertainty about the magnitudes of risks may require a further increment in prices to reduce the risk of bankruptcy.[12] Finally, some risks are so correlated across individuals that risk pooling does not sufficiently reduce aggregate risk to allow actuarially fair prices.[13]

Imagine that, despite these practical limitations, complete and actuarially fair insurance were available for the risk in question. It would be possible for the sponsor of the project to trade the contingent surplus amounts for a certain payment by purchasing sufficient insurance to move along the fair bet line, which represents actuarially fair insurance, to the certainty line. In this way, a certain payment corresponding to the expected surplus could be achieved. For example, returning to Figure 7.3, the project sponsor could guarantee a certain payment of $84, which is larger than the option price of $71.10. In general, *if complete and actuarially fair insurance is available, then the larger of option price and expected surplus is the appropriate measure of benefits.*

This generalization ignores one additional institutional constraint: It is not practical to specify contingency-specific payments that would move an individual from his or her contingent surplus point to other points on his or her willingness-to-pay locus. The impracticality may arise from a lack of either information about the shape of the entire willingness-to-pay locus or the administrative capacity to write and execute contingent contracts—actual taxes and subsidies whose magnitudes depend on the occurrence of events. Yet, if such contracts were administratively feasible *and* the analyst knew the entire willingness-to-pay locus, then the policy could be designed with optimal contingent payments so that the person's postpayment contingent surpluses would have the greatest expected value, which could then be realized with certainty through insurance purchases.

Figure 7.4 illustrates this possibility. In the absence of payments, the person realizes either S_1 or S_2 depending on which contingency occurs. If, in addition to the direct effects of the policy, the person were given a payment equal to $FB_1 - S_1$ if contingency 1 occurred or paid a fee of $S_2 - FB_2$ if contingency 2 occurred, then the person's postpayment contingent surpluses would be given by point FB*. Because it is the point of tangency between the willingness-to-pay locus and a fair bet line, FB* has the largest expected value of any point on the willingness-to-pay locus. Starting at this point, complete and actuarially fair insurance would allow the policy sponsors to move along the fair bet line to the certainty line. The resulting certain payment, $E[FB*]$ would be the maximum certain amount of benefit produced by the payment-adjusted policy.[14]

Thus, *in the unlikely circumstance that optimal contingent payments are feasible, and complete and actuarially fair insurance is available, the expected value of the point on the willingness-to-pay locus that is just tangent to the fair bet line is the appropriate measure of benefits.*

In summary, if the policy under consideration involves costs that are certain and complete and actuarially fair insurance is unavailable, then option price is the appropri-

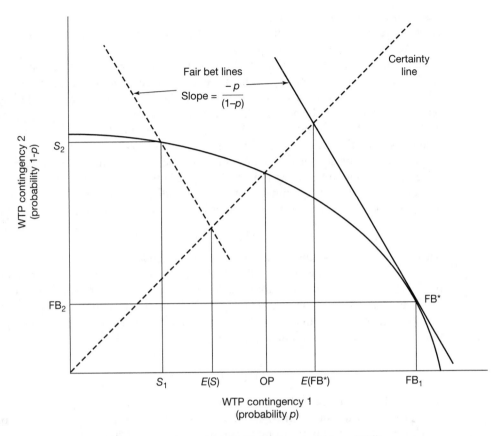

Figure 7.4 Option Price and the Maximum Expected Value of Willingness-to-pay

ate measure of benefits because it allows us to compare certain willingness-to-pay amounts with certain costs. In practice, however, option prices are difficult to measure. Indeed, as will be evident from the discussion of option values in the next section, very specific assumptions about the nature of risks must be made to be able to determine whether option price is larger or smaller than the commonly measured expected surplus.

DETERMINING THE BIAS IN EXPECTED SURPLUS: SIGNING OPTION VALUE

Early attempts to apply CBA to recreational resources such as national parks raised uneasiness about the appropriateness of expected surplus as a benefit measure. In a seminal article dealing with the issue, Burton Weisbrod pointed out that estimates of the benefits of preserving a national park based solely on the benefits accruing to actual visitors do not capture its value to those who anticipate visiting it sometime in the future but actually never do.[15] He argued that these nonvisitors would be willing to pay something to preserve the option of visiting. He called this amount *option value*, which has been interpreted by many as a separate benefit category of relevance to valuing assets, like natural resources, that offer opportunities for future consumption.

Yet CBA requires a more precise definition of option value.[16] The key to formulating it lies in the recognition that option price fully measures a person's *ex ante* willingness-to-pay for a policy in the presence of uncertainty about the benefits that will accrue *ex post*. The uncertainty may arise from a variety of sources, including not only uncertainty about the demand the person will actually have for the goods produced by the policy if it is implemented (Weisbrod's point), but also uncertainty about the quantities, qualities, and prices of the goods, as well as the prices of other goods. Because, even with such uncertainties, it is a full measure of willingness-to-pay, option price includes option value. As previously noted, however, practical limitations usually require analysts to approximate option price with expected surplus. It is now standard to define *option value* as the difference between option price and expected surplus:

$$OV = OP - E[S] \tag{7.1}$$

where OV is option value, OP is the option price, and E[S] is expected surplus. For example, the option value for the dam presented in Table 7.1 is $4.20—the option price of $34.20 minus the expected surplus of $30. The option value of the bridge presented in Table 7.2 is –$12.9—the option price of $71.10 minus the expected surplus of $84.

Rearranging the equation defining option value gives the practical interpretation of option value as an adjustment to expected surplus required to make it equal to option price:

$$OP = E[S] + OV \tag{7.2}$$

where the left-hand side is the certain amount a person is willing to pay, the conceptually correct measure of benefits, and the right-hand side consists of expected surplus, which is what is typically measurable, and option value, which is the amount that would have to be added to expected surplus to make it equal to option price. Though it may seem natural to interpret option value as a distinct benefit category, it is probably better to interpret it as the bias in benefits resulting from measurement by expected surplus rather than option price. Unfortunately, either interpretation requires caution because the sign, let alone the magnitude, of option value is often difficult to determine.

■ EXHIBIT 7.1

In 1980 Richard G. Walsh, John B. Loomis, and Richard A. Gillman combined survey and recreational use data in an effort to estimate the willingness of Colorado households to pay for increments to wilderness designation. They estimated that residents of the state were willing to pay a total of $41.6 million annually for 2.6 million acres. Approximately $6.0 million, or almost 15 percent, of this total was option value.

Source: Richard G. Walsh, John B. Loomis, and Richard A. Gillman, "Valuing Option, Existence, and Bequest Demands for Wilderness," *Land Economics*, 60, no.1 (February 1984), 14–29.

Determining the Sign of Option Value

The sign of option value may be positive or negative, depending on a variety of assumptions concerning the source and nature of risk, the characteristics of the policy being analyzed, and the underlying structure of individual utility. With only a few exceptions, the sign of option value has proven to be theoretically ambiguous. This raises the issue of the usefulness of the concept of option value for even determining the direction of bias when expected surplus is used as an approximation of option price.

Table 7.3 presents an overview of theoretical efforts to sign option value. The earliest studies, listed at the bottom of the table, attempted to determine the sign of option price when the change in the price or quantity of the good being valued is certain, but the demand for the good is uncertain. For example, in the earliest effort to sign option value, Charles J. Cicchetti and A. Myrick Freeman III assumed that there is some probability that a person will have positive demand for the good. Their conclusion that option price is always positive when demand is uncertain was later contradicted by Richard Schmalensee, who showed that the sign was ambiguous under general assumptions.[17]

Subsequent efforts to sign option value without making specific assumptions about individuals' utility functions has produced an unequivocal result only with respect to uncertainty in income. Specifically, in valuing a certain change in the price or quantity of a normal good (quantity demanded increases with increases in income), option value will be negative for a risk-averse person with uncertain income. (Option price is less than expected surplus because the change in price or quantity of the good accentuates the income uncertainty.) Conversely, in valuing a certain change in the price or quantity of an inferior good (quantity demanded decreases with increases in income), option price will be positive for a risk-averse person. As CBA typically involves valuing normal goods, this general result cautions against the tendency to think of option value as a positive adjustment to expected surplus.

On the other hand, with the imposition of a variety of different restrictive assumptions, it appears that for risk-averse persons uncertainty about the quantity, quality, or price of a normal good (supply-side uncertainty) will usually result in a positive option value. For example, Douglas M. Larson and Paul R. Flacco show that if the demand for a normal (inferior) good is linear, semilog, or loglinear in price, then option price is positive (negative) for uncertainty in the price or quality of the good being valued. They also show that uncertainty about the prices of other goods and tastes (demand-side uncertainty) similarly yields positive (negative) option values for normal (inferior) goods for these demand functions.[18]

Overall, the theoretical studies reviewed in Table 7.3 suggest the following general heuristic: *With risk-averse individuals and normal (inferior) goods, treat option value as negative (positive) for income uncertainty, ambiguous for other demand-side uncertainties, and generally positive (negative) for supply-side uncertainties.* Of course, the assumed sign of option value should be consistent with the specific assumptions employed. So, for example, if the empirically estimated demand for the good employs a loglinear functional form with a positive income elasticity, then

TABLE 7.3   THEORETICAL EFFORTS TO DETERMINE THE SIGN OF OPTION VALUE

Study	Assumptions and Conclusions	Comments
Douglas M. Larson and Paul R. Flacco, "Measuring Option Prices from Market Behavior," *Journal of Environmental Economics and Management*, 22, no. 2 (March 1992), 178–198.	(1) Linear, semilog, or loglinear demand functions; uncertainty in own-price, other prices, quality, or tastes: Option value positive for normal goods; option price negative for inferior goods. (2) Linear demand; uncertainty about income; normal or inferior goods: Option value is zero. (3) Semilog or loglinear demand; uncertainty about income; normal or inferior goods: Option value is negative.	Assumption of specific functional forms for demand allow signing of option value for nonincome uncertainty. Linear demand implies risk neutrality; semilog and loglinear demands imply risk aversion for normal goods and risk seeking for inferior goods.
Richard C. Hartman and Mark L. Plummer, "Option Value under Income and Price Uncertainty," *Journal of Environmental Economics and Management*, 14, no. 3, (September 1987), 212–225.	(1) Uncertainty in income: Option value is negative for normal goods. (2) Uncertainty in own-price and other prices: Sign of option value is ambiguous.	General in the sense that preferences may depend on contingencies.
Mark L. Plummer and Richard C. Hartman, "Option Value: A General Approach," *Economic Inquiry*, 24, no. 3 (July 1986), 455–471.	(1) Uncertainty in income and risk aversion: Option value is negative for normal goods. (2) Uncertainty in quality and risk aversion: Option value is positive for normal goods. (3) Uncertainty in tastes and risk aversion: Option value ambiguous for more than two contingencies.	Sign of option value for uncertain parameter depends on signs of the changes in surplus and marginal utility with respect to the parameter.
A. Myrick Freeman III, "The Sign and Size of Option Value," *Land Economics*, 60, no. 1 (February 1984), 1–13.	(1) Uncertainty in demand due to exogenous factors; risk aversion: Option value is positive. (2) If probability of demand is low, expected consumer surplus is large, and person is highly risk averse, then option value may be large.	Depends on assumption that marginal utilities and attitudes toward risk independent of exogenous factors; demonstrated for only two contingencies.
Richard C. Bishop, "Option Value: An Exposition and Extension," *Land Economics*, 58, no. 1 (February 1982), 1–15.	(1) Uncertainty in demand: Sign of option value is ambiguous. (2) Uncertainty in supply (price uncertainty): Option value is positive.	Supply-side case demonstrated for only two contingencies.

(Continued)

TABLE 7.3   THEORETICAL EFFORTS TO DETERMINE THE SIGN OF OPTION VALUE (Continued)

Study	Assumptions and Conclusions	Comments
Richard Schmalensee, "Option Demand and Consumer's Surplus: Valuing Price Changes under Uncertainty," *American Economic Review*, 62, no. 5 (December 1972), 813–824.	Uncertainty in demand: Sign of option value is ambiguous.	Sign depends on risk aversion and whether surplus is measured by equivalent or compensating variation.
Charles J. Cicchetti and A. Myrick Freeman III, "Option Demand and Consumer Surplus: Further Comment," *Quarterly Journal of Economics*, 85, no. 3 (August 1971), 528–539.	Uncertainty in demand: Option value is positive.	Overly strong assumptions imply the same utility results under each contingency.

option value would be negative for income uncertainty, positive for other demand-side uncertainties, and positive for supply-side uncertainties.

It should not be surprising that in view of the difficulty in establishing the sign of option value, even less progress has been made in putting bounds on its size relative to expected surplus. Calculations by V. Kerry Smith suggest that the size of option value relative to expected surplus is likely to be greater for assets that have less perfect substitutes.[19] Larson and Flacco derived expressions for option value for the specific demand functions that they investigated, but their implementation is computationally very difficult.[20] Consequently, it is generally not possible to quantify option value using the information from which estimates of expected surplus are typically made.

RATIONALES FOR EXPECTED SURPLUS AS A PRACTICAL BENEFIT MEASURE

Though option price is generally the conceptually correct measure of benefits in circumstances of uncertainty, analysts most often estimate benefits in terms of expected surpluses. As indicated in the preceding discussion of option value, determining even the sign of the bias that results from the use of expected surplus rather than option price is not always possible. In this section we consider the reasonableness of expected surplus as a practical benefit measure.

We present two arguments often made in defense of the use of expected surplus. One argument is based on the consideration of benefits at the aggregate social level. Another argument applies at the level of the individual policy when people face independent risks so that realized net benefits are likely to be close to expected net benefits. We consider each of these arguments in turn.

Expected Values and Aggregate Social Benefits

If society were risk neutral, then choosing policies that individually maximized expected net benefits would be efficient in the sense of maximizing the expected value of society's entire portfolio of policies.[21] If we assume that projects spread costs and benefits broadly over a large population, then the effect of any particular project on the net income of any person is likely to be small. Even if people are riskaverse, their preferences can be reasonably approximated as being risk neutral for such small changes in income. Therefore, aggregation of individual preferences would lead to risk neutrality at the social level so that expected surplus would be an appropriate measure of benefits.[22]

The variable magnitudes and uneven distribution of costs and benefits that often arise from public policies undercut this line of argument, however. Policies of great import may involve large costs and benefits that remain significant at the individual level, even when spread over a large population. Policies that are targeted at specific groups, such as the unemployed, or at geographical regions often impose substantial costs and benefits on specific individuals. Thus, because social risk neutrality is a questionable assumption, this aggregate-level argument for the use of expected surplus is weak.

A related line of argument is based on the assumption that society holds a fully diversified portfolio of policies that allows it to self-insure against the risk of any particular project. In other words, society is able to pool risk across projects so that it effectively has complete and actuarially fair insurance. As discussed earlier, with the availability of such insurance, the larger of option price and expected surplus is the appropriate benefit measure. Thus, benefits would always be at least as large as expected surplus so that any project with positive expected net benefits would be potentially Pareto improving. Of course, the comparison of mutually exclusive policies in terms of expected surpluses could be misleading if any of the projects have option prices larger than expected surpluses.

It is worth noting that this version of the argument does not rely on the collection of policies effectively averaging costs and benefits across individuals as does the first version of the argument. Rather, it relies on an averaging of aggregate net benefits across policies so that the potential Pareto criterion can be met overall, if not at the level of the individual project.

The weakness of this argument is that diversification does not eliminate all risk. As noted in the discussion of the capital asset pricing model in Appendix 5A, a portfolio of policies as broad as even the whole stock market would still involve some systematic risk. For example, imagine adding independent policies with positive expected net benefits to the portfolio. Though the variance of the average net benefits of the policies would approach zero, the variance in total net benefits would actually increase. The variance in total net benefits means that society cannot guarantee that it will realize the total expected value of net benefits. As diversification does not permit fully effective self-insurance, it does not provide a fully satisfactory rationale for the practical use of expected net benefits.

Expected Values and Pooling Risks Across Individuals: Collective and Individual Risk

We next consider the possibility of risk pooling at the level of the individual policy. It is important to make a distinction between collective risk and individual risk.

By *collective risk*, we simply mean that the same contingency will result for all individuals in society. For example, in the context of doing a CBA for a nuclear power plant, the contingencies might be "no accident" and "nuclear accident"—everyone in the geographic area experiences the same realized contingency. The actual realized net benefits can differ substantially from the expected net benefits, because all individuals share either the favorable or the unfavorable outcome, rather than the weighted average of the two. In such circumstances, the world does not offer us a "middle" outcome corresponding to the expected value. Realized net benefits will, therefore, differ substantially from expected net benefits.

In contrast, consider the case of a large number of individuals who have identical preferences and who face the same probabilities of realizing each of the contingencies, but the contingency that each individual realizes is independent of the contingency realized by any other individual. This is a case of *individual risk*. This might occur, for instance, in the context of evaluating an automobile safety device using a model of traffic accidents in which there is some probability that a driver will have a potentially fatal accident for each mile driven. Multiplying the expected net benefits for one individual by the number of individuals yields a measure of expected net benefits for the policy that can appropriately be treated as approximately certain. The reason is that in circumstances of individual risk with large numbers of individuals exposed to the risk, the proportion of individuals realizing each contingency approximates the probability associated with that contingency. In other words, the averaging process tends to produce realizations of net benefits close to those calculated by the expected value procedure.

This averaging is analytically equivalent to the availability of actuarially fair insurance. Thus, *in cases of individual risk, the larger of option price and expected surplus is the appropriate benefit measure*. As with complete diversification, the use of expected surplus as a benefit measure would guarantee that adopted policies were potentially Pareto improving, but would not necessarily lead to the adoption of the most efficient policies in comparisons of mutually exclusive alternatives.

Summary: Expected Surplus as a Practical Measure

How reasonable is the use of expected surplus as a practical benefit measure? Though social risk neutrality argues for expected surplus as the correct benefit measure, its underlying assumptions are not plausible. Somewhat more plausibly, diversification across policies argues for expected surplus as a conservative measure of benefits. That is, benefits can be no smaller than expected surplus. The pooling of individual risks among those affected by a policy argues convincingly for treatment of expected surplus as a conservative measure of benefits. *Overall, these arguments suggest that when neither option prices nor option values can be estimated, analysts can reason-*

ably use expected surplus as an approximate measure of benefits. Yet they should take special care to consider the potential bias in this approach when dealing with cases involving collective risk.

INFORMATION AND QUASI-OPTION VALUE

As noted, the original but narrow motivation for the concept of option value was the notion that individuals often place some value on the option of future consumption. A similar motivation lies behind the concept of quasi-option value—the value of delaying irreversible decisions so that they can be informed by knowledge that becomes available in the future. Like option value, quasi-option value is best thought of as a correction for bias introduced by the method of analysis rather than as a distinct benefit category.

It may be wise to delay a decision if better information will become available in the future. For example, consider the decision of whether or not to develop a wilderness area. We may be fairly certain about the costs and benefits of development to the current generation. We may be very uncertain of the opportunity cost to future generations of losing the wilderness, however. If information will become available over time that will reduce our uncertainty about how future generations will value the wilderness area, then it may be desirable to delay a decision about irreversible development so that we have the opportunity to incorporate the new information into our decision. The expected value of information gained by delaying an irreversible decision is called *quasi-option value*.[23]

Quasi-option value can be quantified by explicitly formulating a multiperiod decision problem that allows for the revelation of information about the value of options in later periods.[24] Though some environmental analysts see quasi-option value as a distinct benefit category for policies that preserve unique assets like wilderness areas, scenic views, and animal species, it is more appropriately thought of as a correction to the calculation of expected net benefits through an inappropriate one-period decision problem. As the calculation of quasi-option value itself requires specification of the proper decision problem, whenever quasi-option value can be quantified, the correct expected net benefits can be calculated directly. Thus, quasi-option value is redundant as a quantitative benefit measure.

As background for an illustration of quasi-option value, Table 7.4 sets out the parameters for a CBA of alternatives for use of a wilderness area. The project value of net benefits from full development (FD) and limited development (LD) are measured relative to no development (ND) for two contingencies. Under the contingency labeled "Low Value," which will occur with a probability p, future generations place the same value as current generations on preservation of the wilderness area. Under the contingency labeled "High Value," which will occur with a probability $1 - p$, future generations place a much higher value than current generations on preservation of the wilderness area. If the Low Value contingency occurs, then FD yields a positive present value of net benefits equal to B_F and LD yields a positive PVNB equal to B_L. If instead the High Value contingency occurs, then FD yields a negative PVNB equal to $-C_F$ and LD yields a negative PVNB equal to $-C_L$. Assume that $B_F > B_L > 0$ and

TABLE 7.4 *EX ANTE* BENEFITS AND COSTS OF ALTERNATIVE
DEVELOPMENT POLICIES

	Preservation Contingencies	
	Low Value	High Value
Full Development (FD)	B_F	$-C_F$
Limited Development (LD)	B_L	$-C_L$
No Development (ND)	0	0
Probability of Contingency	p	$1-p$

Expected Value of Full Development:	$E[\text{FD}] = pB_F - (1-p)C_F$
Expected Value of Limited Development:	$E[\text{LD}] = pB_L - (1-p)C_L$
Expected Value of No Development:	$E[\text{ND}] = 0$
Adopt Full Development if:	$pB_F - (1-p)C_F > pB_L - (1-p)C_L$
	and $pB_F - (1-p)C_F > 0$

$C_F > C_L > 0$ so that FD yields greater net benefits under the Low Value contingency and greater net costs under the High Value contingency than LD.

Imagine that we conduct a CBA assuming that no learning will occur over time. That is, we assume that no useful information will be revealed in future periods. The expected net benefits of FD equal $pB_F - (1-p)C_F$; the expected net benefits of LD equal $pB_L - (1-p)C_L$; and the expected net benefits of ND equal 0. We would simply choose the alternative with the largest expected net benefits.

Now consider the case of *exogenous learning*. That is, we assume that after the first period we discover with certainty which of the two contingencies will occur. Our learning is exogenous in the sense that the information is revealed to us no matter what actions we take.

Figure 7.5 presents a decision tree for the case of exogenous learning. The square box at the extreme left-hand side of the figure represents our initial decision. If we select FD, then we have the same expected value as in the case of no learning— we have made an irreversible decision and, hence, knowing the contingency has no value because we have no decision left to make in period 2. If we select either LD or ND in the first period, then we do have a decision left to make in period 2 after we know which contingency has occurred. The expected values of the LD and ND decisions in period 1 can be found by the method of backward induction introduced in Chapter 6.

Consider LD first. If the Low Value contingency is revealed at the beginning of period 2, then the optimal decision will be to complete the development to obtain net benefits $B_F - B_L$. The present value of this amount is obtained by discounting at rate d. It is then added to B_L, the period 1 net benefits, to obtain the net benefits of LD conditional on the Low Value contingency occurring. If the High Value contingency is revealed at the beginning of period 2, then the optimal decision is to forgo further development so that the net benefits conditional on the High Value contingency occurring consist only of the $-C_L$ realized in period 1. Multiplying these conditional net

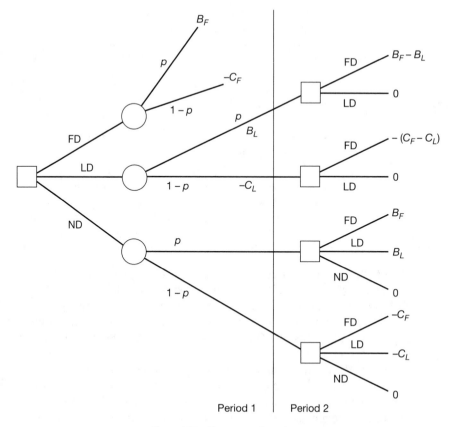

Figure 7.5   Exogenous Learning

benefits by their respective probabilities yields the expected net benefits for limited development in period 1 of $p[B_L + (B_F - B_L)/(1 + d)] - (1 - p)C_L$. Note that it differs from the expected value in the no-learning case by the expected net benefits of the period 2 option, $p(B_F - B_L)/(1 + d)$, which is the quasi-option value of LD.

Next consider the decision ND in period 1. If the Low Value contingency is revealed at the beginning of period 2, then the optimal decision is FD, which has a present value of $B_F /(1 + d)$. If the High Value contingency is revealed at the beginning of period 2, then the optimal decision is ND, which has a present value of 0. Consequently, the expected net benefits from choosing ND in period 1 are $pB_F/(1 + d)$, which equal the quasi-option value of ND.

The middle column of Table 7.5 summarizes the expected values of the period 1 alternatives for the case of exogenous learning.

Figure 7.6 presents a decision tree for the case of endogenous learning. Unlike the case of exogenous learning, information is generated only from development itself. For example, the value placed on preservation by future generations may depend on the risk that development poses to a species of bird that feeds in the wilderness area during its migration. The effect of limited development on the species may

TABLE 7.5   EXPECTED VALUES FOR DECISION PROBLEMS: QUASI-OPTION VALUES (QOV) MEASURED RELATIVE TO NO LEARNING CASE

	No Learning	Exogenous Learning	Endogenous Learning
$E[FD]$	$pB_F - (1-p)C_F$	$pB_F - (1-p)C_F$ QOV = 0	$pB_F - (1-p)C_F$ QOV = 0
$E[LD]$	$pB_L - (1-p)C_L$	$p[B_L + (B_F - B_L)/(1+d)] - (1-p)C_L$ QOV = p $(B_F - B_L)/(1+d)$	$p[B_L + (B_F - B_L)/(1+d)] - (1-p)C_L$ QOV = $p(B_F - B_L)/(1+d)$
$E[ND]$	0	$pB_F/(1+d)$ QOV = $pB_F/(1+d)$	0 QOV = 0

provide enough information to permit a reliable prediction of the effect of full development. If no development is undertaken, then no new information will be available at the beginning of the second period. If full development is undertaken, then new information will be generated but there will be no decision for it to effect.

As shown in the last column of Table 7.5, the expected net benefits for the FD and LD alternatives in the case of endogenous learning are identical to those for the case of exogenous learning. The expected net benefits of ND are zero, however, because there will be no new information to alter the decision not to develop in the future.

Table 7.6 compares the different learning cases for a specific set of parameter values. If we specify the decision problem as one of no learning, then FD has the

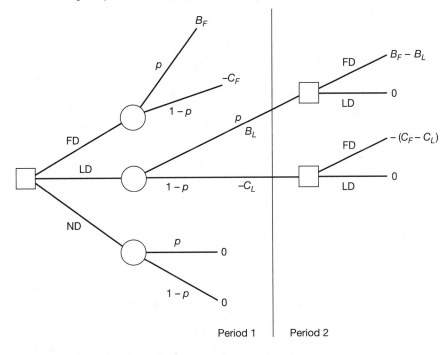

Figure 7.6   Endogenous Learning

TABLE 7.6   NUMERICAL ILLUSTRATION OF QUASI-OPTION VALUE ($ MILLION)

Assumptions:

$B_F = 100$ $C_F = 80$ $B_L = 50$ $C_L = 40$ $p = .5$ $d = .08$	No Learning	Exogenous Learning	Endogenous Learning
$E[FD]$	10.00	10.00	10.00
$E[LD]$	5.00	28.15	28.15
$E[ND]$	0.00	46.30	0.00

largest expected net benefits. Imagine that instead we specify the decision problem as the exogenous learning case. Now ND has the largest expected net benefits. Furthermore, relative to the case of no learning, the quasi-option value of ND is $46.3 million (46.30 – 0) and the quasi-option value of LD is $23.15 million (28.15 – 5).

Now imagine that we specify the decision problem as the case of endogenous learning. LD has the largest expected net benefits. Relative to the case of no learning, the quasi-option value of LD is $23.15 million (28.15 – 5) and the quasi-option value of ND is 0 (0 – 0).

This simple numerical illustration conforms to the common wisdom about quasi-option value: *It tends to be large for no development in cases of exogenous learning and large for limited development in cases of endogenous learning.* It is important to keep in mind, however, that the illustration is based on very stylized models of learning. Differently specified models could yield different rankings and different quasi-option values for the alternatives. Even with this simple model, different numerical assumptions could lead to different rankings of alternatives.

Note that our numerical estimates of quasi-option values in the illustration depended on expected values calculated by comparing what was assumed to be the correct two-period decision problem to a one-period decision problem that incorrectly fails to take account of learning. Of course, if we knew the correct decision problem, then there would be no need to concern ourselves with quasi-option value, as solving the decision problem would lead to the appropriate calculations of expected net benefits. Thus, if we are in a position to calculate quasi-option values, then there is no need to do so.

How should we treat quasi-option value in practice? Two heuristics seem warranted. First, *quantitative quasi-option values should be based on an explicit decision problem that structures the calculation of the expected net benefits.* An explicit decision problem focuses attention on the key assumptions that determine the magnitude of quasi-option value. It also makes it unnecessary to consider quasi-option value as a distinct benefit category. Second, *when insufficient knowledge is available to formulate a decision problem for explicitly calculating the magnitude of quasi-option value, it should be discussed as a possible source of bias rather than added as an arbitrary quantitative adjustment to expected net benefits.* As with other biases, one can ask the question: How big would quasi-option value have to be to affect the ranking of policies?

CONCLUSION

We rarely have much opportunity for inferring option prices directly from observable behavior, though insurance premiums and self-protection investments may convey some useful information about people's willingness to pay for reductions in risk. Contingent valuation provides an alternative approach for directly eliciting option prices through surveys, but it is prone to the problems we discuss in Chapter 11. Consequently, we often have no alternative but to predict policy effects under the specified contingencies, value them with shadow price estimates from observed market behavior, and calculate expected net benefits. These expected net benefits may either understate or overstate the conceptually correct benefits based on option price by an amount called the option value. Unfortunately, signing, let alone quantifying, option price is often not possible.

Quasi-option values take account of the value of being able to act upon future information. As solving a correctly specified decision problem naturally incorporates quasi-option values, they need not be treated as distinct benefits. Quantitative claims about quasi-option values should be based on an explicit decision problem.

EXERCISES FOR CHAPTER 7

1. A large rural county is considering establishing a medical transport unit that would use helicopters to fly emergency medical cases to hospitals. Analysts have attempted to estimate the benefits from establishing the unit in two ways. First, they surveyed a random sample of residents to find out how much they would be willing to pay each year for the unit. Based on responses from the sample, the analysts estimated a total willingness-to-pay of $8.5 million per year. Second, the analysts estimated the dollar value of the improvements in health outcomes and avoided medical costs of users of the unit to be $6.2 million per year.

   Taking the analysts' estimates at face value, specify the following:
   a. The aggregate of individuals' annual option prices for the unit.
   b. The annual total expected gain in social surplus from use of the unit.
   c. The annual aggregate option value for the unit.

2. Imagine that we want to value a cultural festival from the point of view of a risk-averse person. The person's utility is given by $U(I)$ where I is her income. She has a 50 percent chance of being able to get vacation time to attend the festival. If she gets the vacation time, then she would be willing to pay up to S to attend the festival. If she does not get the vacation time, then she is unwilling to pay anything for the festival.

   a. What is her expected surplus if the cultural festival takes place?
   b. Write an expression for her expected utility if the festival does not take place.
   c. Write an expression incorporating her option price, OP, for the festival if the festival takes place. (To do this, equate her expected utility if the festival takes place to her expected utility if the festival does not take place. Also, assume that if the festival does take place, then she makes a payment of OP whether or not she is able to attend the festival.)
   d. Manipulate the expression for option price to show that the option price must be smaller than her expected surplus. (In doing this, begin by substituting $0.5S - \epsilon$ for OP in the

equation derived in 2.c. Also keep in mind that since the person is risk-averse, her marginal utility declines with income.)

e. Does this exercise suggest any generalizations about the benefits of recreational programs when individuals are uncertain as to whether or not they will be able to participate in them?

3. In Chapter 4, the net present value of a hydroelectric plant with a life of 70 years was given as $25.73 million. The net present value of a thermal electric plant with a life of 35 years was found to be $18.77 million. Rolling the thermal plant over twice to match the life of the hydroelectric plant had a net present value of ($18.77 million) + ($18.77 million)/(1 + 0.05)^{35} = $22.17 million.

Now assume that at the end of the first 35 years, there will be an improved second 35-year plant. Specifically, there is a 30 percent chance that an advanced solar or nuclear alternative will be available that will increase the net benefits by a factor of three; a 60 percent chance that a major improvement in thermal technology will increase net benefits by 50 percent; and a 10 percent chance that more modest improvements in thermal technology will increase net benefits by 10 percent.

a. Should the hydroelectric or thermal plant be built today?

b. What is the quasi-option value of the thermal plant?

NOTES

[1]Our discussion in this section is based on Daniel A. Graham, "Cost-Benefit Analysis Under Uncertainty," *American Economic Review*, 71, no. 4 (September 1981), 715–725; V. Kerry Smith, "Uncertainty, Benefit-Cost Analysis, and the Treatment of Option Value," *Journal of Environmental Economics and Management*, 14, no. 3 (May 1987), 283–292; and Charles E. Meier and Alan Randall, "Use Value Under Uncertainty: Is There a 'Correct' Measure?" *Land Economics*, 67, no. 4 (November 1991), 379–389. The latter is the best overview of this topic despite a pedagogically relevant typographical error (the slope of the fair bet line is misstated in several diagrams).

[2]Measuring benefits by persons' *ex ante* willingness-to-pay assumes that they correctly assess and process risks. Lack of information about risks, or biases in processing the information, muddies the comparison between this approach and the expectational approach if the latter involves more accurate risk assessments. For overviews, see Colin F. Camerer and Howard Kunreuther, "Decision Processes for Low Probability Risks: Policy Implications," *Journal of Policy Analysis and Management*, 8, no. 4 (Fall 1989), 565–592, and W. Kip Viscusi, *Fatal Trade-offs: Public and Private Responsibilities for Risk* (New York: Oxford University Press, 1992).

[3]Variance is defined as: $Var[X] = E\{(X - E[X])^2\}$. For a discrete random variable with possible outcomes xi, $i = 1...n$,

$$E[X] = \Sigma x_i p(x_i) \text{ and } Var[X] = \Sigma(x_i - E[X])^2 p(x_i)$$

where $p(xi)$ is the probability of the ith outcome occurring.

In the case of the payoffs from the dam given in Table 7.1,

$$E[X] = (.5)(110)+(.5)(100) = 105$$

$$\text{and } Var[X] = (.5)(110 - 105)^2 + (.5)(100 - 105)^2 = 25$$

[4]Formally, let m_i be the person's wealth under contingency i and let Z be an indicator of whether or not the policy under consideration is adopted ($Z = 0$ if not adopted; $Z = 1$ if adopted). The person's utility

under contingency i can be written as $U(m_i, Z)$. The person's surplus (willingness-to-pay) for the project given that contingency i occurs, S_i, satisfies the equation:

$$U(m_i - S_i, 1) = U(m_i, 0)$$

The expected value of the person's contingent surpluses is $E(S) = p_1 S_1 + p_2 S_2$ in the case of two contingencies.

[5]Continuing with the notation from note 4, points on the willingness-to-pay locus, (w_1, w_2), satisfy the following equation:

$$p_1 U_1(m_1 - w_1, 1) + p_2 U_2(m_2 - w_2, 1) = EU$$

where $EU = p_1 U_1(m_1, 0) + p_2 U_2(m_2, 0)$ is the person's expected utility without the project.

[6]Two aspects of the fair bet line are worth noting. First, a fair bet line can be drawn through any point. Thus, for example, if we wanted to know which point on the willingness-to-pay locus has the largest expected value, then we would find the point that is just tangent to a fair bet line. Second, if insurance were available in unlimited quantity at an actuarially fair price, then the person could actually move from any point on the willingness-to-pay locus along a fair bet line to the certainty line by buying insurance. The near consensus that option price is the appropriate benefit measure is based on the reasonable assumption that complete and actuarially fair insurance markets generally do not exist in the real world.

[7]The intersection corresponds to the solution of the following equations:

$$E(S) \quad = p_1 x_1 + p_2 x_2 \text{ (expected value line)}$$

$$x_1 \qquad = x_2 \text{ (certainty line)}$$

$$p_1 \qquad = 1 - p_2$$

where x_1 defines the location of points on the vertical axis and x_2 defines the location of points on the horizontal axis. Solving these equations gives $E(S) = x$, where x is the point of intersection.

[8]For a general introduction to the theory of insurance, see Isaac Ehrlich and Gary S. Becker, "Market Insurance, Self-Insurance, and Self-Protection," *Journal of Political Economy*, 80, no. 4 (July/August 1972), 663–648.

[9]Mark V. Pauly, "The Economics of Moral Hazard: Comment," *American Economic Review*, 58, no. 3 (June 1968), 531–537.

[10]Philip J. Cook and Daniel A. Graham, "The Demand for Insurance and Protection: The Case of Irreplaceable Commodities," *Quarterly Journal of Economics*, 91, no. 1 (February 1977), 141–156.

[11]One way to get high risks to reveal themselves is to offer two insurance options: one that gives full coverage at a premium that is actuarially fair for high risks and another that gives only limited coverage at a premium that is actuarially fair for low risks. If the level of coverage under the latter option is sufficiently low, then high risks will be better off revealing themselves to get the full coverage. The result is a so-called *separating equilibrium* in which both risk groups honestly reveal themselves. The information is gained, however, at the cost of limiting coverage to good risks. See Michael Rothschild and Joseph Stiglitz, "Equilibrium in Competitive Insurance Markets: An Essay on the Economics of Imperfect Information," *Quarterly Journal of Economics*, 90, no. 4 (November 1976), 629–650.

[12]J. David Cummins, "Statistical and Financial Models of Insurance Pricing and the Insurance Firm," *Journal of Risk and Insurance*, 58, no. 2 (June 1991), 261–301.

[13]Jack Hirshleifer and John G. Riley, *The Analytics of Uncertainty and Information* (New York: Cambridge University Press, 1992).

[14]The difference between $E[FB^*]$ and $E[S]$ is called the *option premium*. Unlike option value, it is always positive. See Dennis C. Cory and Bonnie Colby Saliba, "Requiem for Option Value," *Land Economics*, 63, no. 1 (February 1987), 1–10. Unfortunately, the extreme assumptions of complete and

actuarially fair insurance, knowledge of the entire willingness-to-pay locus, and the feasibility of contingent-specific payments give the notion of option premium little practical relevance to CBA.

[15]Burton A. Weisbrod, "Collective Consumption Services of Individual Consumption Goods," *Quarterly Journal of Economics*, 78, no. 3 (August 1964), 71–77.

[16]The possibility of *double counting* benefits with this formulation was soon pointed out by Millard F. Long, "Collective-Consumption Services of Individual-Consumption Goods," *Quarterly Journal of Economics*, 81, no. 2 (May 1967), 351–352.

[17]Robert Anderson later showed that the contradictory results arose because of additional assumptions of Cicchetti and Freeman that had the unattractive consequence of guaranteeing the option buyer a certain utility level no matter which contingency arose. Robert J. Anderson, Jr., "A Note on Option Value and the Expected Value of Consumer's Surplus," *Journal of Environmental Economics and Management*, 8, no. 2 (June 1981), 187–191.

[18]As discussed in Chapter 10, empirical estimation of demand equations usually involves at least income and own-price as explanatory variables for quantity. If the sign of the estimated coefficient of income is positive (negative), then the good is normal (inferior).

[19]V. Kerry Smith, "A Bound for Option Value," *Land Economics*, 60, no. 3 (August 1984), 292–296.

[20]Their expressions require not only estimates of the parameters of the demand equations, but also fairly complicated expectations over the parameters that are treated as uncertain.

[21]To say that society is risk neutral implies that there is a social welfare function that ranks alternative distributions of goods among individuals. That is, it gives a "score" to each possible distribution such that a distribution with a higher score is preferred by society to a distribution with a lower score. Aggregation of individual preferences, however, cannot guarantee a social welfare function that satisfies minimally desirable properties. See Tibor Scitovsky, "The State of Welfare Economics," *American Economic Review*, 51, no. 3 (June 1951), 301–315. More generally, see Kenneth J. Arrow, *Social Choice and Individual Values*, 2nd ed. (New Haven, CT: Yale University Press, 1963).

[22]Kenneth J. Arrow and Robert C. Lind, "Uncertainty and the Evaluation of Public Investment Decisions," *American Economic Review*, 60, no. 3 (June 1970), 364–378.

[23]The concept of quasi-option value was introduced by Kenneth J. Arrow and Anthony C. Fisher, "Environmental Preservation, Uncertainty, and Irreversibility," *Quarterly Journal of Economics*, 88, no. 2 (May 1974), 312–319.

[24]Jon M. Conrad, "Quasi-Option Value and the Expected Value of Information," *Quarterly Journal of Economics*, 44, no. 4 (June 1980), 813–820; Anthony C. Fisher and W. Michael Hanemann, "Quasi-Option Value: Some Misconceptions Dispelled," *Journal of Environmental Economics and Management*, 14, no. 2 (June 1987), 183–190.

8

EXISTENCE VALUE

Within the CBA framework, people's willingness-to-pay for a policy change comprehensively measures its social benefits. Though analysts sometimes attempt to elicit willingness-to-pay amounts through contingent valuation surveys (see Chapter 11), they more often make inferences about them from observations of people's behaviors (see Chapters 9 and 10). The behaviors usually involve changes in consumption of a good whose price or quantity is affected by the policy change, or changes in consumption of substitutes for or complements of the good. For many, perhaps most, applications of CBA, analysts can reasonably assume that social surplus changes estimated on the basis of observable changes in the consumption of goods conceptually capture the entire willingness-to-pay. Yet in some applications of CBA, especially those involving changes in unique natural resources, people may be willing to pay for the existence of goods that they themselves will never "consume." Correctly conceptualizing and measuring such *existence values* poses an extremely difficult challenge to the application of CBA to many environmental policies.

In this chapter, we consider existence value as a category of benefit. It is often lumped together with option value and quasi-option value under the heading of *nonuse* benefits. As discussed in Chapter 7, however, option and quasi-option values are better thought of as adjustments to standard benefit measures to take account of various aspects of uncertainty rather than as distinct categories of benefits. In contrast, existence value is a meaningful benefit category, though one that poses definitional problems. After framing existence value as a benefit category, we discuss the theoretical and empirical problems analysts face in measuring it.

USE AND NONUSE VALUE

The notion that people may place a value on the very existence of "unique phenomena of nature" that they neither visit, nor anticipate ever visiting, was introduced into the CBA literature almost 30 years ago by John V. Krutilla.[1] Consider, for example, a wilderness area that provides habitat for rare game animals. Hunters might be willing to pay to preserve the wilderness area because it either lowers the price or increases the quality of hunting. Naturalists might be willing to pay to preserve the area because it provides a desirable area for hiking or bird watching. Nearby residents may be willing to pay to preserve the area because it provides scenic beauty and prevents commercial development that they find undesirable. People who enjoy nature films may be willing to pay to preserve the area because it provides a unique setting for filming rare species. All of these people value the area because they make use of it in some way. Yet one can imagine that some other people might be willing to pay to preserve the area even though they do not use it in any of these ways. In commonly used terminology, this latter group of people is said to derive *nonuse value* from the wilderness area.

While most economists accept the general idea that people may derive value from mere knowledge of the existence of unique assets such as scenic wilderness, animal species, or works of art, clearly defining nonuse value has turned out to be so very complicated that there is as yet no clear consensus on its precise meaning.

One complication is the difficulty of drawing a sharp line between use and nonuse. In terms of standard consumer theory, any good that a person values is an argument in his or her utility function. The good need not involve any observable activity by the person to secure its value. The quantity of a pure public good like national defense, for instance, is "consumed" by individuals, however passively. Existence value can also be thought of as a pure public good.[2] It is nonrivalrous—the value one person derives from it does not diminish the values derived by others. It is nonexcludable—no one can be excluded from deriving value from the quantity of the good, which is provided commonly to all. Viewed as a public good, it seems more appropriate to describe existence value as "passive use" rather than "nonuse."

Yet, how passive must the "consumption" be to distinguish use from nonuse? It is probably safe to say that merely thinking about the good does not constitute use as the term is commonly understood. What about discussing the good with other people? Consumption now involves observable behavior, the consumption of a complementary good, time, but most economists would probably consider it nonuse. Consuming films and photobooks based on the good, however, probably crosses the line between use and nonuse because it leaves a behavioral trace in the markets for these complementary goods. These distinctions hinge not just on the intrinsic attributes of the good, but also on our ability to observe and value behavior. Thus, in actual application, distinguishing between use and nonuse is not a purely conceptual issue with a clear resolution.

Another complication, which we consider in more detail in Appendix 8A, arises because individuals can derive both use and nonuse value from an asset. A person's willingness-to-pay for preservation of the wilderness area may be motivated by the anticipation of hunting and the pleasure of knowing that future generations will be able to enjoy it as well. While the person's total willingness-to-pay is conceptually clear, the division between these two categories of value is ambiguous because the order of valuation is generally relevant. One ordering in this case is to elicit first the person's willingness-to-pay for use and then, taking this amount as actually paid, to elicit the person's willingness-to-pay for nonuse. The other possible ordering is to elicit first the person's willingness-to-pay for nonuse and then, taking this amount as actually paid, elicit the person's willingness-to-pay for use. The orderings will yield the same total willingness-to-pay, but they probably will yield different values for use and nonuse. Obviously, the ordering problem blurs the boundary between use and nonuse.

Finally, the nonuse category raises issues of motivation typically avoided by economists. If nonuse does not leave a behavioral trace, then its value can only be discovered empirically through stated rather than revealed preferences.

A theory about the motivations behind nonuse value can help guide the formulation and interpretation of questions for eliciting stated preferences. For example, a possible motivation for nonuse value is altruism toward either current people or future generations. Yet, it makes a difference whether the altruism is either individualistic or paternalistic. A concern about the general utility levels of others is *individualistic altruism*; a concern about the consumption of specific goods by others is *paternalistic altruism*. For example, giving money to homeless alcoholics is consistent with individualistic altruism, while contributing to a program that gives them only meals is consistent with paternalistic altruism. If the analyst believes that individualistic altruism is the motivation for existence value, then it is important that respondents be given sufficient context to understand the implications of provision of the good on the overall wealth of others. Because the targets of altruism generally bear some share of the costs of the provided goods, individualistic altruism generally results in lower existence values than paternalistic altruism.[3]

With these caveats in mind, we offer Table 8.1 as a framework for thinking about existence value as a benefit category.

Consider first use benefits. The most obvious benefit category is *rivalrous consumption* of goods, such as trees for wood products, water for irrigation, and grasslands for cattle grazing. As markets usually exist for rivalrous goods, they are the category most amenable to valuation through the estimation of demand schedules and consumer surplus.

TABLE 8.1   TAXONOMY OF BENEFITS: POSSIBLE PARTITIONING OF TOTAL WILLINGNESS-TO-PAY

Type	Benefit Category	Example
Use	Rivalrous consumption Nonrivalrous consumption: direct Nonrivalrous consumption: indirect	Logging of old-growth forest Hiking in wilderness Watching a film of wilderness area
Nonuse	Pure existence value: good has intrinsic value Altruistic existence value: gift to current generation Altruistic existence value: bequest to future generation	Perceived value of natural order Others hiking in wilderness Future others hiking in wilderness

The other use categories are for nonrivalrous goods. Those consumed onsite, such as hiking and bird watching that do not interfere with other users or uses, are labeled *direct nonrivalrous consumption*. Though rarely traded in markets, such goods can often be valued by observing the travel and time costs people are willing to bear to consume them. (See Chapter 10.) In alternative taxonomies of benefits, this category is sometimes labeled *nondestructive consumption*.

Indirect nonrivalrous consumption takes place offsite. For example, a person may derive value from watching a film about wildlife in a particular wilderness area. Expenditures of time and money on off-site nonrivalrous consumption provide some information for estimating its value, though much less reliably than for the other use categories.

Consider next nonuse benefits. Three categories of existence value can be distinguished in terms of motivation. The first, *pure existence value*, arises because people believe the good has intrinsic value apart from its use. For example, some people might be willing to pay to preserve a wilderness area because they think that it is right that some natural habitats exist for rare animal species.

The remaining two categories are based on altruism. Some people may be willing to pay to preserve a wilderness area, for instance, because they get pleasure from knowing that it is used by others. Generally, the motivation for such *altruistic existence value* is paternalistic in the sense that it is driven by the desire for others to consume this particular good, rather than by the desire to increase their consumption overall. It may be based on the belief that exposure to nature, art, or historical sites is intrinsically good, or perhaps on the desire to share with others a type of experience one has found to be emotionally enriching. When the altruism is directed toward future generations, the good is said to have a *bequest value*. People get pleasure from knowing that those not yet born will be able to use (and nonuse!) the good. Just as people often wish to leave their children a share of the wealth they have accumulated, they may want to bequeath them access to unique goods as well.

THE MEASUREMENT OF EXISTENCE VALUE

Despite the difficulty economists have in clearly defining existence value as a benefit category, few economists would deny that sometimes people are willing to pay a total amount for the preservation of assets that exceeds their willingness-to-pay for their use, or anticipated possible use. Yet, many economists believe that the method of measurement currently available, the contingent value survey, lacks sufficient reliability for existence values to be reasonably included in CBA. As we consider contingent valuation in detail in Chapter 11, our discussion here raises only the general issues most relevant to the measurement of existence value.

Directly Eliciting Total Value

One way to avoid some of the conceptual problems in defining existence value is to measure willingness-to-pay for a policy change holistically rather than disaggregating it into component parts. In the context of contingent valuation, the analyst poses questions aimed at getting respondents to state their willingness-to-pay amounts based on consideration of *all* their possible motivations for valuing policy changes. The total value revealed through this *structured conversation* is each respondent's benefit from the policy change.

The viability of this approach obviously depends on the analyst's ability to structure a meaningful conversation. The analyst must convey a full description of the policy effect being valued. Considerably more context must be provided in the valuation of effects on nonuse than effects on use. People typically know their own current levels of use as a starting point for valuing marginal changes. They are less likely to know the total stock of a good that has nonuse value. Yet their valuation of marginal changes in the good is likely to depend on how much they think is currently available. For example, people who think that a particular species lives only in one particular wilderness area are likely to place a much higher value on the preservation of that area than if they knew that the species lived in several other already protected areas. Indeed, one can imagine that, given enough information and time for reflection, some people may place a zero or negative value on the existence of more of some good when its quantity is above some threshold. One may place a negative value on policies that increase the number of deer in an area, for instance, if their number is already so large as to threaten other species.

Existence value based on altruism poses special problems for the conversation. When individuals are concerned only about their own consumption, it is reasonable to separate costs from benefits. Each can be estimated separately and combined to find net benefits. Altruistic values, however, may depend on the distribution of both costs and benefits. Respondents thus need to know who is likely to use the good being valued and who is likely to bear the costs of preserving it. Failure to include the latter may inflate existence values if it leads to respondents not taking into account all the effects on others.

Let us assume that these concerns, along with the more general problems of contingent valuation discussed in Chapter 11, are adequately addressed so that analysts can be confident that they have correctly elicited individuals' total willingness-to-pay amounts for the policy change under consideration. If their sample of respondents included all the people with standing, then these total valuations would suffice for completing the CBA. Often, however, analysts wish to combine benefits estimated from behavioral data with existence value estimates from a relatively small sample drawn from people with standing. As already noted, partitioning respondents' total willingness-to-pay into use and nonuse values is sensitive to the ordering of categories. If nonuse values from the sample are to be added to use values estimated by other methods to get total benefits, then it is important that questions be asked so as to elicit nonuse values after respondents have considered and reported their use values.

In contrast to use, nonuse does not occur in easily defined geographic markets. Aggregate existence values are very sensitive to the geographic assumptions made in extrapolating from survey samples to the population with standing.[4] People appear to place a higher existence value on resources in closer proximity.[5] Using average existence values estimated from local samples to obtain aggregate existence values for a more geographically extensive population may be inappropriate. Indeed, the question of geographic extrapolation appears to be one of the most controversial aspects of the use of existence values in damage assessment cases.[6]

As a final point, note that as long as the conversation leads respondents to consider all the sources of uncertainty relevant to their valuation of the policy change, their total willingness-to-pay amount is an option price. It is thus fully inclusive of option value so that no adjustments for uncertainty are required.

■ EXHIBIT 8.1

Based on survey data, K.G. Willis estimated existence values for three nature sites of special scientific interest in Great Britain. Consumer surplus associated with use of the sites appeared to account for only about 10 to 12 percent of people's total willingness-to-pay. Option value accounted for a comparable percentage. The remaining portion of willingness-to-pay consisted of existence (pure and bequest) value. Only if the nonuse benefits were included did conservation of these areas appear to have positive net benefits.

Source: K.G. Willis, "Valuing Non-Market Wildlife Commodities: An Evaluation and Comparison of Benefits and Costs," *Applied Economics*, 22, no. 1 (January 1990), 12–30.

Behavioral Traces of Existence Value?

Many economists would be more comfortable measuring existence value through the observation of related behavior. As a pure public good, however, its behavioral trace is likely to be so very weak that considerable ingenuity will be required to find ways of measuring it through nonconversational methods. Nevertheless, the history of the development of increasingly sophisticated methods for measuring benefits offers some hope that a way will be found.

Bruce Madariaga and Kenneth McConnell suggest one line of investigation.[7] They note that people are willing to pay to join such organizations as the Sierra Club and the Audubon Society. Some part of their membership fees can be thought of as voluntary contributions for a public good, the preservation of wilderness areas. Ways of making inferences about existence values from the patterns of contributions to such organizations have yet to be developed.

More sophisticated models of individual utility may also provide some leverage on the measurement of existence value. For example, Douglas Larson notes that public goods are sometimes complements of, or substitutes for, private goods.[8] If investigators are willing to impose assumptions about the form of the demand for market goods and the nature of the complementarity between market goods and existence values, then they may be able to make inferences about the magnitudes of the existence values from observation of the consumption of the market goods. Larson also suggests that explicitly treating time as a constraint in utility maximization may open up possibilities for measurement based on people's allocations of time.

Should Existence Value Be Included in CBA?

A growing number of efforts to estimate existence values through surveys can be found in the literature.[9] The particular estimates are often controversial. More generally, the desirability of the effort to incorporate existence values has been debated.[10]

Should existence values be used in CBA? The answer requires a balancing of conceptual and practical concerns. On the one hand, recognizing existence values as pure public goods argues for their inclusion. On the other hand, given the current state of practice, estimates of existence values are very uncertain. This trade-off suggests the following heuristic: *Although existence values for unique and long-lived assets should be estimated whenever possible, costs and benefits should be presented with and without their inclusion to make clear how they affect net benefits.* When existence values for such assets cannot be measured, analysts should supplement CBA with discussion of their possible significance for the sign of net benefits.

CONCLUSION

As CBA is increasingly applied to environmental policies, concern about existence values among analysts will almost certainly grow. Unless methods of measurement improve substantially, however, deciding when and how to include existence values in CBA will continue to be difficult. By being aware of the limitations of these methods, analysts can be better producers and consumers of CBA.

APPENDIX 8A

EXPENDITURE FUNCTIONS AND THE PARTITIONING OF BENEFITS

Policies that have multiple effects pose conceptual problems for the aggregation of benefits. In most situations, we approximate willingness-to-pay by summing the changes in social surplus associated with each of the effects. In general, however, this procedure tends to overestimate total willingness-to-pay. In this appendix, we introduce some notation for formally representing the measurement of utility changes from policies with multiple effects.[1] We then use a stylized numerical example to show the ambiguity in the partitioning of benefits among the various effects.

Imagine that a person has a budget B and also has a utility function U that depends on the quantities of goods X_1, X_2, ..., X_n. Assume that the prices of these goods are p_1, p_2, ..., p_n, respectively. The problem facing the consumer is to choose the quantities of the goods that maximize U such that $p_1 X_1 + p_2 X_2 + ... + p_n X_n \leq B$. Let U^* be the maximum utility that the person can obtain given B and the prices of the goods. We can construct an expenditure function, $e(p_1, p_2, ..., p_n; U^*)$, which is defined as the minimum dollar amount of budget necessary to obtain utility U^* at the given prices. Obviously, for the original set of prices that we used to find U^*, $e(p_1, p_2, ..., p_n; U^*) = B$.

Assume that we instituted a policy that increased the price of the first good from p_1 to q_1. Associated with this new price is the expenditure function $e(q_1, p_2, ..., p_n; U^*) = B'$, where B' is greater than B because the person must be given more budget to keep the utility equal to U^* in the face of the higher price. A measure of the consumer surplus loss from the price increase is given by

$$e(q_1, p_2, ..., p_n; U^*) - e(p_1, p_2, ..., p_n; U^*)$$

which equals $B' - B$. This amount equals the compensating variation for the price change as discussed in Chapter 3.[2]

Imagine now that X_1 and X_2 are goods, perhaps existence value and hiking, provided to the person by a particular wilderness area. How would we use the expenditure function to value the wilderness area, given the original budget and set of prices?

We want to know how much compensation we would have to give to the person to restore his or her utility level to U^* after making X_1 and X_2 equal zero. In terms of the expenditure function, we do this by setting p_1 and p_2 sufficiently high so that the person's demand for X_1 and X_2 is "choked off" at zero quantities. Assume that p_{1c} and p_{2c} choke off demand. To get the total value of the wilderness area to the individual, TV, we calculate how much additional budget we would have to give the person to return him or her to the original utility level:

$$TV = e(p_{1c}, p_{2c}, ..., p_n; U^*) - e(p_1, p_2, ..., p_n; U^*)$$

which is an unambiguous and correct measure of the person's willingness-to-pay for the wilderness area.

Now consider how we might partition TV into its two components associated with X_1 and X_2. One way would be to first value X_1 and then X_2. We can express this by adding and subtracting $e(p_1, p_{2c}, ..., p_n; U^*)$ to the equation for TV to get the following equation:

$$TV = [e(p_{1c}, p_{2c}, ..., p_n; U^*) - e(p_1, p_{2c}, ..., p_n; U^*)]$$
$$+ [e(p_1, p_{2c}, ..., p_n; U^*) - e(p_1, p_2, ..., p_n; U^*)]$$

where the first line represents the willingness-to-pay to obtain X_1 at price p_1 and the second line represents the willingness-to-pay to obtain subsequently X_2 at price p_2.

The other possible partition is to first restore X_2 at price p_2 and then restore X_1 at price p_1. It is expressed by the following equation:

$$TV = [e(p_{1c}, p_{2c}, ..., p_n; U^*) - e(p_{1c}, p_2, ..., p_n; U^*)]$$
$$+ [e(p_{1c}, p_2, ..., p_n; U^*) - e(p_1, p_2, ..., p_n; U^*)]$$

where the first line represents the willingness-to-pay to obtain X_2 at price p_2 and the second line represents the willingness-to-pay to subsequently obtain X_1 at price p_1.

These alternative partitionings will not in general yield the same willingness-to-pay amounts for X_1 and X_2. Typically, the willingness-to-pay for a good will be greater if the good is introduced in the partitioning sequence earlier rather than later. The rough intuition behind this result is that a good will be relatively less valuable at the margin if it is added to an already full bundle of goods.

If one can measure TV directly, then this ambiguity in partitioning is of little concern.[3] In most circumstances, however, analysts attempt to construct TV from independent estimates of separate benefit categories. In terms of expenditure functions, what is commonly done can be expressed as follows:

$$\text{TB} = [e(p_{1c}, p_{2c}, ..., p_n; U^*) - e(p_1, p_{2c}, ..., p_n; U^*)]$$
$$+ [e(p_{1c}, p_{2c}, ..., p_n; U^*) - e(p_{1c}, p_2, ..., p_n; U^*)]$$

where the first line is the compensating variation for making *only* X_1 available, the second line is the compensating variation for making *only* X_2 available, and TB is the total estimated benefits. In general, TB does not equal TV. TB systematically overestimates TV. The overestimation tends to increase as the number of benefit components increases.[4]

We next illustrate these concepts with the stylized numerical example presented in Table 8.A1. The model assumes that the person's utility, U, depends on three goods: E, the size of the wilderness area (existence); X, a particular use of the wilderness area such as hiking; and Z, a composite good that represents all goods other than E and X. It also depends on the parameter Q, an index of the quality of the wilderness area. The person has a budget of $B = 100$ and faces prices for E, X, and Z of $p_e = \$.50$, $p_x = \$1$, and $p_z = \$2$, respectively.[5] The quantities of E, X, and Z that maximize utility for the parameter values listed in the table can be found through numerical methods to be $E = 9.89$, $X = 30.90$, and $Z = 32.08$.[6] The utility from this combination of goods, U^*, equals 38.93.

The expenditure function follows directly. Obviously, the budget that gives $U^* = 38.93$ is just the budget of $100 in the optimization. Therefore, we can write the expenditure function for the initial position as

$$e(p_e = 0.5, p_x = 1, p_z = 2; Q = 1; U^* = 38.93) = 100$$

Before illustrating the partitioning problem, it may be helpful to consider how expenditure functions can be used to find compensating variations for independent policy effects. Consider, for instance, how one can find the compensating variation for a reduction in the price of X from $1 to $.50. The procedure involves finding the expenditure function,

$$e(p_e = 0.5, p_x = 0.5, p_z = 2; Q = 1; U^* = 38.93) = 63.25$$

by asking what budget amount would allow the person to obtain the original utility at the lower price. The compensating variation for the price reduction is just the difference between the values of the expenditure function with the lower price, $63.25, and the value of the original expenditure function, $100. Therefore, the compensating variation is −$36.75. In other words, the person's budget could be reduced by $36.75 after the price reduction without any loss of utility.

Now consider how one could value a policy that would increase the quality index, Q, by 10 percent. The expenditure function for the quality improvement relative to the initial position is

$$e(p_e = 0.5, p_x = 1, p_z = 2; Q = 1.1; U^* = 38.93) = 94.45$$

TABLE 8.A1 AN ILLUSTRATION OF THE PARTITIONING PROBLEM

Utility Function	$U(E, X, Z; Q) = QE^{\gamma} + QX^{\beta} + Z^{\theta}$ where E is the quantity of wilderness that exists, X is the use level of the wilderness, Z is a market good, and Q is an index of quality of the wilderness.
Budget Constraint	$B = p_e E + p_x X + p_z Z$ where B is the available budget, and p_e, p_x, and p_z are the respective prices of E, X, and Z.
Optimization Problem	Maximize $L = U + \lambda[B - p_e E - p_x X - p_z Z]$ where λ is the marginal utility of money.
Numerical Assumptions	$Q = 1$; $\gamma = 0.5$; $\beta = 0.75$; $\theta = 0.9$; $p_e = 0.5$; $p_x = 1$; $p_z = 2$; $B = 100$
Solution Values	$E = 9.89$; $X = 30.90$; $Z = 32.08$; $\lambda = .318$ $U(9.89, 30.90, 32.08; 1) = 38.93 = U^*$ $e(p_e, p_x, p_z; Q; U^*) = e(0.5, 1, 2; 1; 38.93) = 100$
Expenditure Functions	Wilderness area not available: $e(\infty, \infty, 2; 1; 38.93)$ $\quad = 116.95$ Wilderness existence, no use: $e(0.5, \infty, 2; 1; 38.93)$ $\quad = 111.42$ Wilderness use only: $e(\infty, 1, 2; 1; 38.93)$ $\quad = 105.04$
Existence-Use Partition TV = 16.95	Existence value $= e(\infty, \infty, 2; 1; 38.93) - e(0.5, \infty, 2; 1; 38.93)$ $= 116.95 - 111.42 = 5.53$ Use value $= e(0.5, \infty, 2; 1; 38.93) - e(0.5, 1, 2; 1; 38.93)$ $= 111.42 - 100 = 11.42$
Use-Existence Partition TV = 16.95	Use value $= e(\infty, \infty, 2; 1; 38.93) - e(\infty, 1, 2; 1; 38.93)$ $= 116.95 - 105.04 = 11.91$ Existence value $= e(\infty, 1, 2; 1; 38.93) - e(0.5, 1, 2; 1; 38.93)$ $= 105.04 - 100 = 5.04$
Independent Summation TB = 17.44	Existence value $= e(\infty, \infty, 2; 1; 38.93) - e(0.5, \infty, 2; 1; 38.93)$ $= 116.95 - 111.42 = 5.53$ Use value $= e(\infty, \infty, 2; 1; 38.93) - e(\infty, 1, 2; 1; 38.93)$ $= 116.95 - 105.04 = 11.91$

which indicates that the compensating variation for the quality improvement is −$5.55 ($94.45 − $100), indicating that the original utility could be otained with a smaller budget.

Returning to the initial position, let us now consider the total value of wilderness, TV, and the two ways of partitioning it between existence and use. We choke off consumption of E and X by setting their prices at infinity. This yields the expenditure function,

$$e(p_e = \infty, p_x = \infty, p_z = 2; Q = 1; U^* = 38.93) = 116.95$$

which implies that the wilderness area has a total value of $16.95 ($116.95–$100). If we partition first by existence and then by use, we calculate

$$e(p_e = 0.5, p_x = \infty, p_z = 2; Q = 1; U^* = 38.93) = 111.42$$

which implies an existence value of \$5.53 (\$116.95 – \$111.42) and a use value of \$11.42 (\$111.42 – \$100).[7] If instead we partition first by use and then by existence, we calculate

$$e(p_e = \infty, p_x = 1, p_z = 2; Q = 1; U^* = 38.93) = 105.04$$

which implies a use value of \$11.91 (\$116.95 – \$105.04) and an existence value of \$5.04 (\$105.04 – \$100).[8] Thus, we see that the sequence of valuation makes a difference: Existence and use are each larger when they are valued first rather than second.[9]

Finally, consider the independent summation of benefits. Existence is valued as in the existence-use sequence and use is valued as in the use-existence sequence. Thus, we would estimate the total value of the wilderness to be \$17.44 (\$5.53 + \$11.91), which exceeds the correct compensating variation by \$.49 (\$17.44 – \$16.95).

In summary, the partitioning of benefits between existence and use is conceptually ambiguous when the same individuals derive both values from a policy change. More generally, policies that affect people's utilities in multiple ways are prone to overestimation of willingness-to-pay when each effect is valued independently as a separate benefit category.

EXERCISES FOR CHAPTER 8

1. Imagine a wilderness area of 200 square miles in the Rocky Mountains. How would you expect each of the following factors to affect people's willingness-to-pay for its preservation?
   a. The size of the total wilderness area still remaining in the Rocky Mountains.
   b. The presence of rare species in this particular area.
   c. The level of national wealth.
2. An analyst wishing to estimate the benefits of preserving a wetland has combined information obtained from two methods. First, she surveyed those who visited the wetland—fishers, duck hunters, and bird watchers—to determine their willingness-to-pay for these uses. Second, she surveyed a sample of residents throughout the state about their willingness-to-pay to preserve the wetland. This second survey focused exclusively on nonuse values of the wetland. She then added her estimate of use benefits to her estimate of nonuse benefits to get an estimate of the total value of preservation of the wetland. Is this a reasonable approach? [Note: In responding to this question assume that there was virtually no overlap in the persons contacted in the two surveys.]

NOTES

[1]John V. Krutilla, "Conservation Reconsidered," *American Economic Review*, 57, no. 4 (September 1967), 777–786 at p. 784.

[2]Charles Plourde, "Conservation of Extinguishable Species," *Natural Resources Journal*, 15, no. 4 (October 1975), 791–797.

[3]Bruce Madariaga and Kenneth E. McConnell, "Exploring Existence Value," *Water Resources Research*, 23, no. 5 (May 1987), 936–942.

[4]For an overview, see V. Kerry Smith, "Nonmarket Valuation of Environmental Resources," *Land Economics*, 69, no. 1 (February 1993), 1–26.

[5]Ronald J. Southerland and Richard G. Walsh, "The Effect of Distance on the Preservation Value of Water Quality," *Land Economics*, 61, no. 3 (August 1985), 281–291.

[6]Raymond J. Kopp and V. Kerry Smith, "Benefit Estimation Goes to Court: The Case of Natural Resource Damage Assessment," *Journal of Policy Analysis and Management*, 8, no. 4 (Fall 1989), 593–612.

[7]Bruce Madariaga and Kenneth E. McConnell, "Exploring Existence Value," *Water Resources Research*, 23, no. 5 (May 1987), 936–942.

[8]Douglas M. Larson, "On Measuring Existence Value," *Land Economics*, 69, no. 1 (Winter 1992), 116–122.

[9]See, for example, David S. Brookshire, Larry S. Eubanks, and Alan Randall, "Estimating Option Prices and Existence Values for Wildlife Resources," *Land Economics*, 59, no. 1 (February 1983), 1–15; Richard G. Walsh, John B. Loomis, and Richard A. Gillman, "Valuing Option, Existence, and Bequest Demands for Wilderness," *Land Economics*, 60, no. 1 (February 1984), 14–29; Kevin J. Boyle and Richard C. Bishop, "Valuing Wildlife in Benefit-Cost Analysis: A Case Study Involving Endangered Species," *Water Resources Research*, 23, no. 5 (May 1987), 943–950; K.G. Willis, "Valuing Non-Market Wildlife Commodities: An Evaluation and Comparison of Benefits and Costs," *Applied Economics*, 22, no. 1 (January 1990), 13–30; and Thomas H. Stevens, Jaime Echeverria, Ronald J. Glass, Tim Hager, and Thomas A. More, "Measuring the Existence Value of Wildlife: What Do CVM Estimates Really Show?" *Land Economics*, 67, no. 4 (November 1991), 390–400.

[10]See, for example, Donald H. Rosenthal and Robert H. Nelson, "Why Existence Value Should *Not* Be Used in Cost-Benefit Analysis," *Journal of Policy Analysis and Management*, 11, no. 1 (Winter 1992), 116–122; and Raymond J. Kopp, "Why Existence Value *Should* Be Used in Cost-Benefit Analysis," *Journal of Policy Analysis and Management*, 11, no. 1 (Winter 1992), 123–130.

APPENDIX NOTES

[1]A more formal treatment can be found in Alan Randall, "Total and Nonuse Values," in *Measuring the Demand for Environmental Quality*, John B. Braden and Charles D. Kolstad, eds. (New York: North-Holland, 1991), 303–321. The original analysis of the importance of the sequence of valuation can be found in J.R. Hicks, *A Revision of Demand Theory* (Oxford, United Kingdom: Clarendon Press, 1956), 169–179.

[2]Though we use compensating variation as a measure of the dollar value of utility here because we find it most intuitive, equivalent variation, which measures welfare changes relative to the utility level after the price change, is generally considered a superior money metric for utility because it provides an unambiguous ordinal measure for ranking price changes. See George W. McKenzie, *Measuring Economic Welfare: New Methods* (New York: Cambridge University Press, 1983).

If $U\sim$ is the utility after the price change, then the equivalent variation is

$$e(q_1, p_2, ..., p_n; U\sim) - e(p_1, p_2, ..., p_n; U\sim)$$

where $e(q_1, p_2, ..., p_n; U\sim) = B$.

Compensating and equivalent variation typically differ by a small amount due to income effects. In the case of quantity changes of public goods, however, the size of their difference also depends on the availability of close substitutes for the public good. See W. Michael Hanemann, "Willingness-To-Pay and Willingness-To-Accept: How Much Can They Differ?" *American Economic Review*, 81, no. 3 (June 1991), 635–647.

[3]Of course, the value of TV will depend on whether it is measured in terms of compensating variation or equivalent variation.

[4]John P. Hoehn and Alan Randall, "Too Many Proposals Pass the Benefit Cost Test," *American Economic Review*, 79, no. 3 (June 1989), 544–551.

[5]If E is a public good, then we would interpret p_e as the tax per unit of E that the person pays. As everyone would have to consume the same quantity, the person would not be able to choose the value of E so that the optimization of utility would be over only X and Z.

[6]The partial derivatives of L with respect to E, X, Z, and λ give four equations in four unknowns. Although these *first-order conditions* cannot be solved analytically, they can be rearranged so that E, X, and Z are each expressed as a function of λ and parameters. A solution can be found by guessing values of λ until a value is found that implies values of E, X, and Z that satisfy the budget constraint.

[7]If we assume that E is fixed at its initial level, the more realistic case in evaluating an existing wilderness area, then the existence value equals only $5.47. It is smaller than in the example because the person does not have the opportunity to purchase more E when X is not available. This assumption changes neither the TV nor the existence value as estimated by the use-existence partition.

[8]It may seem strange to partition in this way because one would normally think of existence as being a prerequisite for use. Some types of uses, however, could be provided without maintaining existence value. For example, through stocking it may be possible to provide game fishing without preserving a stream in its natural form.

[9]Using equivalent variation rather than compensating variation as the consumer surplus measure leads to the following:

$$e(p_e = \infty,\ p_x = \infty, p_z = 2; Q = 1; U{\sim} = 33.81) = 100.00$$
$$e(p_e = 0.5,\ p_x = 1, p_z = 2; Q = 1; U{\sim} = 33.81) = 84.10$$
$$e(p_e = \infty,\ p_x = 1, p_z = 2; Q = 1; U{\sim} = 33.81) = 89.00$$
$$e(p_e = 0.5,\ p_x = \infty, p_z = 2; Q = 1; U{\sim} = 33.81) = 94.68$$

$\text{TV}_{ev} = 100.00 - 84.10 = 15.90$

Existence-use partition:	existence value	=	100.00	–	94.68	= 5.32
	use value	=	94.68	–	84.10	= 10.58
Use-existence partition:	use value	=	100.00	–	89.00	= 11.00
	existence value	=	89.00	–	84.10	= 4.90
Independent summation:	existence value	=	100.00	–	94.68	= 5.32
	use value	=	100.00	–	89.00	= 11.00

$\text{TB}_{ev} = 16.32$

9

ESTIMATING IMPACTS
FROM DEMONSTRATIONS

Throughout this book, we have emphasized that the key concept in valuing the positive and negative outcomes (impacts) of a policy is willingness-to-pay as measured by changes in social surplus. To estimate changes in social surplus, we needed to know the shape of relevant supply and demand curves. Earlier, we typically assumed that these were known. In practice, however, these curves are usually unknown. The analyst has to either estimate them in order to give precise measures of benefits and costs or find an alternative means of valuing policy impacts.

Analysts in fact typically face a continuum of possibilities. At one end of this continuum are policy impacts on commodities that are traded in well-functioning, competitive markets. At the other end are policy impacts on goods that are rarely traded in markets—impacts, for example, on health and safety, pollution levels, and access to scenic areas. In between are impacts on commodities that are traded in markets with important distortions such as monopoly power, information asymmetries, and externalities.

Where markets work well, analysts know at least one point on the demand and supply curves, represented by the observed intersection of market price and quantity exchanged, but still have to estimate these curves to measure either existing social surplus or changes in social surplus. Remember from Chapter 3 that changes in social surplus are approximated by areas, such as triangles, rectangles, and trapezoids. Conceptually, estimation can be done using relatively standard econometric techniques, but only when suitable data are available.

As we have seen, however, the rationale for much CBA is that markets are nonexistent or imperfect. In these situations, the analyst may not have even one point on the appropriate demand or supply curve, which makes it particularly difficult to estimate the impacts.

Nonetheless, as we show in this and the next three chapters, all is not lost! These chapters describe practical ways to estimate the impacts of a policy when estimates of the appropriate demand and supply curves are not readily available. In this chapter, we focus on estimating benefits and costs on the basis of *demonstrations* or *pilot programs*. (We use the two terms interchangeably; both remind us that the purpose of the project is to learn whether the program "works.")

The chapter first presents a brief discussion of using demonstration projects to obtain estimates of benefits and costs. It then explores alternative ways in which these demonstrations might be structured. The remainder of the chapter shows the value of demonstrations by describing their use in cost-benefit analyses of employment and training programs. The observed impacts of employment and training demonstrations have been extensively used in conducting CBAs. The chapter concludes by examining actual CBAs of employment and training demonstration programs that were targeted at welfare recipients.

WHY CONDUCT DEMONSTRATION PROJECTS?

In Chapter 1, we noted that the fourth of the basic steps in conducting CBAs is to predict impacts over the life of a project. Demonstration projects can help in doing this. They provide a straightforward method for measuring impacts in the case of proposed programs that provide services to people—for example, health, education, training, employment, housing, and welfare programs. The method works by setting up a small-scale replica or demonstration of the proposed program. To understand why demonstration projects are almost exclusively limited to testing programs that provide people-oriented services, just think about how to pilot test a proposed physical investment, such as a new dam, on a small-scale, pilot basis.

The idea behind demonstration projects is to see if the tested program works before it is adopted on a widespread basis. *Ex post* findings from the demonstration can be plugged into an *ex ante* analysis that computes benefits and costs for the full-scale program. For example, parameters estimated from the Seattle–Denver negative income tax experiment, a prominent demonstration program, have been used to predict the costs and benefits of proposed changes in the U.S. welfare system.[1]

An advantage of conducting a CBA of a demonstration project is that if it turns out that certain aspects of the program need adjustment, this can be done before the program is implemented on a widespread basis. Even more importantly, if it turns out that the program is a bad idea because costs exceed benefits, it can be scrapped before it is expanded and interest groups form to protect it.

Although the small scale of pilot projects offers important advantages, there are also potential disadvantages. First, the impacts of a small-scale demonstration program may not readily translate to a fully implemented large-scale program. For example, while it may be fairly easy to find jobs for graduates of a demonstration program that retrains unemployed workers as electricians if the program has only a few graduates, doing this may be far more difficult if large numbers of unemployed persons graduate from a full-scale program and seek employment in the same geographic area.

A second and related disadvantage of small-scale demonstration programs is uncertainty concerning their *external validity*. That is, there is no assurance that findings from the evaluation, even though valid for the group of persons who participated in the demonstration program, can be generalized to any other group. The reasons for this is that personal and community characteristics interact in complex ways with the services provided by a demonstration program. As a result, the program may more effectively serve some persons than others. For example, findings for a training program for unemployed male blue-collar workers who live in a community with low unemployment may provide little information concerning how well the program would work for unemployed female welfare recipients who live in a community with high unemployment. For this reason, some demonstration programs are tested on a variety of different groups in different locations.

ALTERNATIVE EVALUATION DESIGNS

CBAs of pilot projects require comparisons between alternatives: The existing environment is compared to the proposed program being tested by the demonstration, and impact is measured as differences in outcomes between the two situations. The term *internal validity* refers to whether this measured difference can be attributed to the program being evaluated. Internal validity, in turn, depends on the particular way in which the comparison between the existing environment and the proposed program is made. There are numerous ways in which this comparison can be made. Researchers usually refer to the specific scheme used for making comparisons in order to measure impacts as an *evaluation design*.

Diagrams that represent five commonly used evaluation designs,[2] as well as brief summaries of the advantages and disadvantages of each of these designs, appear in Table 9.1. In these diagrams, the symbol 0 represents an outcome measurement point, X represents a treatment point, and R indicates that subjects were assigned randomly to treatment and control groups.

The evaluation designs that are listed in Table 9.1 are not the only ones that exist. There are numerous others. But these designs provide a good sampling of the major alternatives. So that we can make our discussion of them as concrete as possible, we assume that they all pertain to alternative ways in which a pilot program for training the unemployed might be evaluated. In this context, "being in the treatment group" means enrollment in the training program.

Design 1: Classical Experimental Design

Design 1 is a classical experimental design. The symbols indicate that unemployed persons are randomly allocated between a treatment group and a control (or comparison) group. Members of the treatment group can receive services from the pilot training program, while persons in the control group cannot. The way this might work in actual practice is that once the pilot program is put into place, unemployed persons are notified of its existence. Some of these persons apply to participate in it. A computer

TABLE 9.1   FIVE COMMONLY USED EVALUATION DESIGNS

Type	Structure	Major Advantages	Major Disadvantages
Design 1: Comparison of Net Changes Between Treatment and True Control Groups	$R: O_1 \ X \ O_2$ ――― $R: O_3 \quad O_4$	Random assignment guards against systematic differences between control and treatment groups so highest internal validity.	Direct and ethical costs of random assignment; as with all evaluations of demonstrations, external validity may be limited.
Design 2: Comparison of Posttreatment Outcomes Between True Control and Treatment Groups	$R: X \ O_2$ ――― $R: \quad O_4$	Random assignment guards against systematic differences between control and treatment groups so high internal validity.	Direct and ethical costs of random assignment; danger that a failure of randomization will not be detected.
Design 3: Simple Before/After Comparison	$O_1 \ X \ O_2$	Often feasible and relatively inexpensive; reasonable when factors other than treatment are unlikely to affect outcome.	Does not control for other factors that may cause change.
Design 4: Comparison of Posttreatment Outcomes Between Quasi-Control and Treatment Groups	$X \ O_1$ ――― O_2	Allows for possibility of statistically controlling for factors other than treatment.	Danger of sample selection bias—systematic differences between treatment and quasi-control groups.
Design 5: Comparison of Net Changes Between Treatment and Quasi-Control Group	$O_1 \ X \ O_2$ ――― $O_3 \quad O_4$	Allows for possibility of statistically controlling for factors other than treatment; permits detection of measureable differences between treatment and quasi-control groups.	Danger of sample selection bias—systematic differences between treatment and quasi-control group in terms of nonmeasurable differences.

O—observation
X—treatment
R—random assignment

Source: Based on notation introduced by Donald T. Campbell and Julian Stanley, *Experimental and Quasi-Experimental Designs for Research* (Chicago: Rand McNally College Publishing Company, 1963).

is used, in effect, to flip a fair coin: Heads the applicant is selected as a member of the treatment group and, consequently, becomes eligible to participate in the program; tails the applicant becomes a member of the control group. Controls are not eligible to participate in the program but can receive whatever other services are available for the unemployed.

The procedure just described for establishing treatment and control groups is called *random assignment*.[3] Random assignment evaluations of pilot projects of social programs—for instance, a training program—are often called *social experiments*.

To see how well the pilot program works, data on outcomes are collected for both the treatment group and the control group, both before the treatment is administered and afterward. Members of the experimental and control groups are compared by using the data that are collected. For example, the earnings of the two groups can be compared sometime after the training is completed to measure the size of the program's impact on earnings.[4]

Of the five design schemes summarized in Table 9.1, design 1 is the best for many types of evaluations. Its major advantage is the use of random assignment. Because of random assignment, the characteristics of people in the treatment and control groups should be similar, varying only by chance alone. As a result, random assignment helps assure the evaluation of internal validity; that is, members of the experimental groups can be directly compared in terms of such outcomes as earnings, and any differences that are found between them can be reasonably attributed to the treatment.

Sometimes, however, random assignment may be impractical or infeasible.[5] One reason for this is the resources required to assign individuals randomly to treatment and control groups. Generally, however, these resource costs are quite small.

A second reason concerns the notion of experimenting on human beings. For example, randomization implies that some persons—those assigned to the comparison group—will be denied services under the demonstration program. It is important to recognize, however, that if a program has only limited resources, some potential program participants will inevitably be denied services, and random assignment (which operates very much like a lottery) may be as fair a way to do this as any. A more serious ethical issue is raised by the possibility that some experimental treatments may actually harm some members of the treatment group. For example, as cost-benefit findings reported later in this chapter indicate, some training programs have actually been found to reduce the incomes of participants.

A third reason is pertinent in the case of demonstration programs that are expected to obtain their impacts through communitywide effects. For example, a training program that is available to *all* unemployed persons in a particular community will become well known to both the unemployed and employers. As a result, the attitudes of the unemployed toward entering training and the decisions of employers concerning hiring the graduates of training programs could both be affected. Such effects are unlikely to occur in the case of a random assignment experiment in which only a subset of the unemployed are allowed to participate.

Design 2: Classical Experimental Design Without Baseline Data

Design 2 is similar to design 1 in that random assignment is also used to allocate individuals between the treatment and control groups, and both are referred to as *experimental designs*. The difference between the two designs is that collection of pretreatment, baseline information on members of the treatment and control groups is not part of design 2, but is part of design 1. The problem with not collecting pretreatment information is that there is no way of checking whether the treatment and control groups are basically similar or dissimilar.

For the comparison between the two groups to measure program effects accurately, the groups should, of course, be as similar as possible. But, as previously mentioned, they could be dissimilar by chance alone. This is more likely if each group only has a few hundred members, as is sometimes the case in social experiments. It is also possible that those running an experiment fail to implement the random assignment process correctly. If information is available on pretreatment status—for example, on pretreatment earnings—statistical adjustments can be made to make the comparison between the treatment and the control groups more valid. Hence, there is usually less certainty concerning internal validity with design 2 than design 1.

Design 3: Before and After Comparison

Design 3 is by far the worst of the five designs, relying as it does on a simple *before and after comparison* of the same group of individuals. For example, the earnings of a group of individuals that went through a training program are compared with their earnings before going through the program. The problem with this design is that there is no information on what would have happened without the program. Consequently, there is no way to ensure internal validity. For example, the average earnings of people going into a training program are likely to be very low if most of these people are unemployed at the time of entry. That, perhaps, is why they decided to go into the program in the first place. Even without the program, however, they might have found jobs eventually. If so, their average earnings would have gone up over time even if the program did not exist. With a before and after comparison, this increase in earnings would be incorrectly attributed to the program.

Before and after comparisons do offer certain advantages, however. They provide a comparatively inexpensive way of conducting evaluations. Moreover, when valid information is not available for a control group, a before and after comparison may be the only feasible way of conducting an evaluation. Such a comparison is obviously most valid when nonprogram factors are not expected to affect the outcomes of interest (for example, earnings) or can be taken into account through statistical adjustments.

Design 4: Nonexperimental Comparison Without Baseline Data

Design 4 is based on a comparison of two different groups, one that has gone through a program and the other that has not. Membership in the two groups is not determined by random assignment, however. For example, the comparison group could be made up of people who originally applied for training but ultimately decided not to participate. Because such a comparison group is not selected through random assignment, it is sometimes called a *quasi-control group.* As previously discussed, use of a quasi-control group may be necessary when obtaining a comparison group through random assignment seems to be costly, raises serious ethical issues, or would cause potentially important community effects to be ignored.

Unfortunately, with this design there is no means of controlling for those differences between the two groups that existed prior to the treatment and, hence, no way to ensure internal validity. Perhaps, for example, at the time of application for training, those who ultimately went through the program had been unemployed for a longer period of time than persons in the comparison group, suggesting that in the absence of training they would have fared worse in the job market than members of the comparison group. But if at the end of training, it is observed that they actually did just as well as persons in the comparison group, this suggests the training had an impact: It pulled the trainees up even with the comparison group. However, with design 4, there is no way to know the difference in the length of unemployment prior to training. As a result, it would just be observed that after training members of the treatment group were doing no better than people in the comparison group. This finding is subject to a bias known as *sample selection bias* that results because systematic differences between the treatment and quasi-control group are not, indeed cannot be, taken into account. In this instance, sample selection bias is quite important because it could lead to the incorrect conclusion that the training made no difference.

Design 5: Nonexperimental Comparison With Baseline Data

Design 5 utilizes both a treatment group and a control group. In addition, both pretreatment and posttreatment data are collected. This provides information on how the treatment group differed from the comparison group prior to the training. This information can be used in a statistical analysis to control for pretreatment differences between the treatment and control groups. For this reason, design 5 offers greater opportunity to obtain internal validity than either designs 3 or 4.

Even so, because this design does not randomly assign individuals to the treatment and control groups, a major problem occurs if people in the treatment and the comparison groups differ from one another in ways that cannot be measured readily. Then it becomes very difficult to adjust statistically for differences between the two groups. Perhaps, for example, unemployed persons who enter training are more motivated than unemployed persons who do not. If so, they might receive higher earnings over time even without the training. If analysts cannot somehow take account of this difference in motivation—in practice, sometimes they can, but often they cannot—they may incorrectly conclude that higher posttraining earnings received by the trainees are due to the training when, in fact, they are really due to greater motivation on the part of the trainees. In the evaluation literature, such a situation creates a threat to internal validity that is known as the *selection problem*.[6]

The occurrence of selection problems can be greatly reduced by using design 1 or 2. The reason is that when random assignment is used, people assigned to the treatment group should not differ from members of the comparison group in terms of characteristics such as motivation except by chance alone. Because of this advantage, an increasing number of demonstration projects that embody experimental designs have been conducted over the past several decades.[7] Indeed, the federal government has spent around $1 billion conducting design 1 studies since the late 1960s.[8] However, large numbers of demonstrations that utilize nonexperimental designs, such as designs 3, 4, and 5, also continue to be conducted.

CBAs OF DEMONSTRATION PROJECTS

Although numerous demonstrations of programs that provide services to people have been conducted, formal CBAs have been carried out for only a minority of them. Sometimes the evaluations of particular demonstrations have focused instead on only one or two outcomes of interest. For example, demonstrations in the housing or health areas might be mainly concerned with whether the tested program could be adminis-tered effectively or whether housing or health status improved, and thus no attempt may be made to measure other benefits and costs associated with the program. In a few relatively rare instances, demonstrations have been used to estimate demand and supply relationships. Though these estimates can be used in CBAs, the demonstrations themselves were not subjected to CBA. Two especially important examples of such demonstrations are described in Exhibits 9.1 and 9.2.

■ **EXHIBIT 9.1**

How the consumption of medical care changes as a function of the cost of care to those who use it is central to many public policy questions, especially those pertaining to uni-versal health insurance. Between 1974 and 1977, the federal government funded a social experiment, the Rand Health Insurance Experiment, at six sites. Analysis of data from this experiment by Willard Manning and colleagues suggests that the price elasticity of demand for health-care services is in the range of –0.1 to –0.2.

Source: Willard G. Manning, Joseph P. Newhouse, Naihua Duan, Emmett B. Keeler, Aileen Leibowitz, and Susan Marquis, "Health Insurance and the Demand for Medical Care: Evidence from a Randomized Experiment," *American Economic Review*, 77, no. 3 (June 1987), 251–277.

■ **EXHIBIT 9.2**

During the late 1960s and early 1970s, the U.S. government funded four income main-tenance experiments, which focused on how income transfers affected the supply of labor (equivalently the demand for leisure) of low-income persons. Data from these experiments were used to obtain estimates of wage and income elasticities. Based on averages of separate estimates from the numerous studies that have relied on data from these experiments, Gary Burtless reported the following elasticity values:

	Married Men	Married Women	Single Mothers
Compensated Wage Elasticity	0.09	0.24	0.14
Uncompensated Wage Elasticity	–0.02	0.17	–0.04
Income Elasticity	–0.11	–0.07	–0.18

Source: Gary Burtless, "The Work Response to Guaranteed Income: A Survey of Experimental Evidence," in *Lessons from the Income Maintenance Experiments*, ed. Alicia Munnell (Boston: Federal Reserve Bank of Boston, 1986), 22–52.

CBAs OF EMPLOYMENT AND TRAINING DEMONSTRATIONS: AN INTRODUCTION

Interestingly, almost all the demonstrations that have been subjected to CBA have test-ed programs that attempt to increase the employment or earnings of unemployed or low-skilled workers. In recent years, many of these demonstrations have focused on the welfare population. The services provided by these demonstration programs have varied considerably but have included job search assistance, remedial education, vocational training, subsidizing private-sector employers in exchange for hiring program participants, and the direct provision of public-sector jobs to participants. Although the individual programs that provide such services often differ greatly from one another, such programs are often referred to as *employment and training (E&T) programs.*

Because existing CBAs of demonstrations are almost exclusively limited to those that test various combinations of E&T services, the chapter next discusses issues that arise in conducting CBAs of E&T demonstrations. Then these issues are further examined in the context of actual findings from a set of politically influential CBAs of E&T demonstrations that targeted welfare recipients and were conducted during the 1980s.

THE CBA FRAMEWORK IN THE EDUCATION
AND TRAINING CONTEXT

The basic CBA accounting framework has been described in previous chapters. However, different policy areas have developed variations of the basic CBA framework that address issues specific to each area. The particular accounting framework that is used today in conducting most CBAs of E&T programs was developed during the late 1970s and early 1980s. A stylized version of this framework appears in Table 9.2. Although details concerning the specifics of the framework vary somewhat from one E&T CBA to another, depending upon the specific nature of the services provided, the table lists those benefit and cost components that are typically measured.

This framework offers several advantages: It is readily understandable to policymakers; by displaying benefits and costs from the perspectives of both participants and nonparticipants, it suggests some of the distributional implications of the program being evaluated; and, possibly most important, because measures of each cost-benefit component listed in Table 9.2 can actually be obtained from demonstration data, it is operationally feasible. Indeed, as will be seen, it is far easier to find shortcomings in the framework than to suggest practical alternatives to it.

Table 9.2 presents the benefit and cost impact categories of a stylized E&T demonstration. Plus signs indicate anticipated sources of benefits and minus signs anticipated sources of costs from different perspectives. The first column (*A*) shows aggregate benefits and costs from the perspective of society as a whole. The remaining columns show the distribution of benefits and costs to the two groups that are typically relevant in assessing E&T programs: participants or clients served by the demonstration program (*B*); and nonparticipants, including taxpayers who pay for the program (*C*).

Benefits and costs to society are simply the algebraic sum of benefits and costs to participants and to nonparticipants because society is the sum of these two groups. Hence, the table implies that if a demonstration program causes transfer payments received by participants (e.g., unemployment compensation or AFDC receipts) to decline, this should be regarded as a savings or benefit to nonparticipant taxpayers; a

TABLE 9.2   STYLIZED COST-BENEFIT FRAMEWORK OF E&T DEMONSTRATIONS

	Society (A) (B + C)	Participant (B)	Nonparticipant (C)
Output Produced by Participant			
In-Program Output	+	0	+
Gross Earnings	+	+	0
Fringe Benefits	+	+	0
Participant Work-Related Expenditures			
Tax Payments	0	−	+
Expenditures on Child Care, Transportation, etc.	−	−	0
Use of Transfer Programs by Participants			
AFDC Payments	0	−	+
Other Transfer Payments	0	−	+
Program Operating Costs	+	0	+
Use of Support Programs by Participants			
Support Services Received by Participants	−	0	−
Allowances Received by Participants	0	+	−
Program Operating Costs	−	0	−

cost to program participants (albeit one that may be offset by earnings), and neither a benefit nor a cost to society as a whole but simply income transferred from one segment of the population to another.

This approach is consistent with the standard one used in CBA. As we have seen, in standard CBA "a dollar is a dollar," no matter to whom it accrues. Thus, in Table 9.2, a dollar gained or lost by an E&T participant is treated identically to a dollar gained or lost by a nonparticipant. Consequently, if an E&T program caused the transfer dollars received by participants to fall, this would be viewed as not affecting society as a whole because the loss to participants would be fully offset by benefits to nonparticipants in the form of reductions in government budgetary outlays.

Typically, however, E&T participants have much lower incomes, on average, than nonparticipants. For reasons that will be discussed in detail in Chapter 14, a case can be made for treating the gains and losses of low-income persons differently than those of higher-income persons. In particular, it can be argued that a *distributional weighting* scheme be used in which the gains and losses of relatively low-income persons, such as E&T participants, would be given a weight greater than one and those of higher-income persons, such as nonparticipants, a weight of only one. Once this weighting is completed, *distributionally weighted* social benefits and costs can then be computed. The obvious practical problem with the weighting approach, however, is that the values of the weights that should be used are unknown. As a consequence, CBAs of E&T demonstrations typically do not engage in weighting. Instead, as can be seen in Table 9.2, they simply lay out the results so that the distributional consequences of a particular program can be observed.

Table 9.2 divides the benefits and costs associated with E&T demonstrations into four major categories. The first two of these categories pertain to effects that result if a demonstration increases the work effort or productivity of participants—for example, by providing them work in a public-sector job where they perform useful services, providing them skill training, or helping them find private-sector employment through job search assistance. On the one hand, the value of the output they produce will rise, which in the private sector should be reflected by increases in earnings and fringe benefits. On the other hand, if hours at work rise, expenditures on child care and transportation will also increase. And if earnings rise, tax payments will also increase. The third major cost-benefit category in Table 9.2 pertains to decreases in dependency on transfer payments that may result from an E&T program. Such reductions in dependency should cause both the amount of payments distributed under transfer programs and the cost of administering these programs to fall. The fourth major category refers to expenditures on support services for program participants. Obviously, such expenditures increase when a demonstration program is implemented. However, this increase will be partially offset because participants in the demonstration programs no longer need to obtain similar services from existing programs.

Three of the subcategories listed in Table 9.2 are interrelated and require clarification: participant expenditures on child care, transportation, and so forth; support services received by participants; and allowances received by participants. The first of these subcategories refers to total job-required outlays by E&T participants on such items as child care, transportation, and uniforms. The subcategory of support services pertains to the direct provision of such goods by a government agency, and the allowances subcategory refers to government reimbursement of job-required expenditures by participants. *All* program-induced increases in job-required expenditures should be treated identically: as resource costs to society engendered in producing goods and services. Table 9.2 reflects this philosophy. Of course, to the extent the government directly provides support services to participants, client outlays for this purpose will be smaller. In a CBA, this should be reflected by a smaller dollar amount appearing under the participant expenditures on job-related outlays and a larger dollar amount appearing under the subcategory of support services received by participants.

Benefits and costs that are sometimes referred to as *intangible effects* but are rarely, if ever, actually estimated in evaluations of E&T programs do not appear in Table 9.2. Examples of intangible effects include the values of leisure forgone and satisfaction gained from substitution of work for transfer payments. Almost by definition, such impacts are very difficult to measure. In the next section, we examine the implications of not measuring them.

CONCEPTUAL ISSUES IN CONDUCTING CBAS OF EDUCATION AND TRAINING DEMONSTRATIONS

We now turn to a number of limitations of the accounting framework illustrated in Table 9.2. As will be seen, these arise from the fact that the framework is not completely consistent with the theoretical concepts discussed in Chapter 3. Because these limitations can result in incorrect policy conclusions, it appears useful to compare some of the operational measures of benefits and costs typically used in conducting CBAs of E&T demonstrations with their conceptually correct counterparts. In doing this, it is helpful to examine measures of benefits and costs associated with E&T programs separately from the participant and the nonparticipant perspectives, keeping in mind that social benefits and costs are simply the algebraic sum of benefits received and costs incurred by these two groups.

The Participant Perspective

Two alternative measures. The standard E&T framework, as Table 9.2 suggests, estimates participant net benefits as net changes in the incomes of program clients—that is, as increases in earnings minus decreases in transfer payments and increases in work-related expenditures that result from participation in the program. However, as Chapter 3 emphasizes, the conceptually appropriate measure is net changes in the surplus of program participants, not net changes in their incomes. As will be seen, the difference between these two measures can be substantial.

The extent to which the two measures diverge depends on the precise mechanism through which E&T programs influence earnings. For instance, E&T programs may either increase the hourly wage rates of participants (e.g., by imparting new skills) or increase the hours they work (e.g., by aiding in job search or increasing the obligations that must be met in exchange for transfer payments). Numerous E&T demonstrations have been found to increase hours worked. Meaningful impacts on wage rates are more rare but have occurred. In the discussion that follows, we compare the two alternative measures of net benefits from the perspective of several different hypothetical E&T participants, each of whom is assumed to respond differently to the program.

The first participant is represented in Figure 9.1. Curve S is the labor supply schedule of this participant, an individual who is assumed to have successfully participated in an E&T program that increased her market wage from W_0 to W_1.[9] As a result, the individual increases her hours of work from h_0 to h_1. In the diagram, area A represents the increase in both participant surplus and earnings that would have resulted from the wage increase even if the participant had not increased her hours. Area B represents an additional increase in both participant surplus and earnings, one resulting from the increase in hours that actually takes place. Finally, area C represents a further increase in earnings that results from the hours increase. However, this last increase in earnings is fully offset by the individual's loss of leisure.[10] Hence, no change in participant surplus is associated with it. Consequently, although areas A, B, and C are counted as benefits when using the net income change measure of E&T effects, only A and B are counted in the conceptually more correct net surplus change measure.

In Figure 9.1, the first E&T participant was assumed to be in equilibrium both before entering the program and upon completing the program; that is, it was assumed that at both points, she was able to work the number of hours she desired to work at her market wage. Many E&T participants, however, are not in equilibrium prior to

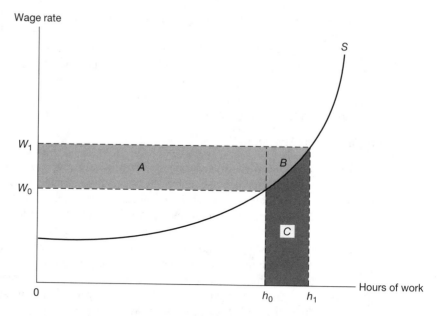

Figure 9.1 Welfare Change Resulting from an Induced Wage Increase

entering a program. Indeed, many persons participate in E&T specifically because they are unemployed.

Such a situation is assumed to face the second participant, an individual who is represented in Figure 9.2. In this figure, the individual has a market wage of W_0 prior to entering E&T but is able to obtain only h_0 hours of work instead of the desired h_1 hours. Assume now that, although participating in E&T does not affect the participant's market wage, it does permit him to increase his hours of work from h_0 to h_1. As a result of this hours increase, the participant enjoys an earnings increase equal to areas $A + B$, but a surplus increase equal to only area A. Thus, once again, the net income change measure of E&T benefits is larger than the conceptually more appropriate net surplus change measure.

Our findings for these first two E&T participants imply that while any earnings increases that result from wage increases should be fully credited to the program, only part of earnings increases resulting from hours increases should be credited. In Figure 9.3, we turn to a more complex situation facing a third E&T participant: a welfare recipient who, as a condition for receiving her welfare grant, is required to work at a public-sector job for h^* hours each month, where h^* is determined by dividing her grant amount by the minimum wage. Such an arrangement, which is becoming an increasingly common requirement for receiving welfare, is often referred to as *work-fare*. The welfare recipient's market wage is assumed to equal W^m, the minimum wage, while curve S_0 represents her supply schedule in the absence of workfare. (Ignore curve S_1 for the moment.) Figure 9.3 implies that in the absence of workfare, W_0^r, the welfare recipient's reservation wage (i.e., the lowest wage at which she would be willing to work) would exceed her market wage. Thus, she would choose not to work.

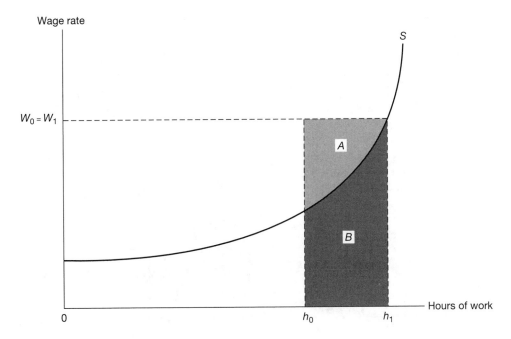

Figure 9.2   Welfare Change Due to an Induced Increase in Hours Worked

Now imagine that the welfare recipient is enrolled in workfare in two distinct steps. In the first step, her welfare grant is withdrawn. This loss of income would cause her labor supply curve to shift to the right from S_0 to S_1. As a consequence, her reservation wage would fall from W_0^r to W_1^r, a value below the minimum wage. In the second step, she is offered the opportunity to work h^* hours at a public-sector workfare job at a wage of W^m. In other words, she is given the opportunity to earn back her welfare grant, which in the diagram corresponds to the rectangular area $W^m a h^* h_0$.[11] Because W^m exceeds W_1^r, the participant represented in Figure 9.3 would prefer workfare to not working at all.

If the welfare recipient accepts the workfare offer, then the net income change and net surplus change measures of program impacts have quite different implications. Assuming she has no opportunities to work in addition to h^*, her net income would be unchanged from what it was prior to the program; consequently, the measure based on changes in net income would imply that she is no worse off. However, the net surplus change measure does imply that she is worse off. Specifically, her net surplus would decline by an amount represented by the area $W_1^r c h^* h_0$, an amount equal to the value that the recipient places on her lost leisure. Looked at somewhat differently, the participant's enrollment in workfare engenders both a cost (the initial loss of the welfare grant, which corresponds to area $W^m a h^* h_0$) and a benefit (the surplus gain from accepting the workfare job, which is represented by area $W^m a c W_1^r$).[12] As is apparent from Figure 9.3, the cost is larger than the benefit. The difference between the two once again corresponds to area $W_1^r c h^* h_0$, the participant's net loss from participating in workfare.

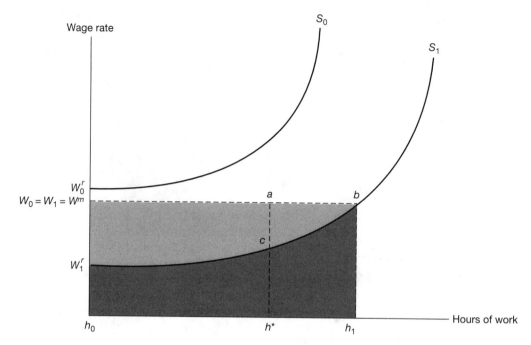

Figure 9.3   Welfare Change Due to Workfare

So far, the focus has been on benefits received by and costs incurred by welfare recipients while they are participating in workfare. Now let us consider a different situation: The benefits and costs associated with a participant move from welfare to a regular private-sector job. This is, of course, one of the major objectives of programs such as workfare, and Figure 9.3 implies that the program would in fact have the desired effect on the participant. Although in the absence of the workfare she would prefer not to work at all, given a choice between participating in workfare (point a) or working at a regular minimum-wage job (point b), the participant would select the latter. By restricting her hours to h^*, workfare causes the participant to be "off her labor supply curve." Only by finding a regular job can she work h_1 hours, the number of hours she would desire to work at the minimum wage. In actual practice, the participant might move directly from welfare to the job upon being confronted with the workfare requirement or, alternatively, she might first participate in workfare while seeking private-sector employment.

A comparison of the net income change measure of workfare's impact on a participant who moves directly to private-sector employment with the corresponding conceptually correct net surplus change measure yields an interesting finding. On the one hand, the net income change measure implies that the participant represented in Figure 9.3 enjoys a net gain. Her transfer payments fall from $W^m a h^* h_0$ to zero, but her earnings increase from zero to $W^m b h_1 h_0$, resulting in a net increase in income of $a b h_1 h^*$. On the other hand, the participant suffers a net loss of surplus because her gain from working, area $W^m b W_1{}^r$, is exceeded by the value of her lost transfer payments, area $W^m a h^* h_0$. Thus, under the circumstances represented in Figure 9.3, the net income change measure suggests a conclusion that is the diametrical opposite from that implied by the conceptually more correct net surplus change measure.

Procedures for computing participant surplus changes from estimates of earnings changes.   In measuring the impacts of E&T programs from the participant perspective, three rules can be drawn from the preceding analyses of the three illustrative E&T participants. First, the full value of reductions in transfer payments should be counted as a cost to E&T participants. Second, the full value of increases in earnings that result from wage rate increases should be counted as a benefit to E&T participants. Third, only part of the value of earnings increases that result from hours increases should be counted as a benefit to E&T participants; namely, the part that represents an increase in participant surplus should be counted, while the part that is offset by reductions in leisure should not.

In conducting CBAs of E&T demonstrations, the first two of these rules are straightforward to implement. Implementing the third rule, however, requires an estimate of the percentage of earnings changes attributable to hours increases that should be counted. Table 9.3 provides estimates of percentage values that can be used for this purpose.

To illustrate the use of Table 9.3 in CBA, consider a hypothetical E&T participant whose work hours increase from 1,000-per year to 2,000 per year as a result of participating in the program. Thus, $h_0 / h_1 = 0.5$. Assume that the participant's postprogram market wage (W_1) equals \$4. Consequently, the 1,000-hour increase results in an increase in annual earnings of \$4,000. Further assume that the participant's postprogram reservation wage $(W_1{}^r)$ equals \$1. Hence, $W_1{}^r / W_1 = 0.25$. Finally, assume that at his postprogram wage rate and hours, the participant's supply of labor is completely inelastic $(\varepsilon = 0)$. In other words, the participant does not adjust his hours to small changes in W_1. Given these assumptions, Table 9.3 implies that only about 46 percent of the \$4,000 earnings increase (\$1,840), corresponds to an increase in participant surplus. The remaining \$2,160 simply offset the participant's lost leisure.

The percentage values found in Table 9.3 can be clarified by reference to Figure 9.4. They were computed by dividing the surplus increase resulting from the increase in hours from h_0 to h_1 (i.e., area abc) by the increase in earnings attributable to the same change in hours (area abh_1h_0).[13] An examination of Figure 9.4 suggests that area abc will increase in size relative to area abh_1h_0, causing the fractions appearing in Table 9.3 to increase in value; the greater the program effect on hours of work (i.e., the smaller h_0 / h_1), the smaller the reservation wage is relative to the market wage (i.e., the smaller $W_1{}^r / W_1$), and the less elastic the labor supply of E&T participants (i.e., the smaller the value of ε). These relations are all reflected by the values appearing in Table 9.3.

Table 9.3 can be used in CBAs of E&T demonstrations to determine the fraction of an earnings increase attributable to an increase in participant surplus by following a five-step sequence:[14]

TABLE 9.3 ALTERNATIVE ESTIMATES OF THE PERCENTAGE OF EARNINGS INCREASES ATTRIBUTABLE TO HOURS INCREASES THAT RESULTS IN AN INCREASE IN E&T PARTICIPANT SURPLUS

h_0/h_1	W_1^r/W_1 0	.25	.5	.75
$\varepsilon = 0$				
0	78.5	58.9	39.3	19.6
.25	71.7	53.8	35.9	17.9
.50	61.4	46.1	30.7	15.4
.75	45.3	34.0	22.7	11.3
.90	29.4	22.0	14.7	7.3
$\varepsilon = 0.1$				
0	76.3	57.7	38.7	19.5
.25	68.8	52.2	35.1	17.8
.50	57.4	43.9	29.7	15.1
.75	39.8	31.0	21.3	11.0
.90	23.8	18.4	12.9	6.9
$\varepsilon = 0.25$				
0	73.7	56.0	37.9	19.3
.25	65.3	50.0	34.1	17.5
.50	52.9	40.9	28.3	14.8
.75	34.2	27.1	19.4	10.5
.90	17.3	14.3	10.9	6.3
$\varepsilon = 0.5$				
0	70.0	53.5	36.6	19.0
.25	60.5	46.7	32.4	17.0
.50	46.8	37.7	26.1	14.1
.75	27.5	22.3	16.7	9.7
.90	12.3	10.4	8.3	5.4

Parameter Definitions:

h_0 = hours of work of program participants in the absence of E&T.
h_1 = postprogram hours of work of program participants.
W_1^r = postprogram reservation wage of program participants who find jobs.
W_1 = postprogram market wage rate of program participants who find jobs.
ε = compensated wage elasticity at h_1 and W_1.

Source: Computed by authors. See text for an explanation.

1. Partition the earnings increases attributable to E&T between that part resulting from increases in wage rates and that part resulting from increases in hours worked.

2. Divide participant hours in the absence of the E&T program (h_0) by postprogram participant hours (h_1).

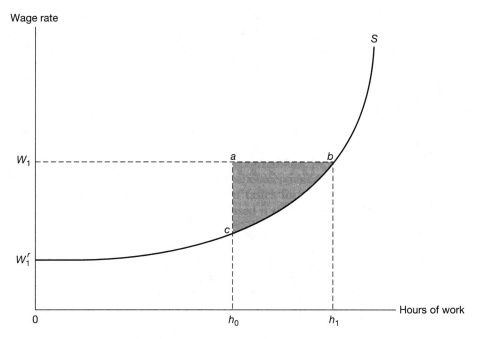

Figure 9.4 The Relation Between Hours Increases and Increases in E&T Client Surplus

3. Divide the postprogram reservation wage rate (W_1') by the postprogram wage rate (W_1).
4. Determine the value of the wage elasticity (ε) at post-program hours and the postprogram wage rate.[15]
5. Multiply the earnings increase attributable to the E&T-induced increase in hours, as obtained in step 1, by the appropriate percentage value from Table 9.3, as determined in steps 2–4.

Completing several of these steps requires a specific effort to obtain the necessary data from the E&T demonstration program being subjected to CBA. For example, the value of h_1 can be obtained by examining the hours of work of members of the treatment group after they have completed the E&T demonstration program. Similarly, the value of h_0 can be obtained by observing the hours of members of the comparison group. The value of W_1 can be obtained by observing the wage rates of working members of the treatment group after they have completed the program. Values for ε can be obtained from existing estimates based on data from the income maintenance experiments alluded to in Exhibit 9.2. Findings from these experiments, which are summarized in Exhibit 9.2, suggest that ε equals 0.09 for married men, 0.24 for mothers in two-parent households, and 0.14 for mothers in single-parent households.

The most difficult of the required values to obtain is that for W_1', the postprogram reservation wage of E&T participants. In principle, this could be done by simply asking E&T participants the lowest wage at which they would be willing to work. However, there is evidence that the responses to survey questions concerning reservation wages are sensitive to precisely how the questions are phrased.[16] Moreover, at least two different studies have found that the ratio of reservation wages reported in surveys of unemployed persons to the wages these persons received on their most recently held jobs is approximately one.[17] One reasonable interpretation of this finding is that unemployed persons tend to answer questions about their reservation wage on the basis of the wage that they expect to receive on the next job and this expected wage simply reflects the wage that they received on their most recent previous job. As Figure 9.4 shows, the value of the reservation wage needed for our purposes, in contrast, is the lowest wage at which nonemployed E&T participants would be willing to relinquish their first hour of nonwork time. Obtaining this value obviously requires very carefully designed survey questions.

The Nonparticipant Perspective[18]

This section discusses the following categories of benefits and costs that accrue to nonparticipants: intangible benefits, benefits from in-program output, and costs resulting from the displacement of public-sector and private-sector workers.

Intangible benefits received by nonparticipants. The preceding section emphasized that in measuring the benefits and costs of E&T programs to participants it is changes in their surplus that should be estimated rather than changes in their money income. Thus, the effects on participant surplus of E&T-induced reductions in participant leisure time should be taken into account.

The same concept applies in measuring benefits and costs of E&T programs to nonparticipants. In particular, it seems plausible that E&T programs that are targeted at welfare recipients and that succeed in reducing the leisure time of these persons may increase the utility of some nonparticipants, especially those who pay the taxes needed to support the welfare system. This is an intangible benefit of E&T programs to nonparticipants that should in principle, be taken into account in conducting CBAs of these programs, although given the practical difficulty of measuring the magnitude of this benefit, it has never been done.[19]

Benefits from in-program output. Many, although far from all, E&T programs involve the provision of public-sector jobs. Perhaps the best-known example of this is the Works Projects Administration (WPA), which operated in the United States during the Great Depression and was intended to absorb some of the massive number of workers who were unemployed during this period. More recently, the Comprehensive Employment and Training Act provided as many as 750,000 public-sector jobs for unemployed persons during the late 1970s. At present, as discussed earlier, welfare recipients in some states are required to perform work at government and nonprofit agencies in exchange for their payments.

How should the value to taxpayers of the in-program output produced by E&T participants be assigned to public-sector jobs? Ideally, this would be done by determining what taxpayers would be willing to pay for this output. Typically, this is infeasible, however, because the output is not purchased in market transactions. Consequently, an alternative approach is used to determine what the labor resources required to produce the output would have cost if purchased on the open market. This is consistent with the procedures used for measurement of public-sector output in the national income accounts. However, in CBAs of E&T demonstrations, evaluation of output on the basis of resource cost is complicated by the fact that the agencies that "employ" E&T participants usually pay nothing for the services of these people. Therefore, the wage rate that would have been paid to similar workers hired in the open market to do the work performed by the participants is used instead. Once an appropriate wage rate is determined, the basic calculation involves multiplying the number of hours E&T participants work by this wage and perhaps adjusting to account for differences between the average productivity of the E&T workers and workers hired in the open market.

The procedure just described can result in an estimate that either overstates or understates the true value of the in-program output produced by E&T participants. The reasons for this can be seen by examining a key assumption that implicitly underlies this valuation method: The decisions of the public-sector agencies that employ E&T workers closely reflect the desires of taxpayers. More specifically, an analogy is implicitly drawn with the behavior of private-sector firms and consumers under perfect competition, and it is assumed that the amount that an agency would be willing to pay to employ an additional worker corresponds to the value that taxpayers would place on the additional output that the worker could potentially produce. Although this is not an appropriate place to assess the perfect competition analogy or discuss the extent to which bureaucratic behavior reflects taxpayer preferences, it should be obvious that a rather strong assumption is required to value output produced by E&T workers.

The implications of this assumption can be explored by use of Figure 9.5, which depicts the demand curve for workers by a public-sector agency that might potentially be assigned E&T participants and the supply curve the agency faces in hiring workers in a competitive labor market. In using this diagram, let us first examine a situation in which the assumption that bureaucratic behavior reflects taxpayer preferences is valid and then one where it is not.

In Figure 9.5, the horizontal line, S, represents the supply curve, which is set at the level of the market-determined wage that must be paid to each regular worker hired by the agency; and the downward sloping line, D, represents the demand curve, which is assumed to slope downward as a result of diminishing returns and (as implied by the assumption about bureaucratic behavior) because the agency prioritizes its tasks so that, as its budget expands, successively less important services are performed. (Ignore curve D^* for the moment.) This demand curve reflects the willingness-to-pay for workers by the agency and, in keeping with the assumption concerning bureaucratic behavior, the area under this curve is presumed to measure the value to taxpayers of output produced by workers hired by the agency.

Figure 9.5 indicates that in the absence of E&T workers the agency would hire R regular workers; but if P E&T participants were assigned to the agency, a total of

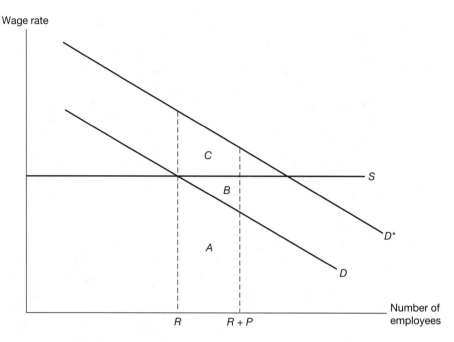

Figure 9.5 Demand for Workers by a Public-Sector Agency

$R + P$ workers would be employed. Thus, if the bureaucratic behavior assumption is valid, the value to taxpayers of the output added by the E&T workers would equal area A.

Unfortunately, however, area A typically cannot be directly measured. The reason for this is that the output produced by public-sector agencies is rarely sold in market transactions and, consequently, the agency's demand curve depicted in Figure 9.5 cannot actually be observed. However, even though government and nonprofit agencies that "employ" E&T participants pay nothing for the services of these people, the area under the supply curve between R and $R + P$ can be valued by simply determining the wages that would have to be paid to similar workers hired on the open market to do the work performed by E&T participants. Consequently, it is the area under the supply curve—that is, area A *plus* area B—that is usually used in practice as the measure of the value of in-program participant output. As a glance at Figure 9.5 suggests, the size of the resulting overstatement of the value of the output produced by E&T participation, which is represented by area B, depends upon the slope of the agency demand curve.

So far, we have assumed that agency bureaucratic behavior simply reflects the value that taxpayers would place on the agency's output. Let us now look at one of the numerous possible situations where this is not the case.[20] The specific example we examine is one in which the agency, perhaps because of budget constraints resulting from the public goods characteristics of whatever services it provides, produces less output than taxpayers collectively desire. These circumstances are represented in Figure 9.5 by two demand curves. As before, curve D indicates *agency* willingness-to-pay for workers, but the value that *taxpayers* place on the output produced by the agency is now represented by the area under demand curve D^*. Consequently, the value of the additional output produced by the P E&T participants provided the agency now equals area A plus area B plus area C. Thus, under these circumstances, the measure based on the supply curve of the output produced by E&T workers, which as previously indicated equals area A plus area B, understates the true value by an area equal to C.

Costs from public-sector labor displacement.   So far, our discussion has been based on the assumption that the E&T workers made available to a public-sector agency would simply be added to the regular work force that the agency would hire in the absence of the program. This need not be the case. The agency might instead substitute E&T workers for regular workers. In terms of Figure 9.5, this behavior on the part of the agency, which is usually referred to as *displacement*, would mean that agency employment would increase by less than the P number of workers provided by E&T. Indeed, with 100 percent displacement, the agency's work force would remain at R, rather than increase to $R + P$. Consequently, at first blush, it would appear that displacement leads to overstatement of the value of output produced by E&T participants.

The issue is actually a bit more subtle and complex, however. If the displaced workers have a similar risk of joblessness as E&T participants, then increases in output produced by E&T participants assigned to public-sector agencies may be entirely offset by losses in the output formerly produced by the displaced workers. This need not be the case, however, if the E&T participants are exceptional in terms of lack of skills or if they face exceptional barriers to labor market access. Moving such persons directly into jobs under these circumstances will change the characteristics of the general pool of unemployed in ways that may allow a reduction in the net incidence of joblessness, especially if local labor market conditions are tight. Thus, to the extent that E&T participants are unskilled relative to those they replaced, the labor market consequences will differ from a simple one-for-one replacement.

Costs from private-sector labor displacement.   A major objective of most E&T programs is to increase the unsubsidized private-sector employment of program participants. To the extent these efforts are successful, some participants undoubtedly end up in jobs that would otherwise have been held by nonparticipants. If, as a result, these nonparticipants become unemployed or accept lower-wage jobs, their earnings obviously fall. This earnings reduction, which is another type of displacement effect, is potentially a cost of E&T programs to nonparticipants, a cost that typically is not measured in CBAs of these programs.

Here, again, the net effect on employment depends in part upon the consequences for the local labor market of the resulting change in the composition of the pool of unemployed. It also depends upon local labor market conditions during the demonstration period. For example, if local unemployment is low, then it should be relatively easy for displaced nonparticipants to find alternative job opportunities. Consequently, any private-sector displacement effects should be small. But if unemployment is high and local labor market conditions are loose, displacement effects could be substantial.

CHOOSING PREDICTION PARAMETERS

In using the cost-benefit framework illustrated in Table 9.2, it is necessary to take account of the fact that some benefits and costs of E&T programs are likely to extend beyond the demonstration period. For example, as a result of having participated in an E&T demonstration, some individuals could potentially enjoy increased earnings but pay higher taxes, incur greater job-required expenses, and receive fewer transfer payments over the remainder of their working lives. These streams of future benefits and costs must be incorporated into the CBAs of the demonstrations. Doing this requires that four important parameters be specified: the social discount rate, the time horizon, the decay rate, and the shadow price of capital. The social discount rate has already been discussed in detail in Chapters 4 and 5. The remaining three parameters are discussed in turn in the following three subsections.

The Time Horizon

As described in Chapter 4, the time horizon is the period over which benefit and cost streams are estimated. In CBAs of E&T programs, benefits and costs beyond the specified time horizon are assumed equal to zero, that is, to have zero terminal value. One procedure for determining the length of the period in CBAs of E&T programs is to subtract the age of program participants at the time they entered the program from the age at which they are expected to retire from the work force. Sometimes, however, a shorter, somewhat arbitrarily selected time horizon—for example, five years—is used instead. Doing this is simply an acknowledgment on the part of analysts that because they do not possess crystal balls, uncertainty increases the further one attempts to extrapolate beyond the demonstration period. Basing a CBA of an E&T demonstration on a short time horizon, however, is likely to understate E&T benefits relative to E&T costs, as at least one of the major potential benefits—earnings improvements—may persist well beyond five years, while the major cost—operating expenditures—does not.

This understatement of benefits relative to costs may be substantial. The figures that follow show the present discounted value of an improvement of $1 in annual earnings under alternative assumptions concerning the length of the time horizon over which the improvement persists and the value of the discount rate.

	DISCOUNT RATE	
TIME HORIZON	5%	10%
5 years	$4.33	$3.79
10 years	7.72	6.15
20 years	12.46	8.51
30 years	15.37	9.43

These figures have two important implications. First, it is evident that the magnitude of benefit and cost estimates are quite sensitive to the choice of the time horizon. For example, if a 5 percent discount rate and a five-year time horizon are used for extrapolation purposes, the present value of an improvement of $1 in earnings equals $4.33. But if a 5 percent discount rate and a 20-year time horizon are used instead, the present value equals $12.46, almost a threefold increase. Second, projections of benefits and costs become increasingly sensitive to the choice of the discount rate, the longer the value of the time horizon that is used. Hence, if a short time horizon is used, cost-benefit findings are less likely to be sensitive to the choice of a discount rate than if a long time horizon is used.

The Decay Rate

A decay rate is necessary in extrapolating E&T effects that persist beyond the demonstration period in order to take account of the possibility that the size of these effects may change over time. For example, it is usually argued that programs that provide training or job placement for low-wage workers initially may give them a competitive advantage in the labor market, but this advantage may decay over time. In the case of training, however, one could alternatively argue that doors are opened on the job that allow participants to obtain additional training after leaving an E&T program and, consequently, the program's effects on earnings will grow over time.

Unfortunately, only very limited empirical evidence exists as to whether the earnings effects of E&T programs tend to grow or decay over time, let alone the magnitude of the actual rate of decay or growth. Thus, the choice of an appropriate decay rate is one of the more problematic aspects of CBAs of E&T demonstrations.[21]

Once values for the discount rate, time horizon, and decay rate, are chosen, equations (4A.5) and (4A.7) in Appendix 4A can be used to compute net present values. In using these formulas, care must be taken to use a negative value for g if it is determined that the effects of the E&T demonstration will decay over time and a positive value for g if it seems likely that these impacts will grow over time. For benefit and cost components that neither grow nor shrink over time, g should, of course, be set equal to zero.

The Shadow Price of Capital

As indicated in Chapter 5, in addition to the discount rate, the time horizon, and the decay rate, there is yet another parameter that should in principle be taken into account in projecting benefit and cost streams of E&T programs: the shadow price of capital. This parameter allows the benefits and costs of public-sector programs that cause additions or reductions in private-sector investment to be treated differently than those that result in additions or reductions in private-sector consumption. As discussed in Chapter 5, the reason this differential treatment is appropriate is that a dollar of program costs that would have been used for private-sector consumption in the absence of the program displaces only one dollar of consumption, but a dollar of forgone investment would have engendered a stream of future returns. If discounted at the social rate of time preference, then the present value of this stream of returns would have exceeded one dollar. Similarly, a dollar of program benefits that is directly consumed can only increase consumption by one dollar, but if the dollar is used instead for private-sector investment, the present value of the resulting stream of returns will also exceed one dollar. Thus, dollars of E&T costs that would have otherwise been used to make private-sector investments and dollars of E&T benefits that stimulate private-sector investments will be undervalued unless multiplied by the shadow price of capital. To the best of our knowledge, however, this has not been done in any CBAs of E&T programs. Later in this chapter, we demonstrate how sensitive findings from some actual CBAs of E&T demonstrations are to some alternative assumptions about the shadow price of capital.

A CASE STUDY: CBAs OF WELFARE-TO-WORK DEMONSTRATIONS

During the 1970s and 1980s, many states conducted demonstrations that had the objective of reducing dependency on transfer payments among welfare recipients by enhancing their employability. Similar to other E&T demonstrations, the components of these *welfare-to-work* programs varied among the demonstrations but usually included one or more of the following: assessment of basic skills, structured job search, training and education, and subsidized employment in the public or private sector.

Many of the welfare-to-work demonstrations have been subjected to CBA. CBAs of a particular subset of demonstrations conducted during the 1980s, the Work/Welfare Demonstrations, exerted considerable influence on the Family Support Act of 1988, a major piece of welfare reform legislation. Much of this influence resulted from the fact that by 1988 many observers, particularly those in the policy-making community, had concluded on the basis of analyses of the Work/Welfare Demonstrations that welfare-to-work programs are cost-beneficial.[22] The Work/Welfare Demonstrations were targeted at participants in the Aid for Families with Dependent Children (AFDC) program, a major welfare program. The CBAs of these demonstrations, which were based on the classical experimental design denoted as design 1 earlier in the chapter, were conducted by the Manpower Demonstration Research Corporation (MDRC), a well-known nonprofit research firm.[23]

CBA Results

Table 9.4 presents summary results from MDRC's CBAs of the Work/Welfare Demonstrations. These estimates should be viewed as program impacts on a typical member of the treatment group in each of the listed demonstrations. The estimates in the table are reported separately for one-parent (AFDC-R) and two-parent (AFDC-U) households and, when available, for new AFDC applicants and prior AFDC recipients. Parentheses are used to indicate when benefits or costs are in the opposite direction from that intended by the demonstration programs—for example, when net remuneration from employment declines or amounts of transfer payments increase.

The first three columns in the table present estimated benefits and costs from the participant perspective and the next four from the nonparticipant perspective. Columns A and D, respectively, report total net gains (or losses) from these two perspectives, while columns B, C, E, F, and G provide information on the benefit and cost components that together account for these gains (or losses). For example, column B reports the estimated *net* gain by participants from employment under each demonstration program—that is, estimates of the sum of increases in earnings, fringe benefits, and any work-related allowances paid under the program less the sum of tax payments and participant job-required expenditures on child care and transportation. Column C indicates changes in AFDC and other transfer benefits received by participants. Column E presents MDRC's valuations of in-program output. Column F is the sum of tax increases paid by participants, reductions in transfer payments paid to participants, and reductions in transfer program operating costs, all of which may be viewed as benefits to nonparticipants. Column G shows the government's cost of operating the treatment programs. Finally, column H, which is computed by summing

TABLE 9.4   SUMMARY OF COST-BENEFIT ESTIMATES FROM MDRC EVALUATIONS OF WORK/WELFARE DEMONSTRATIONS

	Participant Perspective			Nonparticipant Perspective				
	Net Present Value (A=B–C)	Net Gains from Employment	Loss in Transfer Payments	Net Present Value (D=E+F–G)	Value of In-program Output	Tax- Transfer Gains	Program Service Costs	Net Social Gain (or Loss) (A+D)
	A	B	C	D	E	F	G	H
AFDC-R								
APPLICANTS								
San Diego EPP/EWEP:								
Job search only	$ 644	$1,323	$ 679	$ 452	($3)	$ 965	$ 510	$1,096
Job search/CWEP	798	1,874	1,076	1,156	205	1,529	578	1,954
San Diego SWIM	(880)	1,140	2,020	1,633	180*	2,153	700	753
Virginia	1,134	1,698	564	667	41	879	253	1,801
West Virginia	(481)	(407)	74	389	542	25	178	(92)
RECIPIENTS								
San Diego SWIM	725	3,158	2,433	1,698	180*	2,586	1,068	2,423
Virginia	574	982	408	190	145	593	548	764
West Virginia	80	157	77	873	1,059	115	301	953
New Jersey	1,262	2,278	1,016	1,069	(9)	1,591	513	2,331
Maine	3,182	4,497	1,315	(418)	680	894	1,992	2,764
APPLICANTS AND RECIPIENTS								
Cook County:								
Job search only	(420)	145	565	475	1	601	127	55
Job search/CWEP	(34)	311	345	362	100	420	158	328
Baltimore	1,739	1,939	200	74	390	513	829	1,813
Arkansas	(449)	410	859	944	20	1,082	158	495

TABLE 9.4   SUMMARY OF COST-BENEFIT ESTIMATES FROM MDRC EVALUATIONS OF WORK/
WELFARE DEMONSTRATIONS (Continued)

	Participant Perspective			Nonparticipant Perspective				
	Net Present Value (A=B–C)	Net Gains from Employ-ment	Loss in Transfer Payments	Net Present Value (D=E+F–G)	Value of In-program Output	Tax-Transfer Gains	Program Service Costs	Net Social Gain (or Loss) (A+D)
	A	B	C	D	E	F	G	H
AFDC-U								
APPLICANTS ONLY								
San Diego EPP/EWEP:								
Job Search only	(1,196)	375	1,571	1,229	(5)	1,777	543	33
Job search/CWEP	(1,443)	129	1,572	1,414	354	1,732	672	(29)
San Diego SWIM	543	2,083	1,540	1,577	267*	1,970	660	2,120
RECIPIENTS ONLY								
San Diego SWIM	(921)	2,178	3,099	2,487	267*	3,242	1,025	1,566
APPLICANTS AND RECIPIENTS								
Baltimore	(1,233)	(2,017)	(784)	(1,856)	280	(1,599)	537	(3,089)

Notes: See text for detailed explanation of table.

*Separate estimates of the value of in-program output for applicants and recipients not provided for San Diego.

Negative net gains or increases in transfer payment amounts.

Sources: The following final reports on the individual Work/Welfare Demonstrations, all of which were published by the Manpower Demonstration Research Corporation, New York, New York: P. Auspos, G. Cave, and D. Long, *Maine: Final Report on the Training Opportunities in the Private Sector Program*, April 1988; S. Freedman, J. Bryant, and G. Cave, *New Jersey: Final Report on the Grant Diversion Project*, November 1988; D. Friedlander, G. Hoerz, J. Quint, and J. Riccio, *Arkansas: Final Report on the WORK Program in Two Counties*, September, 1985; D. Friedlander, G. Hoerz, D. Long, and J. Quint, *Maryland: Final Report on the Employment Initiatives Evaluation*, December 1985; D. Friedlander, M. Erickson, G. Hamilton, and V. Knox, *West Virginia: Final Report on the Community Work Experience Demonstrations*, September 1986; D. Friedlander, S. Freedman, G. Hamilton, and J. Quint, *Illinois: Final Report on Job Search and Work Experience in Cook County*, November 1987; B. Goldman, D. Friedlander, and D. Long, *California: Final Report on the San Diego Job Search and Work Experience Demonstration*, February 1986; G. Hamilton and D. Friedlander, *Final Report on the Saturation Work Initiative Model in San Diego*, 1989; J. Riccio, G. Cave, S. Freedman, and M. Price, *Virginia: Final Report on the Virginia Employment Services Program*, August 1986.

the benefit-cost components reported in columns B, C, E, F, and G, presents the overall CBA results.

As can be seen from column H, 16 of the 19 reported estimates indicate overall net gains and only three imply net losses. It is this preponderance of positive values that impressed the policy community. Taken at face value, these findings imply that the policies tested in the Work/Welfare Demonstrations generally resulted in positive social net gains. Yet, any final assessment depends upon whether the estimates reported in column H are sensitive to the assumptions MDRC used to derive them. This issue is investigated later.

Distributional Results

One of the most striking findings from Table 9.4 is that of the nineteen reported sets of CBA estimates, seventeen imply net gains for nonparticipants, but only ten indicate net gains for participants. The reason for the nine instances of net losses among participants, which occur disproportionately among the two-parent AFDC-U households, is suggested by a comparison of columns B and C. Some of the demonstration treatments did not result in sufficiently large gains from employment to offset participant losses in transfer payments. Thus, as Table 9.4 implies, in eight of the nine instances, nonparticipants gained at the expense of participants. In one demonstration, that for Baltimore's AFDC-U population, both groups were apparently made worse off. Nine of the ten remaining sets of CBA estimates imply that the demonstration treatment made both participants and nonparticipants better off; the tenth, those for Maine, indicate that participants actually gained while nonparticipants suffered losses.

The total net gains and losses for participants and nonparticipants that are implied by columns A and D are not especially large. For example, a program that resulted in a net participant or nonparticipant gain of $1,000 per treatment group member (a figure that is larger than most of those appearing in either column A or D) and enrolled 1 million AFDC recipients each year (a figure that seems improbably large) would produce a total annual gain of $1 billion, a gain that may be compared to the budgetary cost of AFDC, which is currently around $25 billion per year.[24]

Extrapolations of Benefits and Costs: The Baltimore Options Program

As pointed out earlier, some of the benefits and costs of E&T demonstrations are likely to continue well after the demonstration has ended. To incorporate these future benefit and cost streams into CBAs, assumptions have to be made concerning the social discount rate, the time horizon, and the decay rate. Thus, the findings reported in Table 9.4 reflect MDRC's assumptions about each of these parameters. For example, in obtaining these findings, MDRC consistently used a 5 percent discount rate and a five-year time horizon. For the decay rate, however, MDRC often selected several alternative values and examined whether its findings were sensitive to these alternatives. The exact values used for this purpose varied among the studies but usually included a decay rate of zero, which implied no decay, and often also included a rate of infinity, which implied that no benefits or costs extended beyond the demonstration period. In addition, the actual rate of decay that occurred during the demonstration period was sometimes used, as was an annual rate of 22 percent, which was obtained from a 1980 national study of the WIN program conducted by Ketron, Incorporated.[25] In no case did MDRC use a negative decay rate—that is, a rate that implied that benefits or costs grow rather than decline over time. As will be seen, however, there is some evidence from MDRC's own data that growth rather than decay did in fact occur in some of the Work/Welfare Demonstrations.

Table 9.5 presents cost-benefit findings for one of the Work/Welfare Demonstrations: the Baltimore Options program. These particular results were selected because they could be obtained from two separate sets of published estimates: one that appeared in MDRC's 1985 final report for the Baltimore Options program;[26] and one from a 1987 supplemental report that updated the original estimates by obtaining information on the earnings and transfer receipts of members of the treatment and control groups after the demonstration ended and, hence, shortened the length of time over which extrapolation was required.[27] This is the only instance with which we are familiar in which MDRC has updated its initially published CBA estimates. By comparing the two sets of estimates, one can obtain some sense of how sensitive the CBA results are to incorrect assumptions concerning the rate of decay.

The estimates appearing in Table 9.5 pertain to the participant perspective and are averaged over all members of the Baltimore Options AFDC-R treatment group. Three pairs of columns are displayed, one for each of the three alternative assumptions that MDRC made concerning decay rates. The left column in each pair is taken from MDRC's originally published estimates and the right column from the updated estimates.

In Table 9.5, some variation is apparent across the three pairs of columns, but even greater differences occur within each pair. These differences between the original and updated estimates are attributable to the fact that at least during the extended

TABLE 9.5   SIX ALTERNATIVE ESTIMATES OF BENEFITS AND COSTS PER BALTIMORE OPTIONS PROGRAM TREATMENT GROUP MEMBER: REPORTED FROM PARTICIPANT PERSPECTIVE

	Lower Estimates		Middle Estimates		Upper Estimates	
	Original Estimates	Updated Estimates	Original Estimates	Updated Estimates	Original Estimates	Updated Estimates
Earnings and fringe benefits	$491	$1,277	$930	$1,886	$1,272	$2,021
Tax payments	−81	−172	−247	−269	−343	−290
Out-of-pocket work expenditures	−21	−25	−24	−26	−24	−26
AFDC payments	−29	−52	−100	1	−148	13
Other transfer payments	−111	−174	−225	−211	−297	−213
Allowances and support services	190	220	213	234	213	234
Net gain	439	1,074	547	1,615	673	1,739

Notes: All estimates are based on a time horizon of five years. Lower estimates represent only observed program impacts and, thus, do not include estimates of future impacts. That is, there is no extrapolation beyond the observation period. Middle estimates include estimates of future benefits and costs that are based on an assumed annual decay rate of 22 percent. Upper estimates include estimates of future benefits and costs that are based on an assumed zero decay rate. Original estimates are based on a demonstration period of around 1.5 years and an extrapolation period of about 3.5 years. Updated estimates are based on a demonstration period of around three years and an extrapolation period of about two years.

Source: Original estimates are from Table 6.7 of the Daniel Friedlander, Gregory Hoerz, David Long, and Janet Quint, *Maryland: Final Report on the Employment Initiatives Evaluation* (New York: Manpower Demonstration Research Corporation, Decembe 1985). Updated estimates are from Table A.7 of Daniel Friedlander, *Maryland: Supplementary Report on the Baltimore Options Program* (New York: Manpower Demonstration Research Corporation, October 1987).

data collection period, even an assumption of a zero decay rate for the earnings impact of the Baltimore Options program was overly pessimistic. As it turned out, the earnings differences between the treatment and comparison groups in Baltimore continued to grow during the extended data collection period. This is one example of a *forecasting error*, a common CBA problem, which is discussed in some detail in Chapter 15.

Given the absence of good evidence concerning decay rates, MDRC's strategy of examining the sensitivity of their findings to alternative rates was a good one. It is important to recognize, however, that the amount of variance observed in these sensitivity tests was severely restricted by the very short five-year time horizon upon which they are all based. Nevertheless, as Table 9.5 attests, this variation is far from eliminated.

SENSITIVITY OF THE WORK/WELFARE FINDINGS TO ALTERNATIVE ASSUMPTIONS

As indicated earlier, numerous methodological issues arise in measuring the benefits and costs of E&T demonstrations. Consequently, measuring the benefits and costs of the Work/Welfare Demonstrations inevitably required that MDRC make a number of assumptions. In this section, we examine how sensitive MDRC's findings are to three of the more important of these assumptions. (In Chapter 14, we consider the sensitivity of the results to changes in assumptions on distributional weights.) By conducting these sensitivity tests, we hope to illustrate the role that some of the issues discussed earlier play in conducting actual CBAs of E&T programs, as well as provide some idea of how much confidence can be placed in MDRC's findings for the Work/Welfare Demonstrations.

Sensitivity to Alternative Assumptions About In-Program Output

For reasons discussed in detail earlier, MDRC's estimates of in-program output values could be either overstated or understated. Here we focus only on the implications of a possible overstatement, which is perhaps the more likely of the two possibilities.

Findings from a sensitivity test of this possibility are reported in the first two columns of Table 9.6. Column 1 simply duplicates the social net gain estimates reported in column H of Table 9.4. In keeping with the possibility that the in-program output values incorporated into column 1 are overstated, column 2 is based on the extreme assumption that in-program output should be valued at zero, but is otherwise computed on the same basis as column 1. As suggested by a comparison of these two columns, except for the West Virginia demonstration, the estimates of social net gains and losses are quite insensitive to this assumption.

Sensitivity to Changes in the Shadow Price of Capital

Chapter 5 suggests that in principle dollars of program costs that represent forgone private-sector investment and dollars of program benefits that are used for investment purposes should be multiplied by the value of the shadow price of capital. Columns 3–5 of Table 9.6 test how sensitive the CBA findings for the Work/Welfare Demonstrations are to doing this. The value of the shadow price of capital that we use

TABLE 9.6   SENSITIVITY TESTS OF ESTIMATED NET SOCIAL GAINS (OR LOSSES) FROM THE WORK/WELFARE DEMONSTRATIONS

	Unadjusted Net Social Gain (or Loss) [B–C+E+F–G]	Net Social Gain (or Loss) *if* Value of In-program Output = 0 (B–C+F–G)	Net Social Gain if Shadow Price of Capital = 2.0 and—		
			$S_c = S_n = .15$; Nonparticipant tax-transfer gains reduce taxes; program service costs increase taxes [1.15(B–C)+E+ 1.15(F–G)]	$S_c = 0, S_n = .15$; Nonparticipant Tax-transfer gains reduce taxes; program service costs increase taxes [B–C+E+ 1.15(F–G)]	$S_c = 0, S_n = 15$; Nonparticipant tax-transfer gains reduce national debt; program service costs increase national debt [B–C+E+ 2.0(F–G)]
	1	2	3	4	5
AFDC-R					
APPLICANTS					
San Diego I					
Job Search Only	$1,096	$1,099	$1,261	$1,164	$1,551
Job Search + CWEP	1,953	1,748	2,216	2,097	2,905
San Diego II	753	573	839	971	2,206
Virginia	1,801	1,760	2,065	1,895	2,427
West Virginia	(92)	(634)	(187)	(115)	(245)
RECIPIENTS					
San Diego II	2,423	2,243	2,759	2,651	3,941
Virginia	764	619	857	771	809
West Virginia	953	(106)	937	925	767
New Jersey	2,331	2,340	2,682	2,493	3,409
Maine	2,763	2,083	3,077	2,599	1,666
APPLICANTS AND RECIPIENTS					
Cook County					
Job Search Only	55	54	63	126	529
Job Search + CWEP	328	228	362	367	590
Baltimore	1,813	1,423	2,026	1,766	1,497
Arkansas	495	475	566	634	1,419
AFDC-U					
APPLICANTS					
San Diego I					
Job Search Only	33	38	39	218	1,267
Job Search + CWEP	(29)	(383)	(86)	130	1,031
San Diego II	2,120	1,853	2,398	2,317	3,430
RECIPIENTS					
San Diego II	1,566	1,299	1,757	1,896	3,780
APPLICANTS AND RECIPIENTS					
Baltimore	(3,089)	(3,369)	(3,594)	(3,409)	(5,225)

S_c = Savings rate of clients.
S_n = Savings rate of nonparticipants.
Source: Table 9.4 [Letters in brackets in the column headings indicate the columns from Table 9.4 that were used in the computations.]

for this purpose is 2.0. The 2.0 figure may be interpreted as implying that the forgone stream of returns from each dollar of private-sector investment displaced as a result of a public-sector program and each dollar of program benefits used for investment purposes have a present discounted value of around $2.00. The 2.0 shadow price figure is implied by Table 5.1, given the following assumptions: (1) the marginal rate of time preference is equal to 1.5 percent; (2) the gross pretax rate of return on capital in the private sector is equal to 19.6 percent; (3) the gross savings rate is equal to 15 percent; and (4) the depreciation rate of private-sector capital is 10 percent. The basis for each of these assumptions, as well as the formula used to compute the shadow price, can be found in Chapter 5.

To use the shadow price of capital for CBA purposes, it is necessary to determine the fraction of each program benefit that is invested in the private-sector and the fraction that is directly consumed. Similarly, it is necessary to determine the fraction of each cost that displaces private-sector investment and the fraction that displaces private-sector consumption. For the Welfare/Work Initiative Demonstrations, the values of these fractions are not self-evident. Thus, the estimates in columns 3–5 of Table 9.6 are based on three alternative sets of assumptions, each of which is described in turn.

For purposes of column 3, we begin by assuming that in-program output, which was mostly in the form of services, was entirely consumed. Consequently, this assumption implies that private-sector savings and investment were unaffected by in-program output. We further assume that, except for in-program output, 15 percent of any increases in income enjoyed by either participants or nonparticipants will be saved and, hence, invested in the private-sector, and the remaining 85 percent will be consumed. Similarly, we also assume that 15 percent of any decreases in the incomes of either participants or nonparticipants will displace private-sector savings and investments, and the remaining 85 percent will displace private-sector consumption. These assumptions are consistent with the assumption that the savings rate is equal to 0.15 and imply that, with the exception of in-program output, any increases or decreases in the incomes of either participants or nonparticipants should be multiplied by $[1(0.85) + 2.0(0.15)] = 1.15$. Finally, we assume that any increases in taxes paid by participants or reductions in transfers received by program participants as a result of the demonstration programs are used to reduce the taxes and, hence, increase the incomes of nonparticipants and that program service costs are paid by increasing the taxes of nonparticipants.

To compute column 4, we modify only one of the assumptions made in computing column 3. Rather than assuming that 15 cents of a dollar received by welfare participants is invested, we instead assume, somewhat more realistically we believe, that the entire dollar is consumed. In other words, we assume that, given their low incomes, the savings rate of welfare participants is zero; however, we continue to assume that the savings rate of nonparticipants is 0.15. Thus, while increases or decreases in the incomes of nonparticipants are multiplied by 1.15, changes in the incomes of participants are multiplied by 1.0.

With one important exception, column 5 is based on the same assumptions as column 4. It is assumed that rather than being used to reduce the taxes of nonparticipants, increases in taxes paid by participants and reductions in transfers received by participants are instead used to reduce the national debt. Similarly, it is assumed that rather than paying for program service costs by increasing taxes, the national debt is increased instead. This assumption should be viewed as somewhat unrealistic, if for no other reason than the fact that program service costs, reductions in participant welfare receipts, and increases in participant tax payments would affect state as well as federal budgets. However, the assumption is a useful one for conducting a sensitivity test, for it implies that if there is full employment in the economy and if the savings rate is insensitive to interest rates, each dollar increase in the national debt displaces one dollar of private-sector investment and that each dollar reduction in the national debt increases private investment by one dollar. Thus, instead of multiplying nonparticipant benefits and costs by 1.15, as we do in computing column 4, to compute column 5, we multiply by 2.0, the full shadow price of capital.

By now, it should be apparent that the estimates presented in columns 3–5 of Table 9.6 are based on a large number of assumptions, many of which are tenuous. Thus, these estimates should be considered as only illustrative. Nonetheless, a comparison of columns 3, 4, and 5 with column 1 strongly suggests that in most instances ignoring the shadow price of capital will cause the social net gains of programs such as those tested under the Welfare/Work Demonstrations to be understated. For example, 14 of the 19 estimates appearing in column 4, estimates that in our judgment are based on a more realistic set of assumptions than those reported in either column 3 or column 5, are more positive than their counterparts in column 1. Most of these differences, however, are small. Moreover, there is only one sign change. And that change is from a very small negative value to a small positive value. Thus, while estimates of the magnitude of social net gains from the Work/Welfare Demonstrations seem somewhat sensitive to using the shadow price of capital in their computation, conclusions concerning whether there is a positive payoff from such programs are not.

Sensitivity to Alternative Assumptions About Subtracting Losses in Leisure from Earnings Gains

An analysis presented earlier in this chapter implies that if participants value the time they must relinquish in order to either participate in E&T activities or take paid employment—time that economists usually refer to as *leisure*—net gains for participants in E&Ts would be overstated (or, alternatively, net losses understated) by the results reported in the first column of Table 9.4. This possibility is explored in Table 9.7, which presents estimates of net social gains for a subset of the Work/Welfare Demonstrations that are adjusted on the basis of values found in Table 9.3 and the procedure outlined earlier in the chapter.

Some of the information required by this procedure is not reported in the original CBAs of the Work/Welfare Demonstrations, but can be found in a subsequent follow-up study of several of the demonstrations by Daniel Friedlander and Gary Burtless.[28] However, this study focuses on only recipients of AFDC-R and is limited to only a subset of the Work/Welfare Demonstrations. It is these programs that are listed in Table 9.7.

TABLE 9.7   SENSITIVITY OF FINDINGS FROM THE WORK/WELFARE DEMONSTRATIONS TO TAKING ACCOUNT OF THE VALUE TO CLIENTS OF LOST LEISURE

	Unadjusted Net Social Gain [B–C+E+F–G]	$h_0/h_1 = .25$ $W^r_1/W_1 = .25$ [(.522B)–C+E+F–G]	$h_0/h_1 = .5$ $W^r_1/W_1 = .25$ [(.439B)–C+E+F–G]	$h_0/h_1 = .25$ $W^r_1/W_1 = .75$ [(.178B)–C+E+F–G]	$h_0/h_1 = .5$ $W^r_1/W_1 = .75$ [(.151B)–C+E+F–G]
	I	II	III	IV	V
AFDC-R					
APPLICANTS					
San Diego SWIM	$ 753	$ 208	$ 113	($184)	($215)
Virginia	1,801	989	848	405	359
RECIPIENTS					
San Diego SWIM	2,423	913	651	(173)	(258)
Virginia	764	295	213	(43)	(70)
APPLICANTS AND RECIPIENTS					
Baltimore*	1,813	1,350	1,269	1,016	990
Arkansas	495	299	265	158	147

Net Social Gain (or Loss) if $\varepsilon = 0.1$ and —

*The calculations of columns II–V for Baltimore differed from that for the other site since, unlike the other sites, there was evidence that only half the Baltimore earnings impact should be adjusted for lost leisure. For example, the column II estimate for Baltimore was computed by using the following formula: [1/2(.528B)+1/2B–C+E+F–G].

Source: Table 9.4.: The letters in the brackets at the top of each column identify the columns from Table 9.4 that were used in the calculations.

The five steps required by the procedure described earlier are listed again for convenience, followed by a discussion of how the values needed to complete each step were selected:

1. **Partition the earnings increases attributable to E&T between that part resulting from increases in wage rates and that part resulting from increases in hours.** The study by Friedlander and Burtless indicates that as much as half the demonstration impact on earnings in Baltimore, but little if any of the impact on earnings in the other three sites, resulted from increases in the wage rates received by members of the treatment group. In other words, at least half the earnings impact in Baltimore and virtually all the earnings impact at the other three sites appeared attributable to increases in the hours worked by treatment group members. Thus, in computing the estimates reported in Table 9.7, it was assumed that 50 percent of the estimated earnings impact in Baltimore and 100 percent of the earnings impact in the other three sites should be adjusted to account for lost leisure.

2. **Divide participant hours in the absence of the E&T program (h_0) by post-program participant hours (h_1).** As mentioned earlier, MDRC extrapolated

benefits and costs for the Work/Welfare Demonstrations over a five-year time horizon. According to Friedlander and Burtless's findings, about three-fourths of the hours increase in Virginia can be attributed to hours worked by members of the treatment group who would not have worked at all during this five-year period. The comparable figures for Baltimore, Arkansas, and San Diego are one-third, one-half, and two-thirds, respectively.[29] These findings suggest that those persons whose hours were increased as a result of the demonstration program would have worked relatively few hours in the absence of the program and, consequently, that the ratio of h_0 to h_1 is fairly small. Thus, in computing the estimates appearing in Table 9.7, two alternative values were used for h_0/h_1, a lower bound of 0.25 and an upper bound of 0.5.

3. **Divide the postprogram reservation wage rate (W_1') by the postprogram wage rate (W_1).** In computing the estimates reported in Table 9.7, we used the following two alternative values for W_1'/W_1: an upper bound of .75 and a lower bound of .25. The wide range between these two values reflects our uncertainty concerning the ratio. The numerator of the ratio is the wage that would have just induced those demonstration participants who found work to enter the work force, while the denominator is the wage these persons actually received. Unfortunately, neither findings from the Work/Welfare Demonstrations nor other sources provide direct information about the value of W_1'. It is apparent, however, that the value of the ratio W_1'/W_1 must be less than one, since those who accept a job must obtain a wage that exceeds their reservation wage. It also appears likely that the ratio substantially exceeds zero. Few persons are likely to be willing to work for a zero wage.

4. **Determine the value of the wage elasticity (ϵ) at postprogram hours and the postprogram wage rate.** Table 9.3 suggests that the estimates in Table 9.7 should not be very sensitive to small changes in the value selected for ϵ. Thus, to compute the estimates reported in Table 9.7, we use only one value for ϵ, 0.1. As indicated earlier, this value is roughly consistent with findings from the income maintenance experiments for mothers in single-parent households.

5. **Multiply the earnings increase attributable to the E&T-induced increase in hours, as obtained in step 1, by the appropriate percentage value from Table 9.3, as determined in steps 2–4.** Based on the assumptions described in steps 2–4, the following percentage values were selected from Table 9.3.

Assumptions	Percentage Values
$\varepsilon = 0.1$, $W_1'/W_1 = .25$, $h_0/h_1 = .25$	52.2
$\varepsilon = 0.1$, $W_1'/W_1 = .25$, $h_0/h_1 = .50$	43.9
$\varepsilon = 0.1$, $W_1'/W_1 = .75$, $h_0/h_1 = .25$	17.8
$\varepsilon = 0.1$, $W_1'/W_1 = .75$, $h_0/h_1 = .50$	15.1

To compute the adjusted net social gain estimates appearing in Table 9.7, the earnings impact estimates reported in column B of Table 9.4 were multiplied by the foregoing percentage values. Because of the evidence that only about half of the earnings impact in Baltimore should be adjusted for lost leisure, only half of the earnings estimate for Baltimore was multiplied by the percentage values, while the other half was fully counted. In the remaining sites, the entire earnings estimate was multiplied by the percentage values.

We turn now to the findings in Table 9.7. The first column in this table shows the unadjusted net gain estimates that are also reported in column H of Table 9.4. Net gain estimates that have been adjusted on the basis of the four alternative sets of assumptions described in steps 2–4 to reflect the costs associated with reductions in the leisure time of program participants are reported in columns II–V.

A comparison of the first column with the remaining four columns in Table 9.7 indicates that the estimates of net social gains and losses are quite sensitive to adjustments that account for losses of leisure, with most of them becoming substantially smaller even when they are based on the lower-bound assumptions for the values of W_1^r/W_1 and h_0/h_1. If it is assumed that the reservation wages of welfare recipients are large relative to the wages they actually receive when they go to work, then several of the net gain estimates that were initially positive take on small negative values. Nonetheless, it is important to recognize that none of these estimates turn negative until rather extreme assumptions are made about participant reservation wages. Thus, perhaps the most reasonable conclusion to draw from Table 9.7 is that the major implication of unadjusted net gain estimates in the first column, (i.e., that the programs listed in the table had positive impacts on society as a whole), is fairly robust to adjustments for lost leisure.

In assessing the findings reported in Table 9.7, two additional points should be kept in mind. First, the net gain estimates that are reported in the table are only adjusted for leisure that is lost through paid employment. The leisure of Work/Welfare participants was also reduced to the extent they participated in program activities, but data on time spent in these activities are not available. Thus, further adjustments to take these additional losses of leisure into account were not feasible.

Second, as pointed out earlier, it is likely that programs that reduce the leisure time of welfare recipients may, as a result, increase the utility of the nonrecipient taxpayers who support the welfare system. The dollar value of this increase in utility is also not taken into account in Table 9.7. However, although most nonrecipient taxpayers, if asked, would probably express a desire to see welfare recipients employed, the appropriate CBA question is how much they are willing to pay for this. It is less obvious that the collective willingness-to-pay of nonrecipients for reductions in the leisure time of recipients is of large magnitude.

One additional finding from Table 9.7 of considerable interest is that once the adjustment for the loss of leisure associated with program-induced increases in work hours is made, the largest estimated net social gains are associated with the Baltimore program. Of the programs listed in Table 9.7, this program was the only one oriented toward the goal of increasing enrollee employment in better-paying jobs. The other programs were more oriented toward increasing hours at work. Moreover, the Baltimore program offered education and training services. The San Diego SWIM program also offered such services, but only after participants completed job search and three months of workfare participation. In Baltimore, in contrast, participants could go directly into education and training activities if they so chose and open slots existed. The Virginia and Arkansas programs made little use of such services, focusing instead on job search and, to a lesser extent, on workfare.

CONCLUSION

The analysis presented in this chapter suggests that CBAs of E&T demonstrations are more difficult both to conduct successfully and interpret than they may first appear, even when the demonstrations utilize a classical experimental design. Nevertheless, they can provide useful insights. For example, MDRC's CBAs of the Work/Welfare Demonstrations suggest that the net *social* gains from the tested programs were generally positive but modest. However, because of the relatively short time horizons and the conservative assumptions concerning decay rates used in their computation, and the fact that the shadow price of capital concept was ignored, these estimated gains may well be understated. Moreover, the sensitivity tests presented in this chapter suggest that the finding that the Work/Welfare Demonstrations resulted in positive social gains is quite robust with respect to alternative assumptions. However, the sensitivity tests did indicate that the magnitude of the net social gains is quite sensitive to taking the value of reductions in the leisure time of demonstration participants into account.

EXERCISES FOR CHAPTER 9

1. Using the scheme shown in Table 9.1, diagram the evaluation design used in each of the following demonstration programs.

   a. To evaluate a government training program that provides low-income, low-skilled, disadvantaged persons job-specific training, members of the target population are randomly assigned to either a treatment group that is eligible to receive services under the program or to a comparison group that is not. Data are collected on the earnings, welfare receipts, and so forth of both groups during the training period and for two years thereafter.

   b. To evaluate a government training program that provides low-income, low-skilled, disadvantaged persons job-specific training, members of the target population who live in the counties in the eastern half of a large industrial state are assigned to a treatment group that is eligible to receive services under the program, while members of the target population who live in the counties in the western half of the state are assigned to a comparison group that is not. Information is collected on the earnings, welfare receipts, and so forth of both groups for one year prior to the beginning of training, during the training period, and for two years thereafter.

   c. To evaluate a government training program that provides low-income, low-skilled, disadvantaged persons job-specific training, information is collected on the earnings, welfare receipts, and so forth of those persons who receive training. This information is collected for the year prior to the beginning of training, during the training period, and for two years thereafter.

2. Consider a government training program that provides low-skilled men job-specific training. To evaluate this program, members of the target population were randomly assigned to either a treatment group that was eligible to receive services under the program or to a comparison group that was not. Using this evaluation design, the following information was obtained:

   - Members of the treatment group were found to remain in the program an average of one year, during which time they received no earnings, but were paid a tax-free stipend of $5,000 by the program to help them cover their living expenses. During the program year, the average annual earnings of members of the control group were $10,000, on which they paid taxes of $1,000. During the program year, the welfare and unemployment compensation benefits received by the two groups were virtually identical.
   - Program operating costs (not counting the stipend) and the cost of services provided by the program were $3,000 per trainee.
   - During the two years after leaving the program, the average annual earnings of members of the treatment group were $20,000, on which they paid taxes of $2,000. During the same period, the average annual earnings of members of the control group were $15,000, on which they paid taxes of $1,500.
   - During the two years after leaving the program, the average annual welfare payments and unemployment compensation benefits received by members of the treatment group were $250. During the same period, the average annual welfare payments and unemployment compensation benefits received by members of the control group were $1,250.
   - During the two-year postprogram follow-up period, members of the treatment group worked 2,000 hours per year, on average, while members of the control group worked 1,500 hours per year, on average.
   - A typical member of the treatment group who found work was able to obtain a wage that was twice as high as the wage at which he would have just been willing to accept employment.

   a. Using a 5 percent discount rate, a zero decay rate, and a five-year time horizon, compute the present value of the net gain (or loss) from the program from the trainee, nonparticipant, and social perspectives. In doing this, ignore program impacts on leisure and assume that all benefits and costs accrue at the end of the year in which they occur.

   b. Once again ignoring program impacts on leisure, recompute the present value of the net gain (or loss) from the program from the trainee, nonparticipant, and social perspectives, assuming that at the end of the two-year follow-up period program impacts on earnings and transfer payments begin to decay at the rate of 20 percent each year.

   c. Using a wage elasticity value of 0.1, adjust the estimate of the trainee net benefits that you obtained in 2.a to take account of the impact of the program on their leisure.

3. Perhaps the most careful effort to measure the effects of compensatory preschool education was the Perry Preschool Project begun in Ypsilanti, Michigan in 1962. Children, mostly three years old, were randomly assigned to treatment (58 children) and control (65 children) groups between 1962 and 1965. Children in the treatment group received two academic years of schooling before they entered the regular school system at about age five, while children in the control group did not. The project collected information on the children through age 19, an exceptionally long follow-up period. Using information generated by the study, analysts estimated that two years of preschool generated social net benefits (1988 dollars) of $13,124 at a discount rate of 5 percent. [For a more complete account, see W. Steven Barnett, "Benefits of Compensatory Preschool Education," *Journal of Human Resources*, 27, no. 2 (Spring 1992), 279–312.]

    a. Before seeing results from the project, what would be your main methodological concern about such a long follow-up period? What data would you look at to see if the problem exists?

    b. Benefit categories beyond the age of 19 included crime reduction, earnings increase, and reductions in welfare receipts. If you were designing the study, what data would you collect to help measure these benefits?

4. Five years ago a community college district established programs in ten new vocational fields. The district now wants to phase out those programs that are not performing successfully and retain those programs that are performing successfully. To determine which programs to drop and which to retain, the district decides to perform cost-benefit analyses.

    a. What perspective or perspectives should be used in the studies? Are there any issues concerning standing?

    b. Using a stylized cost-benefit framework table, list the major benefits and costs that are relevant to the district's decision and indicate how each affects different pertinent groups, as well as society as a whole. Try to make your list as comprehensive and complete as possible, while avoiding double counting.

    c. What sort of evaluation design should the district use in conducting its CBAs? What are the advantages and disadvantages of this design? Is it practical?

    d. Returning to the list of benefits and costs that you developed in 4.b., indicate which of the benefits and costs on your list can be quantified in monetary terms. How would you treat those benefits and costs that cannot be monetized?

    e. What sort of data would be required to measure those benefits and costs that can be monetized? How might the required data be obtained?

NOTES

[1]David H. Greenberg and Marvin B. Mandell, "Research Utilization in Policymaking: A Tale of Two Series (of Social Experiments)," *Journal of Policy Analysis and Management*, 10, no. 4 (Fall 1991), 633–656.

[2]This method of diagramming evaluation designs was developed a number of years ago by Donald Campbell and Julian Stanley, *Experimental and Quasi-Experimental Designs for Research* (Chicago: Rand-McNally, 1963).

[3]On randomization problems, see Leslie L. Roos, Jr., Noralou P. Roos, and Barbara McKinley, "Implementing Randomization" *Policy Analysis*, 3, no. 4 (Fall 1977), 547–559.

[4]Sometimes a problem occurs when some members of the two groups cannot be located for purposes of collecting postprogram information on outcomes or refuse to provide the information. This problem, which can occur with all five of the sample designs listed in Table 9.1 and which is known as *sample attrition*, can bias the impact estimates if those who can and cannot be located systematically differ from one another in terms of the postprogram outcome measures. For example, those who can be located may have higher earnings, on average, than those who cannot be located.

[5]For discussions of issues and problems that arise in conducting social experiments, see Gary Burtless, "The Case for Randomized Field Trials in Economic and Policy Research," *The Journal of Economic Perspectives*, 9, no. 2 (Spring 1995), 63–84 and James S. Heckman and Jeffrey A. Smith, "Assessing the Case for Social Experiments," *The Journal of Economic Perspectives*, 9, no. 2 (Spring 1995), 85-110.

[6]The name stems from the fact that in the absence of random assignment people select themselves to participate or not participate in a program on the basis of such unobservable characteristics as motiva-

tion. If appropriate statistical adjustments cannot be made to control for this—and as the text indicates, sometimes this is possible and sometimes it is not—a sample selection bias results. For further information on the selection problem and econometric techniques that are used to attempt to adjust for it, see G.S. Maddala, *Introduction to Econometrics* (New York: Macmillan Publishing Co., 1988); G.S. Maddala, *Limited-Dependent and Qualitative Variables in Econometrics* (New York: Cambridge University Press, 1983); and Christopher H. Achen, *Statistical Analysis of Quasi-Experiments* (Berkeley, CA: University of California Press, 1986).

[7]For a comprehensive survey of social experiments conducted from the late 1960s up to the mid-1980s, see David H. Greenberg and Philip K. Robins, "The Changing Role of Social Experiments in Policy Analysis," *Journal of Policy Analysis and Management*, 5, no. 2 (Winter 1986), 340–362. For two- to three-page summaries of each of the known 63 social experiments that were completed in the United States prior to August 1990, see David Greenberg and Mark Shroder, *Digest of the Social Experiments* (Madison, WI: Institute for Research on Poverty, University of Wisconsin, Special Report #52, May 1991).

[8]Greenberg and Robins, "The Changing Role of Social Experiments in Policy Analysis," 340–362.

[9]For simplicity, we assume that wage changes resulting from E&T programs engender only substitution effects, not income effects. Hence, curve S corresponds to both the participant's compensated and uncompensated labor supply curve. For reasons discussed in Appendix 3A, changes in social surplus should in principle be measured using compensated curves—that is, curves that incorporate substitution, but not income effects. We maintain the assumption of zero income effects throughout this analysis. We discuss the implications of doing this later.

[10]The word *leisure*, as commonly used by economists and as used here, refers to all activities that take place outside the labor market. Many of these activities (e.g., child care, home repair, and education) may, of course, be quite productive.

[11]Because the hours the recipient is required to work are computed by dividing her welfare grant by the minimum wage (i.e., $h^* = \text{grant}/W^m$), are her grant equals $W^m h^*$, a value that in Figure 9.3 is represented by area $W^m a h^* h_0$.

[12]Notice that because the supply curve first shifts from S_0 to S_1, and then, in response to this shift the participant adjusts her labor supply, the surplus gain is measured using S_1 rather than S_0.

[13]Computing the magnitude of area abc requires an assumption about the shape of the labor supply curve between points c and b. The assumption we make is that this segment of the supply curve corresponds to a segment of an ellipse. The lowest point on this ellipse occurs at $W_1{}^r$, while point S is located one-quarter of the way around the circumference of the ellipse. The distance between $W_1{}^r$ and c depends upon the value of h_0, the number of hours that E&T clients would work in the absence of the program. The distance between S and b is determined by the value of ε, the wage elasticity at point b.

If $h_0 = 0$, $W_1{}^r = 0$, and $\varepsilon = 0$, area $abh_1h_0 = W_1h_1$ and area $abc = 0.25\pi(W_1h_1) = 0.785W_1h_1$. In other words, area abc equals one-quarter the area of an ellipse with a width equal to $2h_1$ and a length equal to $2W_1$. Dividing area abh_1h_0 into area abc and multiplying by 100 produces the 78.5 percent figure found in the upper left-hand corner of Table 9.3. The formulas used to obtain the remaining values in the table are derived in David Greenberg, "The Leisure Bias in Cost-Benefit Analyses of Employment and Training Programs," unpublished paper, 1995.

[14]Later in this chapter, we illustrate how Table 9.3 can be used in assessing findings from existing CBAs of E&T demonstrations.

[15]As mentioned in footnote 9, throughout this analysis, it has been assumed that E&T participation results in zero income effects. Hence, in using Table 9.3, it is the value of the *compensated* wage elasticity that should be determined. Although the procedure outlined in the text does not allow for nonzero income effects, a sensitivity analysis conducted by David Greenberg ("The Leisure Bias in Cost-Benefit Analyses of Employment and Training Programs") suggests that the errors resulting from ignoring this possibility will be small.

[16]Harry Holzer, "Black Youth Nonemployment: Duration and Job Search" in *The Black Youth Employment Crisis*, Richard Freeman and Harry Holzer, eds. (Chicago: University of Chicago Press, 1986).

[17]Harry J. Holzer, "Reservation Wages and Their Labor Market Effects for Black and White Male Youth," *The Journal of Human Resources*, 21, no. 2 (Spring 1986), 157–177; and R. Jones, "The Relationship Between Unemployment Spells and Reservation Wages as a Test of Search Theory," *The Quarterly Journal of Economics*, 103, no. 4 (October 1988), 741–765. Both studies examined a number of different subgroups. The ratio of reservation wages to previously received wages was between 0.9 and 1.1 for almost all of the subgroups of unemployed persons examined. Holzer's findings were based on the following question: "What would the wage or salary [on the specific job you are looking for] have to be for you to be willing to take it?" Jones's findings are based on a somewhat different question: "What is the lowest amount in take-home pay that you would be prepared to accept from a new job?"

[18]This section borrows heavily from David Greenberg, "Conceptual Issues in Cost-Benefit Analysis of Welfare-to-Work Programs," *Contemporary Policy Issues*, 10, no. 4 (October 1992), 51–63.

[19]One approach that might be used to attempt to do this is contingent valuation, a topic that is taken up in Chapter 11.

[20]For a review of what bureaucrats actually maximize, see David L. Weimer and Aidan R. Vining, *Policy Analysis: Concepts and Practice*, 2nd ed. (Englewood Cliffs, NJ: Prentice Hall, 1992), pp. 131–138.

[21]Using five years of follow-up information on women who had received training under the Manpower Development and Training Act, Orley Ashenfelter found that the program's earnings effect decayed at an annual rate of 5 percent for black women, but grew at an annual rate of 7 percent for white women [Orley Ashenfelter, "Estimating the Effects of Training Programs on Earnings," *Review of Economics and Statistics*, 60, no. 1 (February 1978), 47–57]. Not only are the divergent results for black and white women difficult to reconcile, but in a reanalysis of Ashenfelter's data, Howard Bloom ["Estimating the Effect of Job Training Programs Using Longitudinal Data: Ashenfelter's Findings Reconsidered," *Journal of Human Resources*, 19, no. 4 (Fall 1984), 544–556] obtained quite different results. Unlike Ashenfelter's study, few evaluations of E&Ts have been based on more than one, two, or three years of follow-up information. Moreover, the few evaluations that have used follow-up data covering a longer time period have obtained mixed results. For example, in a five-year follow-up of four welfare-to-work experiments, Daniel Friedlander and Gary Burtless (*Five Years After: The Long-Term Effects of Welfare-to-Work Programs*, New York: Russell Sage Foundation, 1995) found that by year 5 the earnings impact had decayed in three of the demonstrations, but not in the fourth.

[22] For example, see Ron Haskins, "Congress Writes a Law: Research and Welfare Reform," *Journal of Policy Analysis and Management*, 10, no. 4 (Fall 1991); Erica Baum, "When the Witch Doctors Agree: The Family Support Act and Social Science Research," *The Journal of Policy Analysis and Management*, 10, no. 4 (Fall 1991); and Peter Szanton, "The Remarkable 'Quango': Knowledge, Politics, and Welfare Reform," *Journal of Policy Analysis and Management*, 10, no. 4 (Fall 1991).

[23]Descriptions of the Work/Welfare Demonstrations, as well as the CBA findings from these demonstrations, can be found in the following reports published by the Manpower Demonstration Research Corporation, New York, NY: P. Auspos, G. Cave, and D. Long, *Maine: Final Report on the Training Opportunities in the Private Sector Program*, April 1988; S. Freedman, J. Bryant, and G. Cave, *New Jersey: Final Report on the Grant Diversion Project*, November 1988; D. Friedlander, G. Hoerz, J. Quint, and J. Riccio, *Arkansas: Final Report on the WORK Program in Two Counties*, September, 1985; D. Friedlander, G. Hoerz, D. Long, and J. Quint, *Maryland: Final Report on the Employment Initiatives Evaluation*, December 1985; D. Friedlander, M. Erickson, G. Hamilton, and V. Knox, *West Virginia: Final Report on the Community Work Experience Demonstrations*, September 1986; D. Friedlander, S. Freedman, G. Hamilton, and J. Quint, *Illinois: Final Report on Job Search and Work Experience in Cook County*, November 1987; B. Goldman, D. Friedlander, and D. Long, *California: Final Report on the San Diego Job Search and Work Experience Demonstration*, February 1986; G. Hamilton and D. Friedlander, *Final Report on the Saturation Work Initiative Model in San Diego*, 1989; J. Riccio, G. Cave, S. Freedman, and M. Price, *Virginia: Final Report on the Virginia Employment Services Program*, August 1986.

[24]U.S. House of Representatives, Committee on Ways and Means, *Overview of Entitlement Programs*, (Washington, DC: U.S. Government Printing Office, 1993), p. 616, Table 1.

[25]Ketron, Incorporated, *The Long-Term Impact of WIN II: A Longitudinal Evaluation of the Employment Experiences of Participants in the Work Incentive Program* (Wayne, PA: Ketron, 1980).

[26]Daniel Friedlander, Gregory Hoerz, David Long, and Janet Quint, *Maryland: Final Report on the Employment Initiatives Evaluation* (New York: Manpower Demonstration Research Corporation, December 1985).

[27]Daniel Friedlander, *Maryland: Supplemental Report on the Baltimore Options Program* (New York: Manpower Demonstration Research Corporation, October 1987).

[28]Daniel Friedlander and Gary Burtless, *Five Years After: The Long-Term Effects of Welfare-to-Work Programs* (New York: Russell Sage Foundation, 1995).

[29]Almost all the remaining increases in hours at all four sites appear to have resulted from reductions in the number of weeks that members of the treatment group who would have worked during the follow-up period even in the absence of the demonstration program needed to find their initial job during the follow-up period.

10

ESTIMATING AND VALUING IMPACTS FROM OBSERVED BEHAVIOR

The key concept for valuing policy impacts in terms of willingness-to-pay is change in social surplus. As discussed in Chapter 3, measurement of changes in social surplus is straightforward when we know the shapes and positions of the supply and demand curves in the relevant markets. Recall that with known supply and demand equations, changes in social surplus are represented by areas, often as simple triangles and trapezoids. In practice, however, these curves are usually not known. Rather, analysts have to discover them or find alternative ways to measure benefits and costs. In the last chapter, we discussed how such information can be gathered from demonstrations and social experiments. In this chapter, we consider how to estimate benefits and costs by making use of observations of behaviors when there is no demonstration or social experiment. While contingent valuation methods, which are discussed in Chapter 11, rely on surveys, the methods discussed in this chapter are based on preferences revealed through behavior.

For goods traded in well-functioning markets, we can usually observe at least one piece of information—the market clearing price. We may also be able to observe the aggregate quantity bought and sold, so that we have the point of intersection of the demand and supply curves. Based on this observed price and quantity, and similar observations from different regions or time periods in which prices and quantities differ, we may be able to estimate the market demand and supply curves using fairly standard econometric techniques.

In the public sector, however, it is usually more complicated. After all, the rationale for many public policies and the desirability of evaluating them with CBA are that either markets for certain "goods," like pollution, do not exist or markets exist but are distorted by imperfect competition, externalities, or asymmetric information, as discussed in Chapter 3. Furthermore, in applying CBA to proposed but not yet implemented policies, we obviously have no track record upon which to base our predictions and valuations of future effects. Indeed, we may have no experience with similar programs from which to draw guidance. In these situations, the analyst may not have even one point on the appropriate demand or supply curve, which makes it particularly difficult to obtain estimates of the curves. Nonetheless, as we show in this chapter, all is not lost!

Accurate estimation of changes in social surplus usually requires knowledge of entire demand and supply curves. Sometimes, though, the total change in consumer surplus can be estimated from knowledge of the marginal social benefit or the marginal social cost of one more unit of the good or service affected by the policy being evaluated. In a perfect market, the current price measures both the marginal social cost and the marginal social benefit of an additional unit of a good or service. When market failure leads to a divergence between market price and marginal social cost or marginal social benefit, analysts try to obtain an estimate of what the market price would be if the relevant good were traded in a perfect market. As discussed in Chapter 3, such an estimate is called a *shadow price*. The major focus of this chapter is on various methods for estimating shadow prices.

Practical methods to value impacts based on observed behavior include: (1) the use of project revenues as the measure of benefits; (2) the estimation of benefits from observation of some points on the demand curve; (3) the market analogy method; (4) the intermediate good method; (5) the use of differences in asset values; (6) the hedonic price method; (7) the travel cost method; and (8) the defensive expenditures method. Some of these methods involve estimation of the whole demand or supply curve, while others provide only an estimate of the shadow price.

In this chapter, we focus more on changes in consumer surplus than on changes in producer surplus. Many changes in producer surplus are either offset by changes in consumer surplus (a transfer) or are, in practice, negligible. There are two major exceptions. One pertains to unemployed labor, which we have discussed in detail in Chapters 3 and 9. The other, which we touch on only in passing at several points in this chapter, arises when the government intervenes in otherwise efficient markets for capital, foreign exchange, land, and other productive assets. Nevertheless, our emphasis on estimating changes in consumer surplus enables us to cover the topics likely to be relevant to the most common CBA applications.

PROJECT REVENUES AS THE MEASURE OF BENEFITS

To private-sector producers of goods or services, project revenues are a natural measure of benefits. As we pointed out in earlier chapters, however, revenues are not synonymous with social benefits. In Chapter 3, we showed that when there are no market imperfections, the social benefits of a project equal the revenues *plus* changes in social surplus. Considering only revenues misses changes in social surplus, which may constitute all of the benefits if the policy does not involve the government either selling a good or taxing or subsidizing to correct a market failure.

Of course, it is theoretically correct to treat revenues as benefits in cases where changes in social surplus equal zero. Consider, for example, a public project that exports all of its output. In this case, the consumer surplus accrues to foreigners and, therefore, should not be counted if the analyst is restricting standing to the nation. The North East Coal Development Project, which we discussed in Chapter 4, is an example. It would supply coal to Japanese customers only. As Table 4.8 shows, there were no anticipated consumer surplus benefits for Canadians. The primary beneficiaries (besides the Canadian federal government) were anticipated to be the mining and transportation companies, which would enjoy producer surpluses, legitimately computed as the differences between their revenues and their costs. Thus, when there are no domestic consumers, there are no changes in consumer surpluses, so that revenues theoretically equal gross benefits.

Another correct use of "revenues as benefits" occurs when the government sells a good in an undistorted market without affecting the market price. For example, a government may have surplus office equipment that it sells in sufficiently small quantities that the market price of similar equipment does not change. This is just the reverse of the opportunity cost case discussed in Chapter 3 where government purchases do not affect price in an undistorted market. The assumption of a negligible effect on price is likely to be more reasonable for goods traded in larger, typically national, markets than for goods traded in smaller, typically local, markets. It is also likely to be more reasonable for homogeneous goods, such as surplus equipment, than for heterogeneous goods, such as land, which may differ from one parcel to another.

Unfortunately, the government often sells goods when markets are distorted or where it has a large impact on the price of the good. For example, electricity may not be available to residents of a remote village in a developing country unless the government sponsors the construction of an electric power transmission line. Here government introduction of electricity reduces the price from effectively infinity to the user fee it charges. In these situations, revenues are a poor measure of benefits.

DIRECT ESTIMATION OF THE DEMAND CURVE

It is sometimes possible to make inferences about the demand curve for a good by observing the quantity demanded at different prices. We consider here three possibilities. First, we know only one point on the demand curve, but we also have an estimate of either the elasticity or slope of the demand curve from previous research. Second, we know a few points on the demand curve which we can use as a basis for predicting another point of relevance to our valuation. Third, we have a sufficient number of observations of prices and quantities so that we can apply econometric methods to estimate the entire demand curve.

Using One Point with an Elasticity or Slope Estimate

Many municipalities charge annual fees for household refuse collection that do not depend on the quantity of refuse disposed of by households. Typically, the cost of disposing of each individual household's refuse is shared equally among all households.

Each household faces a marginal private cost (MPC) of refuse disposal that is only a negligible fraction of the marginal social costs (MSC) of the household's garbage—if there are n households, then each household experiences a marginal private cost of MSC/n, which for large n is effectively zero. This divergence between MPC and MSC leads to an excess of refuse disposal from the social perspective. Raising the marginal private cost would reduce the quantity of refuse disposed of by households and thereby reduce the social surplus loss from excess refuse disposal.

Imagine that you have been asked to measure the social benefits that would result if a town, Wasteville, which currently does not charge households by volume for the collection of refuse, imposes a fee of $1 per 30-gallon container. That is, households would be charged $1 for each such container put at the curbside for emptying by the sanitation department. The fee would raise the marginal private cost from zero to $1 per 30 gallons of waste.

From the sanitation department's records, you find that the refuse disposal rate is currently 2.60 pounds per person per day (lb/p/d) and the marginal social cost of each ton of refuse collected is approximately $120 per ton, or $0.06/lb. (One ton equals 2,000 pounds in North America.) This is the sum of the marginal collection costs of $40 per ton and the tipping fee for landfill usage of $80 per ton. As a 30-gallon container holds about 20 pounds of waste, the fee of $1 per container implies a price of about $0.05/lb. Though the fee still leaves the marginal private cost (price) below the marginal social cost, you expect it to produce a gain in social surplus by reducing the amount of waste generated.

To measure the social surplus gain, however, you require the demand curve. You know only one point on the demand curve: 2.60 lb/p/d at a price equal to zero. To go any further, you must find a way of estimating the rest of the demand curve. Lacking any additional information, you might simply make a plausible "guess" that the price elasticity of demand for refuse disposal is between 0 and −1. This wide range would leave you very uncertain about the magnitude of the gain in social surplus!

Borrowing elasticities or slopes. If you went to a research library or used the bibliography at the end of this book, however, then you might turn up a study that would give you an empirically based estimate of the price elasticity of demand for refuse disposal. (The use of secondary sources is explored in Chapter 12.) Indeed, Robin R. Jenkins provides such a study.[1] Jenkins based her estimation on data from nine U.S. communities, which employed a variety of refuse fees linked to volume, ranging from zero in three communities to between $0.25 and $1.73 per 30- to 32-gallon container in the other six, over the period from 1980 to 1989. She applied econometric methods to estimate a price elasticity of the demand for residential refuse disposal of −0.12. Making use of this elasticity is a bit complicated for reasons that we discuss later. Fortunately, however, she also reported the estimated slope for a demand curve for refuse disposal that is linear in price. Specifically, she estimated that each dollar increase in the price charged for a 30- to 32-gallon container reduces waste by 0.40 lb/p/d. Thus, using her estimate leads to a prediction that if Wasteville imposed a fee of $1 per container ($0.05/lb), then residential waste disposal would fall by 0.40 lb/p/d to a level of 2.20 lb/p/d.

Figure 10.1 shows the demand curve implied by Jenkins's slope estimate. It goes through the status quo point of 2.60 lb/p/d at zero dollars per pound (point *c*) and the predicted point of 2.20 lb/p/d at $0.05 per pound (point *d*). This demand curve can be used to estimate social surplus losses. The area of the larger triangle *abc*, $0.0144/p/d, is the social surplus loss at zero price, and the area of the smaller triangle *aed*, $0.0004/p/d, is the social surplus loss at the price of $0.05/lb. The area of trapezoid *debc*, which equals the difference in the areas of these triangles, is the reduction in social surplus loss, $0.0140/p/d due to the price increase from zero to $0.05/lb. If the population of Wasteville is 100,000 people, then the annual gross benefit of the container fee is ($0.0140/p/d)(365 days)(100,000 persons) = $511,000.

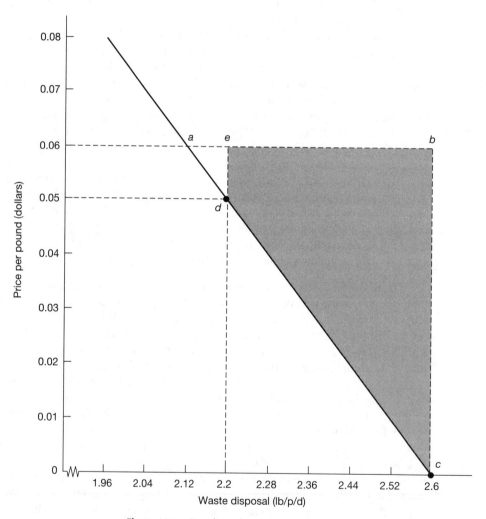

Figure 10.1   Social Surplus Gain from Refuse Fee

In extracting elasticity or slope estimates from research reports, it is important to consider issues of *internal validity* and *external validity*. Internal validity involves the sort of evaluation design issues discussed in Chapter 9, as well as issues related to the proper use of econometric techniques that we take up when discussing how to estimate demand curves from multiple observations. External validity concerns the appropriateness of using estimates made from data collected at other times, in other places, and with different populations. Holding the level of internal validity constant, we expect external validity to be higher, the greater the similarity between the circumstances in which we wish to apply the research results and those under which it was conducted. In the previous example, for instance, the closer Wasteville is in economic, policy, demographic, and geographic characteristics to the communities in Jenkins's sample, the more confident we can be that her estimate of elasticity is an appropriate basis for making predictions about changes in waste disposal that would result from introducing a volumetric user fee in Wasteville. We would be less confident in her estimate if it had been based on data from the 1960s or 1970s rather than the 1980s because there would have been more time for unmeasured variables, such as the level of environmental awareness or recycling infrastructure, to have changed.

■ EXHIBIT 10.1

Erik Lichtenberg and David Zilberman wished to estimate the costs and benefits of government regulations that reduced pesticide use in agriculture. Their study covered three important crops: corn, cotton, and rice. There have been numerous empirical studies of price elasticities in agricultural markets. After reviewing this literature, they came up with "consensus values" for the elasticity of supply of 0.3 (corn), 0.5 (cotton), and 0.8 (rice), and for the elasticity of demand of –0.5 (corn), –0.41 (cotton), and –0.43 (rice). The supply and demand functions for all three crops were assumed to have constant-elasticity forms.

Source: Erik Lichtenberg and David Zilberman, "The Welfare Economics of Price Supports in U.S. Agriculture," *American Economic Review*, 76, no. 5 (1986), 1135–1141.

Functional forms. An important practical question also arises: What is the *correct interpretation* of the reported elasticity or slope? In order to answer this question, it is necessary to know the functional form of the model used to estimate the slope or elasticity. Two functional forms are most common: a linear demand curve and a constant elasticity of demand curve.

Linear functional forms assume that the demand curve can be written as:

$$q = \alpha_0 + \alpha_1 p + \alpha_2 x \qquad (10.1)$$

where, q is the quantity demanded at price p, x represents some nonprice variable that may affect demand, α_0 is the quantity that would be demanded when all of the variables equal zero, α_1 indicates the change in the quantity demanded for a unit change in price, and α_2 indicates the change in the quantity demanded for a unit change in the nonprice variable. In practice, several nonprice variables are often included, each with an associated coefficient. If we hold the nonprice variables constant, then α_1

is the slope of the demand curve represented by equation (10.1), and $1/\alpha_1$ can be interpreted as the slope of the *inverse demand curve*—that is, the demand curve that is typically drawn in a graph with price on the vertical axis and quantity on the horizontal axis. We expect $\alpha_1 < 0$, so that the demand curve and the inverse demand curve are both downward sloping.

The price elasticity of demand implied by the linear demand function in equation (10.1) is:

$$\xi = \alpha_1 p/q \qquad\qquad (10.2)$$

which varies with both price and quantity.[2] Thus, a linear demand curve implies a nonconstant price elasticity of demand. In extracting elasticity estimates from research that uses a linear demand schedule as a functional form, therefore, we must also extract the price and quantity at which the stated elasticity was calculated.

If Jenkins had not reported her estimate of α_1 directly, we could use equation (10.2) to recover it from her report of her elasticity estimate and the price and quantity at which she calculated it. Her stated price elasticity estimate, -0.12, was calculated at the average price charged by those communities in her sample that had nonzero fees, \$0.81/container, and the average residential waste disposed of by the communities in her sample, 2.62 lb/p/d.[3] Using equation (10.2), we can recover the estimated α_1 needed for measuring changes in social surplus if we know ξ, and the price and quantity for which it was calculated:

$$\alpha_1 = \xi q/p = (-0.12)(2.62)/(0.81) \cong -0.40$$

The general point is that *when elasticity estimates are based on linear functional forms, construction of linear demand curves for measuring changes in social surplus requires recovery of either the elasticity with the price and quantity at which it was calculated or the direct estimate of the slope itself.*

A simple constant-elasticity functional form is:

$$q = \beta_0\, p^{\beta_1} x^{\beta_2} \qquad\qquad (10.3)$$

where, q is quantity demanded, p is price, and x is some other variable that may affect demand, such as income or gender. More variables can be included as additional terms with exponents.[4] The slope of a constant-elasticity demand function equals $\beta_1 q/p$, which varies with p and q.[5] The price elasticity of demand, however, equals β_1 no matter what values are taken by p and q.[6]

The constant-elasticity functional form implies a demand curve that is asymptotic to both the price and quantity axes. That is, as price becomes infinite, the quantity demanded approaches zero, and as price approaches zero, the quantity demanded approaches infinity. As we are most often interested in the region of the demand curve near some price that is finite and greater than zero, and the estimates of elasticities are based on data in this range, these asymptotic extremes are usually not relevant to our analysis.

Notice that the constant-elasticity demand function given by equation (10.3) can be converted into a linear function by taking the logarithms, denoted $\ln()$, of both sides:

$$\ln(q) = \ln(\beta_0) + \beta_1(p) + \beta_2\ln(x) \tag{10.4}$$

This functional form is linear in the logarithms of all variables. It is straightforward to estimate the parameters of this model by ordinary least squares, as we will discuss later.

As an illustration of how to use a price elasticity estimate assuming a constant-elasticity demand curve, imagine that a community (not Wasteville) currently charges a refuse collection fee of $0.05/lb at which waste disposal is 2.25 lb/p/d, and that we find a study that reports a constant-elasticity estimate of the price elasticity of demand of –0.15. Using this estimate of β_1 and our status quo point, which is labeled point a in Figure 10.2, we can solve for β_0:

$$\beta_0 = (2.25)/(0.05)^{-0.15} \simeq 1.44$$

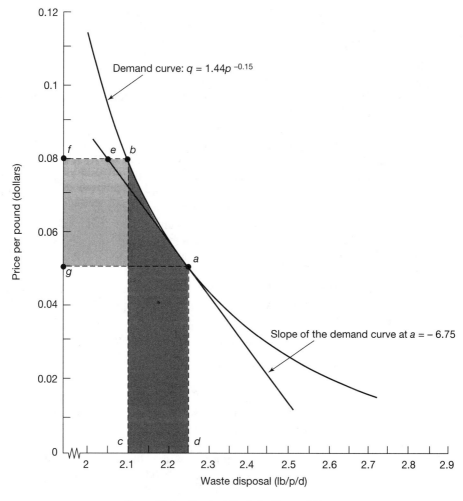

Figure 10.2 Constant Elasticity Demand Curve

which gives us $q = 1.44 \, p^{-0.15}$ as the underlying demand curve for our application. We can use this curve to predict the reduction in waste disposal that would result if collection fees were raised to \$0.08/lb. Following the curve until price equals \$0.08/lb, we find that waste disposal would fall to 2.10 lb/p/d. This point is labeled as point b in Figure 10.2.

Note that our estimate of $\beta_0 = 1.44$ will generally differ from the original estimate of β_0 obtained by the researchers from which we took our price elasticity estimate. This difference arises because we force the demand curve to pass through point a, our known data point, while the original, estimated equation probably will not pass through point a.

An alternative, slightly easier way to predict the reduction in the quantity of waste disposal uses the estimated elasticity to approximate the slope of the demand curve. At point a the slope of the demand curve is $(-0.15)(2.25)/(0.05) = -6.75$. Therefore, a change in price from \$0.05/lb to \$0.08/lb would change the quantity of waste by approximately:

$$\Delta q = -6.75(0.05 - 0.08) = -0.20 \text{ lb/p/d}$$

which would lead us to predict that waste disposal would fall to 2.05 lb/p/d due to the price increase (point e in Figure 10.2).

The discrepancy in the predicted levels of waste disposal at the higher price results because of the difference between *point elasticities* and *arc elasticities*. The point elasticity is the exact elasticity at a particular point, while the arc elasticity is an approximate elasticity for a finite change. For small changes in price, the two methods give approximately the same reduction. But for large price changes, like the 60 percent price change in this example, the two methods can differ substantially. If we are fairly confident in the estimated demand curve, then we should recover its formula and use the first method to predict changes in quantities. The second method is a linear approximation to the first method. The more curvature in the demand curve, the worse the approximation becomes.

In order to estimate the change in consumer surplus or the change in social surplus resulting from an increase in the price from \$0.05 to \$0.08, we must calculate the area under the demand curve over this range. The exact area under a constant-elasticity demand curve from quantity q_0 to quantity q_1 is given by:

$$\text{Area} = (1/\beta_0)^{1/\beta_1} \, [q_1{}^{\rho} - q_0{}^{\rho}] \, / \, \rho \qquad (10.5)$$

where $\rho = [1+(1/\beta_1)]$.[7] For example, applying this formula to measure the area under the demand schedule in Figure 10.2 from 2.10 lb/p/d to 2.25 lb/p/d yields an area \$0.0097/p/d. This area is the darker-shaded area $abcd$. Alternatively, we could approximate the area as a trapezoid by assuming a straight line between the status quo point (point a) and the predicted point (point b), with c and d being the other corners of the trapezoid. This method would lead to an estimated area of \$0.00975/p/d, a slight overestimation. In practice, imprecision in our empirical estimates of elasticities usually swamps the error resulting from linear approximation of areas. Thus, such approximations are usually reasonable. Nevertheless, we use the formula in equation (10.5) in the remainder of this example.

The change in consumer surplus resulting from the price increase is obtained by subtracting the reduction in fee payments due to the reduction in quantity [($0.05/lb)(2.25 lb/p/d – 2.10 lb/p/d) = $0.0075/p/d] from the area under the curve ($.0097/p/d) and adding the increase in fee payments on the remaining quantity [($0.08 – $0.05)(2.10 lb/p/d) = $0.063/p/d]. Hence, the overall loss in consumer surplus equals $0.0652/p/d.[8] Of course, the additional consumer payments for the remaining quantity ($0.063/p/d) would be fully offset by additional revenues to the municipality's government.

Estimation of social surplus change requires knowledge of the marginal social cost. If it were $0.08/lb, then the net social surplus gain would simply be the savings in social cost from reduced waste disposal [($0.08)(2.25 lb/p/d – 2.10 lb/p/d) = $0.012/p/d] minus the loss of value consumers suffer from this reduction ($0.0097/p/d), which equals $0.0023/p/d, or an annual amount for a population of 100,000 of $0.0023 × 365 × 100,000 = $83,950.

A difficult complication arises when we wish to use an elasticity estimated with a constant-elasticity functional form to predict the effect of raising a price from zero to some positive level. As the constant-elasticity demand curve is inconsistent with an observation of zero price, there is no fully satisfactory way to make use of the elasticity estimate. We are forced to postulate some other functional form that goes through the status quo point and use the constant-elasticity estimate as a rough guide for specifying its parameters. This expediency should be thought of at best as no more than an informed guess that can serve as the starting point for sensitivity analysis.

Extrapolating from a Few Points

Recent policy or other fortuitous (at least from the analyst's perspective) changes often provide a basis for predicting the impacts of future policy changes. For example, imagine that we wish to predict the effect of a fare increase on bus ridership. If the last increase of $0.25 resulted in 1,000 fewer riders per day, then it may be reasonable to assume that a further increase of $0.25 would have a similar effect. Here we are treating the observations as if they resulted from a simple before and after quasi-experimental design.

Two considerations are important in determining the appropriateness of extrapolating from the effects of a previous change.

The first consideration concerns the validity of attributing the previous change in outcome to the change in the policy variable. "History" poses threats to the internal validity of our quasi-experiment. In attributing the change in outcome to the policy change, we are implicitly assuming that no other variables of relevance to the outcome changed over the period of time under consideration. For example, the fall in bus ridership might have resulted in part from the opening of a major new highway that reduced the effective price of driving a private vehicle, a substitute for riding the bus. If this were the case, then it is unlikely that a similar change in fare would produce as large a reduction in ridership as did the previous fare change.

The second consideration concerns the assumed functional relationship between the outcome and the policy variable. Linear functional forms can produce very different predictions than constant-elasticity functional forms, for instance. This is illustrated in Figure 10.3. Imagine that two years ago, when residents of Wasteville were charged $0.01/lb for refuse, they disposed of 2.52 lb/p/d (point *a*), and that last year, after the fee was raised to $0.025/lb, they disposed of only 2.40 lb/p/d (point *b*). How much will waste disposal decline in Wasteville if the fee is raised further to $0.05/lb? If we fitted a linear demand curve to the two points, then we would predict that waste will fall by 0.20 lb/p/d to 2.20 lb/p/d (point *c*). If, instead, we fitted a constant-elasticity demand curve to the two points, then we would predict that waste will fall by a

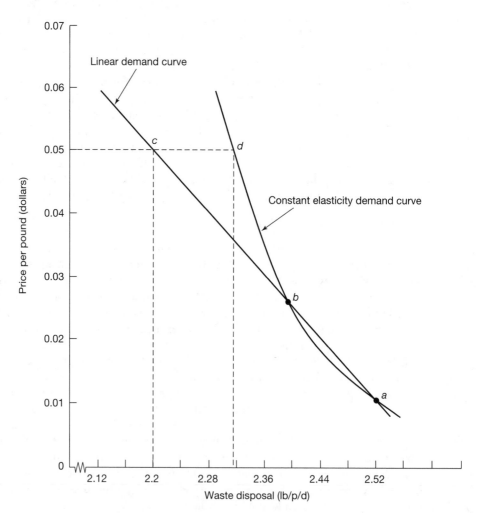

Figure 10.3   Imputing a Demand Curve from Two Points

smaller amount, 0.09 lb/p/d, to 2.31 lb/p/d (point *d*).[9] Note that each of these functional forms fits the two observed data points equally well—perfectly!

The story in Figure 10.3 illustrates a very important point: *The further we extrapolate from past experience, the more sensitive are our predictions to assumptions about functional form.* In the absence of theoretical guidance or other empirical evidence, we have no basis for choosing between the two widely different predictions shown in Figure 10.3.

In order to control for changes in other variables and gain greater confidence about the appropriate functional form, we need more observations and econometric techniques to extract information from them.

Econometric Estimation with Many Observations

If many observations of quantities demanded at different prices are available, then it may be possible to use econometric techniques to estimate demand schedules. The linear regression model typically serves as the starting point for such efforts. We assume here that the reader is familiar with the basic concepts of linear regression. Readers unfamiliar with these concepts, or desiring to review them, should read Appendix 10A before continuing with this section or reading the later section on hedonic pricing. We limit the coverage here to identifying the most important general issues that analysts should keep in mind when they estimate demand curves. Readers not already familiar with the technical points should consult any basic econometrics text for fuller treatment.[10]

Model specification. The starting point for econometric estimation of demand curves is a mathematical model relating explanatory or so-called independent variables, such as price and income, to the dependent variable, quantity demanded.[11] By including a particular explanatory variable, we control for its effect on the dependent variable. Even though we may not have a substantive interest in some of the explanatory variables, if they are theoretically related to demand, then they should be included in the estimated model in order to "control" for their effects on the dependent variable. Ideally, the model should include all variables that theoretically affect demand. This would allow us to isolate the independent effects of variables we do care about, such as the effects of prices and income on quantity demanded. In reality, however, the list of included variables is usually quite limited for three general reasons.

First, measures of variables that are theoretically important may not be available at reasonable cost. For example, the demand for waste disposal may depend on attitudes toward recycling that we cannot measure without specialized surveys, which may be too costly given available resources.

Second, some variables may have relatively small expected effects. For example, the demand for a good depends not just on its own price (*own-price elasticity*) but also on the prices of complements and substitutes (*cross-price elasticities*). Usually it is reasonable to expect that the own-price elasticity is large relative to cross-price elasticities, so that one might think that the latter can reasonably be ignored. Occasionally, however, cross-price elasticities may be large and potentially policy relevant. For example, the demand for bus rides may depend importantly on the price of parking in the central city. Previous empirical research may provide some guidance for deciding which prices of substitutes and complements should be included in the model.

Third, variables may be excluded because they are too highly correlated with other explanatory variables—the problem of multicollinearity—or because they have little variation in the sample. In either case, it may not be possible to estimate their coefficients with precision.

The seriousness of excluding a theoretically important variable depends on the degree to which it is correlated with a variable whose coefficient we require for predicting policy effects. If an excluded variable is not correlated with an included variable, then excluding it will not bias the estimated coefficient of the included variable. Of course, if a theoretically important variable is excluded, then the overall fit of the model, measured by its R^2, will be poorer and the precision of the estimated coefficients will be lower. If the excluded and included variables are correlated, however, then the estimate of the coefficient of the included variable will be biased because it incorporates part of the effect of the excluded variable with which it is correlated. The bias depends on both the degree of correlation between the included and excluded variables, and the true coefficient of the excluded variable; if either is very small, then the bias is likely to be small.[12] But if neither is small, the bias may be large.

After identifying the theoretically important and practically available variables, the next task is to specify a functional form. As previously discussed, linear and constant-elasticity forms are the most commonly used. Sometimes we have theoretical reasons for choosing between them; other times we simply see which fits the observed data better.

Translating equation (10.1) into a regression model is straightforward. All we have to do is add an error term. Note that although this is a linear model, it can be specified in terms of nonlinear functions of the explanatory variables. For example, by adding the square of price as an explanatory variable along with price itself, we allow for a nonlinear demand curve. Also we can allow for the possibility of different demand curves for different subgroups in our sample by introducing interaction terms. For example, if we suspect that men have a steeper demand curve for beer than women, we could create a new variable that is the product of the dummy variable (or indicator variable) for gender (say, "0" for men and "1" for women) and price. We would then interpret the coefficient of price as the slope of the demand curve for men, and the sum of the coefficient of price and the coefficient of the price-gender interaction variable as the slope of the demand curve for women. The general point is that we can have quite complicated functional forms within the basic linear specification that can be estimated with ordinary least squares (OLS), which is described in Appendix 10A.

We can also apply OLS to the constant-elasticity functional form. Imagine, for example, that we wish to estimate the price elasticity of demand for electricity from a random sample of households that face different prices because they are located in different jurisdictions. Let Q equal the quantity of electricity consumed during some time period by a household, P equal the price paid by the household during that time period, I equal the household's income, and S equal the number of individuals in the household. We could specify the following constant-elasticity functional form:

$$Q = \alpha P^{\beta} I^{\theta} S^{\phi} e^{\epsilon} \tag{10.6}$$

where α, β, θ, and ϕ are parameters to be estimated, e is the base of the natural logarithm, and ϵ is the unobserved random error. Though OLS cannot be directly applied to this equation, it can be applied to the equation that results from taking the natural logarithm, denoted by $\ln()$, of both sides of equation (10.6):

$$\ln(Q) = \ln(\alpha) + \beta\ln(P) + \theta\ln(I) + \phi\ln(S) + \epsilon \tag{10.7}$$

Because equation (10.7) results from taking the logarithm of both sides of equation (10.6), it is sometimes referred to as a log-log or log-linear specification. As we know the values of Q, P, I, and S, we can calculate the values of $\ln(Q), \ln(P), \ln(I)$, and $\ln(S)$, which we treat as variables in a regular OLS regression. All of the parameter estimates can be interpreted in the standard way, noting that the constant is an estimate of $\ln(\alpha)$ rather than α. Thus, the coefficient of the variable $\ln(P)$ is an estimate of the price elasticity of demand and the coefficient of the variable $\ln(I)$ is an estimate of the income elasticity of demand.

Types of data. The availability of data is usually the limiting factor in estimating demand curves. Researchers sometimes have sufficient resources to assemble their own data through random sampling of observations across appropriate units, such as individuals or governmental jurisdictions, or over time, often by month, quarter, or even year. More often, however, resource limitations force researchers to rely on *convenience samples*, that is, data that happen to be available at acceptable cost. Though analysts sometimes have opportunities to assemble their own sets of data, often through sampling administrative records or program clients, they are typically limited to published sources, routine records, or data collected by researchers for other purposes. Nevertheless, it is worthwhile to review briefly the major considerations in the choice of data and their implications for demand estimation.

The first major consideration is the level of aggregation. Individual-level data measure the behavior of persons, families, households, or other consuming units. Aggregate-level data measure the combined behaviors of consumers in groups, usually organized by geographic jurisdictions or demographic characteristics.

Individual-level data potentially provide a close congruence between data and theory. Consumer theory is based on models of utility maximization by individuals. Measuring theoretically important variables, such as income, can often be done directly with individual-level data. In contrast, in using aggregate-level data, a mean or median typically serves as the measure of income, perhaps leading to less precise estimates of income elasticity because actual household incomes vary around the aggregate-level measure. Individual-level data, however, are often not available. Aside from the difficulty of gathering them, there are also some situations in which theoretically important variables cannot be observed at the individual level. In estimating the "demand" for criminal acts, for example, an important theoretical variable is their "price," which depends on the perceived probability of arrest. We cannot directly observe the probability of arrest that an individual perceives, but we can assume that it is related to the objective probability, which can be estimated as the fraction of crimes that result in arrest within the region or among a group of individuals.

In moving from lower to higher levels of aggregation, we risk masking policy-relevant variations in demand. For example, imagine that the elasticity of demand for cigarettes is higher for teenagers than for adults, but that we estimate an overall elasticity using data that aggregate across these two groups. Then, the resulting elasticity estimate might be approximately a weighted average of the elasticities for adults and teenagers, with the weights depending on their relative proportions in the aggregation. If so, then using it as the teenage price elasticity would lead to a prediction of too small an effect of an increase in the cigarette tax on teenage smoking.

The second major consideration in selecting data concerns the choice between *cross sections* and *time series*. Cross sections involve observations of variables for a number of comparable units at a particular time, while time series involve making repeated observations of variables for a particular unit over time. For example, if we wished to determine the price elasticity of demand for wine, we might take advantage of different excise tax rates across states. Using observations for each of the fifty states for a particular year, we would regress per capita consumption on differences in after-tax retail prices and other variables that we expect to affect demand, such as average levels of income and education. Alternatively, if the real price of wine has varied over time, we might estimate an elasticity by regressing yearly national per capita consumption on the real price and other variables such as per capita income. Cross-sectional and time series data are prone to different types of econometric problems and yield coefficients that have somewhat different interpretations.

Cross sections generally provide estimates of long-run elasticities, while time series provide estimates of elasticities corresponding to the time unit of the observations and, therefore, usually correspond to short-run elasticities. In estimating elasticities from cross sections, we usually assume that the variations in demands across units reflect long-run adjustments to previous price changes. Thus, we obtain estimates of long-run elasticities. Only if we make our observations shortly after a major price change would we interpret the elasticity obtained from a cross section as a short-run elasticity. In estimating elasticities from time series, we observe responses to price changes occurring as frequently as the unit of time. Consequently, annual data give estimates of annual elasticities, and monthly data give estimates of monthly elasticities. For most goods, monthly elasticities would be interpreted as short run. Annual elasticities, however, may be either short run or long run, depending on the extent to which full adjustment to price changes requires changes in capital goods, location, and other factors that consumers alter gradually.

In general, we expect short-run elasticities to be smaller in absolute value than long-run elasticities. For example, based on a review of 120 empirical studies, P.B. Goodwin found an overall average price elasticity of demand for motor fuel of –0.48, with an average short-run elasticity of –0.27, and an average long-run elasticity of –0.71 from time series studies and –0.84 from cross-sectional studies.[13] He also reports average elasticities of the demand for automobile "traffic" with respect to motor fuel prices based on time series studies: short run, –0.16; long run, –0.33.[14]

Cross sections and time series tend to involve different econometric problems. Cross sections, especially when they consist of units of different sizes, often have error terms with different variances—the *heteroscedasticity* problem. For example, the variance in the number of accidental deaths from fire is likely to be larger in New York City than in a much smaller city such as Utica, New York. If we estimate the model by OLS when the variances of the error terms are unequal, then the OLS estimates of the coefficients will be unbiased, but their calculated standard errors are smaller than the true standard errors. That is, the reported precision of OLS estimates is overly optimistic. If the relative sizes of the variances of the error terms are known, then estimating through *generalized least squares* (GLS) gives more precise estimates of coefficients than OLS. Discussions of tests for detecting heteroscedasticity and of alternatives to OLS estimation in its presence can be found in almost any econometrics text.

Time series data also suffer from a common problem with the error term. Remember that the effects of excluded explanatory variables are incorporated into the error term. If an excluded variable tends to change gradually over time, then it may produce correlation between successive error terms. This is one example of the more general problem of *autocorrelation*, which often exists in one form or another in time series data. It has similar effects to heteroscedasticity: OLS coefficient estimates, though unbiased, are not as precise as reported, and more precise estimates can be made through GLS if the pattern of autocorrelation is known. By far the most widely used test for autocorrelation is the Durbin-Watson statistic, which should always be a component of time series analysis. Discussions of detecting autocorrelation and correcting for it can be found in econometrics texts.

It is also possible to pool cross-sectional and time series data, say by using data from each state for each of a number of years. Though modeling with pooled time series and cross-sectional data can be quite complex and cannot be discussed here, three points are worth noting. First, pooled data provide a rich source of information. Second, pooled data are vulnerable to the econometric problems encountered with both cross-sectional and time series data. Third, cross-sectional problems are most likely to dominate for pools that are wider than longer (more units than time periods), while time series problems are most likely to dominate for pools that are longer than wider (more time periods than units).

Identification.   In a perfectly competitive market, we expect price and quantity to arise from the simultaneous interaction of supply and demand. Changes in price and quantity can result from shifts in the supply curve, the demand curve, or both. In the absence of variables that affect only one side of the market, it may not be possible to estimate separate supply and demand curves. Indeed, if quantity supplied and quantity demanded depended only on price, then the two equations of our model would look identical! How can we identify which is the demand curve and which is the supply curve? This is one example of the problem of *identification*. It occurs in multiple-equation models where some variables, such as price and quantity, are determined simultaneously. Such variables are called *endogenous* variables. In contrast, variables that are determined outside of the model are called *exogenous* variables.

Consider a competitive and unregulated market for wheat. If rainfall affects the supply of wheat but not the demand for wheat, then including rainfall in the supply equation but not in the demand equation identifies the demand equation. The reason is that changes in rainfall result in systematic shifts in supply but not demand, which will trace out the demand curve. Similarly, if income affects demand but not supply, then including it in the demand equation but not in the supply equation allows us to look at systematic shifts in the demand curve, which will trace out the supply curve. In general, a two-equation model will be identified if there is one exogenous variable that belongs in the first equation but not in the second equation, and another exogenous variable that belongs in the second equation but not in the first equation. By "belong," we mean that it has a nonzero coefficient; and by "not belong," we mean that it has a zero-coefficient. The zero-coefficient conditions are most important. One cannot identify a model by excluding an exogenous variable from an equation that in theory belongs in that equation.

Identification of demand curves tends to be less of a problem in the markets typically of interest to cost-benefit analysts than in markets generally. One reason is that CBA often deals with markets that are subject to exogenous government interventions. For example, the demand for cigarettes is probably easily identified in cross-sectional analysis because differences in state excise taxes shift the supply curve by different amounts.

Of course, the identification problem does not arise if in fact the model consists of only one equation, with one endogenous variable and the remaining variables all being exogenous. In some markets, the government either provides the product or service, as is often the case with municipal waste disposal, or regulates the prices charged, as is the case with electricity. When government supplies a good or effectively sets price, there is no supply curve, price is exogenous, and we avoid the identification problem. Indeed, some transportation researchers have begun to worry that the deregulation of the last decade in many industries will make identification of models more difficult in the future![15]

When should analysts worry about the identification problem? A key consideration is whether price can be reasonably treated as exogenous. If it can, perhaps because it is set by a government agency, then identification is unlikely to be a problem. If it is endogenous, then there is a potential identification problem and this topic, as well as methods of simultaneous equation estimation, should be consulted in an econometrics text.

Confidence intervals.   The standard errors of the estimated coefficients of an OLS model can be used to construct confidence intervals for the coefficients. A 95 percent confidence interval is commonly interpreted as there being a 95 percent chance that the true value of the coefficient lies within the interval. Strictly speaking, this is an incorrect interpretation. The correct interpretation is that if we were to repeat our estimation procedure with new draws of data many times, confidence intervals calculated by this procedure would cover the true value of the coefficient about 95 percent of the repetitions. Nevertheless, the confidence interval provides some guidance for sensitivity analysis based on the results from our one draw of data. Most analysts would consider it reasonable to treat the ends of a 95 percent confidence interval as best and worst cases.

    Prediction versus hypothesis testing. As a final point on estimating demand curves, it is important to keep in mind the distinction between hypothesis testing and estimation for purposes of prediction. Social scientists are typically interested in testing hypotheses specified in terms of one or more coefficients in a regression model. If the estimated coefficients are not statistically significantly different from zero, then social scientists do not reject the null hypothesis that their variables have no effect on the dependent variable. In other words, there is not a statistically convincing case that the variables have any effect.

    As cost-benefit analysts, however, we do not always have the luxury of ignoring statistically insignificant coefficients. We must make a prediction. *Even if a coefficient is not statistically significant at conventional levels, we should not treat it as zero in estimation or prediction.* Indeed, if we were to use only the statistically significant coefficients from an estimated model, we would bias our prediction. Eliminating these variables and reestimating the model may or may not be appropriate depending on the theoretical strength of their inclusion in the original model.

    When a coefficient is required for predicting a policy impact, we may have no alternative to using its estimate even if is not statistically significant. We may not be very confident in the value of the coefficient, but if it is the only estimate available, we have no choice but to use it. In such cases, our sensitivity analysis should reflect the imprecision of our estimate.

MARKET ANALOGY METHOD

As we have already noted, many government projects produce goods that are not sold in well-functioning markets. Drawing market analogies and using the econometric methods discussed in this section often make it possible to estimate demand curves for such goods as public campsites, public university education, government-provided home care, public adoption services and other publically provided goods that are similar to goods produced by the private sector and sold in well-functioning markets. The prices in these markets often provide information about the value of publicly provided goods, even if the government gives them away or charges recipients prices set on the basis of administrative or political criteria. Even where there are not well-functioning legal markets, there may be *black markets*. For example, there are no legal private-sector adoption services in some countries. Nevertheless, in such situations analysts may be able to turn to the black market to obtain rough estimates of the value of such services.

    We can use prices in analogous markets as a measure of the value of the publicly provided good or we can use price and quantity information to estimate a demand curve for the publicly provided good. The former approach is used when data to estimate the demand curve are limited or where analysts want a "quick and dirty" estimate. We deal with each of these in turn. Following these sections, we discuss using market analogy methods to value time and lives saved.

Using Only Price or Market Expenditures of an Analogous Good

Consider, for example, a local government project that provides housing for 50 families. The local government may charge a nominal rent of $150 per month so that government revenue equals $7,500 per month (50 units at $150/month each). No occupying family would have a willingness-to-pay of less than $150 per month, but many of them would be willing to pay more than $150 per month and, therefore, the benefits of this project would be larger than $7,500 per month.

Suppose that comparable units in the private sector rent for $500 per month. If we take this market price as the shadow price for the publicly-provided units, then the total monthly benefits of publicly-provided housing would be $25,000 per month (50 units at $500/month each). In other words, the revenue that would be generated by the units in the private sector would be the social benefits of the publicly provided housing.

Is the market price for similar housing a reasonable shadow price for the government-provided housing units? In an efficient private market, those who buy units of the good directly demonstrate a willingness-to-pay equal to or greater than the market price. The willingness-to-pay for the marginal unit supplied is just equal to the market price. In the case of government allocation at other than the market price, however, there is no guarantee that those who receive units of the good value them as highly as do purchasers in the private market. Indeed, *the market price of a comparable good is an appropriate shadow price for a publicly provided good only if it equals the average amount that users of the publicly provided good would be willing to pay.* For the housing project this would be unlikely. If the private housing market were efficient, then families willing to pay the market price, or more, for the public housing would have already found housing in the private sector. Assuming the occupants of public units have lower than average incomes, they are likely to be willing to pay more than the amount charged by the government but less than the market price. Thus, the total monthly benefits would be somewhere between $7,500 per month and $25,000 per month.

The revenue for comparable private housing units would not necessarily be an upper bound on benefits if the publicly provided housing were poorly targeted. If units were allocated to people with higher than average income who would have purchased similar private units in the absence of the allocation, then the market price would be a lower bound on their willingness-to-pay. Ironically, from the CBA perspective, in the absence of any market failures, the more poorly targeted public housing units are, the higher their benefits! This is a case where distributional weights, as discussed in Chapter 14, are potentially appropriate.

This example highlights a general point that should be kept in mind when dealing with an "average" shadow price when values actually differ across different groups of users. Suppose, for example, an analyst wants to value a highway improvement that saves travel time. One way to do this is to multiply the total time saved by the shadow price of a unit of travel time. Yet, some people, such as business executives, value time savings more than other people, such as vacationers. To take account of these different valuations, an analyst can multiply the time saved by each group of travelers by the value of a unit of travel time to that group, and then sum these products across groups. Such a calculation generally gives a more accurate estimate of the aggregate value of time than simply applying a single shadow price to the total number of hours saved.

Using Price and Quantity of an Analogous Private-Sector Good to Estimate the Demand Curve for a Publicly Provided Good

Suppose a municipal government wants to measure the gross benefits of a swimming pool that it owns and operates. Currently, the municipality does not charge an admission fee and the pool receives 300,000 visitors per year, shown as point *a* in Figure 10.4. In a comparable municipality, a privately operated swimming pool, which charges $1 for admission, receives 100,000 visitors per year (point *b*). Assuming a linear demand curve that passes through these two points, we can estimate the gross benefits of the municipal pool as $(1.5)(300,000)/2 = $225,000.

Notice that using revenues at the private pool ($100,000) would underestimate benefits. This figure excludes the consumer surplus of those willing to pay more than the $1 admission fee, the area of triangle *bcd*, as well as the consumer surplus of those willing to pay something less than $1, the area of triangle *abe*.

How reasonable is it to interpret the observed price and quantity at the private pool as a point on the demand curve for the municipal pool? The answer depends on the similarity of the two facilities and their markets. Only if they are similar in terms of such things as changing room facilities, hours of business, the friendliness of the staff, levels of crowding, and populations of potential users is the observed point on the demand curve for the private facility a reasonable prediction of a point on the demand curve for the municipal pool. If these assumptions do not hold, then explicit estimation of the demand curve is preferable.

Using the Market Analogy Method to Value Time Saved

Researchers have used the market analogy method to obtain a shadow price for time saved, an important impact of transportation projects, such as highway improvements, and other projects that affect the amount of time people spend waiting in line, such as the hiring of more clerks in an unemployment insurance office. (Estimates of the value of time are discussed at length in Chapter 12.) An obvious analogy is the labor market, where people sell their time for wages. In theory, the social value of an additional hour of work equals the wage rate. Furthermore, all other things being equal, when people can choose the number of hours they work, and there is no unemployment, the wage rate (net of taxes but including benefits) also equals the marginal

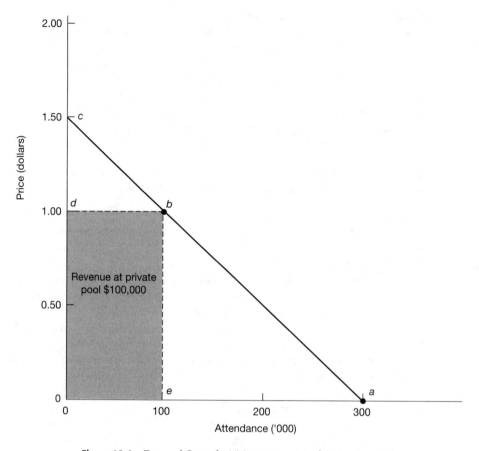

Figure 10.4 Demand Curve for Visits to a Municipal Swimming Pool

value of their time. In other words, the value of an additional hour of leisure to the person enjoying it equals the wage rate. Thus, the value of a project that saves one-half hour for a person who earns $20 per hour, both to society and to that person, is $10. However, there are some serious problems in using the wage rate to value time saved by government projects.

Setting the value of time saved equal to the wage rate is relatively easy. Unfortunately, the wage rate is only a first approximation to the social value of an hour saved. In practice, people who work at dirty dangerous jobs are paid more than people who work in clean safe jobs, yet they may value a marginal hour of leisure time equally. Therefore, the wage rate should be adjusted to take into account the different attributes of different jobs. Also this approach assumes that people would be willing to pay as much as their market wage in order to save an hour traveling or waiting in line. But some people like traveling, while others do not. For those who derive consumption value from traveling through spectacular scenery, such as along the Banff to

Jasper highway, the value of an hour of travel time saved should be set at less than the wage rate. Indeed, some people are willing to pay for the experience of traveling itself. (Consider, for example, the "busman's holiday.") For such reasons, analysts usually value an hour of travel time saved for recreational travelers at a fraction of the average wage rate.

A second type of problem with this method is that it assumes people do not work while they are traveling or waiting in line. This may be incorrect. The notebook computer, for example, facilitates working while people are flying. If people do work while they are traveling or waiting in line, then an hour of time saved is worth less than the wage rate. Of course, this does not apply to truck drivers who are obviously working while they are driving. For them, it does make sense to value their time saved at their wage rate.

Another reason the wage rate may not be an appropriate shadow price for time saved is that it assumes that working hours are flexible, ignoring structural rigidities or market and government failures in the labor market. With an upward sloping supply curve of labor, the more hours someone works, the more highly he or she values leisure. In practice, however, a person may not be able to adjust easily the number of hours worked. Other structural rigidities result in unemployment. Minimum wages and the monopoly power of unions or other factors may distort the labor market. Consequently, everyone who wants to work at the market wage may not be able to find work at that wage. Finally, for some people, such as retirees, no wage rate can be observed.

Using the wage rate as the shadow price also assumes that firms pay their employees the marginal social value of their output. This assumption may be invalid for a number of reasons. For example, if the firm has market power that allows it to raise the price of its products above the competitive level, then it obtains rents. If it shares these rents with employees in the form of higher than market wages, then the wage rate will overestimate the marginal social value of the workers' output. Of course, if an industry generated negative (positive) externalities, then the wage rate would exceed (be less than) the marginal social value of an hour saved.

Because of the serious nature of these problems, therefore, valuing time saved at the wage rate is only a first approximation to its social value. Later in this chapter, we present better methods for valuing time saved.

Using the Market Analogy Method to Value a Life Saved

Valuing life is a highly contentious issue. Society often spends fortunes to rescue trapped miners or to give heart transplants to specific individuals. Yet it may not spend money to make obvious gains in mine safety or to reduce the risk of heart disease. In order to make efficient allocation of resources in the health care area, or to determine the benefits of projects that save lives, analysts require a monetary value of a life saved.

Forgone earnings method.   Early approaches by economists to value life followed a similar approach to the one discussed earlier concerning the value of time. Specifically, if one accepts that a person's value to society for one hour equals that person's wage, then one might reason that the value of that person to society for the rest of his or her lifetime equals the present value of his or her future earnings. One would thus conclude that the value of a life saved equals that person's discounted future earnings. This is the *forgone earnings method* of valuing a life saved.[16] It is currently used by the courts in some U.S. states and in some other countries to award compensation in cases involving death due to negligence. On average, this method generates a higher value for saving the life of people with higher incomes than for people with lower incomes. It also generates higher values for younger people than for older people and for men than for women.

The forgone earnings method provides an unsatisfactory shadow price for lives saved for reasons similar to those discussed previously concerning the value of time saved. It assumes full employment, although the method can easily be adjusted to reflect expected lifetime earnings given average employment expectations. It also assumes people are paid their marginal social product, while often they are not. As homemakers and volunteers are often not paid at all for their services, the method unreasonably values their lives at zero.

A more fundamental problem with the forgone earnings method, however, is that it ignores individuals' willingness-to-pay to avoid or reduce the risk of their own deaths. This point was made clearly by Thomas Schelling, who observed "[t]here is no reason to suppose that a person's future earnings . . . bear any particular relation to what he would pay to reduce some likelihood of his own death."[17]

Schelling also distinguished between the deaths of identifiable individuals and *statistical deaths*. A safety improvement to a highway, for example, does not lead to the saving of the lives of a few individuals who can be identified *ex ante*, but rather to the reduction in the risk of death (or injury) to all users of the highway. In order to value the benefit of proposed safety improvements, analysts should ascertain how much people are willing to pay for reductions in their risk of death that are of the same order of magnitude as the reduced risk that would result from the proposed safety improvements. Such reasoning has led to a series of consumer purchase and labor market studies that have attempted to value life. We outline the general approach in the following sections and present a review of estimates of the value of life in Chapter 12.

Consumer purchase studies.   Suppose airbags are not standard in the car you have decided to buy. (Of course, this was the case until a few years ago.) For $220, however, you can purchase and install an airbag at the time you purchase your car, thereby increasing your survival rate from use of the car from p to $p+\omega$. Would you buy the airbag? This choice problem is represented diagrammatically as a decision tree in Figure 10.5. If a person is indifferent between the two alternatives, then he or she values the upper-branch alternative exactly the same as the lower-branch alternative. Consequently,

$$(p + \omega)V(\text{life}) - \$220 = pV(\text{life})$$

$$(p + \omega)V(\text{life}) - pV(\text{life}) = \$220$$

$$\omega V(\text{life}) = \$220$$

$$V(\text{life}) = \$220/\omega$$

Suppose $\omega = 1/10,000$; that is, if 10,000 people buy airbags, then one statistical life will be saved. Therefore,

$$V(\text{life}) = (\$220)/(1/10,000) = \$2,200,000$$

This method has been applied not only to the purchase of airbags but also to the purchase of other safety-enhancing devices—for example, smoke detectors and fire extinguishers.

Labor market studies. Labor market studies examine the additional wage people require in compensation for exposing themselves to greater risk of death on the job. Suppose, for example, one type of construction job has a 1/1,000 greater chance

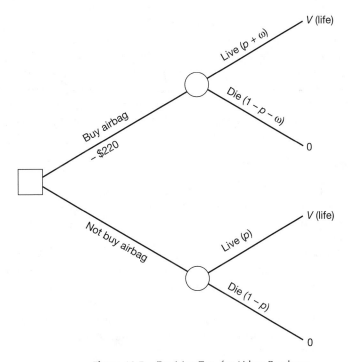

Figure 10.5   Decision Tree for Airbag Purchase

of fatal injury in a year than another type of construction job. Further suppose that the riskier job offers a salary that is $2,000/year higher than the safer job. If workers are indifferent between the two types of job, this implies:

$$1/1,000 * V(\text{life}) = \$2,000$$

$$V(\text{life}) = \$2 \text{ million}$$

In general, the imputed value of life that is obtained from labor market studies varies according to the initial level of risk and the additional level of risk people are asked to assume. This reflects the fact that the value of additional amounts of safety declines as the level of safety increases.

One problem with this method is that it assumes workers have full information concerning risks on their job. For example, in addition to knowing that the chance of dying in a risky type of job is 1/1,000 higher than in the less risky type of job, construction workers have to know what this means. Evidence, which we discuss at further length in Chapter 11, suggests that people suffer from cognitive biases that limit their ability to make rational judgments and decisions in such situations. For example, there is fairly strong evidence that people underestimate the occurrence of low-probability "bad" events.[18] People often think that a bad outcome is so unlikely that it could never happen to them. Yet, people in more risky jobs are indeed more likely to die than people in less risky jobs. Where people suffer from such cognitive biases, labor market studies will tend to underestimate the value of a life saved.

Other problems with this method are that it assumes markets are efficient and that all other variables are held constant. In practice, wage differences may depend partially on the relative bargaining power of unions or on the different characteristics of the different jobs or on different characteristics of workers at different jobs. Indeed, this method suffers from many of the same type of problems that affect the quality of the estimates obtained by using the market analogy method to value time saved.

INTERMEDIATE GOOD METHOD

Some government projects produce intermediate goods, that is, goods that are used as inputs to some other *downstream* activity. For example, a government irrigation project may provide water for farmers that is used as in input to the production of avocados. Where the intermediate good—water—is sold in a well-functioning market, it may be possible to estimate the market demand curve for it using econometric methods. But, if not, we have to impute its value. The intermediate good method estimates the benefit of the project based on its *value added* to the downstream activity. Specifically, the value of the irrigation project can be measured by the increase in the incomes of avocado farmers. In general, the annual benefit of an upstream project can be inferred from the change in the annual incomes of the downstream businesses, thus:

$$\text{Benefit} = \text{NI(with the project)} - \text{NI(without the project)}$$

The total benefit of the irrigation project can be estimated by discounting these benefits over the life of the project.

The intermediate good method can be used to value the benefits of education or training programs. Investment in the skills and abilities of human beings improves the stock of *human capital*, possibly the most valuable national asset. Much of the spectacular economic successes of Japan and Switzerland, for example, both of which are relatively poor in terms of physical natural resources, can be attributed to their investments in human capital. The intermediate good method measures the benefit of such investments by comparing the average incomes of those who have been trained to those who have not. For example, the average annual benefit of a program to increase the number of people earning college degrees equals the difference between the average income of people with a college degree and the average income of people with less than a college degree. The total benefit of the program is found by discounting the annual benefits over the expected working life and multiplying by the number of participants.

One potential problem with this method is that it assumes that differences in income capture all benefits of a project. However, some intermediate goods, such as education, may be partially "final" goods. That is, in addition to having investment value, they may also have consumption value. Some people enjoy being educated and would pay for education even if it had no impact on their expected earnings. People's willingness-to-pay for this enjoyment should also be included as a benefit. Because the intermediate good method does not include the consumption value of the good being valued, it underestimates (overestimates) the value of goods that have positive (negative) consumption benefits.

Care must be taken in application of the intermediate good method to avoid *double counting*. If a shadow price for an intermediate good can be found in some other way, then its contribution to the value of downstream production should not be counted as an additional benefit. The demand curve for the water provided by an irrigation project, for example, fully reflects the value of its various uses. If the benefits of the irrigation water were estimated based on this demand curve, then counting the increased income of avocado farmers as additional benefits would be incorrect.

USING DIFFERENCES IN ASSET VALUES

Projects sometimes affect the prices of assets such as land and capital. The impacts of these projects are said to be *capitalized* into the market value of the assets. Observed increases (decreases) in asset values can often be used to estimate the benefits (costs) of projects. For example, returning to the irrigation project to provide water to avocado farms, if the farms are the only users of the irrigation water and the market for farm land is undistorted, then the full present value of the irrigation project will capitalize into the market value of avocado farms. Observing changes in asset values is a relatively quick and easy method for estimating benefits in *ex post* CBA. Changes in asset values resulting from similar, previously implemented projects can also often provide the basis for predicting the benefits of a proposed project.

A common application of the asset value method involves using differences in housing prices to impute values to particular attributes of the house or its environment, including externalities such as noise.[19] For example, the difference in price between a house with a view and a house with no view provides an estimate of how much households are willing to pay for a view. The difference between the average price of houses in a neighborhood with many parks and the average price of houses in neighborhoods with few parks provides an estimate of how much homeowners are willing to pay for parks.[20] Of course, similar to the other methods discussed earlier, this method assumes that houses are comparable in all other respects, and that no other factor affects differences in house prices.

Recently, *event studies,* which examine changes in the price of stocks, have become an increasingly important method of estimating the costs or benefits to shareholders of an *event,* such as a new program, policy, or regulation.[21] The advantages of using stock prices are that new information concerning policy changes is quickly and efficiently capitalized into the stock price and that the change in the stock price provides an unbiased estimate of the value of a policy change to shareholders. A practical advantage is the availability and accessibility of computer-readable stock price data.

In an event study, researchers estimate the *abnormal return* to a security, which is the difference between the return to a security in the presence of an event and the return to the security in the absence of the event. Usually, researchers estimate daily abnormal returns for each day during an *event window,* that is, for the period during which the event is assumed to be affecting stock prices. Because the return to the security in the absence of the event is unobservable during an event period, it must be inferred. Changes in the prices of other stocks in the market can be used as a basis for inference.[22]

The estimated daily abnormal returns can be aggregated to obtain the *cumulative abnormal return* during the event window. This measures the total return to shareholders that can be attributed to the event. If the event is a proposed policy change, then the cumulative abnormal returns can be used to obtain an *ex ante* estimate of the *expected* impact of the policy on producer surplus, provided the analyst can quantify the market's estimate of the probability that the policy change will be adopted.

THE HEDONIC PRICING METHOD

The market analogy, intermediate good, and asset value methods of benefit estimation described in the preceding sections potentially have several limitations. Most importantly, these benefit valuation methods potentially suffer from the *omitted variable* problem and *self-selection* bias. The *hedonic pricing model* often provides a way to overcome these limitations.

The Omitted Variable Problem

Many benefit valuation methods suffer from the omitted variable problem. Consider, for example, using the intermediate good method to value irrigation. Ideally, analysts should compare the incomes of the same farmers if the irrigation project is built with the incomes of the same farmers if the project is not built. In practice, if the project is built, analysts cannot directly observe what the farmers' incomes would have been without the project. To infer what their incomes would have been without the project, one common assumption is that it equals the incomes of the farmers before the project was built (a before-and-after design) or the incomes of similar farmers who did not get water from the project (a nonexperimental comparison group design). The before-and-after design is reasonable only if all other variables that affect farmers' incomes remain constant. Often, however, important variables, such as weather conditions, crop choices, taxes and subsidies, change simultaneously so that incomes observed before the project are not good estimates of what incomes would have been if the project had not been implemented. The comparison group design is reasonable only if the comparison group is similar to the farmers in all important respects relevant to income except the impacts of the project.

In the education example, incomes may vary with intelligence, socioeconomic background, and gender, as well as with different levels of education. Similarly, some labor market studies to value life assume that the difference in wages of workers reflects only the difference in risk on the job and not other factors, such as differences in the bargaining power of different unions. Similarly, the price of a house typically depends on many factors, such as its distance from the central business district, as well as whether it has a scenic view. All of these other factors should be taken into account; otherwise, as we discussed earlier in the section on model specification, the estimated effects of the variables we are interested in may be biased.

Self-Selection Bias

Several of the methods described previously in this section also have a tendency to be subject to self-selection bias. For example, some people like to take risks and might even be willing to accept a lower than normal salary in order to work at some kinds of more risky jobs. Risk-seeking people self-select into dangerous jobs. One possible result of this is that there may be only very small observed wage premiums for dangerous jobs. Clearly, though, risk seekers are not representative of society as a whole. Consequently, the observed wage differential may underestimate the average amount that members of society would be willing to pay to reduce risks and, hence, may lead to underestimates of the value of a life saved.

Hedonic Regression[23]

The hedonic regression method attempts to overcome the omitted variable and self-selection problems. Suppose that we want to value scenic views; more specifically, suppose we want to estimate each household's willingness-to-pay for changes in the "level" of a scenic view. The hedonic regression method consists of two steps. The first step focuses on estimating the additional cost of houses with marginally better views, controlling for other variables that affect house prices. The second step estimates the willingness-to-pay for a better view, controlling for income and other socioeconomic factors. From this information, we can calculate the change in consumer surplus resulting from projects that improve or worsen the views from some houses. The hedonic price method can be used to value an attribute, or a change in an attribute, whenever its value is capitalized into the price of assets, such as houses.

To begin, the hedonic regression method relates the price of an asset to all of the *attributes* (or characteristics) that theoretically affect its value.[24] The price of a house, for example, depends on such attributes as the level (quality) of its view, its distance from the central business district (CBD), its floor space, its lot size, the number of bathrooms, as well as various characteristics of its neighborhood, such as school quality. A general model could be written as follows:

$$\text{House price} = f(\text{level of view, distance to CBD, lot size,} \qquad (10.8)$$
$$\text{house characteristics, neighborhood characteristics})$$

This equation is called a *hedonic price function* or *implicit price function*.[25] Holding all other variables constant, the change in the price of a house that results from a unit change in any particular attribute (more formally, the slope of house price with respect to the attribute) is called the *hedonic price, implicit price,* or *rent differential* of the attribute. In a well-functioning market, the hedonic price can naturally be interpreted as the additional cost of purchasing a house that is marginally better in terms of a particular attribute. For example, the slope of this hedonic price function with respect to the level of the view measures the additional cost of buying a house with a slightly better (higher-level) view. Sometimes hedonic prices are referred to as *marginal hedonic prices* or *marginal implicit prices*. While these terms are technically more correct, we will not use them in order to make the explanation as easy to follow as possible.

Usually analysts assume the hedonic price function has a multiplicative functional form, similar to equation (10.6), implying that house prices increase as the level of the view increases, but at a decreasing rate. For example, an analyst might specify the following hedonic pricing model:

$$P = \beta_0 \text{CBD}^{\beta_1} \text{SIZE}^{\beta_2} \text{VIEW}^{\beta_3} \text{NBHD}^{\beta_4} e^{\epsilon} \qquad (10.9)$$

where P is the house price, CBD measures the distance of the house from the central business district, SIZE denotes the floor space of the house, VIEW measures the level of its view, and NBHD is a variable indicating in which of two possible neighborhoods the house is located. Each parameter, β, is an elasticity measuring the proportional change in house prices that will result from a proportional change in the associated attribute.

The hedonic price of a particular attribute is the slope of equation (10.8) with respect to that attribute. In general, the hedonic price of an attribute may be a function of all of the variables in the hedonic price equation.[26] Let r_v denote the hedonic price of a view from a house; then, using the hedonic price model given by equation (10.9):[27]

$$r_v = \beta_3 \frac{P}{\text{VIEW}}$$

$$(10.10)$$

In this model, the hedonic price of a view depends on the value of the parameter β_3, and the price of the house and the view from the house, both of which vary from one observation to another. Plotting the hedonic price against the level of the view provides a downward sloping curve, which implies that the implicit price of a scenic view declines as the level of the view increases.

These points are illustrated in Figure 10.6. The top panel shows a hedonic price function, with house prices increasing as the level of scenic view increases, but at a decreasing rate. Thus, the slope of this constant-elasticity curve, r_v, decreases as the level of the view increases. The bottom panel shows how the slope of the hedonic price function, r_v, declines as the level of the view increases.

In order to estimate the hedonic price from a model such as equation (10.9), analysts usually take the natural logarithms, ln, of both sides to obtain:

$$\ln(P) = \ln\beta_0 + \beta_1\ln(CBD) + \beta_2\ln(SIZE) + \beta_3\ln(VIEW) + \beta_4\ln(NBHD) + \epsilon \quad (10.11)$$

As we discussed earlier, the parameters of this equation, the βs, may be estimated by ordinary least squares. Substituting the estimated β_3 (the estimated coefficient of the view variable), the price of the house, and the level of the view into equation (10.10) provides an estimate of the hedonic price of the view for that house.

In a well-functioning market, utility-maximizing households will purchase houses so that their willingness-to-pay for a marginal increase in a particular attribute equals its hedonic price. Consequently, in equilibrium, the hedonic price of an attribute can be interpreted as the willingness-to-pay of households for a marginal increase in that attribute. The graph of the hedonic price of a scenic view, r_v, against the level of view is shown in the lower panel of Figure 10.6. Assuming all households have identical incomes and tastes, this curve can be interpreted as a household inverse demand curve for a scenic view.

But, as we discussed earlier in this section, households differ in their incomes and tastes: Some people are willing to pay a considerable amount of money for a more scenic view, while others are not. To account for different incomes and tastes, analysts should estimate the following willingness-to-pay function (inverse demand curve) for a scenic view:

$$r_v = W(VIEW, Y, Z) \quad (10.12)$$

where Y is household income and Z is a vector of household characteristics that reflects tastes—for example, socioeconomic background, race, age, and family size. Three willingness-to-pay functions, denoted W_1, W_2, and W_3, for three different households are drawn in the lower panel of Figure 10.6. Equilibria occur where these functions intersect the r_v function. Thus, when incomes and socioeconomic characteristics differ, the r_v function is the locus of household equilibrium willingnesses-to-pay for a scenic view.

Using the methods described in Chapter 3 and illustrated earlier in this chapter, it is straightforward to use equation (10.12) to calculate the change in consumer surplus to a household due to a change in the level of scenic view. These changes in indi-

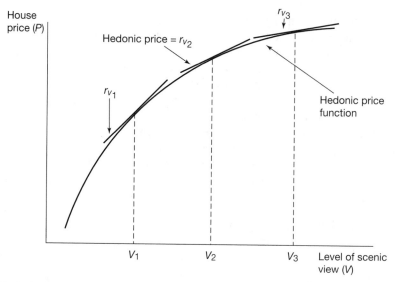

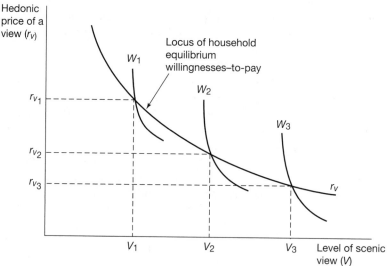

Figure 10.6   Hedonic Price Method

vidual household consumer surplus can be aggregated across all households to obtain the total change in consumer surplus.

In theory, the hedonic pricing method can be used to value incremental changes in the level of many goods that are not traded in markets, such as externalities and public goods.[28] In practice, there are six potential problems. One is that people must know and understand the full implications of the externality or public good. For example, in order to use the hedonic pricing method to value pollution, families should know, prior to the purchase of their house, the level of pollution to which it is exposed and should also know the effect of different pollution doses on their health. Second, it is important that equation (10.11) includes as explanatory variables the attributes that households really do value, not more readily obtainable but incorrect proxies. In econometrics, this problem is referred to as the *errors in variables* problem. Third, if the hedonic pricing model, equation (10.8), is in fact linear, then the hedonic price of each attribute is constant, which would make it impossible to estimate the inverse demand function, equation (10.12). Fourth, there should be many different houses so that families can find an optimal "package," that is, a house with just the right combination of attributes. In other words, there should be sufficient variety so that families can find a house that permits them to reach an "equilibrium." This would be a problem, for example, if a family hates pollution and wants a small house, but all of the houses in pollution-free areas were large. Fifth, there may be multicollinearity problems in the data. To use the same example, if expensive houses were large and located mainly in areas free of pollution, while inexpensive houses were small and located mainly in polluted areas, it would be difficult to estimate separate hedonic prices for pollution and size. Sixth, the method assumes that market prices adjust immediately to changes in attributes and in all other factors that affect demand or supply.

■ **EXHIBIT 10.2**

Dean Uyeno, Stanley Hamilton, and Andrew Biggs used the hedonic regression method to estimate the cost of airport noise in Vancouver, Canada. They estimated the following hedonic price equation:

$$\ln H = \beta_0 + \beta_1 NEF + \sum_{j=2}^{k} \beta_j \ln X_j + \varepsilon$$

where $\ln H$ is the log of residential property value, NEF is a measure of noise level (ambient noise levels are in the NEF 15-25 range, "some" to "much" annoyance occurs in the NEF 25-40 range, and "considerable" annoyance occurs above NEFs of 40), and X_j are house characteristics ($j=2, \ldots ,k$).

Their results show that Vancouver International Airport generates noise costs that capitalize into residential house and condominium prices. For detached houses in Richmond with NEFs of 25 or higher, the "noise depreciation sensitivity index" (i.e., the estimated coefficient of the noise variable) was 0.65 percent, which implies that houses very close to the airport with NEFs of 40 are 9.75 percent cheaper than houses far from the airport with NEFs of 25. In aggregate, the social cost of noise from Vancouver International Airport amounts to about $15 million in 1987 Canadian dollars. The estimated noise depreciation sensitivity is broadly consistent with previous studies, leading the authors to conclude that "the similarity of results spanning several decades and several Western countries would seem to suggest a broad and long-lived consensus on the issue (of the impact of airport noise on property values) . . . " (p. 14).

Source: Dean Uyeno, Stanley W. Hamilton, and Andrew J.G. Biggs, "Density of Residential Land Use and the Impact of Airport Noise," *Journal of Transport Economics and Policy*, 27, no. 1 (1993), 3–18.

Using Hedonic Regression Methods to Value Life

The simple forms of consumer purchase and labor market studies to value life that we have described previously may be biased due to omitted variables or self-selection problems. For example, labor market studies to value life that examine *fatality risk* (the risk of death) often omit potentially relevant variables such as *injury risks* (the risk of injury). These problems may be reduced by following the hedonic regression procedure to find the hedonic prices of various job attributes. For example, a researcher might estimate the following regression model to find the hedonic price of fatality risk:

$$\ln(\text{wage rate}) = \beta_0 + \beta_1 \ln(\text{fatality risk}) + \beta_2 \ln(\text{injury risk})$$

$$+ \beta_3 \ln(\text{job tenure}) + \beta_4 \ln(\text{education}) \tag{10.13}$$

$$+ \beta_5 \ln(\text{age}) + \epsilon$$

The inclusion of injury risk, job tenure, education, and age in the regression model controls for variables that affect wages and would bias the estimated coefficient of β_1 if they were excluded. Using the procedure demonstrated in the preceding section, the analyst can convert the estimate of β_1 to a hedonic price of fatality risk and can then estimate individuals' willingness-to-pay to avoid fatal risks. Most of the empirical estimates of the value of life that are reported in Chapter 12 are obtained from labor market and consumer product studies that employ models similar to the one presented in equation (10.13).

TRAVEL COST METHOD[29]

Suppose we want to estimate the demand for a recreational site so that we can measure its value to consumers. In general, we expect that a person's demand for such a good, q, depends on its price (p), the price of substitutes (p_s), the person's income (Y), and variables that reflect the person's tastes (Z):

$$q = f(p, p_s, Y, Z) \tag{10.14}$$

The travel cost method (TCM) recognizes that the full price paid by persons for a good such as a visit to a recreational site is more than just the admission fee. It also includes the costs of traveling to and from the site. Among these travel costs are the opportunity cost of time spent traveling, the operating cost of vehicles used to travel, the costs of accommodations for overnight stays while traveling or visiting, and parking fees at the site. The sum of all of these costs gives the total cost of a visit to the site. This total cost is used as an explanatory variable in place of the admission price.

The clever insight of the TCM is that while admission fees are usually the same, and often zero, for all persons, the total cost faced by each person varies because of differences in the travel cost component. Consequently, usage also varies, thereby allowing researchers to make inferences about the demand curve for the site. It is worth emphasizing that when total cost replaces price in equation (10.14), this equation is not the usual demand curve that gives visits as a function of the price of admission. As we will show, however, we can use the TCM to estimate the usual market demand curve.

Most applications of the TCM have been to value recreational sites.[30] If the "market" for visits to a site is geographically extensive, then different potential visitors bear very different travel costs depending on their proximity to the site. The resulting differences in total cost, and the differences in the rates of visits that they induce, provide a basis for estimating a demand curve for the site.

Estimating the demand for a particular recreational site with the TCM is conceptually straightforward. First, select a random sample of households within the market area of the recreational site. Second, survey these households to determine their numbers of visits to the site over some period of time, all of their costs from visiting the site, their costs of visiting substitute sites, their incomes, and other of their characteristics that may affect demand. Third, specify a functional form for the demand schedule and estimate it using the survey data.

Zonal Travel Cost Method

With the *zonal travel cost method*, researchers survey actual visitors at a site rather than potential visitors. This is often more feasible and less expensive than surveying potential visitors. Also the level of analysis shifts from the individual, or household, to the area, or zone, of origin of visitors—hence, the term *zonal travel cost method*.

Zonal TCM requires the analyst to specify the zones from which users of the site originate. Zones can easily be formed by drawing concentric rings around the site on a map. Ideally, households within a zone should face similar travel costs as well as have similar values of the other variables, including the price of substitutes, income, and tastes. If residents within a zone have quite different travel costs, then zones should be redrawn. In practice, analysts often use local government jurisdictions as the zones because they facilitate the collection of data on populations and demographic characteristics within zones.

Assuming a constant-elasticity functional form leads to the following regression model that can be estimated by OLS:

$$\ln(V/POP) = \beta_0 + \beta_1 \ln(\bar{p}) + \beta_2 \ln(\bar{p}_s) + \beta_3 \ln\bar{Y} + \beta_4 \ln\bar{Z} + \varepsilon \quad (10.15)$$

where V is the number of visits from a zone per period, POP is the population of the zone; and $\bar{p}$, $\bar{p}_s$, $\bar{Y}$, and $\bar{Z}$, denote the average values of p, p_s, Y, and Z in each zone, respectively.

Note that the quantity demanded is expressed as a visit rate. An alternative specification is to estimate demand in terms of the number of visits, V, but to include population, POP, on the right-hand side of the regression equation. Although both specifications are plausible, the specification in equation (10.15) is less likely to involve heteroscedasticity (which we discuss in Appendix 10A) and, therefore, more likely to be appropriately estimated by OLS.

Using estimates of the parameters in equation (10.15), it is possible to estimate the change in consumer surplus associated with a change in the admission price to a site, the total consumer surplus associated with the site at its current admission fee, and the average consumer surplus per visit to the site. We illustrate how to do this using a simple example for a hypothetical recreational wilderness area.

Assume there are only five relevant zones from which people travel to the recreational site. To avoid unnecessary complications, we assume that demand depends directly only on total price, not on income, the prices of substitutes, or any other variable.

The basic data for the illustration are presented in Table 10.1. In this example, the value of time for residents from different zones varies considerably due to different income levels. (For estimates of the value of time used in CBA, see Chapter 12.) Zone A is adjacent to the recreational area. Residents in Zone A can, on average, pack up their equipment, drive to the site (2 kilometers on average), park, and walk to the entrance in approximately one-half hour. Assuming the opportunity cost of their time is $9.40/hr and marginal vehicle operating costs are 15 cents/km, their total travel costs are $10 per round trip. Adding the admission fee of $10 per day yields a total cost of $20. On average, these local residents make 15 visits each season. Zone B is about 30 km away, requiring two hours of total travel time (including driving, parking, walking, loading, and unloading vehicles) for a round trip. Assuming the value of time for residents of zone B is $5.50/hr and they travel individually, total costs per trip are $30. On average, zone B residents make 13 visits per season. Zone C is about 90 km away, requiring two hours of total travel time in each direction. Assuming the value of their time is $10.35/hr on average, and that travel costs are shared between two people in each vehicle, total costs per person are approximately $65. On average, zone C residents make six trips per year. Zone D residents live on the other side of the metropolitan area and, on average, make three trips per season. Assuming that their average wage rate is $8/hr and that two persons travel per vehicle, their per person cost is $80 per round trip. Zone E residents have to cross an international border. Though the distance is only slight-

TABLE 10.1   ILLUSTRATION OF THE TRAVEL COST METHOD

Zone	Travel Time (hours)	Travel Distance (km)	Average Total Cost per Person ($)	Average Number of Visits per Person	Consumer Surplus per Person	Consumer Surplus per Zone ($ thousands)	Trips per Zone (thousands)
A	0.5	2	20	15	525	5,250	150
B	1.0	30	30	13	390	3,900	130
C	2.0	90	65	6	75	1,500	120
D	3.0	140	80	3	15	150	30
E	3.5	150	90	1	0	0	10
Total						10,800	440

ly further than from zone D, it takes almost one-half hour to get through customs and immigration. The average zone E wage is \$8/hour. Assuming two persons per vehicle, the per person cost is \$90 per round trip.

The data for average total cost (TC) and average visits per person (V) are represented graphically in Figure 10.7 for zones A through E. In this example, the equation $TC = 95 - 5V$ fits these data perfectly. (In practice, our data are unlikely to fall perfectly on a line—regression analysis would be used to fit a line.) This equation is the individual's inverse demand curve: It shows how much a person is willing to pay for each trip. For this recreational area, an individual is willing to pay \$90 for the first trip, \$85 for the second trip, . . . , \$20 for the fifteenth trip.

Different individuals face different prices for their trips depending on their zone of origin—it is cheaper for those who live closer. Therefore, the consumer surplus varies according to the zone of origin. The consumer surplus for a particular trip from a particular zone equals the difference between how much someone is willing to pay for that par-

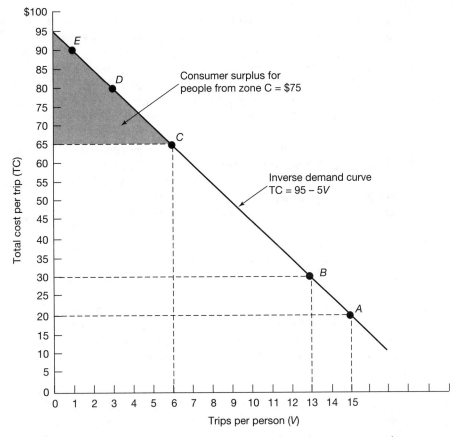

Figure 10.7   Inverse Demand Curve for Trips by Individuals to a Recreational Area

ticular trip, given by the point on the inverse demand curve, and how much they actually pay for that trip *from that zone*. For example, people from zone C are willing to pay $80 for their third trip, but they actually pay only $65 for that trip, yielding a consumer surplus of $15 for that trip.

The total consumer surplus for someone from zone C is obtained by summing the consumer surpluses associated with each trip across all trips ($90 − 65 = $25 for the first trip, $85 − 65 = $20 for the second trip, and $15, $10, $5, and $0 for the third, fourth, fifth, and sixth trips, respectively), which equals $75. This amount is represented by the area of the shaded triangle in Figure 10.7.[31] Similarly, the consumer surplus is $525 per person for people from zone A, $390 for people from zone B, $75 for people from zone D, and $0 for people from zone E. These amounts are presented in column 6 of Table 10.1. Clearly, people who live closer to the recreational site enjoy a larger consumer surplus from it than people who live further away.

From this information and knowledge of the populations of each zone, we can calculate the total consumer surplus per season and the average consumer surplus per visit for the site.

Suppose zones A, B, D, and E have populations of 10,000 people, while zone C has a population of 20,000 people. The consumer surplus per zone is obtained by multiplying the consumer surplus per person in a zone by the population of that zone, as shown in column 7 of Table 10.1. Adding across all zones yields the total site consumer surplus of $10.8 million. Adding admission fees of $4.4 million indicates that the annual benefit of the site to all visitors equals $15.2 million. If the government decided to use the site for some completely different purpose, such as logging, this would be a measure of the lost annual benefits.

The total number of visits to the recreational area is 440,000, as shown in column 8 of Table 10.1. Dividing the total consumer surplus by the total number of visits gives an average consumer surplus per trip of $24.55. If we now add the admission fee, then we obtain the *average demand price* per trip, which is the average maximum amount a visitor would pay for a trip to the site. In this example, the average demand price is $34.55.

An alternative approach to estimating total consumer surplus is to construct a *market inverse demand curve* for the site. That is, determine the total number of visits as a function of the admission fee. This demand curve can then be used to estimate aggregate consumer surplus in the usual way.

Returning to the example, we can rewrite the individual's inverse demand curve, $TC = 95 − 5V$, to obtain a visit demand schedule which gives the number of visits for an individual as a function of total cost: $V = 19 − 0.2TC$. As we stated previously, this is not the usual demand curve, which gives total visits as a function of the admission fee.

To obtain the market demand curve we proceed as follows. To begin, we know two points on the market demand curve. At an admission price of $10, the current admission fee, there are 440,000 visits. Now consider how high admission fees can be raised until demand is choked off and falls to zero. At the current price of $10, people from zone A have the largest consumer surplus per trip of $70 for their first trip. Therefore, if the admission price were increased by slightly more than $70 (from $10) to say $85, then demand would be choked off and would fall to zero. Thus, we know the intercept of the market inverse demand curve: At a price of $85 demand would be zero. The price of admission at which demand would fall to zero is called the *choke price*. Note that we can easily obtain the choke price by subtracting the travel cost of using the site by users from zone A (travel cost = total cost – admission fee), which equals $10, from the intercept of the individual inverse demand curve, which equals $95.

We can find other points on the market demand curve by assuming that the admission fee is increased or decreased and then predicting the visit rate from each zone at the new price. Aggregating across all zones give us the predicted total number of trips at the new price. Suppose, for example, the admission fee were raised by $10 to $20, so that TC would increase by $10 dollars. Using the coefficient of TC in the visit demand equation indicates that the number of visits per person would fall by two for each zone. Thus, the predicted number of visits would be 13 for zone A, 11 for zone B, 4 for zone C, 1 for zone D, and –1 for zone E. As negative visits are not possible, we set the number of visits per person for zone E to zero. Now we multiply the predicted visit rate for each zone by its population and sum these products to obtain the total number of visits demanded at the new price. For the new admission fee of $20, the number of visitors is 330,000 per season. This is a second point on the market demand curve.

Other points on the market demand curve can be obtained in the same way. With a sufficient number of points, the market demand curve can be sketched to the desired level of accuracy. The annual consumer surplus for the site is the area between the curve and the current admission fee from zero visits to 440,000 visits.

Limitations of the TCM

The usefulness of the TCM is limited in a number of ways. One limitation is that the TCM provides an estimate of the willingness-to-pay for the entire site rather than for specific features of a site. As we often wish to value improvements at a site that change its features, the basic TCM does not provide the needed information. However, if the residents of zones can choose from among a number of alternative recreational sites with different attributes, then it may be possible to use the *hedonic travel cost method* to find attribute prices.[32] This method treats the total cost of visiting a particular site from a particular zone as a function of both the distance from that zone to the site *and* various attributes of the site. Its application raises a number of issues beyond those previously discussed in the context of the basic hedonic model. Therefore, before attempting to apply the hedonic method in this context, we recommend consulting sources that deal with it specifically in the travel cost context.[33]

Another limitation of the TCM is that it is restricted to the analysis of sites to which people from different zones have quite different travel costs. If an analyst tried to use this method to value a civic theater where most attendees lived nearby, then it probably would not work well because there would probably be too little variation in travel cost among attendees and, hence, too little variation in total cost. Without variation in total cost, there is no leverage for estimating a demand curve.

Estimation of the market demand curve assumes that people respond to changes in price regardless of its composition. Thus, for example, people respond to, say, a $5 increase in the admission price in the same way as a $5 increase in travel cost. This presumes that people have a good understanding of the impact of changes in the prices of fuel, tires, and repairs on their marginal travel cost.

The TCM also raises a number of analytical problems in its application, many of which concern measuring the price of a visit to the site.[34] Perhaps the most obvious problem is the estimation of the opportunity cost of travel time, which we have previously discussed.[35] Even defining and measuring travel costs raises some difficult issues. Some analysts include the time spent at the site, as well as the time spent traveling to and from it, as components of total price. If people from different zones spend the same amount of time at the site, and if the opportunity cost of their time is similar, then it does not matter whether the time spent at the site is included or not—both the height of the demand curve and total price shift by the same amount for each consumer so that estimates of consumer surplus remain unchanged. If, however, people from different zones have different opportunity costs for their time, or if they spend different amounts of time at the site, then including the cost of time spent at the site would change the price facing persons from different zones by different amounts and, thereby, change the slope of the estimated demand curve.

Another problem arises because recreation often requires investment in fairly specialized equipment such as tents, sleeping bags, wet-weather gear, canoes, fishing rods, and even vehicles. The marginal cost of using such equipment should be included in total price. Yet, estimating the marginal cost of using capital goods is often difficult. As with time spent at the site, however, these costs can be reasonably ignored if they are approximately constant for visitors from different zones.

Multiple-purpose trips also pose an analytical problem. People may visit the recreational site in the morning and, for example, go river rafting nearby in the afternoon. Sometimes analysts exclude visitors with multiple purposes from the data they use to estimate the demand curve. Including visitors with multiple purposes is usually desirable if costs can be appropriately apportioned to the site being valued. If the apportionment is arbitrary, however, then it may be better to exclude multiple users.

A similar problem results because the journey itself may have value. The previous discussion assumes implicitly that the trip is undertaken exclusively to get to the recreation site and travel has no benefit per se. If the journey itself is part of the reason for the visit to the site, then the trip has multiple purposes. Therefore, part of the cost of the trip should be attributed to the journey, not the visit to the recreation site. Not doing so would lead to overestimation of site benefits.

A more fundamental problem is that the travel cost variable may be endogenous, not exogenous. One neighborhood characteristic some people consider when making their residential choices is its proximity to a recreational area. People who expect to make many visits to the recreational area may select a particular neighborhood (zone) partially on account of the low travel time from that neighborhood to the recreational area. If so, the number of trips to a particular recreational area and the price of these trips will be determined simultaneously. Under these circumstances equation (10.15) may not be identified, a problem which we discussed earlier in this chapter. Also, the travel cost variable may not be independent of the error term, thereby leading to ordinary least squares estimates that are biased and inconsistent.

Another econometric problem is that the dependent variable in the estimated models is *truncated*. Truncation arises because the sample is drawn from only those who visit the site, not from the larger population which includes people who never visit the site. Application of ordinary least squares to the truncated sample would result in biased coefficients.

Finally, there may be an omitted variable problem. If the price of substitute recreational sites varies across zones or if tastes for recreation varies across zones, then the estimated coefficients may be biased if the model does not control for these variables. As previously discussed, bias results when an excluded variable is correlated with an included variable.

■ **EXHIBIT 10.3**

Kerry Smith and William Desvousges use the travel cost method to estimate the average household value of a trip to recreational sites along the Monongahela River and the average household value of improving the water quality. Their estimates of travel costs assume the marginal cost of operating an automobile was $0.08 per mile in 1976. For the time cost component of travel cost, they set the value of time equal to the wage rate in a person's particular occupation, which ranged from $2.75 per hour for female farmers to $7.89 per hour for male professional, technical and kindred workers in 1977 dollars. Smith and Desvousges estimate many models including the following relatively simple travel cost model (*t*-statistics in parentheses):

$$\ln V = \quad -3.928 \qquad -0.051TC \quad + 0.00001Y \quad + 0.058DO \qquad (R^2 = 0.225)$$
$$\quad (-3.075) \qquad (-2.846) \qquad (1.109) \qquad (3.917)$$

where Y denotes income and DO is the percent saturation of dissolved oxygen in the water. Based on this model, the authors estimate that the average annual value per household of visiting recreational sites on the Monongahela River is $3.53[36], the average annual value of improving the water quality from boatable to game fishing would be $7.16, and the average annual value of improving the water quality from boatable to swimming would be $28.86 in 1981 dollars.

Source: V. Kerry Smith and William H. Desvousges, *Measuring Water Quality Benefits* (Boston: Kluwer Nijhoff Publishing, 1986), especially pp. 270–271.

DEFENSIVE EXPENDITURES METHOD [37]

If you live in a smoggy city, then you may find that the windows of your house often need cleaning. Imagine that you hire someone to clean your windows periodically. The cost of this action in response to the smog is termed a *defensive expenditure*. Suppose the city passes an ordinance that reduces the level of smog so that your windows do not get as dirty. You would now have to spend less on window cleaners. The reduction in defensive expenditures—the defensive expenditures avoided—has been suggested as a measure of the benefits of the city ordinance. Similarly, the costs of a policy change might be measured by the increase in defensive expenditures.

This method is an example of a broad class of *production function methods*. In these methods, the level of a public good or externality (e.g., smog) and other goods (window cleaners) are inputs to some production process (window cleanliness). If the level of the public good or externality changes, then the levels of the other inputs can be changed in the opposite direction, allowing the quantity of output produced to remain the same. For example, when the negative externality of smog is reduced, less labor is required to produce the same level of window cleanliness. The change in expenditures on the substitute input is used as a measure of the benefit of reduction of the public good or externality.

Suppose that the demand curve for window cleaning is represented by the curve labeled D in Figure 10.8. Let S_0 represent the supply of window cleaning services initially, that is, prior to the new ordinance. The initial equilibrium price and quantity of window cleaning services are denoted by P_0 and Q_0, respectively. The effect of the new ordinance is to shift the supply curve for window cleaning down and to the right: Because there is less smog, windows are easier to clean, so that more windows can be cleaned for the same price. At the new equilibrium, the price of window cleaning is P_1 and the quantity of window cleaning is Q_1. The change in consumer surplus is represented by the area of the trapezoid P_0abP_1.

If households continued to consume the same quantity of window cleaning after the price shift as they did before the price shift, Q_0, then the benefit of the ordinance would be represented by the rectangle P_0acP_1. This would be the amount by which consumers reduce their defensive expenditure. Consumers, however, would not maintain their consumption levels at Q_0, but would increase their consumption of window cleaning to level Q_1. Individuals would spend area bQ_1Q_0c on the purchase of $Q_1 - Q_0$ additional units of window cleaning at a price of P_1. The net change in spending on window cleaning services equals the area of rectangle P_0acP_1 *minus* the area of rectangle bQ_1Q_0c. As one can see from Figure 10.8, however, the gain in consumer surplus equals the area of trapezoid P_0abP_1.

The important point is that the net change in spending on window services may be quite small. Indeed, if the demand curve were a constant-elasticity demand curve, with an elasticity equal to 1, there would be no change in total expenditure on cleaning services at all! Yet, there are obviously positive benefits to consumers. In general, *the reduced spending on defensive expenditures will underestimate the benefits of cleaner air or whatever benefit is being estimated.*[38]

There are at least four additional problems with the defensive expenditures method. First, it assumes implicitly that individuals quickly adjust to the new equilibrium. It may actually take some time for individuals to adjust their purchases to return to equilibrium where the marginal cost of the substitute input equals its marginal benefit. Second, a defensive expenditure may not remedy the entire damage so that reductions in this expenditure do not fully measure benefits. For example, expenditures on

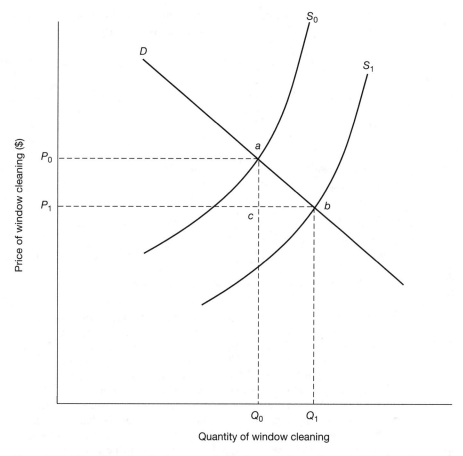

Figure 10.8   The Effect of an Ordinance Reducing Smog on Expenditures for Window Cleaning

window cleaning do not "avoid" the whole problem of smog. Smog also leads to dirtier shirts and to health problems. Defensive expenditures avoided on these items should also be included. Third, the defensive expenditures may have benefits other than remedying damage. For example, the professional cleaning necessitated by the smog may result in cleaner windows than one would otherwise achieve. Fourth, not all of the defensive measures are purchased in markets. Some people clean their own windows—reductions in their opportunity costs should also be included as benefits.

■ **EXHIBIT 10.4**

Charles W. Abdalla, Brian A. Roach, and Donald J. Epp measured the costs of groundwater degradation in the small Pennsylvania borough of Perkasie (population 7,877) using the defensive expenditures method. They conducted mail and telephone surveys to gather information from a sample of residents on the actions they took in response to trichloroethylene (TCE) contamination of one of the borough's wells between December

1987 and September 1989. They estimated the total costs, including both monetary costs and time expenditures, of each of five defensive actions:

Category of Cost	Cost Based on Value of Leisure Time Equal to Minimum Wage ($)[a]	Cost Based on Value of Leisure Time Equal to Individual Wage Rate ($)[a]
Increased Purchases of Bottled Water	11,100	11,100
New Purchases of Bottled Water	17,300	17,300
Home Water Treatment Systems	4,700	4,700
Hauling Water	12,500	34,000
Boiling Water	15,600	64,100
Total	61,200	131,200

[a]Costs in original rounded to nearest hundred dollars.

Note that the costs of hauling and boiling water are very sensitive to the assumed opportunity cost of leisure. The researchers interpreted these total costs as a lower-bound estimate of the true cost of the contamination to residents because of the generally conservative nature of the defensive expenditures method.

A specific factor suggesting that these defensive expenditures represent a lower bound is that only 43 percent of residents were aware of the TCE contamination despite notification laws! Moreover, not all residents who knew about the contamination took defensive measures. Nevertheless, those who had more information about the contamination, those who perceived the cancer risk to TCE to be higher, and those who had children between 3 and 17 years old in the household were, other things equal, more likely to take defensive action than those who did not. Among those who took defensive action, having a child under 3 years of age seemed to be the most important factor influencing the intensity of the defensive actions taken.

Source: Charles W. Abdalla, Brian A. Roach, and Donald J. Epp, "Valuing Environmental Quality Changes Using Averting Expenditures: An Application to Groundwater Contamination," *Land Economics*, 68, no. 2 (1992), 163–169.

CONCLUSION

This chapter describes the major methods currently used in CBA for estimating benefits and costs by utilizing information on revealed preference that is obtained from sources other than demonstrations or social experiments. Some methods are not discussed as we believe that they are too advanced for this book. Perhaps most notably, we have not discussed the use of random utility models or probabilistic choice models to estimate demand, an approach that is quite important in the transportation area.[39]

Also we do not discuss recent methods that estimate demand curves by combining survey data with data on observed behavior.[40] Nevertheless, the methods covered here provide a rich set of tools for practical CBA.

APPENDIX 10A

AN INTRODUCTION TO MULTIPLE REGRESSION ANALYSIS[1]

Linear regression provides a manageable way to control statistically for the effects of several explanatory variables.[2] Its use requires us to assume that the effects of the various explanatory variables on the dependent variable are additive. That is, the marginal effect on the dependent variable of a unit change in any one of the explanatory variables remains the same no matter what the values of the other explanatory variables are. We can express a linear regression model in mathematical form:

$$y = \beta_0 + \beta_1 x_1 + \beta_2 x_2 + \ldots + \beta_k x_k + \epsilon$$

where y is the dependent variable, $x_1, x_2, \ldots x_k$ are the k explanatory or independent variables, $\beta_0, \beta_1, \beta_2 \ldots \beta_k$ are parameters (coefficients) to be estimated, and ϵ is an error term that incorporates the cumulative effect on y of all the factors not explicitly included in the model. The basic model assumes that the explanatory variables are nonrandom and measured without error.

The intercept parameter, β_0, also called the *constant*, is the expected value of y if all the explanatory variables equal zero. The other parameters, $\beta_1, \beta_2 \ldots \beta_k$, which are called *slope* parameters, measure the marginal impacts of the explanatory variables on the dependent variable. If, for instance, we were to increase x_1 by one unit while holding the values of the other explanatory variables constant, y would change by an amount β_1. Similarly, each of the other coefficients measures the marginal effect of a unit change in its variable on the dependent variable.

Imagine that we set the values of all the explanatory variables except x_1 equal to zero. We could then plot y against x_1 in a two-dimensional graph. The equation $y = \beta_0 + \beta_1 x_1$ would represent the true regression. The slope of the line is β_1, the magnitude of the change in y that will result from a unit change in x_1, other things being equal. We do not expect that the actual observations will lie exactly on the line. The vertical distances of the observed points from the line will equal the random error, represented in our model by ϵ. If the values of ϵ are small, the true regression line fits the data well in the sense that the actual observations are close to it.

Estimating the Parameters

How should we go about fitting the line? The most commonly used procedure is the method of ordinary least squares (OLS). When we have only one explanatory variable, so we can plot our data on a two-dimensional graph, the OLS procedure picks the line for which the sum of squared vertical deviations from the estimated line to the observed data is smallest.

Suppose we denote the OLS estimates of the parameters by "hats": $\hat{\beta}_0$, $\hat{\beta}_1, \hat{\beta}_2, ..., \hat{\beta}_k$ then we can write the estimated regression model:

$$y = \hat{\beta}_0 + \hat{\beta}_1 x_1 + \hat{\beta}_2 x_2 + ... + \hat{\beta}_k x_k$$

For the ith observation $(y_i, x_{i1}, x_{i2}, ..., x_{ik})$, the predicted value of the dependent variable is:

$$\hat{y}_i = \hat{\beta}_0 + \hat{\beta}_1 x_{i1} + \hat{\beta}_i x_{i2} + ... + \hat{\beta}_k x_{ik} \qquad i = 1, ..., n$$

and the ith *prediction error* or *residual* is:

$$\hat{\epsilon}_i = y_i - \hat{y}_i \qquad i = 1, ..., n$$

Thus, the residual is the observed value of the dependent variable minus the value we would predict for the dependent variable based on our estimated parameters and the values of our explanatory variables. OLS selects the parameter estimates to minimize the sum of squares of these residuals.[3]

Multicollinearity

As long as the number of observations in our sample exceeds the number of coefficients that we are trying to estimate, $n > k$, the commonly available regression software packages will usually enable us to use computers to find the OLS fitted coefficients. However, when one explanatory variable can be written as a linear combination of the others, we have a case of *extreme multicollinearity*. A less severe but more common form of the problem occurs when the explanatory variables in our sample are highly correlated. This condition, called *multicollinearity,* is not a problem with the specification of our model, but with the data we have available to estimate it. If two variables are highly correlated, positively or negatively, OLS has difficulty identifying their independent effects on the dependent variable. As a result, the estimates of the parameters associated with these variables will not be very reliable. The sum of their estimated coefficients will be closer to the sum of their true coefficients than will be either individual coefficient estimate to its true value. One way to deal with multicollinearity is to add new observations to our sample that lower the correlation between the individual variables. Unfortunately, we often have no choice but to work with the data that are already available.

Properties of OLS Estimates

The estimates of coefficients that we obtain from OLS will generally have a number of very desirable properties. If the explanatory variables are all uncorrelated with the error term (ϵ), and if the expected value of the error term is zero, then our coefficient estimators will be *unbiased.*[4] (Note: An *estimator* is the formula we use to calculate a particular estimate from our data.) To understand what it means for an estimator to be unbiased, we must keep in mind that our particular estimate depends upon the errors actually realized in our sample of data. If we were to select a new sample, we would realize different errors and hence different coefficient estimates. When an estimator is unbiased, we expect that the average of our estimates across different samples will be very close to the true coefficient value. For example, if the price of gasoline had no true effect on quantity of gasoline demanded, then we would almost certainly estimate its coefficient to be positive or negative rather than exactly zero. Repeating OLS on a large number of samples and averaging our estimates of the coefficient of gasoline price, however, would generally yield a result very close to zero. Indeed, by adding more and more samples, we could get the average as close to zero as we wanted.

Our average will not be close to zero, however, if gasoline price is correlated with a variable excluded from our model that does have an effect on quantity demanded. If this is the case, gasoline price stands as a proxy for the excluded variable. Other things equal, the stronger the true effect of the excluded variable on quantity demanded, and the higher the absolute value of the correlation between gasoline price and the excluded variable, the greater will be the bias in the coefficient of gasoline price. Our estimates of the price coefficient would include the indirect affect of the excluded variable.

We might not worry that much about the bias if we knew that it would approach zero as we increase sample size. (If the variance of the estimator also approached zero as we increased sample size, we would say that the estimator is *consistent*.) Although OLS estimators are consistent for correctly specified models, correlation with an important excluded variable makes an estimator inconsistent.

Statistical Significance and Hypothesis Testing

Unfortunately, we usually only have a single sample for estimating coefficients. How do we decide if an estimate deviates enough from zero for us to conclude that the true value of the parameter is not zero? Making the fairly reasonable assumption that the error term for each observation can be treated as a draw from a normal distribution with constant variance, the OLS estimators will be distributed according to the Student's t distribution.[5] That is, we can interpret the particular numerical estimate of a coefficient as a draw from a random variable distributed as a Student's t distribution centered around the true value of the coefficient. (The OLS estimator is the random variable; the actual estimate based on our data is a realization of that random variable.)

Knowing the distribution of the OLS estimator enables us to interpret the *statistical significance* of our coefficient estimate. We determine statistical significance by asking the following question: How likely is it that we would observe a coefficient estimate as large as we did if the true value of the coefficient were zero? We answer this question by first assuming that the true value of the coefficient is zero (the null hypothesis) so that the distribution of our estimator is centered around zero. We then standardize our distribution to have a variance of one by dividing our coefficient estimate by an estimate of its standard error (a by-product of the OLS procedure). The resulting number, called the t-ratio, can then be compared to critical values in tabulations of the standardized Student's t distribution found in the appendix of almost any statistics text. For example, we might decide that we will reject the null hypothesis that the true value of the coefficient is zero if there is less than a 5 percent probability of observing a t-ratio (in absolute value sense) as large as we did if the null hypothesis is true. (The probability we choose puts an upward bound on the probability of falsely rejecting the null hypothesis.[6])

The Student's t distribution is tabulated by degrees of freedom. In the basic OLS framework, the degrees of freedom are the total number of observations minus the number of coefficients being estimated. As the degrees of freedom become larger, the Student's t distribution looks more like a standardized normal distribution.

It is important to also note the difference between a one-tailed and a two-tailed test. Because the standardized Student's t is a symmetric distribution centered on zero, a 5 percent test usually involves setting critical values so that 2.5 percent of area lies under each of the tails (positive and negative). A one-tailed test, appropriate, for example, when the null hypothesis is that the true coefficient value is zero or less than zero, puts the entire 5 percent in the positive tail.

To carry out this test, we look in the standardized tabulations of the Student's t distribution for the critical value corresponding to 5 percent. If the absolute value of our estimated t-ratio exceeds the critical value, then we reject the null hypothesis and say that our estimated coefficient is statistically significantly different from zero.

Most regression software saves us the trouble of looking up critical values in tables by directly calculating the probability under the null hypothesis of observing a t-ratio as large as that estimated. To do a classical test of hypothesis on the coefficient, we simply see if the reported probability is less than the maximum probability of falsely rejecting the null hypothesis that we are willing to accept. If it is smaller, then we reject the null hypothesis.

The square of the correlation between the actual and predicted values of the dependent variable, R^2, is commonly used as a measure of the goodness-of-fit of a regression. It provides a value between zero and one that measures the percentage of variation in the dependent variable explained by the estimated model. It can be used to help select between alternative model specifications when theory is ambiguous, or to test alternative theories. It should not be used in making comparisons across samples, however, because it depends on the particular values of the explanatory variables in each of the samples

EXERCISES FOR CHAPTER 10

1. Day care services in a small midwestern city cost $30 per day per child. The high cost of these services is one reason why very few mothers who are on welfare work; given their low potential wages, virtually no welfare mothers are willing to pay these high costs. To combat this problem, the city establishes a new program: In exchange for their welfare benefits, a group of welfare recipients is required to provide day care for the children of other welfare recipients who obtain private-sector employment. The welfare mothers who use these day

care services are required to pay a fee of $3 per day per child. These services prove very popular; 1,000 welfare children receive them each day and an additional 500 welfare children are on a waiting list to receive them. Do the mothers of the 1,000 children who receive services under the program value these services at $30,000 ($30 x 1,000) a day, $3,000 a day ($3 x 1,000), or at a value that is greater than $3,000 but less than $30,000? Explain.

2. Consider the example presented in Figure 10.3. Imagine that the current price of waste disposal is $0.025/lb and the average waste disposal is 2.40 lb/p/d. As noted in the diagram, when the price was previously $0.01/lb, the average waste disposal was 2.52 lb/p/d. Assume that the marginal social cost of waste disposal is $0.06/lb, that marginal social costs are constant with respect to quantity, and that the town has a population of 100,000.

   a. Fitting a linear demand curve to the two observed points, calculate the annual net benefits of raising the price of waste disposal to $0.05/lb.

   b. Fitting a constant-elasticity demand curve to the observed points, calculate the annual net benefits of raising the price of waste disposal to $0.05/lb.

3. A worker, who is typical in all respects, works for a wage of $10,000 per year in a perfectly safe occupation. Another typical worker does a job requiring exactly the same skills as the first worker, but in a risky occupation with a known death probability of 1 in 1,000 per year, and receives a wage of $12,000 per year.

   What value of a human life for workers with these characteristics should a cost-benefit analyst use?

4. (Regression software required.) An analyst was asked to predict the gross social benefits of building a public swimming pool in Dryville, which has a population of 70,230 people and a median household income of $31,500. The analyst identified 24 towns in the region that already had public swimming pools. She conducted a telephone interview with the recreation department in each town to find out what fee it charged per visit (FEE) and how many visits it had during the most recent summer season (VISITS). In addition, she was able to find each town's population (POP) and median household income (INCOME) in the most recent census. Her data are as follows:

	VISITS	FEE	INCOME	POP
1.	168,590	0	20,600	36,879
2.	179,599	0	33,400	64,520
3.	198,595	0	39,700	104,123
4.	206,662	0	32,600	103,073
5.	170,259	0	24,900	58,386
6.	209,995	0.25	38,000	116,592
7.	172,018	0.25	26,700	49,945
8.	190,802	0.25	20,800	79,789
9.	197,019	0.25	26,300	98,234
10.	186,515	0.50	35,600	71,762
11.	152,679	0.50	38,900	40,178
12.	137,423	0.50	21,700	22,928
13.	158,056	0.50	37,900	39,031
14.	157,424	0.50	35,100	44,685
15.	179,490	0.50	35,700	67,882

	VISITS	FEE	INCOME	POP
16.	164,657	0.75	22,900	69,625
17.	184,428	0.75	38,600	98,408
18.	183,822	0.75	20,500	93,429
19.	174,510	1.00	39,300	98,077
20.	187,820	1.00	25,800	104,068
21.	196,318	1.25	23,800	117,940
22.	166,694	1.50	34,000	59,757
23.	161,716	1.50	29,600	88,305
24.	167,505	2.00	33,800	84,102

Exercise 4: Swimming Pool Data for 24 Towns

    a. Show how the analyst could use these data to predict the gross benefits of opening a public swimming pool in Dryville and allowing free admission.

    b. Predict gross benefits if admission is set at $1.00 and Dryville has marginal excess marginal burden of 0.25. In answering this question, assume that the fees are used to reduce taxes that would otherwise have to be collected from the citizens of Dryville to pay for expenses incurred in operating the pool.

5. (Spreadsheet software required.) Happy Valley is the only available camping area in Rural County. It is owned by the county, which allows free access to campers. Almost all visitors to Happy Valley come from the six towns in the county.

    Rural County is considering leasing Happy Valley for logging, which would require that it be closed to campers. Before approving the lease, the county executive would like to know the magnitude of annual benefits that campers would forgo if Happy Valley were to be closed to the public.

    An analyst for the county has collected data for a travel cost study to estimate the benefits of Happy Valley camping. On five randomly selected days, he recorded the license plates of vehicles parked overnight in the Happy Valley lot. (As the camping season is 100 days, he assumed that this would constitute a 5 percent sample.) With cooperation from the state motor vehicle department, he was able to find the town of residence of the owner of each vehicle. He also observed a sample of vehicles from which he estimated that each vehicle carried 3.2 persons (1.6 adults), on average.

    The following table summarizes the data he collected:

Town	Miles from Happy Valley	Population (thousands)	Number of Vehicles in Sample	Estimated Number of Visitors for Season	Visit Rate (Visits per 1,000 People)
A	22	50.1	146	3,893	77.7
B	34	34.9	85	2,267	65.0
C	48	15.6	22	587	37.6
D	56	89.9	180	4,800	53.4
E	88	98.3	73	1,947	19.8
F	94	60.4	25	666	11.0
Total				14,160	

Excersie 5: Travel Data

In order to translate the distance traveled into an estimate of the cost campers faced in using Happy Valley, the analyst made the following assumptions. First, the average operating cost of vehicles is $0.12 per mile. Second, the average speed on county highways is 50 miles per hour. Third, the opportunity cost to adults of travel time is 40 percent of their wage rate; it is zero for children. Fourth, adult campers have the average county wage rate of $9.25 per hour.

The analyst has asked you to help him use this information to estimate the annual benefits accruing to Happy Valley campers. Specifically, assist with the following tasks:

a. Using the preceding information, calculate the travel cost of a vehicle visit (TC) from each of the towns.

b. For the six observations, regress visit rate (VR) on TC and a constant. If you do not have regression software available, plot the points and fit a line by sight. Find the slope of the fitted line.

c. You know that with the current free admission, the number of camping visits demanded is 14,160. Find additional points on the demand curve by predicting the reduction in the number of campers from each town as price is increased by $5 increments until demand falls to zero. This is done in three steps at each price: First, use the coefficient of TC from the regression to predict a new VR for each town. Second, multiply the predicted VR of each town by its population to get a predicted number of visitors. Third, sum the visitors from each town to get the total number of predicted visits.

d. Estimate the area under the demand curve as the annual benefits to campers.

NOTES

[1] Robin R. Jenkins, *The Economics of Solid Waste Reduction: The Impact of User Fees* (Brookfield, VT: Edward Elgar Publishing Company, 1993).

[2] $\xi \equiv (\partial q/\partial p)(p/q) = \alpha_1 p/q$, where $\partial q/\partial p = \alpha_1$ is the partial derivative of the quantity demanded with respect to price.

[3] Jenkins, *The Economics of Solid Waste Reduction: The Impact of User Fees,* pp. 88–90, 101.

[4] For example, a recent study uses a constant-elasticity model with "tipping fee," "manufacturing income," and "construction employment" as independent variables to estimate an elasticity of disposal demand with respect to tipping fees of –0.11 for communities in the region around Portland, Oregon, over a seven-year period; see James G. Strathman, Anthony M. Rufolo, and Gerard C.S. Mildner, "The Demand for Solid Waste Disposal," *Land Economics,* 71, no. 1 (1995), 57–64.

[5] To demonstrate, note that $\partial q/\partial p = \beta_1 \beta_0 p^{\beta_1-1} x^{\beta_2} = \beta_1 \beta_0 p^{\beta_1} x^{\beta_2}/p = \beta_1 q/p$.

[6] $\xi = (\partial q/\partial p)(p/q) = (\beta_1 q/p)(p/q) = \beta_1$.

[7] The area is calculated by integrating the inverse demand function from q_0 and q_1, that is, as $\int p dq = \int (q/\beta_0)^{1/\beta_1} dq$ with q_0 and q_1 as the limits of integration. This formula assumes that any variables other than price in the original model are held constant.

[8] An easier way to estimate the change in consumer surplus (area *abfg*) is to integrate the demand curve between p_0 and p_1, that is, $\Delta CS = \int q dp = \int \beta_0 p^{\beta_1}$ with p_0 and p_1 as the limits of integration. In fact, $\Delta CS = (p_1 q_1 - p_0 q_0)/(1 + \beta_1)$. Therefore, in this example, $\Delta CS = (.08 \times 2.1 - .05 \times 2.25)/(1 - .15) = \$.0653$, which differs slightly from the number in the text due to rounding errors.

[9] Solve for β_0 and β_1 as follows: $\beta_1 = \ln(q_0/q_1)/\ln(p_0/p_1) = -0.053$, where $\ln$ is the natural logarithm, and $\beta_0 = q_0/(p_0^{\beta_1}) = 1.97$.

[10]For an excellent treatment of the econometric issues raised in this section, see William H. Greene, *Econometric Analysis*, 2nd ed. (New York: Macmillan, 1993). For a recent review of some major econometrics textbooks, see Clive W.J. Granger, "A Review of Some Recent Textbooks of Econometrics," *Journal of Economic Literature*, 32, no. 1 (1994), 115–122.

[11]For an introduction to demand estimation, see William F. Barnett, "Four Steps to Forecast Total Market Demand," *Harvard Business Review*, 88, no. 4 (July–August 1988), 28–38. For examples of demand estimation in different industries, see Thomas F. Hogarty and Kenneth G. Elzinga, "The Demand for Beer," *Review of Economics and Statistics*, 54 (May 1972), 195–198, and Patricia L. Pacy, "Cable Television in a Less Regulated Market," *Journal of Industrial Economics*, 34, no. 1 (September 1985), 81–91.

[12]If the regression equation contains more than one explanatory variable, then the bias in the coefficient of a particular variable depends on the *partial correlation* between that variable and the omitted variable, controlling for all other variables in the regression.

[13]P.B. Goodwin, "A Review of New Demand Elasticities with Special Reference to Short and Long Run Effects of Price Changes," *Journal of Transport Economics and Policy*, 26, no. 2 (May 1992), 155–170 at p. 157.

[14]Ibid., pp. 158–159.

[15]Tae Moon Oum, W.G. Waters, II, and Jong-Say Yong, "Concepts of Price Elasticities of Transport Demand and Recent Empirical Estimates," *Journal of Transport Economics and Policy*, 26, no. 2 (May, 1992), 139–154 at p. 153.

[16]The *net output method* of valuing a life subtracts the value of a person's own consumption from his or her forgone earnings. It measures the benefit or cost the individual contributes to or imposes on the rest of society. The courts' use of this method to measure the loss to survivors of someone's death is somewhat arbitrary but perhaps reasonable. However, it is inappropriate in CBA to use this method to value a life saved. One reason is that the value of the person's own consumption is a benefit to society because the individual is a member of society. Another reason is that it ignores the life cycle of earnings: While a person's net output will be close to zero over an entire lifetime, it will be negative for retired people. For an overview of the net output method, see John J. Lawson, "The Value of Transport Safety," Final Report, Transport Canada Report No. 10569, 1989.

[17]Thomas C. Schelling, "The Life You Save May Be Your Own," in *Economics of the Environment: Selected Readings*, 3rd ed., eds. Robert Dorfman and Nancy S. Dorfman (New York: W.W. Norton, 1993), pp. 388–408 at p. 402.

[18]For a review, see Colin F. Camerer and Howard Kunreuther, "Decision Processes for Low Probability Events: Policy Implications," *Journal of Policy Analysis and Management*, 8, no. 4 (1989), 565–592.

[19]See, for example, Jon P. Nelson, "Airports and Property Values: A Survey of Recent Evidence," *Journal of Transport Economics and Policy*, 14, no. 2 (1981), 37–52.

[20]See T.D. Schroeder, "The Relationship of Local Public Park and Recreation Services to Residential Property Values," *Journal of Leisure Research*, 14, no. 3 (1982), 223–234.

[21]See, for example, Anthony E. Boardman, Ruth Freedman, and Catherine Eckel, "The Price of Government Ownership: A Study of the Domtar Takeover," *Journal of Public Economics*, 31, no. 3 (December 1986), 269–285; John C. Ries, "Windfall Profits and Vertical Relationships: Who Gained in the Japanese Auto Industry from VERs?" *Journal of Industrial Economics*, 61, no. 3 (September 1993) 259–276; Paul H. Malatesta and Rex Thompson, "Government Regulation and Structural Change in the Corporate Acquisitions Market: The Impact of the Williams Act," *Journal of Financial and Quantitative Analysis*, 28, no. 3 (September 1993), 363–379.

[22]There are many ways to estimate what the return would have been in the absence of the event. For a discussion of the different methods, see Stephen J. Brown and Jerold B. Warner, "Measuring Security Price Performance," *Journal of Financial Economics*, 8, no. 3 (1980), 205–258.

[23]Sherwin Rosen developed the theory for estimating hedonic prices; see Sherwin Rosen, "Hedonic Prices and Implicit Markets: Product Differentiation in Pure Competition," *Journal of Political Economy*, 82, no. 1 (1974), 34–55.

[24]The basic idea behind hedonic regression was introduced in Kelvin L. Lancaster, "A New Approach to Consumer Theory," *Journal of Political Economy*, 74, no. 1 (1966), 132–157.

[25]In general, the hedonic price function can be written: $P = p(C_1, C_2, \ldots, C_k, N_1, \ldots, N_m)$, where C_j ($j=1, \ldots, k$) denote k attributes of the house and N_j ($j=1, \ldots, m$) denote m neighborhood characteristics.

[26]Formally, the hedonic price for C_1 given the general hedonic regression model presented in the previous footnote equals $\partial P/\partial C_i = f(C_1, \ldots, C_k, N_1, \ldots, N_m)$.

[27]See footnote 5 for derivation of this equation.

[28]The seminal work on this topic, which actually preceded the formal development of the hedonic pricing method, is Ronald G. Ridker and John A. Henning, "The Determinants of Residential Property Values with Special Reference to Air Pollution," *Review of Economics and Statistics*, 49, no. 2 (1967), 246–257. For a review of studies that have attempted to use the hedonic method to estimate willingness-to-pay for reductions in particulate matter in air, see V. Kerry Smith and Ju-Chin Huang, "Can Markets Value Air Quality? A Meta-Analysis of Hedonic Property Value Models," *Journal of Political Economy*, 103, no. 1 (1995), 209–227. For an application to the value of life, see Paul Portney, "Housing Prices, Health Effects, and Valuing Reductions in Risk of Death," *Journal of Environmental Economics and Management*, 8, no. 1 (1981), 72–78.

[29]This method is often referred to as the Clawson method, or the Knetsch–Clawson method. However, it is now attributed to Harold Hotelling; see Harold Hotelling, "Letter," *An Economic Study of the Monetary Evaluation of Recreation in the National Parks* (Washington, DC: National Park Service, 1949). For some of the earlier descriptions on this method see Marion Clawson, "Methods of Measuring the Demand for and Value of Outdoor Recreation," Reprint No. 10, (Washington, DC: Resources for the Future, 1959); Marion Clawson and Jack L. Knetsch, *Economics of Outdoor Recreation* (Baltimore: Johns Hopkins Press, 1966); and Jack L. Knetsch and Robert K. Davis, "Comparisons of Methods of Recreation Evaluation," in *Water Research*, eds. Allen V. Kneese and Stephen C. Smith (Baltimore: Johns Hopkins Press, 1966), pp. 125–142.

[30]For an interesting and novel application of the TCM, see Charles J. Cicchetti, A. Myrick Freeman III, Robert H. Haveman, and Jack L. Knetsch, "On the Economics of Mass Demonstrations: A Case Study of the November 1969 March on Washington," *American Economic Review*, 61, no. 4 (September 1971), 719–724.

[31]Note that computing the area of the triangle using the formula ($95–$65)(6)/2 = $90 provides a slight overestimate of the consumer surplus, while using the formula ($90–$65)(6)/2 = $75 provides the correct answer. In effect, if we treat the intercept as $90 instead of $95, we obtain the correct answer. The problem arises because the number of visits is a discrete variable, while the equation for the inverse demand function is continuous.

[32]Gardner Brown, Jr. and Robert Mendelsohn, "The Hedonic Travel Cost Model," *Review of Economics and Statistics*, 66, no. 3 (1984), 427–433.

[33]For more detail, see Nancy G. Bockstael, Kenneth E. McConnell and Ivar Strand, "Recreation," in *Measuring the Demand for Environmental Quality*, eds. J.B. Braden and C.D. Kolstad (Amsterdam: Elsevier, 1991), pp. 227–270, and V. Kerry Smith and Yoshiaki Kaoru, "The Hedonic Travel Cost Model: A View From the Trenches," *Land Economics*, 63, no. 2 (1987), 179–192.

[34]Alan Randall, "A Difficulty with the Travel Cost Method," *Land Economics*, 70, no. 1 (1994), 88–96.

[35]See also John R. McKean, Donn M. Johnson, and Richard G. Walsh, "Valuing Time in Travel Cost Demand Analysis: An Empirical Investigation," *Land Economics*, 71, no. 1 (1995), 96–105.

[36]Strictly speaking, Smith and Desvousges estimated the willingness-to-pay to avoid decreasing the water quality from the current boatable levels to levels that would preclude all recreational use.

[37]This method is also referred to as the avoided cost method. For a recent review of the use of this method to measure groundwater values, see Charles Abdalla, "Groundwater Values from Avoidance Cost Studies: Implications for Policy and Future Research," *American Journal of Agricultural Economics*, 76, no. 5 (1994), 1062–1067.

[38]The accuracy of using changes in defensive expenditures on a substitute to measure the benefits of changes in the levels of externalities or public goods depends on how these goods enter the individual's utility function and on the relationship between these goods and the market for the substitute. For more discussion of this issue, see Paul N. Courant and Richard Porter, "Averting Expenditure and the Cost of Pollution," *Journal of Environmental Economics and Management*, 8, no. 4 (1981), 321–329. Also see Winston Harrington and Paul Portney, "Valuing the Benefits of Health and Safety Regulation," *Journal of Urban Economics*, 22, no. 1 (1987), 101–112.

[39]These models are also referred to as qualitative response models. See, for example, G.S. Maddala, *Limited-Dependent and Qualitative Variables in Econometrics* (Cambridge: Cambridge University Press, 1983) and Kenneth Train, *Qualitative Choice Analysis* (Cambridge, Mass: MIT Press, 1986).

[40]See, for example, David A. Hensher and Mark Bradley, "Using Stated Preference Response Data to Enrich Revealed Preference Data," *Marketing Letters*, 4, no. 2 (1993), 139–152

APPENDIX NOTES

[1]This appendix is adapted from David L. Weimer and Aidan R. Vining, *Policy Analysis: Concepts and Practice*, 2nd ed., (Englewood Cliffs, NJ: Prentice Hall, 1992), pp. 392–396.

[2]For clear introductions, see Eric A. Hanushek and John E. Jackson, *Statistical Methods for the Social Sciences* (New York: Academic Press, 1977); and Christopher H. Achen, *Interpreting and Using Regression* (Beverly Hills, CA: Sage Publications, 1982).

[3]Formally, OLS minimizes $\sum_{i=1}^{n} \hat{\epsilon}_i^2$

[4]The OLS estimators are also *efficient*. Here efficiency means that among all estimators whose formulas are linear in the dependent variable, the OLS estimator of a coefficient has the smallest variance. It therefore has the greatest "power" for rejecting the null hypothesis that a coefficient is zero.

[5]The *central limit theorem* tells us that the distribution of the sum of independent random variables approaches the normal distribution as the number in the sum becomes large. The theorem applies for almost any starting distributions with finite variances. If we think of the error term as the sum of all the many factors excluded from our model and, furthermore, we believe that these excluded factors are not systematically related to one another or to the included variables, then the central limit theorem suggests that the distribution of the error terms will be at least approximately normal.

[6]Falsely rejecting the null hypothesis is referred to as Type I error. Failing to reject the null hypothesis when in fact the alternative hypothesis is true is referred to as Type II error. We usually set the probability of Type I error at some low level, such as 5 percent. Holding sample size constant, the lower we set the probability of a Type I error, the greater the probability of a Type II error.

11

CONTINGENT VALUATION: USING SURVEYS TO ELICIT INFORMATION ABOUT COSTS AND BENEFITS

Economists are generally much more comfortable observing individuals' valuations of goods and services through their behavior in markets than eliciting their valuations through survey questionnaires. They prefer to observe purchasing decisions because these decisions directly reveal preferences, whereas surveys elicit statements about preferences. Nevertheless, for some public goods there are simply no, or very poor, market proxies or other means of inferring preferences from observations. In such circumstances, many analysts have concluded that there may be no alternative to asking a sample of people about their valuations.

In CBA, surveys are normally referred to as *contingent valuation* (CV) methods (or sometimes hypothetical valuation surveys) because respondents are not actually required to pay their valuations of the good.[1] In this chapter, we review the uses of CV (including the criticisms of these uses) and discuss the strengths and weaknesses of particular CV methods.

THE ROLE OF CONTINGENT VALUATION

The primary use of CV is to elicit people's willingness-to-pay (WTP) for changes in quantities of goods. A wide range of goods including water quality at recreation sites, trees near subdivisions, goose hunting, and outdoor recreation has been valued with CV surveys.[2] Such agencies as the National Park Service and the U.S Bureau of Reclamation commonly use CV surveys to value recreation and wildlife opportunities. Yet, CV surveys have also been used to value more complex and abstract "goods," such as reductions in hazardous wastes, spotted owl habitat, and lives saved.[3] Valuing the use or potential use of goods with CV is relatively uncontroversial. Valuing nonuse with CV is highly controversial, both for the conceptual reasons discussed in Chapter 8 and the additional survey problems discussed later in this chapter.

In spite of the controversy, the use of CV as a method for estimating costs and benefits (especially benefits) is growing rapidly. Indeed, recently the federal courts have held that surveys of citizens' valuations have "rebuttable presumption" status in cases relating to CBA.[4]

OVERVIEW OF CONTINGENT VALUATION METHODS

In this section, we describe the six major CV methods. As researchers are constantly adapting and combining these methods, the following discussion should be read as broadly illustrative rather than definitive.

The general approach of all the methods is as follows. First, a sample of respondents from the population with standing is asked questions about their valuations of some good. Second, their responses provide information that enables analysts to estimate the respondents' willingness-to-pay (WTP) for the good. Third, these WTP amounts are extrapolated to the entire population. If the respondents are a random sample of the population, then their average WTP would simply be scaled up to reflect their proportion in the population.

As CV surveys are expensive to conduct, analysts may wish to extrapolate the results of existing surveys to different populations. The characteristics of these populations usually do not match those of the population that was previously sampled. For example, the populations may differ in terms of income, access to alternative goods, or other factors that may be relevant to their demands for the good. Reasonable extrapolation requires that these differences be controlled for statistically.[5] Therefore, analysts increase the chances that their CV surveys will have use beyond their own CBAs by collecting and reporting information about the characteristics of their samples, including WTP amounts for subsets of the sample, even when such information is unnecessary for their own studies.

Open-Ended Willingness-to-Pay Method

The first and earliest method to be used is the *open-ended willingness-to-pay question* approach. Here respondents are simply asked to state their maximum WTP for the good that is being valued.[6] The question might be formulated as follows: "What is the most that you would be prepared to pay in additional federal income taxes to guarantee that the Wildwood wilderness area will remain closed to development?" This method had dropped out of favor in CBA because analysts feared "unrealistic" responses unless respondents were given some initial "guidance" on valuations. As evidence has mounted, however, that such "guidance" is subject to *starting point bias*, which can bias respondents' answers, open-ended questions have made a comeback. Open-ended questions are now widely used in conjunction with other CV methods, as they are not prone to starting point bias. Thus, open-ended questions provide a check on the extent of starting point bias introduced by other methods.

Closed-Ended Iterative Bidding Method

The second method is the *closed-ended iterative bidding* approach. Respondents are asked whether they would pay a specified amount for the good that has been described. If respondents answer affirmatively, then the amount is incrementally increased. The procedure continues until the respondent expresses unwillingness to pay the amount specified. Similarly, if respondents answer negatively to the initial amount specified, the interviewer lowers the amount by increments until the respondent expresses a WTP.[7]

The initial question for determining WTP typically starts with something like the following: "Now suppose the costs to clean the Kristiansand Fjord were divided on [sic] all taxpayers in the whole of Norway by an extra tax in 1986. If this extra tax was 200 kronor for an average taxpayer, would you then be willing to support the proposal?"[8] In this CV survey the interviewer set the initial price at 200 kronor. If a respondent indicates a willingness to pay this initial price, then the interviewer raises the price by 200 kronor and asks the question again. The interviewer keeps going until the respondent gives a negative answer. Similarly, if the initial response is negative, then the interviewer incrementally drops the price by 200 kronor until the respondent gives a positive response. Although iterative bidding was the most common method in use until very recently, there is considerable evidence that its results are highly sensitive to the initially presented, or starting, value.

Contingent Ranking Method

The third method is the *contingent ranking*, or *ranked choice*, method. Here respondents are asked to rank order specific feasible combinations of quantities of the good and monetary payments. For example, respondents choose on a continuum between a low level of water quality at a low tax-price and a high level of water quality at a high tax-price. The combinations are ranked from most preferred to least preferred.[9] The rankings are then statistically aggregated and used to estimate WTP. Contingent ranking implies an ordinal ranking procedure in contrast to the iterative bidding procedure that requires cardinal evaluation. Typically tasks that require only ordinal information processing—that is, a ranking rather than a precise specification of value—are considerably easier for respondents to perform.[10] This is a valuable attribute in the CV context where information processing complexity is often high. Of course, this method involves a trade-off between respondent understanding and the amount of information gained.

Dichotomous-Choice Method

The fourth method is the *dichotomous-choice*, or *referendum*, method.[11] In this approach, a sample of individuals receives randomly assigned prices for the good in question. Each respondent receives one randomly drawn price. Respondents are then asked to state whether they would be willing to pay for a specific outcome (e.g., closing the Wildwood wilderness area to development) at the offered price ("yes" means willing to pay and "no" means not willing to pay); in other words, they are made a "take it or leave it" offer. There is no iteration in this process. The dollar amounts that are presented to respondents vary over a range selected by the analyst. Accept/reject respondent probabilities can then be calculated for each dollar amount offered.[12]

Figure 11.1 shows the distribution of responses to dollar offers in the form of a histogram. Specific dollar offer amounts are shown on the horizontal axis ranging from the lowest dollar price offered ($X = \$0$) to the highest price offered ($X = \$100$) in $5 increments. The vertical axis measures the percentage of respondents who answer "yes" to the amount offered them. In this example, almost all of the respondents who are offered the specified outcome at $X = \$0$, state they would accept it. About 75 percent of respondents who are offered the outcome for $30 indicate that they would accept it at this price. We can interpret the responses in terms of the probability that a randomly drawn member of the sample of respondents is willing to pay a specific amount. For example, the probability a randomly drawn respondent would pay at least $30 for the specified outcome is about 0.75.

A curve can be fitted to the histogram to estimate the probability a randomly drawn respondent is willing to pay X or less. This function is downward sloping, reflecting the fact that typically the probability a randomly drawn respondent will say

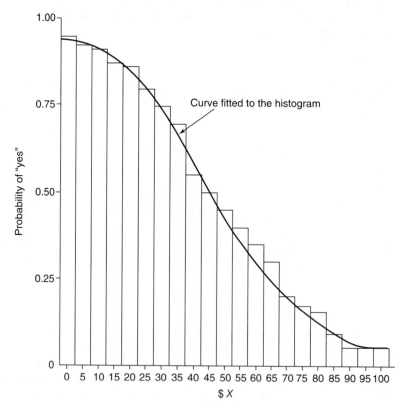

Figure 11.1 Histogram of Dichotomous Choice Responses

"yes" decreases as X increases. One minus this probability can be interpreted as the *cumulative distribution function* for the maximum amount that a respondent would pay.

The fitted curve in Figure 11.1 may be viewed as the demand curve of a randomly drawn (i.e., average) member of the sample, while the histogram may be viewed as a rough approximation of this demand curve. The difference between the demand curve in Figure 11.1 and the more standard demand curve is that instead of the curve indicating the quantity of a good the individual would be willing to purchase at each price, the curve indicates the probability that the individual would be willing to pay for the specified outcome at each price.[13] As in the case of a standard demand curve, the area under the curve in Figure 11.1 provides an estimate of the individual's willingness-to-pay.

As long as the values of X are evenly spread, the histogram can be readily used to obtain a rough estimate of the average individual's willingness to pay by applying a simple formula:

$$\text{WTP} = v \sum_{k=0}^{N} [\text{probability of acceptance at price } kv]$$

where v is the interval between prices (i.e., the width of the individual bars in the histogram) and N is the number of values of X (i.e., the number of bars). In other words, the area covered by the bars, the approximate WTP for an average member of the sample, can be computed by simply summing the heights of the bars and multiplying by the bar width.

Better estimates than those obtained by this method can usually be made by estimating a statistical model for predicting the probability that an individual with specific characteristics will accept an offer of size kv. The estimated model, usually a logistic regression, allows the analyst to sketch the relationship between offer price and the probability of acceptance for individuals with specific characteristics. The area under this curve estimates the mean willingness-to-pay for these individuals.[14] It can be estimated through numerical methods.[15] The statistical model can be used to estimate a probability-of-acceptance curve for each identified group within the sample. It is, therefore, possible to estimate a WTP for an average member of each of these groups as the area under each group's probability-of-acceptance curve. *To find the aggregate WTP for the entire population, multiply the mean for each group by the size of that group in the population with standing and sum across groups.*[16]

Because this method only tells one whether a given respondent's valuation is greater or less than the offered amount, sample sizes need to be large in order to achieve reasonable levels of precision. For small samples, the true value of WTP may be considerably different from the observed value of WTP. One recent estimate is that approximately 66 percent more observations are needed with this method.[17] On the other hand, "take it or leave it" questions are even easier than ranking questions for respondents to answer and they are the closest approximation to market-like transactions.

Some analysts have recently experimented with *double dichotomous-choice* questions to reduce the need for large samples. In this version of the method, depending on the answer to the first offer, a second offer is made that is either double (if yes) or half (if no) the first offer. This provides considerably more information than the standard single-offer version without, it has been argued, adding serious bias.[18] Moreover, this version retains most of the information processing simplicity of "take it or leave it."

Payment Card with Comparative Tax Prices

The fifth method is the *payment card with comparative tax prices*. After describing the good to be valued, respondents are presented a card that shows tax-prices for a range of other publicly provided goods, such as education or national parks. These tax-prices are the prices faced by individuals in the same tax bracket as the respondent. For example, the card might show the specific dollar amount—say $9—which an individual with an income of $30,000 pays per annum for national parks. Respondents are then asked to express their WTP for the good in question, usually with an open-ended question. The idea is that information on other goods provides some "grounding" and stimulus to clear thinking without providing any particular starting point for valuation of the good that is under investigation. Any anchoring that does occur is likely to be related to the particular tax-prices that are presented, encouraging respondents to think realistically about their WTP.

Payment Card with a Range of Prices for the Good

The sixth method is the *payment card with a range of prices for the good*. In this use of the payment card, the interviewer explains a particular, specified change in the good in question and provides a card with a range of dollar values (for example, $0, $5, $10, $15, $20, $25, $50, $75, $100, $150, $200, $250, $300, $350, $400, $450, $500, $550, $600, $750, or more). The respondent is then asked to select the maximum value he or she is willing to pay for the change. This method provides some context on potential relevant prices and their range for respondents while avoiding an explicit starting value. Another advantage of this method is that it can easily be structured to reduce bias resulting from the use of interviews as responses can be placed in an envelope anonymously.

   This method was used in the Nestucca oil spill CV survey. Respondents were asked: "[What is] the most your household would be willing to pay in total in higher prices for programs that prevent all oil spills, like those described above, in the Pacific Northwest over the next five years?" Respondents were then given a payment card that contained dollar figures ranging from $0 to over $5,000 and asked to circle their valuation. Respondents were asked to explain their answers and also to allocate their answers to various spill categories ranging from "very small" to "large."[19]

   Either payment card method requires less complex information processing than open-ended or iterative bidding, but more than rank ordering or dichotomous-choice methods. While neither payment card method presents a particular dollar starting value, it is not clear that they avoid all problems of the broader anchoring bias (to be discussed later) because respondents are given a range of values to structure their thinking. It is reasonable to assume, however, that the payment card with comparative tax-prices is less prone to anchoring problems because prices for the good in question are not shown.

PAYMENT VEHICLE

Almost all CV exercises specify a *payment vehicle*, or bid vehicle, which describes how the costs of providing the good will be paid. (This should not be confused with the payment card method; all the methods described previously require a payment vehicle.) Payment vehicles include taxes paid into a fund specifically earmarked for the good, increased utility bills, higher income or sales taxes, and higher product prices. Specifying a payment vehicle helps ensure that respondents perceive the questions as "real." In order to increase the realism of CV surveys, researchers generally try to specify a payment vehicle that is as close as possible to the actual one that would be used were supply of the good to proceed.

There has been considerable debate in the CV literature as to whether differences in the WTP of respondents due to differences in payment vehicles should be treated as a bias. Kenneth Arrow and others argue that respondents are being asked to value all elements of a project, which include the method of payment; therefore, respondent preferences on payment methods are not biased.[20] Other analysts argue that if specific payment vehicles, such as taxes, introduce "protest" valuations, then such outliers should be excluded from the estimation of aggregate WTP. Currently, it is standard practice to eliminate protest outliers from estimation of WTP. Protest bidders can often be screened out by their answers to specific questions designed to identify them.

ALTERNATIVE CONTACT PROCEDURES: IN-PERSON, PHONE, MAIL

There are three major procedures for conducting surveys: in-person interviews, telephone interviews, and mail questionnaires. Each has strengths and weaknesses, and each raises different methodological issues. None of the three procedures is unequivocally superior to the others.

For most purposes, telephone interviews appear to be as valid as mail questionnaires and in-person interviews. The main disadvantage of telephone interviews in the CV context stems from the fact that visual aids cannot be included (although, of course, they can be mailed out in advance).[21] This is a disadvantage because, as we will see, considerable effort is usually put into making complex issues both real and understandable. Photographs, drawings, and maps are often useful for this purpose.

Mail questionnaires may be preferable in contexts in which respondents feel social pressure to overstate or understate WTP because they are usually more anonymous than either telephone or in-person interviews. On the other hand, mail questionnaires typically have substantially lower response rates than the other procedures. Another advantage of both telephone and mail methods is that they are considerably cheaper than in-person interviewing.

CRITICISMS OF CV

Some critics argue that CV has such serious weaknesses that it should only be used as a last resort. Other critics contend that it is so seriously flawed when used to value either complex goods or nonuse impacts that it should not be used at all for these purposes.[22] It has been pointed out that the summation of average valuations over a broad range of projects to improve the environment would *exhaust* the budget of average individuals.[23] These difficulties are discussed at length later in this chapter. In addi-

tion, CV faces the normal problems associated with all surveys: sampling, nonresponse, and interviewer biases. We deal with these issues relatively briefly because
they are common problems in any kind of survey studies.

In the remainder of this chapter, we review general issues relating to surveys,
and then discuss specific problems relevant to CV in depth. We then review the empirical evidence on the accuracy of contingent valuation methods, including a brief
review of the advantages and disadvantages of the different methods. Finally, we present some heuristic checklists for analysts preparing or reviewing CV instruments.

GENERAL SURVEY ISSUES

The three potential biases of surveys that are most relevant to CV are sample bias,
nonresponse bias, and interviewer bias. Here we simply overview aspects of these
biases that are particularly relevant to CV.

Sample Bias

In almost all survey situations, questions can only be asked of a small number of people relative to the target population. The topic of sample design is concerned with how
to select the sample to include in the survey from among the target population.[24] In
almost all cases, the sample is selected by a probability mechanism, which produces
a *random sample*. In a random sample, each individual has a known probability of
being drawn from the population. *Simple random samples* give each individual in the
target population the same probability of being sampled.

If a given sample is appropriately selected and administered, then sample biases can be avoided. Advances in probability sampling techniques have been such that
findings based on samples of approximately a thousand people can be representative
of the entire population of the United States. However, approximately the same sample size may also be necessary for much smaller populations. Additionally, there is
considerable evidence that the observed distributions of WTP in CV are highly
skewed toward extreme values. For this reason, CV samples should be larger than
samples drawn for many other purposes to obtain reliable estimates of population
means. This is especially true for the dichotomous-choice method.

For CV purposes, *the relevant target population is usually all individuals with
standing who are affected by the project*. Unfortunately, this heuristic begs the question of who is "affected." For many projects, this is apparent. But often it is not, especially in addressing environmental issues. In some contexts there is congruence
between payers and those who benefit. In practice, "the greater the divergence
between those who pay and those who benefit, the more problematic it becomes to
choose the correct population."[25]

There are several major issues involved in assessing who is affected. First, all
those "users" directly affected by the project should be included. The term *users* is in
quotes because we mean it in a specific way. Those who would directly utilize the
good in question are, of course, users. But so too are individuals who suffer direct neg-

ative impacts that they would pay to avoid. For example, nearby residents of a duck hunting reserve who dislike the noise are as much users as the duck hunters. Potential users should also be included. As discussed in Chapter 7, in situations involving uncertainty, the option price that an individual would be willing to pay for a good may differ from his or her expected surplus. So even people who never actually consume the good may value it.

Second, it is important for "users" to understand whether they are being asked to estimate WTP just for themselves or as a representative for their whole household. This distinction is important in extrapolating from the sample to the target population.

Third, an explicit decision should be made concerning the inclusion of nonuse benefits. As discussed in Chapter 8, either users or nonusers may derive existence value from a project. Conceptually, existence value should be included as a component of benefits. For environmental goods, CV surveys that either sample nonusers or estimate existence values of users typically yield much higher aggregate WTP estimates than those that include only use benefits. However, there is considerable disagreement on the validity of using CV surveys to estimate nonuse benefits. The paramount question is: Can existence value be accurately estimated? The short answer, as we discuss later in the chapter, is probably no. As CV methods improve, however, this answer may change.

Fourth, the geographic *spread* or *reach* of the sample should be wide enough to capture all affected individuals. There is increasing recognition that decisions concerning the geographic definition of the relevant "market" can drive the outcomes of many CBAs, especially if nonusers are included.[26]

■ **EXHIBIT 11.1**

In a recent court case, the plaintiffs conducted a CV survey to estimate the natural resource damage caused by a mine. They surveyed residents of both the county (Eagle County) and the state (Colorado) in which the mine was located. Based on their surveys, they estimated past damages were $50.8 million and future expected damages would be between $15 and $45 million. The defendants sampled a much smaller group within Eagle County that they believed had been directly affected by pollution from the mine; they assumed that residents in the rest of Colorado did not bear costs from the mine. Although the per unit values of both sides were similar (for example, on the value of a day's fishing), the defendants' estimate of total past and future expected damage was approximately $240,000, less than 1 percent of the plaintiffs' estimate. "The discrepancies in these respective aggregate estimates arise from the plaintiff's assumption that. . . there would be a much larger number of people experiencing gains with the restoration." (p. 605).

Source: Raymond J. Kopp and V. Kerry Smith, "Benefit Estimation Goes to Court: The Case of Natural Resource Damage Assessments," *Journal of Policy Analysis and Management*, 8, no. 4 (1989), 593–612.

An important sampling question relates to the exclusion of responses. It has been suggested that three categories of respondents should be excluded in estimating WTP: (1) respondents who reject the whole notion of placing a value on the good in question, or of paying for the good in a certain way (this has already been discussed);

(2) respondents who refuse to take the exercise seriously; and (3) respondents who clearly demonstrate that they are incapable of understanding the survey.[27] In practice all three types of respondents are assumed to provide either zero valuations or extremely high valuations. Sometimes such respondents can be directly identified by their answers to specific questions intended to screen them from the sample. Respondents who provide extreme values are known as *outliers*. Outliers are normally handled in CV in one of two ways. First, valuations that are above some prespecified threshold or that are above a specified percentage of the respondent's income are simply eliminated. Second, high valuations are reduced to some maximum plausible amount.[28]

Nonresponse Bias

An appropriate sampling design can usually eliminate most sample bias. Yet, bias can still remain if some individuals do not respond to the survey. Nonresponse bias is a serious problem in almost all survey research. Nonresponse problems have grown over the last twenty years as the public has been asked to give time to more surveys and has become suspicious (sometimes with good reason) of the motives of many "survey researchers." If nonresponse is purely random, then it can be dealt with by increasing the sample size. But there is evidence that nonresponse is usually not random.[29]

There are two major types of nonresponse problems: refusal to respond and unavailability to respond. In CV contexts, the major methods of dealing with refusal to respond are to highlight the legitimacy of the exercise (e.g., by stressing government or university affiliations) or to offer various response incentives. Where unavailability biases the sample, researchers typically account for underrepresentation and overrepresentation in the sample when extrapolating to the target population.[30]

Interviewer Bias

To minimize interviewer bias, it is important to ensure that CV respondents do not perceive that any particular answer is preferred by the interviewer. Evidence suggests that when subjects are in novel situations, they are highly prone to both intended and unintended cues, especially when respondents perceive that the stakes in the interview are small relative to the importance of getting on well with the interviewer.[31] Either in-person or telephone interviewing in the CV context requires considerable training, often up to two days. It is also usually desirable to monitor interviews through random reinterviewing. In the case of telephone interviews, extension lines permit silent monitoring of interviews while they are in progress.

CONTINGENT VALUATION PROBLEMS

Surveying opinions is not an exact science. CV surveys are even less exact!

Specific CV survey difficulties stem from several sources. First, CV inevitably raises questions that are more novel and complex than those raised in other survey situations. This poses problems of hypotheticality (we use this as a catchall word to cover all problems of understanding, meaning, context, and familiarity). Hypotheticality appears to be particularly severe when respondents have not, and will not, "consume" the good in some way. Frequently, hypotheticality and nonuse occur simultaneously in CV surveys. Second, CV raises questions of neutrality. Third, for certain methods, judgmental biases may arise in response to certain kinds of questions (including whether the question is framed as willingness-to-pay or as willingness-to-accept). Not all these problems necessarily create biases (i.e., a systematic tendency to overvalue or undervalue the goods in question), but all of them do raise questions about the validity and reliability of CV as a procedure. Some specific CV methods appear to be more prone to biases than others. Fourth, CV specifically asks about WTP, raising the potential for biases related to strategic behavior (misstatements intended to influence some outcome) and the specified payment vehicle.

Hypotheticality, Meaning, and Context Problems

A major concern in CV design is whether respondents are truly able to understand and contextualize the questions they are being asked and, consequently, whether they can accurately value the good in question. Issues relating to the valuation of the supply of many publicly provided goods are complex and highly contextual. CV questions can be contrasted to many other types of questions for which meaning is not an issue. (For example, "who do you intend to vote for in the next election?")

Questions of hypotheticality and meaning can be thought of as problems of specifying exactly what is the good or commodity in question. Understanding the good or the project that produces it is difficult for respondents because they often are not familiar with either. Attitudes (as expressed in the CV survey) are unlikely to correspond to the behavior that would occur if the project were actually implemented when respondents are presented with questions about goods or projects that they really do not understand.[32] When a project (or the good itself) has multiple attributes, these all need to be explained to respondents: "Unless [an attribute is] specified explicitly (and comprehensively), evaluators must guess its value and, hence, what the offer really means. If they guess wrong, then they risk misrepresenting their values."[33]

This problem, however, has to be seen in context. Individuals also differentially value attributes of market goods: Some individuals may value a mountain bike mostly for prestige reasons and others for transportation purposes. The evidence also suggests that people find it difficult to value the attributes of new and unfamiliar products in market contexts.[34]

Additional problems arise in CV if the perceptions of the good by respondents are not independent of the quality or quantity of the information provided. Given that the quantity and quality of information that can be provided when describing complex goods are virtually unlimited, there is no clear standard. Recently, several commentators have emphasized that there is hardly any evidence that hypotheticality per se introduces bias into CV.[35] But in the presence of hypotheticality certain kinds of bias may be more likely.

The importance of hypotheticality varies enormously across different CBA contexts. But CV is likely to be most useful in contexts in which goods are difficult to define, such as projects involving environmental impacts. When it is difficult to specify potential physical impacts, it is also likely to be difficult for respondents to understand what these impacts mean.

Hypotheticality and lack of realism can be reduced in a number of ways. *Clearly specifying the project and the impacts of increments of goods increases the likelihood of correspondence between attitudes and behavior; so too does providing explicit detail about the payment vehicle.* Visual aids such as photographs, maps, and diagrams often assist in understanding. One important class of visual aids useful in reducing hypotheticality is known as *quality ladders*. An example of a quality ladder is described in Exhibit 11.2. Quality ladders help respondents understand both what the status quo is in terms of quality, and what particular increments of quality mean.

■ **EXHIBIT 11.2**

A "water quality ladder" has been used in several CBAs to help respondents understand how differing levels of toxins, dissolved solids, water clarity, and other factors affect water quality. In their CBA of water quality improvements to the Monongahela River, V. Kerry Smith and William Desvousges included a picture of a ladder with a 0-to-10 scale and the following interviewer instructions:

(*Interviewer: Read the following.*) Generally the better the water quality the better suited the water is for recreation activities and the more likely people will take part in outdoor recreation activities on or near the water. Here is a picture of a ladder that shows various levels of water quality. (*Interviewer: Give respondent water quality ladder.*)

The top of the ladder stands for the best possible quality of water. The bottom of the ladder stands for the worst possible water quality. On the ladder you can see the different levels of the quality of the water. For example: (*Interviewer: Point to each level—E, D, C, B, A—as you read the statements that follow*).

Level E (*Interviewer: Point.*) is so polluted that it has oil, raw sewage, and other things like trash in it; it has no plant or animal life and smells bad.

Water at level D is okay for boating but not fishing or swimming.

Level C shows where the water is clean enough so that gamefish like bass can live in it.

Level B shows where the water is clean enough so that people can swim in it safely.

And at level A, the quality of the water is so good that it would be possible to drink directly from it if you wanted to.

(*Interviewer: Now ask the respondent to use the ladder to rate the water quality in the Monongahela River on a scale of 0 to 10 and to indicate whether the ranking was for a particular site, and if so, to name it.*)

Source: V. Kerry Smith and William H. Desvousges, *Measuring Water Quality Benefits* (Boston, MA: Kluwer Academic, 1986), p. 87.

Baruch Fischhoff and Lita Furey have suggested a checklist for evaluating CV instruments in terms of the likelihood that respondents will understand the questions they are being asked.[36] It requires the analyst to assess the comprehensiveness of information with respect to the good, the specification of the payment vehicle, and the social context. In assessing the adequacy of information on the good and value measures, they stress the need to provide information on both substantive and formal components. The substantive aspect of the good deals with why someone might value it (basically its attributes), while the formal aspect of the good concerns how much they value it (once they understand its attributes).

In practice, *the only effective way to minimize hypotheticality and meaning problems in CV surveys is to devote extensive effort to developing detailed, clear, informative, and highly contextual materials and to pretest these materials extensively on typical respondents.*

Neutrality

While the previous section indicated that lack of clear meaning does not necessarily pose a bias problem, lack of neutrality is certain to do so. As CBA deals with increasingly controversial and complex topics, the neutrality of the CV questionnaire becomes an increasingly important issue. Neutrality has come to the fore as litigants in (especially environmental) court cases have conducted their own CV surveys.

Meaning and neutrality issues often intersect in ways that are extremely difficult to disentangle. For example, in a recent study, Daniel Hagen, James Vincent, and Patrick Welle surveyed 1,000 U.S. households by mail concerning the value of preserving the spotted owl.[37] Of the total, 409 questionnaires were returned. Some of the information that respondents were given included the following: " . . . a scientific committee concluded that logging should be banned on some forest lands to prevent the extinction of the Northern Spotted Owl . . . "and "a second group of independent scientists examined this study and agreed with these conclusions." The survey also included the comment that: "the well-being of the northern spotted owl reflects the well-being of the entire old-growth forest eco-system" (p. 18).

In a review of spotted owl CV studies in general, and the Hagen et al. study in particular, William McKillop criticized this framing of the issue. He argues that the survey did not include many relevant facts and that, specifically, respondents should have been told the following:[38]

- the "committee of scientists" focused almost exclusively on old-growth habitat for spotted owls and largely ignored the fact that many are found in second-growth timber stands;

- logging was already prohibited on considerable areas of old-growth timberland, and these acres were likely to increase in the course of normal national forest planning;

- the *Endangered Species Act* is an unusually severe measure that gives the United States Fish and Wildlife Service extensive powers to declare not only a species, but also subspecies and localized populations of plants and animals that may not be physically distinguishable from other members of the species, as endangered;

- the Act does not provide scientific standards for defining a species or subspecies or a localized population, and does not require that scientific methods be used to determine if subspecies are genetically different from each other;

- respondents were not informed that Hagen et al. estimated the habitat reservation program would cost U.S. citizens between $32.5 billion and $78.3 billion;

- respondents were not made aware of the severity of the economic impacts that were estimated at the time of the survey, such as a reduction in timber harvest equivalent to the amount of lumber needed to build 750,000 homes, and an employment loss of as many as 93,000 jobs if timber harvesting was banned in critical habitat areas on both public and private land; and

- respondents were not told that decreased timber output in the Western United States would have adverse national and global environmental effects as a result of the use of non-wood substitutes or increased harvesting in areas (such as tropical forests) with more fragile ecosystems.

In sum, McKillop argues that the spotted owl issue was not presented accurately or neutrally to respondents. He further argues that this issue is simply too complicated to be addressed by CV surveys.

There are no simple answers to the neutrality problem. But an inevitable conclusion is that one has to be especially cautious in interpreting the results of CV surveys that have been prepared by either parties to litigation or advocacy groups. At a practical level, *neutrality can best be ensured by pretesting the survey instrument with substantive experts who have "no axe to grind" in terms of the specific project that is being considered.* If neutral experts cannot be found, then pretesting with opposing advocates is desirable.

Decision Making and Judgment Biases

While it is reasonable to assume that individuals can make rational judgments about their valuations of goods in most market situations, evidence suggests that in certain circumstances they may not be able to do so. This is even more likely to occur in the context of CV surveys, because judgment rather than decision making is involved and because there are not opportunities to learn from "mistakes" (we discuss the evidence on this issue later in the chapter).[39] More formally, in such circumstances, there is a tendency for individuals to violate the assumptions of utility maximization. In the context of functioning markets, violation of these assumptions causes *decision-making biases* that can result in irrational purchases (or lack of purchases). These decision-making errors can be thought of as a type of market failure.[40] In the context of CV, the term *judgment bias* rather than decision-making bias is applicable because the respondent is not actually purchasing the good in question.

Both decision-making and judgment biases appear to be most serious for activities or projects that would generate small changes in the probabilities of (already) low-probability events that have "catastrophic" costs if they occur (for example, activities that might cause a marginal change in the probability of a nuclear power plant accident).[41] Fortunately, researchers and analysts rarely have to rely solely on CV estimates in such contexts. For example, they can use value-of-life estimates derived from other methods in which these biases are less endemic (see Chapter 12).

Some of the major judgmental biases to which individuals are particularly prone include: (1) availability bias, whereby individuals estimate the probabilities of events by the ease with which occurrences can be recalled—more salient instances, such as those covered by the media, are more likely to be recalled; (2) representativeness or conjunction bias, whereby individuals judge the probabilities of events on the basis of their plausibility—people perceive the probability of an event as being higher as more detail is added, even though the detail is irrelevant; (3) optimism bias, whereby people believe that they can beat the objective odds; (4) anchoring bias, whereby individuals do not fully update their probability assessments as new information becomes available; (5) hindsight bias, whereby individuals believe, after an event occurs, that it was more predictable than it actually was; (6) status quo bias, whereby individuals stick with the status quo even when it is inexpensive to experiment or when the potential benefits from changing are large, and (7) probability assessment biases, whereby people tend to overestimate small probabilities and underestimate large probabilities.[42]

Many of these violations of the expected utility hypothesis can be explained by the fact that, when dealing with complex information, people tend to use simplifying (nonutility-maximizing) heuristics or "rules of thumb." Essentially, people "frame" problems consistently, but the framing does not correspond to maximization of expected utility.

One conceptual framework for explaining violations of the expected utility hypothesis is *prospect theory*.[43] Prospect theory, which is particularly relevant to CV issues, suggests that individuals deviate from expected utility maximization in the following ways: They value gains and losses from a reference point rather than valuing net wealth. Moreover, people are risk averse toward gains and risk seeking toward losses (known as *loss aversion*). As a result, a loss and a gain of the same size would leave people worse off. This may stem from an *endowment effect*, whereby individuals have a greater psychological attachment to things they currently possess.[44]

Several of these effects can be summarized in a prospect theory value function, which is illustrated in Figure 11.2. In this figure, the vertical axis measures value and the horizontal axis measures losses and gains. The figure shows three things. First, people start from a reference point from which changes are measured as losses or gains. Second, individuals are risk averse with respect to potential gains (i.e., they prefer a smaller certain gain over a larger probable gain, when the expected values of the two alternatives are the same). Individuals are also risk seeking with respect to potential losses (i.e., they prefer a larger probable loss to a smaller certain loss, when the expected values of the two alternatives are the same). In Figure 11.2 this is represented by the concave gain function and the convex loss function. Third, losses loom larger than gains of equal size. This is represented in the figure as the loss function being steeper for losses than for gains from the reference point.

The biases suggested by prospect theory are particularly relevant to CV for a number of reasons. Anchoring via reference points are always present. Even if open-ended questions are used to eliminate starting point bias, payment vehicles and other descriptive detail may introduce anchoring indirectly. Furthermore, detailed descrip-

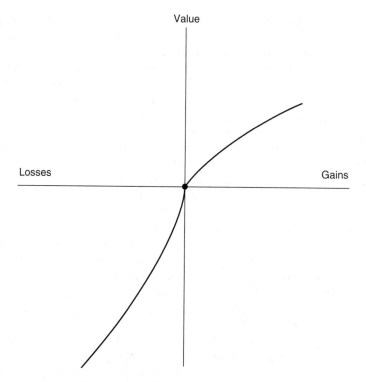

Figure 11.2 A "Loss Aversion" Value Function

Source: Daniel Kahneman and Amas Tversky, "Prospect Theory: An Analysis of Decision Under Risk," *Econometrica*, 47, no. 2 (1979) 263–291, Figure 3, p. 279.

tions may evoke availability bias. Finally, as we discuss later, CV questions can sometimes be plausibly framed as either involving gains or losses.

Empirical research suggests that the most serious judgment problems actually found in CV results relate to *noncommitment bias*, *order effects* (sometimes described as sequencing effects), *embedding effects* (sometimes described as whole/part effects or inclusiveness effects), and *starting point bias*.

Noncommitment bias.[45]   It is well recognized in the marketing literature that respondents to surveys tend to overstate their willingness to purchase a product that is described to them.[46] This does not appear to be a strategic response (an issue discussed later), but rather can be thought of as either a form of optimism bias or a form of anchoring bias (e.g., "this product must be valuable because they are asking me about it and describing it in such detail") in a context in which potential consumers do not engage in any learning. It is likely to be quite unconscious. The bias can flourish, of course, because the respondent does not actually have to commit money.

One recent set of experiments has attempted to test for noncommitment bias. The researchers conclude that "hypothetical WTP is consistently and significantly higher than the WTP that reflects real economic commitments."[47]

It is very difficult to test for noncommitment bias when dealing with nonuse values. One indirect way of testing for the bias is to introduce elements to the survey that encourage respondents to think more carefully about their income and their budget constraints. Michael Kemp and Christopher Maxwell have developed a "top-down disaggregation method" to do just this.[48] Top-down disaggregation attempts to mitigate noncommitment bias by raising awareness of budget constraints. After asking respondents to state initially their total WTP, they were questioned specifically about comparative valuations. For example, after respondents were asked about their WTP to avoid a specified oil spill, they were then asked about their valuations of environmental protection versus reduction in crime, homelessness, and other social problems. They were also asked about their valuations for different kinds of environmental protection (wilderness areas versus groundwater quality, rainforest protection, and other environmental goals). At the next level, they were asked to evaluate various kinds of wilderness area protection (reduction in harm from human-caused problems versus natural degradation and other destructive processes). At the end of this top-down disaggregation process, respondents were again asked their WTP. The result was WTP values several hundred times smaller than the WTP values from the initial open-ended questions.

Order effects.   George Tolley and Alan Randall found that survey respondents' estimates of the value of improved visibility in the Grand Canyon were greatly affected by the order in which the issue was raised.[49] Other studies have also found important order effects. Consider, for example, a study that asked some respondents to value preserving seals and then whales, while others were asked to value preserving whales and then seals. Seal values were considerably lower when the seal question was asked after the whale question.[50]

These findings could be explainable in terms of either an income effect, a substitution effect, or a combination of both. The rationale for an income effect is as follows: If someone has expressed a positive WTP to pay for the first good in a sequence of goods, then that person has less income to spend on the second good in the sequence. Critics of CV, however, have observed that the steep declines in WTP as a good moves down in order cannot be fully explained by income effects since these should be relatively small.[51]

Substitution effects, as for example between seals and whales, could be quite large and consequently they can be important in CBA, especially in terms of assessing the aggregate impacts of projects. If people engage in extensive substitution, then the net aggregate benefits from a project may be smaller than predicted. For example, if a resident of Chicago agrees to contribute to a project that cleans the air in Chicago and is then offered a project that preserves visibility in the Grand Canyon, the value of the Grand Canyon project may be decreased because of the substitution effect.

The issue of whether substitution effects could account for much of the order inconsistency in CV surveys of nonuse values is still undecided.[52] Critics argue that the phenomenon is explained neither by income nor by substitution effects, but it instead demonstrates that respondents cannot really understand these kinds of questions. Hence, they inevitably engage in judgment heuristics that usually cause them to overstate valuations. Thus, it seems unlikely that income and substitution effects provide a complete explanation for order effects.

Embedding effects.   A fundamental axiom of economics is that individuals value more of a good more highly than less of it. If CV respondents' valuations are only slightly higher for large changes in the amount of the good offered than for small changes, then the validity of their responses becomes a concern. But research indicates that individuals cannot readily distinguish between small and large quantities in their valuations of a good when the different quantities are *embedded* in one another. For example, William H. Desvousges and colleagues found that different samples of respondents value 2,000 migratory birds approximately the same as 200,000 birds, and small oil spills much the same as much larger oil spills (given that these are different samples, it does not directly test whether given individuals prefer more to less).[53] Two additional examples of embedding are described in Exhibit 11.3. It is unlikely that declining marginal utility can explain all or even most of the absence of different valuations for different quantities of goods.

■ EXHIBIT 11.3

Daniel Kahneman and Jack L. Knetsch report that residents of Toronto expressed willingness-to-pay increased taxes to prevent a drop in fish stocks in all Ontario lakes that was only slightly larger than their expressed WTP to preserve fish stocks in a small area of the province. This is implausible.

   The same researchers studied the impact of embedding by specifying a good very broadly to one sample of respondents (environmental services that included "preserving wilderness areas, protecting wildlife, providing parks, preparing for disasters, controlling air pollution, insuring water quality, and routine treatment and disposal of industrial wastes") and asking their WTP for this bundle; a considerably narrower subset to a second sample of respondents ("to improve preparedness for disasters" with a subsequent allocation to go to "the availability of equipment and trained personnel for rescue operations"); and an even narrower good to a third sample ("improve the availability of equipment and trained personnel for rescue operations"). They found that the differences in WTP among the three samples were not large.

Source: Daniel Kahneman and Jack L. Knetsch, "Valuing Public Goods: The Purchase of Moral Satisfaction," *Journal of Environmental Economics and Management*, 22, no. 1 (1992), 57–70. (For a critique of this study, see V. Kerry Smith, "Comment: Arbitrary Values, Good Causes, and Premature Verdicts," *Journal of Environmental Economics and Management*, 22, no. 1 (1992), 71–89.)

When dealing with nonuse values, embedding is probably the most worrisome problem identified by critics of CV. It goes to the very heart of welfare economics. Critics argue that the empirical evidence suggests that in these contexts respondents are not actually expressing their valuations, but instead are expressing broad moral attitudes to environmental issues—a "warm glow" or "moral satisfaction."[54]

Starting point bias.   Prospect theory identifies anchoring as a common behavioral response to being asked to make complex judgments. A problem arises in CV when starting values are presented to respondents. The iterative bidding method is particularly prone to this problem because this method provides respondents with a specific initial starting "price."[55] Consider, for example, the Kristiansand Fjord study mentioned earlier in the chapter. It was found that a range starting at 200 kronor and progressing to 2,000 kronor produced different valuations than a range between 0 kronor and 2,000 kronor, even when there were no bids between 0 and 200 kronor.[56]

The dichotomous-choice question format is intended to eliminate starting point bias. It has been argued, however, that "responses to dichotomous-choice questions are very strongly influenced by starting-point bias because respondents are likely to take initial cues of resource value from the solicited contribution amount (e.g., assuming it to be his/her share of the needed contribution)."[57] Moreover, there is at least some empirical evidence to support the contention that the dichotomous-choice method is subject to starting point bias.[58]

Hypotheticality bias versus judgment bias. In the last resort it is almost impossible to disentangle hypotheticality issues from various forms of judgment bias in nonuse contexts—they are essentially two different sides of the same coin. Hence, the same approach is required to minimize both—an effort to present the project or good in question as concretely as possible, at the lowest level of disaggregation as possible, and with as much realism concerning budget constraints as possible. Neutrality problems also appear to be generic to CV. But this problem is less worrisome because it can be made reasonably transparent with good research protocols.

WTP Versus WTA

Economic theory implies that if individuals behave rationally, and if markets are working efficiently, then it should make little difference whether respondents to a CV survey are asked their WTP for receiving a good or their willingness-to-accept (WTA) the loss of a comparable good.[59] Similarly, it should make little difference whether they are asked their WTP to prevent a loss or their WTA a comparable loss.

As we have already discussed, considerable evidence suggests that individuals demand considerably greater monetary compensation to give up things that they already possess than they are willing to pay to acquire the same exact item. In experiments that actually require people to trade goods for money, as well as in other contexts, it has been found that required WTA amounts range from a ratio of four times to fifteen times greater than WTP amounts.[60] Similar differences have also been found in CV studies, even with a well-specified market good. There is evidence that this difference between WTP and WTA is attributable to loss aversion.[61]

There is also considerable evidence, however, that as the subjects in experiments become more experienced, differences between WTP and WTA shrink considerably, usually as a result of decreases in WTA amounts.[62] Yet, other experimental evidence suggests that for nonmarket goods with imperfect substitutes the divergence between WTP and WTA persists even with experience.[63] In any event, CV survey contexts—which are typically "one-shot" affairs—do not present opportunities for learning. Moreover, they often involve nonmarket goods with no close substitutes.

Some commentators have argued that stated preferences are preferences and that, if respondents are actually being asked to give up something, then the relevant formulation is WTA. (Notice, that this is similar to the Arrow argument, which was previously mentioned, concerning payment vehicles.) But even in a context in which something is being given up, analysts still have to decide whether to treat WTA as a judgment bias problem that requires "adjustments." In view of the fact that experiments show learning effects in some contexts and, as discussed later, WTP amounts are much closer to estimates derived from methods based on revealed preferences, the usual procedure is to use WTP estimates. This rule is applied even in cases in which WTA questions fit the facts better than WTP questions—for example, as when the project involves the respondent giving up a good, such as a scenic view, that he or she currently consumes. The heuristic is, therefore, *that WTP question formats rather than WTA question formats should be used in CV in almost all cases.*

In thinking about WTP and WTA, one additional point should be kept in mind: We are concerned only about differences between the two *for the same individual.* The fact that *different* individuals have differing WTPs and WTAs is what makes markets work and presents no problem to CV.

The Strategic Behavior (Honesty) Problem

Will respondents answer honestly when asked about their WTP? It is frequently argued that respondents in CV surveys have incentives to behave strategically, that is, to answer dishonestly. In most other survey contexts, in contrast, respondents do not have strong incentives to behave strategically. An analogy is often drawn between strategic behavior in CV studies and free riding in the provision of public goods. The potential for strategic behavior in CV, however, is actually more varied than the free-riding characterization suggests.

Strategic behavior can take one of two forms. First, if survey respondents believe that they will actually have to pay their stated WTP, and they also believe that the good will be provided regardless of their particular response to the survey, then they may underbid, or free ride. It is individually rational to underbid because respondents believe that they will receive the good whatever they bid. Second, survey respondents may overbid if they believe that this bid will influence either the provision, or the level of provision, of the good, but that they will not actually have to pay this amount.

In practice, the former problem is not likely to be serious because most people realize that it is never certain that a good will be provided. The latter problem is potentially more serious because it is quite likely that many individuals believe that they cannot be, and will not be, held to their valuations. Both the rationality and the extent of free riding have been the subject of intense debate and experimentation in economics. Clearly the extent of free riding depends on what respondents believe will happen in response to their bids.

A framework for understanding strategic behavior. Robert Mitchell and Richard Carson point out that rational behavior is a function of respondents' *perceived* payment obligation and their expectations about the provision of the good.[64]

Depending on the specifics of the survey, as well as other factors, respondents may believe that their payment obligation (PAYOB) will be the actual amounts they offer (PAYOB actual), more or less than the amounts they offer (PAYOB uncertain), or some specific exogenous amount (PAYOB exogenous). Concerning the provision of the good (PROV), they could believe either that it is contingent on their response to the survey (PROV contingent) or that it will be provided regardless of their response (PROV certain).

Thus, given the two variables, there are six combinations of possible beliefs. Respondents do not have incentives to free ride with all, or even with most, of these six belief combinations, although other kinds of systematic distortions can be expected to result from some. If respondents believe "PAYOB actual" and "PROV contingent," then they have a strong incentive to be truthful. If respondents believe "PAYOB uncertain" and "PROV contingent," then their incentives are variable but weak. Much will depend on the specific structure of their beliefs and probability estimates of various outcomes. Mitchell and Carson argue that this belief structure is quite common in CV surveys because, although respondents can be convinced that provision is contingent on their level of valuation, it is much harder to convince them that their payment obligation will be the actual amount they offer or, indeed, any particular fixed amount. Where respondents believe "PAYOB exogenous" and "PROV contingent," those who value the good have a strong incentive to overbid, as they believe that this will influence the provision of the good but not raise the amount they have to pay for it.

When respondents believe that provision is likely no matter how they respond to the questions (PROV certain), there are typically, but not always, incentives to free ride. Classic strong incentives to free ride are found when "PROV certain" is combined with "PAYOB actual" for obvious reasons. There are also incentives to attempt to free ride when "PROV certain" is combined with "PAYOB uncertain," but they are reduced by uncertainty as to whether underbidding will actually do any good. Finally, with "PROV certain" and "PAYOB exogenous," both variables are unaffected by responses. Respondents, therefore, have an incentive to minimize their effort in responding to the survey, as they believe that their response will make no difference. In view of the cynicism toward governments that exists, it would not be surprising if this type of belief structure is common.

How important is free riding in practice?   This question can be addressed at two levels: How important is free riding in general in public policy? How important is it specifically in the contingent valuation context? With respect to the former, the empirical evidence (including experimental evidence) suggests that the extent of free riding is highly influenced by such contextual variables as the size of the affected population and the degree of social "control" that others can exercise over free riders.[65] For example, one recent study found that there is considerable free riding in the case of public broadcasting and that, as expected, the problem was greatest for stations with larger populations.[66] With respect to the importance of free riding in the context of CV, advocates argue that free riding, or other forms of strategic behavior, are not serious problems. Primarily, they note that "good practice" in conducting CV is to be careful not to suggest that the project will be provided regardless of valuations, thereby avoiding the severest free-riding incentives.[67]

Conclusion about the importance of strategic behavior. While in theory strategic behavior might be expected to be a serious problem in CV, in practice it probably is not. It is likely to be most serious for use in contexts at the state or local level where respondents are most likely to believe that they can derive an advantage from specific WTP responses. Yet, in most contexts, respondents are likely to manifest strategic behavior by providing extreme valuations, and in most studies these are eliminated.

HOW ACCURATE IS CONTINGENT VALUATION?

It is possible to test the accuracy of CV WTP estimates in a number of ways.[68] The first method is to compare CV values to those generated by other indirect methods. CV use values have been found to be approximately the same as those derived from travel cost studies.[69] They have also been found to be reasonably similar to prices derived from hedonic price regressions[70] and to the market prices of substitutes.[71] Wesley Magat and W. Kip Viscusi tested whether respondents' WTP for risk reductions associated with an insecticide and toilet bowl cleaner were consistent with standard economic theory or subject to the kinds of judgment biases described earlier. In general, they did not find strong evidence of bias.[72]

The second type of comparison, one that is more common and more appropriate, is between respondents' CV statements and their actual behavior when they participate in an experiment that utilizes a simulated or constructed market for the good in question.[73] Results from studies that have used experimental techniques to examine CV accuracy typically suggest that CV valuations of WTP relying on open-ended and dichotomous-choice methods approximate actual market transactions, although there is some tendency for overvaluation.[74] In assessing these experiments, it is useful to keep in mind that the simulated market only approximates the workings of a real market; for example, there is only one opportunity to buy the good. In addition, the experiments have only been conducted in contexts in which respondents clearly derive use value from the good. Richard Bishop and Thomas Heberlein at the University of Wisconsin have conducted a number of experiments along these lines. The example presented in Exhibit 11.4 is typical of these experiments.

■ **EXHIBIT 11.4**

A wildlife area in Wisconsin is periodically opened to hunting. Hunters require a special permit to participate in these hunts. The permits are issued free to the winners of a lottery. For the 1984 lottery, a large number of applications were received. As a result of the lottery, 150 permits to hunt were issued.

To measure WTA, half of these hunters also received a letter explaining the study and a check made out in their name. To cash these checks, the hunters had to relinquish their permits. The denominations of the checks, which ranged randomly from $18 to $518, corresponded to the dichotomous-choice method described earlier. The other half of the hunters received a similar letter with a hypothetical payment offer drawn from the same range as the first half. They were asked if they would have been willing to give up their permits for the hypothetical amounts stated in their letters.

To measure WTP, 150 unsuccessful lottery participants were selected at random. Again, 75 received a letter explaining that a hunting permit was available if they paid the amount specified in the letter. The amounts covered the same range as described previously. The other 75 were asked the same question hypothetically. That is, they were asked the CV question rather than given the opportunity to reveal their preferences through purchases.

Looking first at WTP, the results indicated that the CV valuations ($35) were only slightly higher than those measured through revealed preference ($31), a difference that was not statistically significant. These results suggest that noncommitment bias was not a major problem in this context. But, consistent with the findings discussed earlier, WTA valuations were much higher than WTP valuations. Furthermore, the CV valuations ($420) were considerably higher than those actually revealed by check cashing ($153).

Source: Richard C. Bishop and Thomas A. Heberlein, "The Contingent Valuation Method," pp. 81–104, in *Economic Valuation of Natural Resources: Issues, Theory, and Application*, eds. Rebecca L. Johnson and Gary V. Johnson (Boulder, CO: Westview Press, 1990).

John Loomis has investigated how consistent household CV valuations are over time. Though not a direct test of accuracy, his investigation is relevant because consistency is a prerequisite for accuracy. He surveyed both visitors and the general public's WTP for recreational, option, existence, and bequest values derived from Mono Lake in California. Identical surveys were administered to the same individuals eight or nine months apart. The results were virtually identical.[75]

Though the evidence tends to suggest that CV is plausible in "use" contexts, the jury is still "out" in terms of nonuse values, given the ordering, embedding, noncommitment, and starting point problems discussed previously. Obviously, given the nature of nonuse values, it is much more difficult to elicit WTP from observed behavior. Nonetheless, it may not be impossible to do so. For example, as noted in Chapter 8, voluntary contributions to environmental causes might serve as the basis for estimation. Market-like experiments might also be used.[76] For example, individuals who have expressed WTP for nonuse could be given the option of returning none, part, or all of the checks sent to them by experimenters. Successfully implementing such experiments would be extremely difficult with current levels of knowledge, however.

The Potential for Calibration

It has long been recognized in marketing research that it may be necessary to *calibrate* respondents' valuations of goods in various ways to get more accurate estimates of their WTP.[77] As noted earlier, noncommitment bias is a well-recognized problem in marketing research when individuals are asked to express their valuations of market goods. Kenneth Arrow has concluded, "A hypothesis to be explored is that, if the results of CVs for nonuse values were suitably calibrated, they would provide useful and reliable estimates."[78] Testing Arrow's hypothesis may be one of the most valuable areas of future research on CV.

The Accuracy of Different CV Methods and Proneness to Biases

Richard Bishop and Thomas Heberlein have conducted experiments comparing the size of valuations from open-ended WTP questions and closed-end iterative bidding formats (again, this is in a "use" context). They conclude that:

> These experiments indicate that contingent values for willingness to pay may be somewhat high, but for open-ended and dichotomous-choice questions the difference was not large enough to be statistically significant . . . Bidding seems to introduce a substantial upward bias . . . Contingent compensation demanded tended to produce excessive values when an open-ended question was asked and values that were biased substantially upward compared to values obtained from actual cash transactions when dichotomous-choice questions were used.[79]

Other researchers have also addressed this issue. V. Kerry Smith and William Desvousges compared the valuations from four CV methods in their study of improvements in the quality of water in the Monongahela River. Their analysis suggests that starting point bias is important with iterative bidding: A low starting point ($25) generated lower valuations than other methods, while a high starting point ($125) produced valuations higher than other methods. Open-ended questions and payment card questions produced fairly similar valuations. Overall, mean valuations from different CV methods ranged from $7 to $36 for one water quality change, from $4 to $31 for another change, and from $11 to $51 for a third change.[80]

William Desvousges and his colleagues have compared open-ended question responses with dichotomous-choice responses to the same questions. They found that in some contexts the differences in the mean WTP valuations were not statistically significant, but in other contexts they were. They also found the dichotomous-choice method generated a considerable number of very high valuations.[81] This is consistent with findings that dichotomous-choice responses produce high variances so that relatively large samples are required to achieve precision.

These findings can be combined with the prior discussions about CV problems and biases to develop some conclusions concerning both CV in general and specific CV methods in particular. Certain problems and biases are generic to all forms of CV: most clearly, neutrality problems, noncommitment bias, embedding effects, and order effects. While noncommitment bias is definitionally generic to CV, it also appears to be exacerbated by iterated bidding, which seems to encourage a form of "winner's curse" or "bidding frenzy" similar to that found in auction contexts.

The major strengths and weaknesses of each CV method are summarized in Table 11.1.

HEURISTICS FOR THE DESIGN AND USE OF CV SURVEYS

Several experts in CV have suggested overall criteria for evaluating CV instruments. Ronald Cummings, David Brookshire, and William Schulze, for example, suggest five criteria for evaluating instruments. First, respondents should understand and be famil-

TABLE 11.1   A SUMMARY OF THE STRENGTHS AND WEAKNESSES OF DIFFERENT CV ELICITATION METHODS

Elicitation Method	Major Strengths	Major Specific Weaknesses	Generic Weaknesses
Open-Ended WTP Method	No starting point bias. May directly measure exactly what researcher wants to know. A good check when used in conjunction with other methods.	High information complexity leads to unrealistic responses in hypothetical situations.	
Closed-Ended Iterative Bidding Method	Bidding provides "thinking time" to elicit maximum WTP, as desired.	Sensitive to starting value. "Bidding frenzy" may lead to some very high valuations.	
Contingent Ranking Method	Ordinal ranking requires low information complexity. Links quantities to prices, reducing hypotheticality.	Ordinal responses cannot be aggregated. Requires analyst to have statistical skills. Anchoring bias and highly dependent on the specified alternatives. Requires fairly large sample sizes.	Apply to most survey methods: sample selection bias; nonresponse bias; outliers; unintended interviewer biases.
Dichotomous-Choice Method	"Take it or leave it" choices reduce hypotheticality and approximate the market. Small strategic bias; very small starting point bias.	Less information per respondent so large samples are needed. Requires analyst to have statistical skills.	Apply especially to CV methods: hypotheticality bias; payment vehicle; noncommitment bias; order bias; embedding bias; strategic bias.
Payment Card With Comparative Tax-Prices	Encourages realistic assessment of WTP, thus reducing hypotheticality and noncommitment bias.	Moderate to high information complexity. May be too sensitive to particular comparisons. Anchoring bias. Often requires personal interviews.	
Payment Card With a Range of Prices for the Good	Moderately low complexity. Low interview bias.	Anchoring bias. Often requires personal interviews.	

iar with the good that is being valued. Second, respondents should have, or be given, experience in both valuation and the choice procedure. Third, there should be as little uncertainty as possible about the details of the project. All three of these concerns can best be addressed by attempting to reduce hypotheticality—for example, by employing quality ladders, by stressing realistically and concretely the substitution possibilities, and by presenting gains (benefits) in percentage terms as well as in absolute terms. Fourth, WTP rather than WTA should be used for valuation purposes. Fifth, attempts should be made to avoid anchoring and starting point bias.[82] Open-ended questions and payment cards with comparative tax-prices are two methods that minimize these problems and dichotomous-choice questions at least "dampen" them.

Heuristics for Using Estimates From Previous CV Studies

Because CV surveys are inevitably complex and expensive, many analysts will be more concerned with using values derived from existing CV studies than they will be in going out and doing CV surveys themselves. In a recent examination of alternative environmental regulatory policies for dealing with water pollution, Ralph Luken illustrates how existing CV estimates can be "plugged in" to a CBA. Specifically, he extrapolates previous CV valuations of benefits from the Monongahela River studies discussed earlier in this chapter. His analysis provides a useful example of how to use *plug-in* values.[83] He is careful to specify which studies and which specific estimates he is using; the specific assumptions he makes in the extrapolations; the quality changes that are involved; the distinction between use and any nonuse components; and finally, any potential remaining biases. He also performs sensitivity analysis.

CONCLUSION

Contingent valuation is now relatively uncontroversial in "use" contexts, although it may overestimate use values. Its accuracy in nonuse contexts is much more controversial, yet it is in this context where its potential usefulness may be the greatest. Doubts about the accuracy of CV in nonuse contexts stem from the problems of hypotheticality and the attendant judgment biases that appear to flourish in this context. Strategic bias, on the other hand, does not appear to be a major problem and neutrality bias can be minimized by use of appropriate survey techniques. Probably the most important topics for future CV research are the directional biases in particular methods and the development of techniques that allow reliable calibration.

EXERCISES FOR CHAPTER 11

1. The construction of a dam that would provide hydroelectric power would result in the loss of two streams: one that is now used for sport fishing; and another that does not support game fish but is part of a wilderness area.
   a. Imagine that a contingent valuation method is used to estimate the social cost of the loss of each of these streams. Would you be equally confident in the two sets of estimates?
   b. Consider two general approaches to asking contingent valuation questions about the streams. The first approach attempts to elicit how much compensation people would require to give up the streams. The second approach attempts to elicit how much people would be willing to pay to keep the streams. Which approach would you recommend? Why?

2. A number of residents of Dullsville have complained to the mayor that the center of town looks shabby compared to the centers of many other nearby towns. At the mayor's request, the Parks Department has put together a proposal for converting the town square parking lot into a sitting park with flower displays—it modeled the design on a similar park in the neighboring town of Flowerville. The annualized cost of installing and maintaining the park, and relocating parking to nearby Short Street, would be about $120,000. With about 40,000 households paying property taxes, the project would cost an average household about $3 per year.

   You have been asked to give advice about conducting a survey to measure the benefits of the project.

   a. The Parks Department proposes conducting a telephone survey. Does this seem like an appropriate survey vehicle?

   b. How might a random sample be drawn for a telephone survey?

   c. Write a statement that could be read by the interviewer to describe the project.

   d. Write questions to implement the open-ended WTP method.

   e. Propose a procedure for implementing the dichotomous-choice method.

3. Consider a project that would involve purchasing marginal farmland that would then be allowed to return to wetlands capable of supporting migrant birds. Researchers designed a survey to implement the dichotomous-choice method. They reported the following data:

Stated Price (annual payment in dollars)	Fraction of Respondents Accepting Stated Price (percent)
0	98
5	91
10	82
15	66
20	48
25	32
30	20
35	12
40	6
45	4
50	2

What is the mean willingness-to-pay for the sampled population?

NOTES

[1]CV overviews include: Ronald G. Cummings, David S. Brookshire, and William D. Schulze, *Valuing Environmental Goods: An Assessment of the Contingent Valuation Method* (Totowa, NJ: Rowman & Allanheld, 1986); Robert C. Mitchell and Richard T. Carson, *Using Surveys to Value Public Goods: The Contingent Valuation Method* (Washington, DC: Resources for the Future, 1989); Richard C. Bishop and Thomas A. Heberlein, "The Contingent Valuation Method," in *Economic Valuation of Natural Resources: Issues, Theory, and Application*, eds. Rebecca L. Johnson and Gary V. Johnson (Boulder, CO: Westview Press, 1990), pp. 81–104.

[2]William H. Desvousges, V. Kerry Smith, and Ann Fisher, "Option Price Estimates for Water Quality Improvements: A Contingent Valuation Study for the Monongahela River," *Journal of Environmental Economics and Management*, 14, no. 3 (1987), 248–267; Richard C. Bishop and Thomas A. Heberlein, "Measuring Values of Extra-Market Goods: Are Indirect Measures Biased?" *American Journal of Agricultural Economics*, 61, no. 5 (1979), 926–930; M.W. Jones-Lee, M. Hammerton, and P.R. Philips, "The Value of Safety: Results of a National Survey," *Economic Journal*, 95, no. 377 (1985), 45–72.

[3]For an example, see Gretchen J. Burger, "Application and Assessment of the Contingent Valuation Method for Federal Hazardous Waste Policy in the Washington, D.C. Area," Ph.D. dissertation, University of New Mexico, Albuquerque, 1984.

[4]Raymond J. Kopp, Paul R. Portney and V. Kerry Smith, "The Economics of Natural Resource Damages after *Ohio v. U.S. Dept. of the Interior*," *Environmental Law Reporter*, 20, no. 4 (1990), 10,127–10,131.

[5]On this point see, Daniel McFadden and Gregory Leonard, "Issues in the Contingent Valuation of Environmental Goods: Methodologies for Data Collection and Analysis," in *Contingent Valuation: A Critical Assessment*, ed. J.A. Hausman (New York: North-Holland, 1993), pp. 165–208.

[6]For an example of this approach, see J.C. Horvath, *Southeastern Economic Survey of Wildlife Recreation*, 2 vols., (Atlanta, GA: Environmental Research Group, Georgia State University, 1974).

[7]For an example, see David Brookshire, Berry Ives, and William D. Schulze, "The Valuation of Aesthetic Preference," *Journal of Environmental Economics and Management*, 3, no. 4 (December 1976), 325–346.

[8]James L. Regens, "Measuring Environmental Benefits with Contingent Markets," *Public Administration Review*, 51, no. 4 (July/August 1991), 345–352.

[9]For an example, see V. Kerry Smith and William H. Desvousges, *Measuring Water Quality Benefits* (Boston, MA: Kluwer Nijhoff Publishing, 1986), Chapter 6.

[10]Baruch Fischhoff and Louis A. Cox, Jr., "Conceptual Framework for Regulatory Benefits Assessment," in *Benefits Assessment: The State of the Art*, eds. Judith D. Bentkover, Vincent T. Covello, and Jeryl Mumpower (Boston, MA: D. Reidel Publishing Co., 1986), pp. 51–84.

[11]For an example using this method, see John Loomis, *Integrated Public Lands Management* (New York: Columbia University Press, 1993), pp. 276–279.

[12]For more detail on this method, see Bishop and Heberlein, "Measuring Values of Extra-Market Goods," pp. 89–91. On the technical issues relating to interpreting the function as utility and how to deal with truncation, see W. Michael Hanemann, "Welfare Evaluations in Contingent Valuation Experiments with Discrete Responses," *American Journal of Agricultural Economics*, 66, no. 3 (1984), 332–341.

[13]The formula for computing the WTP of the average member of the sample can be derived more formally if some additional notation is introduced. (Note that this derivation involves approximating the expected value of WTP.) Assume that the offer prices are 0, v, $2v$, $3v$, . . . Nv, where v is the interval between prices, and Nv is the maximum price offered. For example, if the offer prices were 0, \$10, \$20, \$30, . . . , \$200, then $v = \$10$ and $N = 20$. Let $F[X]$ be the fraction of respondents offered price X who accept the offer—this is the height of the bar in the histogram that sits above X. In order to calculate the expected value of WTP, we require the probability that each offer price is the *maximum* amount that a respondent would be willing to pay. We can approximate this for offer amount \$$kv$ with the expression:

$$F[kv]-F[(k+1)v] \text{ for } k=0,1,...,N-1$$

which is roughly the probability of a respondent accepting \$$kv$ minus the probability of accepting a larger offer price, \$$(k+1)v$. The mean WTP (that is, the WTP of a randomly selected respondent) is then approximately the sum of the products of maximum payments times their probabilities:

$$E[WTP] = NvF[Nv]+ (N-1)v\{F[(N-1)v] - F[Nv]\}+ (N-2)v\{F[(N-2)v] - F[(N-1)]\}+ \ldots + 0\{F[0] - F[v]\}$$

Collecting terms yields the simple expression:

$$E[WTP] = v\sum_{k=0}^{N} F[kv]$$

[14]A complication arises because the statistical model usually assumes an infinite range for x. In practice, surveys use offer prices with a finite range, usually bounded from below at zero. Averaging over this finite range will miss some of the probability assumed by the statistical model. A correction to help account for this truncation bias involves rescaling the distribution to account for the missing areas in the tails of the distribution. See Kevin J. Boyle, Michael P. Welsh, and Richard C. Bishop, "Validation of Empirical Measures of Welfare Change: Comment," *Land Economics*, 64, no. 1 (February 1988), 94–98.

[15]The area under the curve can be estimated through numerical integration. The procedure involves approximating the area with rectangles through the following steps. First, divide the range of X into equal segments of width v. Second, calculate the probability of acceptance at each of these points. Third, find the average acceptance value for adjacent pairs of points. Fourth, multiply each of these averages by v. Fifth, sum all these products to get the estimate of the area. Any desired degree of accuracy can be obtained by choosing a sufficiently small value of v.

[16]For an overview of the statistical issues in estimating aggregate WTP from such models, see Timothy Park, John B. Loomis, and Michael Creel, "Confidence Intervals for Evaluating Benefits Estimates from Dichotomous Choice Contingent Valuation Studies," *Land Economics*, 67, no. 1 (February 1991), 64–73.

[17]Anna Alberini and Richard T. Carson, "Efficient Threshold Values for Binary Discrete Choice Contingent Valuation Surveys and Economic Experiments," Working Paper, Department of Economics, University of California, San Diego, 1990.

[18]Trudy A. Cameron and Michelle D. James, "Efficient Estimation Methods for Use with 'Closed-Ended' Contingent Valuation Survey Data," *Review of Economics and Statistics*, 69, no. 2 (1987), 269–276.

[19]Robert Rowe, William D. Schulze, W. Douglas Shaw, David Schenk, and Lauraine G. Chestnut, "Contingent Valuation of Natural Resource Damage Due to Nestucca Oil Spill," prepared for the Dept. of Wildlife, WA, Ministry of Environment, BC, and Environment Canada by RCG/Hagler, Bailly Inc., June 1991.

[20]See "The Review Panel's Assessment," pp. 180–204, Kenneth Arrow, "Comments" at pp. 180–185, in Cummings, Brookshire and Schulze, *Valuing Environmental Goods: An Assessment of the Contingent Valuation Method*.

[21]See Norman Bradburn, "Response Effects," pp. 289–328, at pp. 293–298, in *Handbook of Survey Research*, eds. Peter H. Rossi, James D. Wright and Andy B. Anderson (Orlando, FL: Academic Press, 1983).

[22]The most comprehensive criticisms of CV can be found in Hausman, ed., *Contingent Valuation: A Critical Assessment*.

[23]William D. Schulze, Ronald G. Cummings, and David S. Brookshire, "Methods Development in Measuring Benefits of Environmental Improvements", vol. II, (Washington, DC: Report to U.S. EPA, 1983).

[24]For overviews, see Martin Frankel, "Sampling Theory," pp. 21–67, and Seymour Sudman, "Applied Sampling," pp. 145–194 in Rossi, Wright, and Anderson, *Handbook of Survey Research*; for issues specifically relevant to CV, see Steven F. Edwards and Glen D. Anderson, "Overlooked Biases in Contingent Valuation Surveys: Some Considerations," *Land Economics*, 63, no. 2 (1987), 168–178.

[25]Richard T. Carson, "Constructed Markets," in *Measuring the Demand for Environmental Quality*, eds. John B. Braden and Charles D. Kolstad (New York: Elsevier Science Publishers, 1991), p. 152.

[26]For an example of an attempt to estimate the extent of a recreational market, see V. Kerry Smith and Raymond J. Kopp, "The Spatial Limits of the Travel Cost Recreational Demand Model," *Land Economics*, 56, no. 1 (February 1980), 64–72.

[27]Desvousges, Smith and Fisher, "Option Price Estimates for Water Quality Improvements."

[28]Alan Randall, John P. Hoehn, and George S. Tolley, "The Structure of Contingent Markets: Some Results of a Recent Experiment," paper presented at the American Economic Association Annual Meeting, Washington, DC, 1981.

[29]F.L. Filion, "Estimating Bias Due to Non-response in Mail Surveys," *Public Opinion Quarterly*, 39, no. 4 (1975–6), 482–492.

[30]For a review, see John B. Loomis, "Expanding Contingent Value Sample Estimates to Aggregate Benefit Estimates: Current Practices and Proposed Solutions," *Land Economics*, 63, no. 4 (1987), 396–402.

[31]Robert Rosenthal and Ralph L. Rosnow, eds., *Artifacts in Behavioral Research* (New York: Academic Press, 1969), especially William J. McGuire, "Suspiciousness of Experimenters' Intent," pp. 13–57.

[32]For an extensive discussion of the attitude-behavior nexus, see Mitchell and Carson, *Using Surveys to Value Public Goods: The Contingent Valuation Method*, pp. 175–187.

[33]Baruch Fischhoff and Lita Furey, "Measuring Values: A Conceptual Framework for Interpreting Transactions with Special Reference to Contingent Valuation of Visibility," *Journal of Risk and Uncertainty*, 1, no. 2 (1988), 147–184, at pp. 179–180.

[34]In marketing, the technique called *conjoint analysis* is used to elicit consumer valuations for new, unfamiliar goods. For a review, see Daniel McFadden, "The Choice Theory Approach to Market Research," *Marketing Science*, 5, no. 4 (1986), 275–297.

[35]For a discussion of this point, see Cummings, Brookshire, and Schulze, *Valuing Environmental Goods: An Assessment of the Contingent Valuation Method*, pp. 43, 253.

[36]Fischhoff and Furey, "Measuring Values: A Conceptual Framework for Interpreting Transactions with Special Reference to Contingent Valuation of Visibility," Table 1, p. 156.

[37]Daniel A. Hagen, James W. Vincent, and Patrick G. Welle, "The Benefits of Preserving Old-Growth Forests and the Northern Spotted Owl," *Contemporary Policy Issues*, 10, no. 2 (1992), 13–16. A second CV study of the spotted owl that can be critiqued on neutrality grounds is Jonathan Rubin, Gloria Heland, and John Loomis, "A Benefit-Cost Analysis of the Northern Spotted Owl: Results from a Contingent Valuation Survey," *Journal of Forestry*, 89, no. 12 (1991), 25–30.

[38]William McKillop, "Use of Contingent Valuation in Northern Spotted Owls Studies: A Critique," *Journal of Forestry*, 90, no. 8 (1992), 36–37.

[39]Ed Bukszar, "Does Overconfidence Lead to Poor Decisions? A Comparison of Decision Making and Judgment Under Uncertainty," paper presented at the Annual Conference of Judgment and Decision Making, Washington, DC, November 7, 1993.

[40]See David L. Weimer and Aidan R. Vining, *Policy Analysis: Concepts and Practice* 2nd ed. (Englewood Cliffs, NJ: Prentice Hall, 1992), pp. 85–86.

[41]For a review of this issue, see Colin F. Camerer and Howard Kunreuther, "Decision Processes for Low Probability Events: Policy Implications," *Journal of Policy Analysis and Management*, 8, no. 4 (1989), 565–592.

[42]For an extensive review of biases and the various theories behind them see Camerer and Kunreuther, "Decision Processes for Low Probability Events: Policy Implications."

[43]Daniel Kahneman and Amos Tversky, "Prospect Theory," *Econometrica*, 47, no. 2 (1979), 263–292. Many of the violations of expected utility hypothesis that can be explained by prospect theory can also be explained by assuming people maximize expected utility but employ Bayesian updating of probabilities; see W. Kip Viscusi, "Prospective Reference Theory: Toward an Explanation of the Paradoxes," *Journal of Risk and Uncertainty*, 2, no. 3 (September 1989), 235–263.

[44]Richard H. Thaler, "Towards a Positive Theory of Consumer Choice," *Journal of Economic Behavior and Organization*, 1, no. 1 (1980), 39–60.

[45]It may seem somewhat artificial to separate hypotheticality from noncommitment bias. However, as emphasized earlier, hypotheticality does not appear to generate upward or downward bias, while, as we will see, noncommitment does appear to bias valuations upward.

[46]See, for example, Linda F. Jamieson and Frank M. Bass, "Adjusting Stated Intention Measures to Predict Trial Purchase of New Products: A Comparison of Models and Methods," *Journal of Marketing Research*, 26, no. 3 (1989), 336–345; F. Thomas Juster, *Anticipations and Purchases* (Princeton, NJ: Princeton University Press, 1964).

[47]Helen R. Neill, Ronald G. Cummings, Philip T. Ganderton, Glenn W. Harrison, and Thomas McGuckin, "Hypothetical Surveys and Economic Commitments," *Land Economics*, 70, no. 2 (1994), 145–154; Kalle Seip and Jon Strand, "Willingness to Pay for Environmental Goods in Norway: A Contingent Valuation Study with Real Payment," *Environmental and Resource Economics*, 2, no. 1 (1992), 91–106.

[48]For more detail, see Michael A. Kemp and Christopher Maxwell, "Exploring a Budget Context for Contingent Valuation Estimates," pp. 217–265, in Hausman, ed., *Contingent Valuation: A Critical Assessment*.

[49]George Tolley and Alan Randall, "Establishing and Valuing the Effects of Improved Visibility in the Eastern United States," (Washington, DC: Report to the U.S. EPA, 1983).

[50]Karl C. Samples and James R. Hollyer, "Contingent Valuation of Wildlife Resources in the Presence of Substitutes and Complements," pp. 177–192, in Johnson and Johnson, eds., *Economic Valuation of National Resources: Issues, Theory, and Application*.

[51]See Peter A. Diamond, Jerry A. Hausman, Gregory K. Leonard, and Mike Denning, "Does Contingent Valuation Measure Preferences? Experimental Evidence," pp. 43–85, in Hausman, ed., *Contingent Valuation: A Critical Assessment*.

[52]See the heated argument between Peter Diamond and Richard Carson, in Hausman, ed., *Contingent Valuation: A Critical Assessment*, pp. 87–89.

[53]William H. Desvousges, F. Reed Johnson, Richard W. Dunford, Sara P. Hudson, and K. Nicole Wilson, "Measuring Natural Resources Damages with Contingent Valuation: Tests of Validity and Reliability," in Hausman, ed., *Continget Valuation: A Critical Assessment*, pp. 91–159.

[54]Daniel Kahneman and Jack L. Knetsch, "Valuing Public Goods: The Purchase of Moral Satisfaction," *Journal of Environmental Economics and Management*, 22, no. 1 (1992), 57–70, pp. 64–68.

[55]Kevin J. Boyle, Richard C. Bishop, and Michael P. Walsh, "Starting Point Bias in Contingent Valuation Bidding Games," *Land Economics*, 16, no. 2 (1985), 188–194.

[56]Regens, "Measuring Environmental Benefits with Contingent Markets," pp. 347–348.

[57]Walter J. Mead, "Review and Analysis of State-of-the-Art Contingent Valuation Studies," pp. 305–332 in Hausman, ed., *Contingent Valuation: A Critical Assessment*.

[58]See Trudy A. Cameron and D.D. Huppert, "Referendum Contingent Valuation Estimates: Sensitivity to the Assignment of Offered Values," *Journal of the American Statistical Association*, 86, no. 416 (1991), 910–918.

[59]But recently Michael Hanemann ["Willingness to Pay and Willingness to Accept: How Much Can They Differ?" *American Economic Review*, 81, no. 3 (1991), 635–647] has argued that there is no reason why WTA should not be considerably larger than WTP in certain circumstances. He points out, for example, that one cannot pay more than one's income year after year to save one's own life, but there may be no finite offer that could make one willingly give up one's life.

[60]Jack Knetsch and J.S. Sinden, "Willingness to Pay and Compensation Demanded: Experimental Evidence of an Unexpected Disparity in Measures of Value," *Quarterly Journal of Economics*, 99, no. 3 (1984), 507–521; Shelby Gerking, Menno De Haan, and William Schulze, "The Marginal Value of Job Safety: A Contingent Valuation Study," *Journal of Risk and Uncertainty*, 1, no. 2 (1988), 185–199; Wesley Magat and W. Kip Viscusi, *Informational Approaches to Regulation* (Cambridge, MA: MIT Press, 1992).

[61]Timothy McDaniels, "Reference Points, Loss Aversion, and Contingent Values for Auto Safety," *Journal of Risk and Uncertainty*, 5, no. 2 (1992), 187–200.

[62]Don L. Coursey, John J. Hovis, and William D. Schulze, "The Disparity between Willingness to Accept and Willingness to Pay Measures of Value," *Quarterly Journal of Economics*, 102, no. 3 (1987), 679–690; Jason F. Shogren, Seung Y. Shin, Dermot J. Hayes, and James B. Kliebenstein, "Resolving the Differences in Willingness to Pay and Willingness to Accept," *American Economic Review*, 84, no. 1 (1994), 255–270; Wiktor L. Adamovicz, Vinay Bhardwaj, and Bruce McNab, "Experiments on the Difference Between Willingness to Pay and Willingness to Accept," *Land Economics*, 64, no. 4 (1993), 416–427.

[63]Shogren, Shin, Hayes, and Kliebenstein, "Resolving the Differences in Willingness to Pay and Willingness to Accept."

[64]Mitchell and Carson, *Using Surveys to Value Public Goods: The Contingent Valuation Method*.

[65]See R. Mark Isaac, James Walker, and Susan Thomas, "Divergent Evidence on Free Riding: An Experimental Examination of Possible Explanations," *Public Choice*, 43, no. 2 (1984), 113–149; Oliver Kim and Mark Walker, "The Free Rider Problem: Experimental Evidence," *Public Choice*, 43, no. 1

(1984), 3–24; G. Marwell and R. Ames, "Economists Free Ride, Does Anyone Else? Experiments on the Provision of Public Goods," *Journal of Public Economics*, 15, no. 3 (1981), 295–310.

[66]Linda Goetz, T.F. Glover, and B. Biswas, "The Effects of Group Size and Income on Contributions to the Corporation for Public Broadcasting," *Public Choice*, 77, no. 2 (1993), 407–414.

[67]See Mitchell and Carson, *Using Surveys to Value Public Goods: The Contingent Valuation Method*, pp. 154–158, for further reasons; see also John P. Hoehn and Alan Randall, "A Satisfactory Benefit Cost Indicator from Contingent Valuation," *Journal of Environmental Economics and Management*, 14, no. 3 (1987), 226–247.

[68]For an overview of this issue and a listing of relevant studies, see V.K. Smith, "Nonmarket Valuation of Environmental Resources: An Interpretive Appraisal," *Land Economics*, 69, no. 1 (1993) pp. 1–26, pp. 8–14, and Table 1.

[69]See William K. Desvousges, V. Kerry Smith, and Matthew P. McGivney, "A Comparison of Alternative Approaches for Estimating Recreation and Related Benefits of Water Quality Improvements," (Report to U.S. EPA, Research Triangle Institute, 1983); Christine Sellar, John R. Stoll, and Jean-Paul Chavas, "Validation of Empirical Measures of Welfare Change: A Comparison of Nonmarket Techniques," *Land Economics*, 61, no. 2 (1985), 156–175; Smith and Desvousges, *Measuring Water Quality Benefits*, compare of CV to "simple" travel cost methods.

[70]David S. Brookshire, Mark A. Thayer, William D. Schulze, and Ralph C. d'Arge, "Valuing Public Goods: A Comparison of Survey and Hedonic Approaches," *American Economic Review*, 72, no. 1 (1982), 165–177.

[71]Mark A. Thayer, "Contingent Valuation Techniques for Assessing Environmental Impacts: Further Evidence," *Journal of Environmental Economics and Management*, 8, no. 1 (1981), 27–44.

[72]Magat and Viscusi, *Informational Approaches to Regulation*, Ch. 7.

[73]For a listing of such studies, see Carson, "Constructed Markets," pp. 121–126.

[74]Coursey, Hovis, and Schulze, "The Disparity Between Willingness to Accept and Willingness to Pay Measures of Values"; Mark Dickie, Ann Fisher and Shelby Gerking, "Market Transactions and Hypothetical Demand Data: A Comparative Study," *Journal of the American Statistical Society*, 82, no. 398 (1987), 69–75.

[75]John Loomis, "Test-Retest Reliability of the Contingent Valuation Method: A Comparison of General Population and Visitor Responses," *American Journal of Agricultural Economics*, 71, no. 1 (1989), 76–84.

[76]For a discussion of this possibility, see Douglas M. Larson, "On Measuring Existence Value," *Land Economics*, 69, no. 3 (1993), 377–388.

[77]An example of such calibration is Donald G. Morrison, "Purchase Intentions and Purchase Behavior," *Journal of Marketing*, 43 (1979), 65–74. "It is possible to improve prediction accuracy by measuring and using perceptions that affect and modify the relationship between stated intentions and trial purchase for new products," in Jamieson and Bass, "Adjusting Stated Intention Measures to Predict Trial Purchase of New Products," p. 344.

[78]Kenneth Arrow, "Contingent Valuation of Nonuse Values: Observations and Questions," pp. 479–483, p. 483 in Hausman, *Contingent Valuation: A Critical Assessment*.

[79]Bishop and Heberlein, "The Contingent Valuation Method," p. 97.

[80]Smith and Desvousges, *Measuring Water Quality Benefits*, Table 105, p. 271.

[81]Desvousges, Johnson, Dunford, Hudson, and Wilson, "Measuring Natural Resources Damages with Contingent Valuation: Tests of Validity and Reliability."

[82]Summarized from "Comparison Studies: What Is Accuracy," pp. 71–109 and "reference operating conditions," Table 13.1, p. 230, in "Summary and Conclusions," pp. 205–236 in Cummings, Brookshire, and Schulze, *Valuing Environmental Goods: An Assessment of the Contingent Valuation Method*.

[83]Ralph A. Luken, *Efficiency in Environmental Regulation: A Benefit-Cost Analysis of Alternative Approaches*, (Boston, MA: Kluwer Academic Publishers, 1990), pp. 45–53; more detail on Luken's use of plug-in values is provided in Chapter 12.

12

SHADOW PRICES
FROM SECONDARY SOURCES

Policy analysts typically face time pressure and resource constraints. They naturally wish to do cost-benefit analysis with the least redundant effort, at the lowest opportunity cost, and without getting into estimation issues beyond their competence. Anything that legitimately lowers the cost of doing CBA increases the likelihood that any particular CBA will be worth doing. That is, it increases the chance that a CBA of doing a CBA will be positive! The most straightforward way to reduce the analytic cost of a CBA is to use as many preexisting shadow prices, or *plug-ins*, as possible.

Three kinds of shadow prices can be found in the literature. First, applied economists have devoted considerable effort to estimating values that are typically used in CBA. Examples include the value of a unit of time, the value of life, or the (negative) value of particular types of crime. After necessary adjustments such as the conversion from nominal to real dollars, these per-unit values can be directly used as shadow prices in CBA.

Second, applied economists have also estimated a whole range of price elasticities, cross-elasticities, and income elasticities for specific goods that can be used by the CBA analyst. Frequently, these empirical estimates have been summarized in surveys of the empirical literature.[1] These elasticities can be used by analysts to project policy impacts. As they are based on the responses of people to similar price changes in the past, they provide an empirically grounded basis for predicting the responses to proposed price changes. For example, how consumers responded to a price increase for water in New Mexico can be reasonably used to estimate how they will respond to a similar price increase in Arizona. In addition to own-price elasticities, estimates of cross-price elasticities, which identify changes in the demand for a good that are likely to result from changes in the prices of other goods, though less often available, are frequently very useful. For example, are transportation and various forms of communications (such as telecommuting and teleconferencing) complements or substitutes?[2] These cross-elasticities are important to transport planners and policy analysts who are estimating the costs and benefits of transport capital investments, assessing expected consumers' responses to price changes, or forecasting changes in demand for transportation. Existing estimates of income elasticities can also be very useful, especially when policies have strong distributional effects. Unfortunately, elasticity estimates are scattered widely throughout the academic literature. Therefore, analysts must garner them from the economic and policy journals on an ongoing basis.

Third, some CBAs also provide per-unit impact estimates that can be "recycled." For example, in their CBA of the Jobs Corps program David Long, Charles Mallar, and Craig Thornton expected that one of the benefit categories would be reduced crime. They estimated the per-crime cost of a range of felonies.[3] These estimates, with updating, may still be reasonably used in some circumstances. Similarly, as we saw in Chapter 11, Ralph Lukin reused estimates previously developed by Kerry Smith and William Desvousges in their study of the Monongahela River in his CBA of alternative EPA water regulations.[4]

In this chapter, we focus on the most commonly used per-unit plug-ins: the value of life, the cost of various kinds of injuries (including those resulting from road crashes), the cost of crime, and value of time. For our purpose, *value* and *cost* can be used interchangeably, but we stick with common nomenclature—that is, we refer to "the value of (a lost) life" and "the cost of injury." We also provide brief reviews of a few other per-unit values such as those for recreational activities. We provide these values as illustrations of how you may wish to extract per-unit values for CBAs of other impacts, such as education or noise pollution.

Our aim is to survey the relevant literature and to provide a "best estimate" of the value of each of the shadow prices we consider. Of course, more detail on these values can be found in the cited studies. Unless otherwise specified, we report the discounted present value of cost per person, as costs may occur over a long period, even the remaining life of an individual. Costs per person are the easiest plug-ins to use in CBA. Finally, we consider how analysts can sometimes use results from previous CBAs to do qualitative CBA.

THE VALUE OF LIFE

Researchers have used several of the benefit estimation techniques that we described in earlier chapters of this book to estimate the value of life. These techniques either indirectly estimate the "price" people are willing to pay to take, or accept, certain risks by observing their behaviors in markets for commodities that embody risks (Chapter 10), or directly elicit these amounts with hypothetical survey questions (Chapter 11). The most common and widely accepted of the market-based techniques are those that examine how much of a wage premium people working in risky jobs must be given to compensate them for the additional risks. Our purpose here is not to revisit the methodological issues raised by use of these techniques, but to summarize the empirical estimates of the value of life. We do this while keeping in mind that people have varying preferences for risk, just as they do for everything else; any aggregate figure is an average that must be compared to the risk profile of that of the actual population in the particular CBA. We draw on recent overviews of the evidence provided by Ted Miller, by Ann Fisher, Lauraine Chestnut and Daniel Violette, and by W. Kip Viscusi.[5]

The Miller Survey of Value-of-Life Estimates

Ted Miller reviewed 49 studies that estimated the value of life using criteria such as the quality of the survey design, sample size, and inclusion of appropriate risk variables. He then summarized the value-of-life estimates from the 29 studies that best satisfied these criteria. All estimates are in 1985 after-tax dollars and are computed with a consistent discount rate.

The studies estimate the value of life in one of four ways. The first set of 15 studies derives its estimates on the basis of wage premia for risky jobs; these studies produce values ranging from $1 million to $3 million. Four studies are based on consumers' willingness to pay for safety features (safer cars and smoke detectors), houses in less polluted areas, or life insurance; they produce a range of values from $1.1 million to $2.3 million. Four studies are based on individual behavior with respect to decisions concerning the use of pedestrian tunnels and seatbelts, speed choice when driving, and driver travel time; valuations range from $1 million to $3.10 million. Finally, four studies use contingent valuation methods to survey individuals about their willingness to invest in specific ways to increase health and safety. Consistent with our conclusions in the contingent valuation chapter, these studies produce somewhat higher values, ranging from $2 million to $2.6 million.

The mean value of life across the 29 studies is $1.95 million, with a standard deviation of $0.5 million. Miller concludes that there is enough consistency across the studies to suggest that this mean is quite plausible. He points out that the evidence also suggests that individuals value life similarly whether the risk is largely voluntary (for example, auto driving behavior) or involuntary (for example, the risk of a nuclear accident) and whether the potential death is slow and painful or sudden and quick.

The Fisher, Chestnut, and Violette Survey of Value-of-Life Estimates

These authors review 21 studies reporting estimates of the value of life. They convert all estimates to 1986 dollars and provide both the range for each estimate of the value of life from each study and a specific "judgmental best estimate."[6] Additionally, they also report an estimate of the mean level of risk considered in each study. Knowing the mean level of risk is useful because individuals' valuation of risk reduction (or safety increase) tends to increase with the level of risk, as discussed in Chapter 10.

They divide the 21 studies that they review into five categories: early low-range wage-risk estimates, early high-range wage-risk estimates, new wage-risk estimates, new contingent valuation studies, and consumer market studies. They conclude: "The most defensible empirical results indicate a range for the value-per-statistical-life estimates of $1.6 million to $8.5 million. . .On balance, we place more confidence in the lower end of the range."[7]

The Viscusi Survey of Value-of-Life Estimates

W. Kip Viscusi provides the most extensive review of both the conceptual framework and the empirical literature on the value of life. Here we concentrate on his assessment of the empirical literature. He reviews three sets of studies: those concerning wage premia for risky jobs, other revealed preference approaches, and surveys.

Viscusi summarizes the empirical results of 24 labor market studies, which are reported in (December) 1990 dollars. He cautions:

> As the implicit value-of-life estimates. . .indicate, the estimated wage-risk trade-off varies considerably across data sets and methodologies. Some heterogeneity is expected. The value of life is not a universal constant, but reflects the wage-risk trade-off pertinent to the preferences of the workers in a particular sample. The mix of workers in these samples is quite different. The majority of the estimates. . .are in the $3 million–$7 million range. . .The wage-risk relationship is not as robust as is, for example, the effect of education on wages.[8]

Viscusi reviews seven revealed preference studies based on other than labor market behavior. As he points out, these studies are probably somewhat less reliable than labor market studies because the latter allow one to distinguish risk levels across individuals, while other revealed preference methods do not. For example, we normally do not know whether individuals purchasing smoke detectors live in apartments that are "firetraps" or modern apartments with built-in sprinklers. Additionally, some of these studies can only provide information on the lower bound of the value of life because discrete purchase decisions do not force individuals to reveal their total willingness-to-pay, only whether they will pay more than a given price.[9] These studies provide widely varying estimates of the value of life—from $0.07 million to $4 million. However, he argues that the study that provides the most reliable estimate is Scott Atkinson and Robert Halvorsen's analysis of the purchase of safety features on new automobiles. This study includes the car purchase price (equivalent to the wage in the labor studies) and explanatory variables such as other product characteristics, characteristics of the purchasers, and the risk. The study estimates the value of life at $4 million, at the top of the range for this group of studies.[10]

Finally, Viscusi reviews six survey, or contingent valuation, estimates of the value of life. Surveys have some advantages over other methods.[11] However, the range of values this method produces is wide, ranging from $0.1 million to $15 million.

THE COST OF INJURIES

A major report has recently been prepared for Congress on the cost of injuries. This report, prepared by Dorothy Rice, Ellen MacKenzie, and associates, provides detailed estimates of costs for injuries from different causes and of three levels of severity.[12] Their estimates incorporate medical and rehabilitation costs and forgone earnings (including an imputed value for household labor) but, unfortunately, do not include pain and suffering and other dimensions of unhappiness that people would pay to avoid. They also do not include property damage losses and other related costs, such as court costs—their study was only concerned with the financial cost of injuries, rather than the social cost of any activity associated with the injury. Thus, the human capital approach adopted in the study leads to a very conservative estimate of the social cost of injuries as it ignores disutility resulting from pain and suffering. (This problem is discussed in the section on using the market analogy method to value a life saved in Chapter 10.) Therefore, we also summarize evidence on the cost of injury reviewed by W. Kip Viscusi. As Viscusi reviews labor market studies, the estimates he summarizes focus on individual willingness-to-pay, which do include the disutility of pain and suffering.

The Rice and Associates Estimates of the Cost of Injuries

The average costs per person per type of injury (in 1985 dollars) are as follows: motor vehicle injuries, $9,062; falls, $3,033; firearm injuries, $53,831; poisonings, $5,015; fire injuries and burns, $2,619; drownings and near drownings, $64,993; and "other," $1,187. The report notes that almost one-quarter of the total (discounted) lifetime cost occurs more than one year after the injury occurs.

Their report also calculates costs for three levels of severity of injury (in 1985 dollars): fatalities (including later fatalities directly attributable to the injury), $317,189; injuries requiring hospitalization, $34,116; and injuries not requiring hospitalization, $518. The average cost of an injury across all three levels of seriousness was $2,772.

The Viscusi Survey of Cost-of-Injury Estimates

W. Kip Viscusi has reviewed the evidence on the cost of nonfatal work-related injuries (in the same article as his value-of-life estimates, discussed earlier in this chapter). He was able to compute cost-of-injury estimates from 14 labor market studies conducted between 1978 and 1991. Unfortunately, the individual studies cover a wide range of nonfatal injury circumstances. For example, some studies only examined injuries that resulted in some degree of job interruption, while others included less serious injuries. Some studies used average injury risk rates for industries, while others used workers' (subjective) assessment of risk. Some studies controlled for wage differences due to loss-of-life risks, while others did not. Additionally, of course, mean injury risk rates varied considerably across the studies (from 0.03 to 0.10 per year). Because work-related injuries may be of different severity and type than other kinds of injuries, these estimates cannot be directly compared to estimates based on injuries in general.

Viscusi's conclusion (in 1990 dollars) is that "most of the estimates based on data for all injuries regardless of severity are clustered in the $25,000–$50,000 range. . .the value of lost workday injuries is in the area of $50,000, or at the high end of the range for estimates for the implicit value of injuries overall."[13]

THE COST OF MOTOR VEHICLE CRASHES AND INJURIES

Reduced injuries and reduced automobile costs are common potential impacts of transportation projects, such as better road lighting, more appropriate speed limits, or vehicle safety features. Here we examine estimates of the cost of vehicle crashes in the United States (Ted Miller) and the cost of serious road injuries in the United Kingdom (Transport Research Laboratory).

The Miller Estimates of the Cost of Motor Vehicle Crashes

Ted Miller has estimated the comprehensive costs of U.S. motor vehicle crashes.[14] The cost of motor vehicle crashes is not synonymous with the cost of injuries because motor vehicle crashes typically engender many costs, such as vehicle damage costs and additional time travel costs for other motorists, that the typical injury does not. Holding other things constant, therefore, one would expect the average cost of a motor vehicle crash to be higher than the average injury cost. Additionally, of course, vehicle crashes are also likely to have a distribution of injury severity that differs from the aggregate distribution.

Miller includes in his cost estimates medical and emergency services, lost wages and household production, workplace disruption, insurance administration costs, the cost of legal proceedings (but not the income transfers resulting from settlements), and the lost quality of life. Thus, these estimates differ methodologically from the cost-of-injury estimates calculated by Dorothy Rice and her colleagues, which only included "monetary" losses and, hence, did not include lost quality of life, including pain and suffering, inferred from individuals' willingness-to-pay to avoid injuries.

Miller reports his estimates in two formats. The first is a fully monetized "cost per crash" figure that can be directly plugged into a CBA. The value of life was set at $2.2 million per life (for use with all other dollar figures which are in 1988 dollars). Nonfatal quality of life losses were calculated by first multiplying the value of fatal risk reduction by the ratio of the years of functional capacity lost through the injury to years lost in a fatality, and then subtracting the monetary component of this value, namely, the value of wages and household production that was lost due to the injury.

Second, Miller reports estimates in a quantitative figure—years of life and functioning lost—which can be used in a cost-effectiveness measure as it quantifies, but does not monetize, the value of life or injuries. Thus, for example, on average, crash injuries involving lower extremities, such as pelvis and hip, resulted in 6.5 years of functional loss. This latter approach reflects the fact that some decision makers are uncomfortable monetizing the value of life or the cost of injuries. (Cost-effectiveness analysis is explained in detail in Chapter 13.)

Miller classifies crash injuries in two ways. First, by region of the body in decreasing order of severity: spinal cord, brain, lower extremity, upper extremity, trunk/abdomen, other head, face and neck, and minor external. Second, by "threat to life severity," which is estimated using the Abbreviated Injury Scale (AIS) of the Most life-threatening injury (thus, MAIS). Here we only report the summary findings by region of the body (in 1988 dollars): spinal cord, $1,459,042; lower extremity,

$142,330; brain, $84,592; upper extremity, $55,335; trunk/abdomen, $42,124; face, other head, other neck, $16,288; and minor external, $3,950. The average cost of non-fatal crashes for all body regions is $39,905, while the average cost per fatal crash is $2,385,090.

Miller points out that not using comprehensive cost measures (in other words, measuring incorrectly) can seriously distort public policy decision making. If injury costs are underestimated, then the benefits of safety-enhancing road improvements are lowered relative to the benefits of time-saving road improvements. The result is that it can appear that it is better to be dead than to be stuck in traffic![15] This is usually not the case when the numbers are estimated correctly.

The Transport Research Laboratory Estimate of the Cost of Serious Road Injuries

In 1989, the United Kingdom Department of Transport commissioned a number of studies of the cost of serious road accidents. These studies adopted a WTP approach.[16] Two random samples of households were drawn: one using standard contingent valuation procedures and the other using "standard gamble" questions. The contingent valuation questions asked respondents how much they would be willing to pay for a hypothetical safety feature that would reduce the risk of given injuries by a specific amount and that had to be purchased annually.

In the standard gamble format, respondents were asked to suppose that they had suffered a road injury, which, if treated in the standard way, would have a given prognosis. They were then asked to suppose that an alternative treatment would return them to normal health if successful—a result that is better than that produced by the standard treatment—but which, if unsuccessful, would result in a prognosis worse than that associated with the standard treatment. As described in Chapter 13 in more detail, the purpose of such questions is to determine the risk of treatment failure at which they would be indifferent between accepting and rejecting the treatment.

The researchers found that the contingent valuation questions produced estimates that were between 1.5 and 10.5 times higher than the standard gamble method. They conclude that, in this case, the standard gamble estimates are superior.[17] As a result of this work, the U.K. Department of Transport has set a figure of £74,480 for the cost of a "serious" nonfatal road accident (1992 pounds), including all economic costs.

THE COST OF CRIME

Many programs in criminal justice and education have as one of their projected impacts the reduction of crime among the population that is "treated." In order to estimate the benefits of such programs, it is first necessary to estimate the number of crimes of each type that will be avoided (N_{CT}) and to place a dollar value on each crime type avoided (C_{CT}). Obviously, crime types vary enormously in the extent to which they impose social costs—robbery is much more costly than jaywalking. The benefits of avoided crime are the sum of the discounted value of N_{CT}

times C_{CT}. Ideally, N_{CT} is estimated using an experimental design as described in Chapter 9. Of course, this is an expensive experiment to conduct, as one is interested in the number of crimes avoided over an extended period. Additionally, one must estimate C_{CT}. Here it is quite common to use estimates from secondary sources.

We provide evidence from three sources: estimates of violent crime by Ted Miller, Mark Cohen, and Shelli Rossman; estimates of the costs of firearm injuries from Wendy Max and Dorothy Rice; and estimates of the costs of a variety of crimes by David Long, Charles Mallar, and Craig Thornton.[18]

The Miller Estimates of the Cost of Violent Crime

Ted Miller and his colleagues provide estimates of the costs of the violent crimes of rape, robbery, assault, and murder. They seek to measure the total cost of these crimes; for our purpose, we are interested in their per-crime cost estimates. They include three kinds of cost in their total cost measure: (1) direct costs, such as the costs of medical care, mental health and emergency response services, and insurance administration; (2) the opportunity costs from forgone productivity, estimated as forgone wages, fringe benefits, and housework; and (3) the costs of pain and suffering. They do not include the costs of lost property or costs incurred to prevent future crime.

Their first set of cost estimates shows the cost per crime victim, where all crimes resulted in some degree of physical injury (with murder treated as a separate category). The second set of cost estimates is for "cost per victimization associated with completed or attempted crime." This includes crimes where there may be no physical injuries—for example, attempted crimes and arson. Value-of-life estimates were derived from a literature review along the lines described earlier. The costs of nonfatal injuries were estimated by multiplying estimates of the loss in quality-adjusted life years (QALYs) by the value of a life lost per year (derived from the value-of-life estimates). Quality-of-life losses were rated on a "functional capacity loss" scale that included cognitive, mobility, sensory, cosmetic, pain, and daily functioning losses, as well as a work-related disability dimension.[19]

The victim injury costs per physically injured victim (in 1989 dollars) were: rape plus other injury, $60,376; robbery, $24,947; assault, $22,314; arson, $49,603; and murder, $2,387,054. As already mentioned, the second set of costs (victim injury cost per crime) includes some crimes in which there was no *physical* injury. In general, one would expect this to produce lower average crime costs. However, this method allocates murder costs to the crime, usually assault, that underlies it. Thus, for example, the costs of a murder occurring during a robbery would be allocated to the robbery. In general, this would be expected to raise the average cost per crime. The resulting cost figures are (in 1989 dollars): rape, $47,424; robbery, $19,486; assault, $14,738; and arson, $24,714. These costs are the C_{CT} noted previously. The latter figures are lower, suggesting that including only crimes with physical injuries raises mean estimated costs more than allocating murder to crimes.

The Cost of Firearm Injuries: Max and Rice

Wendy Max and Dorothy Rice provide estimates of the cost of firearm injuries. It is important to recognize that this is not a cost-of-crime estimate; many firearm injuries are accidental. However, as most firearm injuries do arise from crime, we review the estimates here. Their estimate of costs has two components: (1) direct costs such as medical and hospital, rehabilitation, medication, and transportation costs; (2) indirect costs resulting from lost productivity (including the value of household labor). Indirect costs include morbidity costs (estimated as the value of days lost from injury or as the years of life lost from injury-related disability) and mortality costs (estimated as either the monetary value of lost future output or the years of life lost from premature death).

The estimates are for three classes of firearm injury: those resulting in fatalities, those resulting in hospitalization, and those not requiring hospitalization. Before presenting their estimates, it is important to note that their method is likely to produce very conservative estimates of the cost of firearm injuries. They do not include psychological costs of injuries (which one would expect to be an important component of total individual costs) and they use forgone earnings rather than willingness-to-pay in estimating the (lost) value of life.

Max and Rice find that the average total cost per injured person is as follows (in 1990 dollars): all types of firearm injuries, $53,831; fatal injuries, $373,520; injuries requiring hospitalization, $33,160; and injuries that do not require hospitalization, $458. They also find that fatal injuries result in an average decrease in life of 35.7 years per injured person. Nonfatal injuries that require hospitalization reduce the average longevity of the injured person by 2.87 years, while injuries that do not require hospitalization lead to a 0.01-year reduction.

Cost-of-Crime Estimates: Long, Mallar, and Thornton

David Long, Charles Mallar, and Craig Thornton estimate shadow prices for a wide variety of crimes, including murder, assault, robbery, burglary, larceny, motor vehicle theft, and drug violations. They estimate three major components of crime cost: criminal justice system costs, the costs of personal injury and property damage, and losses associated with stolen property. Criminal justice system cost estimates were based on the probability and cost of each arrested person passing through the various stages of the criminal justice system: police custody, arraignment, detention, trial, and incarceration. Personal injury medical costs and property damage costs were estimated from data collected in the National Crime Panel Survey. Specifically, the cost per victimization was multiplied by the ratio of victimizations to arrests to estimate a "per capita arrest cost." The value of stolen property was estimated as follows. The researchers found that thieves were only able to realize 35 percent of the value of stolen goods. They, therefore, treated 35 percent of the value of stolen goods as a transfer (from property owners to thieves) and multiplied the dollar value of stolen property by 0.65 to estimate the social cost of stolen property. One could certainly argue, however, that it is inappropriate to give thieves standing.

Adding these three cost components, their estimates of cost per arrest for each crime were as follows (in 1977 dollars): murder, $24,767; assault, $2,732; robbery, $12,087; burglary, $5,892; larceny and motor vehicle theft, $2,618; drug law violations, $2,618; other personal crimes, $756; other miscellaneous crimes, $919; and unspecified crimes, $2,048.

THE VALUE OF TIME

Time is a valuable commodity; as the saying goes, "time is money." Time spent traveling, which individuals would be willing to pay to avoid, is a cost. Change in travel time is an important component of many CBAs, most obviously those concerned with transportation. Though rarely a dominating cost or benefit, changes in waiting time can nonetheless be an important cost or benefit in many nontransportation projects as well. For example, queuing time is an important cost of any policy that rations goods such as gasoline or services such as medical care.

In practice, almost all of the empirical literature on time cost has been concerned with estimating the value of travel time. This is normally referred to as the *value of travel time savings* (VTTS), reflecting the fact that in transportation projects time changes usually are benefits. We use this terminology, even though time change impacts in other types of CBA may be costs. Also keep in mind that travel time costs may only provide a rough guide to other time costs; people, for example, usually experience considerably greater disutility from waiting time than from "pure" travel time. Indeed, waiting time disutility may be orders of magnitude larger than travel time disutility.[20]

There is a large empirical literature on VTTS that has been reviewed by several researchers. Many of these are on a country-specific or regional basis. Typically, these have been commissioned by the relevant government and have led to the adoption of a standard VTTS. For example, there have been recent reviews of the VTTS evidence in the United Kingdom, Canada, New Zealand, the Netherlands, the United States, and for developing countries.[21]

We primarily rely here on a review of the literature by W.G. Waters II.[22] Waters reviewed the estimates of VTTS from 56 empirical studies conducted between 1974 and 1990. These studies comprise both revealed preference approaches and contingent valuation studies. Revealed preference approaches include a wide range of situations: route choice decisions where there are different costs (for example, toll roads versus nontoll roads); mode choice decisions (bus or car travel versus faster but more costly airline travel); speed choice decisions (where faster speeds involve higher operating costs); and location choice decisions (hedonic methods that isolate the impact of commuting time on land values). Survey methods are increasingly being used to estimate VTTS because they allow researchers to gather data of direct relevance to determining willingness-to-pay.

As is the normal procedure in the VTTS literature, Waters presents the results as a percentage of the (hourly) wage rate rather than as a dollar figure. He found as much as a tenfold variation in estimates from his literature review. As with other estimates described in this chapter, the studies cover a wide range of circumstances. Waters partitions these studies in a number of ways. He aggregates the 32 studies that focus on commuting trips and (after eliminating some outliers) calculates the mean value at 48 percent of the wage rate with a median of 40 percent. When this is reduced to the 15 North American automobile commuting studies, Waters calculates a mean of 59 percent (54 percent with the elimination of outliers) and a median of 42 percent. The 17 non-North American auto commuting studies generate a mean of 38 percent. Waters concludes that a shadow price between approximately 40 to 50 percent of the wage rate is appropriate for auto commuting.[23]

This conclusion is broadly consistent with that of Herbert Mohring and his colleagues regarding all intracity transit travel time: "[W]age earners with annual incomes greater than about US$30,000 value an hour of time in intracity transit at about half their equivalent hourly wage rates."[24] Governments have usually mandated the use of rates of between 40 percent and 60 percent of the hourly wage rate in CBA. The U.S. Federal Highway Administration currently uses 60 percent as the VTTS for highway projects, while Transport Canada recommends 50 percent for nonwork time savings.[25]

In interurban travel contexts, it is usually useful to divide travel time savings between work time and leisure, with work time valued at the relevant wage rate and leisure valued somewhat less than the value of commuting time. But again, valuations vary widely: the ratio of VTTS for work and nonwork ranges from 1:1 to over 5:1.[26]

Should estimates be adjusted for the different time preferences of different income groups? From the CBA perspective, the answer is clearly "yes." If the analyst has information about the income of prospective project users, then income-specific estimates should be used if they are available. Waters has also reviewed those studies that have examined the relationship between VTTS and income.[27] He finds that VTTS increases with income but not proportionally. He suggests that a convenient rule of thumb for the relationship is a square root rule. Using such a rule when income is above the average, the VTTS rises more slowly than does income. For example, if income goes up fourfold, the VTTS only doubles.[28]

THE VALUE OF RECREATION BENEFITS

Over the last 20 years there has been a vast number of studies that estimate the value of various kinds of recreation. These studies generally use the travel cost or the contingent valuation method.

A comprehensive review of recreation values has been conducted by Cindy Sorg and John Loomis.[29] Unfortunately, this review was conducted in 1984 and there has been no comprehensive review since, although there is a large number of more recent individual estimates based on more sophisticated estimation techniques. In order to facilitate comparisons, Sorg and Loomis reported all values in 1982 dollars per "activity-day." They excluded studies for which it was not possible to calculate such a value. They made several adjustments, which were approved by an expert panel, to facilitate comparison. The major adjustments were: the conversion of "value per trip" to value per activity-day; the addition of time travel costs to other travel costs for studies that had not included this element (a 30 percent upward adjustment); an adjustment for the fact that differences in travel costs alter the probability of participation—essentially the demand for specific recreational activities is more inelastic than actually estimated (the downward adjustment in predicted use ranged from zero for highly specialized activities to 30 percent for nonspecialized activities); an adjustment to include the value to out-of-state visitors, where this value had not been included and where it was deemed likely to be important as, for example, in the case of big game hunting (a 15 percent upward adjustment); an adjustment to contingent valuation studies that had not excluded protest bids (a 15 percent upward adjustment).

Sorg and Loomis report activity-day estimates for a large number of recreational activities. They do not, however, provide a single "best estimate" for each activity. Therefore, we report the adjusted activity-day ranges for each recreational activity. The values are (in 1982 dollars, rounded to the nearest dollar): salmon and steelhead sport fishing, $26 to $99 (six studies); big game hunting, $18 to $132 (15 studies); camping, $6 to $26 (ten studies); downhill skiing, $24 (one study); cold water fishing, $9 to $68 (15 studies); warm water fishing, $15 to $26 (five studies); saltwater fishing, $41 to $90 (one study, two different methodologies); hiking, $8 to $46 (six studies); motorized boating, $6 to $43 (three studies); motorized travel, $7 (one study); nonmotorized boating, $6 to $33 (five studies); picnicking, $7 to $29 (five studies); small game hunting, $16 to $43 (four studies); upland game hunting, $37 (one study); water fowl hunting, $16 to $85 (seven studies); water sports, $10 to $27 (five studies); and wilderness recreation, $13 to $74 (five studies). The authors point out that their adjustments considerably reduce the range of estimates and also that, as is the case with other empirically derived estimates in this chapter, many of the differences in estimates can be explained by quality differences (for example, rarity in the particular jurisdiction).

■ **EXHIBIT 12.1**

Ralph Luken wished to estimate the costs and benefits of (technology-based) water pollution standards introduced by the Clean Water Act of 1972. However, there were no existing estimates of WTP for improvements in the water quality of the rivers in question. Therefore, he utilized WTP estimates from existing studies as a basis for his estimates of the value of improvements in water quality.

He initially considered eight existing studies that might provide plug-in values. Five of the existing studies used the contingent valuation method, two studies used the travel cost method, and the eighth study was a user participation study. Luken eliminated five of the studies because their focus was not similar to the sites he was considering. These five studies dealt with water systems, such as those on a large western lake and a western river basin. His sites, in contrast, were generally eastern rivers with local recreation usage. Therefore he focused on three studies: one on the Charles River in Boston and two on the Monongahela River in Pennsylvania. The Monongahela studies estimated benefits for three levels of improvement in water quality (from boating to fishing, from fishing to swimming, and from boating to swimming), while the Charles River study only examined improvements in water quality from boating to swimming (i.e., the biggest "jump" in quality). The summarized values as annual WTP per household (1984 dollars) are as follows:

River	Water Quality Change		
	Boat–Fish	Fish–Swim	Boat–Swim
Monongahela (contingent valuation)	$25–40	$14–23	$40–64
Monongahela (travel cost)	$8	$10	$18
Charles (contingent valuation)	—	—	$74

Unfortunately, these benefit categories did not directly map into the benefit categories Luken was using, which covered five quality improvement levels: U = Unusable, B = Boatable, R = Rough fishing, G = Game fishing, and G* = Superior game fishing. Luken assumed that the travel cost method provided lower-bound estimates (because they include only use valuations) and the contingent valuation estimates provided upper-bound estimates (as they include nonuse as well as use valuations). As shown next, he also included intrause estimates to reflect smaller benefit improvements. His plug-in values are as follows:

VALUES FOR WATER QUALITY BENEFITS

(WILLINGNESS-TO-PAY PER HOUSEHOLD PER YEAR) ($1984)

Initial Water Quality	Final Water Quality	Lower Bound	Upper Bound
U	U	$1–3	$9–18
U	B	$5	$35
U	R	$15	$50
U	G	$20	$80
U	G*	$25	$90
B	B	$2–4	$8–15
B	R	$8	$30
B	G	$15	$50
B	G*	$20	$60
R	R	$3–5	$6–13
R	G	$10	$25
R	G*	$15	$35
G	G	$3–6	$5–10
G	G*	$12	$20

Although the purpose of this exhibit is to illustrate the use of secondary sources, it is interesting to note that in using these values, Luken generally found that costs exceed benefits.

Sources: Frederick W. Gramlick, "The Demand for Clear Water: The Case of the Charles River," *National Tax Journal*, 30, no. 2 (1977), 183–195; Ralph A. Luken, *Efficiency in Environmental Regulation* (Boston, MA: Kluwer Academic Publishers, 1990), pp. 45–50, pp. 88–90; V. Kerry Smith and William H. Desvousges, *Measuring Water Quality Benefits* (Boston, MA: Kluwer-Nijhoff Publishing, 1986); V. Kerry Smith, William H. Desvousges and Ann Fisher, "A Comparison of Direct and Indirect Methods for Estimating Environmental Benefits," Working Paper No. 83–W32, Vanderbilt University, Nashville, TN, 1984.

A SUMMARY OF VALUATIONS

Table 12.1 contains summary estimates for most of the values discussed in this chapter. As such summary estimates inevitably involve some arbitrariness, we provide a brief explanation of the suggested valuations. The values are presented either as a dollar value per person in 1990 U.S. dollars or as a fraction of either value of life or wage rate.

The range suggested in Table 12.1 for the value of life is of $2 to $3 million (1990 dollars). While taken from Miller, this range is also quite close to Fisher and colleagues' lower-bound estimate, which is the one in which these authors express the greatest confidence. The upper end of the range corresponds to Viscusi's lower-bound estimate, which is the one in which he expresses the greatest confidence.

Motor vehicle accident costs are also summarized. Because Rice and MacKenzie's estimates only cover monetary costs, they are not directly comparable to Viscusi's summary of injury costs. Therefore, we provide both. Additionally, Viscusi's estimates cannot be directly reported in terms of a severity index. For summary purposes, we arbitrarily assume that Viscusi's lower-bound estimate ($25,000) represents an average of less serious injuries, while his upper-bound estimate ($50,000) represents an average of more serious injuries. The Rice and MacKenzie estimates are least useful for injuries that eventually prove fatal, as monetary costs are likely to be only a small fraction of total social costs. However, their estimate of the cost of hospitalization injuries is not much lower than Viscusi's upper-bound estimate in equivalent-year dollars.

Motor vehicle crash injury costs are reported as a fraction of the value of life. This illustrates the alternative method of reporting injury costs. The 1.08 coefficient for fatal crashes illustrates that if a relatively conservative estimate of the value of life is used (in this case Miller's value of life), motor vehicle crashes resulting in death can produce costs that are higher than "average" value-of-life estimates.

Because the estimates of the cost of crime either cover different crimes or deal with different specific circumstances (firearms injuries), we summarize all three studies discussed in the text. The only case in which there is more than one estimate for the same crime is robbery. These two estimates are extremely close in same-year dollars.

For the value of travel time, we suggest using 45 percent of the wage. This reflects a midrange for both Waters and Mohring, although government agencies have tended to prescribe use of a somewhat higher ratio.

USING PREVIOUS CBAs TO DO QUALITATIVE CBA

In some situations it may not be feasible or necessary to collect original data in order to produce "cost-benefit-like" analysis. This can occur when previous CBAs consistently demonstrate that a particular type of project has or has not produced positive net benefits. In these circumstances, often the most useful product that the analyst can produce is a literature review of relevant CBAs. A useful precursor to such reviews is for the analyst to build a bibliography that is germane to the particular policy area of interest.[30]

TABLE 12.1   SOME RULES OF THUMB FOR "QUICK AND DIRTY" CBA

Shadow Price	Value	Comments
Value of Life	(1990 US$) $2 to $3 million	Most appropriate for North American applications; conservative estimate
Monetary Injury Costs per Person (Rice and MacKenzie): 1) Eventually fatal 2) Hospitalized/nonfatal 3) Nonhospitalized/nonfatal	(1990 US$) 1) $385,000 2) $41,000 3) $600	Figures for monetary costs only
Per Person Cost of Injury (Viscusi): 1) Less serious 2) More serious	(1990 US$) 1) $25,000 2) $50,000	Based on WTP studies
Motor Vehicle Crash Injuries (Miller): 1) Spinal cord 2) Brain 3) Lower extremity 4) Upper extremity 5) Average for nonfatal crash 6) Average for fatal crash	As fraction of value of life: 1) 0.66 2) 0.04 3) 0.06 4) 0.03 5) 0.02 6) 1.08	Based on Miller's estimates of value of life
Average Victim Cost per Crime (Miller): 1) Rape 2) Robbery 3) Assault 4) Arson	(1990 US$) 1) $64,000 2) $26,000 3) $24,000 4) $52,000	Only crimes that included some physical injury
Per Person Cost of Firearm Injuries (Max and Rice): 1) Fatal injuries 2) Injuries requiring hospitalization 3) Injuries not requiring hospitalization	(1990 US$) 1) $374,000 2) $33,000 3) $500	Not WTP
Per Person Cost of Crime (Long, Mallar, and Thornton) 1) Robbery 2) Burglary 3) Larceny 4) Drugs	(1990 US$) 1) $27,000 2) $13,000 3) $6,000 4) $6,000	Relatively old study, but good methodology
Value of Travel Time Saved: 1) Intraurban (usually commuting) travel 2) Work time	As fraction of wage rate: 1) 0.40 to 0.50 2) Equal to wage rate	High variance among studies

EXERCISES FOR CHAPTER 12

1. A 40-mile stretch of rural road with limited access is used primarily by regional commuters and business travelers to move between two major interstate highways. The legal speed limit on the road is currently 55 miles per hour (mph) and the estimated average speed is 61 mph. Traffic engineers predict that if the speed limit were raised to 65 mph and enforcement levels were kept constant, the average speed would rise to 70 mph.

   Currently, an average of 5,880 vehicles per day use the stretch of road—approximately half are commuters and half are business travelers. Traffic engineers do not expect that a higher speed limit will attract more vehicles. Vehicles using the road carry, on average, 1.6 people. Traffic engineers predict that raising the speed limit on this stretch of road would result in an additional 52 vehicle crashes involving, on average, 0.1 fatalities annually. They also predict that operating costs would rise by an average of $0.002 per mile per vehicle (in 1990 dollars).

   The average hourly wage in the county in which the majority of users of the road work is $12.20 (in 1990 dollars).

   Estimate the annual net benefits of raising the speed limit on the road from 55 mph to 65 mph. In doing this, test the sensitivity of your estimate of annual net benefits to several alternative estimates of the value of time savings and the value of life that you have selected from the chapter.

2. Analysts estimate that the expansion of the capacity of the criminal courts in a city would require about 7,200 additional hours of juror time. The average wage rate in the county is $10/hour. A recent survey by the jury commissioner, however, found that the average wage for those who actually serve on juries under the present system, who are also currently employed, is only $6/hour. The survey also found that about one-third of those who actually serve on juries under the existing system do not hold jobs—for example, they are homemakers, retirees, or unemployed.

   a. What shadow price should the analysts use for an hour of jury time?
   b. About a quarter of jurors do not receive wages from their employers while on jury duty. How does this affect your choice of the shadow price?

NOTES

[1]For example, Tae Hoon Oum, W.G. Waters II, and Jong-Say Yong surveyed over 60 studies of own-price elasticities of transport demand, "Concepts of Price Elasticities of Transport Demand and Recent Empirical Estimates," *Journal of Transport Economics and Policy*, 26, no. 2 (1992), 139–154. A companion survey by Philip Goodwin reviews empirical estimates of public transit and auto usage, "A Review of New Demand Elasticities with Special Reference to Short and Long Run Effects of Price Changes," *Journal of Transport Economics and Policy*, 26, no. 2 (1992), 155–169.

[2]For example, one recent study suggests that transportation and communications are substitute;, see E.A. Selvanathan and Saroja Selvanathan, "The Demand for Transport and Communication in the United Kingdom and Australia," *Transportation Research - B*, 28B, no. 1 (1994), 1–9.

[3]David A. Long, Charles D. Mallar, and Craig V. Thornton, "Evaluating the Benefits and Costs of the Jobs Corps," *Journal of Policy Analysis and Management*, 1, no. 1 (Fall 1981), 55–76.

[4]Ralph A. Luken, *Efficiency in Environmental Regulation: A Benefit-Cost Analysis of Alternative Approaches* (Boston, MA: Kluwer Academic Publishers, 1990).

[5]Ted R. Miller, *Narrowing the Plausible Range Around the Value of Life* (Washington, DC: The Urban Institute, 1989); Ann Fisher, Lauraine G. Chestnut, and Daniel M. Violette, "The Value of Reducing Risks to Death: A Note on New Evidence," *Journal of Policy Analysis and Management*, 8, no. 1 (Winter 1989), 88–100; W. Kip Viscusi, "The Value of Risks to Life and Health," *Journal of Economic Literature*, 31, no. 4 (December 1993), 1912–1946.

[6]The authors either use the original authors' "best estimate" or make a judgment based on the original study.

[7]Fisher, Chestnut, and Violette, "The Value of Reducing Risks to Death: A Note on New Evidence," pp. 96, 98.

[8]Viscusi, "The Value of Risks to Life and Health," pp. 1930–1931.

[9]This is analogous to the dichotomous-choice method discussed in Chapter 11. With the dichotomous-choice method, this problem is dealt with by offering different individuals different prices. This does not normally occur in markets.

[10]Scott E. Atkinson and Robert Halverson, "The Valuation of Risks to Life: Evidence from the Market for Automobiles," *Review of Economics and Statistics*, 72, no. 1 (February 1990), 332–340.

[11]See Viscusi, "The Value of Risks to Life and Health," at pp. 1937–1938 for a discussion of the advantages of surveys.

[12]Dorothy P. Rice, Ellen J. MacKenzie, and associates, *Cost of Injury in the United States: A Report to Congress*, (San Francisco, CA: Institute for Health and Aging, University of California and Injury Prevention Center, The Johns Hopkins University, 1989).

[13]Viscusi, "The Value of Risks to Life and Health," p. 1935.

[14]Ted R. Miller, "Costs and Functional Consequences of U.S. Roadway Crashes," *Accident Analysis and Prevention*, 25, no. 5 (1993), 593–607.

[15]Ascribed by Miller, *Narrowing the Plausible Range Around the Value of Life,* 1993, p. 605, to Ezra Hauer (no cite).

[16]The studies are summarized in Deirdre O'Reilly, Jean Hopkin, Graham Loomes, Michael Jones-Lee, Peter Philips, Kate McMahon, Dawn Ives, Barbara Sobey, David Ball, and Ray Kemp, "The Value of Road Safety: U.K. Research on the Value of Preventing Non-Fatal Injuries," *Journal of Transport Economics and Policy*, 28, no. 1 (January 1994), 45–60.

[17]For their reasoning, see O'Reilly et al., "The Value of Road Safety," pp. 52–53.

[18]Ted R. Miller, Mark A. Cohen, and Shelli Rossman, "Victim Costs of Violent Crime and Resulting Injuries," *Health Affairs*, 12, no. 4 (1993), 186–197; Wendy Max and Dorothy P. Rice, "Shooting in the Dark: Estimating the Cost of Firearm Injuries," *Health Affairs*, 12, no. 4 (1993), 171–185; Long, Mallar and Thornton, "Evaluating the Benefits and Costs of the Jobs Corps."

[19]See Miller, "Costs and Functional Consequences of U.S. Roadway Crashes."

[20]Herbert Mohring, John Schroeter, and Paitoon Wiboonchutikula, "The Values of Waiting Time, Travel Time, and a Seat on a Bus," *Rand Journal of Economics*, 18, no. 1 (Spring 1987), 40–56.

[21]United Kingdom: C. Sharp, "Developments in Transport Policy, The Value of Time Savings and of Accident Prevention," *Journal of Transport Economics and Policy*, 22, no. 2 (1988), 235–238; Canada: J.J. Lawson, *The Value of Passenger Travel Time for Use in Economic Evaluation of Transport Investments* (Ottawa, Ontario: Transport Canada, 1989); New Zealand: Ted Miller, "The Value of Time and the Benefit of Time Saving," presented to the National Roads Board, New Zealand, and the Federal Highway Administration, U.S. Dept. of Transportation (Washington, DC: Urban Institute, 1989); United States: Texas Transportation Institute, "Value of Time and Discomfort Costs, Progress Report on Literature Review and Assessment of Procedures and Data," Technical Memorandum for NCHRP, pp.7–12; Miller (this footnote); Netherlands and developing countries: J. Bates and S. Glaister, "The Valuation of Time

Savings for Urban Transport Appraisal for Developing Countries: A Review," report prepared for the World Bank, 1990.

[22]W.G. Waters II, "Variations in the Value of Travel Time Savings: Empirical Studies and the Values for Road Project Evaluation," Working Paper, Faculty of Commerce, University of British Columbia, October 1993.

[23]Ibid., p. 10.

[24]Mohring, Schoreter, and Wiboonchutikula, "The Values of Waiting Time, Travel Time, and a Seat on a Bus," p. 40.

[25]Waters, "Variations in the Value of Travel Time Savings," p. 13.

[26]Ibid., p. 11.

[27]W.G. Waters II, "The Value of Travel Time Savings and the Link with Income: Implications for Public Project Evaluation," *International Journal of Transport Economics*, 12, no. 3 (October 1994), 243–253.

[28]A VTTS_Y that varies with income Y can be written as:

$$\sqrt{(Y/\overline{Y}} \; \bullet \; \overline{\text{VTTS}}$$

where $\overline{Y}$ is the mean income level and $\overline{\text{VTTS}}$ is the VTTS for the mean income group. Thus, for incomes that are only half of the average, VTTS is 0.71 of that for average incomes, rather than 0.5.

[29]Cindy F. Sorg and John B. Loomis, *Empirical Estimates of Amenity Forest Values: A Comparative Review*, General Technical Report RM-107 (Fort Collins, CO: Rocky Mountain Forest and Range Experiment Station, Forest Service, USDA, 1984).

[30]A representative sample bibliography by sector is presented at the end of this book.

13

COST-EFFECTIVENESS ANALYSIS
AND COST-UTILITY ANALYSIS

Cost-effectiveness analysis (CEA) and cost-utility analysis (CUA) are commonly used alternatives to CBA.[1] These methods are potentially useful when analysts seek efficient policies but face certain constraints that prevent them from doing CBA. Three constraints are common. First, analysts may be unwilling or unable to monetize the most important policy impact. This constraint arises most frequently in the evaluation of alternative policies that save lives: Many people are willing to predict the numbers of lives saved by alternative programs but are unwilling to place a dollar value on a life saved. The second constraint arises when analysts recognize that a particular effectiveness measure does not capture all of the social benefits of each alternative, and some of these other social benefits are difficult to monetize. In using CBA, analysts face the burden of monetizing all impacts. If the effectiveness measure captures "most" of the benefits, it may be reasonable for analysts to use CEA to avoid the burden of conducting a CBA. The third constraint arises when analysts deal with intermediate goods whose linkage to preferences is not clear. For example, the exact contribution of different types of weapon systems to overall national defense is often unclear. In such situations, CBA is not possible, but CEA may give useful information concerning the relative efficiency of alternatives.

Even though both CEA and CUA have been widely used by analysts working in a number of policy areas, especially health and defense, they are not applied consistently. There is great variation in a number of practices, such as the specification of alternative policies, the justification of effectiveness measures, the inclusiveness of cost measures, and the discounting of effectiveness over time. Indeed, one recent review of the application of CEA and CUA to the evaluation of health policies found that approximately half of the studies examined were of less than adequate quality.[2]

CEA compares (usually mutually exclusive) alternatives on the basis of their costs and a single quantified but not monetized effectiveness measure, such as number of lives saved per dollar. Though there is no conceptual reason why costs cannot be measured comprehensively, in practice analysts most often measure them narrowly as budgetary costs. For example, CEA might include hospital salaries and supplies but might not include clients' waiting time. Except where otherwise noted, our discussion in this chapter refers to CEA as it is commonly practiced, that is, with this usually overly narrow specification of cost.

If budgetary cost happens to equal opportunity cost exactly, *and* the effectiveness measure is the only impact for which people are willing to pay, *and* the scale of the alternatives being compared is the same, then the rankings of alternatives by CEA and CBA will be identical. As discussed in Chapters 1 and 2, however, CBA not only produces a ranking of alternatives, it also reveals whether the highest-ranked or any of the other alternatives increase efficiency. CEA produces a ranking but does not provide explicit information about whether there would be positive net social benefits associated with any of the alternatives being considered. However, *if all alternatives are mutually exclusive, and the status quo is among the alternatives, sharing similar scale and patterns of costs and benefits, then CEA does select the most efficient policy.*

In many situations, the effectiveness measure selected by analysts (or decision makers) for use in CEA does not correspond to social benefits as measured in CBA, which are ultimately based on the willingness-to-pay (WTP) of individuals. We can reasonably infer in many circumstances that individuals would demonstrate WTP for incremental units of "effectiveness" such as "lives saved." In other circumstances, however, the inference of WTP is more tenuous. For example, "number of addicts treated" may or may not be an approximate measure for such benefits as reductions in street crime and the other negative externalities of drug abuse. While analysts cannot avoid making estimates of WTP in doing CBA, even if they must rely on shadow prices from secondary sources, they often do not make an explicit connection between WTP and the effectiveness measure used in CEA. To highlight this problem, some authors distinguish between intermediate outputs, such as "patients appropriately treated," where the value may not be clear, and final outputs, such as "lives saved," for which people are more clearly willing to pay. Michael Drummond and his colleagues argue that "[i]ntermediate outputs are admissible, although care must be taken to establish a link between these and a final health output, or to show that the intermediate outputs themselves have some value. . .In general, though, one should choose an effectiveness measure relating to a final output."[3]

Cost-utility analysis also relates budgetary costs to a single benefit measure, but its benefit measure is a construct made up of several (usually two) benefit categories. For example, the benefit measure may be quality-adjusted life-years. If analysts use *either* additional years of life per dollar cost, *or* a quantitative index of improved quality of life per dollar cost, they are doing CEA. The rationale for CUA is that *both* the number of additional years *and* the quality of life during those years are important benefit categories. Thus, if the alternatives under consideration have two related quantified (but not monetized) benefits, or a benefit with two distinct dimensions that can be quantified, CUA comes a step closer than CEA to the full treatment of benefits provided by CBA through WTP.

Keep in mind that CEA and CUA do not necessarily take account of all *social* costs. *Indeed, most CEA and CUA studies consider only budgetary costs and exclude other social costs.*[4] In many studies, it is also unclear whether budgetary costs are based on marginal costs (the appropriate measure) or on average costs (which might differ widely from marginal costs).[5] When alternatives have different opportunity costs that fall outside of measured costs, CEA and CUA may yield rankings that differ from those that would result from CBA.

COST-EFFECTIVENESS ANALYSIS

There are two basic ways to create cost-effectiveness ratios. For decision-making purposes, there are two ways to impose constraints to facilitate comparison of policy alternatives involving projects with different scales. There are also adjustments that can be made to make CEA closer to CBA.

The Two CEA Ratios

As CEA does not monetize benefits, it inevitably involves two different metrics: cost in dollars and an effectiveness measure—for example, lives saved, tons of carbon monoxide reduced, or children vaccinated. Because one cannot add or subtract noncommensurable metrics, one cannot obtain a single measure of net social benefits from the two metrics. One can only compute the ratio of the two measures as a basis for ranking alternative policies. Obviously, this can be done in two ways.

First, one can measure cost-effectiveness in terms of cost per unit of outcome effectiveness, for example, cost per life saved. To compute this, one takes the ratio of the budgetary cost of each alternative i, denoted by C_i, to the effectiveness (or benefit) of that alternative, E_i:

$$CE_i = C_i / E_i \qquad (13.1)$$

This CE ratio can be thought of as the average cost per unit of effectiveness. The most cost-effective project has the lowest average cost per unit of effectiveness. Thus, *projects should be rank ordered from the most cost-effective (those with the smallest CE ratio) to the least cost-effective (those with the largest CE ratio).*

Second, cost-effectiveness can be calculated as the ratio of the outcome effectiveness units per unit of budgetary cost, or:

$$EC_i = E_i / C_i \qquad (13.2)$$

It is important to be aware that, rather confusingly, some authors call *this* EC ratio the cost-effectiveness ratio. This EC ratio can be thought of as the average effectiveness per unit of cost. The most cost-effective project has the highest average effectiveness per unit of cost. Thus, *projects should be rank ordered from the most cost-effective (those with the largest EC number) to the least cost-effective (those with the smallest EC number).*

Both cost-effectiveness measures involve computing for each alternative the ratio of the input to the output. Thus, they are measures of technical efficiency. As we discuss in the sections that follow, differences across policy alternatives in terms of scales of project, as well as the fact that cost-effectiveness measures often omit important social costs and benefits, frequently make them poor measures of allocative efficiency.

CEA Where Scale Problems Are Irrelevant: Identical Program Budgets or Identical Program Effectiveness

One may feel uneasy about selecting policy alternatives on the basis of their cost-effectiveness ratios. This intuition is correct. Ratios do not take into account the different scales of projects, a reason discussed in Chapter 2 for avoiding benefit-cost ratios.

If, however, *all* of the policy alternatives have the same cost, then there is no scale difference. If, in addition, the cost-effectiveness ratio is inclusive of all social costs and benefits, then CEA does rank alternatives in terms of allocative efficiency. Table 13.1 compares three alternative projects (one of which might be the status quo) for saving lives. The only (measured) costs are budgetary costs (in millions of dollars) and the effectiveness criterion is the number of lives saved. In this case the CE ratio reveals the average cost per life saved. Of course, in this simple example one does not even need to compute cost-effectiveness ratios: by "eye-balling" the table, one can easily observe that alternative C saves the most lives. Computing the cost-effectiveness ratio simply confirms this. It does not matter whether the ratio is calculated as cost per life saved or as lives saved per (million) dollars. Because all alternatives involve the same level of expenditure, they can be thought of as different ways of spending a *fixed budget*.

Similarly, scale is not a problem if the level of effectiveness is constant across all alternatives. This is illustrated in Table 13.2, which shows three alternatives for saving the same number of lives, namely, 10. Here, alternative A is best. Again, it does not matter whether the ratio is calculated as cost per life saved or as lives saved per (million) dollars. Situations in which the level of effectiveness is constant across alternatives, or is treated as constant, can be thought of as different ways of achieving a *fixed effectiveness*.

TABLE 13.1   COST-EFFECTIVENESS ANALYSIS WITH FIXED (IDENTICAL) COSTS

	ALTERNATIVES		
Cost and Effectiveness	A	B	C
Cost Measure (budget cost)	$10M	$10M	$10M
Effectiveness Measure (number of lives saved)	5	10	15
CE Ratio (cost per life saved)	$2.0M	$1.0M	$0.67M*
EC Ratio (lives saved per million dollars)	0.5 life	1.0 life	1.5 lives*

*CE ratio or EC ratio of the most cost-effective alternative

TABLE 13.2   COST-EFFECTIVENESS ANALYSIS WITH FIXED (IDENTICAL) EFFECTIVENESS LEVELS

Cost and Effectiveness	ALTERNATIVES		
	A	B	C
Cost Measure (budget cost)	$5M	$10M	$15M
Effectiveness Measure (number of lives saved)	10	10	10
CE Ratio (cost per life saved)	$0.5M*	$1.0M	$1.5M
EC Ratio (lives saved per million dollars)	2 lives*	1 life	0.66 life

*CE ratio or EC ratio of the most cost-effective alternative

Note that in the case of fixed effectiveness, CEA corresponds to a simple cost-minimization problem (minimize dollars),[6] while in the fixed-budget case CEA corresponds to a simple effectiveness-maximization problem (maximize lives saved). Both tables contain examples of *dominated alternatives*—by holding one dimension constant, they ensure that the alternative with the best cost-effectiveness ratio dominates on one dimension and is exactly the same on the other dimension. It is possible that one alternative can dominate another even if they have neither the same cost nor the same effectiveness, as long as it is superior on both dimensions. Clearly, dominated alternatives should not be selected. If an alternative dominates all others, then it should be selected.[7]

Modifying CEA to Deal with Scale Differences

Large scale differences among alternatives potentially distort choice. The simple example in Table 13.3 illustrates this. It shows a choice between two mutually exclusive alternatives, A and B. Clearly, if we used a cost-effectiveness ratio, then we would choose alternative A. Yet, if we look more closely at alternative B, we see that it would save a large number of lives at the relatively low "price" per life saved of $0.5 million per life—much less than the shadow prices reviewed in Chapter 12. It is therefore likely that a CBA would show alternative B has larger net benefits. (Of course, we cannot be certain of this without valuing all costs and benefits.) Given that CEA was probably proposed in the first place because analysts were unwilling to monetize lives saved, how can CEA be used sensibly as a decision rule without monetizing lives saved?

TABLE 13.3   THE PROBLEM WITH THE CE RATIO WHEN SCALE DIFFERS

Cost and Effectiveness	ALTERNATIVES	
	A	B
Cost Measure (budget cost)	$1M	$100M
Effectiveness Measure (number of lives saved)	4	200
CE Ratio (cost per life saved)	$250,000*	$500,000
EC Ratio (lives saved per million dollars)	4.0 lives*	2.0 lives

*CE ratio or EC ratio of the most cost-effective alternative

In order to make CEA more useful for decision making, decision makers sometimes specify a minimum acceptable level of effectiveness, denoted $\bar{E}$. There are two common ways of imposing such a constraint.

First, we could select the project that meets the constraint at the lowest cost:

$$\text{Minimize } C_i$$

$$\text{s.t.}^8 \quad E_i > \bar{E}$$

Here the analyst or decision maker has decided on a minimum level of effectiveness and selects the least costly alternative to achieve it. The decision maker is acting as if he or she does not value additional units of effectiveness. This might apply, for example, to alternative ways of ensuring that children receive minimum amounts of fluoride to protect their teeth. It might also apply to some national defense activities, although in these examples, additional units of effectiveness above $\bar{E}$ are probably worth something to decision makers.

Second, we could select the most cost-effective alternative that satisfies the effectiveness constraint:

$$\text{Minimize } CE_i$$

$$\text{s.t.} \quad E_i > \bar{E}$$

This rule generally leads to higher levels of effectiveness and higher costs than the first rule.

An alternative way to constrain choice is to specify a maximum budgetary cost, denoted $\bar{C}$. Again there are two alternative decision rules for selecting the best project subject to this constraint.

First, we could select the project that yields the largest number of units of effectiveness, subject to the budget constraint:

$$\text{Maximize } E_i$$

$$\text{s.t.} \quad C_i < \bar{C}$$

The problem with this approach is that it ignores incremental cost savings. In other words, cost savings beyond $\bar{C}$ are not valued.

Second, we could select the alternative project that most cost-effectively meets the imposed budget constraint:

$$\text{Minimize } CE_i$$

$$\text{s.t.} \quad C_i < \bar{C}$$

This rule places some weight on incremental cost savings and is more likely to result in the selection of a project with less than the minimum cost.

An Illustration of the Different CE Rules

Imagine that each of the ten mutually exclusive and exhaustive projects shown in Table 13.4 are intended to save lives. The expected number of lives saved for each project are given in column 2, and the expected budgetary cost in millions of dollars for each project is in column 3. The "basic" cost-effectiveness ratio (cost per life saved) appears in column 4. Using the standard CE formula, projects can be ranked from most cost-effective to least cost-effective: project E is most cost-effective, followed by B, J, I, A, C, G, H, D, and F. Dominated projects can be eliminated from the choice set at the outset to simplify the analysis: Project D can be eliminated because it is dominated by project C, and projects C and F can be eliminated because they are dominated by project A. The most cost-effective alternative is project E. For this project, the average cost of a life saved is $2.0 million.

Project E, however, saves the fewest lives. Project B saves twice as many lives as project E and costs only $24 million more. Which project is better? This question illustrates the problem of different scales. Preferably, we would like the option of performing 2.2 project E's. This would be superior to project B, but it is not feasible because the projects are mutually exclusive and exhaustive.

This example illustrates that if we are prepared to monetize the value of a life saved, as in CBA, we can get closer to determining which alternative is the most allocatively efficient. Specifically, if a life saved is valued at more than $2.4 million, then project B is preferred to project E; if a life saved is valued at between $2.0 million and $2.4 million, then project E is preferred to project B; on the other hand, if a life saved is valued at less than $2.0 million, then no project at all is preferred to either project E or project B.

Now, suppose that the decision maker specifies that he or she wishes to save a minimum of 50 lives. The cheapest acceptable alternative is project H, but the most

TABLE 13.4   DIFFERENT VERSIONS OF COST-EFFECTIVENESS ANALYSIS

Projects	Lives Saved	Budget Cost ($M)	CE Ratio (Cost per life saved ($M/life saved)	Budget Cost of Projects that Save at Least 50 Lives	CE Ratio of Projects that Save at Least 50 Lives	Lives Saved of Projects that Cost No More Than $250M	CE Ratio of Projects that Cost No More Than $250M
(1)	(2)	(3)	(4)	(5)	(6)	(7)	(8)
A	100	250	2.5	250	2.5*	100*	2.5
B	20	44	2.2	—	—	20	2.2
C	100	300	3.0	300	3.0	—	—
D	50	300	6.0	300	6.0	—	—
E	10	20	2.0*	—	—	10	2.0*
F	100	900	9.0	900	9.0	—	—
G	60	210	3.5	210	3.5	60	3.5
H	50	200	4.0	200*	4.0	50	4.0
I	40	100	2.5	—	—	40	2.5
J	45	110	2.4	—	—	45	2.4

* CE ratio, budget cost, or effectiveness of the most efficient alternative.

cost-effective acceptable alternative is project A. Which is preferable? Note that project A costs $50 million more than project H, but it saves 50 more lives. The cost of these extra lives saved is only $1 million per life, on average. Saving these additional lives is more cost-effective than even project E, but it is 25 percent more expensive than project H. The choice depends on the decision maker's willingness to trade additional lives saved for additional budgetary cost. Thus, even though CEA is often proposed as a way of avoiding monetization of some benefit, analysts or decision makers must often make trade-offs between costs and a nonmonetized benefit in order to make decisions.

The same type of problem arises if a budget constraint is imposed. Now the analyst should select either the project that yields the greatest benefit subject to the cost constraint or the most cost-effective project that satisfies the cost constraint. If the decision maker specifies a maximum budgetary cost of $250 million, project A saves the most lives, but project E is the most cost-effective. Again, to choose between projects A and E, the decision maker must consider trade-offs between additional lives saved and additional budgetary costs.

Technical versus Allocative Efficiency: Omitted Costs and Benefits

CEA almost invariably omits impacts that would be included in CBA. Indeed, CEA typically considers only one measure of effectiveness. Projects often have multiple benefits, however. For example, regulations that save lives may also reduce injuries or illnesses. On the cost side, as we have stressed previously, most CEA studies consider only budgetary costs. Relevant nonbudgetary opportunity costs may be omitted. To get a better measure of allocative efficiency, these costs and benefits should be taken into consideration. One way to get closer to doing this—that is, to reach a "halfway house" between standard CEA and CBA—is to compute the following ratio:

$$\tilde{CE} = \frac{\text{social costs} - \text{other social benefits}}{\text{effectiveness}} \quad (13.3)$$

If the numerator can be fully valued and monetized, then this adjusted CE ratio incorporates all the impacts that would be included in a CBA.

Most likely, however, CEA was selected in the first place because some social costs and benefits could not be monetized. Obviously, the omission of a particular category of social cost or benefit from the numerator could very well alter the ranking of alternatives. The danger of obtaining an arbitrary ranking increases as alternatives become less similar in terms of the inputs they require and the impacts they produce. Moreover, the transparency of CEA is also reduced because cost no longer has a simple interpretation (budgetary dollars) and decision makers must rely on the judgment of analysts about what social costs and benefits to include. For these reasons, *moving all the way to CBA with extensive sensitivity analysis is often a better analytical strategy overall than expanding the scope of measured costs in CEA.*

COST-UTILITY ANALYSIS

The greatest use of cost-utility analysis occurs in the evaluation of health policies. In CUA the (incremental) costs of alternative policies are compared to the health changes, usually measured in *quality-adjusted life-years* (QALYs), that they produce. CUA is most useful when a trade-off must be made between quality of life (morbidity) and length of life (mortality). In principle, however, CUA could be used with any two distinct dimensions of health status. CUA can be thought of as a form of CEA employing a more complex effectiveness measure; all of the previous discussion about decision rules thus applies. The rationale for distinguishing CUA is that considerable analytical effort has gone into the specific issues relating to developing QALYs.

The Meaning of Life—Quality-Adjusted Life-Years, That Is!

As QALYs involve two distinct variables—quality and quantity—the analyst must designate how these variables are to be defined and combined. This is a problem in *multiattribute decision making*. Consider, for example, the effects of three mutually exclusive alternative prenatal programs. Under the status quo, no babies with a particular condition are born alive. Prenatal alternative A will result in five babies being born alive per year, but with permanent, serious disabilities. Prenatal alternative B will result in only two live births, but with only low levels of disability. Before we can compare the costs of these alternatives to their effectiveness, we first have to make quantity and quality commensurate.

The general form of the problem is shown in Table 13.5. The columns show additional years of life ranging from a low of Y_1 to a high of Y_5. The rows show health status ranging from the worst (health state H_1), to the best (health state H_5). For simplicity, assume that alternatives A and B and the status quo involve the same costs and that there is no uncertainty about the longevities and health status they will yield. Suppose that the status quo (denoted SQ) gives Y_1H_1 (the fewest years of life in the worst health status), while alternative A achieves Y_3H_3 and alternative B achieves Y_4H_2. Clearly, the status quo is dominated, but how should we choose between alternatives A and B? Before answering this question, we must look more closely at the definition of health status.

TABLE 13.5 THE BASIC QALY FORMAT

Health Status (H)	Additional Years of Life (Y)				
	Y_1	Y_2	Y_3	Y_4	Y_5
H_1	Y_1H_1 SQ	Y_2H_1	Y_3H1	Y_4H_1	Y_5H_1
H_2	Y_1H_2	Y_2H_2	Y_3H_2	Y_4H_2 B	Y_5H_2
H_3	Y_1H_3	Y_2H_3	Y_3H_3 A	Y_4H_3	Y_5H_3
H_4	Y_1H_4	Y_2H_4	Y_3H_4	Y_4H_4	Y_5H_4
H_5	Y_1H_5	Y_2H_5	Y_3H_5	Y_4H_5	Y_5H_5

Defining States of Health Status

Defining health status is complex. Health states are normally defined by CUA researchers in collaboration with clinicians familiar with variations in health—whether in relationship to particular diseases, injuries, and mental states, or to health in general. This reliance on experts is based on the assumption that neither the public nor potential treatment subjects are likely to have enough information and knowledge to formulate health states. Most often experts formulate health status indexes for specific diseases or illnesses.

George Torrance and his colleagues, however, have developed a comprehensive four-dimensional classification system with the following dimensions: physical function (mobility and physical activity); role function (ability to care for oneself); social-emotional function (emotional well-being and social activity), and "health problem" (including physical deformity).[9]

Paul Kind and his colleagues have developed a disability ranking based on two dimensions: disability level and the level of distress.[10] Their disability levels are: no disability, slight social disability, severe social disability or slight work performance impairment, choice of work or work performance seriously limited, unable to work or continue education, confined to chair or wheelchair, confined to bed, and unconscious. Their distress levels are: none, mild, moderate, and severe.

Formulating a Health Status Index

How are different health states scaled to form an index? How are changes in the index traded against additional years of life? Obviously, the usefulness of CUA depends on the validity of the methods used to answer these two questions. In the CUA literature, efforts to answer these questions are referred to as measuring the *utilities*, or *utility values*, of a sample of individuals.[11]

There are three common methods of deriving utilities of health status: the health rating method, the time trade-off method, and the standard gamble method. The methods vary in the extent to which they correspond to the economic concept of utility.[12]

Health rating method.   Generally, analysts derive *health rating* from questionnaires or interviews with health experts or potential subjects of treatment, members of society in general, or on the basis of their own expertise. Respondents are presented a scale with well-defined extremes. For example, the scale may assign "death" a value of 0 and "health" a value of 1. Intermediate health states are described in detail to the respondents, who are then asked to locate each state between the end points, 0 and 1. If there are three intermediate health states described to an individual corresponding to "seriously disabled," "moderately disabled," and "minimally disabled," an individual might, for example, assign values of 0.15, 0.47, and 0.92 to these states, respectively.

This rating scale concerns only the health state dimension in Table 13.5. It does not directly provide a method for trading off health states with additional years. However, assuming that health status and longevity have independent effects on utility, the scale values can be directly merged with years of life to get QALYs, which can then be used as an effectiveness measure. The two other methods we review scale the health index and can analyze the trade-offs between the health states and years.

The time trade-off method. In the *time trade-off method*, respondents are asked to compare different combinations of length and quality of life. The typical comparison is between a longer life of lower health status and a shorter life with a higher health status. Figure 13.1 illustrates such a comparison. The horizontal axis measures additional years of life (Y) and the vertical axis measures health status (H). Respondents might be asked to compare some status quo point, say R, representing health status H_2 and additional years of life Y_1, with an alternative point, say S, representing health status H_1 and additional years of life Y_2. If a respondent is indifferent between the two points, then he or she is willing to give up H_2-H_1 units of health quality in return for Y_2-Y_1 additional years of life. This pattern of trade-offs can provide a basis for rank ordering the cells in Table 13.5.

This method assumes implicitly that additional years of life are valued equally, that is, there is no discounting of health years.

The standard gamble method. In the *standard gamble* approach, respondents are presented with a decision tree along the lines described in Chapter 6. Respondents are offered a choice between two alternatives. Alternative C has two possible outcomes: either a return to normal health for N additional years (occurring with probability p) or immediate death (occurring with probability $1 - p$). Alternative C might be an operation that has probability $1 - p$ of failure (death), but which, if successful, will

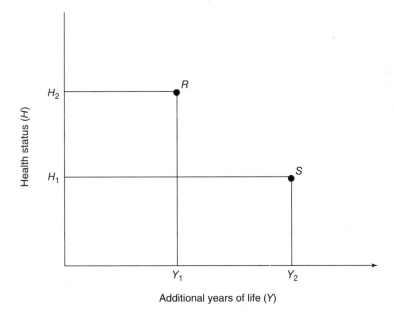

Figure 13.1 Time Trade-Off Example

return the patient to normal health for *N* years. Alternative D guarantees the patient *t* additional years with a specified level of health impairment. This choice is shown in Figure 13.2. The probability *p* is varied until a respondent is indifferent between alternatives C and D. When using a health status index ranging from 0 (death) to 1 (normal health for *N* years), the *p* at which a respondent is indifferent can be interpreted as that respondent's utility from alternative D.

The issues relating to QALYs are not all resolved. One problem is the issue of discounting additional years of life (the *Y* axis in Table 13.5). The basic idea that individuals have positive discount rates relating to additional years is widely accepted, but there is considerable controversy over the theory, measurement and level of the appropriate discount rate.[13] We touched briefly on some of these issues in Chapter 5. One obvious problem when thinking about discounting health is that individuals cannot trade near (far) health years for far (near) health years. While many of the issues remain unresolved, it is problematic to discount costs but not to discount health years. The reason is that the cost-effectiveness ratio would improve if we delayed the health expenditure until the following year.[14]

■ **EXHIBIT 13.1**

Barbara McNeil and her colleagues conducted a study of laryngeal cancer treatment. First, the authors constructed a health status index for respondents in which 25 years of additional life (the full life expectancy for a 50-year-old male) with normal speech was assigned a value of 100 and immediate death was assigned a value of 0. Second, respondents were offered a choice between (1) a gamble with a 50 percent chance of survival for 25 additional years and a 50 percent chance of death in a few months (which we value as zero), and (2) a specified certain number of years of impaired survival (*t*) ranging between 0 and 25 years. The number of certain years offered with impairment (the lower

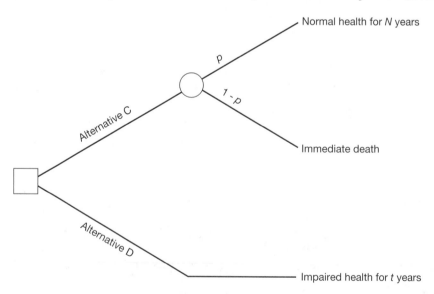

Figure 13.2   The Standard Gamble Method

branch in Figure 13.2) was varied until an individual was indifferent between the two branches. If an individual was indifferent when the value of the lower branch was seven years, for example, then seven additional years of certain life with impairment was assigned a value of 50 on the health status index. Additional gambles were offered to determine the periods of certain survival with impairment that would be assigned health status indexes of 25 and 75.

One of their findings was that executives and firefighters (males, with an average age of 40 years) would trade off 14 percent of their life expectancy to avoid artificial speech. Although most respondents would accept some decrease in life-years to avoid artificial speech, virtually none would accept any decrease in years when only five years or less of certain survival were offered.

Source: Barbara J. McNeil, Ralph Weichselbaum, and Stephen G. Pauker, "Speech and Survival: Tradeoffs Between Quality and Quantity of Life in Laryngeal Cancer," *New England Journal of Medicine*, 305, no. 17 (October 22, 1981), 982–987.

Some Caveats on CUA

As these preference elicitation methods are based on questionnaires, many of the issues discussed in Chapter 11 with respect to contingent valuation are also relevant to QALY methods. For example, samples drawn from the general public tend to be more prone to the hypotheticality problems described in Chapter 11—respondents simply have not thought very much about these kinds of issues. This problem can be ameliorated somewhat by providing detailed descriptions of the various health states and the expected changes in years of life. Additionally, in practice, convenience samples rather than random samples are often drawn from the general population. Unfortunately, respondents who are potential treatment candidates because they are already ill may have incentives to exaggerate the "utility" they would receive from better health states. Finally, of course, either type of sample may be subject to framing (and neutrality) effects inherent in the questionnaire approach. Therefore, a utility elicitation instrument should be subjected to the same kind of validity checks as a contingent valuation instrument. In spite of all these caveats, there is evidence that different samples—whether the general public, potential treatment candidates, or physicians—as well as different sexes, ages, and races, do not vary much in their responses, either in terms of ranking health states or making trade-offs.[15]

A second type of problem arises from the fact that different utility derivation techniques produce different weightings. One recent survey, for example, found that six different methods to assess preferences did not correlate well.[16]

THE USE OF LEAGUE TABLES

CEA and CUA usually compare mutually exclusive projects. By definition, this means that the alternative projects address the same problems—for example, alternative methods of breast cancer screening. Yet, both CEA and CUA have been used to make rankings *across* policies that are not mutually exclusive. *League tables* draw on multiple CEA or CUA studies to rank policies sharing the same cost-effectiveness measure, usually "cost per life saved." John Morrall III, for example, has developed a league table of regulations intended to save lives. He found that regulations ranged in their cost-effectiveness from a cost per life saved of $100,000 (steering column protection regulation) to a cost per life saved of $132 million (cattle feed regulation).[17] CUA league tables are usually used to "compare" investments in different kinds of health treatments.[18]

How useful are league tables? Comparisons of mutually exclusive projects inherently control for some of the differences in the measurement of cost and effectiveness. There can be no such presumption when comparing studies across different authors, using different data, and somewhat different methodologies. Different studies may measure costs differently, they may omit different costs, some may include other social benefits, and they may differ considerably in scale. These problems apply even more so to CUA studies because different methodologies are used to calculate QALYs and, as discussed earlier, different QALY methodologies do not necessarily produce consistent results.

Karen Gerard's caution on the use of league tables is appropriate:

> [A]s more and more studies were read in the course of the investigation, it became striking how many not only placed their results in some standard QALY league table. . .but also purported to present their results as 'favourable.' It is unlikely to be the case that all of these studies can have 'favourable' results.[19]

Thus, caution is warranted in using league tables as guides for policy choice.

CONCLUSION: WHEN IS CEA CLOSE TO CBA?

CEA is closest to CBA when budgetary costs approximate social costs, when the effectiveness measure "captures" most of the social benefits, and when alternative projects are of similar scales. When there are significant nonbudgetary social costs or significant other categories of benefits, CEA is not close to CBA. When they are close, CEA may be less expensive and more transparent than CBA. When they are not close, analysts have three options. First, they should, if they can, do CBA. Second, they can move to a more qualitative evaluation method. Third, they can try to incorporate significant nonbudgetary social costs and other categories of benefits into cost-effectiveness measures.

EXERCISES FOR CHAPTER 13

1. A public health department is considering five alternative programs to encourage parents to have their preschool children vaccinated against a communicable disease. The following table shows the cost and number of vaccinations predicted for each program:

Program	Cost ($)	Number of Vaccinations
A	20,000	2,000
B	44,000	4,000
C	72,000	6,000
D	112,000	8,000
E	150,000	10,000

a. Ignoring issues of scale, which program is most cost-effective?

b. Assuming that the public health department wishes to vaccinate at least 5,000 children, which program is most cost-effective?

c. If the health department believes that each vaccination provides social benefits equal to $20, then which program should it adopt?

2. Analysts wish to evaluate alternative surgical procedures for spinal cord injuries. The procedures have various probabilities of yielding the following results:

Full recovery (FR)—the patient regains full mobility and suffers no chronic pain.

Full functional recovery (FFR)—the patient regains full mobility but suffers chronic pain that will make it uncomfortable to sit for periods of longer than about an hour and will interfere with sleeping two nights per week, on average.

Partial functional recovery (PFR)—the patient regains only restricted movement that will limit mobility to slow-paced walking and will make it difficult to lift objects weighing more than a few pounds. Chronic pain is similar to that suffered under full functional recovery.

Paraplegia (P)—the patient completely loses use of legs and would, therefore, require a wheelchair or other prosthetic for mobility, and suffers chronic pain that interferes with sleeping four nights per week, on average. Aside from loss of the use of his or her legs, the patient would regain control of other lower body functions.

a. Describe how you would construct a quality-of-life index for these surgical outcomes by offering gambles to respondents. Test your procedure on a classmate, friend, or other willing person.

b. Assume that the index you construct on the basis of your sample of one respondent is representative of the population of patients. Use the index to measure the effectiveness of each of three alternative surgical procedures with the following distributions of outcomes:

| | Surgical Procedures | | |
	A	B	C
FR	.10	.50	.40
FFR	.70	.20	.45
PFR	.15	.20	.10
P	.05	.10	.05

c. Imagine that the surgical procedures involved different life expectancies for the various outcomes. Discuss how you might revise your measure of effectiveness to take account of these differences.

NOTES

[1] For a discussion of other less comprehensive techniques, such as cost minimization, see Michael Drummond, Greg L. Stoddart, and George W. Torrance, *Methods for the Economic Evaluations of Health Care Programmes* (Oxford: Oxford University, 1987), pp. 7–9 and 39–73.

[2] Karen Gerard, "Cost-Utility in Practice: A Policy Maker's Guide to the State of the Art," *Health Policy*, 21, no. 3 (1992), 249–279, at p. 271–275.

[3] Drummond, Stoddart, and Torrance, *Methods for the Economic Evaluations of Health Care Programmes*, p. 76.

[4]Gerard found that approximately 90 percent of the health studies she reviewed only looked at direct budgetary costs, "Cost-Utility in Practice," p. 263.

[5]Ibid., pp. 263–264.

[6]See, for example, Karin V. Lowson, M.F. Drummond, and J.M. Bishop, "Costing New Services: Long-Term Domiciliary Oxygen Therapy," *The Lancet*, no. 8230 (May 1981), 1146–1149.

[7]Dominant alternatives tend to be rare but they can occur. For an example, see Russell D. Hall, Jack Hirsh, David L. Sackett, and Greg L. Stoddart, "Cost-Effectiveness of Primary and Secondary Prevention of Fatal Pulmonary Embolism in High-Risk Surgical Patients," *Canadian Medical Association Journal*, 127, no. 10 (November 15, 1982), 990–995.

[8]The term *s.t.* means "subject to."

[9]George W. Torrance, Michael H. Boyle, and Sargent P. Horwood, "Application of Multi-Attribute Utility Theory to Measure Social Preferences for Health Status," *Operations Research*, 30, no. 6 (1982), 1043–1069.

[10]P. Kind, R. Rosser, and A. Williams, "Valuation of Quality of Life: Some Psychometric Evidence," in *The Value of Life and Safety*, ed. M.W. Jones-Lee (Amsterdam: Elsevier/North Holland, 1982), 159–170.

[11]For a detailed review of this issue, see Debra G. Froberg and Robert L. Kane, "Methodology for Measuring Health-State Preferences - I: Measurement Strategies," *Journal of Clinical Epidemiology*, 42, no. 4 (1989), 345–354.

[12]For an overview and discussion of this issue, see Debra Froberg and Robert L. Kane, "Methodology for Measuring Health-State Preferences - IV: Progress and a Research Agenda," *Journal of Clinical Epidemiology*, 42, no. 7 (1989), 675–685.

[13]Amiram Gafni, "Time in Health: Can We Measure Individuals' 'Pure Time Preference'?" *Medical Decision Making*, 15, no. 1 (1995), 31–37; Donald A. Redelmeier, Daniel N. Heller and Milton C. Weinstein, "Time Preference in Medical Economics: Science or Religion?" *Medical Decision Making*, 13, no. 3 (1993), 301–303; Magnus Johannesson, Joseph Pliskin, and Milton C. Weinstein, "A Note on QALYs, Time Trade-off and Discounting," *Medical Decision Making*, 14, no. 2 (1994), 188–193.

[14]Emmett B. Keeler and Shan Cretin, "Discounting of Life-Saving and Other Nonmonetary Effects," *Management Science*, 29, no. 3 (March 1983), 300–306. However, this is not a paradox per se because, as we have shown, a CE ratio never tells us whether a project has positive social value and hence, should be implemented—whether this year or next year.

[15]David L. Sackett and George W. Torrance, "The Utility of Different Health States as Perceived by the General Public," *Journal of Chronic Diseases*, 31, no. 11 (1978), 697–704; Froberg and Kane, "Methodology for Measuring Health-State Preferences," p. 681.

[16]See J.C. Hornberger, D.A. Redelmeier, and J. Peterson, "Variability Among Methods to Assess Patients' Well-Being and Consequent Effect on a Cost-Effectiveness Analysis," *Journal of Clinical Epidemiology*, 45, no. 5 (1992), 505–512. For more on the debate over how well different methods get at utility, see A.J. Culyer and Adam Wagstaff, "QALYs versus HYEs," *Journal of Health Economics*, 11, no. 3 (October 1993), 311–323 and Amiram Gafni, Stephen Birch, and Abraham Mehrez, "Economics, Health and Health Economics: HYEs versus QALYs," same issue, pp. 325–329.

[17]John F. Morrall III, "A Review of the Record," *Regulation* (November/December 1986), pp. 25–34.

[18]See, for example, Alan Williams, "Economics of Coronary Artery Bypass Grafting," *British Medical Journal*, 291, no. 6491 (August 3, 1985), 326–329.

[19]Gerard, "Cost-Utility in Practice," p. 274.

14

DISTRIBUTIONALLY WEIGHTED COST-BENEFIT ANALYSIS

Government policies, programs, and projects typically affect individuals differently. Thus, in conducting CBAs, analysts often report benefits and costs for separate categories of people. The relevant classification of individuals into groups for this purpose depends, of course, on the specific policy under evaluation. Some examples include: consumers versus producers versus taxpayers; program participants versus nonparticipants; citizens (of a nation or a state or a city) versus noncitizens; and high-income persons versus low-income persons.

Once individuals are divided into categories, the first issue that must be decided is whether each group will be given standing in the CBA.[1] For example, in conducting a CBA of U.S. regulatory policy on acid rain, a decision must be made as to whether to give standing to Canadians affected by acid rain resulting from manufacturing in the United States.

Given this decision, costs and benefits may be reported separately for each group receiving standing. But how is this information to be utilized in making a decision concerning the policy that has to be analyzed?

Throughout this book, we have emphasized use of the Kaldor-Hicks potential compensation test in reaching such decisions. In using this test, benefits and costs are simply summed across all groups with standing to determine whether total benefits are larger than total costs and, hence, whether the policy should be adopted. This test examines benefits and costs from the perspective of society as a whole, where "society" is composed of all groups with standing. Indeed, the implicit philosophy behind the Kaldor-Hicks potential compensation test is that, given standing, it does not matter who receives the benefits from a government program or who pays the costs ("a dollar is a dollar regardless of who receives or pays it"), as long as there is a net gain to society as a whole—in other words, as long as the program is efficient in terms of potential Pareto improvement. Strict use of the Kaldor-Hicks test means that information on how benefits and costs are distributed among groups is ignored in decision making.

In making actual policy decisions, however, the way in which benefits and costs are distributed among various groups is seldom ignored. In fact, this consideration can have a major influence over whether a policy is politically acceptable. Hence, in actual decision making, a dollar received or expended by a member of one group may not be treated as equal to a dollar received or expended by a member of another group.

In this chapter, we focus on the role of the distribution of benefits and costs among groups in using CBA for decision making.[2] We first examine the economic rationale for treating dollars received or expended by various groups differently in CBA. We then consider approaches for doing this in practice.

DISTRIBUTIONAL JUSTIFICATIONS FOR INCOME TRANSFER PROGRAMS

The rationale suggested by economists for treating dollars received or expended by various groups differently in CBA is mainly limited to situations in which low-income persons are helped (or hurt) by a program more than other persons.[3] Political decision makers may, of course, treat dollars received or expended by various groups differently, even if their income levels are similar. They may, for example, be influenced by differences among groups in voting behavior or campaign contributions. Economists, however, typically argue for treating dollars received or expended by various groups similarly unless they differ in terms of income or wealth.[4] Consequently, in the remainder of this chapter, we focus on CBAs of policies that have differential effects on groups that differ by income—for example, projects that are located in underdeveloped regions or programs that are targeted at disadvantaged persons.

To illustrate such a policy, consider a hypothetical program that taxes high-income persons in order to provide income transfers to low-income persons. The tax component of this program is illustrated in Figure 14.1.[5] For purposes of discussion, assume that the market represented in this graph is for a luxury good, such as yachts, that is only purchased by the rich. In the absence of the tax, equilibrium in this market would occur at a price of P_1 and a quantity of Q_1. If an excise tax of t is levied against each unit of output, then the supply curve would shift up by this amount as suppliers attempted to pass along to consumers the additional cost the tax imposes upon them.

Using the approach implied by the Kaldor-Hicks rule, a distributional analysis of the costs and benefits associated with this tax would look like this:

	BENEFITS	COSTS
Producers		$C + D$
Consumers		$A + B$
Transfer Recipients	$A + C$	
Society		$B + D$

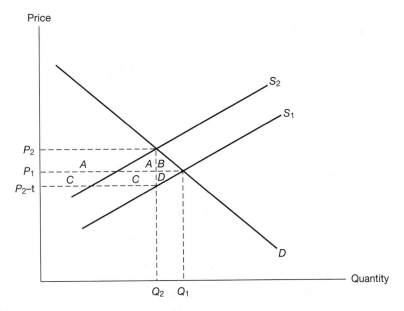

Figure 14.1 An Excise Tax on a Luxury Good

Source: Adapted from Arnold C. Harberger, "On the Use of Distributional Weights in Social Cost-Benefit Analysis," *Journal of Political Economy*, 86, no. 2, Part 2, (April 1978), S87–S120; Figure 1, p. 589.

Thus, a deadweight loss equal to areas *B + D* would result from the tax. In addition to this deadweight loss, there are two off-graph social costs that also would result from our hypothetical transfer program:

1. Administering both the tax and the transfer parts of the program would require the use of social resources.

2. Some of those receiving the transfer would probably work less or stop working entirely, thereby reducing the goods and services available to society. In fact, there is considerable evidence that this is exactly what occurs under existing welfare programs.[6] Only part of this loss would be offset by the gains in leisure to transfer recipients (see Chapter 9). The remaining residual is a second source of deadweight loss.

It should be obvious that this program would never pass the Kaldor-Hicks test. It must instead be justified on distributional grounds. In other words, one would have to argue that giving a low-income person a dollar warrants taking more than a dollar away from a higher-income person. Apparently, this distributional argument has some force because programs such as AFDC and food stamps, which transfer income from higher-income to lower-income persons do in fact exist. Hence, it appears that society is willing to sacrifice some efficiency in order to provide assistance to low-income persons.

The importance of this for CBA analysis is that it implies that, in practice, a dollar of benefits received or a dollar of costs incurred by a low-income person is sometimes given greater weight in assessing government programs than a dollar of benefits received or a dollar of costs incurred by a higher-income person. How can this be justified?

THE CASE FOR TREATING LOW- AND HIGH-INCOME GROUPS DIFFERENTLY IN CBA

In the economics literature, there are at least three arguments for giving dollars received or paid by low-income persons greater weight in CBA than dollars received or paid by higher-income persons:

1. Income has diminishing marginal utility.
2. The income distribution should be more equal.
3. The "one man–one vote" principle should apply.

We discuss each of these arguments in turn.

Diminishing Marginal Utility of Income

The first argument is based on the standard assumption in economics that each additional dollar an individual receives provides less utility than the preceding dollar. A corollary of this assumption is that a dollar received or a dollar of cost incurred by a high-income person has less of an impact on his or her utility than it would on a low-income person's utility. For that reason, the argument suggests, it should count less in a CBA.[7]

This argument can be summarized algebraically as follows:

$$\Delta u_l/\Delta y_l > \Delta u_h/\Delta y_h \qquad (14.1)$$

where $\Delta u_i/\Delta y_i$ is the marginal private utility of income of individual i, l indicates a low-income person, and h a high-income person.

Income Distribution Should Be More Equal

The second argument for giving dollars received or paid by the poor greater weight in CBA than dollars received or paid by the rich is premised on the assertion that the current income distribution is less equal than it should be and social welfare would be higher if it were more equal.[8] There are several possible bases for such an assertion. The first is that a highly unequal distribution of income may result in civil disorder, crime, and riots. More equality in income may reduce these threats to the general social welfare. Second, it can be argued that there is some minimum threshold of income that is so low that no one can (or, to preserve human dignity, should have to) live below it. This suggests that the income distribution be made more equal by truncating it at the minimum threshold through income floors. Third, some relatively well-off persons may receive utility if the circumstances facing the worse-off members of society at the bottom of the income distribution improve. Certain types of charitable giving, such as contributions to the Salvation Army, provide some evidence for the existence of this form of altruism. Finally, it is possible that some persons value greater income equality in and of itself.[9]

If for any of these reasons society prefers greater income equality than current-ly exists, then a dollar increase in the income of a low-income person would result in a larger increase in the welfare of society as a whole than would a dollar increase in the income of a high-income person. Note that this would be true even if the margin-al utility of income was not diminishing and, consequently, a dollar increase in the income of high- and low-income persons resulted in equal increases in the utilities of these persons. Each of the justifications listed in the previous paragraph suggests that society as a whole (or at least some relatively well-off members of society) becomes better off if those at the bottom of the income distribution gain relative to those in the rest of the distribution. Thus, the first and second arguments are quite distinct from one another.

Stated algebraically, the second argument implies that

$$\Delta SW/\Delta y_l > \Delta SW/\Delta y_h, \text{ even if } \Delta u_l/\Delta y_l = \Delta u_h/\Delta y_h \qquad (14.2)$$

where ΔSW refers to the change in aggregate social welfare and $\Delta SW/\Delta y_i$ is the mar-ginal effect on social welfare of a change in income that is received by individual i.[10]

This argument confronts the Kaldor-Hicks test quite directly. It implies that there are some projects and programs that fail the Kaldor-Hicks test but should nonetheless be adopted if they redistribute income in a way that makes the income distribution more equal. In other words, the argument suggests that some programs that are inefficient should be undertaken if they increase income equality sufficiently. This also implies, of course, that some projects that make the income distribution less equal should not be undertaken, even though the Kaldor-Hicks test implies that they are efficient.

The "One Person–One Vote" Principle

This argument begins by noting that the benefits and costs of government programs to consumers are appropriately measured as changes in consumer surplus. Then it goes on to point out that because high-income persons have more income to spend than low-income persons, the measured impacts of policies on their consumer surplus will typically be larger and, hence, will be of greater consequence in a CBA based strictly on the Kaldor-Hicks rule.

This is illustrated by Figure 14.2, which compares the demand schedules of a typical high-income consumer and a typical low-income consumer for a good. If the good is a normal good, that is, if demand for the good increases as income increases, then the demand schedule of the high-income consumer will be to the right of that of the low-income consumer, as the diagram shows. Now if a government policy increas-es the price of the good, say from P_1 to P_2, both consumers will bear the cost of that increase in the form of a loss in consumer surplus. However, the loss suffered by the high-income consumer (areas $A + B$) will be greater than the loss borne by the low-income consumer (area A alone). As a result, a CBA will give more weight to the impact of the policy on the high-income consumer than on the low-income consumer.

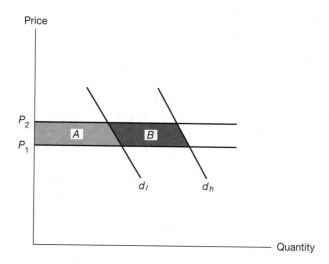

Figure 14.2   Changes in Consumer Surplus for High- and Low-Income Consumers

The final part of the argument suggests that in a democracy, low-income persons should have as much influence over decisions on whether to undertake public projects as high-income persons. In other words, it is argued that "since the principle of 'one man, one vote' is deeply embedded in the concept of democracy," measures of changes in consumer surplus for different persons should be adjusted to what they would be if everyone had the same income.[11] For example, we would count the impact of the price change on the low-income person represented in the diagram at about double what we would count the impact on the high-income person, in effect, equalizing the "votes" of the two individuals.[12]

DISTRIBUTIONAL WEIGHTS

In principle, various groups can be treated differently in a CBA by using *distributional weights*. As will be seen, distributional weights are just numbers, such as 1, 2, or 1.5, which are intended to reflect the value placed on each dollar paid out or received by each group. For example, the highest-income group might be given a value of 1, while a lower-income group could be given a value of 2, implying that a dollar received by the member of the low-income group is valued in the CBA at twice that of a dollar received by the high-income group.

Distributional weights can be incorporated into a CBA through a slight modification of the net present value formula:

$$\text{NPV} = \sum_{j=1}^{m} [W_j \sum_{t=0}^{\infty} \frac{b_{t,j} - c_{t,j}}{(1+r)^t}] \tag{14.3}$$

where W_j is the distributional weight for group j, $b_{t,j}$ are the real benefits received by group j in period t, $c_{t,j}$ are the real costs imposed on group j in period t, m is the number of groups, and r is the real social discount rate.

The idea behind this formula is simple. The persons affected by the government policy are divided into as many groups as seems appropriate. Each group is then given a distributional weight. The net present value for each group is then computed and multiplied by its weight. These weighted net present values are then added together to obtain an overall net present value. Note that in CBAs that rely strictly on the Kaldor-Hicks rule, W_j is implicitly set equal to 1 for all groups.

To illustrate the use of distributional weights, consider the following simple numerical example, a welfare program that costs the nonpoor $10 billion and raises the incomes of the poor by $8 billion:

$$b^{\text{poor}} = \$8 \text{ billion} \qquad c^{\text{nonpoor}} = \$10 \text{ billion}.$$

This program obviously would not pass the standard Kaldor-Hicks test. It is inefficient. But imagine that distributional weights have been developed that imply that a dollar received by a poor person is worth 50 percent more than a dollar received by a nonpoor person. That is:

$$W^{\text{poor}} = 1.5 \qquad W^{\text{nonpoor}} = 1.$$

In this case, the costs and the benefits of the program would be multiplied by the appropriate weights:

$$(1.5)(\$8 \text{ billion}) - (1)(\$10 \text{ billion}) = +\$2 \text{ billion}.$$

Thus, with the weights, the program passes muster; but without them, it does not.

DETERMINING DISTRIBUTIONAL WEIGHTS

The obvious difficulty with implementing this approach is determining appropriate weights for each group. The weights should, of course, be consistent with the rationale for using them. However, of the three arguments for using weights presented earlier, only the one based on the one man–one vote principle suggests an approach that could potentially be used in practice for valuing the weights of various groups, and even in this case, the information requirements are substantial. Among the required information is the average income level of each relevant group, an estimate of the *income elasticity of demand* for each good affected by the government policy being evaluated (i.e., the percentage change in the quantity demanded of each good that results from a 1 percent increase in income), and an estimate of the market demand curve for each affected good. Given this information, the consumer surplus of the average member of each group could then be computed. These estimates could, in turn, be used to derive distributional weights for each group that are consistent with the one man–one vote principle.[13]

To develop weights that are consistent with the remaining two arguments, information is needed on $\Delta u/\Delta y$ (the marginal private utility of income) and $\Delta \text{SW}/\Delta y$ (the marginal effect on social welfare of a change in income) for a typical member of each group of interest. For example, a set of distributional weights could be developed that is consistent with the diminishing marginal utility of income argument *if* we knew that a $100 increase in income increased the utility of rich people by, say, two units and the utility of poor people by three units by simply computing weights on the basis of the ratio of the marginal utility values. Thus, W_j would be set equal to 1 for rich persons and to 1.5 for poor persons. Similarly, a set of distributional weights that is consistent with the argument that the income distribution should be more equal could be developed if we knew that a $100 increase in the income of a typical poor person increased social welfare by two units, but the same increase in the income of a typical rich person increased social welfare by only one unit.

Unfortunately, such information is not available and there is no known way to obtain it. First, utility is a subjective concept that defies cardinal measurement.[14] Indeed, most economists eschew any explicit interpersonal comparisons of utility for this reason. But in the absence of interpersonal comparisons of utility, it is not possible to develop a system of relative distributional weights that is consistent with the diminishing marginal utility of income argument. Second, there is no general consensus among members of society concerning the specific relationship between a given change in the income levels of individuals and social welfare, except that most persons would, perhaps, agree that the relation is positive and its magnitude is larger for low-income than high-income persons. Without such a consensus, however, it is not possible to develop distributional weights that are consistent with the greater income equality argument.[15]

POLITICALLY DETERMINED WEIGHTS

Given these problems in deriving distributional weights, how can distributional issues be actually handled in CBA? One possibility is to use contingent valuation techniques to determine distributional weights. Distributional weights, after all, can be viewed as a type of shadow price, an effort to measure benefits and costs in terms of their true social value. To the best of our knowledge, however, no attempt has so far been made to do this. If such an attempt were made, it would, of course, be subject to the limitations of contingent valuation described in Chapter 11.

Another approach is to derive distributional weights on the basis of revealed political behavior. For example, Otto Eckstein suggested that marginal income tax rates might be used to determine weights for different income classes.[16] For instance, families with annual incomes between $15,000 and $30,000 face a marginal tax rate of 15 percent under the U.S. income tax, while families with over $30,000 in income face a marginal tax rate of between 28 percent and 33 percent. One might infer that in establishing these tax rates society, or at least Congress, felt that at the margin taxing away 15 cents from a low-income person was as painful as taxing away around 30 cents from a higher-income person. Taking this one step further, one could infer that the political process has implied that dollars paid out or received by moderate-income families under a government program should be weighted twice as heavily as dollars paid out or received by families at the top of the income distribution.

Although weighting schemes based on tax rates have been used in CBA, such schemes raise serious issues.[17] One problem is that tax rates do not only reflect what

Congress thinks the relative value of a dollar to different income groups should be. For example, Congress may be afraid to set tax rates too high because of concern that high rates will create work and investment disincentives. In addition, Congress may use the progressive federal income tax to offset the fact that other taxes, such as state sales taxes, tend to be regressive. Indeed, it might be better to base weighting schemes on the total tax system than on the federal income tax alone.

An alternative to using marginal tax rates to derive distributional weights is to use public expenditure decisions instead.[18] To illustrate, consider two projects, A and B. If project A has a higher net present value than project B—that is, $NPV^A > NPV^B$—yet project A is rejected and B is undertaken, this suggests that decision makers must have viewed project B as at least as desirable as project A on nonefficiency grounds. One possible explanation is that project B provides greater net gains to low-income persons than does project A (that is, $NPV_l^A < NPV_l^B$), while higher-income persons would be better off under project A ($NPV_h^A > NPV_h^B$).

If these conditions hold and the values of NPV_l^A, NPV_l^B, NPV_h^A, and NPV_h^B are known, then it is possible to derive distributional weights by solving the following two simultaneous equations for W_l and W_h:[19]

$$W_l \cdot NPV_l^A + W_h \cdot NPV_h^A = NPV^A$$

$$W_l \cdot NPV_l^B + W_h \cdot NPV_h^B = NPV^A \tag{14.4}$$

The second equation is based on the premise that because decision makers selected project B over project A, even though NPV^A was actually larger that NPV^B, they must have implicitly used a set of weights that allowed them to treat project B *as if* it had a net present value that was *at least* as high as NPV^A. The weights are derived by treating the two projects as if, once weighted, they were of exactly equal value in the eyes of the decision makers.

The estimates of W_l and W_h should provide a reasonable approximation of the implicit weights that decision makers used in deciding between the two projects. Unfortunately, however, the estimates may reflect other factors than only the concern of decision makers over the trade-off between efficiency and distributional equity. Considerations related to electoral prospects, for example, may very well have been more important in determining the decision.

A PRAGMATIC APPROACH TO WEIGHTING

Given the enormous practical problems with obtaining a defensible set of distributional weights, we suggest that their use be limited to only those CBAs where distributional issues are of central concern—for example, CBAs of programs targeted at disadvantaged groups or at impoverished areas within countries, states, or cities. Even then, it may often be possible to use an approach that highlights the importance of the distributional implications associated with the policy being analyzed without requiring that any particular set of distributional weights be selected as the "correct" set.

To illustrate the particular approach that we suggest using to do this, we return to the Work/Welfare Initiative Demonstrations that we first described in Chapter 9. As indicated there, these demonstrations were run in a randomized experimental setting during the 1980s to determine the impacts of various combinations of job search, training, and subsidized jobs for AFDC recipients. Because these experimental programs were targeted at welfare recipients—an especially disadvantaged low-income group—both their distributional effects and their effects on economic efficiency are relevant. Thus, CBAs of the Work/Welfare Initiative Demonstrations should take both types of effects into account.

Displaying Unweighted Cost and Benefit Estimates

The first step in doing this is simply to display unweighted program impacts on society as a whole, as well as on pertinent subgroups. This is accomplished in the first three columns in Table 14.1, which simply duplicate total net present value estimates for the Work/Welfare Initiative Demonstrations that were originally reported in Table 9.4.[20] Column 1 reports these estimates from the perspective of program participants, column 2 from the perspective of nonparticipants, and column 3 (which is computed by summing the first two columns) from the perspective of society as a whole.

None of the estimates reported in the first three columns of Table 14.1 are weighted. *Even when distributional weighting is used, unweighted estimates of benefits and costs for society as a whole should always be provided in CBAs. In addition, whenever distributional considerations are important, benefit and cost estimates for relevant subgroups should also be provided,* if it is feasible to do so.

The unweighted net present value estimates reported in the first three columns of Table 14.1 have two especially important implications. First, they indicate that almost all the Work/Welfare Demonstration programs pass the Kaldor-Hicks test. Specifically, 16 of the 19 unweighted net present value estimates for society as a whole, which appear in column 3, are positive. Second, in 6 of the 16 cases that pass the Kaldor-Hicks test, program participants were apparently made worse off by the tested program, while nonparticipants—a group who, on average, enjoys substantially higher-incomes than participants—were made better off. In these instances, a trade-off occurs between economic efficiency and distributional considerations. (A similar trade-off would also arise if a program failed the Kaldor-Hicks test, but participants were made better off. However, this situation did not arise in any of the Work/Welfare Demonstrations.) It is only when such a trade-off occurs that distributional weighting is relevant.

Conducting Sensitivity Tests

Column 4 tests whether the estimates reported in column 3 of Table 14.1 are sensitive to the choice of distributional weights. Thus, in contrast to the unweighted figures appearing in column 3, which are based on the assumption that society values the gains and losses of AFDC recipients and nonrecipients equally, those appearing in column 4 assume that the gains and losses of AFDC recipients are valued by society at

TABLE 14.1   SENSITIVITY OF THE WORK/WELFARE INITIATIVE DEMONSTRATION ESTIMATES TO THE USE OF DISTRIBUTIONAL WEIGHTS

	Net Present Value From Participant Perspective	Net Present Value From Nonparticipant Perspective	Unweighted Social Net Present Value [Col 1 + Col 2]	Social Net Present Value *If* Participant Distributional Weight = 2 [2 x Col 1 + Col 2]	Estimates of Internal Weights for Participants [Col 2/Col 1]
	1	2	3	4	5
AFDC-R					
APPLICANTS					
San Diego EPP/EWEP:					
Job search only	$644	$452	$1,096	$1,740	NA
Job search/CWEP	798	1,156	1,954	2,751	NA
San Diego SWIM	(880)	1,633	753	(127)	1.86
Virginia	1,134	667	1,801	2,935	NA
West Virginia	(481)	389	(92)	(573)	NA
RECIPIENTS					
San Diego SWIM	725	1,698	2,423	3,148	NA
Virginia	574	190	764	1,338	NA
West Virginia	80	873	953	1,033	NA
New Jersey	1,262	1,069	2,331	3,593	NA
Maine	3,182	(418)	2,764	5,945	NA
APPLICANTS AND RECIPIENTS					
Cook County:					
Job search only	(420)	475	55	(365)	1.13
Job search/CWEP	(34)	362	328	294	10.64
Baltimore	1,739	74	1,813	3,552	NA
Arkansas	(449)	944	495	46	2.10
AFDC-U					
APPLICANTS ONLY					
San Diego EPP/EWEP:					
Job search only	(1,196)	1,229	33	(1,163)	1.03
Job search/CWEP	(1,443)	1,414	(29)	(1,472)	NA
San Diego SWIM	543	1,577	2,120	2,663	NA
RECIPIENTS ONLY					
San Diego SWIM	(921)	2,487	1,566	642	2.70
APPLICANTS AND RECIPIENTS					
Baltimore	(1,233)	(1,856)	(3,089)	(4,322)	NA

NA: Not Applicable

Source for columns 1–3: Table 9.4.

twice those of nonrecipients. In other words, participants are given a distributional weight of 2 and nonparticipants a weight of 1. Although these weights are obviously arbitrary—as previously stressed, we do not know the actual relative values that society places on dollars received and paid out by participants and nonparticipants—in our judgment, it seems likely that they overstate society's generosity toward AFDC recipients and thus test whether the net social gain and loss estimates are sensitive to a rather extreme assumption.

A comparison of columns 3 and 4 indicates that this assumption causes ten of these estimates to become larger and nine smaller. More importantly, however, only three change sign. Although all three of these sign changes are from positive to negative—that is, from a net gain to net loss—in two cases, the originally estimated net gain was well under $100. Hence, it appears that conclusions concerning whether most of the Work/Welfare Initiative Demonstrations listed in the table were cost-beneficial to society are not very sensitive to the choice of distributional weights.

Computing Internal Weights

Column 5 in Table 14.1 is based on the computation of *internal weights*, an alternative to the approach used in column 4 for distributional weighting. This scheme works best if there are just two pertinent groups, one of which is relatively disadvantaged (e.g., participants in the Work/Welfare Demonstrations) and the other relatively advantaged (e.g., nonparticipants in the demonstrations).

Internal distributional weights are derived by first setting the weight for the advantaged group equal to unity and then computing the weight for the disadvantaged group by dividing the estimated net present value for the advantaged group by the estimated net present value for the disadvantaged group. The idea is similar to that behind the computation of internal rates of return. Instead of somehow selecting weights, one finds the weights at which the program being analyzed would just break even, in other words, the weights at which the net present value for society as a whole would equal zero. Viewed a bit differently, the internal weight for the disadvantaged group indicates the dollars of costs incurred by the advantaged group per dollar of benefits received by the disadvantaged group, if the former is made worse off by the program and the latter better off, or the dollars of benefits received by the advantaged group per dollar of costs incurred by the disadvantaged group, if the former is made better off and the latter worse off.

In Table 14.1, we compute internal weights for Work/Welfare Demonstration participants by dividing column 2 by column 1. We do this, however, only when there is a trade-off between efficiency and distribution, that is, when column 1 and column 3 are of the opposite sign. In all other instances (i.e., when columns 1 and 3 are both positive or both negative), a trade-off between efficiency and distribution does not exist and, consequently, distributional weighting is not germane. As a trade-off between efficiency and distribution only occurred in six instances in the Work/Welfare Demonstrations, only six internal weights for program participants appear in column 5 of Table 14.1.

Each of these six values indicates the weight at which a demonstration program would just break even. Thus, if the "true" weight for participants is larger than their internal weight, programs with positive unweighted social net present values would fail to break even once their distributional implications were taken into account and programs with negative unweighted social net present values would more than break even. However, because the "true" weight for participants is unknown, policymakers would have to make a judgmental decision as to whether dollars of benefits or costs to participants should be given a higher or lower value than that implied by the computed internal weights. Indeed, one advantage of internal weighting is that it makes the trade-off between efficiency and distribution explicit for policymakers.

For example, in all six of the cases for which internal weights are computed in Table 14.1, program participants were worse off under the demonstration programs, but the unweighted social net present value estimate was positive. Thus, all six programs pass the Kaldor-Hicks test, even though they make the distribution of income less equal. If policymakers believed that dollars lost to participants in the Work/Welfare Demonstrations should be valued at, say, 25 percent more than dollars gained by nonparticipants, this would imply that two of these six programs failed to break even and, hence, should be discontinued even though they passed the Kaldor-Hicks test. If they instead valued dollars lost to participants at three times more than dollars gained by nonparticipants, then this would imply that five of the six programs failed to break even. Thus, they would conclude that five of the programs that passed the Kaldor-Hicks test actually had a negative payoff once their adverse effects on the income distribution were taken into account. But is a weight for participants as high as 3 plausible? We consider this issue next.

Obtaining Upper-Bound Values for Distributional Weights

It was pointed out earlier in this chapter that pure transfer programs inevitably fail the Kaldor-Hicks test—each dollar of transfer benefits costs nonrecipients more than a dollar. However, it has been argued that transfer programs can be used as a standard to which other types of programs that redistribute income can be compared.[21] Specifically, the argument suggests that if a nontransfer program makes the disadvantaged better off, but results in a loss of efficiency, then it should not be accepted if a transfer program that results in a smaller loss in efficiency can potentially be used instead. By the same token, if a nontransfer program makes the disadvantaged worse off but results in gains in efficiency, then it should be accepted if there is a transfer program that can potentially compensate the disadvantaged for their losses without fully offsetting the gains in efficiency from the nontransfer program.

This approach requires that internal weights that are derived similarly to the six values that appear in the last column of Table 14.1 be obtained for transfer programs. This has been done by Edward M. Gramlich, who suggests that setting the internal weight for nonrecipients to unity, the internal weight for transfer recipients is on the order of 1.5 to 2. In other words, Gramlich found that it costs taxpayers around $1.50 to $2.00 for each dollar transferred to a recipient under a transfer program.[22] As

Gramlich indicates, although these estimates should be considered rough and tentative, if one accepts them as being of the right order of magnitude, then it can be argued that distributional weights for the disadvantaged should never be set above 1.5 or 2.

Consider, for example, a nontransfer program that costs the advantaged $2.50 for every dollar of benefits received by the disadvantaged. Gramlich's estimates imply that every dollar received by the disadvantaged under a transfer program would cost the advantaged only $1.50 to $2.00. Thus, in principle, a transfer program could be used instead to make the disadvantaged just as well off as the nontransfer program but at a lower cost to the advantaged. Thus, not only does the nontransfer program have a negative unweighted net social present value, it is inferior to a simple transfer program for redistributing income to the disadvantaged.

Now consider a program that provides the advantaged $2.50 of benefits for every dollar of costs incurred by the disadvantaged. Under these circumstances, each dollar lost under the program by the disadvantaged could, in principle, be reimbursed through a transfer program at a cost to the advantaged of only $1.50 to $2.00. Hence, this program not only has a positive unweighted net social present value, the disadvantaged also can be compensated for their losses without completely offsetting the gains in efficiency from the program.

The argument just presented implies that distributional weights assigned to the disadvantaged should not exceed 1.5 or 2 in value. Higher weights would imply acceptance of inefficient programs that are also inferior to simple transfer programs for redistributing income and rejection of efficient programs that allow the advantaged to enjoy net gains even when the disadvantaged could be fully compensated through income transfers for losses they suffer. Thus, the argument suggests that the two programs in Table 14.1 that have internal weights well in excess of 2 should definitely be accepted, while the two that have internal weights that are close to 2 should probably also be accepted, even though all four programs have adverse effects on the income distribution.

Note, however, that this argument is very similar in spirit to the one underlying the Kaldor-Hicks rule. Both are based on the *potential* use of transfer payments to compensate losers under a policy, while leaving winners better off than they would be in the absence of the policy. Nothing, however, requires that these transfer payments actually be made.

CONCLUSION

This chapter focuses on the use of distributional weighting to take account of the fact that many policies have divergent impacts on different income groups. Given the absence of generally accepted sets of distributional weights, we suggests that *the use of distributional weights should be limited to policies that meet both of the following conditions: (1) they are targeted at the disadvantaged; (2) they result in reductions in overall social efficiency but make low-income persons better off; or they increase social efficiency but make low-income persons worse off.*

There may, in fact, be relatively few policies that meet both of these conditions. Those policies that do might be subjected to sensitivity tests based on a plausible range of weights. Or alternatively, internal weights might be computed, thereby providing policymakers with information on which to base their choice of distributional weights. In either case, however, a cogent argument can be made for not allowing the distributional weights for low-income groups to be set much more than 50 percent to 100 percent above those for higher-income groups.

EXERCISES FOR CHAPTER 14

1. A city is about to build a new sanitation plant. It is considering two sites, one located in a moderately well-to-do neighborhood and the other in a low-income neighborhood. Indeed, most of the residents in the latter neighborhood live below the poverty line. The city's sanitation engineer is adamant that "the city needs the new plant and it has to go somewhere." However, he is indifferent as to which neighborhood it is located in. The plant would operate at the same cost and as efficiently in either neighborhood, and about as many people would be affected by the air pollution emitted by the plant. The city hires an economist to study the two sites. The economist finds that the plant would cause a considerably larger fall in average property values in the well-to-do neighborhood than in the low-income neighborhood, given the more expensive homes that are located in the former. Consistent with this, a contingent valuation study that the economist conducts finds that willingness-to-pay to avoid the sanitation plant is substantially higher in the well-to-do neighborhood than in the low-income neighborhood.

   The residents of the poor neighborhood strongly prefer that the plant be built in the well-to-do neighborhood. In the face of the economist's findings, what sort of arguments might they make?

2. Cost-benefit analyses have been conducted of six proposed projects. None of these projects are mutually exclusive and the agency has a sufficient budget to fund those that will make society better off. The findings from the CBAs are summarized here in millions of dollars:

	Net Social Benefits	Net Group I Benefits	Net Group II Benefits
Project A	$2	$2	$0
Project B	6	8	−2
Project C	4	12	−8
Project D	−1	−3	2
Project E	−2	−1	−1
Project F	−2	4	−6

   Group I consists of households with annual incomes over $15,000, while Group II consists of households with annual incomes under $15,000.

   a. According to the net benefit rule, which of these projects should be funded?
   b. For which of the projects might distributional considerations be an issue?
   c. Compute internal distributional weights for the projects you selected in 2.b. Using these weights, indicate the circumstances under which each project might actually be undertaken.

d. Recompute social net benefits for the six projects using a distributional weight of 1 for Group I and a distributional weight of 2 for Group II. Using these weight-adjusted net social benefit estimates, indicate the circumstances under which each project might actually be undertaken. In doing this, assume that the distributional weight for Group II is an upper bound—that is, it probably overstates society's true generosity toward low-income households.

NOTES

[1]For a further discussion of standing in CBA, see Chapter 2.

[2]For a more general discussion of the role of distributional considerations in assessing policy initiatives, see Alphonse G. Holtmann, "Beyond Efficiency: Economics and Distributional Analysis" in *Policy Analysis and Economics*, ed. David L. Weimer (Boston, MA: Kluwer Academic Publishing, 1991), 45–64.

[3]It would be better to distinguish among the persons or families affected by government programs in terms of their wealth (i.e., the value of their stock of assets), rather than in terms of their income (the observed flow of payments they receive in exchange for the labor, capital, and land that they provide the production process). For example, two households may have similar income, but if one owns a house and the other does not, their standard of living may be quite different. However, income is usually used instead of wealth in categorizing individuals or families because it is more readily measured.

[4]An exception sometimes occurs in conducting CBAs in less developed countries, however. Because of the paucity of funds for investment in such countries, some economists argue that each dollar of increase or reduction in savings that results from a project should count more heavily in conducting a CBA of the project than each dollar of increase or reduction in consumption. [See, for example, Anandarup Ray, *Cost-Benefit Analysis: Issues and Methodologies* (Baltimore: Johns Hopkins University Press, 1984), 15–17.] In principle, however, the relative importance of savings and consumption can be taken into account by using the shadow price of capital approach to discounting, which is described in Chapter 5.

[5]This diagram was adapted from Arnold C. Harberger, "On the Use of Distributional Weights in Social Cost-Benefit Analysis," *Journal of Political Economy*, 86, no. 2 (1978), S87–S120, University of Chicago Press.

[6]See Robert Moffitt, "Incentive Effects of the U.S. Welfare System: A Review," *Journal of Economic Literature*, 30, no. 1 (March 1992), 1–61, and the references cited therein.

[7]Martin Feldstein's discussion of technical issues in computing distributional weights is premised on this argument. See Martin S. Feldstein, "Distributional Equity and the Optimal Structure of Public Prices," *The American Economic Review*, 62, no. 1 (1972), 32–36.

[8]Arnold Harberger's classical examination of distributional weighting ("On the Use of Distributional Weights in Social Cost-Benefit Analysis") can be viewed as a critical assessment of whether this assertion provides a basis for conducting distributionally weighted CBA.

[9]As discussed by Aidan R. Vining and David L. Weimer, "Welfare Economics as the Foundation for Public Policy Analysis: Incomplete and Flawed but Nevertheless Desirable" *The Journal of Socio-Economics*, 21, no. 1 (1992), 25–37; John Rawls, *A Theory of Justice* (Cambridge, MA: Harvard University Press, 1971), and others have provided a more philosophical basis than the reasons listed here for greater income equality.

[10]The first two arguments can be derived more formally by specifying a social welfare function. To illustrate, we specify a very simple social welfare function in which individual utility depends upon income, total social welfare depends upon a linear combination of individual utilities, and the possibility of interdependent utility (i.e., one person's utility being affected by the gains or losses of others) is ignored:

$$SW = f[u_1(y_1). \ldots, u_i(y_i). \ldots, u_n(y_n)]$$

where n is the total number of individuals in society.

Totally differentiating the social welfare function yields the following expression:

$$dSW = \sum_{i=1}^{n} [(\partial SW / \partial u_i) (\partial u_i / \partial y_i) dy_i]$$

where dy_i represents the change in income resulting from a government policy.

The first argument implies that $\partial u_l / \partial y_l > \partial u_h / \partial y_h$, while the second argument implies that $\partial SW / \partial u_l > \partial SW / \partial u_h$. Thus, together the two arguments imply that $(\partial SW / \partial u_l) (\partial u_l / \partial y_l) > (\partial SW / \partial u_h) (\partial u_h / \partial y_h)$.

[11]D.W. Pearce, *Cost-Benefit Analysis*, 2nd ed. (New York: St. Martin's Press, 1983), 64–66.

[12]From the perspective of social choice theory, this is a somewhat naive view of democracy. See William H. Riker, *Liberalism Against Populism* (San Francisco: Freeman, 1982).

[13]For an illustration of how this might be done in practice, see D.W. Pearce, *Cost-Benefit Analysis*, p. 71.

[14]For a brief overview, see Amartya Sen, *On Ethics and Economics* (New York: Basil Blackwell, 1987). For a more detailed discussion, see Robert Cooter and Peter Rappoport, "Were the Ordinalists Wrong About Welfare Economics?" *Journal of Economic Literature*, 22, no. 2 (June 1984), 507–530.

[15]In principle, a set of weights that is consistent with both the diminishing marginal utility of income and the greater income equality arguments could be derived by simply setting them equal to $(\partial SW / \partial u)(\partial u / \partial y)$ for the average member of each group of interest and then dividing the resulting values for each group by the value for the highest-income group. However, finding values for $(\partial SW / \partial u)(\partial u / \partial y)$ is subject to the same informational problems mentioned in the text. Moreover, the term itself was derived in footnote 10 by first arbitrarily specifying a simple social welfare function that did not allow for interdependencies in utility and in which social welfare depends upon a linear combination of individual utilities. As noted in the text, general agreement on the form of the social welfare function does not exist. For example, utilities are probably interdependent and the social welfare function could very well be nonlinear.

[16]Otto Eckstein, "A Survey of the Theory of Public Expenditure Criteria" in *Public Finances: Needs, Sources and Utilization*, ed. James M. Buchanan (Princeton, NJ: Princeton University Press, 1961), pp. 439-494.

[17]For example, see Robert H. Haveman, *Water Resource Investment and the Public Interest* (Nashville, TN: Vanderbilt University, 1965); and V.C. Nwaneri, "Equity in Cost-Benefit Analysis: A Case Study of the Third London Airport," *Journal of Transport Economics and Policy*, 4, no. 3 (1970), 235–254.

[18]This approach was first developed by Burton A. Weisbrod, "Income Redistribution Effects and Benefit-Cost Analysis" in *Problems in Public Expenditure Analysis*, ed. S.B. Chase (Washington, DC: Brookings Institution, 1968), 177–208.

[19]The empirical analysis in Weisbrod's 1968 paper is actually somewhat more complex than suggested in the text. For example, Weisbrod analyzed four water resource projects considered by the U.S. Corps of Engineers. Of these projects, the one with the highest estimated NPV was rejected, while the other three were accepted. Thus, Weisbrod used four equations to estimate weights for four separate subgroups (rich whites, poor whites, rich nonwhites, and poor nonwhites).

[20]Table 9.4 also provides estimates of the individual benefit and cost components of the various Work/Welfare Demonstrations.

[21]This argument was apparently first made by Arnold C. Harberger, "On the Use of Distributional Weights in Social Cost-Benefit Analysis."

[22]Edward M. Gramlich, *A Guide to Benefit-Cost Analysis*, 2nd ed. (Englewood Cliffs, NJ: Prentice Hall, 1990), pp. 123–127. Gramlich bases his conclusion on his own "simple analysis" and on findings from a a general equilibrium computer simulation conducted by Edgar Browning and William Johnson ["The Trade-Off between Equality and Efficiency," *Journal of Political Economy*, 92, no. 2 (April 1984), 175–203]. Both analyses are examples of attempts to compute the marginal excess burden associated with taxes, which was discussed in Chapter 3.

15

HOW ACCURATE IS CBA?

In Chapter 1 we observed that CBA can be useful for decision making. In practice, such usefulness depends on the accuracy of CBA. One way to examine the accuracy of CBA is to perform analyses of the same project at different times and to compare the results. We suggested in Chapter 1 that *ex ante/ex post* (*EA/EP*) comparisons and *ex ante/in medias res* (*EA/IMR*) comparisons are most valuable for learning about the accuracy of CBA. However, we provided few details. We now return to this subject in more detail.[1]

An *ex ante* CBA is performed when the decision is made about whether or not to proceed with a proposed project. We refer to this time as year 0, that is, $t = 0$. An *ex post* (*EP*) analysis is performed after all impacts of the implemented project have been realized. This may take many years, even centuries. Suppose that, in fact, all impacts have occurred by year T, then an *ex post* CBA is one performed in year t, where $t \geq T$. An *in medias res* (*IMR*) analysis is performed in year t, where $0 < t < T$. Thus, an *IMR* or *EP* CBA is done as if it were an *EA* CBA, but using more recent data. The main difference between these classes of CBA is that, as time passes, there is generally less uncertainty about the impacts and more accuracy about the actual NPV of the project.

Accuracy of CBA depends on how well the analyst performs the nine steps we present in Chapter 1. Each step is subject to errors. The most important ones for decision makers relate to specifying the impact categories, predicting the impacts, and valuing the impacts. For evaluation purposes we should add measurement error, which does not arise in *EA* by definition, but may occur in *IMR* or *EP* studies. Difficulties associated with the other steps, while they occur frequently enough, should be avoidable by an analyst with a good training in the concepts of CBA. In this chapter, then, we consider only omission errors, forecasting errors, measurement errors, and valuation errors.

In general, these errors decline as CBAs are performed later, but they never reach zero. Thus, CBAs performed toward the end of a project are more accurate than those performed earlier, but even later studies contain errors. This chapter illustrates the presence of these errors in CBA by providing a detailed example of a highway project that has been the subject of three separate CBAs performed at different times—one *ex ante*, one *in medias res*, and one *ex post*.

The estimates of net benefits differ considerably across the studies. Contrary to what might have been expected, the largest source of the difference was not errors in forecasts, nor differences in evaluation of intangible benefits, but from major differences in declared and actual construction costs of the project. Thus, the largest errors arose from what most analysts would have thought were the most reliable figures entered into the CBA.

SOURCES OF ERRORS IN CBA STUDIES

Errors in CBA studies may arise for many reasons. They may result from the manager's bureaucratic lens, as we discussed in Chapter 1.[2] Some errors in CBA studies appear to be disingenuous or strategic, that is, resulting from self-interest. There is considerable evidence that managers systematically overestimate benefits and underestimate costs; see, for example, Exhibit 15.1.[3] Strategic bias of this sort is widespread among managers and does not appear to be limited to the public sector.[4] For example, Nancy Ryan found that recent nuclear projects have experienced "awe-inspiring" cost overruns, some attributable to strategic underestimation of costs.[5]

■ EXHIBIT 15.1

Political and bureaucratic actors not only directly underestimate costs and overestimate benefits of their favored alternative. They also overestimate the costs and underestimate the benefits of alternatives they do not favor. John Kain documents the use of such "straw men" alternatives by Houston's regional transit authority in its consideration of a new urban light rail system. He shows how it made its preferred rail alternative appear better by "goldplating" the all-bus alternatives. For example, it overestimated the capital costs of the bus-way alternatives in one report by 70 percent.

Source: John F. Kain, "The Use of Straw Men in the Economic Evaluation of Rail Transport Projects," *American Economic Review: Papers and Proceedings*, 82, no. 2 (May 1992), 487–493.

Where CBAs are performed by independent analysts, as was the case for our highway example, one would not expect to encounter this type of bias. Consequently, this section focuses on other potential causes of errors. As the source(s) of many errors are unobservable, it is often impossible to disentangle the separate effect of each source. This is endemic, for example, where benefits are overestimated and costs underestimated. Who knows the extent to which such errors result from optimism bias or strategic bias?

Omission Errors

Analysts may exclude some impact category completely because they think it is too unlikely to occur. This problem is quite likely where a project is highly technical and there are genuine disagreements about the physical impacts. There is, for example, much uncertainty concerning the fundamental scientific relationships concerning global warming.[6] The scientific literature pertaining to many environmental issues, from dioxins to the marbled murrelet, is sparse or controversial. Analysts may find themselves in the middle of a "battle of the experts," not knowing with certainty the impacts of various policy alternatives. For our highway example, we would be surprised if there were problems of this particular sort.

Double counting is the converse of omission and, consequently, can be considered in this section. One way analysts double count benefits is by including benefits that arise in both the primary market *and* a secondary market, for example, including both time saved and increases in house prices. As we discuss in Chapter 3, benefits (or costs) in secondary markets should not be included when prices equal social marginal costs.

While omission errors may be present in any CBA at any time, we would expect them to decline over time. Undoubtedly, as a project progresses, more knowledge comes to light concerning the actual impact categories. Thus, omission errors are likely to be less frequent in CBAs performed later.

Forecasting Errors

Forecasting errors in CBA can arise from inherent difficulties (due, for example, to the difficulty of predicting technological change), cognitive biases, changing project specifications, and for strategic reasons. Forecasting beyond a few months is often inaccurate whatever the context.[7] The difficulty of accurate forecasting generally increases as projects are more complex, unique, further in the future, and involve unknown cause-and-effect relationships.[8]

The impacts of some government projects are relatively easy to predict because they are of low complexity, are not unique, and are easily comparable to previous projects. Small road improvements, for example, typically fall into this category. In contrast, major projects such as the Chunnel (Channel Tunnel between England and France) are complex, not easily compared to previous projects, and have impacts that extend far into the future.

Unknown cause-and-effect relationships frequently arise when there is uncertainty concerning fundamental scientific relationships, as discussed previously. They also arise when a government attempts a new project and analysts cannot be certain how affected individuals will respond. Evidence suggests, for example, that some individuals tend to react to new rules and regulations with "offsetting behavior," which attenuates the anticipated benefits of risk-reducing regulations.[9]

In the presence of uncertainty, there is scope for cognitive biases. A few categories of cognitive bias have been discussed previously in the CBA context. In particular, some CBA analysts recognize that people systematically underweight low-probability "bad" events. Thus, people on flood plains do not buy sufficient flood insurance.[10] At the same time, as lottery purchases indicate, people may overweight low-probability "good" events. Indeed, there is a large literature concerning the importance of cognitive perceptions on decision making and information processing that has not found its way into mainstream CBA. Charles Schwenk provides a recent summary of the effect of cognitive biases on decision making, which one can reasonably assume also pertains to forecasting.[11] The main conclusion of this literature is that cognitive biases may lead to severe and systematic errors of forecast and judgment, with an overall tendency toward overoptimism.

Forecasting errors also arise due to changing project specifications. Large and complex projects are invariably modified when underway, often as a result of irresistible "evolutionary" adaption by front-line employees.[12] Sometimes these changes are quite substantial. For example, changing regulatory requirements contributed significantly to construction cost overruns of nuclear power plants.[13] When projects are modified, *EA/EP* comparisons may, in effect, compare "apples and oranges."

There is a tendency to assume that forecasting errors do not arise in *EP* analysis because all impacts have been realized. But the analyst must still compare what did happen to what would have happened in the absence of the project—the counterfactual. While analysts may know what did happen (subject to measurement error), they must estimate what would have happened if the project had not been implemented. In general, though, *EP* forecasting uncertainty is less than *EA* forecasting uncertainty.

Measurement Errors

There is also a tendency to assume that once an event (impact) has occurred, all uncertainty associated with the impact is removed. But, in practice, events are often observed, recorded, or interpreted inaccurately. The extent of this problem depends largely on the quality of the measurement equipment (technology) and on the ability of statistical or econometric methods to make inferences in the presence of measurement errors (methodology). These problems have received little specific attention within the CBA literature. One possible explanation is that they are perceived as being of relatively little importance compared to other problems. Another reason is that current statistical methods for handling measurement error are complex, have stringent data requirements, or require strong underlying assumptions.

Valuation Errors

The reality of CBA, as we discuss in Chapter 12, is that accurate monetary estimates of the social value (i.e., shadow prices) of many impacts are scarce. While estimates of the value of injuries are reasonably good, there remains a wide range of plausible estimates for valuations of other impacts of the highway, such as time saved and lives saved. Obtaining appropriate shadow prices is particularly difficult for projects in developing countries.[14]

Valuation errors also arise due to unanticipated relative price changes. (In a way, this is a forecasting error rather than a valuation error.) This type of error can have significant impacts, especially on large infrastructure development projects.

THE DISTRIBUTION OF NET BENEFITS OVER TIME

These different types of error have different impacts on estimated net benefits. Furthermore, these errors have different impacts at different times. This section examines how the distribution of net benefits changes over time.

Suppose NB_t denotes the present value (in year 0 dollars) of the net benefits of a project at time t. NB_t is a random variable with a probability density function, $f_t(NB_t; \mu_t, \sigma_t)$, where μ_t is the mean and σ_t is the standard deviation. *Ex ante*, the distribution of the present value of net benefits, NB_0, has a large variance. Over time some impacts are realized—nature "rolls the dice" on some impact variable(s)—for example, the initial volume of traffic. Consequently, the distribution of NB_t changes over time. The mean, μ_t, may increase or decrease relative to the *EA* mean, μ_0. It may sometimes be above NB_T, the actual net benefits of the project, and sometimes below NB_T, but it will tend to approach NB_T over time. In contrast, the variance monotonically decreases over time, although it never equals zero.

These changes in the distribution of NB_t over time are represented graphically in Figure 15.1. Here, the present value of net benefits has an approximate normal distribution, which is a reasonable assumption for any project with many impacts. As t increases, the distribution of NB_t changes, its mean tends to move closer to NB_T and its variance decreases. As t approaches T, NB_t converges toward NB_T, which is represented by the vertical line in Figure 15.1.

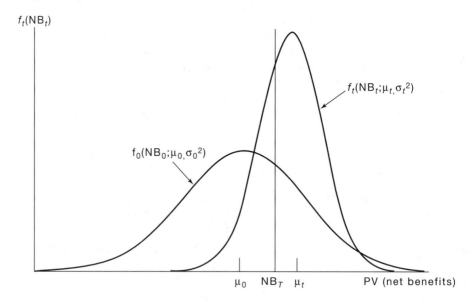

Figure 15.1   Illustrative Probability Density Functions of the Present Value of Net Benefits at Time 0, Time t, and the Actual Net Benefits, NB_T.

Source: Same as Table 15.1, page 435.

Now consider the effects of changing the time when a CBA is conducted on omission, forecasting, valuation, and measurement errors. While omission errors may always be present, we expect they would decline over time. Similarly, as impacts occur, some forecasting errors are reduced or eliminated. Of course, as we discussed earlier, there may be some forecasting errors in an *EP* study due to the problem associated with predicting the counterfactual events—what would have happened if the project had not been implemented. Even if forecasting errors are reduced over time, there may still be measurement errors, although, of course, measurement errors are generally smaller than forecasting errors. Valuation errors may shrink over the life of a particular project but, given the state of existing methodologies, they are most likely to be still present in an *EP* study. Thus, in summary, as t increases, the variance of the estimate of the present value of net benefits will decrease, although it will never equal zero: Uncertainty is reduced but never completely resolved.

Whether estimates of the present value of net benefits are consistently above or below NB_T, that is, whether estimators are systematically positively or negatively biased depends on whether omission, forecasting, measurement, or valuation errors are systematically biased (as well as on the size of these biases relative to other errors). Obtaining estimates of net benefits over time and comparing the results provide clues about the magnitude of the different types of errors in a CBA and about the presence of systematic biases. With such knowledge analysts may be able to provide better information about the precision of their estimates in similar situations.

SUMMARY OF THE CBAS OF THE COQUIHALLA HIGHWAY

The Coquihalla Highway is a four-lane toll road, which improves access to the interior of British Columbia (B.C.) from Vancouver; see Figure 15.2. Alternate routes are generally two-lane, with occasional sections of passing lanes. Congestion and safety concerns on alternate routes were important factors in the decision to build the new highway. Construction was performed in three phases. Phase I, which extends for 115 kilometers from Hope to Merritt, was completed in May 1986. Phase II, which extends for another 80 kilometers from Merritt to Kamloops, was completed in September 1987. Phase III extends east from Merritt for 108 kilometers to Peachland (near Kelowna), and was completed in October 1990.

Three CBAs of the Coquihalla Highway are summarized in Table 15.1. All were performed by independent analysts from the perspective of 1984 when the initial decision was made, but using the information available at the time the CBA was conducted. Each study took a global perspective; that is, everyone had standing, both Canadians and Americans! All assumed there would be tolls set at the toll levels that were used initially. All CBAs were compared to the "status quo" (no new highway in this region) alternative. Furthermore, all used a 7.5 percent real social discount rate with a discounting period of 20 years, the assumed life of the project. Benefits and costs were expressed as present values in 1984 Canadian dollars. It is important to note that the *EA* study was performed on the first two phases only, while the other two studies were performed on all three phases.

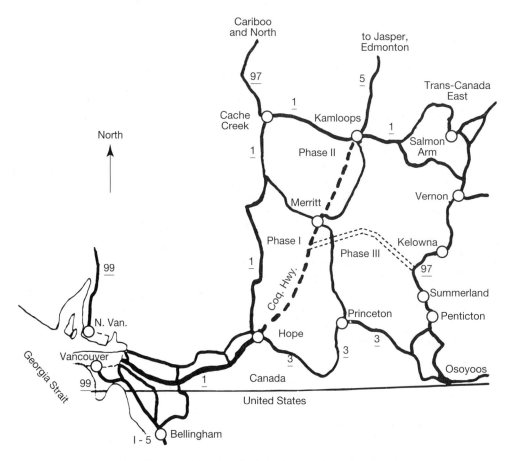

Figure 15.2 Map of the Coquihalla Highway and Nearby Routes

Source: Same as Table 15.1, page 435.

The first CBA was conducted by Waters and Meyers, henceforth WM, in June 1986.[15] This is essentially an *EA* study, although Phase I was just opening at that time. The authors used "information and forecasts developed before the highway was built as this is more relevant to assessing the original decision to build the highway."[16] The WM impact categories, as listed in Table 15.1, are self-explanatory. Note that since the CBAs were performed from the global perspective, there is no impact category for toll revenues, which are transfers. WM calculated the present value of the net benefit of the project to be $40.2 million in 1984 dollars.

The second study was conducted by Wendy L. Mallery, hereafter MLY, in December 1987.[17] At that time, Phases I and II had been completed, but Phase III had not. MLY had access to actual traffic data (sixteen months for Phase I and one month for Phase II) and published estimates of actual construction costs. Thus, MYL's study is an early *IMR* CBA.

TABLE 15.1   THREE CBAs OF THE COQUIHALLA HIGHWAY

| | Waters and Meyers Phases I and II | Mallery Phases I, II, and III | Boardman, Mallery, and Vining Phases I, II, and III |
	Ex Ante	In Medias Res	Ex Post
PROJECT BENEFITS:			
Time and operating savings	$290.7	$417.6	$900.3
Safety benefits	36.5	51.5	203.1
Reduced congestion on alternative routes	14.1	29.7	56.6
Terminal value after 20 years	53.3	140.6	147.8
Total Benefits	$396.6	$639.4	$1,307.8
PROJECT COSTS:			
Construction	$338.4	$702.6	$837.2
Toll collection	8.4	8.4	8.4
Maintenance and snow removal	7.6	56.6	67.9
Total Costs	$354.4	$767.6	$913.5
NET BENEFITS	$40.2	($128.2)	$394.3

Note: All figures are present values expressed in millions of 1984 Canadian dollars, discounted at 7.5%, assuming a project life of 20 years.

Source: Anthony E. Boardman, Wendy L. Mallery, and Aidan R. Vining, "Learning from *Ex Ante/Ex Post* Cost-Benefit Comparisons: The Coquihalla Highway Example," *Socio-Economic Planning Sciences*, 28, no. 2 (June 1994), 69–84, Table 2, p. 77. Reprinted with kind permission from Elsevier Science Ltd, The Boulevard, Langford Lane, Kidlington OX5 19GB, UK.

The most recent study by Anthony Boardman, Wendy L. Mallery, and Aidan Vining, hereafter BMV, was completed in March 1993, although some impacts were estimated earlier.[18] Despite the fact that this study was conducted somewhat early in the project's life, we will treat it as an *EP* study.

ANALYSIS OF THE DIFFERENCES AMONG THE CBAs

Omissions

It could be argued that there were omission errors in all three studies. No study considered the opportunity cost of the land occupied by the highway. This land was owned by the provincial government and even analysts have a tendency to treat publicly owned land as "free," which, of course, is incorrect. In fact, the land did not have a high opportunity cost and so excluding it did not have a large impact on the NPVs.

There is considerable controversy over the highway's environmental impacts. Though there is no separate impact category for environmental damage in any of the three studies, the cost of constructing underpasses, which allow animals to cross the highway safely, careful timing of construction activity, and special efforts to repair any encroachment of rivers were included in construction costs. All studies assumed implicitly that, after taking these actions, additional environmental impacts would be negligible. Environmentalists, however, contend the actual environmental impacts (e.g., wild animal road kills, wildlife and fish habitat destruction) are quite large.

None of the CBAs includes benefits associated with regional development. Such indirect, local benefits are generally viewed in CBA as transfers from other areas, not real benefits. However, analysis of indirect effects becomes complicated in the presence of externalities. Recently, there has been an economic boom in Kelowna, which exceeded expectations. This may be partly attributable to agglomeration effects or positive network externalities.[19] If so, it would be legitimate to treat part of the regional development benefits as real.

Forecasting Differences

Traffic volume data on the Coquihalla and other routes.   Estimates of traffic volume are likely to be the most crucial forecast in a highway CBA because they directly affect many of the benefit categories. Traffic levels are difficult to predict; they may change over the life of the project as potential consumers "learn" about the advantages and disadvantages of the highway, as population distributions change, and as consumer tastes change.

WM obtained aggregate annual traffic forecasts by applying recent traffic growth patterns to a British Columbia Ministry of Transportation forecast for 1986, and allowing for an "EXPO 86" traffic bulge. They then disaggregated the data into different origin-destination groups for three categories of vehicles (trucks, passenger vehicles–work, and passenger vehicles–leisure). For each group, they estimated the proportion of diverted, undiverted, or generated traffic.[20] Price-sensitive diversion rates were used to account for the impact of tolls on the Coquihalla.

MLY used actual Coquihalla traffic counts from May 1986 (when Phase I opened) to September 1987 (when Phase II opened). For subsequent years, MLY produced three different NPVs, assuming a 1 percent, 3 percent, and 5 percent annual traffic growth. The 3 percent rate is used in Table 15.1. Accordingly, total vehicle traffic (at the toll booth) in the years 2000 and 2005 was projected to be 2.85 million and 3.65 million, respectively. MLY estimated the annual average daily traffic allocations on alternative routes for 1984–87 based on actual average summer daily traffic counts.[21] This historical information was used to estimate a diversion rate of 30 percent for Highway 3 traffic to the Coquihalla after the completion of Phase III.

BMV draw on four sources of data: (1) Toll booth receipts for the years 1986–90 were broken out by the following vehicle classes: motorcycles, passenger vehicles, two-axle, three-axle, four- to five-axle, and six-axle or more trucks;[22] (2) Perusal of April 1991 traffic counts at the Coquihalla toll booth and on the Okanagan Connector (Phase III) shows completion of Phase III increased Coquihalla traffic by about 40 percent. (3) Data were obtained from counters on all alternative routes for 1985–89. (The summer traffic counts for each highway section were then adjusted to account for seasonality: Summer traffic was 1.25 to 1.9 times the annual average daily traffic.)

(4) Ministry of Transportation origin-destination surveys were used to estimate that 90 percent of passenger vehicles were leisure travelers, while 10 percent were business travelers. Based on these data, and assuming a 5 percent annual growth rate (after completion of Phase III), BMV project annual Coquihalla traffic volumes of 4.03 million and 5.14 million vehicles for the years 2000 and 2005, respectively.

It is impossible to determine the accuracy of the traffic volume forecasts of WM's *EA* study because they did not present them, nor did they specify the growth rate. Backward induction suggests that WM only slightly overestimated initial use but seriously underestimated future traffic volumes. MLY used actual data for the initial year and then estimated a growth rate of 3 percent, while actual growth has been about 5 percent. She predicted that the opening of Phase III would increase the traffic base by 20 percent, but preliminary evidence suggests it increased by about 40 percent. BMV's *EP* study projections for the years 2000 and 2005 are 41 percent higher than MLY's estimates.

Time and distance savings on the Coquihalla.   One would expect that time and distance savings per trip would not vary by very much among the studies. In fact, they did vary, as shown in Tables 15.2A and 15.2B. Differences in distance are due to changes in the final design as well as use of different sources to measure distance. Differences in time saved are due to differences in distance saved and different assumptions about the speeds traveled on different routes.

Reduced congestion on alternative routes.   WM estimated that, due to the Coquihalla, through vehicles on the old routes saved 20 minutes during congested periods. They assumed local traffic saved less, proportional to the number of cars diverted to the new highway. MLY also used the 20-minute saving. BMV followed a different approach, assuming users of alternative routes would save 2 kph in 1986, and 5 kph from 1987 onward. Highways 1 and 3 savings were calculated for all years; Highways 3A and 97 savings were included for 1991 onward.

Accident rates.   WM calculated safety benefits resulting both from reduced distance traveled and from traveling on a safer highway. To estimate safety benefits

TABLE 15.2A   DISTANCE SAVED PER COQUIHALLA TRIP (KILOMETERS)

Trip	Waters and Meyers *Ex Ante*	Mallery *In Medias Res*	Boardman, Mallery, and Vining *Ex Post*
Phase I:			
Hope to Merritt	N/A[a]	87	112
Phases I and II:			
Hope to Kamloops	72	83	107
Phases I and III:			
Hope to Peachland	N/A	77	53

TABLE 15.2B   TIME SAVED PER COQUIHALLA TRIP (MINUTES)

Trip	Waters and Meyers _Ex Ante_	Mallery _In Medias Res_	Boardman, Mallery, and Vining _Ex Post_
Phase I:			
Hope to Merritt	N/A[a]	102	108
Phases I and II:			
Hope to Kamloops	72	89	120
Phases I and III:			
Hope to Peachland	N/A	100	79

[a]N/A = Not available or not applicable.

Source: Anthony E. Boardman, Wendy L. Mallery, and Aidan R. Vining, "Learning from _Ex Ante/Ex Post_ Cost-Benefit Comparisons: The Coquihalla Highway Example," _Socio-Economic Planning Sciences_, 28, no. 2 (June 1994), 69–84, Tables 3A and 3B, p. 79. Reprinted with kind permission from Elsevier Science Ltd, The Boulevard, Langford Lane, Kidlington OX5 19GB, UK.

from reduced distances, they multiplied the predicted 130 million vehicle-kilometers saved by the accident rates for fatal, injury, and property-damage-only accidents on two-lane highways determined by Radnor Pacquette and Paul Wright.[23] To estimate benefits resulting from a safer road, they multiplied the estimated 313 million vehicle-kilometers traveled on the Coquihalla by one-third of the accident rate—their estimate of the accident rate reduction due to using a four-lane divided highway versus the existing highway. MLY followed a similar approach but, for benefits due to a safer road, she used the higher accident rate reductions implied by Pacquette and Wright, which ranged from 35 to 50 percent, depending on the severity of accident. BMV obtained accident rate data by severity from the ministry.

The Coquihalla saves lives. The fatal accident rate of the Coquihalla is about 50 percent lower than on alternate routes, a higher reduction than WM assumed, but similar to MLY's estimate. Furthermore, actual fatal accident rates on all routes in British Columbia are higher than WM or MLY assumed. Consequently, more lives are saved due to reduced distance driving than either WM or MLY predicted. Relative to other routes, the Coquihalla has a lower injury rate, but higher property-damage-only rate. Nonetheless, because both of these types of accident rates are also higher in British Columbia than anticipated, the shorter Coquihalla generates much higher safety benefits than projected.[24]

Estimation/Measurement Differences

Maintenance expenses.   At the time of the _EA_ study, the Maintenance Services Branch's estimates of annual maintenance and snow removal costs ranged between $2,500 and $7,500 per lane-kilometer. WM selected a number near the low end of this range but interpreted the figures as per kilometer rather than per lane-kilometer, resulting in an estimate of $2,600 per _kilometer_. In contrast, MLY estimated $7,000 per *lane-kilometer* for Phase I, and $5,000 per *lane-kilometer* for Phases II and III. As the highway was 80 percent four-lane highway and 20 percent six-lane highway, MLY's maintenance and snow removal estimates are far higher than WM's estimates. BMV made a largely unsuccessful attempt to isolate actual maintenance expenses. One problem was that the ministry maintained appropriate data by district, not by highway. To complicate matters, in 1988, the ministry privatized highway maintenance. The two major contractors for the Coquihalla were reluctant to reveal their costs as they were bidding on new tenders. BMV's discussions did reveal that, due to poor quality control in construction, some older sections already required resurfacing and ditch cleaning costs were large. Ultimately, BMV used an estimate of $6,000 per lane-kilometer, the average of the two figures used by MLY. There was one difference, however, stemming from the record-breaking snowstorms over the 1990–91 winter. To account for the "once in 10, 20, or 50 year" snowstorms that can severely affect the Coquihalla, maintenance and snow removal costs were arbitrarily increased in each of two, randomly chosen years. Overall, this approach is not entirely satisfactory; but it highlights that, like *EA* analyses, *EP* analyses can suffer from measurement error.

Construction costs. WM performed their study after Phase I was completed. Consequently, forecasting construction costs was not an issue, but as we will see, measuring these costs was problematic. Based on the best available estimates, WM estimated the present value (in 1984 dollars) of construction costs for Phases I and II were equal to $338.1 million.

Soon after completion of the highway, rumors circulated of higher costs. On November 7, 1987, the *Vancouver Sun* published estimates of undiscounted total costs of $570 million for Phase I and II and $270 million for Phase III. Based on these figures, MLY estimated the present value of construction costs at $507.9 million for Phases I and II, and $194.7 million for Phase III. BMV's construction cost estimates are based on the MacKay Commission, a Commission of Inquiry that was formed when it became publicly known that the Coquihalla had cost much more than originally anticipated.[25] MacKay concluded that "differences between costs and estimates of the Coquihalla Highway. . .system are due to. . .lack of proper budgeting, monitoring cost-control and reporting systems" (p. xi), and observed "[t]he current method of reporting highway capital spending. . .by individual contracts, by Electoral Districts, and on an annual basis. . .has served to disguise the true cost of major projects" (p. xi). MacKay also commented that "The Ministry's cost reporting system for capital works is fragmented and inconsistent" (p. xx). Based on MacKay, BMV estimated that the present value of construction costs was $837 million, that is, $135 million higher than MLY. The difference between BMV's estimate and the estimates in the earlier studies is due probably as much to strategic biases as to anything else.

During BMV's enquiries on actual construction costs, one ministry official estimated that MacKay's total Coquihalla construction cost figures were "out" (underestimated) by as much as 300 percent. Uncertainties undoubtedly remain even after the events. Doubling construction costs would be a rough way of accounting for work that was hidden or lost in general accounts, and for increases in indirect ministry overhead costs due to the Coquihalla.

One should not go too far, however. While BMV's estimate of $837.2 million may underestimate total construction costs, a significant part of the cost overruns for Phase I can be attributed to the political pressures to speed up completion in time for EXPO 86. These additional costs should be attributed to the EXPO 86 project, not to the Coquihalla Highway.

Valuation Differences

Value of vehicle operating cost savings and value of time saved. The three studies were quite similar in terms of how they valued time savings. Specifically, each assumed that business travelers value an hour of their time at the average gross wage for British Columbia hourly and salaried employees, while leisure travelers value their time at 25 percent of this rate. All studies also made similar assumptions about the number of passengers in each vehicle. Based on a perusal of estimates from the ministry, BMV assumed 2.2 passengers per leisure vehicle and 1.2 passengers per business vehicle. As far as we know, the other studies used similar estimates.

The studies differed, however, in the estimated gross wage rates and in the vehicle operating costs. Consider, for example, the estimates pertaining to a trip from Hope to Kamloops. WM estimated vehicle operating cost savings per Coquihalla trip at $7.00 for automobiles and $33.50 for large trucks. Estimated time savings were $8, $14.40, and $16.80 per trip for leisure vehicles, business vehicles, and trucks, respectively. MLY calculated vehicle operating cost savings at $9.66 per automobile trip and at $46.73 per truck trip. Time savings were calculated as $6.58 per leisure trip, $20.25 per business-auto trip, and $22.35 per truck trip.[26] BMV's estimates were considerably higher. Based largely on data provided by Trimac Consulting Services, BMV estimated time *and* vehicle operating cost savings at $27.50 per leisure trip, $46.80 per business trip, and $86.50 for a five-axle semi-trailer trip in 1987 dollars.[27]

Value of safety benefits. WM valued fatalities, injuries, and property-damage-only accidents at $500,000, $11,000, and $2,000, respectively. MLY used slightly higher valuations: Saved fatalities, injuries, and property-damage-only accidents were valued at $550,000, $12,000, and $2,000, respectively. Since 1984 there has been considerable work on this topic. Valuations of avoided fatalities vary considerably, as we discus in Chapter 12, but current valuations are considerably higher than was thought appropriate in 1984. Based on the most recent research at the time of their study, BMV used $2.2 million (1984 Canadian dollars) for the value of an avoided fatality.[28]

Terminal value. As discussed in Chapter 4, in theory, with a discounting period of 20 years, the terminal value equals the present value of the net benefits of the project from the twenty-first year to infinity. The obvious difficulty is in making projections that far into the future. Future costs, for example, will depend critically on the actual depreciation rate of the highway, which is partially endogenous in so far as it varies with use. The Maintenance Services Branch has suggested that highways similar to the Coquihalla are generally not reconstructed or relined for 40 to 50 years, and not repaved for about 15 years.

The method used here was to base the terminal value on the initial construction cost. WM calculated the terminal value as of the year 2005 to be 75 percent of the present value of the initial construction costs. MLY used 85 percent of initial construction costs, due partially to the high proportion of Coquihalla construction costs, such as rock cutting and sand blasting, that needed to be done only once in its life. BMV used 75 percent.

CONCLUSIONS ARISING FROM THE IMR, EP VERSUS EA COMPARISONS

Did the EA and IMR Analyses Have Overall Predictive Capability?

Contrasting an *EP* analysis with earlier CBAs of the same project provides an opportunity to assess the predictive capability of *EA* analysis. This is a critical element in determining the value of *EA* CBA. The NPV estimates of $40 and –$128 million for the earlier studies differ significantly from the NPV of $394 million for the *EP* study. Given that total costs were under $1 billion, the overall order of magnitude of error in estimation is large. Importantly, this aggregate difference understates actual differences in the earlier studies for two reasons. First, some benefits and costs erred in the same direction, thereby tending to cancel each other. For example, the *EP* study had higher construction costs, but also had higher time and operating savings benefits than the previous studies. Second, some errors offset one another within an impact category. For example, concerning safety benefits, the Coquihalla accident rate was higher than predicted, but highway ridership and accident rates elsewhere were also higher than forecast.

One comparison study alone cannot tell us everything about the general accuracy of CBA. Are such aggregate prediction errors prevalent in other CBAs? If they are, it is troubling. One might argue that this particular project raises more problems than is typical, but we think not. This project is *relatively* straightforward; after all, it is a highway, not a high-tech, mega project. Another possibility is that the cost underestimation problem (partly due to regional rather than project-specific budgeting) is specific to "wild and woolly" British Columbia. Again, we do not think so. Several non-British Columbia bureaucratic readers acknowledge that their agencies routinely hide project budget items in other accounts.

Other Lessons from this Comparison Study

This exercise is somewhat humbling. One lesson is that *EA* CBA is difficult to do precisely. Accuracy depends on omission, measurement, forecasting, and valuation errors (as well as other types of errors). In this study, there are examples of all four types of errors. As noted previously, some errors cancel out. Often, however, errors compound one another. For example, estimation of *EA* travel benefits requires estimates of both total time saved and the valuation of time. In turn, time saved depends on both the estimated number of vehicles and time saved per vehicle. When two or more terms with error are multiplied, the error in the resulting product can be quite large.

At least in other contexts, economists tend to anticipate forecasting errors, especially those associated with benefits. In this example, however, there were also large differences in measurement error (e.g., construction costs) and valuation (e.g., value of life). The *EA* CBA relied on announced estimates of total costs and did not attempt to reanalyze cost estimates. Although independent estimates of project costs are not easy to obtain, the *EA/EP* comparison highlights the importance of not passively accepting announced cost estimates of projects. Researchers should attempt to generate at least rough independent estimates.

Of course, research on the value of life is independent of construction of the Coquihalla. We expect that in the future economists will narrow the range in their estimates of the appropriate value of life to use in CBA. In general, valuation errors are less likely to occur as CBA matures and progresses technically.

Despite the difficulty of identifying the source of errors in *EA* studies, we found evidence of a variety of sources. Uniqueness played a part. For example, actual maintenance costs were much higher than was originally forecasted, based on average provincial costs. Other forecasting errors were purely random, for example, underestimation of the usage levels. Project specifications also changed. Strategic biases by bureaucrats and politicians probably accounted partially for the low cost estimates in the *EA* study. And there were analysts' procedural errors; for example, WM erred in using maintenance costs per kilometer, rather than maintenance costs per lane-kilometer.

In conclusion, the main lesson illustrated here is the importance of periodically conducting *EA/EP* comparisons. This may seem trivial, but it is almost totally ignored in the cost-benefit analysis literature. If *EA* studies were mandatory, should one in five be subject to *IMR* or *EP* comparison to the *EA* analysis? This chapter provides a template for how to do such comparison analyses.

NOTES

[1]The chapter draws upon Anthony E. Boardman, Wendy L. Mallery and Aidan R. Vining, "Learning from *Ex Ante/Ex Post* Cost-Benefit Comparisons: The Coquihalla Highway Example," *Socio-Economic Planning Sciences*, 28, no. 2 (June 1994), 69–84.

[2]See also Anthony Boardman, Aidan Vining, and W.G. Waters, II, "Costs and Benefits Through Bureaucratic Lenses: Example of a Highway Project," *Journal of Policy Analysis and Management*, 12, no. 3 (Summer 1993), 532–555.

[3]For example, see Leonard Merewitz, "Cost Overruns in Public Works," in *Benefit-Cost and Policy Analysis, 1972*, eds. W.A. Niskanen, A.C. Harberger, R.H. Haveman, R. Turvey, and R. Zeckhauser (Chicago: Aldine Publishing Company, 1973), pp. 277–295.

[4]This bias has been found in a wide range of corporations by Stephen W. Pruitt and Lawrence J. Gitman, "Capital Budgeting Forecast Biases: Evidence from the *Fortune* 500," *Financial Management*, 16, no. 1 (Spring 1987), 46–51.

[5]Nancy E. Ryan, "Policy Formation in a Politically Charged Atmosphere: An Empirical Study of Rate-base Determination for Recently Completed Nuclear Power Plants," paper presented at the 14th Annual APPAM Research Conference, 1992, at p. 3.

[6]William E. Colglazier, "Scientific Uncertainties, Public Policy, and Global Warming: How Sure Is Sure Enough?" *Policy Studies Journal*, 19, no. 2 (Spring 1991), 61–72.

[7]For recent reviews see, for example, Spyros Makridakis, "The Art and Science of Forecasting: An Assessment and Future Directions," *International Journal of Forecasting*, 2, no. 1 (1986), 15–39; Kenneth F. Wallis, "Macroeconomic Forecasting: A Survey," *Economic Journal*, 99, no. 1 (1989), 28–61; and K. Holden, D.A. Peel, and J.L. Thompson, *Economic Forecasting: An Introduction* (Cambridge: Cambridge University Press, 1990).

[8]Jeffrey L. Pressman and Aaron Wildavsky, *Implementation* (Berkeley: University of California Press, 1973).

[9]Robert S. Chirinko and Edward P. Harper, Jr., "Buckle Up or Slow Down? New Estimates of Offsetting Behavior and Their Implications for Automobile Safety Regulation," *Journal of Policy Analysis and Management*, 12, no. 2 (Spring 1993), 270–296.

[10]Howard Kunreuther, Ralph Ginsberg, L. Miller, Philip Sagi, Paul Slovic, B. Borkan, and N. Katz, *Disaster Insurance Protection: Public Policy Lessons* (New York: John Wiley, 1978); and Colin F. Camerer and Howard Kunreuther, "Decision Processes for Low Probability Events: Policy Implications," *Journal of Policy Analysis and Management*, 8, no. 4 (Fall 1989), 565–592.

[11]Charles R. Schwenk, "The Cognitive Perspective on Strategic Decision Making," *Journal of Management Studies*, 25, no. 1 (January 1988), 41–55. See also J.E. Russo and P.J. Schoemaker, "Managing Overconfidence," *Sloan Management Review*, 33, no. 2 (Winter 1992), 7–17.

[12]E. Hutchins, "Organizing Work by Adaption," *Organization Science*, 2, no. 1 (1991), 14–39.

[13]Oak Ridge National Laboratory, *Prudence Issues Affecting the U.S. Electric Utility Industry*, Oak Ridge, TN, 1987.

[14]I.M.D. Little and J.A. Mirrlees, "Project Appraisal and Planning Twenty Years On," *Proceedings of the World Bank Annual Conference on Development Economics 1990*, 1991, 351–391.

[15]W.G. Waters, II and Shane J. Meyers, "Benefit-Cost Analysis of a Toll Highway—British Columbia's Coquihalla," *Journal of the Transportation Research Forum*, 28, no. 1 (1987), 435–443.

[16]Ibid., 435–443.

[17]Wendy L. Mallery, "A Cost-Benefit Analysis of the Coquihalla Highway," class paper for J.M. Munro, Simon Fraser University, December 1987.

[18]Boardman, Mallery, and Vining, "Learning from *Ex Ante/Ex Post* Cost-Benefit Comparisons."

[19]A positive network externality arises where the utility one person derives from the consumption of a good increases with the number of other people consuming the good. For example, the benefit of having a telephone increases with the number of other people who have telephones that are connected to the same network. For a comprehensive analysis of network externalities, see Michael A. Katz and Carl Shapiro, "Network Externalities, Competition and Compatibility," *American Economic Review*, 75, no. 3 (June 1985), 424–440. In the context of regional development, the idea is that there may be regional positive externalities that arise when a region reaches a critical mass, or agglomeration, in terms of the nature, depth, and breadth of its economic activity. Michael Porter uses the related concept of *clustering* to explain the comparative advantage of nations in international competitiveness; see Michael E. Porter, *The Comparative Advantage of Nations* (New York: The Free Press, 1990).

[20]Diverted traffic refers to traffic that would have gone on the old routes but now travels on the Coquihalla. Undiverted traffic refers to traffic that continues on the old routes despite the existence of the Coquihalla. Generated traffic refers to traffic that would not have made the trip by road at all without the

Coquihalla, but now does so because the effective price is lower. These travelers may have gone by air or train, or done something completely different.

[21]These numbers were then adjusted by the estimated ratio of average summer to average annual traffic.

[22]Total traffic data were obtained for 1986 to 1990. Traffic data by vehicle class were obtained for the period April 1987 to March 1991, and estimated for 1986 and part of 1987. The traffic data thus cover three full years of Phase II operation from Hope to Kamloops and a few months of Phase III operation from Hope to Peachland. The *EP* study excludes motorcycles, which comprise less than 1 percent of total annual Coquihalla traffic.

[23]Radnor J. Pacquette and Paul H. Wright, *Highway Engineering* (New York: Wiley & Sons, 1979) at p. 73. In an earlier version of their paper, WM used an expected death rate of 0.027 per million vehicle-kilometers based on historical data for British Columbia.

[24]MLY based her projections on Pacquette and Wright (p. 73), who estimated the accident rates on a divided highway are 0.0155, 0.168, and 0.304 (per million vehicle-kilometers) for fatalities, injuries, and property damage only, respectively.

[25]Douglas L. MacKay, Commissioner, *Report of the Commission Inquiry into the Coquihalla and Related Highway Projects*, Province of British Columbia, December 1987.

[26]MLY used the average April 1986 gross wage for all B.C. industries for hourly and salaried employees, from the Statistics Canada publication, *Monthly Employment Earnings and Hours*, as the business hourly wage.

[27]Trimac Consulting Services Limited, *Operating Costs of Trucks in Canada*, 1988 and 1986 editions, prepared for the Motor Carrier Branch, Surface Transport Administration, Transport Canada (Ottawa, Ontario: Minister of Supply and Services, 1986, 1988).

[28]See Chapter 12 for a review of value-of-life estimates.

A Selected Cost-Benefit Analysis Bibliography

This bibliograpy provides representative CBA studies in a number of substantive areas. Instructors who adopt this book as a text will receive a more comprehensive bibliography upon request to the publisher. Others may obtain a copy at the cost of reproduction and mailing by writing to Professor Aidan Vining, Faculty of Business Administration, Simon Fraser University, Burnaby, B.C., Canada V5A 1S6.

TABLE OF CONTENTS

1. AGRICULTURE

Borcherding, T., and G.W. Dorosch, *The Egg Marketing Board: A Case Study of Monopoly and Its Social Cost*. Vancouver, B.C.: The Fraser Institute, 1981.

Graham, J.D., C.A. Webber, and R.J. MacGregor, "A Regional Analysis of Direct Government Assistance Programs in Canada and Their Impacts on the Beef and Hog Sectors," *Canadian Journal of Agricultural Economics*, 36, no. 4, part 2 (1988), 915–928.

Henze, A., and J. Zeddies, "EC Programmes, Economic Effects and Cost Benefit Considerations on Adjustments in EC Agriculture," *European Review of Agricultural Economics*, 15, no. 2/3 (1988), 191–210.

Klein, K.K., and F.P. Jeffer, "Economic Benefits From the Alberta Warble Control Program," *Canadian Journal of Agricultural Economics*, 35, no. 2 (1987).

Krystynak, R.H.E., "An Economic Assessment of 2,4-D in Canada: The Case of Grain," *Canadian Farm Economics*, 18, no. 1 (1983), 7–30.

McLeod, P.B., E.J. Roberts, and G.J. Syme, "Willingness to Pay for Continued Government Service Provisions: The Case of Agriculture Protection Services," *Journal of Environmental Management*, 40, no. 1 (1994), 1–16.

Norton, G.W., V.G. Ganoza, and C. Pomereda, "Potential Benefits of Agricultural Research and Extension in Peru," *American Journal of Agricultural Economics*, 69, no. 2 (1987), 247–257.

Reichelderfer, K.H., "Externalities and the Returns to Agricultural Research: Discussion," *American Journal of Agricultural Economics*, 71, no. 2 (1989), 464–465.

Sampson, J.A., and C.D. Gerrard, "Government Interventions and the Production of Wheat in Saskatchewan and North Dakota: An Empirical Analysis," *Canadian Journal of Agricultural Economics*, 35, no. 1 (1987).

Ulrich, A., W.H. Furtan, and A. Schmitz, "The Cost of a Licensing System Regulation: An Example From Canadian Prairie Agriculture," *Journal of Political Economy*, 95, no. 1 (1987), 160–178.

van Kooten, G.C., W.P. Weisensel, and E. de Jong, "Estimating the Costs of Soil Erosion in Saskatchewan," *Canadian Journal of Agricultural Economics*, 37, no. 1 (1989), 63–75.

2. AIR POLLUTION

Adams, R.M., D.M. Adams, J.M. Callaway, C. Chang, and B.A. McCarl, "Sequestering Carbon on Agricultural Land: Social Cost and Impacts on Timber Markets," *Contemporary Policy Issues*, 11, no. 1 (1993), 76–87.

Adams, R.M., J.M. Callaway, and B.A. McCarl, "Pollution, Agriculture, and Social Welfare: The Case of Acid Deposition," *Canadian Journal of Agricultural Economics*, 34, no. 1 (1986), 3–19.

Adams, R.M., and B.A. McCarl, "Assessing the Benefits of Alternative Ozone Standards on Agriculture: The Role on Response Information," *Journal of Environmental Economics and Management*, 12, no. 3 (1985), 264–276.

Adams, R.M., T.D. Crocker, and N. Thanavibulchai, "An Economic Assessment of Air Pollution Damages to Selected Annual Crops in Southern California," *Journal of Environmental Economics and Management*, 9, no. 1 (1982), 42–58.

Adams, R.M., S.A. Hamilton, and B.A. McCarl, "The Benefits of Pollution Control: The Case of Ozone and U.S. Agriculture," *American Journal of Agricultural Economics*, 68, no. 4 (1986), 886–893.

Anderson, R.C., and B. Ostro, "Benefits Analysis and Air Quality Standard," *Natural Resources Journal*, 3, no. 3 (1983), 566–575.

Atkinson, S., and D. Lewis, "A Cost-Effectiveness Analysis of Alternative Air Quality Control Strategies," *Journal of Environmental Economics and Management*, 1, no. 3 (1974), 237–250.

Bailey, M.J., "Risks, Costs and Benefits of Fluorocarbon Regulation," *American Economic Review Papers and Proceedings*, 72, no. 2 (1982), 247–250.

Bayless, M., "Measuring the Benefits of Air Quality Improvement: A Hedonic Salary Approach," *Journal of Environmental Economics and Management*, 9, no. 1 (1982), 81–99.

Brady, G.L., B.T. Bower, and H.A. Lakhani, "Estimates of the National Benefits and Costs of Improving Ambient Air Quality," *Journal of Environmental Management*, 16, no. 3 (1983), 191–210.

Brown, D., and M. Smith, "Crop Substitution in the Estimation of Economic Benefits Due to Ozone Reduction," *Journal of Environmental Economics and Management*, 11, no. 3 (1984), 347–360.

Cline, W.R., *The Economics of Global Warming*, Washington DC: Institute for International Economics, 1992.

Crocker, T.D., and J.L. Regans, "Acid Deposition Controls—A Benefit-Cost Analysis: Its Prospects and Limits," *Environment Science and Technology*, 19, no. 2 (1985), 112–116.

Farber, S., and A. Rambaldi, "Willingness to Pay for Air Quality: The Case of Outdoor Exercise," *Contemporary Policy Issues*, 11, no. 4 (1993), 19–30.

Fraas, A., and A. McGartland, "Alternative Fuels for Pollution Control: An Empirical Evaluation of Benefits and Costs," *Contemporary Policy Issues*, 8, no. 1 (1990), 62–74.

Freeman, A.M., III, "On Estimating Air Pollution Control Benefits from Land Value Studies," *Journal of Environmental Economics and Management*, 1, no. 1 (1974), 74–83.

Garcia, P., B.L. Dixon, J.W. Mjelde, and R.M. Adams, "Measuring the Benefits of Environmental Change Using a Duality Approach: The Case of Ozone Air Pollutants," *Journal of Environmental Economics and Management*, 13, no. 1 (1986), 69–80.

Gerking, S., and W. Schulze, "What Do We Know About Benefits of Reduced Mortality from Air Pollution Control?" *American Economic Review*, 71, no. 2 (1981), 228–234.

Giannias, D.A., "Consumer Benefit From Air Quality Improvements," *Applied Economics*, 21, no. 8 (1989), 1099–1108.

Haigh, J.A., D. Harrison, Jr., and A. Nichols, "Benefit-Cost Analysis of Environmental Regulation: Case Studies of Hazardous Air Pollutants," *Harvard Environmental Law Review*, 8, no. 2 (1984), 395–434.

Harrison, D., Jr., and D.L. Rubinfeld, "Hedonic Housing Prices and the Demand for Clean Air," *Journal of Environmental Management*, 5, no. 4 (1978), 81–102.

Joyce, T.J., M. Grossman, and F. Goldman, "An Assessment of the Benefits of Air Pollution Control: The Case of Infant Health," *Journal of Urban Economics*, 25, no. 1 (1989), 32–51.

Kopp, R.J., and A.J. Krupnick, "Agriculture Policy and the Benefits of Ozone Control," *American Journal of Agricultural Economics*, 69, no. 5 (1987), 956–962.

Krupnick, A.J., "Costs of Alternative Policies for the Control of Nitrogen Dioxide in Baltimore," *Journal of Environmental Economics and Management*, 13, no. 2 (1986), 189–197.

Krupnick, A.J., and M.A. Walls, "The Cost-Effectiveness of Methanol for Reducing Motor Vehicle Emissions and Urban Ozone," *Journal of Policy Analysis and Management*, 11, no. 3 (1992), 373–396.

McCorriston, S., and I.M. Sheldon, "The Welfare Implications of Nitrogen Limitation Policies," *Journal of Agricultural Economics*, 40, no. 2 (1989), 143–151.

Mendelsohn, R., "An Economic Analysis of Air Pollution from Coal Fired Plants," *Journal of Environmental Economics and Management*, 7, no. 1 (1980), 30–43.

Nelson, J.P., "Residential Choice, Hedonic Prices, and the Demand for Urban Air Quality," *Journal of Urban Economics*, 5, no. 3 (1978), 357–369.

Parks, P.K., and I.W. Hardie, "Least-Cost Forest Carbon Reserves: Cost-Effective Subsidies to Convert Marginal Agricultural Land to Forests," *Land Economics*, 71, no. 1 (1995), 122–136.

Perl, L.J., and F.C. Dunbar, "Cost Effectiveness and Cost-Benefit Analysis of Air Quality Regulations," *American Economic Review*, 72, no. 2 (1982), 208–213.

Regens, J.L., and R.W. Rycroft, *The Acid Rain Controversy*, Pittsburgh, PA: University of Pittsburgh Press, 1988.

Repetto, R., "The Economics of Visibility Protection: On A Clear Day You Can See A Policy," *Natural Resources Journal*, 21, no. 2 (1981), 355–370.

Rowe, R.D., R.C. d'Arge, and D.S. Brookshire, "An Experiment on the Economic Value of Visibility," *Journal of Environmental Economics and Management*, 7, no. 1 (1980), 1–19.

Schulze, W.D., and D.S. Brookshire, et al., "The Economic Benefits of Preserving Visibility in National Parklands of the Southwest," *Natural Resources Journal*, 23, no. 1 (1983), 149–173.

Schwing, R.C., B.W. Southwark, C.R. von Buseck, and C.J. Jackson, "Benefit-Cost Analysis of Automobile Emission Reductions," *Journal of Environmental Economics and Management*, 7, no. 1 (1980), 44–64.

Smith, V.K., and J. Huang, "Can Markets Value Air Quality? A Meta-Analysis of Hedonic Property Value Models," *Journal of Political Economy*, 103, no. 3 (1995), 209–227.

Thomas, V., "Evaluating Pollution Control: The Case of Sao Paulo, Brazil," *Journal of Development Economics*, 19, nos. 1 and 2 (1985), 133–146.

Young, D., and S. Aidun, "Ozone and Wheat Farming in Alberta: A Micro-study of the Effects of Environmental Change," *Canadian Journal of Agricultural Economics*, 41, no. 1 (1993), 27–43.

3. CRIME AND DRUG ABUSE (INCLUDING ALCOHOL)

Anderson, R.W., "Towards A Cost-Benefit Analysis of Police Activities," *Public Finance*, 29, no. 1 (1974), 1–17.

Coate, D., and M. Grossman, "Effects of Alcoholic Beverage Prices and Legal Drinking Ages on Youth Alcohol Use," *Journal of Law and Economics*, 31, no. 1 (1988), 145–171.

Cohen, M.A., "Pain, Suffering, and Jury Awards: A Study of the Cost of Crime to Victims," *Law and Society Review*, 22, no. 3 (1988), 537–555.

Cook, P., and G. Tauchen, "The Effect of Liquor Taxes on Heavy Drinking," *Bell Journal of Economics*, 13, no. 2 (1982), 255–285.

Grant, M.M., and A.W. Williams, eds., *Economics and Alcohol Consumption and Controls*. New York: Gardner Press, 1983.

Gray, C.M., *The Costs of Crime*. Beverly Hills, CA: Sage Publications, 1979.

Greenwood, P., ed., *Intervention Strategies for Chronic Juvenile Offenders*. New York: Greenwood Press, 1988.

Kenkel, D.S., "Drinking, Driving, and Deterrence: The Effectiveness and Social Costs of Alternative Policies," *Journal of Law and Economics*, 36, no. 2 (1993), 3877–3914.

Kimbrough, J., "School-Based Strategies for Delinquency Prevention," in *Intervention Strategies for Chronic Juvenile Offenders*, ed. P. Greenwood. New York: Greenwood Press, 1987, pp. 193–206.

Lee, D.R., "Policing Cost, Evasion Cost, and the Optimal Speed Limit," *Southern Economic Journal*, 52, no. 1 (1985), 34–45.

Levy, D., and N. Sheflin, "New Evidence on Controlling Alcohol Use Through Price," *Journal of Studies on Alcohol*, 44, no. 6 (1983), 929–937.

Lipsey, M., "Is Delinquency Prevention a Cost-Effective Strategy? A California Perspective," *Journal of Research in Crime and Delinquency*, 21, no. 4 (1984), 279–302.

Pogue, T.F., and L.G. Sgontz, "Taxing to Control Social Costs: The Case of Alcohol," *American Economic Review*, 79, no. 1 (1989), 235–243.

Saffer, H., and M. Grossman, "Drinking Age Laws and Highway Mortality Rates: Cause and Effect," *Economic Inquiry*, 25, no. 3 (1987), 403–418.

Schweinhart, L.J., and D.P. Weikart, *Young Children Grow Up: The Effects of the Perry Preschool Program on Youths Through Age 15*, Monograph No. 7. Ypsilanti, Michigan: High/Scope Educational Research Foundation, 1980.

4. ECONOMIC DEVELOPMENT AND INDUSTRIAL POLICY

Grossman, G.M., "Promoting New Industrial Activities: A Survey of Recent Arguments and Evidence," *OECD Economics Studies*, no. 14 (1990), 88–125.

Hufbauer, G.C., and K.A. Elliot, *Measuring the Cost of Protection in the United States*. Washington, DC: Institute for International Economics, 1994.

Leff, N.H., "Externalities, Information Costs, and Social Benefit-Cost Analysis for Economic Development: An Example from Telecommunications," *Economic Development and Cultural Change*, 32, no. 2 (1984), 255–276.

Mynemi, G., J. Dorfman, and G.C. Ames, "Welfare Impacts of the Canada–U.S. Softwood Lumber Trade Dispute: Beggar Thy Consumer Trade Policy," *Canadian Journal of Agricultural Economics*, 42, no. 3 (1994), 261–271.

Warr, P.G., "The Jakarta Export Processing Zone: Benefits and Costs," *Bulletin of Indonesian Economic Studies*, 19, no. 3 (1983), 28–49.

5. EDUCATION AND EMPLOYMENT/TRAINING PROGRAMS

Ashenfelter, O., "Estimating the Effects of Training Programs on Earnings," *Review of Economics and Statistics*, 60, no. 1 (1978), 47–57.

Barnett, W.S., "Benefits of Compensatory Preschool Education," *Journal of Human Resources*, 27, no. 2 (1992), 279–312.

Bas, D., "Cost-Effectiveness of Training in Developing Countries," *International Labour Review*, 127, no. 3 (1988), 355–369.

Borus, M.E., "Assessing the Impact of Training Programs," in *Employing the Unemployed*, ed. E. Ginzberg. New York: Basic Books, 1980, pp. 25–40.

Epp, D.J., "Unemployment and Benefit-Cost Analysis: A Case Study Test of a Haveman-Krutilla Hypothesis," *Land Economics*, 55, no. 3 (1979), 397–404.

Greenberg, D., and M. Wiseman, "What Did the OBRA Demonstration Do?" in *Evaluation Design for Welfare and Training Programs*, eds. I. Garfinkel and C. Manski. Cambridge, MA: Harvard University Press, 1992, pp. 25–75.

Gueron, J.M., *Reforming Welfare With Work*. New York: The Ford Foundation, 1987.

Gueron, J.M., and R.P. Nathan, "The MDRC Work/Welfare Project: Objectives, Status, Significance," *Policy Studies Review*, 4 (1985), 417–432.

Haveman, R.H., "The Dutch Social Employment Program," in *Creating Jobs: Public Employment Programs and Wage Subsidies*, ed. J.L. Palmer. Washington, DC: Brookings Institution, 1978, pp. 241–269.

Kemper, P., and P. Moss, "Economic Efficiency of Public Employment Programs", in *Creating Jobs: Public Employment Programs and Wage Subsidies*, ed. J.L. Palmer. Washington, DC: Brookings Institution, 1978, pp. 277–312.

Lalonde, R., and R. Maynard, "How Precise Are Evaluations of Employment and Training Programs: Evidence From a Field Experiment," *Evaluation Review*, 11, no. 4 (1987), 428–451.

Lane, J., and T. Berry, "A Multi-State Analysis of the Targeted Jobs Tax Credit Programme," *Applied Economics*, 21, no. 1 (1989), 85–94.

Long, D.A., C.D. Mallar, and C.V.D. Thornton, "Evaluating the Benefits and Costs of the Job Corps," *Journal of Policy Analysis and Management*, 1, no. 1 (1981), 55–76.

Psacharopoulos, G., "Returns to Education: an Updated International Comparison," *Comparative Education*, 17, no. 3 (1981), 321–341.

Psacharopoulos, G., "Returns to Education: A Global Update," *World Development*, 22, no. 9 (1994), 1325–1343.

Schiller, B.R., "Lesson From WIN: A Manpower Evaluation," *Journal of Human Resources*, 13, no. 4 (1978), 502–523.

Tines, J., et al., "Benefit-Cost Analysis of Supported Employment in Illinois: A State-Wide Evaluation," *American Journal on Mental Retardation*, 95, no. 1 (1990), 44–54.

Woodbury, S.A., and R.G. Spiegelman, "Bonuses to Workers and Employers to Reduce Unemployment: Randomized Trials in Illinois," *American Economic Review*, 77, no. 4 (1987), 513–530.

Zuidema, T., "Cost-Benefit Analysis in a Situation of Unemployment: Calculating the Decline in Unemployment as a Result of the Realization of a Government Project," *Public Finance Quarterly*, 15, no. 1 (1987), 105–115.

6. ENERGY AND ENERGY CONSERVATION

Anand, S., and B. Nalebuff, "Issues in the Application of Cost-Benefit Analysis to Energy Projects in Developing Countries," *Oxford Economic Papers*, 39, no. 1 (1987), 190–222.

Burkhart, L.A., "Conservation Program Cost-Benefit Analysis—Choosing Among Options," *Public Utilities Fortnightly*, 125, no. 7 (1990), 41–44.

Burwell, C.C., and D.L. Phung, "On the Energy Cost-Effectiveness of Electric Home Heating," *Public Utilities Fortnightly*, 113, no. 6 (1984), 26–31.

Caves, D.W., L.R. Christensen, W.E. Hendricks, and P.E. Schoech, "Cost-Benefit Analysis of Residential Time of Use Rates: A Case Study for Four Illinois Utilities," *Electric Ratemaking*, 1 (1982–1983), 40–46.

Chao, H., and A.S. Manne, "An Integrated Analysis of U.S. Oil Stockpiling Policies," in *Energy Vulnerability*, ed. J.L. Plummer. Cambridge, MA: Ballinger Publishing Company, 1982, pp. 59–82.

Cicchetti, C.J., "The Trans Alaska Pipeline: A Benefit-Cost Analysis of Alternatives," in *Benefit-Cost and Policy Analysis, 1973*, eds. R.H. Haveman, et al. Chicago: Aldine Publishing, 1974, pp. 110–143.

Dixon, J.A., "Selected Policy Options for Fuelwood Production and Use in the Philippines," from materials prepared by E.L. Hyman in *Economic Valuation Techniques for the Environment*, eds. J.A. Dixon and M.M. Hufschmidt. Baltimore and London: The Johns Hopkins University Press, 1986, pp. 163–177.

Frieden, B., and L. Baker, "The Market Needs Help: The Disappointing Record of Home Energy Conservation," *Journal of Policy Analysis and Management*, 2, no. 3 (1983), 432–448.

Friedman, L., and K. Hausker, "Residential Energy Consumption: Models of Consumer Behavior and Their Implications for Rate Design," *Journal of Consumer Policy*, 11, no. 3 (1988), 287–313.

Hartman, R.S., "An Analysis of Department of Energy Residential Appliance Efficiency Standards," *The Energy Journal*, 2, no. 2 (1981), 49–70.

Hausman, J.A., and P. Joskow, "Evaluating the Costs and Benefits of Appliance Efficiency Standards," *American Economic Review*, 72, no. 2 (1982), 220–225.

Horwich, G., H. Jenkins-Smith, and D.L. Weimer, "The International Energy Agency's Mandatory Oil-Sharing Agreement: Tests of Efficiency, Equity and Practicality," in *Responding to International Oil Crisis*, eds. G. Horwich and D. Weimer. Washington, DC: American Enterprise Institute, 1988, pp. 104–133.

Horwich, G., and D.L. Weimer, *Oil Price Shocks, Market Response and Contingency Planning*. Washington, DC: American Enterprise Institute, 1984.

Kalt, J.P., "The Costs and Benefits of Federal Regulation of Coal Strip Mining," *Natural Resources Journal*, 23, no. 4 (1983), 893–915.

Khazzoom, J.D., "Economic Implications of Mandated Efficiency Standards for Household Appliances," *Energy Journal*, 4, no. 1 (1980), 27–40.

Levinson, M., "Alcohol Fuels Revisited: The Costs and Benefits of Energy Independence in Brazil," *Journal of Developing Areas*, 21, no. 3 (1987), 243–257.

MacAvoy, P.W., "The Regulation-Induced Shortage of Natural Gas," *Journal of Law and Economics*, 12, no. 1 (1971), 167–200.

Rosenfeld, A., C. Atkinson, J. Koomey, A. Maier, R. Mowris, and L. Price, "Conserved Energy Supply Curves for U.S. Buildings", *Contemporary Policy Issues*, 11, no. 1 (1993), 45–68.

Rowe, R., M.G. Shelby, J.B. Epel, and A. Michelsen, "Using Oxygenated Fuels to Mitigate Carbon Monoxide Air Pollution: The Case of Denver," *Contemporary Policy Issues*, 8, no. 1 (1990), 39–53.

Sexton, R.J., and T.A. Sexton, "Theoretical and Methodological Perspectives on Consumer Response to Electricity Information," *Journal of Consumer Affairs*, 21, no. 2 (1987), 238–257.

Trane, K.E., "Incentives for Energy Conservation in the Commercial and Industrial Sectors," *The Energy Journal*, 9, no. 3 (1988), 113–128.

Walls, M.A., "Welfare Costs of an Oil Import Fee", *Contemporary Policy Issues*, 8, no. 2 (1990), 176–189.

Wenders, J.T., and R.A. Lyman, "An Analysis of the Benefits and Costs of Seasonal-Time-of-Day Electricity Rates," in Chapter 5 of *Problems in Public Utility Economics Regulation*, ed. M.A. Crew. Lexington, MA: D.C. Heath, 1979, pp. 73–91.

Wenders, J.T., and R.A. Lyman, "Determining the Optimal Penetration of Time-of-Day Electricity Tariffs," *Electric Ratemaking*, 1 (1982), 15–20.

7. FORESTRY

Anderson, F.J., "Ontario Reforestation Policy: Benefits and Costs," *Canadian Public Policy*, 5, no. 3 (1979), 336–347.

Hagen, D.A., J.W. Vincent, and P.G. Welle, "The Benefits of Preserving Old-Growth Forests and the Northern Spotted Owl," *Contemporary Policy Issues*, 10, no. 2 (1992), 13–26.

Hyde, W.F., R.G. Boyd, and B.L. Daniels, "The Impacts of Public Interventions: An Examination of the Forestry Sector," *Journal of Policy Analysis and Management*, 7, no. 1 (1987), 40–61.

Newcomb, K., "An Economic Justification for Rural Afforestation: The Case of Ethiopia," *Annals of Regional Science*, 21, no. 3 (1987), 80–99.

Rosenthal, D.H., and T.C. Brown, "Comparability of Market Prices and Consumer Surplus for Resource Allocation Decisions," *Journal of Forestry*, 83, no. 2 (1985), 105–109.

Rubin, J., G. Helland, and J. Loomis, "A Benefit-Cost Analysis of the Northern Spotted Owl: Results from a Contingent Valuation Survey," *Journal of Forestry*, 89, no. 12 (1991), 25–30.

8. HAZARDOUS WASTE (INCLUDING NUCLEAR POWER AND WASTE)

Gamble, H.B., and R.H. Downing, "Effects of Nuclear Power Plants on Residential Property Values," *Journal of Regional Science*, 22, no. 4 (1982), 457–478.

Grossman, P.Z., and E.S. Cassedy, "Cost-Benefit Analysis of Nuclear Waste Disposal: Accounting for Safeguards," *Science, Technology and Human Values*, 10, no. 1 (1985), 47–54.

Hageman, R.K., "Nuclear Waste Disposal: Potential Property Value Impacts," *Natural Resources Journal*, 21, no. 4 (1981), 789–810.

Nelson, J.P., "Three Mile Island and Residential Property Values: Empirical Analysis and Policy Implications," *Land Economics*, 57, no. 3 (1981), 363–372.

O'Donnell, E.P., and J.J. Mauro, "A Cost-Benefit Comparison of Nuclear and Non-Nuclear Health and Safety Protective Measures and Regulation," *Nuclear Safety*, 20, no. 5 (1979), 525–540.

Payne, B.A., S.J. Olshansky, and T.E. Segel, "The Effects on Property Values of Proximity to a Site Contaminated with Radioactive Waste," *Natural Resources Journal*, 27, no. 3 (1987), 579–590.

Sengupta, M., "The Choice Between Coal and Nuclear Power in India: A Cost-Benefit Approach," *Journal of Energy and Development*, 2, no. 1 (1986), 85–92.

Smith, V.K., and W.H. Desvousges, "The Value of Avoiding a LULU: Hazardous Waste Disposal Sites," *Review of Economics and Statistics*, 68, no. 2 (1986), 293–299.

9. HEALTH AND HEALTH REGULATION

Albritton, R.B., "Cost-Benefits of Measles Eradication: Effects of a Federal Intervention," *Policy Analysis*, 4, no. 1 (1978), 1–22.

Bartel, A., and P. Taubman, "Some Economic and Demographic Consequences of Mental Illness," *Journal of Labour Economics*, 4, no. 2 (1986), 243–256.

Bartel, A.P., and L.G. Thomas, "Direct and Indirect Effects of Regulation: A New Look at OSHA's Impact," *Journal of Law and Economics*, 28, no. 1 (1985), 1–25.

Berger, M.C., et al., "Valuing Changes in Health Risks: A Comparison of Alternative Measures," *Southern Economic Journal*, 53, no. 4 (1987), 967–984.

Birch, S., and C. Donaldson, "Applications of Cost-Benefit Analysis to Health Care: Departure from Welfare Economic Theory," *Journal of Health Economics*, 6, no. 3 (1987), 211–225.

Boyle, M.H., G.W. Torrance, J.C. Sinclair, and S.P. Horwood, "Economic Evaluation of Neonatal Intensive Care of Very-Low-Birth-Weight Infants," *New England Journal of Medicine*, 308, no. 22 (1983), 1330–1337.

Brown, R.A., and C.H. Green, "Threats to Health and Safety: Perceived Risk and Willingness-to-Pay," *Social Science and Medicine*, 15, no. 2, part D (1981), 67–75.

Bunker, J.P., B.A. Barnes, and F. Mosteller, eds., *Costs, Risks and Benefits of Surgery*. New York: Oxford University Press, 1977.

Butler, J.R., and D.P. Doessel, "Measuring Benefits in Health: A Clarification," *Scottish Journal of Political Economy*, 28, no. 2 (1981), 196–205.

Buxton, M.J., and R.R. West, "Cost-Benefit Analysis of Long-Term Haemodialysis for Chronic Renal Failure," *British Medical Journal*, 2, no. 5967 (1975), 376–379.

Cauley, S.D., "The Time Price of Medical Care," *Review of Economics and Statistics*, 69, no. 1 (1987), 59–66.

Chernickovsky, D., and I. Zmora, "A Hedonic Prices Approach to Hospitalization Costs: The Case of Israel," *Journal of Health Economics*, 5, no. 2 (1986), 179–191.

Churchill, D.N., B.C. Lemon, and G.W. Torrance, "A Cost-Effectiveness Analysis of Continuous Ambulatory Peritoneal Dialysis and Hospital Hemodialysis," *Medical Decision Making*, 4, no. 4 (1984), 489–500.

Cummings, J., and F. Weaver, "Cost Effectiveness of Home Care," *Clinics in Geriatric Medicine*, 7, no. 4 (1991), 865–874.

Cummings, J., and F. Weaver, et al., "Cost Effectiveness and Hospital-Based Home Care," in *Quality and Cost Containment in Care of the Elderly*, eds. J. Romeis and R. Coe. New York: Springer Publishing Company, 1991, pp. 159–174.

Dardis, R., S. Aaronson, and Y. Lin, "Cost-Benefit Analysis of Flammability Standards," *American Journal of Agricultural Economics*, 60, no. 4 (1978), 695–700.

Devaney, B., L. Bilheimer, and J. Schore, "Medicaid Costs and Birth Outcomes: The Effects of Prenatal WIC Participation and the Use of Prenatal Care," *Journal of Policy Analysis and Management*, 11, no. 4 (1992), 573–592.

Dewees, D.N., and R.J. Daniels, "The Costs of Protecting Occupational Health: The Asbestos Case," *Journal of Human Resources*, 21, no. 3 (1986), 381–396.

Disbrow, D., "The Costs and Benefits of Nutrition Services: A Literature Review," *Journal of American Dietetic Association*, 89, no. 4 (1989), supplements.

Evans, R.G., and G.C. Robinson, "Surgical Day Care: Measurements of the Economic Payoff," *Canadian Medical Association Journal*, 123, no. 9 (1980), 873–880.

Fisher, G.W., "Willingness-to-Pay for Probabilistic Improvements in Functional Health Status: A Psychological Perspective," in *Health: What Is It Worth? Measures of Health Benefits*, eds. S. Mushkin and D.W. Dunlop. New York: Pergammon Press, 1979, pp. 167–200.

Ginsberg, G.M., and D. Shouval, "Cost-Benefit Analysis of a Nationwide Neonatal Inoculation Programme against Hepatitis B in an Area of Intermediate Endemicity," *Journal of Epidemiology and Community Health*, 46, no. 6 (1992), 587–594.

Goldman, F., and M. Grossman, "The Demand for Pediatric Care: A Hedonic Approach," *Journal of Political Economy*, 86, no. 2, part 1 (1978), 259–280.

Goodwin, P.J., R. Feld, W.K. Evans, and J. Pater, "Cost-Effectiveness of Cancer Chemotherapy: An Economic Evaluation of a Randomized Trial in Small-Cell Lung Cancer," *Journal of Clinical Oncology*, 6, no. 10 (1988), 1537–1547.

Grannemann, T.W., R.S. Brown, and M.V. Pauly, "Estimating Hospital Costs: A Multiple Output Analysis," *Journal of Health Economics*, 5, no. 2 (1986), 107–127.

Hagard, S., and F.A. Carter, "Preventing the Birth of Infants With Down's Syndrome: A Cost-Benefit Analysis," *British Medical Journal*, 1, no. 6012 (1976), 753–756.

Hagard S., F. Carter, and R.G. Milne, "Screening for Spina Bifida: A Cost-Benefit Analysis," *British Journal of Social and Preventive Medicine*, 30, no. 1 (1976), 40–53.

Harrington, W., and P.R. Portney, "Valuing the Benefits of Health and Safety Regulation," *Journal of Urban Economics*, 22, no. 1 (1987), 101–112.

Hartunian, N.S., C.N. Smart, and M.S. Thompson, "The Incidence and Economic Costs of Cancer, Motor Vehicle Injuries, Coronary Heart Disease and Stroke: A Comparative Analysis," *American Journal of Public Health*, 70, no. 12 (1980), 1249–1260.

Hellinger, F.J., "Cost-Benefit Analysis of Health Care: Past Applications and Future Prospects," *Inquiry*, 17, no. 3 (1980), 204–215.

Hull, R., J. Hirsh, D.L. Sackett, and G.L. Stoddart, "Cost-Effectiveness of Clinical Diagnosis, Venography and Noninvasive Testing in Patients With Symptomatic Deep-Vein Thrombosis," *New England Journal of Medicine*, 304, no. 26 (1981), 1561–1567.

Jerrell, J.M., and T. Hu, "Cost-Effectiveness of Intensive Clinical and Case Management Compared With an Existing System of Care, *Inquiry*, 26, no. 2 (1989), 224–234.

Johnson, L.L., *Cost-Benefit Analysis and Voluntary Safety Standards for Consumer Products*. Santa Monica, CA: Rand Corporation, 1982.

Joyce, T.J., M. Grossman, and F. Goldman, "An Assessment of the Benefits of Air Pollution Control: The Case of Infant Health, *Journal of Urban Economics*, 25, no. 1 (1989), 32–51.

Kutner, N.G., "Cost-Benefit Issues in U.S. National Health Legislation: The Case of the End–Stage Renal Disease Program," *Social Problems*, 30, no. 1 (1982), 51–64.

Levin, H.V., "A Benefit Cost Analysis of Nutritional Programs for Anemia Reduction," *World Bank Research Observer*, 1, no. 2 (1986), 219–245.

Logan, A.G., B.J. Milne, C. Achber, W.P. Campbell, and R.B. Haynes, "Cost-Effectiveness of Worksite Hypertension Programme," *Hypertension*, 3, no. 2 (1981), 211–218.

Ludbrook, A., "A Cost-Effectiveness Analysis of the Treatment of Chronic Renal Failure," *Applied Economics*, 13, no. 3 (1981), 337–350.

Mauskopf, J.A., C.J. Bradley, and M.J. French, "Benefit-Cost Analysis of Hepatitis B Vaccine Program for Occupationally Exposed Workers," *Journal of Occupational Medicine*, 33, no. 6 (1991), 691–698.

Neuhauser, D., and A.M. Lewicki, "What Do We Gain from the Sixth Stool Guaiac?" *New England Journal of Medicine*, 293, no. 5 (1975), 226–228.

Paterson, M.L., "Cost-Benefit Evaluation of a New Technology for Treatment of Peptic Ulcer Disease," *Managerial and Decision Economics*, 4, no. 1 (1983), 50–62.

Rosser, R., and P. Kind, "A Scale of Valuations of States of Illness: Is There a Social Consensus?" *International Journal of Epidemiology*, 7, no. 4 (1978), 347–358.

Ruchlin, H.S., et al., "The Efficacy of Second-Opinion Consultation Programs: A Cost-Benefit Perspective," *Medical Care*, 20 (1982), 3–20.

Schoenbaum, S.C., et al., "Benefit-Cost Analysis of Rubella Vaccination Policy," *The New England Journal of Medicine*, 294, no. 6 (1976), 306–310.

Schoenbaum, S.C., et al., "The Swine-Influenza Decision," *The New England Journal of Medicine*, 295, no. 14 (1977), 759–785.

Shukla, R.K., "ALL-RN Model of Nursing Care Delivery: A Cost-Benefit Evaluation," *Inquiry*, 20, no. 2 (1983), 173–184.

Stilwell, J.A., "Benefits and Costs of the Schools' BCG Vaccination Programme," *British Medical Journal*, 1, no. 6016 (1976), 1002–1004.

Strange, P.V. and A.T. Sumner, "Predictive Treatment Costs and Life Expectancy for End Stage Renal Disease," *The New England Journal of Medicine*, 298, no. 7, (1978), February 16, 372–378.

Torrance, G.W., "Measurement of Health State Utilities for Economic Appraisal: A Review," *Journal of Health Economics*, 5, no. 1 (1986), 1–30.

Warner, K.E., and R.C. Hutton, "Cost-Benefit and Cost-Effectiveness Analysis in Health Care: Growth and Composition of the Literature," *Medical Care*, 18, no. 11 (1980), 1069–1084.

Weisbrod, B.A., "Benefit-Cost Analysis of a Controlled Experiment: Treating the Mentally Ill," *Journal of Human Resources*, 16, no. 4 (1981), 523–548.

Weisbrod, B.A., "Costs and Benefits of Medical Research: A Case Study of Poliomyelitis," *Journal of Political Economy*, 79, no. 3 (1971), 527–544.

Williams, A.H., "Economics of Coronary Artery Bypass Grafting," *British Medical Journal*, 291, no. 2 (1985), 326–329.

Williams, A.H., "The Costs and Benefits of Surgery," in *Surgical Review I*, eds. J.S.P. Lumley and J.L. Craven. London: Butterworths, 1978.

Windle, R., and M. Dresner, "Mandatory Child Safety Seats in Air Transport: Do They Save Lives?" *Transportation Research Forum*, 31, no. 2 (1991), 309–316.

Zeckhauser, R., "Measuring Risks and Benefits of Food Safety Decisions," *Vanderbilt Law Review*, 38, no. 3 (1985), 539–569.

10. HOUSING

DeSalvo, J.S., "Benefits and Costs of New York City's Middle Income Housing Programs," *Journal of Political Economy*, 83, no. 4 (1975), 791–806.

Hammond, C.M.H., *The Benefits of Subsidized Housing Programs: An Intertemporal Approach*. Cambridge: Cambridge University Press, 1987.

Kraft, J., and E.O. Olsen, "The Distribution of Benefits From Public Housing," in *The Distribution of Economic Well-Being*, ed. F.T. Juster. New York: National Bureau of Economic Research, 1977.

Olsen, E.O., and D.M. Barton, "The Benefits and Costs of Public Housing in New York City," *Journal of Public Economics*, 20, no. 3 (1983), 299–332.

11. INDUSTRY REGULATION (NOT PROFESSIONAL OR SAFETY)

Anderson, J.E., "The Relative Inefficiency of Quotas," *American Economic Review* 17, no. 1 (1985), 178–190.

Bailey, E.E., D.R. Graham, and D. Kaplan, *Deregulating the Airlines*. Cambridge, MA: MIT Press, 1985.

Barnekov, C.C., and A.N. Kleit, "The Efficiency Effects of Railroad Deregulation in the United States," *International Journal of Transport Economics*, 17, no. 1 (1990), 21–38.

Barth, J.R., J.J. Cordes, and A.M.J. Yezer, "Benefits and Costs of Legal Restrictions on Personal Loan Markets," *Journal of Law and Economics*, 29, no. 2 (1986), 357–380.

Beck, R., C. Hoskins, and G. Mumey, "The Social Welfare Loss from Egg and Poultry Marketing Boards, Revisited," *Canadian Journal of Agricultural Economics*, 42, no. 2 (1994), 149–158.

Benston, G.J., "An Appraisal of the Costs and Benefits of Government-Required Disclosure: SEC and FTC Requirments," *Law and Contemporary Problems*, 41, no. 3 (1977), 30–62.

Bogen, K.D., "The Costs of Price Regulation: Lessons From Railroad Deregulation," *Rand Journal of Economics*, 18, no. 3 (1987), 408–416.

Boorstein, R., and R.C. Feenstra, "Quality Upgrading and Its Welfare Cost in U.S. Steel Imports, 1969–74," in *International Trade and Trade Policy*, eds. Elhanam Helpman and Assaf Razin. Cambridge, MA: The MIT Press, 1991, pp. 167–186.

Boyer, K., "The Costs of Price Regulation: Lessons From Railroad Deregulation," *Rand Journal of Economics*, 18, no. 3 (1987), 408–416.

de Melo, J., and D. Tarr, "Welfare Costs of U.S. Quotas in Textiles, Steel and Autos," *The Review of Economics and Statistics*, 72, no. 3 (1990), 489–497.

DeVany, A.S., W. Gram, T. Saving, and C.W. Smithson, "The Impact of Input Regulation: The Case of Costs and Input Use," *Journal of Law and Economics*, 25, no. 2 (1982), 367–382.

Dinopoulos, E. and M.E. Kreinin, "Effects of the U.S.-Japan Auto VER on European Prices and on U.S. Welfare," *Review of Economics and Statistics*, 70, no. 3 (1983), 484–491.

Feenstra, R.C., "How Costly is Protectionism?" *Journal of Economic Perspectives*, 6, no. 3 (1992), 159–178.

Felton, J.R., "Costs and Benefits of Motor Truck Regulation," *Quarterly Review of Economics and Business*, 18, no. 2 (1980), 7–20.

Gomez-Ibanez, J., R. Leone, and S. O'Connell, "Restraining Auto Imports: Does Anyone Win?" *Journal of Policy Analysis and Management*, 2, no. 2 (1983), 196–219.

Gray, W., "The Cost of Regulation: OSHA, EPA and the Productivity Slowdown," *American Economic Review*, 77, no. 5 (1987), 998–1012.

Hahn, R.W., and J.A. Hird, "The Costs and Benefits of Regulation: Review and Synthesis," *Yale Journal of Regulation*, 8, no. 1 (1991), 233–278.

Hazilla, M., and R. Kop, "Social Cost of Environmental Quality Regulations: A General Equilibrium Analysis," *Journal of Political Economy*, 98, no. 4 (1990), 853–873.

Hofbauer, G.C., D.T. Berliner, and K.A. Elliott, *Trade Protection in the United States: 31 Case Studies*. Washington, DC: Institute for International Economics, 1986.

Ippolito, R.A., "The Effect of Price Regulation in the Automobile Insurance Industry," *Journal of Law and Economics*, 23, no. 1 (1979), 55–90.

Len, G.M., A. Schnitz, and R.D. Knutsen, "Gains and Losses of Sugar Program Policy Options," *American Journal of Agricultural Economics*, 69, no. 5 (1987), 591–608.

Luken, R.A., *Efficiency in Environmental Regulation: A Benefit-Cost Analysis of Alternative Approaches, Studies in Risk and Uncertainty*. Boston: Kluwer, 1990.

Moore, T.G., "U.S. Airline Deregulation: Its Effects on Passengers, Capital and Labor," *Journal of Law and Economics*, 29, no. 1 (1986), 1–2.

Morrison, S., and C. Winston, *The Economic Effects of Airline Deregulation*. Washington, DC: The Brookings Institution, 1986.

Olsen, E.O., "An Economic Analysis of Rent Control in New York City," *Journal of Political Economy*, 80, no. 6 (1972), 1081–1110.

Peltzman, S., "The Effect of FTC Advertising Regulation," *Journal of Law and Economics*, 24, no. 3 (1981), 403–448.

Schmitz, A., and T.G. Schmitz, "Supply Management: The Past and Future," *Canadian Journal of Agricultural Economics*, 42, no. 2 (1994), 125–148.

Schneider, L., B. Klein, and K.M. Murphy, "Governmental Regulation of Cigarette Health Information," *Journal of Law and Economics*, 24, no. 3 (1981), 575–612.

Sloan, F.A., and B. Steinwald, "Effects of Regulation on Hospital Costs," *Journal of Law and Economics*, 23, no. 1 (1980), 81–110.

Smith, A., and A.J. Venables, "Counting the Cost of Voluntary Restraints in the European Car Market," in *International Trade and Trade Policy*, eds. E. Helpman and A. Razin. Cambridge, MA: The MIT Press, 1991, pp. 187–220.

Smith, J.K., "An Analysis of State Regulations Governing Liquor Store Licensees," *Journal of Law and Economics*, 25, no. 2 (1982), 301–319.

Smith, R.L., II, "Franchise Regulation: An Economic Analysis of State Restrictions on Automobile Distribution," *Journal of Law and Economics*, 25, no. 1 (1982), 125–157.

Treda, I., and J. Whalley, "Global Effects of Developed Country Trade Restrictions on Textiles and Apparel," *The Economic Journal*, 100, no. 403 (1990), 1190–1205.

Winston, C., "Welfare Effects of ICC Regulation Revisited," *Bell Journal of Economics*, 12, no. 1 (1981), 232–244.

Winston, C., T.M. Corsi, C.M. Grimm, and C.A. Evans, *The Economic Effects of Surface Rate Deregulation*. Washington, DC: Brookings Institution, 1990.

12. INFORMATION

Moffitt, J., R.L. Farnsworth, L.R. Zavaleta, and M. Kogan, "Economic Impact of Public Pest Information: Soybean Insect Forecasts in Illinois," *American Journal of Agricultural Economics*, 68, no. 2 (1986), 274–279.

Senauer, B., J.K. Kinsey, and T. Roe, "The Cost of Inaccurate Consumer Information: The Case of EPA Gas Mileage," *Journal of Consumer Affairs*, 18, no. 2 (1984), 193–212.

Sexton, R.J., "Welfare Loss From Inaccurate Information: An Economic Model With Application to Food Labels," *Journal of Consumer Affairs*, 15, no. 2 (1981), 214–231.

Sexton, R.J., and T.A. Sexton, "Theoretical and Methodological Perspectives on Consumer Response to Electricity Information," *Journal of Consumer Affairs*, 21, no. 2 (1987), 238–257.

13. MIGRATION

Collier, V.C., and H. Rempel, "The Divergence of Private From Social Costs in Rural-Urban Migration: A Case Study of Nairobi, Kenya," *Journal of Development Studies*, 13, no. 3 (1977), 199–216.

Davies, G.W., "Macroeconomic Effects of Immigration: Evidence from CANDIDE, TRACE, and RDX2," *Canadian Public Policy*, 3, no. 3 (1977), 299–306.

Gerking, S.D., and J.H. Mutti, "Costs and Benefits of Illegal Immigration: Key Issues for Government Policy," *Social Science Quarterly*, 61, no. 1 (1980), 71–85.

Graves, P.E., and P.D. Linneman, "Household Migration: Theoretical and Empirical Results," *Journal of Urban Economics*, 6, no. 3 (1979), 383–404.

Greenwood, M.J., "Research on Internal Migration in the United States: A Survey," *Journal of Economic Literature*, 13, no. 2 (1975), 397–433.

MacMillen, M.J., "The Economic Effects of International Migration: A Survey," *Journal of Common Market Studies*, 20, no. 3 (1982), 245–267.

14. NOISE POLLUTION

Alexandre, A., J. Barde, and D.W. Pearce, "Practical Determination of a Charge for Noise Pollution," *Journal of Transport Economics and Policy*, 14, no. 2 (1980), 205–220.

Gautrin, J.F., "An Evaluation of the Impact of Aircraft Noise on Property Values with a Simple Model of Urban Land Rent," *Land Economics*, 51, no. 1 (1975), 80–86.

Harrison, D. Jr., "The Problem of Aircraft Noise," in *Incentives for Environmental Protection*, ed. Thomas C. Schelling. Cambridge, MA: The MIT Press, 1983, pp. 43–69.

Langley, J.C., Jr., "Adverse Impacts of the Washington Beltway on Residential Property Values," *Land Economics*, 52, no. 1 (1976), 54–65.

McMillan, M.L., et al., "An Extension of the Hedonic Approach for Estimating the Value of Quiet," *Land Economics*, 56, no. 3 (1980), 315–328.

Mieszkowski, P., and A.M. Saper, "An Estimate of the Effects of Airport Noise on Property Values," *Journal of Urban Economics*, 5, no. 4 (1978), 425–440.

Nelson, J.P., "Airport Noise, Location Rent, and the Market for Residential Amenities," *Journal of Environmental Economics and Management*, 6, no. 4 (1979), 320–331.

Nelson, J.P., "Airports and Property Values," *Journal of Transport Economics and Policy*, 14, no. 1 (1980), 37–52.

Nelson, J.P., "Highway Noise and Property Values: A Survey of Recent Evidence," *Journal of Transport Economics and Policy*, 16, no. 2 (1982), 117–138.

O'Byrne, P.H., J.P. Nelson, and J.J. Seneca, "Housing Values, Census Estimates, Disequilibrium, and the Environmental Cost of Airport Noise: A Case Study of Atlanta," *Journal of Environmental Economics and Management*, 12, no. 2 (1985), 169–178.

Pearce, D.W., "Noise Valuation," in *The Valuation of Social Cost*, ed. D.W. Pearce. London: George Allen, 1978, pp. 31–53.

Pennington, G., N. Topham, and R. Ward, "Aircraft Noise and Residential Property Values Adjacent to Manchester International Airport," *Journal of Transport Economics and Policy*, 24, no. 3 (1990), 49–59.

Whitbread, M., "Measuring the Costs of Noise Nuisance From Aircraft," *Journal of Transport Economics and Policy*, 12, no. 2 (1978), 202–208.

15. PARKS, LAKES, RIVERS, AND OTHER RECREATION

Beasley, S.D., W.G. Workman, and N.A. Williams, "Estimating Amenity Values of Urban Fringe Farmland: A Contingent Valuation Approach: Note," *Growth and Change*, 17, no. 4 (1986), 70–78.

Brookshire, D.S., B. Ives, and W.D. Schultze, "The Valuation of Aesthetic Preferences," *Journal of Environmental Economics and Management*, 3, no. 4 (1976), 325–346.

Brown, W., C. Sorhus, B. Chou-Yang, and J.A. Richards, "Using Individual Observations to Estimate Recreation Demand Functions: A Caution," *American Journal of Agricultural Economics*, 65, no. 1 (1983), 154–157.

Burt, O.R., and D. Brewer, "Estimation of Net Social Benefits from Outdoor Recreation," *Econometrica*, 39, no. 5 (1971), 813–827.

Caulkins, P.P., R.C. Bishop, and N. Bouwes, Sr., "The Travel Cost Model for Lake Recreation: A Comparison of Two Methods for Incorporating Site Quality and Substitution Effects," *American Journal of Agricultural Economics*, 68, no. 2 (1986), 291–297.

Clawson, M., and J.L. Knetsch, *Economics of Outdoor Recreation*. Baltimore: Johns Hopkins University Press, 1966.

Darling, A.H., "Measuring Benefits Generated by Urban Water Parks," *Land Economics*, 49, no. 1 (1973), 22–34.

Daubert, J.T., and R.A. Young, "Recreational Demands for Maintaining Instream Flows: A Contingent Valuation Approach," *American Journal of Agricultural Economics*, 63, no. 4 (1981), 666–684.

Dwyer, J.F., H.W. Schroeder, J.J. Louviere, and D.H. Anderson, "Urbanites Willingness to Pay for Trees and Forests in Recreation Areas," *Journal of Arboriculture*, 15, no. 10 (1989), 247–252.

Gum, R.L., and E.W. Martin, "Problems and Solutions in Estimating the Demand for and Value of Rural Outdoor Recreation," *American Journal of Agricultural Economics*, 57, no. 4 (1975), 558–566.

Hanley, N.D., "Valuing Rural Recreation Benefits: An Empirical Comparison of Two Approaches," *Journal of Agricultural Economics*, 40, no. 3 (1989), 361–374.

Harris, B.S., and A.D. Meister, "The Use of Recreation Analysis in Resource Management: A Case Study," *Journal of Environmental Management*, 16, no. 2 (1983), 117–124.

Krutilla, J.V., and C.J. Cichetti, "Evaluating Benefits of Environmental Resources with Special Application to Hells Canyon," *Natural Resource Journal*, 12, no. 2 (1972), 1–29.

Loomis, J.B., "Balancing Public Trust Resources of Mono Lake and L.A.'s Water Right: An Economic Approach," *Water Resources Research*, 23, no. 8 (1987), 1449–1456.

Loomis, J.B., C.S. Sorg, and D.M. Donnelly, "Evaluating Regional Demand Models for Estimating Recreation Use and Economic Benefits: A Case Study," *Water Resources Research*, 22, no. 4 (1986), 431–438.

McConnell, K.E., "Congestion and Willingness to Pay: A Case Study of Beach Use," *Land Economics*, 53, no. 2 (1977), 185–195.

Menz, F.C., and J.K. Mullin, "Expected Encounters and Willingness to Pay for Outdoor Recreation," *Land Economics*, 57, no. 1 (1981), 33–40.

Morey, E.R., "The Demand for Site-Specific Recreational Activities: A Characteristic Approach," *Journal of Environmental Economics and Management*, 8, no. 4 (1981), 345–371.

Schroeder, T.D., "The Relationship of Local Public Park and Recreation Services to Residential Property Values," *Journal of Leisure Research*, 14, no. 3 (1982), 223–234.

Schulze, W.D., and D.S. Brookshire, "The Economic Benefits of Preserving Visibility in the National Parklands of the Southwest," *Natural Resources Journal*, 23, no. 1 (1983), 124–133.

Smith, R.J., "The Evaluation of Recreation Benefits: The Clawson Method in Practice," *Urban Studies*, 8, no. 2 (1971), 89–102.

Walker, J.L., "Tall Trees, People, and Politics: The Opportunity Costs of the Redwood National Park," *Contemporary Policy Issues*, no. 5 (1984), 22–29.

Willis, K.G., and J.F. Benson, "A Comparison of User Benefits and Costs of Nature Conservation at Three Nature Reserves," *Regional Studies*, 22, no. 5 (1988), 417–428.

Willis, K.G., and G.D. Garred, "Valuing Landscape: a Contingent Valuation Approach," *Journal of Environmental Management*, 37, no. 1 (1993), 1–22.

16. PROFESSIONAL REGULATION

Begun, J.W., *Professionalism and the Public Interest: Price and Quality in Optometry.* Cambridge, MA: MIT Press, 1981.

Benham, L., "The Effect of Advertising on the Price of Eyeglasses," *Journal of Law and Economics*, 15, no. 2 (1972), 337–352.

Caroll, S.L., and R.J. Gaston, "Occupational Restrictions and Quality of Service Received: Some Evidence," *Southern Economic Journal*, 47, no. 4 (1981), 959–976.

Feldman, R., and J.W. Begun, "The Effects of Advertising Restrictions: Lessons From Optometry," *Journal of Human Resources*, 13, supplement (1978), 248–262.

Haas-Wilson, D., "The Effect of Commercial Practice Restrictions: The Case of Optometry," *Journal of Law and Economics*, 29, no. 1 (1986), 165–186.

Leffer, K.B., "Physician Licensure: Competition and Monopoly in American Medicine," *Journal of Law and Economics*, 21, no. 1 (1978), 165–186.

Shepard, L., "Licensing Restrictions and the Cost of Dental Care," *Journal of Law and Economics*, 21, no. 1 (1978), 187–201.

White, W.D. "The Impact of Occupational Licensure of Clinical Laboratory Personnel," *Journal of Human Resources*, 8, no. 4 (1978), 91–102.

White, W.D., *Public Health and Private Gain: The Economics of Licensing Clinical Laboratory Personnel*. Chicago: Maaroufa Press Inc., 1979.

17. PUBLIC WORKS (NONTRANSIT)

Blackorby, C., G. Donaldson, R. Picard, and M. Slade, "Expo 1986: An Economic Impact Analysis," Chapter 13 in *Restraining the Economy: Social Credit Economic Policies for B.C. in the Eighties*, eds. R.C. Allen and G. Rosenblath. Vancouver: New Star Books, 1986, pp. 254–278.

Conrad, K. and H. Seitz, "The Economic Benefits of Public Infrastructure," *Applied Economics*, 26, no. 4 (1994), 303–311.

Graves, S.C., M. Horwitch, and E.H. Bowman, "Deep-Draft Dredging of U.S. Coal Ports: A Cost-Benefit Analysis," *Policy Sciences*, 17, no. 2 (1985), 153–178.

Muller, R.A., "Some Economics of the Grand Canal," *Canadian Public Policy*, 14, no. 2 (1988), 162–174.

Shaffer, M., "The Benefits and Costs of Two B.C. Hydro Construction Projects," Chapter 14 in *Restraining the Economy*, eds. R.C. Allen and G. Rosenblath. Vancouver: New Star Books, 1986, pp. 279–296.

Viscencio-Brambila, H., and S. Fuller, "Estimated Effects of Deepened U.S. Gulf Ports on Export-Grain Flow Pattern and Logistics Costs," *Logistics and Transportation Review*, 23, no. 2 (1987), 139–154.

Yochum, G.R., and V.B. Agarwal, "Economic Impact of Port on a Regional Economy: Note," *Growth and Change*, 18, no. 3 (1987), 74–87.

18. R&D

Bozeman, B., and A.N. Link, "Tax Incentives for R&D: A Critical Evaluation," *Research Policy*, 13, no. 1 (1984), 21–31.

Fox, G., "Is the United States Really Underinvesting in Agricultural Research?" *American Journal of Agricultural Economics*, 67, no. 4 (1985), 806–812.

Griliches, Z., "Research Cost and Social Returns: Hybrid Corn and Related Innovations," *Journal of Political Economy*, 66, no. 1 (1958), 419–431.

Mansfield, E., and L. Switzer, "How Effective Are Canada's Direct Tax Incentives for R&D?" *Canadian Public Policy*, 11, no. 2 (1985), 241–246.

Nagy, J.G., and W.H. Furtan, "Economic Costs and Returns From Crop Development Research: The Case of Rapeseed Breeding in Canada," *Canadian Journal of Agricultural Economics*, 26, no. 1 (1978), 1–14.

Nelson, R., "Government Support of Technical Progress—Lessons from History," *Journal of Policy Analysis and Management*, 2, no. 4 (1983), 499–514.

Norton, G.W., and J.S. Davis, "Evaluating Returns to Agricultural Research: A Review," *American Journal of Agricultural Economics*, 63, no. 4 (1981), 685–699.

Norton, G.W., V.G. Ganoza, and C. Pomereda, "Potential Benefits of Agricultural Research and Extension in Peru," *American Journal of Agricultural Economics*, 69, no. 2 (1987), 247–257.

Stranahan, H.A., and J.S. Shonkwiler, "Evaluating the Returns to Postharvest Research in the Florida Citrus-Processing Subsector," *American Journal of Agricultural Economics*, 68, no. 1 (1986), 88–94.

Terleckyj, N., "Direct and Indirect Effects of Industrial Research and Development on the Productivity Growth of Industries," in *New Developments in Productivity Measurements*, eds. J.W. Kendrick and B. Vaccara. Chicago: Chicago University Press for NBER, Studies in Income and Wealth, No. 44, 1980, pp. 359–377.

Widmer, L.R., G. Fox, and G.L. Brinkman, "The Rate of Return to Agricultural Research in a Small Country: The Case of Beef Cattle Research in Canada," *Canadian Journal of Agricultural Economics*, 36, no. 1 (1988), 23–35.

Zentner, R.P., "Returns to Public Investment in Canadian Wheat and Rapeseed Research," in *Economics of Agricultural Research in Canada*, eds. K.K. Klein and W.H. Furtan. Calgary: The University of Calgary Press, 1983, pp. 169–188.

19. RECREATIONAL AND COMMERCIAL FISHERIES

Anderson, L.G., "The Demand Curve for Recreation Fishing with an Application to Stock Enhancement Activities," *Land Economics*, 59, no. 3 (1983), 279–286.

Anderson, D.M., S.A. Shankle, M.J. Scott, D.A. Neitzel, and J.C. Chatters, "Valuing Effects of Climate Change and Fishery Enhancement on Chinook Salmon," *Contemporary Policy Issues*, 11, no. 4 (1993), 82–94.

Cauvin, D., "The Valuation of Recreational Fisheries," *Canadian Journal of Fishing and Aquatic Sciences*, 37, no. 8 (1980), 1321–1327.

Hufschmidt, M.M., and J.A. Dixon, "Valuation of Losses of Marine Produce Resources Caused by Coastal Development of Tokyo Bay," adapted from materials prepared by Y. Hanayama and I. Sano in *Economic Valuation Techniques For the Environment*, eds. J.A. Dixon and M.M. Hufschmidt. Baltimore and London: The Johns Hopkins University Press, 1986, 102–120.

Loomis, J.B., C. Sorg, and D. Donnelly, "Economic Losses to Recreational Fisheries Due to Small-Head Hydro-Power Development: A Case Study of the Henry's Fork in Idaho," *Journal of Environmental Management*, 22, no. 1 (1986), 85–94.

McConnell, K.E., "Values of Marine Recreational Fishing: Measurement and Impact of Measurement," *American Journal of Agricultural Economics*, 61, no. 5 (December 1979), 921–925.

McConnell, K.E., and I. Strand, "Measuring the Cost of Time in Recreation Demand Analysis: An Application to Sportfishing," *American Journal of Agricultural Economics*, 63, no. 1 (February 1981), 153–156.

McConnell, K.E., and V. Duff, "Estimating Net Benefits of Recreational Fishing," *Journal of Environmental Economics and Management*, 2, no. 3 (1976), 224–230.

Meyer, P.A., "Publicly Vested Values for Fish and Wildlife: Criteria in Economic Welfare and Interface with the Law," *Land Economics*, 55, no. 2 (1979), 223–235.

Russell, C.S., and W.J. Vaughan, "The National Recreational Fishing Benefits of Water Pollution Control," *Journal of Environmental Economics and Management*, 9, no. 3 (1982), 328–354.

Samples, K.C., and R.C. Bishop, "Estimating the Value of Variations in Anglers' Success Rates: An Application of the Multiple-Site Travel Cost Method," *Marine Resource Economics*, 2, no. 1 (1985), 55–74.

Sorg, C., et al., "The Net Economic Value of Cold and Warm Water Fishing in Idaho," *Resource Bulletin*, Rocky Mountain Forest and Range Experiment Station, U.S. Forest Service, Fort Collins, Colorado, 1985.

Vaughan, W.J., and C.S. Russell, "Valuing a Fishing Day: An Application of a Systematic Varying Parameter Model," *Land Economics*, 58, no. 4 (1982), 450–463.

Weithman, S., and M. Haas, "Socioeconomic Value of the Trout Fisheries in Lake Taneycomo, Missouri," *Transactions of the American Fisheries Society*, 111 (1982), 223–230.

20. REDISTRIBUTION PROGRAMS

Ballard, C., "The Marginal Efficiency Cost of Redistribution," *American Economic Review*, 78, no. 5 (1988), 1019–1033.

Browning, E.K., "On the Marginal Welfare Costs of Taxation," *American Economic Review*, 77, no. 1 (1987), 11–23.

Caniglia, A.S., "The Economic Evaluation of Food Stamps: An Intertemporal Analysis With Nonlinear Budget Constraints," *Public Finance Quarterly*, 16, no. 1 (1988), 3–30.

Gramlich, E., and M. Wolkoff, "A Procedure for Evaluating Income Distribution Policies," *Journal of Human Resources*, 14, no. 3 (1979), 319–350.

Hu, S.T., and N.L. Knaub, "Effects of Cash and In-Kind Welfare on Family Expenditures," *Policy Analysis*, 2, no. 1 (1976), 71–92.

Jorgenson, D.W. and K. Yun, "The Excess Burden of Taxation in the United States," *Journal of Accounting, Auditing, and Finance*, 6 (1991), 487–508.

Knaub, N.L., "The Impact of Food Stamps and Cash Welfare on Food Expenditures, 1971–1975," *Policy Analysis*, 7, no. 2 (1981), 169–182.

Lermer, G., and W.T. Stanbury, "The Cost of Redistributing Income by Means of Direct Regulation," *Canadian Journal of Economics*, 28, no. 1 (1985), 190–207.

Lewis, H.G., and R.J. Morrison, *Income Transfer Analysis*. Washington, DC: The Urban Institute, 1989.

Mead, L.W., "The Potential for Work Enforcement: A Study of WIN," *Journal of Policy Analysis and Management*, 7, no. 2 (1988), 264–288.

Moffitt, R.A., and K.C. Kehrer, "The Effect of Tax and Transfer Programs on Labor Supply," *Research in Labor Economics*, 4 (1981), 103–150.

Tullock, G., *Economics of Income Redistribution*. Hingham, MA: Kluwer Boston, 1983.

21. TRANSPORTATION/TRANSIT (INCLUDING SAFETY)

Alexander, D.A., "Motor Carrier Deregulation and Highway Safety: An Empirical Analysis," *Southern Economic Journal*, 59, no. 1 (1992), 28–36.

Beggs, S., S. Cardell, and J. Housman, "Assessing the Potential Demand for Electric Cars," *Journal of Econometrics*, 17, no. 1 (1981), 1–20.

Binder, R.H., "Cost-Effectiveness in Highway Safety," *Traffic Engineering*, 46, no. 12 (1976), 26–30.

Blomquist, G., "Economics of Safety and Seat Belt Use," *Journal of Safety Research*, 9, no. 4 (1977), 179–189.

Brems, H., "Light Rail Transit: Cost and Output," *Journal of Urban Economics*, 7, no. 1 (1980), 20–30.

Brent, R.J., "Imputing Weights Behind Past Railway Closure Decisions Within a Cost-Benefit Framework," *Applied Economics*, 7, no. 2 (1979), 157–170.

Castle, G., "The 55 MPH Speed Limit: A Cost-Benefit Analysis," *Traffic Engineering*, 46, no. 1 (1976), 11–14.

Chalk, A.J., "Market Forces and Commercial Aircraft Safety," *The Journal of Industrial Economics*, 36, no. 1 (1987), 61–80.

Claybrook, J., and D. Bollier, "The Hidden Benefits of Regulation: Disclosing the Auto Safety Payoff," *Yale Journal of Regulation*, 3, no. 1 (1985), 87–132.

Clotfelter, C., and J. Hahn, "Assessing the 55 MPH Speed Limit," *Policy Sciences*, 9, no. 3 (1978), 281–294.

Conybeare, J.A.C., "Evaluation of Automobile Safety Regulations: The Case of Compulsory Seat Belt Legislation in Australia," *Policy Sciences*, 12, no. 1 (1980), 27–39.

Crandall, R.W., and J.D. Graham, "Automobile Safety Regulation and Offsetting Behaviour: Some New Empirical Estimates," *American Economic Review Papers and Proceedings*, 74, no. 2 (1984), 328–331.

Crandall, R.C., H.W. Gruenspecht, T.E. Keeler, and L.B. Lave, *Regulating the Automobile*. Washington, DC: The Brooking Institution, 1986.

Davidson, B.R., "A Benefit-Cost Analysis of the New South Wales Railway System," *Australian Economic History Review*, 22, no. 2 (1982), 127–150.

Dodgson, J.S., "Benefits of Changes in Urban Public Transport Subsidies in Major Australian Cities," *Economic Record*, 62, no. 177 (1986), 224–235.

Dodgson, J.S., and N. Topham, "Benefit-Cost Rules for Urban Transit Subsidies: An Integration of Allocational, Distributional and Public Finance Issues," *Journal of Transport Economics and Policy*, 21, no. 1 (1987), 57–71.

Forester, T., R. McNown, and L. Singell, "A Cost-Benefit Analysis of the 55 MPH Speed Limit," *Southern Economic Journal*, 50, no. 3 (1984), 631–641.

Gardner, B.M., and R.O. Goss, "Lifeboats vs. Inflatable Liferafts: A Comparison of Costs and Benefits," in *Advances in Maritime Economics*, ed. R.O. Goss. Cambridge, MA: Cambridge University Press, 1977, pp. 247–287.

Gomez-Ibanez, J.A., and G.R. Fauth, "Downtown Auto Restraint Policies: The Costs and Benefits for Boston," *Journal of Transport Economics and Policy*, 14, no. 2 (1980), 155–168.

Goodman, A.C., "Willingness to Pay for Car Efficiency: A Hedonic Price Approach," *Journal of Transport Economics and Policy*, 17, no. 3 (1983), 247–266.

Goss, R.O., and A.H. Vanags, "The Costs and Benefits of Navigational Aids in Port Approaches," in *Advances in Maritime Economics*, ed. R.O. Goss. Cambridge, MA: Cambridge University Press, 1977, pp. 213–256.

Graham, J.D., and S. Garber, "Evaluating the Effects of Automobile Safety Regulation," *Journal of Policy Analysis and Management*, 2, no. 2 (1984), 206–224.

Graves, S.C., M. Horwitch, and E. Bowman, "Deep-Draft Dredging of U.S. Coal Ports: A Cost-Benefit Analysis," *Policy Sciences*, 17, no. 2 (1984), 153–178.

Greene, D., and K.G. Duleep, "Costs and Benefits of Automotive Fuel Economy Improvement: A Partial Analysis," *Transportation Research-A*, 27, no. 3 (1993), 217–235.

Hanke, S.H., and R.A. Walker, "Benefit-Cost Analysis Reconsidered: An Evaluation of the Mid-State Project," *Water Resources Research*, 10, no. 5 (1974), 898–908.

Hansen, B., and K. Tourk, "The Suez Canal Project to Accommodate Super-Tankers," *Journal of Transport Economics and Policy*, 8, no. 2 (1974), 103–121.

Hartunian, N., C.N. Smart, T.R. Willemain, and P. Zander, "The Economics of Safety Deregulation: Lives and Dollars Lost Due to Repeal of Motorcycle Helmet Laws," *Journal of Health Politics, Policy and Law*, 8, no. 1 (1981), 76–98.

Hettich, W., "The Political Economy of Benefit-Cost Analysis: Evaluating STOL Air Transport for Canada," *Canadian Public Policy*, 9, no. 4 (1983), 478–498.

Horowitz, A.J., "Assessing Transportation User Benefits With Maximum Trip Lengths," *Transportation Planning and Technology*, 6, no. 3 (1980), 175–182.

Jara-Diaz, S.R., "On the Relation Between Users' Benefits and the Economic Effects of Transportation Activities," *Journal of Regional Science*, 26, no. 2 (1986), 379–391.

Jara-Diaz, S.R., and T.L. Friezz, "Measuring the Benefits Derived from a Transportation Investment," *Transportation Research–B*, 16, no. 1 (1982), 57–77.

Jonah, B.A., and J.L. Lawson, "The Effectiveness of the Canadian Mandatory Seat Belt Use Laws," *Accident Analysis and Prevention*, 16, no. 5/6 (1984), 433–450.

Jones-Lee, M.W., M. Hammerton, and P.R. Philips, "The Value of Safety: Results of a National Sample Survey," *Economic Journal*, 95, no. 377 (1985), 49–72.

Joray, P.A., and P.A. Kochanowski, "Inter-Urban Rail Passenger Service—Social Benefits of Retaining the South Shore Railroad (Chicago)," *Logistics and Transportation Review*, 14, no. 1 (1978), 81–89.

Kamerud, D.B., "Benefits and Costs of the 55 MPH Speed Limit: New Estimates and Their Implications," *Journal of Policy Analysis and Management*, 7, no. 2 (1988), 341–352.

Kamerud, D.B., "The 55 MPH Speed Limit: Costs, Benefits, and Implied Trade-Offs," *Transportation Research–A*, 17, no. 1 (1983), 51–64.

Kanemoto, Y., "Cost-Benefit Analysis and the Second Best Land Use for Transportation," *Journal of Urban Economics*, 4, no. 4 (1977), 483–503.

Kanemoto, Y., "General Equilibrium Analysis of the Benefits of Large Transportation Improvements," *Regional Science and Urban Economics*, 15, no. 3 (1985), 343–363.

Keeler, T.E., "Public Policy and Productivity in the Trucking Industry: Some Evidence on the Effects of Highway Investments, Deregulation, and the 55 MPH Speed Limit," *American Economic Review*, 76, no. 2 (1986), 153–158.

Kim, J., and D.S. West, "The Edmonton LRT: An Appropriate Choice?" *Canadian Public Policy*, 17, no. 2 (1991), 173–182.

Krupnick, A.J., and M.A. Walls, *The Cost-Effectiveness of Methanol for Reducing Motor Vehicle Emissions and Urban Ozone Levels*. Washington, DC: Resources for the Future, 1990.

Lave, C.A., "Speeding, Coordination, and the 55 MPH Limit," *The American Economic Review*, 75, no. 5 (1985), 1159–1164.

Lave, L.B., and W.E. Weber, "Benefit-Cost Analysis of Auto Safety Features," *Applied Economics*, 2, no. 4 (1970), 265–275.

Loeb, P.D., "The Efficacy and Cost-Effectiveness of Motor Vehicle Inspection Using Cross-Sectional Data—An Econometric Analysis," *Southern Economic Journal*, 52, no. 2 (1985), 500–509.

Loeb, P.D., and B. Gilad, "The Efficacy and Cost-Effectiveness of Motor Vehicle Inspection: A State Specific Analysis Using Time Series Data," *Journal of Transport Economics and Policy*, 18, no. 2 (1984), 145–164.

Mackie, P.J., and D. Simon, "Do Road Projects Benefit Industry? A Case Study of the Humber Bridge," *Journal of Transport Economics and Policy*, 20, no. 3 (1986), 377–384.

McBride, M.E., "An Evaluation of Various Methods of Estimating Railway Costs," *Logistics and Transportation Review*, 19, no. 1 (1983), 45–66.

Mohring, H., "Maximizing, Measuring and Not Double Counting Transportation Improvement Benefits: A Primer on Closed- and Open-Economy Cost-Benefit Analysis," *Transportation Research-B*, 27, no. 6 (1993), 413–424.

Muller, A., "Evaluation of the Costs and Benefits of Motorcycle Helmet Laws," *American Journal of Public Health*, 70, no. 6 (1980), 586–592.

Nelson, D.E., T.D. Peterson, T.L. Chorba, O.J. Devine, and J. Sacks, "Cost Savings Associated with Increased Safety Belt Use in Iowa, 1987–1988," *Accident Analysis and Prevention*, 25, no. 5 (1993), 521–528.

Obeng, K., "Fare Subsidies to Achieve Pareto Optimality: A Benefit-Cost Approach," *Logistics and Transportation Review*, 19, no. 4 (1983), 367–384.

Obeng, K., "The Economics of Bus Transit Operation," *Logistics and Transportation Review*, 20, no. 1 (1984), 45–65.

Olson, D.D., "A Benefit-Cost Analysis of Improving Alaska's Dalton Highway," *Logistics and Transportation Review*, 22, no. 2 (1986), 141–157.

Orr, L.D., "Incentives and Efficiency in Automobile Safety Regulation," *Quarterly Review of Economics and Business*, 22, no. 3 (1982), 43–65.

Peaker, A., "The Economics of VTOL Aircraft," *Journal of Transport Economics and Policy*, 8, no. 1 (1974), 48–57.

Peltzman, S., "The Effect of Automobile Safety Regulation," *Journal of Political Economy*, 83, no. 4 (1975), 677–725.

Sagner, J.S., "Benefit/Cost Analysis: Efficiency-Equity Issues in Transportation," *Logistics and Transportation Review*, 16, no. 4 (1980), 339–388.

Sawicki, D.S., "Break-Even B-C Analysis of Alternative Express Transit Systems," *Journal of Transport Economics and Policy*, 8, no. 3 (1974), 274–293.

Schwing, R.C., B. Southwark, C. von Buseck, and C.J. Jackson, "Benefit-Cost Analysis of Automobile Emission Reductions," *Journal of Environmental Economics and Management*, 7, no. 1 (1980), 44–64.

Small, K.A., "Estimating Air Pollution Costs of Transport Modes," *Journal of Transportation Economics*, 11, no. 2 (1977), 109–132.

St. Seidenfus, H., "European Ports in the Context of the World Economy and the European Economy: Changes in Sea Transport," *International Journal of Transportation Economics*, 14, no. 2 (1987), 133–138.

Swoveland, C., "Benefit-Cost Analysis of a Proposed Runway Extension," *Management Science*, 27, no. 2 (1981), 155–173.

Talley, W.K., and E.E. Anderson, "An Urban Transit Firm Providing Transit, Paratransit and Contracted-Out Services: A Cost Analysis," *Journal of Transport Economics and Policy*, 20, no. 3 (1986), 353–368.

Taylor, S., and R. Wright, "An Economic Evaluation of Calgary's North-East Light Rail Transit System," *Logistics and Transportation Review*, 19, no. 4 (1983), 351–365.

Viscencio-Brambila, H., and S. Fuller, "Estimated Effects of Deepened U.S. Gulf Ports on Export-Grain Flow Pattern and Logistics Costs," *Logistics and Transportation Review*, 23, no. 2 (1987), 139–154.

Vitaliano, D.F., "An Economic Assessment of the Social Costs of Highway Salting and the Efficiency of Substituting a New De-icing Material," *Journal of Policy Analysis and Management*, 11, no. 3 (1992), 397–418.

Viton, P.A., "On the Economics of Rapid-Transit Operations," *Transportation Research-A*, 14, no. 4 (1980), 243–253.

Wabe, S., and O. Coles, "The Short and Long Run Cost of Bus Transport in Urban Areas," *Journal of Transport Economics and Policy*, 9, no. 2 (1975), 127–140.

Walters, A.A., "The Benefits of Minibuses: The Case of Kuala Lumpur," *Journal of Transport Economics and Policy*, 13, no. 3 (1979), 320–334.

Waters, W.G. II, and Shane J. Meyers, "Benefit-Cost Analysis of a Toll Highway: British Columbia's Coquihalla," *Journal of the Transportation Research Forum*, 28, no. 1 (1987), 434–443.

Watson, G.S., P.L. Zador, and A. Wilks, "The Repeal of Helmet Use Laws and Increased Motorcyclist Mortality in the United States, 1975–1978," *American Journal of Public Health*, 70, no. 6 (1980), 579–585.

Wheaton, W.C., "Residential Decentralization Land Rents and the Benefits of Urban Transportation Investment," *American Economic Review*, 67, no. 2 (1977), 136–143.

Wilson, H.G., "The Cost of Operating Buses in U.S. Cities," *Journal of Transport Economics and Policy*, 11, no. 1 (1977), 68–91.

Woolley, P.K., "C-B Analysis of the Concorde Project," *Journal of Transport Economics and Policy*, 6, no. 3 (1972), 225–239.

22. WASTE DISPOSAL

Bingham, T.M., "Allocative and Distributive Effects of a Disposal Charge on Product Packaging," in *Resource Conservation: Social and Economic Dimensions of Recycling*, D. Pearce and I. Walter. London: Macmillan, 1977.

Dinan, T.M., "Economic Efficiency Effects of Alternative Policies for Reducing Waste Disposal" *Journal of Environmental Economics and Management*, 25, no. 3 (1993), 242–256.

Jenkins, R.R., *The Economics of Solid Waste Reduction: The Impact of User Fees*. Brookfield, VT: Edward Elgar Publishing Company, 1993.

Judge, R., and A. Becker, "Motivating Recycling: A Marginal Cost Analysis," *Contemporary Policy Issues*, 11, no. 3 (1993), 58–68.

Porter, R.C., "A Social Benefit-Cost Analysis of Mandatory Deposits on Beverage Containers," *Journal of Environmental Economics and Management*, 5, no. 4 (1978), 351–375.

Rose, D., "National Beverage Container Deposit Legislation: A Cost-Benefit Analysis," *Journal of Environmental Systems*, 12, no. 1 (1982), 71–84.

Strathman, J.G., A.M. Rufolo, and G.C.S. Mildner, "The Demand for Solid Waste Disposal," *Land Economics*, 71, no. 1 (1995), 57–64.

23. WATER

Boyle, K., G.L. Poe, and J.C. Bergstrom, "What Do We Know About Groundwater Values? Preliminary Implications from a Meta Analysis of Contingent-Valuation Studies," *American Journal of Agricultural Economics*, 76, no. 5 (1994), 1055–1061.

Crouter, J.P., "Hedonic Estimation Applied to a Water Rights Market," *Land Economics*, 63, no. 3 (1987), 259–271.

Decooke, B.G., J.W. Buckley, and S.J. Wright, "Great Lakes Diversions Preliminary Assessment of Economic Impacts," *Canadian Water Resources Journal*, 9, no. 1 (1984), 1–15.

Gibbons, D.C., *The Economic Value of Water*. Washington, DC: Resources for the Future, 1986.

Kanazawa, M., "Pricing Subsidies and Economic Efficiency: The U.S. Bureau of Reclamation," *Journal of Law and Economics*, 36, no. 1 (1993), 205–234.

Kulshreshtha, S.N., et al., "Economic Impacts of Irrigation Development in Alberta Upon the Provincial and Canadian Economy," *Canadian Water Resources Journal*, 10, no. 2 (1985), 1–10.

MacRae, D., Jr., and D. Whittington, "Assessing Preferences in Cost-Benefit Analysis: Reflections on Rural Water Supply Evaluation in Haiti," *Journal of Policy Analysis and Management*, 7, no. 2 (1988), 246–263.

McGuckin, J.T., and R.A. Young, "On the Economics of Desalination of Brackish Household Water Supplies," *Journal of Environmental Economics and Management*, 8, no. 1 (1981), 79–91.

Renzetti, S. "Evaluating the Welfare Effects of Reforming Municipal Water Prices," *Journal of Environmental Economics and Management*, 22, no. 2 (1992), 147–163.

24. WATER POLLUTION

Ashworth, J., J. Papps, and D.J. Storey, "Assessing the Impact Upon the British Chlor-Alkali Industry of the EEC Directive on Discharges of Mercury into Waterways," *Land Economics*, 63, no. 1 (1987), 72–78.

Beck, M.B., and B.A. Finney, "Operational Water Quality Management: Problem Context and Evaluation of a Model for River Quality," *Water Resources Research*, 23, no. 11 (1987), 2030–2042.

Bockstael, N.E., W.M. Hanemann, and C.L. Kling, "Estimating the Value of Water Quality Improvements in a Recreational Demand Framework," *Water Resources Research*, 23, no. 5 (1987), 951–960.

Cohen, M.A., "The Costs and Benefits of Oil Spill Prevention and Enforcement," *Journal of Environmental Economics and Management*, 13, no. 2 (1986), 167–188.

Dasgupta, A.K., and M.N. Murty, "Economic Evaluation of Water Pollution Abatement: A Case Study of Paper and Pulp Industry in India," *India Economic Review*, 20, no. 2 (1985), 231–267.

Desvousges, W.H., V.K. Smith, and A. Fisher, "Option Price Estimates for Water Quality Improvements: A Contingent Valuation Study for the Monongahela River," *Journal of Environmental Economics and Management*, 14, no. 3 (1987), 248–267.

Feenberg, D., and E.S. Mills, *Measuring the Benefits of Water Pollution Abatement*. New York: Academic Press, 1980.

Gardner, R.L., and R.A. Young, "An Economic Evaluation of the Colorado River Basin Salinity Control Program," *Western Journal of Agricultural Economics*, 10, no. 1 (1985), 1–12.

Greenley, D.A., R.G. Walsh, and R.A. Young, "Option Value: Empirical Evidence From a Case Study of Recreation of Water Quality," *Quarterly Journal of Economics*, 96, no. 1 (1981), 657–673.

Grigalunas, T.A., et al., "Estimating the Cost of Oil Spills: Lessons from the Amoco Cadiz Incident," *Marine Resource Economics*, 2, no. 3 (1986), 239–262.

Harris, B.S., "Contingent Valuation of Water Pollution Control," *Journal of Environmental Management*, 19, no. 3 (1984), 199–208.

Hufschmidt, M.M., "Systematic Analysis of Water Pollution Control Options in a Suburban Region of Beijing, China," from a report prepared by F. Guowei, Z. Lansheng, C. Shengtong, and N. Guisheng in *Economic Valuation Techniques For the Environment*, eds J.A. Dixon and M.M. Hufschmidt. Baltimore and London: The Johns Hopkins University Press, 1986, pp. 178–192.

Hufschmidt, M.M., "The Nam Pong Water Resources Project in Thailand," from a paper prepared by R. Srivardhana in *Economic Valuation Techniques For the Environment*, eds. J.A. Dixon and M.M. Hufschmidt. Baltimore and London: The Johns Hopkins University Press, 1986, pp. 141–162.

Kitabatake, Y., "Welfare Costs of Eutrophication-Caused Production Losses: A Case of Aquaculture in Lake Kasumigaura," *Journal of Environmental Economics and Management*, 9, no. 3 (1982), 199–212.

Lichtengerg, E., and D. Zilberman, "Efficient Regulation of Environmental Health Risks: The Case of Groundwater Contamination in California," *Recherche Economics*, 39, no. 4 (1985), 540–549.

Mitchell, R.C., and R.T. Carson, "Option Value: Empirical Evidence from a Case Study of Recreation of Water Quality: Comment," *Quarterly Journal of Economics*, 100, no. 1 (1985), 291–294.

Peshin, H.M., and E.P. Seskin, eds., *Cost-Benefit Analysis and Water Pollution Policy*. Washington, DC: The Urban Institute, 1975.

Raucher, R.L., "A Conceptual Framework for Measuring the Benefits of Ground Water Protection," *Water Resources Research*, 19, no. 2 (1983), 320–326.

Raucher, R.L., "The Benefits and Costs of Policies Related to Ground Water Contamination," *Land Economics*, 62, no. 1 (1986), 33–45.

Russell, C.S., and W.J. Vaughan, "The National Recreational Fishing Benefits of Water Pollution Control," *Journal of Environmental Economics and Management*, 9, no. 3 (1982), 328–354.

Smith, V.K., and W.H. Desvousges, "The Generalized Travel Cost Model and Water Quality Benefits: A Reconsideration," *Southern Economic Journal*, 52, no. 2 (1985), 371–381.

Smith, V.K., and W.H. Desvousges, *Measuring Water Quality Benefits*. Boston, MA: Kluwer Nijhoff Publishing, 1986.

Sutherland, R.J., "A Regional Approach to Estimating Recreation Benefits of Improved Water Quality," *Journal of Environmental Economics and Management*, 9, no. 3 (1982), 229–247.

Sutherland, R.J., and R.G. Walsh, "Effects of Distance on the Preservation Value of Water Quality," *Land Economics*, 61, no. 3 (1985), 281–291.

25. WILDERNESS/WETLANDS/WILDLIFE

Batie, S.S., and C.C. Mabbs-Zeno, "Opportunity Costs of Preserving Coastal Wetlands: A Case Study of a Recreational Housing Development," *Land Economics*, 61, no. 1 (1985), 1–9.

Batie, S.S., and L.A. Shabman, "Estimating the Economic Value of Wetlands: Principles, Method, and Limitations," *Coastal Zone Management Journal*, 10, no. 3 (1982), 255–278.

Clayton, C. and R. Mendelsohn, "The Value of Watchable Wildlife: A Case Study of McNeil River," *Journal of Environmental Management*, 39, no. 2 (1993), 101–106.

Danielson, L.E., and J.A. Leitch, "Private vs. Public Economics of Prairie Wetland Allocation," *Journal of Environmental Economics and Management*, 13, no. 1 (1986), 81–92.

Farber, S.C., "The Value of Costal Wetlands for Protection of Property Against Hurricane Wind Damage," *Journal of Environmental Economics and Management*, 14, no. 2 (1987), 143–151.

Guldin, R.W., "Wilderness Costs in New England," *Journal of Forestry*, 78, no. 9 (1980), 548–552.

Guldin, R.W., "Predicting Costs of Eastern National Forest Wildernesses," *Journal of Leisure Research*, 13, no. 2 (1981), 112–128.

Hyde, W.F., "Developments Versus Preservation in Public Resource Management: A Case Study from the Timber-Wilderness Controversy," *Journal of Environmental Management*, 16, no. 4 (1983), 347–355.

Jaworski, E., and C.N. Raphael, "Economics of Fish, Wildlife, and Recreation in Michigan's Coastal Wetlands," *Coastal Zone Management Journal*, 5, no. 3 (1979), 181–200.

Lakhani, H., "Benefit-Cost Analysis: Substituting Iron for Lead Shot in Waterfowl Hunting in Maryland," *Journal of Environmental Management*, 14, no. 3 (1982), 201–208.

Loomis, J.B., and R.G. Walsh, "Assessing Wildlife and Environmental Values in Cost-Benefit Analysis: State of the Art," *Journal of Environmental Management*, 22, no. 2 (1986), 125–131.

Lynne, G.D., P. Conroy, and F. Prochaska, "Economic Valuation of Marsh Areas for Marine Production Processes," *Journal of Environmental Economics and Management*, 8, no. 2 (1981), 175–186.

McKillop, W., "Wilderness Use in California: A Quantitative Analysis," *Journal of Leisure Research*, 7, no. 3 (1975), 163–178.

Peterson, G.L., and A. Randall, *Valuation of Wildland Benefits*. Boulder, CO: Westview, 1984.

Porter, R.C., "The New Approach to Wilderness Preservation Through Benefit-Cost Analysis," *Journal of Environmental Economics and Management*, 9, no. 1 (1982), 59–80.

Rafsnider, G.T., M.D. Skold, and R.J. Sampath, "Range Survey Cost Sharing and the Efficiency of Rangeland Use," *Land Economics*, 63, no. 1 (1987), 92–101.

Rausser, G.C., and R.A. Oliveira, "An Econometric Analysis of Wilderness Area Use," *Journal of American Statistical Association*, 71, no. 354 (1976), 276–284.

Wetzstein, M.E., R.D. Green, and G.H. Elsner, "Estimation of Wilderness Use Functions for California: An Analysis of Covariance Approach," *Journal of Leisure Research*, 14, no. 1 (1982), 16–26.

AUTHOR INDEX

SUBJECT INDEX